LEMON-AID

NEW CAR GUIDE 1997

LEMON-AID

NEW CAR GUIDE 1997

Phil Edmonston

Stoddart

Published in 1996 by
Stoddart Publishing Co. Limited
34 Lesmill Road
Toronto, Ontario
M3B 2T6

Canadian Cataloguing in Publication Data

The National Library of Canada has catalogued this publication as follows:

Edmonston, Louis-Philippe, 1944-
Lemon-aid new car guide

1982–
Continues in part: Lemon-aid, ISSN 0383-7084.
Includes index.
ISSN 0714-5861
ISBN 0-7737-5828-3 (1997)

1. Automobiles - Purchasing - Periodicals. I. Title.

TL162.E3396 629.2'222'05 C82-031621-0

Typesetting and text design: Wordstyle Productions
Editorial services: Greg Ioannou, Colborne Communications Centre

Printed and bound in Canada

CONTENTS

Part Three/NEW VEHICLE RATINGS
136

American Vehicles
145

Asian Vehicles
309

Introduction
THE *LEMON-AID* PHILOSOPHY

The *Lemon-Aid New Car Guide 1997* is unlike any other auto book on the market. Its main objective is to inform and protect Canadian consumers in an industry known for its pressure tactics, dishonesty, and exaggerated claims.

Fighting corporate fraud carries certain risks. As a consumer advocate, I have sued and been sued (never successfully) by automakers for millions of dollars during my 20-year stint as founder, past president, and member of the non-profit Automobile Protection Association (APA). I'm not easily intimidated and I know where the skeletons are buried.

The book's information is gathered throughout the year from whistle blowers, lawsuits and judgments, as well as confidential manufacturer service bulletins. Consumer complaints from across Canada are investigated, and industry practices as reported by federal and provincial government agencies, consumer groups, and automobile associations are analyzed.

The *Lemon-Aid New Car Guide* follows a 24-year tradition of publicizing abusive auto industry practices and providing hard-to-get information that may save your life—and certainly make you a smarter consumer. And if you're cheated, *Lemon-Aid* can help you to get a refund—and get even. In short, this book's mission is to put you behind the wheel of the safest, most reliable vehicle for the least amount of money and stress.

The 1997 *Guide* makes a critical comparison of '96 and '97 models to determine if improvements and additional safety features justify the higher costs of new models (most don't). Safer, often cheaper and more reliable alternatives are given for each vehicle. Points are given for crash test results that demonstrate that the driver and passengers are well-protected, and also for the availability of essential safety features. Performance comparison tests, a list of essential accessories, and guidelines as to how much profit the dealer makes on each vehicle are only a sampling of the wealth of material that you have at your fingertips.

Lemon-Aid combines test results with owner complaints, Internet and CompuServe postings, and surveys to determine its rating of a particular model. Not all vehicles are test-driven because of time or availability constraints. Vehicles that are test-driven are rented or borrowed from their owners; no manufacturer "freebies" are solicited or accepted.

Please fill out the questionnaire found at the end of this *Guide*, and list the degree of satisfaction or dissatisfaction you have experienced with your new or used vehicle. The information will be compiled and used in the next edition of the *Lemon-Aid New Car Guide.*

Phil Edmonston
November, 1996

Part One

BEWARE THE "SHOWROOM SHAKEDOWN"

Know what you really need

There are about 4000 vehicle dealerships in Canada, and they all want your money—over $20,000 for the average new car or minivan. Before paying these big bucks, you should know what your real needs are and how much you can afford to spend. Don't confuse needs with styling (Do you transport the neighbourhood hockey team? Take long holiday trips?) or the trendy with the essential (Are you serious about off-roading? Will you be towing a trailer?).

Canadians buy more small cars and minivans than do Americans.

You might be surprised to learn that Canadians have different vehicle preferences than do Americans. For example, we are absolutely head over heels in love with minivans and small cars. Sales figures show, for example, that minivans make up about 35 percent of the total Canadian light-truck market compared to 20 percent in the U.S. We spend less because we have less disposable income, making inexpensive small and compact cars and functional minivans the darlings of Canadian sales. In fact, Canada's small and compact cars and minivans account for 61 percent of sales—20 points higher than the U.S. experience.

Most car buyers don't have a clue as to what they really want, and automakers are cashing in on their confusion by overpricing their cars and minivans. These vehicles are loaded up with costly, complicated mechanical and electronic components that compromise their original simplicity and easy repairability. Buyers are forced to purchase vehicles that are over-engineered for their driving requirements or equipped with expensive options needed only for hauling heavy cargo or extended driving vacations. Don't fall for the dealer's "must have" song and dance. Instead, ask yourself the following questions about the kind of vehicle you want and at what price.

What can I afford to spend?
It makes good sense to determine how much money you can spend and then to decide on what vehicles interest you in that price range. Have several models in mind so that you won't be tempted by one that may be overpriced. Use as your benchmark the ratings, alternative models, estimated purchase cost, and residual value figures shown in Part Three. Remember, logic and prudence are the first casualties of showroom hype, so carefully consider your actual requirements and how much you can budget to meet them before comparing models and prices at a dealership. Write down your first, second, and third choices relative to each model and the equipment offered (use the Appendix worksheet found at the back of this *Guide*). Call the dealership and ask for an appointment to be assured of getting a sales agent's complete attention.

What kind of driving am I going to do?
In the city, a small Japanese-made wagon is more practical and less expensive than a minivan. However, if you're going to be doing a lot of highway driving, transporting small groups of people (especially kids), and loading up on accessories, a medium-sized wagon like the Ford Taurus or a small minivan could be the more logical choice considering price, comfort, and reliability. You need an extended minivan or van only if you have to carry at least seven occupants, haul supplies, or get a better view of the road.

Most families who travel less than 20,000 km per year should avoid the smallest and the largest engines available with a given model. Less driving will be accommodated by a smaller engine that offers both economy and performance; more than 20,000 km of driving per year demands the cruising performance, extra power for additional accessories, and durability of a larger engine (a 6-cylinder engine, perhaps). If you spend lots of time on the road, for example for business, you'll definitely need an 8-cylinder powerplant to handle the AC and other power-hungry accessories essential to your driving comfort and convenience. Believe me, fuel savings will be the last thing on your mind if you buy an underpowered car.

Do I feel comfortable in this vehicle?
The advantages of many sports cars and vans quickly pale in direct proportion to your tolerance for a harsh ride, noise, buffeting, limited visibility, and a cramped or cold interior. After falling in love with the showroom image, you'll likely end up hating the vehicle—all the more reason to test-drive your choice over a period of several days to get a real feel for its positive and negative characteristics.

Does it respond to my special needs?
Auto designers have been more preoccupied with putting cupholders in their minivans, for example, than designing them to be safer, more convenient to use, and more comfortable for women and an aging population.

A survey of 2400 women by *Chatelaine* magazine concluded that 77 percent of women play a role in car buying, and 52 percent feel that manufacturers don't adequately consider women's needs in designing vehicles. For example, if men wore skirts it's doubtful that minivans and vans would have such a high step, and if more men hauled their children around it's likely that standard seats would more easily accommodate child safety seats. Other improvements I'd like to see are:

1. Instrument panels that don't house small, complicated, high-effort controls and difficult-to-see gauges. They should have light-coloured faces and dark numerals, with minimal glare from the windshield.
2. Easy entry and exit, with lightweight doors that open wide, wider foot corridors, and flat seats with smooth finishes.
3. Easy-to-engage, foot-operated emergency brakes, vanity mirrors on the driver's side sun visor (women drive too), lots of storage bins, door handles that won't break fingernails and are easy to operate, delayed headlight shutoffs that keep the lights on until you're through the front door, a user-friendly trunk lock with remote control, a low liftover trunk sill, and a lightweight trunk lid.
4. Folding rear seatbacks that open to the trunk and can be locked shut.
5. Radio and temperature controls that are easy to reach and that have more space between the buttons.
6. Automatic childproof door locks.
7. The parking brake positioned so that it won't snag clothing, and seat buttons placed where they don't entangle skirts or rip panty hose.
8. Seatbelts that cross comfortably across the chest.
9. Standardized seatbelts that make it easy to install child safety seats, or safety seats that are integrated into the seat.
10. Small steps on multipurpose vehicles for easier entry/exit.
11. A low front end that gives the driver and passengers a better view of the road.
12. User-friendly gas and brake pedals that can be used while wearing a shoe with heels, and a protective cushion underneath to prevent unsightly and costly shoe back abrasion.

Can I adjust to the different handling characteristics of different vehicles?
Front-drive braking is quite different from braking with a rear drive, and braking efficiency on ABS-equipped vehicles is compromised if you pump the brakes. Also, rear-drive minivans handle like trucks, while full-size vans will scrub the right rear tire during sharp right-hand turns until you get the hang of making wider turns.

What safety features do I want?
Dual airbags, head restraints, beams in the side doors for side collision protection, and a reinforced roof offering increased rollover protection are all likely to become standard features for most 1997 model cars and minivans. If you are of small size, or are likely to carry an infant or child in the front seat, airbags may pose a serious safety hazard to you or your child. Since you can't buy a new car without a driver-side airbag you'll want to choose a vehicle with an adjustable seat that has far enough backward travel to keep you at a safe distance from the airbag's explosive deployment. The child's safety can be assured by getting a vehicle with an airbag shut-off switch (available only in pickups, and other vehicles without rear seating).

Remember too that some vehicles are more crashworthy than others, and that size doesn't always guarantee crash safety. Look up each vehicle's crash rating in Part Three.

Is new better than used?
Yes, if you buy a minivan, a vehicle class known to depreciate slowly. No, if you buy a passenger car. Depreciation will knock off less than one-third of your minivan's value during the first three years of ownership, while the average car will be worth only half its original value over the same period. And once you add federal and provincial taxes, financing costs, maintenance, and a host of other expenses, the yearly outlay for a new car is about twice that of a used car.

Can I get the best for less?
Sometimes a cheaper twin or hybrid model will fill the bill. Twins are those nameplates that are virtually identical in body design and mechanical components, like the Ford Sable/Taurus, GM Beretta/Corsica, and the Chrysler Caravan and Voyager.

Perhaps a hybrid or "captive import" will be more to your liking, and to your pocketbook's. American manufacturers have learned to join the Asian carmakers instead of competing against them, and vice versa. This has resulted in hybrids whose parentage is impossible to nail down but which incorporate a high degree of quality control. Suzuki builds GM's Tracker 4X4 in Ontario, Mazda and Ford churn out Probes in the United States, and Ford's Villager/Quest minivan is a Nissan co-venture.

This Ford Probe, a Best Buy, uses Mazda MX-6 mechanical components.

Sometimes choosing a higher trimline will cost you less when all the standard features are accounted for. (General Motors "special edition" vehicles, for example, could give you all the options you need for much less than if you ordered them separately on a cheaper model.) It's hard to compare value prices with the manufacturer's base price, though, because the base prices are inflated and can be negotiated downward, while cars that are value priced are offered as a "take it or leave it" proposition.

Twins and hybrids are only two of the alternatives; there are plenty of others. Minivans, for example, come in two versions: a base commercial version and a more luxurious model for private use. The commercial version doesn't have as many bells and whistles, but it's more likely to be in stock and will probably cost much less. And if you're planning to convert it, all the extras may just get in the way.

Leasing is an alternative often used to make vehicles appear to be more affordable, but it's more expensive than buying, and for most people the pitfalls may far outweigh any advantages. If you have to lease, keep your losses to a minimum by leasing only for the shortest time possible, and by making sure that the lease is closed-ended (meaning that you walk away from the vehicle when the lease period ends).

If long-term leasing looks to be too expensive, consider purchasing a three- to five-year-old vehicle with 60,000 to 100,000 km on the clock and some of the original warranty left. Such a vehicle is likely to be just as reliable for less than half the cost of one bought new. Parts will be easier to find, independent servicing should be a breeze, insurance premiums will come down from the stratosphere, and if you get a lemon your financial risk is lessened considerably.

Know all the costs

There are a lot of hidden costs in owning a new car or minivan. Automotive magazines don't provide many details about these costs because they don't want to anger their industry sponsors or to direct buyers to used cars, which would undercut new car sales. Car columnists in particular don't want to offend the manufacturers who supply them with free test cars. This is why you don't see most of the motoring press including such important factors as crashworthiness, parts costs and availability, warranty complaints, and depreciation in their new car ratings. Yet this is precisely the information that most buyers want. The exceptions are *AutoWeek*, a spinoff of the fiercely independent *Automotive News*; *Mechanics Illustrated* and its quarterly spinoff *CarSmart*, which have always taken an independent line; and *Consumer Reports*, which spurns paid advertisements.

Don't be taken in by gas mileage figures trumpeted by the manufacturers. They're exaggerated by about 10 percent because vehicles are run under optimum conditions by automakers who submit their test results to the government. Sure, good fuel economy is important, but it's hardly worth a harsh ride, highway noise, sidewind buffeting, anemic acceleration, and a cramped interior. You may end up with much worse gas mileage than advertised and a vehicle that's underpowered for your needs.

Tax advantages

Tax rules for cars and minivans are very complex. Nevertheless, whether you have a full-time job or are self-employed, there's a good chance that you can deduct some of your transportation expenses on your income tax return. It all hinges on the quality of your recordkeeping.

The accounting firm of Price Waterhouse has prepared an inexpensive car benefit and expense kit that makes recordkeeping a snap and costs less than $10. It includes a booklet for employees, another for employers, and a logbook where you can list all the details required by government tax auditors. Order the kit from Price Waterhouse at 20 Queen St. West, Suite 200, P.O. Box 75, Toronto, Ontario, M5H 3V7.

"New" isn't always new

There's no guarantee that the vehicle you finally decide to buy is really new. The odometer may have been disconnected and the vehicle could have been involved in an accident, as was the case with Chrysler cars sold in the late 1980s. Chrysler admitted to disconnecting the odometers on more than 60,000 vehicles. Some of these had been involved in serious accidents, and were repaired and sold as new to unsuspecting Canadian and American buyers. Or, the dealer may have disconnected the odometer and driven the car for several thousand kilometres as a demonstrator. Even if the vehicle hasn't been used it may have been left outdoors for a considerable length of time, causing the deterioration of rubber components; rusting of internal mechanical parts, which leads to brake malfunction and fuel line contamination (hard starting, stalling); and premature body and chassis rusting.

You can check a vehicle's age by consulting the date of manufacture plate found on the driver's side door pillar. If the date of manufacture is 7/96 and you purchased the car in 1996, your car was one of the last 1996 models made before the September changeover to the 1997 models. Exceptions to this rule are those vehicles that are redesigned or relatively new to the market, arriving at dealerships in early spring or midsummer. They're considered to be next year's models, but depreciate more quickly due to their earlier launching (a difference that narrows over time).

Carryovers from previous years generally have fewer problems than vehicles that have been significantly reworked or just introduced to the market. This fact is borne out by a recent J. D. Power study of 74 vehicle launches from 1989-96, which showed that the Big Three's relaunched models had an eight-percent decline in quality, which turned around to a 19 percent quality improvement in the second year.

The Power study showed that GM's 14 newly relaunched/replaced vehicles had more quality problems than their predecessors, but that after a year on the market they had a better quality rating than the models they replaced. Chrysler's relaunched/replaced models also scored lower, with quality improving dramatically over the ensuing two years. Ford was the only American automaker whose relaunched/replaced vehicles were of a higher quality than the vehicles they replaced. Among Japanese automakers, Honda, Toyota, and Nissan posted an average 17 percent decline in their first-year offerings, although this decline was wiped out by an average 19 percent improvement in the next year.

Most vehicles assembled between September and February are called "first series" cars because they were the first off the assembly line for that model year. "Second series" vehicles, made between March and August, incorporate more assembly-line fixes and are built better than the earlier models, which depend on ineffective "field fixes" that may only mask the symptoms until the warranty expires. Both vehicles will sell for the same price, but the post-February one will be a far better buy since it benefits from assembly-line upgrades and rebates. Last year's crop of redesigned Chrysler minivans, for example, won't be as defect-free as are the '97 versions.

This Probe was manufactured in February, 1991, making it a first series '91 model. The second series '91 Probes, made from March through August, were much better. Since these cars were launched in 1989 they've improved markedly in overall reliability and quality control.

There's also the very real possibility that the new vehicle you've just purchased was damaged while being shipped to the dealer, and was fixed by the dealer during the pre-delivery inspection. It's estimated that this happens to about 10 percent of all new vehicles. There's no specific Canadian legislation allowing buyers of damaged vehicles to cancel their contracts. However, Canadian common law jurisprudence allows for cancellation or compensation whenever the delivered product differs markedly from what the buyer expected to receive.

Who Can You Trust?

Deceptive ratings and phony car columnists

Granted, this year's crop of new cars and minivans is more stylish and safe than last year's, but they're also outrageously overpriced. That's why in Part Three I don't recommend any 1996-97 model that doesn't show important safety, quality, performance, or convenience improvements over a less expensive 1996 version.

Once you've established a budget and selected some vehicles that interest you, the next step is to ascertain which ones are rated as reliable and safe. Be wary of the ratings found in some enthusiast magazines; their supposedly independent tests are a lot of baloney. Their test car is supplied by the manufacturer and tuned to just the right specifications. Of course, servicing will be impeccable. Finally, the manufacturer will probably load the car with an assortment of expensive options to compensate for any design faults.

Carmakers can't lose with this rigged test. And if the tester wants other free courtesy cars to drive, the published report had better gloss over the vehicle's defects and hype its mediocre features. Also, if the magazine or newspaper receives advertising from the manufacturer, any criticism that gets through the driver's own self-censorship will be muted by the editor. Another very important reason for discounting these tests is that they don't predict a car's vulnerability to rust, poor servicing, crash forces, or inadequate parts distribution.

When automakers fail to buy a magazine's loyalty with free test cars, trips, and advertising deals, they're not above using blackmail to "goose" the advertising department into bringing the editorial people into line. Toyota boycotted *Road and Track* for almost a year and a half when *R and T*'s February 1991 issue failed to include any Toyota models in its listing of the "10 Best Cars in the World." Former *Car and Driver* publisher David E. Davis, Jr. felt GM's sting a few years back when the company pulled its ads from his *Automobile* magazine after he criticized the company. A subsequent GM memo said that pulling the ads was a way of repaying Davis with "our undying neglect."

The ubiquitous H. Ross Perot, a former GM board member and frequent candidate for the American presidency, unleashed scathing criticism of GM mismanagement in a 1988 *Fortune* story. As a result, GM pulled the magazine off its media list for an eight-page ad insert. *Fortune* didn't flinch, but few Canadian publications could have withstood the loss of that many advertising dollars.

Take the *Montreal Gazette* and the *Windsor Star* as two examples. In a May 18, 1991 story on Chrysler's call for trade restraints on Japanese imports, the *Gazette* rightfully suggested that Chrysler Canada president Yves Landry was a hypocrite for supporting import quotas. The story pointed out that Chrysler, part owner of Mitsubishi, was a large-scale importer of Japanese-made vehicles sold under Chrysler's name as the Colt, Eagle, Laser, and Talon. Chrysler claimed that the story was unfair and yanked all of its advertising from the paper. The *Gazette* stood its ground, although it did publish lots of pro-auto fluff shortly afterward, and Chrysler advertising in the paper has returned to normal.

Compare this with the *Windsor Star*'s strange, unnecessary, and exaggerated apology to car dealers made earlier this year by that paper's publisher, James Bruce. Bruce ran a three-column apology to Windsor-area car dealers for having run a Canadian Press story criticizing Montreal car dealers (that's right, *Montreal*). The story, based on a survey done by APA president George Iny, questioned the honesty of nine auto dealerships that were surveyed in Montreal. Bruce felt that the story might reflect badly on local dealers and insisted that the following apology be run.

Story Failed to Meet *Star's* Standards

. . . On rare occasions a story finds its way into the newspaper which does not meet the high ethical and journalistic standards of balance, fairness and factual accuracy which we set for ourselves at the *Windsor Star*. . . . Although the story did not involve any Essex County dealers, it may have by implication, cast aspersions on their business practices. The story was a discredit to the dealers and employees of members of the Windsor Essex County Dealers Association, who adhere to the highest of ethical standards and provide their customers with first rate standards of service. . . .

Don't look to the automakers or their dealers for helpful information relating to the crashworthiness of the vehicles they manufacture and sell. At Toronto's International Auto Show held in February 1995, Richard Martin, a TVOntario field producer, asked automaker representatives how well their vehicles fared in their own or government-run crash tests. With camera crew in tow, he was rebuffed by a half-dozen automakers who said crash information was unavailable or was given out only by head office. Even after calling each company's head office, no crash data was given out. Surprisingly, Volvo and Saturn, two automakers who claim to put their owners' interests first, refused to provide the requested crash-test information.

Car columnists are no angels either. Although they still claim that their integrity is not for sale, there's no doubt that it can be rented.

CTV's *W5* newsmagazine show confirmed this fact a few years ago when it ran an exposé that showed Canadian car columnists and broadcasters ripping off automakers by demanding $3000 in corporate membership fees to join their Automotive Journalists Association. (Individual memberships cost $100.) Following the CTV broadcast, the *Toronto Star* required its columnists to indicate in a footnote to their articles, when applicable, that their information came from a travel junket, or that a manufacturer-supplied vehicle was used. General Motors of Canada pulled out of the association's "Car of the Year" competition held shortly after the broadcast.

Travel junkets, public relations, and advertising contracts all sweeten the honey pot for these phony journalists.

Honest info

Everybody wants to tell you what to buy—relatives, co-workers, friends, and everyone else who thinks they know what's best for you. After a while you'll get so many conflicting opinions that it'll seem as if any choice you make will be the wrong one. Before making your decision, remember that you should invest a month of research in your $20,000-plus new car-buying project. This includes two weeks for basic research (see below) and another two weeks to actually bargain with dealers to get the right price and equipment. The following sources provide a variety of useful information that will help you to get the best deal.

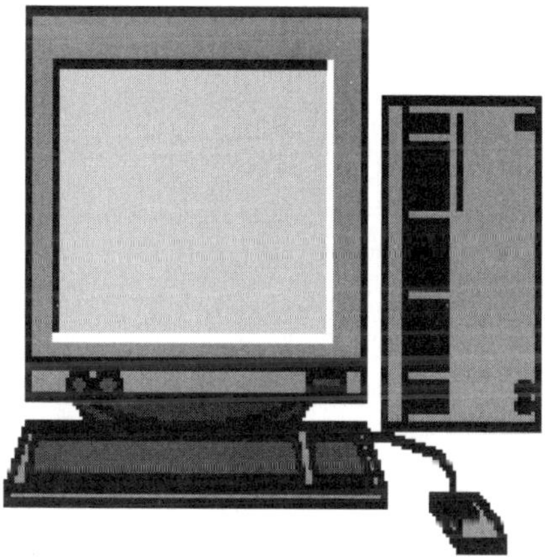

Online services/Internet

Anyone with access to a computer and a modem can now obtain useful information relating to the auto industry in a matter of minutes and at little cost. This is accomplished in two ways: subscribing to one of the three American online services that offer everything from consumer forums to easy Internet access, or going directly to the Internet through a low-cost Canadian "server" and cruising the thousands of sites that interactively summarize the subject matter that's covered or the services offered.

Online services

The three major American online services accessible to Canadians are America Online, CompuServe, and Prodigy. Except for minor differences in the way fees are collected, all three services are similar.

CompuServe, the service I'm most familiar with as a member, offers dozens of auto-related services that simplify buying and owning a car. With the click of a button you can cruise consumer-advocacy message areas (called forums); download (transfer data from a host computer via an electronic link) government auto safety defect probes, recall campaigns, and crashworthiness ratings; and find out what dealer incentives and customer rebates are being paid out by automakers in the States. Subscribers can also access sites in order to shop for a new vehicle or accessories (Canadian prices, though, are rarely given); read online versions of popular American auto magazines, including *Consumer Reports;* and get industry news and reviews. Without a doubt, the liveliest and most informative CompuServe sites are the forums on cars and consumer rights. Watched over, but not censored, by a volunteer system operator (sysop), members post hundreds of messages each week responding to questions ranging from how to keep cats off your car (use an open box of mothballs) to what the particulars are of GM's secret paint warranty (a Chevrolet dealer's warranty administrator actually gave out all the details).

The Internet

Even if you're not a subscriber to one of the online services mentioned above, you can still access plenty of auto information by cruising different Internet sites and bulletin boards.

Although the Internet and World Wide Web are names that are often used interchangeably, the Internet is the largest network of computers in the world—most sharing the TCP/IP protocol for transferring files—while the World Wide Web is the hypertext system (on that network of computers) for locating and accessing Internet resources. The Internet also has various other services, such as Gopher—a powerful search tool that can locate sites around the world.

To get on the Internet you must first find a "server," or service provider, who may be able to access the Internet at a lower cost than the big U.S. systems. Most service providers provide test accounts so that you can try out the service before signing up. This allows you to check the number of phone lines your server has and the accessibility of phone-in technical support.

Competent installation experts are rare because they must be very experienced in hardware, software, and communication problems in a rapidly evolving field. In a worst-case scenario it may cost you up to $150 for installation and some handholding. But you can save much of this cost by using shareware software and a good service provider.

Local newspapers or computer publications are a good place to comparison shop for servers in your area. Before signing up, though, talk to your local college, university, or library to find out if they offer free Internet connections to outsiders, or if they can put you in touch with a "freenet" system run largely by volunteers.

The Web

Web connection is the current state of the art on the Internet, but a monthly charge of $25 for two-hour daily service is typical. There are also flat-rate Internet providers offering unlimited access at rates as low as $15 a month.

Surfing the Web also requires software such as Netscape Navigator, along with a "dial-up" program such as Trumpet Winsock, both of which can be loaded without much trouble. Your service provider (if it's a good one) will have a technical service line you can call for step-by-step help in downloading the software you need. There are also search engines that will list sites on the Web according to subject or name. For example, if you want to find sites related to Chrysler cars, a Web search using Web Crawler will come up with 218 sites. Keep in mind, though, that a poorly installed Netscape Navigator will run v-e-r-y slowly.

The Web's DejaNews service is a great tool for finding problems and experts quickly. The Alexander Law Firm's extensive home page is the site of choice for advocates and consumers. On the other hand, the commercialized home pages can be a trap for the unwary. For example, a leasing association's "free leasing calculator" is the bait for a "lease now" soft-sell.

Usenet

Usenet is a separate network carried by most Internet connections. Like the CompuServe forums, Usenet has newsgroups that are dedicated to specific topics. The World Wide Web's DejaNews service mentioned above is the one to use to find groups in your area of interest.

Listservs

This is the short term for list servers—providers that have automated mailing lists of subscribers who share a common interest. Listservs can be very useful because they send targeted information straight to your E-mail box. You can use them to research everything from high-performance cars to secret car warranties.

Objective publications

The key word here is *objective.* Consumer groups and auto associations are your best bet for independent auto ratings. The following thorough, independent sources of new car buying information are available from your local library: the APA's *Magazine* (a quarterly publication available for $12 from the APA, 292 St. Joseph Blvd. West, Montreal, Quebec, H2V 2N7); the CAA's *Auto Opinion* magazine (published annually), available from the CAA; and the April auto edition of *Consumer Reports* (a monthly available for $35 Cdn. from Consumers Union, 256 Washington St., Mount Vernon, New York, 10551).

Neither the APA's *Magazine* nor *Consumer Reports* carries advertising. The former bases its evaluations on Canadian motorists' complaints, government probes, and reports from independent garages. *CR* rates vehicles from an American perspective through member surveys, government crash tests, and its own testing centre, where vehicles it has purchased anonymously are road tested. All three publications list the MSRP; however, Canadian dealers' higher markup isn't shown and most prices have been boosted by the time these magazines hit the newsstand. Also, the APA's list prices are too broad in range to be useful.

Consumer magazines don't agree on every model, but they're generally very objective in the way they rate vehicles.

AutoWeek, Automotive News, and *Popular Mechanics* are the best trade and special-interest magazines for objective car-buying information. These publications accept carmaker and engine "wonder drug" ads, but they remain relatively independent.

Consumer Reports ratings, extrapolated from Consumers Union's annual U.S. member survey, accurately mirror the Canadian experience. There are two exceptions, however. Components that are particularly vulnerable to our harsh climate usually perform less well than the *CR* reliability ratings indicate; and poor servicing caused by a weak dealer body can make some service-dependent vehicles a nightmare to own in Canada.

Based on 600,000-plus member responses, *CR* lists vehicles that are better or worse than average if owner reports vary from the industry average. Statisticians agree that *CR*'s sampling method has some room for error, but the ratings are good, conservative guidelines for buying a new vehicle that hasn't changed much from year to year. And the ratings have stood up to court challenges from automakers.

The CAA and its ratings are a different kettle of fish. Kind of like the AARP on wheels, the CAA is an efficient, competent organization that has just recently stuck its big toe into the hot water of consumer advocacy, mostly by promoting auto safety. The group spends much of its time starting/towing cars, selling vacations and preparing trip maps, and decrying gasoline taxes. Much like Canada's Better Business Bureaus, whose noble intentions were compromised early on by a mixture of business-led intimidation (the threat of lawsuits and the withdrawal of financial support), the CAA has traditionally treated consumer advocacy with a mixture of fear and benign neglect.

Its annual (every March) *Autopinion* contains mostly general-interest articles from auto industry toadies in addition to auto ratings. Its owner sampling is less than 5 percent of *CR*'s and is declining: 27,700 responses for 1993, and 26,000 for 1994 (these survey results comprised the CAA's 1995 ratings). *Autopinion* gives you a good general idea of those vehicles that have generated the most problems for CAA members, but its conclusions shouldn't be followed unless they're confirmed by another consumer publication. CAA editors paint too broad a stroke for vehicles and model years that have an insufficient number of responses.

What about the APA's semi-annual ratings of new and used cars and my own *Lemon-Aid*'s auto ratings? Don't trust them either without checking other consumer publications. The APA's ratings are based on Canadian consumer complaints and independent garage reports. What it lacks in breadth it makes up for in depth. *Lemon-Aid* does make technical mistakes (I once wrote that one should avoid the GM Astro/Safari 8-cylinder engine forgetting that GM doesn't put an 8-cylinder motor in that model). I also tend to be very dismissive of auto industry hype and, perhaps, place too much emphasis on the 1500 consumer complaints I get each year. I try to balance these shortcomings with a wide variety of objective data that include confidential dealer service bulletins, whistle-blower reports, consumer surveys, and government investigations and tests.

DEGREE OF OWNER SATISFACTION WITH PRESENT VEHICLE

by manufacturer

Manufacturer	Very Satisfied	Moderately Satisfied	Dissatisfied	Total Number of Responses
Chrysler	74.7%	22.6%	2.7%	(4,635)
Ford	68.9%	27.0%	4.1%	(4,555)
General Motors	73.6%	23.7%	2.6%	(8,459)
Overall North American	*72.7%*	*24.3%*	*3.0%*	*(17,649)*
Honda	86.5%	12.9%	0.6%	(1,917)
Hyundai	64.9%	31.2%	3.9%	(362)
Mazda	79.1%	19.2%	1.7%	(949)
Nissan	84.1%	13.9%	2.0%	(799)
Subaru	75.7%	21.5%	2.8%	(247)
Suzuki	66.7%	31.0%	2.4%	(84)
Toyota	87.7%	11.2%	1.1%	(2,592)
Overall Japanese/Asian	*83.9%*	*14.7%*	*1.4%*	*(6,950)*
Alfa Romeo	100.0%	0.0%	0.0%	(2)
Audi	76.5%	20.0%	3.5%	(85)
BMW	79.2%	17.7%	3.1%	(96)
Jaguar	63.2%	31.6%	5.3%	(19)
Lada	66.7%	33.3%	0.0%	(12)
Mercedes-Benz	87.6%	11.2%	1.1%	(89)
Peugeot	77.8%	22.2%	0.0%	(9)
Porsche	100.0%	0.0%	0.0%	(7)
Volkswagen	76.0%	21.0%	3.0%	(692)
Volvo	82.9%	15.7%	1.4%	(293)
Overall European	*78.5%*	*19.0%*	*2.5%*	*(1,304)*
Overall	*76.0%*	*21.4%*	*2.6%*	*(25,903)*

Note: General Motors includes Isuzu, Saab and Saturn

HYUNDAI

Excel 89	Excel 90	Excel 91	Excel 92	Excel 93		Sonata 89	Sonata 90	Sonata 91	Sonata 92	Sonata 93
39	8	11	6	INSUFFIENT DATA	Number of Responses	32	15	18	25	INSUFFIENT DATA
●	○○○	○○○	○○○		Cooling System	●	●●	●●	●●	
○	○○○	●●	○○○		Engine	●●	●	○○○	●	
●●	●●	●●	○○○		Carburation and Fuel System	●●	●●	●	●●	
○	○	●●	○○○		Ignition System	○○	○	●	○○○	
●●	●●	●●	○○○		Exhaust System	●●	●●	●●	●	
●●	○○○	○○○	○○○		Final Drive	●●	●●	●●	○○○	
●●	○○○	○○○	○○○		Transmission	○○	○○○	●●	●●	
○○○	○○○	●●	○○○		Steering	○○	●●	○○○	○○○	
○○	○	●●	○○○		Suspension and Wheels	●●	○○	○○○	○○○	
○	○○	●	○○○		Braking System	○○	○	○○	○	
●●	●●	●	●●		Electrical System	●●	●	○	●●	
●	○	○	○○○		Instruments and Accessories	●	○	●●	●●	
●●	●●	●●	○○○		Body	○○○	○○○	●●	○○	
●	●●	●●	○○○		Interior Trim & Fittings	○○	●●	●	●●	
684	282	693	110		Avg. Mechanical Repair Cost ($)	610	268	231	213	
●	●	●●	○○○		General Appraisal	●	●	●	●●	
54	88	64	83		Would Repeat Purchase of Vehicle (%)	77	87	94	88	
V.S. 57.6%	M.S. 27.3%		DIS. 15.2%		Degree of Satisfaction	V.S. 74.2%		M.S. 21.5%		DIS. 4.3%

Do you really believe the CAA table above that shows Hyundai's Excel and Sonata—two cars decried by most consumer groups as being so low on the quality/reliability totem pole that they've begun to take root—have "satisfied" 84.8 percent and 95.7 percent, respectively, of their owners? (How could the CAA be wrong? Hint: look at the number of owners polled.)

Other research sources

1. Conduct on-the-lot inspections of different vehicles—after business hours so that you don't get harassed—to become familiar with several models you're considering.
2. Talk to private garage mechanics, rental agents, and the leasing manager at work. They get the owner/driver feedback as to durability and reliability, and they don't have any reason to prefer one vehicle over another.
3. Auto shows and dealerships are good places to get the Manufacturer's Suggested Retail Price, specifications, and optional equipment. Brochures can also be useful in court if the car or its equipment don't perform as advertised.

Buy or Lease?

The Canadian auto market peaked in 1988 when 1.54 million cars and light trucks were sold. Since then Canadian car sales have gone south, both figuratively and literally. Canadians aren't buying new cars because they cost too darned much. Instead of doing the right thing—reducing prices and interest rates—automakers are offering deceptive buy-back leases that contain high interest charges hidden in monthly payments that appear to be lower than finance payments.

Why leasing costs more

Lessees pay the full manufacturer's suggested retail price on a vehicle loaded with costly options, plus hidden fees and interest charges that wouldn't be included if the vehicle were purchased instead (see *Schryvers v. Richport Ford* in Part Two). There's also a wide array of restrictions imposed on the leased vehicle. Forget about getting clear information that would permit you to compare the costs of leasing and financing, says DesRosiers Automotive Research Inc., a Toronto consulting firm that studies the leasing industry. DesRosiers found that cheaper cars often cost more to lease than some luxury models. This was confirmed by the Canadian Bankers Association (CBA), after it blasted dealers' leasing contracts for charging interest rates up to 34 percent and called for consumer protection legislation to regulate the industry. In another survey carried out three years ago by *Les Affaires*, a Montreal-based business weekly, more expensive mid range cars and minivans were shown to cost about $3000 more if leased rather than financed for purchase, and luxury cars about $7000 to $9000 more.

Rob Lo Presti, a Toronto-based consumer advocate and leasing consultant, has campaigned tirelessly for more disclosure in leasing contracts. He says that Quebec, Manitoba, and British Columbia are the only provinces with legislation that requires disclosure and limits contract cancellation penalties, but that so far most of the disclosure requirements don't go far enough. Leasing agencies are getting away with legalized highway robbery through outrageously excessive hidden leasing charges and loan rates that are practically usurious.

Most people don't have the time or patience to do the complex calculations that leasing contracts require. For them, Lo Presti has created *CarCalculator*, an easy-to-use program that runs on any computer with DOS 3.3 or higher. It takes the mystery out of leasing, giving you the effective interest rate you're paying, the total cost of the lease, and how it compares with financing—facts guaranteed to frustrate any fast-talking dealer or leasing agent. It costs $29.95 (tax and shipping included) from OrangeSoft, P.O. Box 33518, 1277 York Mills Road, North York, Ontario, M3A 1Z5. Callers may dial 1-800-647-8693 (toll-free in Canada) or 1-416-441-0297. OrangeSoft will also check a leasing quote for $20 ($10 for each additional quote). Call the 1-800 number.

The Obscure Language of Leasing

Until leasing contracts become more comprehensible, follow the brief glossary below that lists some of the legalese and obscure terms found in most leasing contracts.

Acquisition fee: Frequently hidden in the body of the contract, this is an extra charge for what is essentially overhead. Following consumer protests, media criticism of the practice, and an official inquiry by the federal Department of Corporate Affairs, General Motors Acceptance Corporation has tried to justify its acquisition fee in a variety of interesting, though unconvincing ways (see below the confidential GMAC letter to Branch Managers on ways of explaining the charges to customers and the media).

Closed-end lease: This lease protects you from a decline in the vehicle's value when the lease expires. Useful with some cars, but a waste of money with slow-depreciating MPVs.

Disposition fee: Another abusive "extra" for preparing the vehicle for resale at the end of the lease. Don't accept this charge.

Early termination penalty: The fee paid by the customer when the lease is broken (see previous comments).

Excess mileage charge: This fee is charged for mileage that exceeds the cap set in the contract; try to get a cap of 30,000 km per lease year and a rate that's less than 5 cents per kilometre.

Open-end lease: This lease holds the customer responsible for the difference should a vehicle's value fall below the residual value pre-set when the contract was signed. Not a likely prospect with most MPVs.

Residual value: Think of it as the pre-set trade-in value for a leased vehicle. The lower the residual value, the greater your chance of making money if you purchase the vehicle at the expiration of the lease and then sell it privately a year or two later. This is more easily done with MPVs and presupposes that you have an open-end lease.

GMAC Canada Tries to Justify Acquisition Fees (Are You Convinced?)

GENERAL MOTORS ACCEPTANCE CORPORATION OF CANADA, LIMITED

To	All Branch Managers	Address	
From	W.J. Watson	Address	Head Office
Subject	SmartLease Disclosure	Date	April 18, 1994

As leasing becomes more and more popular, consumers and governments are becoming better educated and are scrutinizing leasing very closely. We have a great opportunity to use leasing to generate more business for GM, GMAC and the dealers, however, it must be presented in a very up front, honest way or the repercussions could damage this sensitive relationship with the lessee.

Attached for your interest is an article from the "Money" section of the B.C. Province newspaper. It appears that in the very near future, B.C. will be passing disclosure laws for leasing and we anticipate that other provinces will follow suit. Also attached is an article from the Globe and Mail where for $29.95 you can order a computer program that breaks down a lease payment.

In the past, it has not been required for us to disclose the acquisition fee of $350 and very few people (especially our dealers) are able to explain this fee. As we move into the 1995 Model year, it will be our intention to disclose this acquisition fee in some point of sale material. We will also be encouraging the DMA's to include it in their advertising. We want to lead the industry with disclosure and clarify what might otherwise be misinterpreted. The key to our success will be providing the dealership sales staff with the proper training to be able to explain the acquisition fee to the satisfaction of a potential lessee.

There are some very good reasons why GMAC requires an acquisition fee, which is a direct result of ownership of the vehicle by us and not the lessee. There are also other things that GMAC provides on a lease that we do not provide on a finance contract. The following is a list of some of those items:

- monthly billings mailed to lessee
- insurance follow-up
- third party liability insurance protection
- handling of PST and GST
- costs associated with remarketing of returned vehicles
- GAP protection
- Client Management System

Acquisition fees are an industry standard. G.E. Capital, Nissan, Honda and Mercedes-Benz all charge $350; Toyota and Chrysler charge $325 and Ford charges 1/10 of 1.0% of the Cap Cost per month. In addition, the majority of dealers include an acquisition fee in their leases.

It is critical that all GMAC sales staff understand what is covered in the acquisition fee and that we train the dealership personnel accordingly.

get signature

President

WJW:lm

Att:

Leasing advantages

Leasing can be worthwhile for people who frequently trade in their cars, as it's more convenient and results in less sales tax. This advantage is wiped out, however, if you lease for longer than three years or buy back the car at the end of the lease. In some cases you may be paying too much if you don't lease, since leasing enables you to drive a new vehicle without tying up a bundle of money that you could otherwise invest or use to pay down more costly debt such as charge cards. Leasing may also offer some tax advantages if your car expenses are deductible from gross income. However, the savings may be minimal. According to the accounting firm of Price Waterhouse, in 99 percent of the cases it has examined there wasn't much difference in the tax liability if the vehicle was bought or leased. Your chief consideration shouldn't be the tax savings but the difference between the implicit interest rate in the lease and the financing charge.

Leasing disadvantages

Leased vehicles are usually overpriced, jam-packed with nonessential options, and accompanied by a hefty upfront fee. A leased vehicle's residual value also gives the leasing agent another avenue to rip you off by setting the vehicle's buy-back value at much more than it's likely to be worth. Check the residual values section found in Part Three for a realistic buy-back price for the car or minivan you're thinking of leasing. It's a smart idea to buy additional "gap" insurance to cover the balance owed on the lease if the vehicle is stolen or written off in an accident, but most lessors charge too much for the protection (about $200 is fair). In some cases, the leasing company will throw in gap insurance at no extra cost.

Ask the leasing firm what it's prepared to do if the car turns out to be a lemon. Most companies accept that this happens from time to time and will simply return the car to the manufacturer and get a replacement. But that's not part of the standard agreement, so be sure that such a clause is included in your lease before you sign it. Remember, if your leased car is a lemon, arbitration programs run by the Better Business Bureau and others may refund the purchase price of the vehicle, but not the interest costs.

Here are two other reasons why you may not wish to lease:

- If you drive more than 24,000 km a year (you may be charged from 4 to 15 cents per extra kilometre over that limit).
- If you always seem to have dents or scrapes on your car and can't be bothered getting regular maintenance. The vehicle's value at the end of the lease period is probably the single most important factor in computing whether leasing is to the driver's advantage or not. Responsible leasing firms allow for normal wear and tear on the vehicle during the leasing contract, but rip-off companies count every scratch and you may have to pay a grossly inflated repair bill.

Ford has recently responded to owner and dealer complaints about the definition of what is "normal" wear and tear with the following memo to dealers telling them exactly what should be considered when a leased vehicle is returned.

To Pay or Not to Pay?

Normal Wear and Tear	Excess Wear and Tear
• Dings	• Broken or missing parts
• Minor dents	• Dented body panels or trim
• Small scratches	• Damaged fabric
• Stone chips in the paint finish	• Cracked or broken glass
• Reduced tread on tires	• Poor-quality repairs
	• Unsightly alterations
	• Tire/wheel damage or less than 1/8 inch of tread remaining
	• Mechanical and electrical malfunctions

Unfair lease restrictions

Make sure that the lease allows you to service the vehicle yourself at an independent repair facility. A maintenance lease that ties you to the leasing firm's repair shop can lead to outrageous service charges. Use a less expensive independent repair shop for routine servicing and keep all your receipts to prove that proper maintenance, as required by the manufacturer, was carried out should a warranty dispute arise.

Be wary of unfair restrictions, excessive penalties, and hidden damage charges. Excessive penalty charges for early cancellation of the contract are horrendous. Sometimes lessors will put you on a leasing treadmill by waiving the penalty only if another vehicle is leased. Most impose a 24,000 km per year mileage limit and charge a whopping surcharge on the excess. Also, you may be restricted from driving your vehicle outside Canada or lending it to a third party.

Decoding leasing ads

Take a close look at the small print found in most leasing ads. Pay particular attention to the model year, kind of vehicle (demonstrator or used), equipment, warranty, interest rate, buy-back amount, down payment, security payment, monthly payment, transportation and preparation charges, administration fee, insurance premium, number of free kilometres, and excess kilometre charge.

One final point about leasing. When you take your leased vehicle back at the end of an open lease, make sure that you get some written offers on your vehicle and tell the leasing company or dealer that you expect them to call these buyers. This will save you thousands of dollars by preventing the leasing agency from making a "lowball" bid and forcing you to make up the difference between the residual value and what the leasing company actually gets for the vehicle. (See "Leasing" in Part Two.)

When and Where to Buy

When to buy

The best time to buy a new car or minivan is in the winter, between January and May. Lay low for a couple of months and then return in force in August, when you can double dip from the automakers' dealer incentive and buyer rebate programs, which average about a thousand dollars each. Remember, too, that vehicles made between March and August offer the most quality upgrades. Dealers have very few customers in the dead of winter and most buyers are on vacation or moving during the month of August, so they're anxious to cut prices substantially to keep their inventory and financing costs low. Some carmakers cut special deals in December to boost year-end numbers for specific models—as Ford did with its Sable and Taurus so that it could then proclaim them as outselling Honda's Accord, their closest competitor.

Allow yourself at least two weeks to finalize a deal if you're not trading in your vehicle, and longer if you sell your vehicle privately. Visit the dealer at the end of the month just before closing, when the salesperson will want to make that one last sale to meet that month's quota. If sales have been terrible, the sales manager may be willing to do some extra negotiating.

Try not to buy when there's strike action. It'll be especially tough to get a bargain because there's less product to sell and the dealer has to make as much profit as possible on each sale. Furthermore, work stoppages increase the chance that on-line defects will go uncorrected and the vehicle will be delivered, as is, to product-starved dealers.

Where to buy

Forget about saving money by purchasing a new vehicle in the United States. Although European carmakers offer substantial discounts to Canadians who purchase their cars while in Europe and guarantee that their vehicles will meet Canadian federal safety and emission regulations, American manufacturers don't follow this policy (and it may be impossible to upgrade your vehicle to conform to the Canadian standard). Furthermore, lower prices on American-sourced cars aren't an advantage, due to the higher cost of the American dollar and substantial Canadian sales taxes (GST, provincial sales taxes, and a gas-guzzling surcharge). Servicing may be a problem, since some dealers are reluctant to service cars that they didn't sell. They won't refuse service outright, but they'll certainly put their own customers first and give them "goodwill" warranty coverage before you.

If you fall victim to this blackmail and there's no other dealer nearby to carry out warranty repairs, send a registered letter or a fax to the manufacturer explaining why you'll be getting your warranty inspections done by an independent garage, and that you'll hold the automaker responsible for all warranty repairs refused by the dealer.

Smart new car shoppers *can* save big bucks by buying, or just threatening to buy, from a dealer in another province where competition and geography make for substantially lower prices, transportation, and predelivery fees. Generally, new car prices in Ontario and Quebec are much lower than prevailing prices in eastern and western Canada. The smart thing to do is sell your trade-in in the province where you'll get the most for it and buy in the province where new cars cost the least. This can be done easily by combining your shopping plans with your annual vacation to see the folks.

Relatives can steer you in the right direction based on their own dealer experiences. Once again, though, you may find servicing given with a snarl when you get back home, but this should only be a problem with vehicles that can't be easily serviced by independent garages. And a good dealer doesn't care where his customers bought their cars as long as the warranty work is paid by the automaker.

Good dealers aren't always the ones with the lowest prices. Dealing with someone who gives honest and reliable service is just as important as getting a good price. Check a dealer's honesty and reliability by talking with motorists driving vehicles purchased from that dealer (identified by the nameplate on the trunk). If these customers have been treated fairly they'll be glad to recommend him. You can also ascertain the quality of new car preparation and servicing by renting one of the dealer's minivans or pickups for a weekend or by having your trade-in serviced by the dealer.

How can you tell which dealers are the most honest and competent? Well, judging from the many complaints I receive each year, dealerships in small suburban and rural communities are fairer than big city dealers, because they're more vulnerable to negative word-of-mouth advertising and to poor sales. When their vehicles aren't selling, good service takes up the slack. Prices may be more competitive too because overhead is often much lower than in metropolitan areas.

Dealers selling more than one manufacturers' product line present special problems. Overhead can be quite high, and cancellation of a dual dealership in favour of an exclusive franchise elsewhere is an ever-present threat. Parts availability may also be a problem, because a dealer with two separate car lines must split his inventory, and so may have an inadequate supply on hand.

The quality of new car service is linked directly to the number and competence of dealerships within the network. If the network is weak, parts are likely to be unavailable, repair costs can go through the roof, and the skill level of the mechanics may be questionable. The Japanese automakers have the best overall dealer representation across Canada among foreign manufacturers. European carmakers are almost all crowded into Quebec and Ontario, leaving eastern and western Canada to fend for themselves.

Dealers offering top-quality repairs are able to keep their commercial fleet customers, so if a dealer has a large volume of commercial work, chances are he's giving good service at a reasonable price.

Patronize dealers that shun "shop supplies" charges and use hourly rather than flat-rate time in calculating repair charges. Twenty-four-hour servicing, free loaner cars, and/or a downtown shuttle service make for more convenient servicing. Make sure the free loaner car is spelled out in the sales contract.

It's also a good idea to patronize dealerships that are accredited by auto clubs such as the Canadian Automobile Association affiliates, or consumer groups like the Automobile Protection Association. Auto club accreditation is no iron-clad guarantee of honest or competent business practices, but if you're cheated or become the victim of poor servicing you'll have one more place to take your complaint and apply additional pressure. As well, plaintiffs have won in court by pleading that the auto club is legally responsible for the consequences of the recommendations it makes.

Automobile brokers and vehicle buying services

Throughout this book I've tried to give you all the key information you need to get a good deal when buying a new or used vehicle. I understand that this kind of negotiation isn't for everyone, and offer you the following alternative: an auto broker.

Brokers are independent agents who try to find the new or used vehicle you want at a price below what you'd pay at a dealership, including the extra cost of the broker's services. Broker services appeal to buyers who want to save time and money, while avoiding most of the stress and hassle associated with the dealership experience which, for many people, is like a swim in shark-infested waters.

Automobile brokers are a relatively small part of the car buying scene, even though their numbers have grown perceptibly in the past few years. Because their services are currently unregulated it's difficult to determine how many brokers are operating in any one area, except for Ontario and British Columbia where they're often found through ads placed in newspapers. Brokers get new cars through dealers, while used cars may come from automobile dealers, auctions, private sellers, and leasing companies. Basically, brokers find an appropriate vehicle that meets the client's expressed needs, and then negotiate the purchase (or lease) on behalf of their client. The majority of brokers tend to deal exclusively in new cars, with a small percentage dealing in both new and used vehicles. Ancillary services vary among brokers, and may include such things as comparative vehicle analysis and price research. For example, one Willowdale, Ontario, broker (AutoBuy Advisory Services) often finds itself battling insurance adjusters to get fair settlements for claimants: "We regularly assist clients in obtaining better insurance settlements on total loss claims. Frequently, consumers are uninformed about the value of their vehicles. Claimants often forget to tell their insurers about expensive repairs (done in the months preceding the accident), after-market equipment, and recently purchased items such as new tires/rims, all of which can bolster settlements. We analyse each client's situation and provide the market research and other information needed to win a more equitable settlement."

The cost of hiring a broker ranges anywhere from a flat fee of a few hundred dollars to a percentage of the value of the car. Sometimes a car broker may offer his services for a nominal fee, or even tell the buyer that the service is "free." In such cases it is best to remember that nothing is free in the car business. If the customer isn't paying the fee directly, then the broker's fee is being paid by the dealer, who simply buries that commission in the total price of the car. Ultimately, the customer pays either way. While it's not impossible to get a reasonable deal under such an arrangement, beware that the broker may be unduly biased toward a certain dealer or manufacturer. Reputable brokers are not beholden to any particular dealership or make, and will disclose their flat fee up front or tell the buyer the percentage amount they charge on a specific vehicle.

There are both advantages and disadvantages to using a broker. The advantages are:

- Brokers can save you lots of time. This is particularly true with used cars, because each one is unique and must be approached accordingly. A responsible broker may check out and reject a number of used vehicles before finally recommending one to the buyer.
- Brokers work full time at buying vehicles. Since they deal in volume, they have access to new-vehicle fleet rates. This "fleet price" can translate into thousands of dollars off the manufacturer's suggested list price.
- Most brokers have also had experience working in dealerships, so they understand the rhythm and ploys of negotiations. As negotiators, they have the distinct advantage of being emotionally detached from the purchase in a way the actual purchaser rarely is. They also tend to know current wholesale values of vehicles, so that the buyer doesn't get shortchanged on a trade-in or pay too much for a used car.

The disadvantages of using a broker are minimal. They include:

- Buyers are still reponsible for doing their homework on the type of vehicle they want and the price they're willing to pay. A broker won't necessarily discourage a client from selecting a particular vehicle, but should, at the very least, be able to outline the advantages or disadvantages of a given choice, describe comparable vehicles and their prices, and generally show an in-depth understanding of the car market.

- Buyers are also on their own in making financial arrangements, although a good broker can review the various alternatives, such as bank financing versus the manufacturer's, and should be able to calculate the total purchase or lease cost.

Finding the right broker
Buyers who are looking for a broker should first ask friends and acquaintances if they can recommend one. Word-of-mouth referrals are often the best, because people won't refer others to a service they were dissatisfied with. If a referral isn't an option, try local consumer advocacy organizations, the Yellow Pages, or the local newspapers.

Obviously, buyers should use a broker they trust, but trust must be earned. Ask about the benefits of the buying service above and beyond the usual "locate and negotiate." Does the broker have "industry experience"? Is the broker well informed? Impartial? Empathetic to your needs? The broker should provide full disclosure of all charges related to the service. If the broker seems vague or evasive on this point, hang up and call a different one.

In Quebec, the Automobile Protection Association recommends the Wendman Auto Agency in Westmount and Agence Negocie-Auto in Verdun. For Toronto consumers, both the APA and the Ontario Consumer Action Group recommend AutoBuy Advisory Services, 107 Hendon Ave., Willowdale, Ontario, M2M 1A6. Tel: (416) 590-9902.

Buying clubs

Buying clubs that promise huge savings on purchases, or claim to get new vehicles at dealer's cost, seldom survive close scrutiny. The savings are illusory at best because the so-called wholesale or dealer's cost price is usually no different from the regular retail selling price suggested by the manufacturer.

Some credit union or union buying clubs do a good job in cutting prices on all vehicles. They use their buying clout in a particular region to exact substantial concessions from local dealers. They generally charge minimal membership fees and put their members' interests first.

Safety First

Buying a safe vehicle

According to the U.S. National Highway Traffic and Safety Administration (NHTSA), a new vehicle will be in an average of two accidents from the time it leaves the assembly line (10 percent of all new vehicles sustain some transport damage) to the day it's towed to the junkyard. So crash safety is a major factor that must be taken into consideration when purchasing a new vehicle. NHTSA data show that 51 percent of deaths occur in head-on collisions, 27 percent in side impacts, and barely 4 percent in rear impacts. Rollovers, a frequent occurrence with sport-utility vehicles, are particularly lethal, especially for occupants who are ejected because they're not wearing their seatbelts. They face a fatality rate 25 times greater than passengers who remain strapped into the vehicle.

Women are particularly vulnerable to traffic fatalities and injuries. The number of women who die behind the wheel has increased 62 percent since 1975, while highway deaths among men are dropping. The reasons given for this difference include the fact that women are driving more, they drive smaller cars, they drive more aggressively, are less tolerant of alcohol, and tend to drive on local roads where accident rates are higher.

With these figures in mind, everyone should buy a vehicle equipped with dual airbags for frontal collision protection, anti-lock brakes (ABS), side-door beams that offer side impact protection, head restraints, three-point seatbelts, and roll bars for utility vehicle safety.

Active and passive safety

How safe a vehicle is depends on its active and passive safety features. Active safety components like ABS, 4X4 capability, and specialized suspensions help the driver to avoid accidents. Advocates of active safety stress that accidents are caused by the proverbial "nut behind the wheel" and believe that safe driving courses are the key to fewer accidents. While professional drivers extol the virtues of active safety features, everyday drivers feel safer with passive safety protection.

The theory of active safety has several drawbacks. There is no independent proof that safe driving can be taught successfully. Even if one learns how to master defensive driving techniques there's still no assurance that this training will be of any use in an emergency situation, where panic reflexes kick in. And what about the NHTSA's 1994 study estimating that 41 percent of all fatal accidents are caused by drivers who are under the influence of alcohol or drugs? All the high-performance options and specialized driving courses in the world won't provide much protection for such drivers or their victims. That's why passive safety systems are so effective: they work just as well with skilled and unskilled drivers. This fact hasn't escaped Canadian motorists; when asked by the CAA what safety features they want on their next vehicle, 69.6 percent chose airbags, 62 percent wanted ABS, and 20.5 percent selected traction control. Incidentally, of all the passive safety features one can choose, traction control seems to be the least important because it's so rarely used and its advantages aren't apparent.

Passive safety features have four objectives:

1. They make a vehicle easier to see, or give the driver a greater field of vision (one of the best features of MPVs). Transport Canada says that daytime running lights (DRL) reduce collisions by 11 percent. Yet this fact is conveniently ignored by U.S. car magazines (*AutoWeek*, *Automobile*, and *Car and Driver*), who call this uniquely Canadian safety item "a product of sick minds, the worst idea ever concocted, such a stupid move, I'm tempted to paint over all of them." The final irony is that most of GM's cars sold in the U.S. have DRL.

2. They keep the occupants inside the vehicle in a collision. Restraint systems provide the best means of reducing severe injuries caused by ejection.
3. They keep the occupants from being banged around the interior in a collision. Airbags and head restraints in particular help to prevent injury inside the vehicle by redirecting impact forces in a controlled manner. Rollbars, three-point seatbelts, well-anchored seat assemblies, integrated child safety seats (see "Options"), and reinforced doorlatches are effective in keeping passengers inside their vehicles.
4. They ensure that the vehicle, not the occupants, absorbs most of the impact forces. Volvo's soft front end and Honda's break-away engine mounts are recent examples of structural components that deform in a controlled manner, absorbing crash forces or directing them away from the occupants.

Airbags

I agree that airbags can be scary. I don't like the idea of an explosive charge going off in the steering wheel a foot from my face. On the other hand, as a former emergency medical technician, I prefer having my face smacked or hands scalded than my brains splattered on the windshield or wrapped around the wrap-around dash (see Part Two for a summary of airbag court decisions).

No matter what preferences I may have, airbags are here to stay. Already in an estimated 40 million vehicles in North America, all passenger vehicles are required to have them by 1997, and most automakers have installed dual airbags as standard equipment on their 1996 models. A few companies, including Volvo and Mercedes-Benz, have taken airbag protection a step further by installing standard side-impact airbags and dual airbags in their 1996 cars. Chrysler, Ford, and GM intend to put side-impact airbags in some of their '97 cars and minivans before installing them in 4X4s, vans, and pickups the following year.

Supplemental Inflatable Restraint

Designed to supplement safety belts, the SIR system includes two vital components supplied by Delco Electronics: one or more crash sensors and an electronics module. The module stores enough energy to inflate the air bag during a crash in which the vehicle's power (battery) might be lost. In addition, the module performs diagnostic testing on the SIR system to ensure system readiness. If the SIR system is malfunctioning, the driver will be notified by a warning light located on the instrument panel. The air bag will be deployed when the system detects the equivalent of a frontal impact of 14 mph or above into a fixed barrier. Together with safety belts, air bags provide state-of-the-art occupant protection.

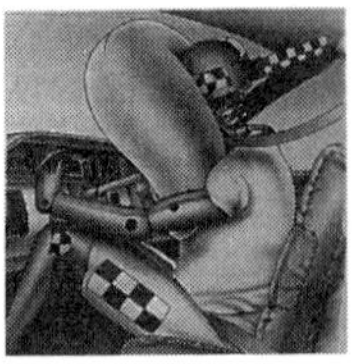

How airbags work

When an impact as low as 20 km/h (12 mph) is sensor-detected, a vehicle's front sensors send an electronic signal that almost instantaneously deploys an airbag or cushion from within the steering hub or underneath the dash. The airbag protects the head and upper torso from serious injury.

Airbags reduce the risk of a seatbelted occupant's death in an accident by 50 percent, compared with 45 percent for a seatbelted occupant with no airbag. That extra 5 percent margin has convinced governments, automakers, insurance companies, and motorists that airbags are a worthwhile investment. There is no proof, on the other hand, that injuries are reduced by airbags. In fact, one Virginia Commonwealth University study found that owners of cars equipped with airbags filed more personal injury claims than did owners of like cars without airbags.

One shortcoming is that airbags are designed to work best with people of "ideal proportions," in crashes at moderate speeds, and with occupants who have their seatbelt and shoulder harness fastened. All bets are off if you're seriously overweight or are involved in a collision at speeds of more than 57 km/h. If you have only your shoulder belt fastened, as is the case with many people who use automatic seatbelts, you risk decapitation.

Several hundred lawsuits have been filed alleging that the device has malfunctioned or caused minor burns, abrasions, and eye trauma. There have been no injuries reported to drivers who wear glasses because of the airbag's "give" and its quick deflation. However, some minor burns on the hands have been reported with airbags that vent propellant gases at points where the hands grip the steering wheel. This design has been improved in the last couple of years to allow additional venting and reduce the chance of burns.

Ford offers a passenger-side airbag disabler (a deactivation switch) on its new pickups for parents using a child safety seat or infant carrier. Without the disabler, a deployed airbag could seriously injure or kill a child.

Thieves are finding airbag theft easier to carry out and more lucrative than stealing car radios or cellular phones. They simply remove four bolts and disconnect the wiring harness (passenger-side airbags are a bit more difficult to remove). Stealing an airbag takes about two minutes and can bring $200 to $300 on the black market—much less than the $1200 charged by automakers. The makers of the Club, an anti theft steering wheel locking bar, now sell the Cap, an airbag cover that works with the Club. Both devices can easily be defeated with a hacksaw in about twenty seconds.

Childproof locks

Especially important in sport-utility vehicles, minivans, and vans, childproof locks consist of a special control that the driver can trip to prevent the rear doors from being unlocked from the inside while the vehicle is in motion. They offer extra safety and convenience.

Child restraint systems

Every year car accidents in Canada kill almost 70 youngsters under age five and injure another 4000. The tragedy of this statistic is that parents ignore it; half of the children riding in vehicles still aren't properly secured compared to the 87 percent of adults who wear seatbelts. Seventy percent of these deaths and injuries could have been prevented if children had been properly belted into a safety seat. In recognition of this fact safety authorities and the courts are cracking down on negligent parents. Provinces with seatbelt laws now require that children, especially infants, travel in an approved safety seat. Drivers who don't protect young passengers may face criminal charges or be held liable for civil damages if a youngster is injured or killed.

Contrary to popular belief, carrying young children on laps in a moving vehicle is not safe. A 20-pound child will be pulled away with a force of over 600 pounds in a 30-mph crash. Accident studies show that unrestrained adults can crush their children against the dashboard during a crash. Even in a relatively minor accident or panic stop, a child can be pulled away with surprising force and hit the dashboard or the floor hard enough to be seriously injured or killed.

There are three types of safety seats for children: infant-only carriers for birth up to about 9 kg (20 lbs.) or 27 inches in height; convertible carriers for children from birth up to 18 kg (40 lbs.) or 40 inches in height; and booster seats for kids weighing between 18 and 27 kg (40 to 60 lbs.). If you're not sure which seat fits your child's weight and height, check the Transport Canada compliance label affixed to the seat.

There are two sizes of infant carriers—those that are designed only for infants weighing up to 7.9 kg (17 lbs.) and others that can handle up to 9 kg (20 lbs.). Infant carriers often do double-duty as rockers and baby feeders. The typical carrier is lined with soft padding, has an internal safety harness, and is anchored by the vehicle's safety belt in the rear seat. Extra padding (a rolled up towel or baby blanket) can be added between the legs or on the sides as long as it's not placed under the harness straps. The baby faces backwards in a semi-reclining position. In an accident, the baby's back absorbs the crash forces rather than its delicate chest and abdomen. These rear-facing infant safety seats should never be used in the front seat of a vehicle equipped with a passenger-side airbag, unless the airbag has a disabler. The force of the airbag inflating is the equivalent of being hit by a vehicle travelling 200 miles per hour. Put the carrier in the rear outboard seats.

Forward-facing seats are anchored to the vehicle's frame by a tether strap, and they too should be used in the rear seat. Extra care is needed to make sure that the seat is installed properly. Convertible models are bulky and much less portable than infant seats, but they can be used for a much longer time. Chrysler's built-in child safety seats are an innovative optional safety feature patented by Ontario-based Magna International Ltd., and are now offered by several other automakers. They're convenient to use and may spare you the expense of a convertible or booster seat. Since they can't be faced to the rear, don't use them to carry infants.

Seatback-integrated child safety seats are effective, convenient, and relatively inexpensive.

A booster seat bridges the gap between a forward-facing seat and the vehicle's standard seatbelt. It consists of a firm cushion that incorporates its own restraining system that ensures the lap belt doesn't ride up. Instead, the belt fits snugly over the child's lap and the shoulder harness doesn't touch the neck. Remember, booster seats used around the house cannot protect your child in a collision. You can discontinue use of the booster seat when the child's height or weight exceeds the compliance label's limits.

Tots that are almost, but not quite, large enough for regular seatbelts may be able to use the "Child Saver," a device that allows adjustment of a three-point seatbelt so that it fits a small child. It sells for under $25 at most auto parts stores.

A variety of child safety seats can be rented from hospitals and provincial safety groups. If you decide to purchase one, be sure to ask the retailer for a registration card. The manufacturer can notify you of a recall that you otherwise might not learn about. Incidentally, all the seats on the market manufactured after October 1981 have been tested to meet Transport Canada's safety standards.

Vehicle size and safety

Insurance Institute for Highway Safety (IIHS) figures show that for every thousand pounds added to a car's mass, driver injury risk is lowered by 34 percent for the unrestrained driver and 25 percent for the restrained driver. This doesn't mean that motorists should drive cars and trucks built like army tanks. In fact, many subcompacts are so well designed to absorb crash forces that they will allow you to walk away from a frontal collision at 57 km/h (35 mph).

Ergonomics

One of the new catchphrases used in rating vehicles is "ergonomics." Simply put, it means making the vehicle's interior user-friendly. For example, can you reach the controls you'll need without strain or taking your eyes off the road? Are the controls just as easy to operate by feel as they are by sight? Can rear seat passengers enter or exit without becoming contortionists, as is the case with many two-door sport-utility vehicles?

To answer these questions, you need to drive the vehicle over a period of time to test how well it responds to the diversity of your driving needs. If this can't be done, you may find out too late that the climate control system keeps you cold in the winter and hot in the summer, or that the handling is more truck-like than you'd wanted. But you can conduct the following showroom test. Adjust the seat to a comfortable setting, buckle up, and settle in. When you look out the windshield and use the rear- and side-view mirrors, do you detect any serious blind spots? Will optional mirrors give you an unobstructed view? Does the seat feel comfortable enough for long trips? Can you reach important controls without moving off the seatback? If so, then your vehicle has been ergonomically designed. If not, shop for something that better suits your requirements.

Head restraints

Offered as a standard feature on front seats, but not in the rear, their main function is to prevent you from breaking your neck during a rear collision when the impact forces snap your head back. Your vehicle's restraints may be either fixed or adjustable. Fixed restraints are preferred, but adjustable ones are acceptable as long as they're adjusted high enough (at ear level). Make sure that rear visibility isn't obstructed by the front or rear head restraints, which surprisingly is the case with some Mercedes models.

Seats and seatbacks

Seat anchorages have to conform to government load regulations (some recalled '96 Chrysler minivans and Cirrus/Stratus models are the exceptions), but the regulations are so minimal that seats can easily collapse or tear loose from their anchorages, leaving drivers and passengers vulnerable in accidents.

Seatback failures are common among all car and MPV model lines except Mercedes-Benz, which has a tougher standard than that required by federal laws. It's not surprising to see seatbacks collapse in low-speed collisions, because the mechanisms that hold them upright fail when they're most needed.

Don't hold your breath waiting for stronger seatback regulations. Canada won't act before U.S. rulemakers propose their own standards, which have already come under intense industry lobbying pressure. Automakers claim that stronger seats would increase injuries when front passengers are slammed into rigid seatbacks during a crash. Safety critics, on the other hand, say that more occupants are seriously injured or killed by collapsing seats when they're thrown into the rear seat or flung from the vehicle.

Seatbelts

Apart from airbags, seatbelts provide the best means of reducing the severity of injury arising from low-speed as well as high-speed frontal collisions. In order to be effective, though, seatbelts must be adjusted properly and be comfortably tight, without undue slack. Unfortunately, this is not always the case and seatbelts rank high for customer complaints that they chafe the neck and don't properly fit children. These problems can be easily and inexpensively corrected by installing a Buckle Buddy seatbelt clip sold for $5.95 by NuZone Products Corp., P.O. Box 200185, Arlington, Texas, 76006; 1-800-772-8339. Some automakers have corrected this problem with adjustable shoulder-belt anchors that allow both tall and short drivers to raise or lower the belt for a snug, more comfortable fit. Look for this important feature in the showroom.

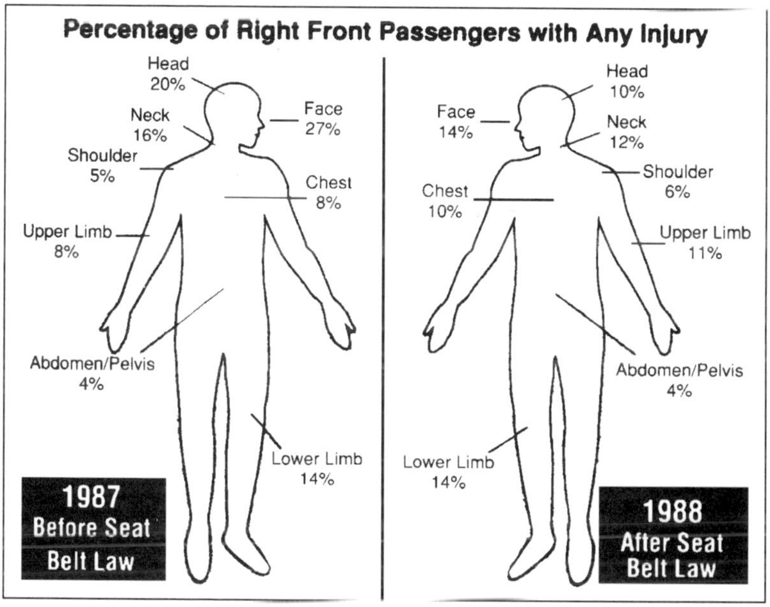

Crashworthiness

All things being equal, a heavier vehicle—including most MPVs except for compact sport-utility vehicles—will fare better in a crash than a light one. GM's recent two-car crash tests confirm this fact dramatically. Its engineers concluded that if two cars collide, and one weighs half as much as the other, the driver in the lighter car is ten times as likely to be killed as is the driver in the heavier one.

The Washington-based IIHS says that vehicles in the midsize and large car class are far safer than smaller ones when crashed at 40 mph—5 mph more than government tests. The IIHS figures show that the fatality rate for the occupants in a small car is roughly twice that of a midsize car, and three times as high as a big car. What's the cutoff point? A wheelbase of at least 105 inches. Vehicles with wheelbases of 105 inches or more have 1.4 or fewer deaths per 10,000 registered vehicles, while those with 104-inch wheelbases or less have 2.1 or more deaths for the same number of registered vehicles.

Choosing an Inexpensive Vehicle

Warranty fact vs. fiction

There's a big difference between warranty promise and warranty performance. All major automakers offer bumper-to-bumper warranties good for the first 3 years/60,000 kilometres. It's becoming an industry standard for car companies to also pay for roadside assistance, a loaner car, or hotel accommodations if your vehicle breaks down under warranty while you're away from home.

The auto industry's more comprehensive warranties have become an important marketing tool featured heavily in advertising campaigns. But, like the performance ads you see on TV, what you think you see is not always what you get. For example, bumper-to-bumper coverage usually excludes tires (GM vehicles are an exception, in that they allow you to claim a refund through the dealer), stereo components, brake pads, clutch disks, and many other expensive components. Furthermore, Canadian warranties are not always honoured in the United States. To really know what the warranty covers on your vehicle, you have to read the fine print. Chrysler, for example, offers a fairly comprehensive powertrain warranty, but major items are excluded and Chrysler is very tightfisted in the interpretation of its obligations (exemplified by its frequent refusal to pay automatic transmission and paint delamination claims on its minivans). Ford, on the other hand, often extends its basic warranty to cover component failures and then publicizes the fact, as it did four years ago when it extended warranty coverage on 1991 Sable and Taurus automatic transmission breakdowns and fuel pump failures; and on paint problems with its 1989-94 4X4s, minivans, vans, and pickups. (Ford is now less forthcoming on its paint defects.)

"Secret" warranties

It seems to me that there are more secret warranties covering 4X4s, minivans, vans, and pickups than one ordinarily sees with passenger cars. This may be due to the greater sophistication and rising number of MPV buyers, or the automakers' fear of losing their commercial clients—I don't know which.

I do know, however, that automobile manufacturers are reluctant to publicize their secret warranty programs because they feel that such publicity would weaken consumer confidence in their products and increase their legal liability. The closest they come to an admission is to send out a "goodwill policy," "special policy," or "product update" service bulletin for dealers' eyes only. These bulletins admit liability and propose free repairs for defects running the gamut from fishy-smelling headliners on Chrysler sport-utilities and minivans to transmission failures on Chrysler, Ford, and GM cars and trucks (see Part Three).

Only those motorists who yell the loudest or threaten to go to small claims court when faced with repairs for defective parts get compensated. Uninformed customers who hesitate to complain are forced to pay for the same repairs.

If you're refused compensation, keep in mind that secret warranty extensions are, first and foremost, an admission of manufacturing negligence. You can usually find them in dealer service bulletins (DSBs) that are sent daily to dealers by automakers. Your bottom-line position should be to accept a pro-rata adjustment from the manufacturer, whereby you share a third of the repair costs between the dealer and automaker. If polite negotiations fail, challenge the refusal in court on the grounds that you should not be penalized for failing to make a reimbursement claim under a secret warranty that you never knew existed!

Getting a DSB summary for your vehicle

If you want your own DSB summary, fill out the Bulletin Search Request found in Appendix IV of this *Guide.*

For a $15 Cdn. fee (this includes computer time and mailing costs), you will be faxed or mailed an exhaustive summary of all DSBs that concern your vehicle. For an additional $5 per DSB, you can then order any number of the DSBs listed in the summary that address your concerns. For example, one summary and one specific DSB would cost $20 Cdn. Remember, there's no extra charge for fax replies. On the other hand, only VISA cards or cheques made out to DSB are accepted.

Confidential dealer service bulletins pave the road to free repairs because they prove that *a part failure is factory related* and *not* normal maintenance; hence, the repair cost should be paid by the dealer and manufacturer, *even if the normal warranty has expired.*

These bulletins are also great guides for warranty inspections (especially the final one). They're written by automakers in "mechanic speak" and are republished in this *Guide* unedited because service managers relate better to them that way and manufacturers can't weasel out of their obligations by claiming that they never wrote such a bulletin.

If your vehicle is out of warranty, show these bulletins to less expensive independent garages to quickly find the trouble, and order the most recent *upgraded* part so that you don't replace one defective part with another.

Because these bulletins are sent out by U.S. automakers, Canadian service managers will sometimes deny, at first, that a bulletin exists; however, when they're shown a copy they usually find the appropriate Canadian part number or DSB in their files. The problem and its solution don't change from one side of the border to another. Imagine American and Canadian tourists being towed across the border because each country's technical bulletins were different. Mechanical fixes do differ in cases where a bulletin is for California only, or relates to a safety or emissions component used only in the U.S. But these cases are rare indeed.

The best way to get DSB-related repairs carried out is by visiting the dealer and showing him the specific DSB covering your vehicle's problems. Direct his attention to all the tech-speak and codes and ask for the Canadian equivalent. If you're refused help:

- Fax the automaker in Canada a copy of the DSB and ask for the appropriate kit or upgraded part number for Canada.
- If the dealer and automaker say that Canadians are excluded, ask why Canadians don't have the same rights as Americans.
- Complain to Transport Canada and your provincial consumer affairs about being refused corrective repairs that are given routinely to American customers.
- Finally, you could visit an American dealer to have the repair carried out during a regularly scheduled vacation trip. Once back in Canada, you can sue the Canadian automaker and its dealer for your costs (including DSB and fax costs) in small claims court, because they gave you the runaround in the first place.

Fuel economy fantasies

Fuel economy figures are supplied by Transport Canada and are based on data supplied by the carmakers who follow U.S. Environmental Protection Administration testing guidelines. These figures can be off by 10 to 20 percent depending on the testing method chosen. In fact, a recent Ford bulletin warns dealers that "very few people will drive in a way that is identical to the EPA tests. . . . These (fuel economy) numbers are the result of test procedures that were originally developed to test emissions, not fuel economy."

If you never quite got the hang of metric fuel economy measurements (like me), use the fuel conversion table below to establish how many miles to a gallon of gas your vehicle provides.

Conversion Table

L/100	m.p.g.	L/100 km	m.p.g.	L/100 km	m.p.g.
5.0	56	7.4	38	12.5	23
5.2	54	7.6	37	13.0	22
5.4	52	7.8	36	13.5	21
5.6	50	8.0	35	14.0	20
5.8	48	8.5	33	15.0	19
6.0	47	9.0	31	15.0	18
6.2	46	9.5	30	17.0	17
6.4	44	10.0	28	18.0	16
6.66	43	10.5	27	19.0	15
6.8	42	11.0	26	20.0	14
7.0	40	11.5	25	21.0	13
7.2	39	12.0	24	23.0	12

Insurance costs

Insurance costs can vary between $500 and $5000 per year, depending on the type of vehicle you own and your own personal statistics and driving habits. Multipurpose vehicles are usually classed in the high-risk category (accident and theft) and therefore usually cost more than passenger cars to insure.

Now that banks are getting into the insurance business they're heating up the competition by offering lower premium payments through independent agents whom they use as go-betweens. The Canadian Imperial Bank of Commerce, for example, says that it offers low insurance premiums by selling directly to the Ontario public, avoiding the 10–12 percent commission that most insurance brokers charge. During its first three and a half weeks of operation, the bank received more than 40,000 inquiries and signed up 1000 customers. The Toronto Dominion Bank also jumped into the Ontario market early last year.

You can cut insurance costs considerably by choosing a vehicle that has the best overall claims record. One good place to find this out is the Vehicle Information Centre of Canada, 175 Commerce Valley Dr. West, Suite 220, Markham, Ontario, L3T 7P6. This non-profit organization has free brochures that show which new and used vehicles have important safety features and how well they perform in real-life accidents reported in Canada.

Rating the dealer network

The more sophisticated and complicated a vehicle's engineering, the more important it is to have service support from the dealer network. Ford Aerostar and GM Astro/Safari minivans, for example, use some old truck technology and so can often be repaired anywhere using parts from independent suppliers. The more complicated VW Eurovan, on the other hand, is severely handicapped by a lack of extensive dealer support.

Sometimes good parts availability exists within a weak dealer body network. This occurs when a vehicle has sold quite well or has been on the market for a long time with few changes, thereby creating a good supply of replacement parts. Nissan/Mercury and Geo/Suzuki dealerships are mutually supportive since they service almost identical vehicles: the Quest and Villager minivans and the Tracker and Sidekick sport-utility vehicles.

Parts and service

Parts for imports are generally no more expensive than parts sold by the major American automakers. But when it comes to captive imports, some American carmakers have been known to charge twice as much for the same part sold by their Japanese partners.

Here are a two tips that may help cut the high cost of repair parts:

- Try to find good-quality rebuilt parts whenever possible. The APA has found that rebuilt parts cost anywhere from one-third to one-half the price of new parts and generally last just as long. A vehicle has to be on the market for at least two years before rebuilt or remanufactured parts become available in sufficient quantities.

- Before authorizing non-warranty repairs at an independent shop, ask the mechanic to compare the parts prices charged by different manufacturers selling the same basic vehicle. For example, a Tracker part may be cheaper at a Suzuki dealership under the Sidekick name than one bought from General Motors.

Even when parts costs aren't deliberately "boosted" by American car manufacturers, prices are unacceptably high. For example, according to the Alliance of American Insurers, the price of original-equipment replacement parts needed to rebuild a multipurpose vehicle is about 2.5 times that of the vehicle's original retail price. In an annual study, a 1991 Jeep Cherokee Sport five-door retailing for $22,000 was rebuilt with Jeep-supplied replacement parts. Total cost? More than $52,000 for the parts alone. No labour was included in the estimate.

Consumers have found that, except for Saturn, American carmakers are more interested in sales than in ensuring that their dealers give honest, competent service. In fact, I can't recall a single occasion where an automaker terminated a dealership's franchise because of odometer tampering or other dishonest dealings, yet the RCMP reports dozens of odometer fraud convictions every year.

A vehicle can incorporate the best engineering in the world, but it will quickly deteriorate and fall into the lemon category if the servicing is lousy, as may be the case with a used Mazda MPV or Chrysler minivan. The servicing problem is more acute with vehicles that are new on the market, and with European and South Korean imports. American manufacturers are generally weak in service support, and General Motors is the best example of this deficiency. Its own records show that 70 percent of its customers switch to other repair outlets when their vehicle warranty expires.

Servicing has been the *bête noire* of European importers. They get low ratings for mishandling customer complaints, inadequate service training, and hiring an insufficient number of service representatives—not to mention the abrasive, arrogant attitude typified by some German automakers and service outlets.

The area where Japanese manufacturers can be faulted most is in the training of service representatives and the delegation of responsibility to them. Service reps are often ill-informed about the strengths and weaknesses of their own products, and their decisions at the service bay level often take an inordinate amount of time to be approved by the head office. Both Mazda and Toyota have admitted that this is a problem and have pledged to make their dealers more sensitive to customer needs, starting this year.

Check servicing costs and the quality of repairs with owners who drive similar models, fleet administrators, and rental car counter attendants. They'll be glad to tell you about servicing problems they've encountered. Be sure to question consumer protection groups about which vehicles generate the most complaints and what mechanical components are the most failure-prone and covered by secret warranties. Owner comments found in online forums and owners' groups listed in collectors' publications and car buff magazines are also helpful in giving you a picture of the overall reliability, parts availability, servicing, and price range for specific models. Remember, the more sophisticated and complicated a vehicle's engineering, the more important it is to have competent service support from the dealer network.

Buying a Reliable Vehicle

The myth of American quality

A lot of controversy surrounds the relative quality control of North American and imported vehicles. Before deciding which manufacturer provides the best quality, forget all the popular mythology about what is made in North America and what is "foreign" made. The see-saw value of the dollar and the yen has led to a rush of foreign automakers moving production facilities to the U.S. and Canada. Surprisingly, this has been accomplished without a corresponding drop in quality control. Toyota's Corolla assembly plant in Cambridge, Ontario, for example, has been rated by J. D. Power and Associates as the highest quality production facility in North America.

Once Mercedes' sport-utility vehicles come on line in Alabama in 1997 a total of ten importers—seven Japanese and three German—will be building "foreign" cars in the U.S. Among the top eight automakers, General Motors has the most vehicles currently being assembled in the U.S. at 83.5 percent, compared to Ford at 81.2 percent and Chrysler at only 66.2 percent. Honda leads the Japanese in having 50.8 percent of its vehicles assembled in the U.S. Adding to the confusion, the North American Free Trade Agreement defines Mexican content as "domestic."

Domestic vs. import

In spite of their improvements over the past several years, American vehicles still don't measure up to the Japanese in quality and technology. This is particularly evident in small pickups, where Toyota, Nissan, and Mazda have the highest reliability and dependability ratings. American firms have copied Japanese production methods and their team approach, but the quality of their vehicles hasn't closed the reliability gap, except in co-ventures like the Ford/Mazda production of the Probe and Ranger, the Nissan/Mercury Villager, or the GM/Suzuki Tracker.

Japanese vehicles are redesigned every three to four years, while American carmakers often wait a decade or longer. The Big Three American automobile manufacturers know that the Japanese and their dealers build, market, and service vehicles to a higher standard than they do. That's why they gave up much of the small 4X4 market to Asian producers in the late 1980s; it was easier and more profitable to buy high-quality Asian products and market them as homegrown.

The yen's roller-coaster ride over the past year and the threat of American trade sanctions have temporarily helped the U.S. auto industry compete with Japanese imports. But no such help is needed in the multipurpose vehicle niche, inasmuch as Asian producers have failed to gain a toehold with minivans, vans, and trucks. Japanese sport-utilities have had excellent sales, but Honda's new Odyssey minivan's sales have been in the basement due to its anemic engine and high cost; sales of existing Japanese minivans are down; and Toyota's four-year-old pickup, the T100, just can't break the GM and Ford truck monopoly in spite of its superior reliability record.

Japanese vehicles are not made better or more quickly because of robotics or overworked, low-salaried workers, as American automakers would like us to believe. Actually, American production costs are now lower than what the Japanese and Europeans pay at home. High manufacturing costs in Japan and Europe (due mostly to high taxes and workers' benefits) are forcing European and Japanese carmakers to locate plants in Canada (a new Honda minivan assembly plant in Ontario is planned for late 1996) and in the U.S., where skilled workers are plentiful. The real reasons for American inferiority are their automakers' inefficient design methods, and production techniques that began with the Model T.

AUTO RANKINGS

***Consumer Reports'* best cars of 1996, based on its testing and reader surveys.**

- Best family sedan — Toyota Camry
- Best inexpensive car — Honda Civic
- Best sport-utility vehicle — Ford Explorer
- Best high-mileage car (fuel economy) — Toyota Tercel
- Most fun to drive — Mazda MX-5 Miata and BMW 318ti hatchback
- Best regardless of price — Mercedes-Benz E320

Results of *Consumer Reports'* auto-reliability surveys for 1995 models, from best to worst:

1. Acura
2. Infiniti
3. Honda
4. Geo
5. Subaru
6. BMW
7. Toyota
8. Mazda
9. Volvo
10. Saturn
11. Nissan
12. Eagle
13. Lexus
14. Lincoln
15. Mercedes
16. Chrysler
17. Oldsmobile
18. Jeep
19. Pontiac
20. Ford
21. Buick
22. Dodge
23. Mercury
24. Plymouth
25. GMC
26. Volkswagen
27. Chevrolet
28. Saab
29. Cadillac

(AP)

European vehicles

European imports have been hit hard by increased Japanese competition throughout all market segments. Even venerable Mercedes-Benz was forced to lay off 30,000 workers several years ago, at the same time that Volkswagen shifted Golf and Fox production to Mexico and Brazil in an effort to beat high labour costs. And it's not only high wages and Japanese competition that have cost jobs. One study suggests that Germany's luxury carmakers are no longer competitive because of their inefficient and costly approach to quality. As well, one MIT report concludes that German carmakers have gotten lazy and now fail to build quality into every step of the production process, as do Japanese manufacturers. Instead, at the end of the assembly line, they waste time and money correcting mistakes that should never have been made in the first place.

In spite of a perceived decline in overall quality, European automakers are still doing quite well because their cars are noted for impressive driving performance, comfort, and a relatively slow rate of depreciation (Audi, Jaguar, Lada, and Saab being the exceptions). Volkswagen has managed to do relatively well by offering a comprehensive warranty and by holding the line on prices in the mid-range where Japanese imports are too pricy and American cars don't perform as well. Luxury and sporty car importers, like BMW and Porsche, have also made a remarkable comeback through price cuts. Peugeot and Fiat have pulled out of the North American market, while Saab and Jaguar losses are paid off by GM and Ford.

European automakers now want some of the high profits and soaring sales of multipurpose vehicles and are consequently doing what was unthinkable a few years ago—launching their own luxury sport-utility and minivan models. Land Rover has already moved into the North American market with its $60,000 U.S. '96 Range Rover and Discovery; Jaguar, a Ford subsidiary, is looking at an Explorer-based luxury SUV selling in the $50,000-plus range; and Mercedes-Benz plans to soon market its All Activity Vehicle, a $35,000 van and sport-utility combo.

Volkswagen's failure-prone and expensive-to-repair Eurovan, on the other hand, hasn't been a serious minivan player for years, and most of VW's pickup variants have been sent back to Europe.

Other Buying Considerations

Front-wheel drive

Front-drives direct engine power to the front wheels, which *pull* the vehicle forward while the rear wheels simply support the rear. The biggest benefit of front-wheel drive (FWD) is foul weather traction. With the engine and transmission up front there's lots of extra weight pressing down on the front-drive wheels, increasing tire grip in snow and on wet pavement. But the weight shifts when you drive up a steep hill or tow a boat or trailer, and you lose the traction advantage.

Although I recommend a number of FWD vehicles in this *Guide*, I don't like them. Granted, front-drives provide a bit more interior room (no transmission hump), more car-like handling, and better fuel economy than do rear-drives, but damage from potholes and fender-benders is usually more extensive, and maintenance costs (especially premature front tire and brake wear) are much higher than with rear drives.

Servicing front-wheel drives can be a real nightmare—and a wallet-buster. Entire steering, suspension, and drivetrain assemblies have to be replaced when only one component is defective. Downtime is considerable, the cost of parts is far too high, and the drivetrain and its components aren't designed for the do-it-yourself mechanic. A new FWD transmission assembly (called a transaxle) can cost about $2000 to repair, compared to $700 for a rear-drive transmission. And having to make such a repair isn't that remote a possibility, particularly if you own a Chrysler minivan or a Ford Sable or Taurus.

Accident repairs are a unique problem. Front-wheel-drive transmissions and steering and suspension components are easily damaged, and alignment difficulties abound. Repair shops need expensive, specialized equipment to align all four wheels and square up a badly smashed unibody chassis. Even if you manage to get all four wheels tracking true the clutch and transaxle can still be misaligned. No wonder many insurance companies prefer to write off an FWD car rather than repair it. And when that happens you wind up eating the difference between what you paid for the vehicle and what the insurance company says your vehicle is worth—minus your deductible, of course.

I also feel that front-drives are unsafe because braking requires a whole new set of reflexes than what we've developed over the years with rear-wheel-drive vehicles. You remember the routine from driving school or from your dad: *When in a skid, pump the brakes lightly and turn into the direction of the skid.* Well, if you pump the brakes of a front-drive in a skid, you've bought the farm.

Let's leave the last word, not to safety researchers and their arcane statistics, but to professional drivers like Alfred LaGasse, executive vice-president of the New York-based International Taxicab and Livery Association. He says that chauffeurs refuse to drive front-wheel-drive vehicles: "The experience of those who've used them has been bad. We have a lot of minor accidents with rear-wheel-drives, but with front-wheel-drive they become serious accidents."

Rear-wheel drive

Rear-drives direct engine power to the rear wheels, which *push* the vehicle forward. The front wheels steer and also support the front of the vehicle. With the engine up front, the transmission in the middle, and the drive axle in the rear, there's plenty of room for larger and more durable drivetrain components. This makes for less crash damage, lower maintenance costs, and higher towing capacities than front-drives.

On the other hand, rear-drives don't have as much weight over the rear wheels as do the front-drives (no, putting cement blocks in the bed or trunk will only void your transmission warranty), and therefore they can't provide as much traction on wet and icy roads unless they're equipped with an expensive traction-control system.

Four-wheel drive

Four-wheel drives direct engine power through a transfer case to all four wheels, which *pull* and *push* the vehicle forward, giving you twice as much traction. The system is activated with either a floor-mounted shift lever or a dashboard button. When the 4X4 drive isn't engaged the vehicle is essentially a rear-drive truck. The large transfer case housing makes the vehicle sit higher, giving you additional ground clearance. Two-wheel RWD vehicles have some of the highest payload and towing capabilities, usually slightly more than four-wheel drives.

Encouraged by the popularity of 4X4 vehicles in North America, many automakers now offer optional four-wheel drive or all-wheel drive on their more moderately priced family sedans, pickups, and minivans—at jacked-up prices. This has created an abundant supply of unsold 4X4 sedans and minivans that are not only overpriced, but promise much more than they actually deliver. Furthermore, customers are quickly turned off by reports of high repair costs, low rust resistance, fragile mechanical components, and government studies that show an increased risk of rollover accidents. Buyers are instead turning to front-drive compacts with manual transmissions and better-traction tires, or two-wheel-drive pickups equipped with winches and large, deep-lugged rear tires.

All-wheel drive

Essentially, this is four-wheel drive *all* the time. Used mostly in minivans, AWD never needs to be deactivated when running over dry pavement and doesn't require a heavy transfer case (although some sport-utilities and pickups do use a special transfer case) that raises ground clearance and cuts fuel economy. AWD-equipped vehicles aren't recommended for off-roading because of their lower ground clearance and their fragile driveline parts that aren't as rugged as four-wheel drive components.

Diesel

Diesel engines become more efficient, and gasoline engines less so, as the engine load increases. This is the main reason why diesels are best used when the driving cycle includes a lot of city driving, with its slow speeds, frequent stops, and long idling times. At full throttle, both engines are essentially equal from a fuel-efficiency standpoint. The gasoline engine, however, leaves the diesel in the dust when it comes to high-speed performance. Many owners of diesel-equipped MPVs are plagued by starting problems, excessive repair costs, and poor road performance. And bear in mind that before the high cost of a diesel purchase can be amortized the average purchaser has to drive between 40,000–50,000 km (25,000–30,000 miles) a year.

What Kind of 1997 Vehicle?

Approximately two-thirds of the vehicles driven on Canadian highways are cars; the rest are multipurpose vehicles that include pickups, trucks, minivans, and vans in all colours, sizes, and body styles. A higher price doesn't guarantee higher quality, or we'd all be driving Jaguars. For example, although you may have your heart set on a luxury import, you may be surprised to learn that some American-built cars can provide as much performance, comfort, and reliability for much less money; or that the same Japanese carmaker offers an almost identical vehicle for a third less under another name (Nissan and Toyota have been playing this game for years with their Infiniti and Lexus models). So compare the advantages and disadvantages of the following vehicle classes, and consider their recommended alternatives, in order to ensure that you get what best suits your driving needs for the cheapest possible price.

Small cars (subcompacts)

Subcompacts are designed for city dwellers who want fuel economy at any price. Mostly front-drives, they offer excellent gas economy (5 to 9.5L/100 km, or 30 to 56 mpg), easy manoeuvrability, and a low retail price. They can carry four passengers, but only two in comfort because rear seating is limited. Engine and road noise are intrusive, and small engines sometimes can't supply enough power to adequately heat the interior or to defrost the windshield. Luggage capacity is minimal. One of the more alarming characteristics of a subcompact's highway performance is its vulnerability to strong lateral winds.

Crash safety is compromised by the small size and weight of these vehicles. Nevertheless, careful engineering for better crashworthiness, and the availability of airbags, have made many subcompacts safer in collisions than some larger cars.

The following small cars are recommended:

Geo Metro
Honda Civic
Mazda Protegé
Nissan Sentra
Suzuki Swift
Toyota Corolla
Toyota Tercel

Compacts

This size of car is a trade-off, providing more comfort and safety with a bit less fuel economy (9.6 to 11.5L/100 km, or 25 to 30 mpg) than a subcompact. These are excellent cars for city and highway driving, since they combine the advantages of a subcompact with those of a larger car and sustain lower-than-average depreciation. Compacts provide adequate passenger space for five people (four in comfort), and a trunk that's usually large enough to meet average baggage requirements. They also stress safety through the use of anti-lock brakes, airbags, transmission/brake interlocks, and three-point seatbelts. Crash protection is well above average.

In this hotly competitive niche, the compact sedan market accounts for 25 percent of all U.S. passenger car sales. The diverse assortment of sedans includes the Ford Contour, Toyota Camry, Honda Accord, and Nissan Altima.

The following compacts are recommended:

Honda Accord **Toyota Camry**
Nissan Altima **VW Golf/Jetta**

Midsize cars

These cars stress comfort and are good highway performers. Gas consumption, however, is high in stop-and-go city driving (14L/100 km or 15 mpg) if a smaller engine isn't chosen. Unfortunately, a smaller powerplant degrades highway performance and overall reliability, and reduces resale value.

Midsize cars offer an interior that can seat six (five in comfort) and that provides lots of space for luggage. High-speed performance isn't spectacular, but piloting the vehicle doesn't require much effort on the driver's part. Gas consumption on the highway may be higher than you'd expect (19L/100 km or 15 to 20 mpg). Crash safety is fair to good, but increased size doesn't always mean better protection.

The following midsize cars are recommended:

Ford Thunderbird/Cougar and Sable/Taurus **Nissan Maxima**
Mazda 929

Large four-door sedans

The quintessential symbol of middle-class motoring, these cars are best suited for extensive highway driving by motorists who can write off relatively high gasoline consumption (19L/100 km, or 15 to 20 mpg), maintenance, and insurance premiums. They fall into two groups: traditional, heavy, V8-equipped rear-drives with mushy suspensions and separate body-on-frame construction; and the more recent, lighter, V6-equipped front-drives embodying unit-body construction. Ford's Crown Victoria/Marquis and GM's Caprice/Roadmaster and Fleetwood are examples of the former, while the Buick LeSabre/Oldsmobile Eighty-Eight and Chrysler LHS/New Yorker are typical of the more contemporary designs.

Owners have to pay a considerable amount of money for these roomy vehicles, but they do deliver comfort, trailer-towing capability (especially the rear-drives), and stability at high speeds. They also depreciate slowly, can usually seat six adults in relative comfort, and incur less damage from front, rear, and side collisions—although recent U.S. government crash tests show that some smaller cars better absorb frontal crash forces.

The Ford Crown Victoria/Grand Marquis/Lincoln Town Car are recommended large sedans.

Sports cars

Sports cars fall into four categories that I have arbitrarily set according to cost and scarcity:

- Entry-level (Mustang, Probe, Camaro, and Talon)
- Mid-level (Honda del Sol and Mazda Miata)
- Upper-level (Chevrolet Corvette and Toyota Supra)
- Exotic-level (Acura NSX, Dodge Viper, Ferrari Testarossa, and Lamborghini DB132-Diablo).

Chrysler's Eagle Talon provides sports car thrills without excessive repair bills.

Common characteristics of sports cars that you're not likely to find touted in brochures are as follows. They're uncomfortably small (cramped interiors can get very warm and there's little cargo space), heavy to steer in city traffic, hard-riding, and difficult to enter and exit. As well, they burn lots of fuel, tend to overheat and stall, offer minimal visibility, are prone to leaks, rattles, and squeaks, and are notoriously unreliable and expensive to service and insure. The sports car market is currently drying up as a result of increased car and fuel prices, the shift in consumer tastes toward sport-utility vehicles, and family cocooning (best exemplified by soaring minivan sales), where a practical family hauler becomes more important than speed and wind blowing through your hair. This means that such marginal sellers as the Acura NSX and Toyota Supra will probably join the discontinued Dodge Stealth, Eagle Laser, Mazda RX-7, Nissan 300SX, Toyota MR2, and Alfa Romeo Spyder during the next few model years. Ford's Mustang and GM's Camaro/Firebird duo will likely benefit the most from this shake-out.

The following sports cars are recommended:

Chrysler Talon	**GM Camaro**	**Mazda MX-6**
Dodge Stealth	**GM Firebird**	**Toyota Celica**
Ford Probe	**Mazda Miata**	

Convertibles

Convertibles went underground for several decades while automakers worked out their crash-safety shortcomings and the motoring public revived its love affair with topless cars. They're now undergoing a resurgence with attractive offerings in almost every marketing niche, including the BMW 318i, Chevrolet Camaro Z28, Ford Mustang GT, Saab 900, and VW Cabrio.

Of this group, the VW Cabrio and Camaro lead the pack with their low initial cost and good reliability/warranty performance. From a safety perspective, the BMW stands out with small rollover bars that deploy automatically if the car flips. Unfortunately, its small 138-hp engine loses steam quickly when mated to an automatic transmission.

The VW and BMW are the most rattle-free ragtops, followed by Saab, Ford's Mustang, and with Chevrolet's Camaro bringing up the rear. Although the Camaro takes top prize for a tacky interior, rattles, and water/wind leaks, its reasonable base price, powerful engine, superior handling, and in-your-face styling more than compensate for body shortcomings.

Luxury cars

Luxury cars fit into two classes, based primarily on price: entry-level models that range from $30,000 to $40,000, and high-end models that can cost a lot more. In the past, the luxury car niche has been a rear-drive market dominated by the Cadillac DeVille and Fleetwood, Ford Lincoln Town Car and Continental, and Chrysler Imperial. During the past two decades, however, buyers have gravitated toward Japanese and European front-drive models. This shift in buyer preference has forced GM, Ford, and Chrysler to downsize and adopt front-drive.

In considering a luxury car, buy equipment and not a nameplate. Most luxury cars are overpriced, yet give you the same level of equipment found on other, less expensive, fully equipped models sold by the same manufacturer. These cheaper versions offer many other advantages: parts are more easily found and priced competitively, and mechanics are more familiar with cars they've been repairing for some time. This is the case with the Nissan Maxima and Toyota Camry. When fully loaded, they offer practically all the features that the Lexus and Infiniti provide but for almost one-third less. Ford's all-equipped Taurus and Sable also compete very well with most luxury cars, and provide an airbag for both the driver and front seat passenger.

Entry-level European and Japanese luxury models have a lower 17–25 percent dealer markup, primarily because increased Japanese competition is cutting into European sales and Asian automakers are compensating for a fluctuating yen by cutting dealer profits.

Luxury Car Markups

Cadillac	26-28+%
Lincoln	27-30%
Infiniti	25-30%

Lexus 25-29%
Audi 23-30%
BMW 17-30%
Mercedes 23-30%

Mercedes and BMW have been particularly successful in holding the line or lowering retail prices by cutting dealer profit margins and using North America as an export base in the future. Audi has a fairly negative image in terms of safety (sudden acceleration), poor reliability (consumer reports) and high parts costs (confirmed by CAA annual surveys). Infiniti and Lexus, however, have a higher degree of overall customer satisfaction and a much lower rate of depreciation. Remember, price is never an infallible indication of quality. Jaguar and Saab build some of the most problem-plagued vehicles on the planet, and even the venerable Rolls-Royce has been hit by a number of lawsuits alleging serious factory-related defects.

Most American-made luxury cars are not as reliable as Japanese models, but they are generally safer in accidents than smaller vehicles, can be repaired almost anywhere, and are often sold for much less than list price. In fact, both Ford and Chrysler have just announced major price cuts on their '97 large-size and luxury cars. Ford's Lincoln-Mercury division says prices for this year's Continental will be slashed almost $2000, while its new Mark VIII will cost only $800 more. GM, on the other hand, has raised prices by about $1200 on its '97 Cadillac Eldorado and Seville lines. GM's dealers are still shaking their heads in disbelief.

European luxury cars are far more comfortable and driver-responsive than American vehicles; however, their prices aren't discounted as often, they aren't easy to service, and parts are relatively rare. The Japanese luxury models have the best overall record for reliability, and their interior ergonomics are outstanding from a comfort and convenience standpoint.

The following luxury cars are recommended:

Acura Legend/TL	**Lincoln Town Car**	**Mercedes 300 series**
Infiniti series	**Mazda 929**	**Nissan Maxima**
Lexus series	**Mazda Millenia**	**Toyota Avalon**

Multipurpose vehicles (minivans, vans, pickups, and 4X4s)

Unlike passenger vehicles, you're likely to spend a lot more money than you'd expect since advertised prices don't include many of the must-have optional features that give MPVs their full utility. Expect to pay an additional 30 percent or more over the advertised price to make your new sport-utility, minivan, van, or truck as convenient and practical as the automakers promise. This means that a $20,000 base price for a bare-bones model can easily escalate to $27,000 for a model with essential—not lavish—performance and convenience features.

Second, take the phrase "car-like handling" with a large grain of salt. Since many of the rear-drive models are built upon a modified truck chassis and use steering and suspension components from their truck divisions, they tend to handle more like trucks than cars despite automakers' claims to the contrary. What you see is not necessarily what you get when you buy or lease a new 4X4, van, or pickup, because multipurpose vehicles seldom come with enough standard features to fully exploit their versatility.

Additional options are usually a prerequisite in order to make them safe and comfortable to drive. Consequently, the term "multipurpose" is a misnomer unless you're prepared to spend multi-bucks to outfit your 4X4, van, or pickup. And even when they're fully equipped these vehicles don't always provide the performance that's touted by automakers.

Front-drives handle better than rear-drives, but the size and weight of MPVs still require a whole new set of driving skills when cornering under moderate speeds, parking, or turning. A moment's inattention can easily lead to a deadly rollover, and the advent of ABS has made drivers so overconfident that they tend to exceed their driving skills or go way beyond their vehicle's safety/performance capabilities.

In addition to fewer designed-in safety features than a car (a gap that will be closed in 1997), heating-defrosting-AC is often inadequate and requires additional optional equipment, the ride can be quite rough without buying an optional suspension, and handling can be tricky. Fuel economy is atrocious with the full-size models.

Third, depreciation savings can be wiped out by higher insurance and maintenance costs (especially with full-size models) and by exorbitant fuel costs. ABS and 4X4 drivetrain components are particularly failure-prone, hard to troubleshoot, and expensive to replace. Consumers Union also confirms that body hardware (windows, locks, doors, trim, etc.), brakes, and shocks tend to fail or wear out sooner on minivans and sport-utility vehicles than on passenger vehicles. Your best protection is to make sure that you know what you need and that you choose a minivan rated in Part Three of this *Guide* as having the lowest rate of depreciation and highest quality/dependability.

Cutting Through the Options Jungle

Dealers make three times as much profit selling options as they do selling most cars (50 percent vs. 15 percent). No wonder their eyes light up when you start perusing their options list. If you must have some options, compare prices with independent retailers and buy where the price is lowest and the warranty is the most comprehensive. Buy as few options as possible from the dealer, since you'll get faster service, more comprehensive guarantees, and lower prices from independent suppliers. Remember, extravagantly equipped vehicles hurt your pocketbook in three ways: they cost more to begin with, they cost more to maintain, and they often consume extra fuel.

Saver or spender? Know your options.

The options you choose in the showroom will affect your car's fuel efficiency for life.

Fuel-saving Options	Options with Little or No Effect on Fuel Economy	Options that Increase Fuel Consumption
• small engine	• space-saver spare tire	• high-performance engine
• small turbocharged engine	• exterior trim packages	• turbocharged V8 engine
• manual transmission	• tinted glass (on cars without air conditioning)	• 4-barrel carburetor on a V8 engine
• overdrive (manual or automatic)	• heavy-duty suspension	• four-wheel drive
• diesel engine		• power brakes
• cruise control		• power steering
• fuel injection		• air conditioning
• fuel economy reminders (shift indicator lights)		• power windows and seats
• block heater, preferably with timer		• heated seats
		• sun roof
		• roof rack

Before buying options separately, consider getting a vehicle in a higher trimline or in a "special edition" format, where the options package includes what you want for a lower price. Another possibility is "value pricing," where automakers like GM will offer a package of options on a bare-bones model. Whichever choice you make, don't buy any unnecessary options if the total cost of the package exceeds what you'd pay for the options if purchased separately.

A heavy-duty battery and suspension and perhaps an upgraded sound system will generally suffice for most multipurpose vehicles; imports already come well equipped. An engine block heater isn't a bad idea, either. It's an inexpensive investment that ensures winter starting. Factory installed in-line heaters are usually more efficient and durable.

It's hard to buy a new vehicle that isn't loaded with unnecessary options. This is particularly evident with sports cars and MPVs. If you're unsure as to what equipment is available on a particular model, don't take the dealer's word for it. Shop around and compare prices with independent suppliers like J. C. Whitney. Their mail order parts catalogue can be ordered by calling 312-431-6102 (Visa and Mastercard accepted).

Smart Options

Air conditioning

Whether or not you choose air conditioning should depend more on where you live and your comfort requirements than on saving money.

Just like buying an underpowered car to save on fuel costs and then regretting its poor performance, your savings will be the last thing on your mind when you're sweltering in your vehicle some summer day.

Air conditioning costs between $800 and $1650, plus a $100 federal excise tax, and may reduce fuel economy by as much as 13 percent. It provides extra comfort, reduces wind noise from not having to roll down the windows, and improves window defogging. But because air conditioning units aren't used year-round they're failure-prone (expect repairs to cost about $1500 during the first five years), easy prey for premature corrosion, and an excellent incubator for airborne bacteria and allergens. If you must have air conditioning, opt for a factory-installed unit. You'll get a longer warranty and reduce the chance that other mechanical components will be damaged during installation.

Anti-lock brakes (ABS)

Anti-lock brakes prevent the wheels from locking when the brakes are applied in an emergency situation, thus reducing skidding and the loss of directional control. An ABS-equipped vehicle is therefore able to stop more quickly under certain road conditions and in a straight line—but it won't necessarily stop you in a shorter distance. This has led to studies showing that the effectiveness of ABS in preventing collisions may be overrated.

On dry pavement, a trained driver can outperform ABS using a technique called "threshold braking," where you feel the brakes beginning to lock and ease up on them before reapplying them again. On wet pavement, braking is so chancy that ABS will outperform threshold braking nearly every time.

Carmakers have created the impression that cars equipped with ABS will stop on a dime, but they don't fully explain how ABS should be used. For example, many drivers don't know that anti-lock brakes require that they do what driving schools have told them not to do—slam on the brakes in a skid.

A particularly important feature of ABS is that it preserves steering control. As you brake near the limit and turn the wheel, ABS will release the brakes if it senses steering-triggered lockup, and back off on the percentage of the time that the brakes are applied. Braking distances will lengthen accordingly, but at least you'll have some steering control. On the other hand, if you start sliding on glare ice, don't expect ABS to help you out very much. The laws of physics, particularly the coefficient of friction, still apply even on ABS-equipped vehicles.

The high cost of ABS maintenance is one disadvantage that few safety advocates mention, but consider the following: 1) original equipment parts costs can run five times higher than regular braking components; and 2) most manufacturers explicitly forbid the use of non-corrosive DOT-5 (silicone) brake fluids in ABS-equipped vehicles. Therefore, to prevent corrosion, the brake fluid needs to be replaced annually.

Although long-term ABS reliability still remains unproven, this is one option that can be a lifesaver. In fact, studies show that while the average driver will go eleven years before having a serious collision involving the deployment of an airbag, anti-lock brakes will probably be required once a year to avoid a serious collision.

Insurance claims, however, aren't very supportive of assertions that ABS prevents collisions. The Washington-based Highway Loss Data Institute's study of identical vehicles equipped and not equipped with ABS found that the frequency of collision claims and their cost were not reduced with ABS. Other studies do show a decrease in crashes, varying between 8 percent (the Markham, Ontario-based Vehicle Information Centre) and 3 percent (General Motors) depending on the road conditions. In view of these conflicting studies, insurance companies are backing away from premium reductions for ABS-equipped vehicles.

Transport Canada is concerned about the hype surrounding ABS effectiveness. Its tests indicate that the safety benefits may be compromised by drivers who are less cautious and who tend to drive more aggressively than others. They accelerate more quickly, drive faster, and apply the brakes later than do drivers using vehicles without anti-lock brakes. This contention was confirmed by a paper presented at the 1993 Proceeding of the Multidisciplinary Road Safety Conference, which concluded that drivers of vehicles equipped with ABS drove up to 8 km/h faster than did people whose cars were not ABS-equipped.

Although the jury is still out in assessing the degree of ABS effectiveness, it's still a viable safety feature when used correctly and in harsh climatic conditions. For maximum effectiveness, it's important that you use the same size and type of tire on all four wheels; otherwise the ABS computer can get confused.

Anti-theft systems

Car break-ins and thefts cost Canadians more than $400 million annually, meaning there's a 1 in 130 chance that your car will be stolen and only a 60 percent chance that you'll ever get it back. No wonder that over one-third of new vehicles are equipped with standard or optional alarms, with a clear preference for fuel cut-off devices and electronic alarms among the four main types of security systems: active and passive units either armed by the driver or self-arming; ignition disablers; parts identification; and security keys.

The most effective theft-deterrent systems are not always the most expensive ones. Don't waste your money on costly anti-theft devices that depend solely upon your car's horn or lights to scare thieves away. They often go off at the wrong time and can be easily deactivated. Furthermore, they frighten the thief away only after the vehicle has been damaged. When it comes to stealing your car's contents, no alarm system can resist a brick through a side window. It takes just twelve minutes for thieves to strip a car seat, radio, and body parts, and few citizens are brave enough to personally stop a theft or testify in court. Your best protection is discretion: take your radio with you or lock it in the trunk, particularly if you own a Japanese or German car with an upgraded sound system.

Steering locks are crude, but they're effective and relatively inexpensive.

Since most cars are stolen by amateurs, the best theft deterrent is a visible device that complicates the job while immobilizing the vehicle and sounding an alarm. For less than $150, you can install both a steering wheel lock and a hidden remote-controlled ignition disabler. These clublike devices cost between $50 and $75, and deter thieves by forcing them to carry a hacksaw and adding about a half-minute to the time it takes to steal the average car (they have to cut through the steering wheel or bust the lock). The Winner's Club is an inexpensive steering wheel lock distributed by Superex (416-497-2850). It's a huge bar that locks the steering wheel without any need to rewire or make other modifications. If your vehicle is stolen, Superex will pay the deductible up to $500. The Nightstick, another steering lock, is carried by Canadian Tire.

Ignition disablers are also inexpensive and very effective. They sell for $30 to $90, depending on their sophistication. The *Electronic Cop* sells for $89.95 and can be purchased from Sequel Security Systems, 853 Sanders Road, Box 278, Northbrook IL 60062 (1-800-215-4100).

Auxiliary lighting

Essential only for serious off-roaders, extra lighting improves safety and makes night driving less fatiguing. In the city, it's a pain in the butt to other drivers who are constantly blinded by the lights' intensity and high placement. Lights should employ strong halogen bulbs, mounted high out of harm's way.

Battery (heavy duty)

The best battery for northern climates is the optional heavy-duty type offered by many manufacturers for about $80. It's a worthwhile purchase, especially for MPVs equipped with lots of electrical options. Most standard batteries last only two winters.

Block heater

Costing about $75, a block heater is an inexpensive investment. Factory-installed in-line models are effective and durable.

Cellular telephone

This is a recommended option mainly because it provides a greater degree of safety for drivers stuck on the side of the road or threatened by smash-and-grab artists. Buy the cheapest hands-free model available from an independent retailer.

The cellular radio telephone industry developed in the late 1970s in response to an intense demand for scarce mobile communication frequencies. The telephone works by sending radio waves to a cell site that's hooked up to a wire-based telephone network. More than a half-million Canadians use cellular phones, bringing about lower prices with the increased competition in phone hardware. After-market units bought through independent suppliers cost less than dealer-supplied phones.

Cellular phones are expensive to operate due to the high rates charged by the phone companies to "carry" calls. Because calls are billed by the minute and according to the distance the caller or receiver is from a given site, charges can vary from $250 to $1000-plus a month for a sales agent who uses it extensively. The temptation to use the car phone for nonessential calls is also hard to resist and expensive in the long run. The average monthly cost for personal calls is about $125. And remember that what's said on a cellular phone can be heard by anyone.

Car phones are a known safety hazard. The American Automobile Association Foundation for Traffic Safety says that a road hazard is 20 to 30 percent more likely to go unnoticed by someone using a car phone than by a driver who gives full attention to driving. This warning is buttressed by another study done at the Rochester Institute of Technology in Rochester, New York, which found that drivers with cellular phones installed in their vehicles run a 34 percent greater risk of having an accident than other motorists. The AAA foundation recommends that drivers use a hands-free phone and keep calls to a minimum.

This console-mounted, dual mode, voice-activated unit is offered by Cadillac.

If the possibility of crashing into someone or contracting brain cancer isn't scary enough (several lawsuits have been filed and lost), how about cellular phones that are real heart-stoppers? The U.S. government is looking into allegations that people with heart pacemakers implanted in their chests may experience pacemaker malfunctions as a result of their cell phones. Safety researchers say that if the phone is placed in close proximity to the chest it may cause the pacemaker to stop, restart, or recalibrate itself. The problem is more apparent with the new digital cellular phones than with the older analog models now most commonly used.

As well, cellular phones aren't particularly efficient in placing emergency calls through the 911 exchange. Rather than going to a central dispatch centre where the caller's location is indicated on-screen, cell phone calls are often routed to other, distant places where staffers may be unfamiliar with the area from which the call originates.

Central locking control

Costing a couple hundred dollars, this option is most useful for families with small children, car poolers, or drivers of multipurpose vehicles who can't slide across the seat to lock the other doors. Look for a remote feature that provides automatic locking and then unlocking when the inside door handle is pulled.

Child safety seat (integrated)

Designed to accommodate any child more than one year old, or weighing over 20 pounds, a child safety seat that's permanently integrated into the seatback takes the fuss out of installing and removing the safety seat and finding some place to store it. When not in use, it quickly folds away out of sight—becoming part of the seatback. Most factory-integrated child seats use a 3-point harness system, but GM's Lumina sedan and Chrysler's '96 minivans employ a 5-point system with a single belt connector that distributes crash forces more evenly across a child's body.

Courtesy lights

This option permits the car's lights to stay on a few seconds after the doors are closed. This is particularly convenient when entering your home if the only outside source of illumination is your car's headlights.

Cruise control

Another convenience feature, automakers provide this $250 to $300 option to motorists who use their vehicles for long periods of high-speed driving. Some fuel is saved due to the constant rate of speed, and driver fatigue is reduced during long trips. Still, the system is particularly failure-prone and expensive to repair, and it can lead to driver inattention and make the vehicle hard to control on icy roadways. As well, malfunctioning cruise control units are one of the major causes of sudden acceleration incidents. Make sure that your vehicle has a transmission/brake interlock before investing in cruise control.

Engines

Choose the most powerful 6-cylinder engine or smallest 8-cylinder available if you're going to be doing a lot of highway driving, or if you plan to carry a full passenger load and luggage on a regular basis. The determining factor for any optional engine choice is the amount of heavy hauling or pulling that the vehicle will perform.

Engine and transmission cooling system (heavy duty)

This relatively inexpensive option provides extra cooling for the transmission and engine. It can extend the life of these components by preventing overheating when heavy towing is required.

Keyless entry (remote)

A safety and convenience option. You don't need to fiddle with the key in a dark parking lot or take off a glove in cold weather to unlock/lock the vehicle. Try to get a keyless entry system combined with anti-theft measures that include an ignition kill-switch or some other disabler.

Mirror options

Power mirrors are particularly convenient on vehicles that have a number of drivers, or on large sedans and wagons, minivans, vans, or trucks.

Paint

Acrylic lacquer or urethane is a good choice. Both are bright, tough, and easily touched up. Clearcoats can be difficult to match. Horizontal stripes help to conceal dings and scratches. Metallic paint is a $300 decorative option that's often poorly applied, expensive, and difficult to match if the car needs some repainting as a result of early rusting or minor collision damage.

Power-assisted windows and seats

Merely a convenience feature with cars, power-assisted windows and seats are a necessity with minivans—crawling across the front seat a few times to roll up the passenger-side window or to lock the doors will quickly convince you of their value. Power seats with memory are particularly useful if a vehicle is driven by more than one person. Automatic window and seat controls currently have few reliability problems, and they're fairly inexpensive to install, troubleshoot, and repair.

Sound system

Remember when it was just called a radio?

A car's sound system may offer a lot of bells and whistles, including an AM/FM radio, cassette, and CD player along with the requisite speakers and amplifiers. Enjoy some real savings by purchasing a complete sound system from an independent retailer. Standard sound systems supplied in moderately priced new vehicles are usually mediocre (GM Delco radios are particularly bad), and their buttons are too complex and way too small for precise tuning. Some welcome exceptions to this rule are the optional systems sold by Bose and Blaupunkt.

When buying a sound system three criteria must be considered: your overall budget, the make of car, and the kind of music that's likely to be played. A simple AM/FM stereo radio with a stereo cassette tape player is sold by GM for less than $500, but most independent aftermarket stores can easily beat GM's price. Sophisticated, personalized car stereos may cost between $500 and $1000, and hi-fi fanatics can spend between $2000 and $9000 for a "total sound system." In addition to getting the best quality sound for the cheapest price, the stereo buyer should look for features that make it easy and safe to operate; for example, radios that automatically seek out stations and cassette decks with automatic reverse, play, and eject.

In budgeting for a stereo sound system, allocate half the money for the speakers. Pare down the scores of available features to what's essential, like a strong FM receiver (under two decibels), separate controls for treble and bass, auto reverse, and a key-auto-eject to protect the tape when the ignition is turned on and off.

The cheapest quality stereo system capable of being upgraded will cost about $250. A stable digital system may cost twice as much, including installation. When installation is charged separately, it should cost about $75. Insist upon listening to the speakers in an audio booth before checking out the system's other features. Many times the "perfect" sound you hear in a showroom will sound less than perfect when played in a new car. This deformation is caused by the acoustical character of each car. Blaupunkt has come up with a $300 solution to this problem with its PSA-108 amplifier and plug-in module that adjust the system's frequency response to the requirements of more than 83 different vehicles. Manipulate the controls to see if proper speaker balance can be achieved with a minimum of effort. Choose components for expandability, compatibility, ease of servicing, and their guarantee. Check out whether repair parts are available and reasonably priced.

CD players

Sales of car CD players exceed a million units annually, including at least 140 separate models. Mail-order discount houses offer them for less than $300. Improved vibration dampening has made the players impervious to potholes. Look for:

- repeat functions that allow you to select a mixture of tracks or repeat a particular track
- anti-theft features that include removing the faceplate or unit
- a CD changer that's mounted in the trunk, which allows you to play many different CD discs.

Speakers

If your factory speakers lack power handling, efficiency, and dynamic range, swap them for after-market units. If the basic stereo player isn't up to par either, buy a new head unit incorporating a noise reduction system, auto reverse, separate bass and treble controls, and AM/FM with electronic presets. Pioneer's KEH 5200 model offers all these features and much more (pre-amp outputs, CD changer, auxiliary output, 25 watts of power, and portability) for about $350.

Factory-installed speakers are usually lousy performers, and options are outrageously priced by carmakers. For example, an after-market CD player priced at $400 would cost about $1200 if installed by the factory or dealer. Dealers often say that only the factory's original equipment can overcome electrical interference or provide the appropriate sound for a vehicle's particular interior configuration. This is baloney.

There are, however, some advantages to having a factory-installed sound system. It's usually guaranteed for a much longer period than an independently installed unit, and the dealer is better equipped than a retailer to remove, ship, and reinstall it. A factory unit will also be more cosmetically attractive and less prone to rattle because it fits better when mounted in the dash and door panels.

Once a stereo system has been purchased, it must be protected from theft. Experts recommend the installation of a slider box for about $80 to $100. It's the size of a textbook and connects the cassette player and radio to the car's wiring when pushed into place. When the car is parked, the box and unit stereo can be removed from the vehicle.

Steering wheel (adjustable)

This option facilitates access to the driver's seat and permits a more comfortable driving position. It's particularly useful if a vehicle will be driven by more than one person.

Suspension (heavy duty)

Always a good idea, this inexpensive option pays for itself in providing additional ride comfort and in extending shock life an extra year or two.

Tires

There are three rules to remember when purchasing tires: First, neither brand nor price is a reliable gauge of performance, quality, or durability. Second, choosing a tire recommended by the automaker may not be in your best interest, since traction and long tread life are often sacrificed for a softer ride and maximum EPA mileage ratings. And third, don't buy any new tire that's older than two years, since the rubber compound may have deteriorated due to poor handling and improper storage (near electrical motors). You can check the date of manufacture on the sidewall.

There are two types of tires: all-season and performance. Touring is just a fancier name for all-season tires. All-season radial tires cost between $90 and $150. They're a compromise, since according to Transport Canada they won't get you through winter with the same margin of safety as will snow tires, and they don't provide the same durability on dry surfaces as do regular summer tires. In low to moderate snowfall areas, however, these tires are adequate as long as they're not pushed beyond their limits.

Mud or snow tires provide the best traction on snowy surfaces, but traction on wet roads is actually decreased. Tread wear is also accelerated by the use of softer rubber compounds. Beware of using wide tires for winter driving; 70-series or wider give poor traction and tend to "float" over snow. Consumers report good performance with Nokia Hakkapellitas snow tires imported from Finland.

Performance tires have a low sidewall profile and a wider and shallower tread. They give good wet and dry traction, but perform poorly on snow and ice. They also wear quickly and tend to give a hard ride. Remember, some sports cars can't be fitted with snow tires unless the rims are changed or a more expensive brand is chosen.

It's a good idea to purchase tires that provide a road hazard warranty. Under the terms of this guarantee the tire dealer or manufacturer will provide compensation for any tire that's found to be defective. Also, don't pay full list for any tire; just as with autos, prices vary considerably among retailers. Make sure, though, that the price includes mounting and balancing. Tire dealers are the best place to find a wide selection of tire brands, models, and sizes, and their salespeople are usually more knowledgeable than they are at dealerships, discount houses, or gas stations.

Which tires are best?

There is no independent Canadian agency that evaluates tire performance and durability. However, the NHTSA has been providing this information for the past decade through tests that rate tread wear, traction, and resistance to sustained high temperatures. The tread wear grade is fixed at a base 100 points and the tire's wear rate is measured after the tire is driven through a course that approximates most driving conditions. A tire rated at 300 will last three times as long as one rated 100.

The following tire ratings come from government tests, consumer comments, and industry insiders.

Goodyear Aquatred: Treadware rated 340, traction A, temperature B. A bit noisy, higher-rolling resistance cuts fuel economy. On the market for three years. Uses a deep, V-shaped water groove down the middle of the tire to dissipate water to each side. Exceptional on wet roads, and works especially well on front-drive cars where the weight is over the front tires. Average performance on dry pavement. Costs about $130; no discounts.

Michelin MX4: Treadware rated 320, traction A, temperature B. Smooth ride and a sharper steering response than Aquatred. Cost: $144 list; often discounted to $100.

Pirelli P300: Treadware rating 460, traction A, temperature B. Above average performer. Cost: $173 list; sells for about $120.

Toyo 800 Plus: Treadware rating 520, traction A, temperature B. A

high-mileage touring tire. Noisy when cornering. Hard ride probably due to high-mileage construction. Doesn't track well when pushed. Six year/unlimited mileage warranty. Cost: $140 list; sells for about $100.
Dunlop D65: Treadware rating 520, traction A, temperature B. The bargain of the group. Corners well, excellent wet braking, good steering response, wanders a great deal over ruts or rough terrain. 128,000 km warranty. Cost: $146 list; sells for $100.
General Hydro 2000: An Aquatred knock-off. Tends to wander over rough terrain. Cost: $142 list; discounted to $100.
Firestone FR680: Treadware rated 400, traction A, temperature B. Substandard wet road performance, firm ride, good dry grip, and quick steering response. 110,000 km limited treadware warranty, and four years of Firestone's Road Hazard Protection. Cost: $149 list; sells for less than $100.

J. D. Power publishes an annual "Original Equipment Tire Satisfaction Study" that rates owners' experiences with tires that were original equipment on their new vehicles. The 1993 survey found that seven of the twelve tiremakers rated failed to meet the industry average for satisfaction. They were (in alphabetical order): Bridgestone, Continental, Dunlop, General, Toyo, Uniroyal, and Yokohama.

Michelin and Pirelli scored highest, while B. F. Goodrich, Firestone, and Goodyear posted average scores. Specific tire models singled out for kudos were the Bridgestone Potenza RE71; Goodyear Eagle GS-C and Eagle GT+4; Michelin MXT4, XGT4, MXV4 (not recommended for driving in the snow), XW4, and XZ4; and Pirelli P5 and P2000.

Trailer-towing equipment

Just because you need a vehicle with towing capability doesn't mean that you have to spend big bucks. The first thing you should do when choosing a towing option is determine if a pickup or small van will do the job and if your tires will handle the extra burden. For most towing needs (up to 900 kg or 2000 lbs.), a passenger vehicle, small pickup, or minivan will work just as well and cost much less than a full-size pickup or van. But if you're pulling a trailer that weighs more than 2000 lbs., most passenger vehicles won't handle the load unless they've been specially outfitted according to the automaker's specifications. Pulling a trailer that weighs more (up to 1800 kg or 4000 lbs.) will likely require a compact passenger van. A full-size van can handle up to 4500 kg (10,000 lbs.), and may be cheaper and more versatile than a multipurpose vehicle that would have to be equipped with a V8 engine and heavy-duty chassis components.

Don't trust the towing limit found in the owner's manual. Carmakers publish tow ratings that are on the optimistic side, and sometimes they're outright wrong.

Carmakers reserve the right to change limits whenever they feel like it, so make any sales promise an integral part of your contract (see "Misrepresentation" in Part Three). A good rule of thumb is to reduce the promised tow rating by 20 percent. In assessing towing weight, consider the cargo, passengers, and equipment of both the trailer and the tow vehicle. Keep in mind that five people and luggage add 450 kg (1000 lbs.) and that a full 227-litre (50 gallon) water tank adds another 225 kg (500 lbs.) to the load. The manufacturer's gross vehicle weight rating (GVWR) takes into account the anticipated average cargo and supplies that your vehicle is likely to carry.

Automatic transmissions are fine for trailering, although there's a slight fuel penalty to pay. Manual transmissions tend to have greater clutch wear from towing than automatic transmissions. Both transmission choices are equally durable if the driver is competent. Ford and Chevrolet/GMC give higher tow ratings to their trucks with automatics than to those with manual transmissions—they know that drivers tend to ride the clutch and generally screw up shifting with a manual. Remember, the best compromise is to shift the automatic manually for maximum performance going uphill, and to maintain control while not overheating the brakes when descending mountains.

Unit-body vehicles (without a separate frame) can handle most trailering jobs as long as their limits aren't exceeded. Front-drives aren't the best choice for pulling heavy loads in excess of 2000 pounds. They lose some steering control and traction with all the weight concentrated in the rear.

Whatever vehicle you choose, keep in mind that the trailer hitch is crucial. It must have a tongue capacity of at least 10 percent of the trailer's weight, otherwise it may be unsafe to use. Hitches are chosen according to the type of tow vehicle and, to a lesser extent, the weight of the load. They fall into the following four classes depending on the weight they can pull:

- Class 1: loads up to 900 kg (2000 lbs.); hooked to the frame or rear bumper of most passenger cars, small pickups, and small vans.
- Class 2: loads up to 1600 kg (3500 lbs.); attached to a car or MPV frame.
- Class 3: loads up to 3400 kg (7500 lbs.); also attached to a car or MPV frame.
- Class 4: loads up to 4500 kg (10,000 lbs.); attached to a pickup or MPV frame or incorporated as fifth-wheel hitches used in the beds of large pickups.

Most hitches are factory installed, even though independents can put them on more cheaply. Expect to pay about $200 for a simple boat hitch and a minimum of $600 for a fifth-wheel version.

Equalizer bars and extra cooling systems for the radiator, transmission, engine oil, and steering are a prerequisite for towing anything heavier than 2000 pounds. Heavy-duty springs and brakes are a big help, too. Separate brakes for the trailer may be necessary to increase your vehicle's maximum towing capacity.

Don't take the dealer's word that a vehicle is capable of pulling a particular trailer. Make the claim a condition of the sale by putting it in the sales contract. Check all claims with the trailer manufacturer for an independent assessment of your vehicle's capabilities.

Transmission: automatic, manual, 5-speed, and overdrive automatic
Most motorists prefer to pay extra to have a transmission that shifts by itself. Nevertheless, this convenience cuts fuel economy, saps the performance of small engines, requires expensive repairs, and makes you less alert to driving conditions. This last point is particularly important, because a manual transmission makes you aware of the traffic flow and requires that you shift gears in anticipation of changes. It demands that you be in total control of the vehicle and results in safer driving.

Dumb Options

Adjustable ride control
Touted as allowing the driver to adjust the ride and handling to all road conditions, this option does very little and can be costly to repair.

Automatic level control
A useless option unless you're planning to carry heavy loads or pull a trailer. It's expensive to repair and not easily adjusted.

Bumper strips and bumper guards
Merely decorative items that give very little real protection from fender-bender accidents.

Electronic instrument read-out
If you've ever had trouble reading a digital watch face or re-setting your VCR you'll feel right at home with this electronic gizmo. Gauges are presented in a series of moving digital patterns that are confusing, distracting, and unreadable in direct sunlight. Often accompanied by a trip computer and a vehicle monitor that computes fuel use and kilometres to empty, indicates average speed, and signals component failures. Figures are frequently in error or slow to catch up.

Foglamps
A pain in the eyes for other drivers, foglamps aren't necessary for most drivers with well-aimed original-equipment headlamps.

Gas-saving gadgets/fuel additives
Because full-sized SUVs, vans, and trucks are notorious fuel-burners, the accessory market has been flooded with hundreds of gas-saving gadgets and fuel additives that purport to make these vehicles less fuel-thirsty. There isn't one on the Canadian market that works, according to Transport Canada, and the use of any of these products is a quick way to render your warranty invalid.

Leather upholstery
An expensive option that's too hot in summer, too cold in winter, too slippery, and tough to clean or repair.

Paint and fabric protectors
The auto industry's equivalent of the "Emperor's New Clothes," I wouldn't give two cents for paint protector products sold by car dealers. Selling for $200 to $300, these "sealants" are a waste of money and add nothing to a vehicle's resale value. Although paint lustre may be temporarily heightened, this treatment is less effective and more costly than regular waxing, and may also invalidate the manufacturer's guarantee.

According to tests carried out by the Consumers' Association of Canada and the Quebec Consumer Protection Bureau, waxing your vehicle regularly is a much better idea than investing in paint protectors. Certain waxes are better than others, as shown in CAC field tests; Nu Finish gave good paint protection for three to six months after each application and did very well in bringing out paint lustre. Surprisingly, Turtle Wax was one of the poorer performers in the CAC study.

Fabric protectors are nothing more than Scotchguard variations, which can be bought in aerosol cans for a few dollars, instead of the $50 to $75 charged by dealers.

Radar detectors and "stealth" devices
Another product that targets van vacationers and sports car enthusiasts, radar detectors are a dumb idea for two reasons: they're illegal in most provinces and most U.S. states and, in many cases, they don't work. The newest wrinkle is an electronic "stealth" cloaking device that claims to generate a frequency that confuses police radar and laser guns. Mounted on the front end of the vehicle, the $400 (tax and installation included) device failed every test carried out by the *Vancouver Province.* Even if it were effective, motorists would have to buy one for the rear end as well since many laser guns are trained on vehicles after they've gone by.

"Rainsense" wiper system
A standard feature on the Cadillac STS, and soon to be offered as an option on other cars, this system automatically activates the wipers in inclement weather. Wipers accelerate, decelerate, pause, and return to Park automatically without driver interface. This is all done by an electronic controller module located on the windshield next to the inside rear view mirror. It senses moisture on the windshield when the infrared beams emitted by the module are deflected by moisture on the windshield surface.

Two questions: Does this device solve a problem that doesn't exist? And I wonder how long it'll last against squeegee-wielding windshield "cleaners" found at some traffic intersections.

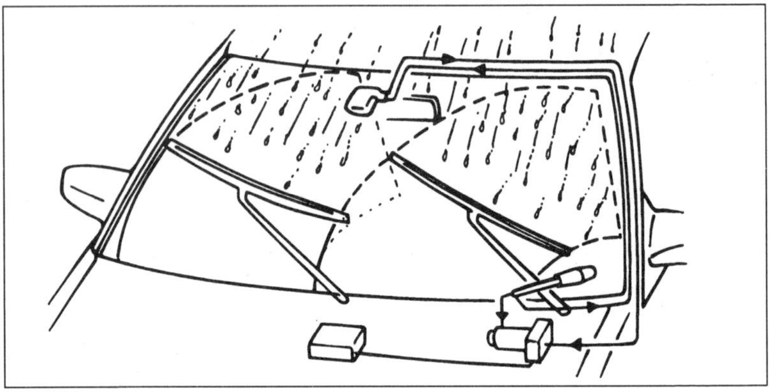

"Rainsense" is nonsense, in my opinion.

Rustproofing

Rustproofing is no longer necessary now that the automakers have extended their own rust warranties up to seven and, in some cases, ten years. In fact, you have a greater chance of seeing your rustproofer go belly-up than having your untreated vehicle ravaged by premature rusting. Even if the rustproofer stays in business, you're likely to get a song and dance about why the warranty won't cover so-called "internal" rusting, or why repairs will be delayed until the sheet metal is actually rusted through. If you live in an area where roads are heavily salted in winter, or in a coastal region, have your vehicle undercoated frequently—paying particular attention to rocker panels (door bottoms) and wheel wells—and keep it out of a heated garage in winter.

Door rocker panels and wheel wells are the first to go.

The high profits earned from rustproofing cars (over 75 percent in some cases) encourage dealers to sell after-market rustproofing, even though automakers like GM and Nissan threaten to void the rust warranty because critical drain holes have become plugged. Most automakers will reject all rust warranty claims where holes have been drilled into their cars by after-market rustproofers.

Sunroof

Unless you live in a temperate region, the advantages of a sunroof are far outweighed by its disadvantages. You're not going to get better ventilation than a good air-conditioning (AC) system would provide, and you'll appreciate that your highway trips aren't accompanied by wind noises, water leaks, and road dust accumulation. Gas consumption is increased, night vision is reduced by overhead highway lights shining through the roof opening, and several inches of headroom can be lost, forcing tall drivers to adopt a hunched-over driving position. Flip-up styles are particularly leak-prone, while electronically-controlled sliding sunroofs often fall prey to short circuits. And without a manual override, your car will be vulnerable to theft and the weather.

Factory installation of a sunroof is far more costly than having it done by an independent—$1000 vs. $250, with little difference in the quality of the job or the warranty.

Tinted glass

Tinting jeopardizes your safety by reducing night vision. On the other hand, it does keep the interior cool in hot weather, reduces glare, and hides the car's contents from prying eyes. Factory applications are worth the extra cost because cheaper after-market products (costing about $100) distort visibility and peel away after a few years. Some tinting done in the U.S. can run afoul of provincial highway codes that require more transparency.

Turbocharging

Turbochargers use exhaust gases to turn a turbine that compresses air to achieve more power from the engine. What works well for long-hauling diesel trucks, though, has resulted in high repair bills for owners of GM, Ford, and Chrysler turbocharged cars (bearing burnouts at 30,000 to 50,000 km and failure after hot shutdowns). Engine seizures have also been reported from excessive heat build-up and oil deterioration.

Automakers claim that failures are rare and blame defects on driver negligence, but J. D. Power and Associates found that 22 percent of the owners it polled had turbocharger failures leading to valve, piston ring, and engine block problems.

Turbocharged motors usually require premium gasoline to give the maximum boost in performance, in addition to more frequent oil and filter changes using expensive "turbo approved" oil. They're also far more complicated in their operation than standard motors and may require parts that aren't readily available at most dealerships and independent garages. And should the shaft bearing fail or the compressor impeller be destroyed by dirt, it will be necessary to rebuild or replace the entire system at a cost of $500 to $800.

Wheels (aluminum)

Standard equipment on many sporty models, alloy wheels are optional on other cars ($160 to $330). They're fragile, frequently leak, corrode easily, and aren't always compatible with snow tires. Unpainted wheels require regular cleaning with acetone and an annual coating with a protective clear spray.

Cutting the Price

Buy by fax—and avoid the "showroom shakedown"

Consumers who want a fair price, loathe haggling, or who are just too busy to visit a number of showrooms have found that dealers will actually bid for their business if an invitation is sent by their personal or company fax. Dozens of *Lemon-Aid* readers have told me how effective buying by fax was in keeping the price down and preventing the showroom song-and-dance routine between the sales agent and sales manager ("he said, she said, they said"). Here's how it's done.

The prospective purchaser sends a fax to area dealerships asking them to give their bottom-line price for a specific make and model, and clearly stating that all final bids must be faxed within a week. Because no salesperson is acting as an intermediary, the dealers' first bids are likely to start off a few hundred dollars less than the suggested retail price. When all the bids are received, the lowest bid is faxed to the other dealers to give them a chance to beat that price. After a week of bidding, the lowest price gets your business.

Here's how one Downsview, Ontario, *Lemon-Aid* reader got the bidding started and subsequently paid 18 percent, or $1995.47, less than the list price of a 1994 Nissan Sentra.

FAX TRANSMISSION
Date: November 30, 1994
To: Joe Blow Motors
Att: President

Dear Sir,

I have decided to buy a new car. What and from whom I buy depends on the responses to this fax.

I have visited dealerships and have brochures for every car I am considering, and am sending this fax to other dealers. It is now a matter of finding the best deal.

I will buy either a Nissan Sentra, Honda Civic, Toyota Corolla or Mazda Protegé. I would like the base model, and the only options that interest me are a full-size spare tire and a block heater. I will accept other features that are already installed, but my decision is going to be based on price. I want a manual transmission, will take either two or four doors, and will accept any color. I will pay by cheque and will not trade in my current car.

Please fax me an offer. Include the price of the car, the price of all options, PDI, freight, GST, PST, all surtaxes (fuel, etc.), your administration fee and the license transfer fee. You should specify the total amount and include the name of the person I should contact if I accept the offer.

Today is November 30, 1994. I will make my selection at the end of the business day on December 7th. When faxing your offer, please phone me first at 555-1212 so I may connect my modem.

I want to buy a car. Do you want to sell one?

Awaiting your earliest convenient response, I remain

Sincerely,
Jane Customer

Several hours after sending this fax, our reader got her first quote. She also received additional bids by phone and mail, including one dealer's promise to beat the lowest price offered. That dealer gave the best price, drove the customer to his dealership, and sold the Sentra.

Be wary of "official" and "no haggle" pricing

New cars and minivans have no "official" selling price, and most dealers will charge as much as the market will bear. If you let them they'll use any pretext they can to boost prices, including a "no dicker sticker" policy. They'll pretend to have abandoned negotiated prices and high-pressure sales tactics in favour of "no haggle prices," where they give the buyer a better deal. But industry figures show that such dealers still average a 14 percent markup over their cost.

Consumer Reports, for example, found that its expert shopper saved a few hundred dollars at a conventional dealership as opposed to one that displayed the dealer's invoice cost and a "no haggle" selling price.

There are several price guidelines, however, and dealers use the one that will make the most profit on each transaction. Two of the more common prices quoted are the Manufacturer's Suggested Retail Price (what the carmaker advertises as a fair price) and the dealer's invoice cost, which indicates how much the dealer claims to have paid for the vehicle. Both price indicators leave considerable room for the dealer's profit margin, along with some extra padding in the form of inflated transportation and preparation charges. If presented with both figures, go with the MSRP because it can be verified by calling the manufacturer. Any dealer can print up an invoice and swear to its veracity.

Canadians who live in rural and western Canada are often faced with car prices that are grossly inflated compared to those charged in major metropolitan areas. A good way to beat this scam without buying out of province is to buy a couple of out-of-town newspapers (the Saturday *Toronto Star* "Wheels" section is especially helpful) and demand that your dealer bring his selling price, preparation, and transportation fees into line with the costs as advertised.

What's a Fair Price?

The dealer's cut

Most new car salespeople are reluctant to give out information on the amount of profit figured into the cost of each new car, but *Automotive News* gave the following markups a few years back. These percentages may vary a bit from year to year, but they're fairly accurate.

Dealer Markup (American Vehicles)

small cars: 8–10%
compacts: 10–15%
midsize cars: 15–20%
large cars: 17–20+%
sports cars: 17–20+%
high-end sports cars: 20–25+%
luxury cars: 25+%
high-end luxury cars: 20+%
minivans: 13-20+%
high-end minivans: 20+%
base pickups: 10–15%
vans and sport-utility vehicles: 15–20%
fully equipped top-of-the-line MPVs: 20–25%

Dealer Markup (Japanese Vehicles)

small cars: 7-8%
compacts: 10-12%
midsize cars: 15%

large cars: 15-17%
sports cars: 17-20%
high-end sports cars: 20-25%
luxury cars: 19-20+%
high-end luxury cars: 20+%
minivans: 20+%
high-end minivans: 25+%
base pickups: 15-20+%
vans and sport-utility vehicles: 25-30%
fully equipped top-of-the-line MPVs: 25-30%

In addition to the dealer's markup, there's a 5 percent carryover allowance on the previous year's vehicles given by Ford and GM, and a holdback allowance of another 2–3 percent. Options are the icing on the cake with their 35–65 percent markup.

Note: Dealers get their holdback rebate in the form of quarterly payments from the manufacturer based on the total list price of the vehicle. Except for Mercedes-Benz and VW, foreign carmakers don't give a holdback to their dealers.

Three steps to a fair price

To come up with a fair price that the dealer will likely accept, add the dealer markup and holdback allowance and multiply the MSRP by that figure. Then offer the dealer one-half of the computed profit. Compute the options separately and sell your trade-in privately. Buyers can more easily knock $1000 to $1500 off a $20,000 base price if they wait until January or February when sales are stagnant, choose a vehicle in stock, and forego unnecessary options.

Remember, the 7 percent GST and provincial sales tax must be paid on the *negotiated* price of a new vehicle and not on its suggested selling price. GST is calculated before subtracting the trade-in value from the purchase price. For example, if you buy a vehicle for $20,000 (plus $200 for transport and PDI), and you have a $5000 trade-in, you must pay 7 percent GST on the $20,200. Taxes that have to be paid are a fuel conservation tax, a $100 federal excise tax on air conditioning, and provincial sales tax calculated on the $20,200 plus the GST. If there's a $1000 rebate, you deduct the amount from your total. You only pay GST and provincial sales tax once, at the point of purchase. You don't pay it each time you make a loan payment.

Once you and the dealer have settled on the vehicle's price, you aren't out of the woods yet. Like a tag-team wrestling match, you will then be handed over to an F&I (financing and insurance) specialist, whose main goal is to convince you to buy additional financing, loan insurance, paint and seatcover protectors, rustproofing, and extended warranties. These items will be presented on a computer screen as costing only "a little bit more each month." Compare the dealer's insurance and financing charges with an independent agency that may offer better rates and better service. Often the dealer gets a kickback for selling insurance and financing, and guess who pays for it? Remember too that if the financing rate looks too good to be true, you're probably paying too much for the vehicle. The F&I closer's hard-sell approach will take all your willpower and patience to resist, but when he gives up, your trials are over.

Don't overpay the sales tax. Make sure that each transaction is treated separately and that the trade-in amount is deducted from the new vehicle price before provincial tax is calculated. The federal 7 percent GST will be charged on the full price of the contract, including all options, and provincial tax is then charged only after the trade-in value has been deducted.

Add-on charges are the dealer's last chance to stick it to you before the contract is signed. Dealer preparation PDI and transportation charges, "documentation" fees, and extra handling costs are ways that the dealer gets extra profits for nothing. Dealer preparation is a once-over-lightly affair, with a car seldom getting more than a wash job and a couple of dollars of gas in the tank. It's paid for by the factory in most cases and, when it's not, should cost no more than 2 percent of the car's selling price. Reasonable transportation charges are acceptable, however they're often inflated by dealers claiming that the manufacturer requires the payment.

Wait until management has approved the vehicle's bottom-line price you've agreed upon before rejecting these add-on charges; otherwise the dealership may try to pad the price to get its normal add-on profit. Negotiate delivery and preparation charges down to a strict minimum. Dealers are particularly adept at boosting these charges, but if you head for the door, they'll relent. Remember, the key to keeping costs down is to sell your trade-in privately (see "Selling Your Trade-In"), keep options to a minimum, and don't accept a high markup for low interest rates or a rebate.

Rebates and discounting

When vehicles are first introduced in the fall they're generally overpriced. Later on, near the end of summer, carmakers offer customer cash rebates of $750 to $3000 and increased dealer cash incentives for almost as much. Incentives are first offered during the winter months and boosted in late summer or early fall when dealer showroom traffic has fallen off. Smart shoppers who buy during these months can shave an additional 10 percent off a vehicle's list price (about $3000 on a $30,000 MSRP) by double-dipping from both of these automaker rebate programs.

In most cases, the manufacturer's rebate is straightforward and mailed directly to the buyer from the automaker. But there are other rebate programs that require a financial investment on the dealer's part. These shared programs tempt dealers to offset losses by inflating the selling price or pocketing the manufacturer's rebate. Therefore, when the dealer participates in the rebate program, demand that the rebate be deducted from the suggested selling price and not from some inflated price concocted by the dealer.

Some rebate ads will include the phrase "from dealer inventory only." If your dealer doesn't have the vehicle in stock, you won't get the rebate. Keep in mind that the manufacturer's rebate is considered to be part of the fair value and is not deductible from the purchase price prior to determining the retail sales tax payable.

Sometimes carmakers will suddenly decide that a rebate no longer applies to a specific model, even though their ads continue to include it. When this happens, take all brochures and advertisements showing your eligibility for the rebate plan to provincial consumer protection officials. They can use false advertising statutes to force carmakers to give rebates to every purchaser who was unjustly denied one.

When buying a heavily discounted vehicle, be wary of "option packaging" by dealers who push unwanted protection packages (rustproofing, paint sealants, and upholstery finishes) or levy excessive charges for preparation, filing fees, loan guarantee insurance, and credit life insurance.

Prevailing market value

A vehicle's stylishness, scarcity, or general popularity can inflate its value considerably. For example, the '96 Dodge Caravan minivan and '97 Ford F-150 series pickup have a prevailing market value that's higher than their suggested selling price, mainly because they're revamped and in short supply. Once sales slow down later in the new year they'll sell at a discount. A good rule of thumb for MPVs that have a high prevailing market value is to wait for their popularity to subside or to purchase the previous year's version. On the other hand, if a vehicle has a lower than usual market value (like the Mazda MPV minivan), find out why it's so unpopular before buying it. (In the Mazda example, the MPV is overpriced and unreliable.) Vehicles that don't sell because of their weird styling are no problem, but poor quality control can cost big bucks.

Accommodation sales

To carry out an accommodation sale, you must first find a buyer for your trade-in and obtain the cooperation of the dealer who will be selling you your new vehicle. The dealer reduces the new car cost by deducting the selling price of the trade-in. This lowers the amount of sales tax you pay on the new car. The buyer of the trade-in pays you through the dealer, and the dealer ends up selling a new car plus receiving an additional small fee (usually $50) for permitting the transaction. The seller pays the dealer's fee and is responsible for any serious problems that the buyer may have with the trade-in.

Leftovers: false bargains?

In the fall, at the beginning of each new model year, most dealers still have a few of last year's cars left. Some are new, some are demonstrators. The factory gives the dealer a 3–5 percent rebate on late-season cars, and dealers will often pass on some of these savings to clients. But are these leftovers really bargains?

They might be, if you can amortize the first year's depreciation by keeping the vehicle for six to ten years. But if you're the kind of driver who trades every two or three years, you're likely to come out a loser by buying an end-of-the-season car. The simple reason is that as far as trade-ins are concerned, a leftover is a used car that has depreciated at least 20 percent. The savings the dealer gives you may not equal that first year's depreciation, a cost you'll incur without getting any of the first year's driving benefits. If the dealer's discounted price matches or exceeds the 20 percent depreciation, then you're getting a pretty good deal. But if the next year's model is only a bit more expensive, and has been substantially improved or is covered by a more extensive, comprehensive warranty, it could represent a better buy than a cheaper left-over.

Ask the dealer for all work orders relating to the car and make sure that the odometer readings follow in sequential order. Remember, most demonstrators have fewer than 5000 km on the ticker and the original warranty has been reduced from the day the vehicle was first put on the road. Have the dealer extend the warranty or lower the price accordingly—about $100 for each month of warranty that has expired. If the vehicle's file shows that it was registered to a leasing agency or any other third party, you're definitely buying a used vehicle disguised as a demo. You should walk away from the sale because you're dealing with a crook.

Mid-year models

Entirely new models often make their debut in mid-summer, and getting any kind of a discount from the dealer for mid-year models is like pulling teeth. Dealers know that a seller's market exists during the first few months of a model's launch, and they're not likely to sell their few sample cars for anything less than full price. Furthermore, you're likely to lose an extra year of depreciation, since over time mid-year vehicles are depreciated back to the beginning of the model year in which they were introduced.

Paying Cash vs. Getting a Loan

The accounting firm of Price Waterhouse says that it may be smarter to borrow the money to purchase a new vehicle even if you can afford to pay cash, because if you use the vehicle for business a portion of the interest may be tax deductible. The cash that you free up can then be used to repay debts that aren't tax deductible, such as a mortgage.

The hidden costs

The effects of the recession continue to take their toll on credit applications. Poor credit risks have resulted in 30 –35 percent of all car loan applications being turned down, compared to 10–15 percent in previous years. Don't get caught short. Decide how much you want to spend and then pre-arrange your loan before you buy the car, so that you'll know in advance if your credit is good enough to qualify for the amount you need. Call various financial institutions to find out:

- the annual percentage rate on the amount you want to borrow and for the duration of your repayment period
- the minimum down payment that the institution requires
- whether taxes and licence fees are considered part of the overall cost, and thus covered by part of the loan
- whether lower rates are available for different loan periods or for a larger down payment
- whether discounts are available to depositors and if so, how long you must be a depositor before qualifying.

Monthly payments and total amount paid for an $7500 loan at various interest rates (APR), for a 36-month loan period

Interest Rate	Monthly Payment	Total Owed	Portion that is Interest
8.9	$238.15	$8573.40	$1073.40
9.9	241.65	8699.40	1199.40
11.0	245.54	8839.44	1339.44
12.5	250.90	9032.40	1532.40
14.0	256.33	9227.88	1727.88
16.0	263.68	9492.48	1992.48

What counts is the total amount you have to pay.

Monthly Payment Per $1000 of Loan Value

Interest Rate	1 Year	2 Years	3 Years	4 Years	5 Years
9%	87.45	45.68	31.80	24.89	20.76
9½%	87.68	45.91	32.03	25.12	21.00
10%	87.92	46.15	32.27	25.37	21.25
10½%	88.15	46.38	32.51	25.61	21.50
11%	88.39	46.61	32.74	25.85	21.75
11½%	88.62	46.85	32.98	26.09	22.00
12%	88.85	47.08	33.22	26.34	22.25
12½%	89.09	47.31	33.46	26.58	22.50
13%	89.32	47.55	33.70	26.83	22.76
13½%	89.56	47.78	33.94	27.08	23.01
14%	89.79	48.02	34.18	27.33	23.27
14½%	90.03	48.25	34.43	27.58	23.53
15%	90.26	48.49	34.67	27.84	23.79

Stretching out the payment time results in lower monthly payments and higher interest costs.

When comparing loans, consider the annual rate and calculate the total cost of the loan offer; that is, how much you will pay above and beyond the total price of the vehicle.

Dealers can finance the cost of a new car at interest rates that are competitive with the banks because of the rebates they get from the manufacturers and some lending institutions. Some dealers, though, mislead their customers into thinking they can borrow money as much as 5 percentage points below the prime rate. Actually they're jacking up the retail price to more than make up for the lower interest charges. Sometimes, instead of boosting the price, dealers reduce the amount they pay for the trade-in. In either case, the savings are illusory.

When dealing with banks, keep in mind that the traditional 36-month loan has now been stretched to 48 and 60 months. Longer payment terms make each month's payment more affordable, but over the long run they increase the cost of the loan considerably. Therefore, take as short a term as possible.

Be wary of lending institutions that charge a "processing" or "document" fee ranging from $25 to $100. Sometimes consumers will be charged an extra 1–2 percent of the loan up front in order to cover servicing. This is similar to lending institutions adding "points" to mortgages, except that with auto loans it's totally unjustified.

Some banks will cut the interest rate if you're a member of an automobile owners association, or if loan payments are automatically deducted from your chequing account. This latter proposal may be costly, though, if the chequing account charges exceed the interest rate savings.

Finance companies affiliated with GM, Ford, and Chrysler have been offering low-interest loans many points below the prime rate. In many cases, this low rate is applicable only to hard-to-sell models or cars equipped with expensive options. The low rate frequently doesn't cover the entire loan period. If vehicles recommended in this book are covered by low-interest loans, then the automaker-affiliated finance companies become a useful alternative to regular banking institutions.

Loan protection

Credit insurance guarantees that the car loan will be paid if the borrower becomes disabled or dies. There are three basic types of insurance that can be written into an installment contract: credit life, accident and health, and comprehensive. Most bank and credit union loans are already covered by some kind of loan insurance, but dealers sell the protection separately at an extra cost to the borrower. For this service the dealer gets a hefty 20 percent commission. The additional cost to the purchaser can be significant. The federal 7 percent GST is applied to loan insurance, but provincial sales tax is exempted in provinces such as Ontario.

Collecting on these types of policies isn't easy. There's no payment if your illness is due to some condition that existed prior to your taking out the insurance. Neither will the policy cover strikes, layoffs, being fired, etc. Generally, credit insurance is unnecessary if you're in good health, have no dependents, and your job is secure.

The Royal Bank has two interesting loan programs. One protects motorists from depreciation losses arising from an accident. For example, if a vehicle is scrapped after an accident, the Royal Bank will reimburse its depreciated value. The other program keeps monthly payments low, except for a final balloon payment.

There are plenty of advantageous programs available elsewhere. Personal loans from financial institutions now offer lots of flexibility. Most offer 100 percent financing (with no down payment), fixed or variable interest rates, a choice of loan terms, and no penalties for prepayment. Precise conditions depend on your personal credit rating. Leasing contracts are less flexible. There's a penalty for any prepayment, and rates are not necessarily competitive. Finally, credit unions can also underwrite new car loans that combine a flexible payment schedule with low rates.

Negotiating the Contract

Any document that requires your signature is a contract. Don't sign anything unless all the details are clear to you and all the blanks have been filled in. Don't accept any verbal promises. Remember, too, that your contract doesn't have to include all the clauses found in the dealer's preprinted form. You and the sales representative can agree to strike some clauses and add others. It's up to you to negotiate the best deal for yourself.

When the sales agent asks for a deposit, make sure it's stated on the contract as a deposit and try to keep it as small as possible (a couple of hundred dollars at the most). If you decide to back out of the deal on a vehicle taken from stock, let the seller have the deposit as an incentive to cancel the contract (believe me, it's cheaper than a lawyer and probably equal to his or her commission).

Scrutinize all references to prices and delivery dates. Delivery can sometimes be delayed three to five months, and you'll have to pay all price increases announced during the interim (3–5 percent) unless you specify a delivery date in the contract that protects the price.

Essential clauses

You can put things on a more equal footing by negotiating the inclusion of as many clauses as possible from the sample contract found on page 76. To do this, write in a "Remarks" section on your contract, and add "See attached clauses, which form part of this agreement." Then attach a photocopy of the "Additional Contract Clauses" printed below and have the sales agent initial as many of the clauses as you can. Although some clauses may be rejected, the inclusion of just some of these clauses can have important legal ramifications later on if you want a full or partial refund.

Additional Contract Clauses

1. **Financing:** This agreement is subject to the purchaser obtaining financing at a rate of _____% or less within ______ days of the date below. Failing notification in writing confirming approval of this financing, the contract is automatically cancelled.
2. **Delivery:** The motor vehicle is to be delivered by _____.
3. **Cancellation: (a)** The purchaser retains the right to cancel this agreement without penalty at any time before delivery of the vehicle by sending a notice in writing to the vendor.
   (b) Following delivery of the vehicle, the purchaser shall have two days to return the vehicle and cancel the agreement in writing, without penalty. After two days and before thirty-one days, the purchaser shall pay the dealer $25 a day as compensation for depreciation on the returned vehicle.
   (c) Cancellation of contract can be refused where the vehicle has been subjected to abuse, negligence or unauthorized modifications after delivery.
   (d) The purchaser is responsible for accident damage and traffic violations while in possession of the said vehicle. The purchaser is also responsible for re-registering the vehicle traded in and obtaining reimbursement of the sales tax. If the traded vehicle has been resold, the vendor will remit the monetary value attributed to the vehicle when it was delivered to the vendor.
4. **Protected Price:** The vendor agrees not to alter the price of the new vehicle, the cost of preparation or the cost of shipping.
5. **Trade-in:** The vendor agrees that the value attributed to the vehicle offered in trade shall not be reduced. An exception may be made when the said vehicle has been significantly modified or has suffered from unreasonable and accelerated deterioration since the signing of the agreement.
6. **Courtesy Car: (a)** In the event the new vehicle is not delivered on the agreed-upon date, the vendor agrees to supply the purchaser with a courtesy car at no cost. If no courtesy vehicle is available, the vendor agrees to reimburse the purchaser the cost of renting a vehicle of equivalent or lesser value than the new car purchased.
   (b) If the vehicle is off the road for more than five days for warranty repairs, the purchaser is entitled to a free courtesy vehicle for the duration of the repair period. If no courtesy vehicle is available, the vendor agrees to reimburse the purchaser the cost of renting a vehicle of equivalent or lesser value.
7. **Work Orders:** The purchaser will receive duly completed copies of all work orders pertaining to the vehicle, including warranty repairs and the original pre-delivery inspection (PDI).
8. **Dealer Stickers:** The vendor will not affix any dealer advertising, in any form, on the purchaser's new vehicle.

______	________________	________________
Date	**Vendor's Signature**	**Buyer's Signature**

The pre-delivery inspection

Many new vehicle orders are screwed up by the factory, so the pre-delivery inspection (PDI) is critical for making sure that corrections are made before taking delivery. Also, because about 10 percent of new vehicles are damaged in transit from the factory, the PDI can spot the damage and the extent of repairs needed. If the repair costs are substantial, the dealer can be forced to exchange the vehicle or give the buyer a rebate. Every auto manufacturer expects the dealer to carry out a PDI on every vehicle sold.

The PDI allowance is figured into the suggested retail price, so whatever you pay the dealer is profit. Dealers who don't get top dollar for a vehicle are tempted to skip the PDI. According to testimony before the U.S. Federal Trade Commission and the U.S. Senate Subcommittee on Antitrust and Monopoly, many dealers deliver vehicles straight from the factory to their customers with only a cursory inspection. This practice wouldn't have such serious consequences if vehicles were delivered from the factory in reasonably good shape. The PDI serves as a last stop to catch the five or so major and minor defects that *Consumer Reports* estimates afflict most new vehicles. If they aren't corrected before delivery, there's a good chance the dealer will charge to fix them later. And if these minor defects aren't caught in time, they can quickly become major failures.

The best way to ensure that the PDI will be done is to write in the sales contract that you'll be given a copy of the completed PDI sheet when the vehicle is delivered to you. Then, with the PDI sheet in hand, verify some of the items that were to be checked. If any items appear to have been missed, refuse delivery of the vehicle. Once you get home, check out the vehicle more thoroughly and send a registered letter to the dealer if you discover multiple major defects.

Selling Your Trade-In

To sell or not to sell?

It doesn't take a genius to figure out that the longer one keeps a vehicle, the less it costs to own—up to a point. The Hertz Corporation has estimated that a compact car equipped with standard options, driven 10,000 miles and traded each year, costs 9.6 cents more a mile than a comparable compact traded after five years. A compact kept for 10 years and run 10,000 miles a year would cost 10.8 cents less a mile than a similar vehicle kept for five years, and a whopping 20.38 cents less a mile than a comparable compact traded in each year. That would amount to a savings of $20,380 over a 10-year period.

Shortly after your vehicle's fifth birthday (or whenever you start to think about trading it in), ask a mechanic to look at it to give you some idea of what repairs, replacement parts, and maintenance work it will need in the coming year. Find out if dealer service bulletins show that it will need extensive repairs in the near future. (See the

Appendix on how to order a bulletin summary.) If it will require expensive repairs, you should trade the car right away; if expensive work isn't necessary, you may want to keep your vehicle. A good yardstick to use is provided by auto owner associations. They estimate that the annual cost of repairs and preventive maintenance for the average car is between $500 and $600. If your vehicle is five years old and you haven't spent anywhere near $3000 in maintenance, it would pay you to invest in your old car and continue using it for another few years.

Consider whether your car can still be serviced easily. If it's no longer on the market, the parts supply is likely to dry up and independent mechanics will be reluctant to repair it.

Don't trade for fuel economy alone. More fuel-efficient vehicles, such as front-drives, offset the savings through higher repair costs. Also, the more fuel-efficient cars may not be as comfortable to drive due to excessive engine noise, lightweight construction, and stiff suspension and torque steer.

Reassess your needs. Does your family growth require a different vehicle? Are you driving less? Are long trips taken less frequently? Let your car rust in peace and pocket the savings if its deteriorating condition doesn't pose a safety hazard or isn't too embarrassing. On the other hand, if you're in sales and are constantly on the road it makes sense to trade every few years, since mechanical reliability is a prime consideration and the increased depreciation costs are mostly tax deductible.

Getting the most for your trade-in

Customers who are on guard against paying too much for a new car often sell their trade-ins for too little. Before agreeing to any trade-in amount, read Part Three of the *Lemon-Aid Used Car Guide 1997* if your trade-in is a passenger car or minivan. For prices on used pickups, vans, or sport-utilities, consult the third edition of the *Lemon-Aid 4X4, Van and Truck Guide.* Both guides give your vehicle's dealer and private selling price in addition to offering a formula to figure out regional price fluctuations. For a small fee, you can also obtain used car prices by calling the Montreal or Toronto office of the Automobile Protection Association (514-273-1733 or 416-964-6774).

Now that you've nailed down your trade-in's approximate value, here are some tips on selling it with a minimum of stress:

- Never sign a new car sales contract unless your trade-in has been sold—you could end up with two cars.
- Negotiate the price from *retail* (dealer price) down to *wholesale* (private sales).
- If you haven't sold your trade-in after two weekends, you might be trying to sell it at the wrong time of year.

Private sales

If you must sell your vehicle and want to make the most out of the deal, consider selling it yourself and putting the profits toward your next purchase. You'll likely come out hundreds of dollars ahead, because buyers will pay more for your vehicle since they won't have to pay the 7 percent GST on a private sale. The most important thing to remember is that there's a large market for used vehicles in good condition in the $4000 to $5000 range. Although most people prefer buying from individuals rather than from used car lots, they may still be afraid that the vehicle is a lemon. By using the following suggestions you should be able to sell your vehicle quite easily.

1. Know its value. Study dealers' newspaper ads and compare them with the prices listed in this book. Undercut the dealer price by $300 to $800 and be ready to bargain down another 10 percent for a serious buyer. Remember, prices can fluctuate wildly depending on which models are trendy, so watch the want ads carefully.
2. Enlist the aid of the salesperson who is selling you your new car. Offer him a couple of hundred dollars if he finds you a buyer. Knowing that one sale hinges on the other and that there's a possibility of making two commissions may work wonders.
3. Put notices on bulletin boards at your office or local supermarkets and place a "For Sale" sign in the window of the car itself. Place a newspaper ad only as a last resort.
4. Don't give your address right away to a potential buyer responding to your ad. Instead, ask for the telephone number where you may call that person back.
5. Don't sell to friends or family members. Anything short of perfection, and you become the local leper.
6. Don't touch the odometer. You may get a few hundred dollars more—and a criminal record.
7. Paint the vehicle. Some specialty shops charge only $300 and give a guarantee that's transferable to subsequent owners.
8. Make minor repairs. This includes a minor tune-up and patching up the exhaust. Again, if any repair warranty is transferable, use it as a selling point.
9. Clean the vehicle. Go to a reconditioning firm or spend the weekend scrubbing the interior and exterior. First impressions are important. Clean the chrome, polish the body, and peel off old bumper stickers. Remove butts from the ashtrays and clean out the glove compartment. Make sure all tools and spare parts have been taken out of the trunk. Don't remove the radio or speakers. The gaping holes will make the vehicle worth much less than the radio or speakers cost. Replace missing or broken dash knobs and window cranks.
10. Change the tires. Recaps are good buys.
11. Let the buyer examine the vehicle. Insist that the vehicle be inspected by an independent garage. Accompany the prospective buyer to the garage.

12. Keep important documents handy. Show prospective buyers the sales contract, repair orders, owner's manual, and all other documents that show how the vehicle has been maintained. Authenticate your claims on fuel consumption.
13. Don't mislead the buyer. If the vehicle was in an accident or some financing is still to be paid, admit it. Any misleading statements may be used later in court against you. It's also advisable to have someone witness the actual transaction in case of a future dispute.
14. Sell to a dealer who sells the same make. He'll give you more because he can sell the vehicle more easily to his customers who shop for a used car.
15. Write an effective ad.

Using the want ads

The most effective want ads give all the basic information, including make, model, year, mileage, optional features, asking price, and whether the price is firm or negotiable. The ad should also give a number where the seller can be reached.

Don't use hyped-up or come-on advertising. An ad that screams in big, bold type "SHARP! MUST SEE TO BELIEVE!" does not inspire confidence. Stick with a more sober ad that gives the information you need to convey without the hoopla. Don't say anything that can be interpreted as a guarantee, and be cautious of such catch-all phrases as "mechanic's special," which is to a car buyer what a "handyman's special" is to a home buyer and can mean anything. Another common error found in used car ads is the innocent misrepresentation of what the vehicle will do from a performance standpoint. Refrain from making fuel economy claims, even if you believe them to be true.

How to write a good want ad

1. Start your advertisement with the make of the vehicle you're selling. State the manufacturer, model name, and year.
2. Give information clearly, including price. Readers react more quickly and favourably when given complete and definite information.
3. Make it easy for the prospect to reach you. Always include your telephone number and state a preferred time for prospects to contact you.
4. Use consecutive insertions for better exposure. A six-day order is best and costs less per insertion.
5. Place yourself in the reader's position. Ask yourself what you would want to know if you were buying a used car.

Want ads that fail usually do so because they're carelessly worded and don't contain enough information to get prompt action. Even an interested reader may pass up an ad that, for example, doesn't include a telephone number where the seller can be reached.

Selling to dealers

Selling to a dealer means that you're likely to get 20 percent less than if you sold your vehicle privately, unless the dealer agrees to participate in an accommodation sale. Most sellers will gladly pay some penalty to the dealer, however, for the peace of mind that comes with knowing that the eventual buyer won't lay a claim against them. This assumes that the dealer hasn't been cheated by the seller. But if the car is stolen, isn't paid for, has had its odometer spun back (or forward to a lower setting), or is seriously defective, the buyer or dealer can sue the original owner for fraud.

Park and sell outlets

Private owners in some parts of Canada have been able to pay a rental fee to an intermediary agency that permits their vehicle to be parked on a public lot where prospective buyers can inspect it and arrange for purchase. This automotive flea-market idea comes from the U.S., where it's very popular because it eliminates the dealer's commission while affording the seller the freedom of not being disturbed at home. Are these rented lots worth the extra expense? Judging by the comments already received, the answer is yes. Your vehicle is accessible, in constant public view, and you don't have to invest a lot of your own time. If you're a prospective buyer make sure that the seller is really a private party, and that the vehicle is paid for by asking to see the original sales contract.

Drawing up the contract

First draw up a bill of sale in duplicate and date it (photocopy the sample contract on the following page). Identify the vehicle (including the serial number), its price, whether a warranty applies, and the nature of the examination made by the buyer. The buyer may ask you to put in a lower price than what was actually paid in order to reduce the sales tax. If you agree to this, don't be surprised when a Ministry of Revenue agent comes to your door. Although the purchaser is ultimately the responsible party, you're an accomplice in defrauding the government. Furthermore, if you turn to the courts for redress your own conduct may be put on trial.

Don't forget to take your licence plates off the car. They're your property and must remain with you once the vehicle has been sold. In most provinces, your vehicle's registration certificate will have a plate portion and a vehicle portion. When the car is sold, the vehicle portion of the permit must be signed by you and given to the buyer. The remaining portion and your plates must be turned into the Ministry of Transportation of your province if you don't intend to buy another vehicle. You'll get a refund for the unexpired time left on your plates. If you decide to buy another car, you can put your old plates on it (if it's a similar class of vehicle), but it has to be re-registered within a short period (usually a week).

Sample Private Contract
Used Vehicles

1. The seller agrees to sell, and the buyer agrees to buy a:
   a) ________________ , b) ________________ .
   Year Serial Number

2. The seller is selling the motor vehicle:
   ❑ without a warranty
   ❑ with the following warranty ______________________ .

3. The buyer;
   ❑ has test driven the motor vehicle
   ❑ has not test driven the motor vehicle.

4. The purchase price in full is $________ .

5. The seller acknowledges receiving from the buyer a deposit in the amount of $_______ .

6. The seller warrants and guarantees that there are no liens, chattel mortgages or security agreements outstanding with respect to the motor vehicle or any equipment and/or accessories and that the motor vehicle and any equipment and/or accessories has/have not been given as collateral on any loan.

7. The seller and the buyer agree that the buyer was allowed to take the motor vehicle for an inspection by a mechanic before the signing of this agreement.

8. The seller warrants to the buyer that to the best of his knowledge:
   a) the odometer reading on the motor vehicle is accurate,
   b) the motor vehicle has not been damaged in a collision, and
   c) there are no outstanding traffic violations with respect to the motor vehicle.

______________ ______________
Date City

______________ ______________
Buyer Seller

Summary

Purchasing a vehicle used saves you the most money. Paying cash or with the biggest down payment you can afford and piling up as many kilometres and years as possible on your trade-in are the best ways to save money when buying a new vehicle. Remember, too, that safety is another consideration that depends largely upon the type of vehicle you choose. Focus on the following objectives.

Buy smart

1. Buy the vehicle you need and can afford, not what someone wants you to buy, or one loaded with options that you'll probably never use.
2. Test-drive your choice by renting it for several days.
3. Buy by fax and avoid the "showroom shakedown."
4. Use an auto broker if you're not confident in your own bargaining skills or lack the time to haggle.
5. Japanese vehicles made in North America, co-ventures with American automakers, and rebadged imports cost less than imports.
6. Some Asian and European imports aren't as reliable as you might imagine (Mazda's MPV minivan and VW's Eurovan are prime examples).
7. Try to avoid leasing. If you must lease, choose the shortest time possible.
8. Ask for at least a 5 percent discount off the MSRP.
9. Order a minimum of options and seek a 30 percent discount.
10. Sell your trade-in privately.
11. Arrange financing before buying your vehicle.
12. Use auto club references to get honest, competent service at a reasonable price.
13. Get extra warranty protection from the automaker if you're buying a model that has a higher than average repair history.
14. Buy in winter or during the month of August to double up on incentive programs.
15. Take your time. Price comparisons and test drives may take a month, but you'll get a better car and price in the long run.

Buy safe

1. A high crashworthiness rating and low rollover potential.
2. Three point belts with belt pre-tensioners and adjustable shoulder belt anchorages.
3. Integrated child safety seats and seat anchors.
4. Standard dual airbags and unobtrusive head restraints.
5. Good visibility.
6. Ergonomic interior with an efficient heating and ventilation system.
7. Test drive for responsive handling, braking efficiency, side wind vulnerability, rear-end slippage, and steering response.

Now that you know what the rules of the game are, Part Two will show you how to fight back when that dream car turns into a nightmare and your dealer tells you to get lost.

Part Two

HOW TO FIGHT BACK

"I deeply regret being forced to sue a company (Chrysler) that I helped build and love so much."

— *Lee Iacocca, explaining why he had to sue Chrysler for refusing to pay him $40 million in stock options, saying he disclosed confidential information about Chrysler to Kirk Kerkorian (12 April 1995)*

If you've bought a lemon, or if you've been forced to pay for repairs that shouldn't be your responsibility, this section will help you get your money back—without going to court or getting frazzled by the broken promises or "benign neglect" of the dealer or private party who sold you the vehicle. But if going to court is your only recourse, you'll find the jurisprudence you need to get an out-of-court settlement or to win your case without spending a fortune on lawyers and research.

Getting Your Money Back

Any sales contract for a new or used vehicle can be cancelled because the vehicle:

- was misrepresented.
- was unfit for the purpose for which it was purchased.
- wasn't reasonably durable, considering its selling price, how well it was maintained, the mileage driven, and the type of driving.
- was seriously defective at the time of purchase.

If the seller says that a minivan can pull a 2000-pound trailer and you discover that it can barely tow half that weight, you can cancel the contract for misrepresentation. The same principle applies to a seller's exaggerated claims concerning a vehicle's off-road capability, fuel economy and reliability, and to "demonstrators" that are in fact used MPVs with false (rolled back) odometer readings.

It's essential that printed evidence and/or witnesses (relatives are not excluded) are available to confirm that the false representation actually occurred. These misrepresentations must concern an important fact that substantially affects the vehicle's performance, reliability, or value.

Some vehicles are meant to be driven hard, but when they fail to live up to the advertised hype sellers often blame the owner for having pushed the vehicle beyond its limits. Therefore, when you seek to set aside the contract, it's essential that you get the testimony of an independent mechanic in order to prove that the vehicle's poor performance isn't caused by negligent maintenance or abusive driving.

Another hurdle to overcome is the "reasonable diligence" rule that requires you to file suit within a reasonable time after purchase or after you've discovered the defect. This delay must not exceed a few months if there have been no negotiations with the seller. If the seller has been promising to correct the defects for some time, or has done some minor repairs while negotiating a final settlement, the delay for filing the lawsuit can be extended.

Consequential damages

It's a lot easier to get the automaker to pay to replace a defective part than it is to be compensated for a missed day of work or a ruined vacation. Manufacturers hate to pay for consequential expenses under the basic warranty, supplementary warranty, or extended warranty because they can't control the amount of the refund. Towing expenses, however, are usually accepted. Courts are more generous, having ruled that all expenses (damages) flowing from a problem covered by a warranty or service bulletin are the manufacturer's/dealer's responsibility under both common law (all provinces except Quebec) and Quebec civil law. Fortunately, when legal action is threatened—usually through small claims court—automakers quickly back down from their refusal to pay consequential damage claims.

Warranties

Every vehicle sold new or used in Canada is covered by a provincial warranty that protects you from misrepresentation and a host of other evils. Furthermore, Canadian law presumes that car dealers, unlike private sellers, are aware of the defects present in the vehicles they sell. That's why dealers are paid their commission. The vehicles they sell are expected to be reasonably durable and merchantable. What is reasonably durable depends on the price paid, miles driven, the purchaser's driving habits, and how well the vehicle was maintained by the owner. Judges carefully weigh all these factors in awarding compensation or cancelling a sale.

The manufacturer's warranty is a legal promise that the product it sells will perform in the normal and customary manner for which it was designed. This promise remains in force, regardless of the number of subsequent owners, as long as the warranty's original time/kilometre limits haven't expired.

1997 WARRANTIES

Manufacturer	Bumper-to-Bumper Yrs./Km	Powertrain Yrs./Km	Emission Components Yrs./Km	Corrosion Yrs./Km	Seatbelts & Airbags Yrs./Km
AUDI	4/100	4/100	5/80	Sur: 4/100 Per: 10/Unlim	Belts: 4/100 Airbags: 4/80
BMW	4/80	4/80	2/40 8/130(A)	Sur: 4/80 Per: 6/unlim	Belts: 4/80 Airbags: 4/80
CHRYSLER, JEEP, EAGLE	3/60	3/60	3/60 8/130(A)	Sur: 1/120 Per: 7/160	Belts: 3/60 Airbags: 3/60
FORD	3/60	3/60	3/60 8/130(A)	Sur: 1/120 Per: 5/Unlim	Belts: 5/80 Airbags: 5/80
Lincoln	4/80	4/80	4/80 8/130(A)	Sur: 4/80 Per: 5/Unlim	Belts: 5/80 Airbags: 5/80
GENERAL MOTORS	3/60	3/60	3/60 8/130(B-C)	Sur: 3/60 Per: 6/160	Belts: 3/60 Airbags: 3/60
Cadillac/ Olds (Aurora)	4/80	4/80	4/80 8/130(B-C)	Sur: 4/80 Per: 6/160	Belts: 4/80 Airbags: 4/80
Saturn	3/60	3/60	3/60 8/130(B-C)	Sur: 3/60 Per: 6/160	Belts: 3/60 Airbags: 3/60
Saab	4/80	4/80	4/80 8/130(B-C)	Sur: 4/80	Belts: 5/Unlim Airbags: 5/Unlim
HONDA/ACURA	3/60	5/100 + M.C.	3/60 8/130(A)	Sur: 3/Unlim Per: 5/Unlim	Belts: 5/100 Airbags: 3/60
HYUNDAI	3/60	5/100 + M.C.	3/60 8/130(A)	Sur: 3/60 Per: 5/Unlim	Belts: 3/60 Airbags: 3/60
JAGUAR	4/80	4/80	2/40 8/130(A)	Sur: 4/80 Per: 6/Unlim	Belts: 4/80 Airbags: 4/80
LADA	3/72	3/72	5/80	Sur: 1/20 Per: 5/Unlim	Belts: 1/20 Airbags: N/A
MAZDA	3/80	5/100 + M.C.	3/80 8/128(A)	Sur: 3/80 Per: 5/Unlim	Belts: 5/100 Airbags: 5/100
MERCEDES-BENZ					
C, E Class	4/80	4/80	4/80 8/130(A)	Sur: 4/80 Per: 5/Unlim	Belts: 4/80 Airbags: 4/80
S, SL Class	4/80	5/120	4/80	Sur: 4/80 Per: 5/Unlim	Belts: 4/80 Airbags: 4/80
NISSAN	3/80	6/100 + M.C.	6/100	Sur: 3/80 Per: 6/Unlim	Belts: Life long Airbags: 6/100
Infiniti	4/100	6/100 + M.C.	6/100	Sur: 4/100 Per: 7/Unlim	Belts: Life long Airbags: 6/100
PORSCHE	2/Unlim	2/Unlim	5/80	Sur: 3/Unlim Per: 10/Unlim	Belts: 2/Unlim Airbags: 2/Unlim
SUBARU	3/60	5/100 + M.C.	3/60 8/130(A)	Sur: 3/Unlim Per: 5/Unlim	Belts: 5/100 Airbags: 5/100
SUZUKI	3/80	3/80	3/80 5/80(B) 8/130(C)	Sur: 1/20 Per: 5/Unlim	Belts: 3/Unlim Airbags: 3/Unlim
TOYOTA/	3/60	5/100 + M.C.	3/60 8/130(A)	Sur: 3/60 Per: 5/Unlim	Belts: 5/100 Airbags: 5/100
Lexus	4/80	6/110 + M.C.	4/80 8/130(A)	Sur: 4/80 Per: 6/Unlim	Belts: 6/110 Airbags: 6/110
VOLKSWAGEN	3/60	3/60	5/80	Sur: 3/60 Per: 6/Unlim	Belts: 3/60 Airbags: 3/60
VOLVO	4/80	4/80	5/80	Sur: 1/Unlim Per: 5/Unlim	Belts: 5/Unlim Airbags: 5/Unlim

M.C.: Major Components
Sur: Surface
Per: Perforation
Unlim: Unlimited
N/A: Not Available

(A) Catalytic converter; electronic control module and onboard emissions diagnostic device
(B) Catalytic converter
(C) Powertrain module

Note: Warranties may vary; all may apply to subsequent owners.

Tires and batteries aren't covered by most car manufacturers' warranties (except for GM), and are warranted instead by the manufacturer on a pro-rated basis. Batteries are covered for at least a year against defects, and then generally for another 24 months on a pro-rated basis. This isn't such a good deal, because the manufacturer is making a profit by charging you the full list price. If you were to buy the same replacement battery from a discount store you'd likely pay less even without the pro-rated rebate. The same principle applies to tires, because you're given a pro-rated rebate on the suggested list price, which almost nobody pays.

Safety restraints, such as airbags and safety belts, usually mirror the basic warranty with coverage extended for the lifetime of the vehicle. After-market products and services—such as gas-saving gadgets, rust-proofing, paint protectors, air conditioning, and van conversions—can render the manufacturer's warranty invalid, so be sure to check with your dealer before purchasing any optional equipment or services from an independent supplier.

How fairly a warranty is applied is more important than how long it remains in effect. The new warranties are useful to consumers who are making claims before provincial small claims courts because they prove that the technology exists to make powertrain components and rust resistance/paint adhesion last far longer than admitted in the past. Once you know what is the normal wear rate for a mechanical component or body part, you can demand proportional compensation when you get less than normal durability—no matter what the original warranty said.

Extended (supplementary) warranties

Extended warranties are the most fun of the entire automobile buying experience. Simply cut your best deal without referring to the warranty. Then tell the sales agent to throw in the warranty. When he says no, just get up and walk out. He'll chase you to the parking lot and you'll get the warranty for free.

Here's what you get: If a part malfunctions or fails, and it's the fault of the vehicle, the dealer or designated repair agency will repair or replace the defective part or parts and bill the automaker or warranty provider for the cost. Still, it's often difficult to collect on these warranties because independent companies not tied to the carmakers frequently go out of business. If a company's insurance policy won't cover your claim, take the dealer to small claims court and ask for the repair cost and the refund of the original warranty payment.

Supplementary Warranties

Supplementary warranties are sold by manufacturers and private companies to cover product defects after the manufacturer's or dealer's warranty has expired. They're particularly popular with MPV buyers, who are given shorter warranty coverage than car owners. It's often difficult for consumers to collect on these supplementary warranties because the independent companies not tied to the carmakers frequently go of business. Furthermore, their warranty contracts are full of legal loopholes that are routinely used to refuse compensation without any justification. Warranty compensation is often refused simply by claiming that there was a lack of proper maintenance, or that the problem is due to normal wear and tear, or that there's evidence of owner abuse.

All these excuses for denying supplementary warranty compensation can be countered by getting an independent expert to confirm that the defects are abnormal and weren't caused by improper maintenance or abusive driving.

When a company closes its doors your recourse is different. When International Warranty went out of business, for example, it left 400,000 Canadian motorists without protection. Customers in this situation who want repair compensation or their money reimbursed should:

- Try to have the repairs done at the dealer's expense.
- Get an itemized receipt if the dealer charges for the repairs.
- Make two copies of the invoice. With covering letters that identify the car and the warranty, send your claim to the dealer and warranty company.
- If a reimbursement or compensation is not forthcoming, sue for one or both before the small claims court.

Emission control warranties

These little-publicized warranties come with all new vehicles and cover the emission control system for up to 8 years/130,000 km. Unfortunately, although owners' manuals vaguely mention the emissions warranty, most don't specify which parts are covered (see the "1997 Warranties" chart above). The U.S. Environmental Protection Agency refused to accept this omission and has ruled that all major motor and fuel-system components are covered. These include fuel metering, ignition spark advance, restart, evaporative emissions, positive crankcase ventilation, engine electronics (computer modules) and catalytic converters, as well as hoses, clamps, brackets, pipes, gaskets, belts, seals, and connectors. In Canada there is no government definition, and it's left up to each manufacturer and the small claims courts to decide which components are covered.

Many of the dealer service bulletins listed in Part Three under *Service Tips* show parts failures that are covered under the emissions warranty. A good example is a recent bulletin applicable to Ford's Ranger. It explicitly states that owners of 1990-92 Rangers and 1991-92 Explorers who experience a loss of power at high engine speeds will get free repairs under the basic warranty, and when it expires, the emissions warranty. Unfortunately, few owners will ever see this bulletin and will end up paying for a repair that is really Ford's responsibility.

Secret warranties

Secret warranties have been around since automobiles were first mass produced. They're set up to provide free repairs to fix performance-related defects caused by substandard materials, faulty design, or assembly-line errors. In 1974, *Lemon-Aid* exposed Ford's J-67 secret rust warranty that covered the company's 1970-74 models. After first denying that it had such a warranty, Ford admitted two years later that it was indeed in place, and negotiated a $2.8-million settlement with this author. And you know what? Twenty-two years later, *Lemon-Aid* presents another Ford secret warranty covering paint defects on its 4X4s, trucks, and minivans.

Carmakers are reluctant to make these warranty programs public because they feel that it would weaken confidence in their product and increase their legal liability. The closest they come to an admission is by sending a "goodwill policy," "product improvement program," or "special policy" service bulletin to dealers. Consequently, only those motorists who yell the loudest when faced with repairs for defective parts get compensated. Uninformed customers who hesitate to complain are forced to pay for the same repairs. The state of Connecticut enacted the first secret warranty law four years ago, introducing a series of disclosure requirements that permit all consumers to benefit from repair "adjustment programs." This law requires automakers to:

- Establish procedures to inform consumers of adjustment programs.
- Notify all eligible consumers by first-class mail within 90 days of adopting a program.
- Implement procedures to assure reimbursement to eligible consumers who incur expenses before learning of the program.
- Notify a consumer within 21 days whether a claim for reimbursement is accepted or rejected.

Violators are subject to prosecution under the state's Unfair Trade Practices Act and may be hit with a cease and desist order or forced to provide restitution of up to $2000. Plaintiffs are also empowered to initiate private lawsuits for additional compensation. Similar bills have passed in Virginia, Maryland, Pennsylvania, and New York. In Canada, provincial legislators have sat on their hands.

If you're refused compensation, keep in mind that secret warranty extensions are an admission of manufacturing negligence. Try to compromise with a pro-rata adjustment from the manufacturer. If polite negotiations fail, challenge the refusal in court on the grounds that you should not be penalized for failing to make a reimbursement claim under a secret warranty that you never knew existed!

Getting free paint repairs

In spite of improvements in overall vehicle safety and quality, General Motors, Ford, and Chrysler sport-utilities, minivans, vans, and pickups have been plagued for almost a decade by serious paint deficiencies. So far this hasn't been as serious a problem with Japanese and European automakers. GM and Ford have had similar paint problems during the past decade: the paint whitens and takes on a chalky colour, or it peels away prematurely during the first five years of ownership.

Paint flaking—or delamination as it's called in the industry—occurs when the top coat of paint separates from the primer coat, mostly along horizontal surfaces and often as a result of intense sunlight. When the paint peels the entire vehicle must be repainted after a new primer resurfacer has been added. For some vehicles, the labour alone can run about 20 hours at a cost of $50 to $75 an hour.

Confidential U.S. dealer service bulletins show us one important benchmark that the auto industry uses to accept or reject secret warranty paint claims. With Corsica and Beretta paint defects, GM lets dealers repaint the entire car at no charge to the owner (up to $650), regardless of whether it was bought new or used. And, as confirmed by GM's Pontiac dealer letter, vehicles as old as six years will be repainted free of charge.

Ford is more generous than GM (at least in theory), although its dealers first need Oakville's authorization. Ford has been repainting 1983-93 cars, minivans, vans, F-series trucks, Explorers, Rangers, and Broncos for free under a little-known "Owner Dialogue" program. Ford says it discontinued the program early last year, but owners who were never alerted to the program's existence and who threaten small claims action are still getting compensation.

Brandishing some of the same internal dealer bulletins mentioned on the following pages, Ford owners have argued convincingly that secret warranty programs are unfair because not everyone has an equal chance of being told they exist. They insist that these programs should be used as compensation to owners for the company's factory negligence—not as so-called "goodwill" marketing tools that can be arbitrarily cut off.

Chrysler's paint problems are more recent and concern 1991-94 minivan paint discolouration and "shadowing"—a blotchy shadow or spotting all over the vehicle. All of Chrysler's '95 lineup of dark-coloured full-size vans and pickups are affected. Vehicles that are kept in a heated garage and then driven in sub-zero temperatures are especially vulnerable.

Chrysler won't be repainting its vehicles with the "shadowing" problem. Instead, the automaker says it will buy back all affected vehicles and sell them at auction as used vehicles—with the paint defect disclosed.

The following chart, based on service bulletins and owner feedback, will give you a better understanding of which vehicles have paint defects, the nature of the defect, and what program is used by the manufacturer to describe the secret warranty that applies.

Company	Problem as stated by the company	Confirmation	Bulletin	Euphemism	Automaker Solution	Limitations
GM						
All vehicles	"Clearcoat degradation," "chalking," "whitening"	*Dealer letter	#331708, "Clearcoat degradation," issued November 1993	Special Policy	Partial repaint/ full repaint	100% up to 6 years (optional 60,000 miles)
1988-92 trucks, vans, 4X4s (blue, grey, silver, and black metallic)	"Delamination," peeling	*Dealer letter	#231054R, "Delamination," issued October 1992	Special Policy	Full repaint	100% up to 6 years (optional 60,000 miles)
Corsica/Beretta	"Delamination," peeling, fading	*Dealer letter	#9034110, "Delamination," issued September 1990	Policy Adjustment	Full repaint (optional	100% up to 6 years 60,000 miles)
Ford						
1983-93 trucks, 4X4s, minivans, vans, all cars**	"Microchecking," peeling, fading, hazing	Ford PR statements to Action Line columnists	#93-8-4, "Microchecking," issued April, 1993	"Owner Dialogue"	Full repaint	100%/ Program discontinued January 1995

Company	Problem as stated by the company	Confirmation	Bulletin	Euphemism	Automaker Solution	Limitations
Chrysler/ Mitsubishi 1995 vehicles/ none made in Canada	"Shadowing"	*Automotive News*, May 8, 1995	None issued	"Goodwill"	Buyback/ Mitsubishi will repaint	None
Chrysler 1989-94 vehicles	"Chalking"	Owner feedback	None issued	"Goodwill"	Repaint	None
1990 Shadow/ Sundance with clearcoat paint	Alkaline spotting, industrial fallout, chemical "etching"	Owner feedback	#23-11-90, issued Sept 10, 1990	"Goodwill"	Partial repaint	Reimbursable*** under the base warranty

** Refers to GM's Pontiac Division dealer letter sent October 16, 1992, signed by Perry S. White, Director of Service/Customer Satisfaction. A follow-up dealer service bulletin (Bulletin No: 57-05-01, "Dealer/Retailer Administration of Case-by-Case individual Goodwill Adjustments") was sent throughout the GM dealer network in April, 1995 giving all dealers authorization to carry out "goodwill" repairs for any problem free of charge, with no mileage limitations or deductible up to two years beyond the vehicle's bumper-to-bumper base warranty. Both documents should be subpoenaed if you go to small claims court.*

*** Broncos, F-series, and Mustangs are named, but Ford has applied the program's parameters to all affected vehicles.*

**** Probably long since expired, which means threatening a small claims action using the Ford and GM parameters as a benchmark as to what is reasonable durability.*

Recall campaigns

Safety- and emissions-recall campaigns confer warranty benefits on owners whereby the manufacturer and dealer are obligated to repair a defect at no charge, no matter how often the vehicle has been sold or what its mileage is. Furthermore, Transport Canada monitors how well carmakers carry out recall campaigns and will intervene if any company stonewalls a legitimate request.

Confidential service bulletins

Technical service bulletins are sent to dealers by carmakers to advise them of the latest secret warranties and to help them quickly diagnose and correct factory defects. These bulletins also disclose a) how much of the repair the dealer can charge back to the manufacturer, and b) which parts are available free of charge. Armed with these bulletins, motorists can use less expensive independent garages to diagnose and repair their vehicles or to negotiate compensation for defects that the bulletins point out are the manufacturer's fault.

The major problem with these bulletins is that they're difficult to get. Dealers and automakers are reluctant to provide this kind of detailed technical information because it allows customers to second-guess a mechanic's work or to buttress their demands for compensation. As long as their involvement isn't disclosed, some dealers will discreetly provide copies of service bulletins to help their customers fight for compensation from the auto manufacturer.

How long should a part last?

Minivan front brakes are known to wear out prematurely because of the extra weight they have to handle. Dealers will repair the brakes only to have the same defect reappear a few thousand kilometres or a few months later (usually when the warranty has expired). Motorists who don't have an expert handy to challenge the dealer's opinion that the defect is not a defect at all but is normal wear and tear may have to pay for expensive repairs. If a part doesn't last as long as estimated, demand a refund from the manufacturer and dealer. Back up your demand with the threat of court action.

Three Steps to a Settlement

Step 1: Informal negotiations

If your vehicle was misrepresented, has major defects, or wasn't properly repaired under warranty, the first thing you should do is give the seller (the dealer or a private party) a written summary, by registered mail or fax, of the outstanding problems and stipulate a time period in which they will be corrected or your money will be refunded. Keep a copy for yourself along with all your repair records. At the beginning, try to work things out informally.

When negotiating with the seller, speak in a calm, polite manner and try to avoid polarizing the issue. Talk about how "we can work together" on the problem. Support your position with independent garage reports, service bulletins, and maintenance records. Let a compromise slowly emerge—don't come in with a hardline set of demands. Don't demand the settlement offer in writing, but make sure you're accompanied by a friend who can confirm the offer in court if it's not honoured (relatives *can* testify in court). Be prepared to act on the offer without delay, so that you won't be blamed for it being withdrawn.

Dealers

If the vehicle was purchased from a dealer, be sure to check all of the sales and warranty documents you were given to see if they conform with provincial laws. Any errors, omissions, or violations can be used to clinch a deal with the dealer in lieu of making a formal complaint, because the dealer could be fined if he's violated provincial protection laws.

If the dealer won't talk with you, write or call the nearest regional office or the manufacturer's head office. The address and telephone numbers can be found in the owner's manual. General Motors, for example, has a toll-free customer hotline (1-800-263-3777) that has been in operation for four years in Oshawa and employs over 30 people (one-third of whom are bilingual) to answer customer inquiries. Don't expect miracles from these people. Each staffer has a guide book showing the appropriate, corporate-approved response for the most frequently asked consumer questions. If you dig too deeply, you'll likely get the cold shoulder or, as one GM owner wrote me, get the receiver hung up in your ear.

If there is a warranty dispute, or if you've found that your service manager can't correct a persistent problem, GM customer relations staff will intervene to set things right, if possible, at the dealership level. Once your name, vehicle identification number (VIN), and dealer's name are punched into the computer, the customer relations rep can tell you if you're eligible for free repairs under a special (i.e., secret) warranty or through a safety/emissions recall campaign. The telephone staff will never mention the phrase "secret warranty," nor will they ever pass you on to someone else who's in charge. Since they were hired to reduce the number of calls their bosses receive, every call that gets through their screening is a black mark against their job performance.

Some dissatisfied GM car owners tell me that the telephone staff have been told to "barter down" owners' requests for warranty compensation involving paint defects and other secret warranty-related problems. Callers are given a "Let's Make a Deal" spiel where the initial offer of 50 percent is often boosted to 75 percent compensation if the customer will agree—at that very moment—to pay 25 percent of the repair. Although these deals are never put in writing (that's when the receiver was hung up on the customer), GM and its dealers usually stick to the agreement made over the phone.

Factory reps

Assuming that the dealer and customer relations couldn't set things right on their own, your next step is to convene a mini-summit where you meet the factory rep and service manager. The factory rep is directly responsible to the manufacturer and has the last word as to what work is covered under warranty. Not unlike the customer relations staff, he's paid to save the company money. Every time he says no, he does his job. When he says yes to warranty coverage, it's because you convinced him he must. This can be done by personally presenting the facts in a confident, forthright manner with as many dealer service bulletins as you can find for support (see Appendix I on how to order your own bulletins). Don't use your salesperson as a runner; he has less pull than you do, and the factory rep can promise him anything and later deny it. Should you see that you're getting nowhere with the factory rep, give him one last chance to make a reasonable offer. Don't threaten him or tip him off to your next move.

Step 2: Send a registered letter or fax

This is the next step to take if the dealer or factory rep refuses your claim. Send the dealer and manufacturer a polite, registered letter that asks for compensation for repairs that have been done or need to be done, insurance costs while the vehicle was being repaired, towing charges, supplementary transportation costs (e.g. taxis and rented cars), and damages for inconvenience.

Specify five days (but allow ten) for either party to respond. If no satisfactory offer is made, file suit in small claims court. Make the manufacturer a party to the lawsuit—especially if the emissions warranty, a secret warranty extension, a safety-recall campaign, or extensive chassis rusting are involved. The sample claim letters shown below can be useful in getting compensation for a defective new or used vehicle or for unsatisfactory repairs. Include a reference in your letter to any court decisions you find in this chapter that support your claim.

Step 3: Mediation and arbitration

If you have a new or used vehicle complaint and the formality of a courtroom puts you off, or if you're not sure your claim is all that solid and don't want to pay legal costs to find out, consider using mediation or arbitration sponsored by the Better Business Bureau, the Automobile Protection Association, the Canadian Automobile Association, or provincial and territorial governments.

Except for Quebec, all provinces and the Northwest Territories have set up the Canadian Motor Vehicle Arbitration Plan (CAMVAP). (This is a spinoff from Ontario's Motor Vehicle Arbitration Program (OMVAP), an arbitration panel that was set up in late 1986 and has since closed down.) Through this new plan, disputes between consumers and automakers that result from alleged manufacturing defects can be put before a third party for arbitration.

CAMVAP offers its services free of charge to new and used car owners. There are no lawyers involved (so no awards need to be split); binding arbitration by a neutral third party can be arranged within a six- to eight-week period; and all negotiations are carried out informally.

Despite OMVAP's respectable track record, consumer advocates criticized the Ontario group for giving less compensation than did the courts, keeping judgments secret, not allowing appeals to the courts, and for its lack of subpoena powers. CAMVAP's shortcomings are similar, but some provinces allow for a "judicial review" of the arbitrator's decision and lawyers can represent claimants.

CAMVAP won't consider personal injury claims, tire defects (except on GM's models), rustproofing product third-party claims, motorhomes, or vehicles used primarily for business purposes. Another big CAMVAP cop-out is its refusal to intervene in disputes between dealers and customers.

Nevertheless, based on its Ontario track record, which has been verified by independent auditors, CAMVAP arbitration is worth serious consideration. Canadian residents who own or lease a defective 1991 or later model vehicle used for non-commercial purposes must first contact their dealer and carmaker to settle the dispute before asking for arbitration. If this doesn't take care of the problem, ask the dealer for the regional CAMVAP phone number and call for an arbitration application form. If the dealer is uncooperative, call CAMVAP toll-free at 1-800-207-0685. If the vehicle is leased, the leasing agency must agree to abide by CAMVAP's decision. Hearings are held within 50 days after the Claim Form and Agreement for Arbitration have been signed by both parties. Decisions are handed down within 21 days of the claim being filed, and automakers have 30 days after that to pay the award. Stephen Moody, CAMVAP's general manager, says that 70 percent of the awards handed down by CAMVAP have been in favour of the consumer. Of course, this self-serving figure can't be checked because CAMVAP puts a gag order on all claimants.

Involving other agencies

Remember, it's not the mediator or arbitrator's fault if you lose your case due to poor preparation. Ask government and independent consumer protection agencies, like those listed below, to evaluate how well you're prepared before going to your first hearing.

Automobile Protection Association
292 St-Joseph Blvd. West, Montreal, Quebec H2V 2N7
160 Pears Ave., Suite 322, Toronto, Ontario, M5R 1T2
Attn: George Iny, President

A non-profit Canadian motorist protection organization, the APA mediates thousands of complaints yearly, mostly for its own members. The group also negotiates class settlements on behalf of motorists across Canada after being alerted to common problems based on the complaints it receives from members and non-members alike.

Consumers Action Group
Robert Salvador
6-2400 Dundas St. West (West Region)
Mississauga, Ontario, L5K 2R8
Tel/Fax: 416-587-0070

The Consumers Action Group is an Ontario-based, non-profit association of consumer advocates that does much more than just complain. Its loosely knit structure allows the group to effectively assist consumers in using the small claims courts and class actions to obtain redress. Volunteers include lawyers, paralegals, and other professionals. They use research, media publicity, lawsuits, and out-of-court settlements to obtain compensation from automakers, manufacturers, dealers, and retailers whenever a product or service violates provincial laws or is deemed to involve fraud or negligence. One CAG member hosts quarterly forums on exposing scams and other nefarious activities carried out by what one CAG lawyer calls "white collar thugs." In the past, the group has successfully taken on airlines, the medical profession, eyeglass manufacturers, food retailers, telemarketers, and a host of other businesses. CAG receives no funding and there is currently no membership fee, but members are expected to help others in cooperative efforts.

Anyone who would like specific information on class actions (only Quebec, Ontario, and British Columbia allow this recourse) should send a self-addressed, stamped envelope to Carole Barrons, CAG (Class Actions).

Center for Auto Safety
2001 South St., NW, Washington, DC 20009
Tel: 202-328-7700
Attn: Clarence Ditlow

Founded by Ralph Nader, this group probes auto safety and consumer protection issues relating to the auto industry. The CFAS can give you full, independent reports on common vehicle defects reported by dissatisfied car owners, and put you in touch with lawyers in your area who have handled cases similar to yours.

Online services/Internet/Websites

America Online and Compuserve are two online service providers with active consumer forums that use experts to answer consumer queries and to provide legal as well as technical advice. The Internet offers the same information, but uses a worldwide database. If you or someone you know is able to create a Website, you might consider using this site to attract attention to your plight and arm yourself for arbitration or court.

Last year, Debra and Edward Goldgehn's 1985 Ford Ranger caught fire and burned completely. The couple's suspicions that it was a factory-related defect were later confirmed by a TV show that reported a series of similar Ford fires. The couple created their own Website called Flaming Fords and began amassing an incredible database containing reports of similar fires, class actions lawsuits, expert witnesses, and actions taken in other countries (for example, Ford had already recalled a number of its vehicles to fix the problem in Canada). Shortly thereafter, Ford USA recalled 8.7 million cars and trucks. Ford says that the Internet pressure was coincidental and not a factor in its decision to recall the vehicles in the States.

Association of

FLAMING FORD

Owners

Do You Own A Flaming Ford?

Click Here to see if you are

a ***Flaming*** Ford Owner!

(Current U.S. Recall Information Included)

Our *BLUE BUTTON* Website Program is Raising Some Eyebrows.

Click Here to find out why!

NEW!

Is Your Ford one of the 8.7 Million Vehicles recalled?

Click Here to find the

Ford, Lincoln or Mercury Dealer nearest you.

Stay tuned to this site for further details

Government consumer affairs

The wind left the sails of the consumer movement a decade ago, leaving provincial consumer affairs offices understaffed and unsupported by the government. This has created a passive mindset among many staffers who are tired of getting their heads kicked in by business and budget-cutters.

Investigation, mediation, and some litigation are the primary areas in which consumer affairs offices can be helpful. Strong and effective consumer protection legislation has been left standing in most of the provinces, and resourceful consumers can use these laws and media coverage to prod provincial consumer affairs offices into action. Furthermore, provincial bureaucrats aren't as well shielded from criticism as are their federal counterparts. A call to your MPP or MLA, or the Minister's executive assistant, can often get things rolling.

Federal consumer protection is a government-created PR myth. Don't expect the reorganized Consumer and Corporate Affairs staffers to be very helpful—they've been de-fanged and de-gummed through budget cuts and a succession of ineffective ministers. Although the revised Competition Act has some bite concerning misleading advertising and a number of other illegal business practices, the federal government has downplayed the Act's usefulness to consumer groups and individual consumers.

Nevertheless, used creatively, the recently beefed-up Competition Act can be a powerful tool for forcing a formal government investigation and prosecution, attracting media attention, and obtaining individual and collective compensation. And, the Act costs little to use.

Earlier this year, the Ontario-based Consumer Action Group grouped together six consumer complainants and successfully used the Competition Act to file a "6-citizen declaration" against a number of auto leasing companies that had allegedly misled the public by not disclosing various hidden fees. When word leaked out that the government was investigating auto leasing (it had no choice—the act requires a formal inquiry), the major automakers and dealer organizations started scrambling over themselves to find ways to disclose the extra charges without losing customers. In the meantime, several provincial governments have pledged to update lease disclosure regulations. Furthermore, lessees can also use the Act to get hidden fees refunded through the small claims courts, regardless of the outcome of the federal probe.

No matter what federal investigators find, the filing of a complaint under the Competition Act alone has resulted in alerting consumers and provincial governments to a longstanding deceptive practice in auto leasing. A copy of the original complaint is printed below as a guide for readers wishing to petition the government to probe other deceptive business practices, or for lessees seeking refunds in small claims court.

Request for Competition Act Investigation

DECLARATION

We declare that we are of the belief that:

Individuals, arranging auto leases on behalf of leasing corporations, have committed, and continue to commit, offences under the Competition Act (the "Act"), and that grounds exist for a Director's inquiry (under Part VIII of the Act) into certain practices related to auto leasing. Hence, we hereby formally request for the Director of Investigation and Research to commence an inquiry as required under Sec. 10(2) of the Act.

We verily believe that these corporations and individuals are committing acts that result in undisclosed and hidden charges being overcharged to consumers, at an average of $400 per lease; and that these deceitful practices adversely affect the majority of car lessees; and that the resulting loss of buying power creates a further stress on the middle-class citizens of this country; and that there is an urgent need for a vigorous and thorough investigation into the misleading practices of the auto leasing industry.

We verily believe that the following major auto leasing companies …

– General Motors Acceptance Corporation of Canada, Limited ("GMAC")
– Chrysler Credit Canada Ltd
– GE Capital Corporation
– Ford Credit Corporation
– Setay Motors Inc. c.o.b. Queenston Leasing (Hamilton, Ont.)

… and various other auto leasing dealers — the names of addresses of which can be readily obtained from the…

> Ontario & Toronto Automobile Dealers Associations
> ("OADA" and "TADA" respectively)
> 85 Renfrew Dr., Markham, Ont., L3R 0N9
> Toll Free Tel 1-800-668-6510 Fax 905-940-6235
> Tel 905-940-6232

… and must be immediately investigated.

We verily believe that the deception can be revealed by investigating the Capital Cost in the lessors' worksheets which were used to calculate monthly lease payments. What we believe is that these hidden Acquisition Fees are being added to the Capital Cost without lessees' knowledge or consent.

We verily believe that the deceptive practices listed herein are widely practiced in Ontario and other provinces that do not have "full leasing disclosure laws."

Sec. 9 **("6-citizen")** **Declaration ... under the Competition Act**

We believe that Mr. Robert (Bob) Pierce — a former Motor Vehicle Dealers' Act Registrar of Ontario — has declared the ethical norm for lessors. However, it is a notorious fact that many lessors today are still are not complying with Mr. Pierce's stated standard of ethics.

FACTS:

1) There are hidden, undisclosed charges in leasing contracts. These fees are commonly referred to as "acquisition" or "administration" fees.
Reference: Paul Timoteo, President, Lease Busters, Mississauga, in a local radio talk show.
Exhibit "A"

2) These hidden charges in car lease contracts cannot be readily ascertained without the aid of specialized software to reveal these hidden charges.
Reference: GMAC's "leaked" memo, par. 2, referring to a *Globe and Mail* article about software that can break down a lease payment.
Exhibit "B"

3) The head of the dealership associations in Ontario indicated that these hidden charges "*ought to be on front of the lease*" and, therefore, should be disclosed to lessors.
Reference: Robert ("Bob") Pierce, CEO of OADA and TADA, in a local radio talk show.
Exhibit "A"

4) A leaked GMAC document and a news article reveal that GMAC has been forced to 'fess up to hidden charges, when journalists blew the lid off hidden acquisition fees.
Reference: "GMAC boss admits leasing confusion."
"Acquisition fee to be revealed: Memo"
The Province Money, May 24, 1994.
Exhibit "C"

5) This deceitful practice is "very common in the industry," and "everybody" (*in the auto leasing business*) is charging "between three and four hundred dollars."
Reference: Paul Timoteo, President, Lease Busters, in a local radio talk show.
Exhibit "A"

We designate Eric Ritter, of 18 Billington Cres., North York, Ont., M3A 1G6, tel 416-391-5835 as the contact person for purposes of this declaration and complaint.

Sec. 9 **("6-citizen")** **Declaration … under the Competition Act**

FEBRUARY 19 1996

To: GEORGE N. ADDY, DIR. OF INVESTIGATION AND RESEARCH
BUREAU OF COMPETITION POLICY
INDUSTRY CANADA
50 VICTORIA ST.,
HULL, QUE
K1A 0C9

From: Eric Ritter
18 Billington Crescent,
North York, Ont., M3A 1G6 Tel: 416-391-5835

RE: REQUEST FOR STATUTORY INVESTIGATION

We are sending by fax, in advance, copies of a duly-sworn, Sec. 9, "6-citizen declaration," invoking the Competition Act's Sec. 10(2) of Part VIII legislative requirement for an investigation to commence into the practices of certain auto leasing companies.

(The originals — along with exhibits, audiotape, and transcripts — will be sent via registered mail forthwith.)

Please acknowledge receipt of this document, and advise what kind of response we could expect, and perhaps, a timeframe as to when results could be expected.

Thank you for your assistance in this matter.

cc: R. Lo Presti (416) 441-0297
Doug Barnett
M. McGowan
P. Edmonston
etc…

Launching a Lawsuit

If the seller agrees to make things right, give him a deadline and then check the repairs by an independent garage. If no offer is made within ten working days, file suit in small claims court. Make the manufacturer a party to the lawsuit only if the original, unexpired warranty was transferred to you; your claim falls under the emissions warranty; or a secret warranty extension, a safety recall campaign, or extensive chassis rusting is involved.

There are small claims courts in most counties of each province, and you can make a claim in the county where the problem occurred or where the defendant lives and carries on business. The first step is to make sure that your claim doesn't exceed the dollar limit of the court. Then you should go to the small claims court office and ask for a claim form. The form includes instructions on how to fill it out properly. Remember, you must identify the defendant correctly. It is a practice of some dishonest firms to change a company's name in order to escape liability; for example, it would be impossible to sue Joe's Garage (1991) if your contract is with Joe's Garage Inc. (1984).

You're entitled to bring any evidence to court that is relevant to the case, including such written documents as a bill of sale or receipt, a contract, or a letter. If your car has developed severe rust problems, take a photograph to court. Have the photographer sign and date the photo. You may also have witnesses testify in court (a family member may act as a witness). It's important to discuss a witness's testimony prior to the court date. If a witness can't attend the court date, he or she can write a report and sign it for representation in court. This situation usually applies to an expert witness, such as an independent mechanic who has evaluated your car's problems.

Be sure to organize your evidence, prepare questions for the witnesses, and write down what you want to tell the court.

Choosing the Right Court

You must decide on the remedy to pursue; that is, whether you want to get a partial refund or to have the sale cancelled. The amount of the refund is determined by estimating the cost of fixing existing mechanical defects plus the cost of prior repairs. Don't exaggerate your losses or claim for repairs that are considered routine maintenance.

Generally, if the cost of repairs or the sales contract falls within the small claims court limit (the limits differ from province to province), the case should be filed there to keep costs to a minimum and to obtain a speedy hearing. Small claims court judgments are not easily appealed. Lawyers aren't necessary, and in some jurisdictions (Quebec, for example) they are formally excluded. Trials are heard usually within a few months, and filing fees are minimal ($25).

If the damages exceed the small claims court limit and there is no way to reduce them, you'll have to go to a higher court—which will be costly. Before rushing off to file a lawsuit before a higher court, consider the following ways you can win your case in a higher court and still wind up losing your shirt.

Lawyers' fees can vary between $500 and $1000 for a simple case that comes to a short trial. These fees must be paid whether the case is won or lost. If you lose, you may have to pay court costs as well.

The first trial isn't likely to take place for two or three years. Then, even if you win, the judgment is likely to be appealed, thus delaying final judgment for another two to four years and boosting each side's legal fees. Once appeals are exhausted and you've won, the judgment will be paid in depreciated dollars supplemented by a low interest rate—if you can collect. Car dealers can avoid judgment by disappearing or closing down and reopening under a new name. It happens quite often, and the courts can do little to stop it.

There are practical problems involved in a suit for cancellation of sale. The court requires that the vehicle be "tendered" back to the seller at the time the lawsuit is filed. This means that the plaintiff is without transportation for as long as the case continues, unless the plaintiff purchases another car in the interim. If the plaintiff loses the case, he or she must take back the old car and pay storage fees. One could go from having no car to having two, one of which is a clunker.

For these reasons, try to stay out of the higher courts and plead the case yourself if at all possible. In some cases, small claims courts can be used creatively to get as much compensation as would be given by a higher court. For example, the hardship of owning a $6000 lemon can be eased if the owner sues the dealer in small claims court for the maximum to cover repairs, insurance, rental cars, inconvenience, etc., which may total $3000. If the court awards this amount, the car can then be sold without the repairs done for about $3000. The customer, therefore, gets back the $6000 with few legal fees to pay after a delay of only a few months. Furthermore, the car can still be used during the lawsuit, because the plaintiff isn't seeking to set the sale aside. If the small claims court rejects such a claim, the car owner has only a $25 filing fee to pay and can still sell the vehicle to reduce his or her loss.

Trial conduct

On the day of the trial, bring in a mechanic to confirm that defects exist and to estimate the cost to repair them. If the repairs have already been carried out, he can explain what caused the defects and justify his bill for repairing them. This should be done by presenting the defective parts, if possible. He must convince the judge that the defects were present at the time the car was sold and not caused by poor maintenance or abusive driving habits.

When the dealer gets on the stand, ask for the exclusion of all witnesses and try to ferret out the following facts:

- When and from whom was the used car last purchased?
- How much was it bought for?
- What was done to recondition the car and at what cost?
- What was the *Red Book* value of the car when first bought from the previous owner and when sold to the plaintiff?

This line of questioning should show the judge the considerable profits the dealer made by buying the car below the market value, by not spending much to recondition it, and by reselling it far above the *Red Book* value.

Before the dealer leaves the stand, get him to confirm whether he or his salespeople made any representations, either verbally or through a newspaper ad, extolling the vehicle's qualities. With witnesses excluded, it's quite likely that the dealer's witnesses will contradict him when their turn comes to testify. Other witnesses who can help the plaintiff's case are the car's previous owner, who can testify as to its deficiencies when sold, and any co-worker or friend of the plaintiff who can testify as to the level of maintenance on the vehicle and how it was driven, as well as describe the seriousness of the defects.

Do's and don'ts

- Do complain to the provincial Transport and Consumer Affairs ministries about possible violations of provincial laws.
- Do bring in the RCMP if you suspect that the odometer has been tampered with.
- Do contact local consumer groups and the Automobile Protection Association for used car jurisprudence and help in mediating the complaint.
- Do publicize any favourable court judgment as a warning to other dealers and as encouragement for other consumers.
- Don't sue a car dealer if he has no money, isn't bonded, is bankrupt, has changed his company, or is willing to negotiate a settlement.
- Don't sign a false sales tax receipt. Crooked car dealers try to get their customers to take a receipt that indicates a selling price far below the price paid.
- Don't threaten or insult the dealer. This will only gain sympathy for him and hurt your own credibility.

In conclusion, it's obvious that buying a used car from a dealer is a risky affair. But through the skillful use of the courts, it doesn't have to be a money-losing experience. Remember, don't delay in filing a claim once it's obvious that no settlement is forthcoming. A lawsuit should be filed no later than three months after the final registered claim letter has been sent.

Dealers in the courtroom

Lawyers often tell their dealer-clients to settle a small claims case out of court because the cost of defence would be prohibitive and the bad publicity could ruin the dealer's business. Also, lawyers know that urging their clients to settle out of court means they never lose a case.

Sometimes a dealer's lawyer will threaten to sue the plaintiff for libel or slander if the case is taken to court. This is a move designed to intimidate. No one can be sued for libel or slander merely for exercising his or her rights before the courts. The dealer, though, can be sued for harassment, and the lawyer can be cited for unprofessional conduct if the threat is carried out.

The dealer's warranty and the provincial warranty exist independently of each other. The provincial warranty requires that the vehicle be "reasonably durable," of "merchantable quality," and "appropriate for the use intended." These principles are sufficiently broad to allow a judge considerable latitude in awarding compensation.

Collecting your winnings

Settlements

You may be asked to sign a document called a "release," which proves that a final settlement has been made. Generally, once you sign the release you can't sue the other person for that particular debt or injury. If you're the debtor, it's very important that you make sure the other person signs the release when you pay him or her. If you're the creditor collecting on the debt, you must sign the release, but don't do so until you've received the money. Also, don't give up any more rights than you have to. Release the debtor from that particular debt, but don't release him or her from all future debts.

As the following example shows, the essential elements of the release are the names of the two people involved, the sum of money that was paid, the nature of the debt (or injury) that was paid off, and the fact that the creditor gives up any present or future rights to sue the debtor on that particular debt.

> I, John Doe, hereby acknowledge the receipt of $300 plus $10 interest from Jane Smith, in full and final satisfaction of all claims, which I may have against her arising from a sale of a used Ford Mustang by me to her on June 30th, 1996, and from all claims arising from a cheque for $300 dated November 30th, 1993, signed by her and payable to me which, was returned to me marked "Not Sufficient Funds."
>
> ________________ ________________
>
> Date John Doe

Deadbeat defendants

Once you win your case the real work begins if you're dealing with a professional crook. You may have to garnishee (seize) part of the defendant's bank account or wages, or ask the sheriff to serve a writ of execution. This writ allows the sheriff to demand full settlement plus court costs and, failing that, to seize the defendant's goods to cover the amount of the judgment. But here's the catch. Property that is needed to earn a living (car, tools, machinery, etc.), household goods, and anything encumbered by a lien are exempt from seizure.

Professional deadbeats can tell the sheriff that practically everything they own is exempt, and it will take another action before the regular courts, at the plaintiff's expense, to have the defendant questioned under oath. If he's found to be lying, he can then be sent to jail for perjury or contempt of court. And the small claims court judgment will remain unpaid.

A number of provinces are putting winning plaintiffs on a "fast-track" enforcement schedule that takes the time and cost out of collecting judgments.

Helpful Court Decisions

Canadian courts have rendered a number of important decisions in favour of motorists seeking damages from automakers, car dealers, insurance companies, and rustproofing firms. By citing relevant cases in your initial claim letter you might avoid having to go to court, since no one wants to waste time and money defending a position that's been rejected in previous cases. If court can't be avoided, use the following judgments to find out the legal points you should raise, the arguments that will probably be used against you, how much compensation is fair, and how judges in your area have ruled in similar cases.

These court judgments cover typical problems that are likely to arise, and have been grouped regionally to reflect the peculiarities of each province. Legal principles applying to Canadian and American law are similar; however, Quebec court decisions may be based on legal principles that don't apply outside that province. Therefore, do what most lawyers do: present all the court judgments that may be helpful and let the presiding judge or the defendant's lawyer sort out those that apply.

Additional court judgments can be found in the legal reference section of your city's main public library or at a nearby university law library. Use the following flow chart to look up specific relevant cases. Ask the librarian for help in choosing the legal phrases that best describe your claim.

Delay (in bringing lawsuit)
Bouchard v. Vaillancourt (1961), C.S., 171. If the seller has defrauded the consumer, delays for initiating a lawsuit are longer than in cases where fraud isn't involved. See also *Ginn v. Canbec Auto* (1976), C.S., 1416; *Lemire v. Pelchat* (1957), R.C.S., 823; *Ennis v. Klassen* 70 D.L.R. (4th), 325.

Damages (Punitive)

Punitive damages allow the plaintiff to get compensation that exceeds his or her losses. Judges sometimes award punitive damages in Canada as a deterrent to those who carry out dishonest or negligent practices; however, these kinds of judgments are more common in the U.S.

Vlchek v. Koshel (1988), 44 C.C.L.T. 314 (B.C.S.C., Van Reg. No. B842974). The plaintiff was seriously injured when she was thrown from a Honda all-terrain cycle she had been riding as a passenger. The court allowed for punitive damages because the manufacturer was well aware of the injuries likely to be caused by the cycle. Specifically, the Court ruled that there is no firm and inflexible principle of law stipulating that punitive or exemplary damages must be denied unless the defendant's acts are specifically directed against the plaintiff. The Court may apply punitive damages "where the defendant's conduct has been indiscriminate of focus, but reckless or malicious in its character. Intent to injure the plaintiff need not be present, so long as intent to do the injurious act can be shown."

See also: *Schryvers v. Richport Ford Sales*, the Supreme Court of British Columbia, NO: C917060, May 18, 1993, Judge Tysoe; *Morrison v. Sharp* (Ont Ct. (Gen. Div.)), 43/548; *Varleg v. Angeloni* (B. C. S. C.), 41/301; *Granek v. Reiter* (Ont. Ct. (Gen. Div.)), 35/741.

- Provincial business practices acts cover false, misleading, or deceptive representations and allow for punitive damages should the unfair practice toward the consumer amount to an unconscionable representation. See C. E. D. (3d) s. 76, pp.140-45. "Unconscionable" is defined as "where the consumer is not reasonably able to protect his or her interest because of physical infirmity, ignorance, illiteracy, or inability to understand the language of an agreement or similar factors."

- Exemplary damages are justified where compensatory damages are insufficient to deter and punish. See *Walker et al. v. CFTO Ltd. et al.* (1978), 59 O. R. (2nd) 104 (Ont. C. A.).

- Exemplary damages can be awarded in cases where the defendant's conduct was "cavalier." See *Ronald Elwyn Lister Ltd. et al. v. Dayton Tire Canada Ltd.* (1985), 52 O. R. (2d) 89 (Ont. C. A.).

- Punitive damages can be awarded for mental distress. See *Ribeiro v. Canadian Imperial Bank of Commerce* (1992), Ontario Reports 13 (3d); *Brown v. Waterloo Regional Board of Comissioners of Police* (1992), 37 O. R. (2d).

- Disregard of the public's interest, lack of preventive measures, and a callous attitude all merit exemplary damages. See *Coughlin v. Kuntz* (1989), 2 C. C. L. T. (2d) (B. C. C. A.).

- The primary purpose of exemplary damages is to prevent the defendant and all others from doing similar wrongs. See *Fleming v. Spracklin* (1921).

Bolduc v. Racicot, April 2, 1982, Quebec Provincial Court (Hauterive), No. 655-02-000364-817, Judge Cloutier. Plaintiff was given a verbal estimate of $500 for repairs, but the garage presented a bill for $1255. The court reduced the bill to $900 with the consent of the plaintiff, and then awarded another $300 as punitive damages against the garage for failing to provide a written estimate, doing more work than was requested, not guaranteeing the work, and not presenting a bill in conformance with the requirements of the Consumer Protection Act.

Defects (Safety Related)

More than 200 million cars have been recalled since 1971 to correct safety-related defects. These cars are usually fixed at no charge. Some used cars, though, may have been defective and never repaired. To find out if your car has been recalled, write the Canadian manufacturer or visit a dealer who can access the manufacturer's computerized recall file (easily done with Ford and GM).

Under Canadian federal legislation (Canadian Motor Vehicle Safety Act, 1971), car companies *do not* have to recall their cars, or fix them free of charge, within a certain period of time. The law stipulates that companies only have to notify owners that their cars can kill them. American legislation requires notification and free correction.

Use the following court decisions as a guide to what you can expect when filing a lawsuit against an automobile manufacturer for safety-related defects.

Airbags

First, let's emphasize the positive: according to the National Highway Traffic Safety Administration, airbags have saved 1500 lives. They also reduce by 25 percent moderate and severe injuries in auto accidents.

Unfortunately, airbags also can kill and injure.

According to the NHTSA, since 1990 airbags have killed 42 people, 23 of them children or infants in the front passenger seat. Another 25,000 people are estimated to have sustained (mostly minor) injuries from airbag deployment between 1988 and 1991. As well, American federal safety regulators have received 3000 reports of airbag malfunctions that have caused late or inadvertent deployment.

All these injuries and deaths have led to hundreds of lawsuits winding their way through American courts. (Canadian court figures are unavailable.) Chrysler is the target of most of these lawsuits, because it was the first company to install airbags as a standard feature and used a Thiokol airbag whose escaping gases would cause first- or second-degree burns to the hands. Used on Chrysler's 1988-91 models, these airbags have vent holes that direct hot gases at the three o'clock and nine o'clock hand positions. In late 1990, the vent holes were relocated to the twelve o'clock position. A class-action lawsuit asking for damages arising from the earlier Thiokol design has been filed in the Court of Common Pleas in Philadelphia County. Coincidentally, a U.S.

national auto safety group, the Insurance Institute for Highway Safety (IIHS), has launched an exhaustive investigation into reports that inflating airbags have seriously injured motorists.

If you're thinking of launching a lawsuit relative to an airbag malfunction keep in mind that these kinds of cases are very difficult to win due to the high costs of experts and the scarcity of judgments won by plaintiffs. In fact, Chrysler hasn't lost a jury award so far in 200 cases filed in the States alleging faulty airbag deployment, although it has settled a few. GM says that it has won 11 out of 12 jury verdicts and has seen most of the 143 cases filed either dismissed or dropped. The company admits that it has settled 15 percent of the actions—most for less than $100,000 US.

Axle

Fuller v. Ford of Canada Ltd. (1978), 2 O.R. (2d), 764. This new 1974 Econoline truck had an axle failure that caused an accident. The Court held both the manufacturer and seller responsible.

Battery

Marin v. Varta Batteries Ltd. (1983) 28 Sask. R. 173; 5 D.L.R. (4th) 427 (Q.B.). An exploding battery caused serious injuries to the plaintiff's face. The battery maker admitted liability, and the Court awarded the plaintiff $21,000 in damages.

Brakes

Marton Properties v. Northbridge Chrysler Plymouth Ltd., March 2, 1979, British Columbia Supreme Court. The plaintiff's used Chrysler had serious brake defects that warranted cancellation of the sale contract. The Court ordered the vehicle returned and the purchase price refunded.

Morschler v. Masser's Garage (1956), 2 D.L.R. (2d), 484. The plaintiff was awarded damages to a third party from a repairer who failed to fix a car's brakes properly.

Phillips v. Ford of Canada and Elgin Motors (1970), 2 O.R., 714. Ford was held responsible for the injuries caused by defective power brakes that would not have been apparent to the plaintiff. The dealer and Ford had a duty to warn the plaintiff that if the power-brake unit failed the back-up brakes would be inadequate.

Santos vs. Chrysler Corporation, Suffolk County Superior Court, February, 1996. The plaintiff's wife and three children were killed when his 1988 Caravan's rear brakes locked as he applied them to avoid rear-ending another vehicle. The jury award for $19.2 million followed Paul Santos's pleading that Chrysler "knowingly built the vehicle with a deadly defect that caused the rear brakes to lock before the front brakes." Chrysler's defence was that Santos drove the Caravan 100 miles with a broken windshield wiper and steered directly into oncoming traffic.

Fires

Brown v. Ford of Canada Ltd. (1979), 27 N.B.R. (2d), 550. The plaintiff's 1977 van suddenly caught fire while under warranty. The Court held the manufacturer only partially negligent, because the plaintiff's son, who was a mechanic, should have spotted the defect.

Chabot v. Ford Motor Company of Canada Ltd. (1983), 39 O.R. (2d) 162. This case contains an excellent and exhaustive review of manufacturer's liability for defectively manufactured vehicles. It establishes liability for losses arising from a defect while the vehicle is being maintained by the dealer. Although the plaintiff couldn't prove that a defective part caused a fire, Judge Eberle's presumption that the 1979 F-250 truck ignited from some sort of manufacturing defect implied that the manufacturer was negligent *(re ipsa loquitur).*

The Court also ruled that Ford breached a fundamental term of the sales contract by providing an unfit vehicle, and also failed to meet its obligations as set by the Manitoba Sale of Goods Act (Ontario Sales of Goods Act R.S.O. 1980 c 462, 5-15).

In his decision the judge made a number of interesting and critical observations about the motives and strategy of a large manufacturer like Ford when preparing for a case and presenting expert evidence.

In cases where companies try to avoid liability through their own limited warranties, or by invoking the exclusions expressed in the warranty, this decision confirms the *Kravitz v. General Motors* decision (which struck down these exclusions under Quebec law) from a common-law standpoint.

See also:

CPR v. Kerr, 49 S.C.R., 33 at 36.

Gougeon v. Peugeot Canada, July 20, 1973, Quebec Superior Court, No. 12736, Judge Kaufman.

Lazanik v. Ford, June 15, 1965, C.S.M. 623-664, Judge Challies.

Parent v. Lapointe (1952), I S.C.R., 381.

Rioux v. General Motors, March 9, 1970, C.S.M. 739-005, 6.

Touchette v. Pizzagalli (1938), S.C.R. 433.

Zelezen v. Model Auto Sales Ltd., November 26, 1971, C.S.M. 722-487, Judge Nichols.

La Paix v. Chrysler Canada, April 5, 1982, Quebec Provincial Court, No. 500-02-040677-796, Judge Prenouveau. A new 1976 Volaré suddenly caught fire while the owner tried to start the car. It had been in use for only 10 months. Chrysler Canada refused all liability, claiming that the fire was probably due to poor starting technique. The Court held Chrysler responsible for $4039 in damages after it was proven that the fire was caused by unburned gasoline catching fire in the muffler.

Racine v. Durand Pontiac-Buick and General Motors, December 15, 1977, Quebec Provincial Court, No. 02-015218-774, Judge Lacoste. The plaintiff claimed $700 for a catalytic converter that exploded. General Motors and the dealer claimed that the explosion was due to poor maintenance and that the 50,000 mile/five-year emissions warranty on the converter didn't cover such maintenance-related defects. The judge disagreed, stating that the catalytic converter exploded due to a defective PCV valve for which General Motors and the dealer had to take responsibility. The fact that the converter could overheat and catch fire whenever the engine was badly tuned caused the judge to suggest that a warning be placed on all General Motors vehicles with the converter. The plaintiff was awarded $700.

Parking gear slippage

General Motors v. Colton, October 17, 1980, Quebec Court of Appeal, No. 500-09-000692-772. A 1970 Oldsmobile parked on the plaintiff's inclined driveway rolled back and injured the owner. Judgment was against General Motors for $29,000.

Rusting undercarriage

McGouey v. Lawson Motors Ltd. (1982), 42 N.B.R. (2d) 225. Seven weeks after buying a used Fiat, the frame collapsed from excessive corrosion. The purchaser was awarded a complete refund of the purchase price and damages.

In *R. v. Ford Motor Company of Canada*, the Federal Ministry of Transport successfully pleaded that rusting of the undercarriage of Ford's 1965-1974 midsize cars was a safety defect.

Seatbelt design/defects

Door-mounted seatbelts, motorized seatbelts, and lapbelts have come under fire during the past decade from safety advocates and the courts after insurance studies and trauma specialists showed that they increase the severity of accident injuries.

Motorized seatbelts

These front seat restraints run along a channel and cross the shoulder when the ignition is turned on. A lapbelt has to be fastened separately. These automatic belts are set so high above the door frame that they're uncomfortable to wear and a nightmare to adjust. Their most serious shortcoming, however, is that they give the driver a false sense of security, and the separate lapbelt often goes unfastened (the U.S. government says that only 29 percent of the people with motorized seatbelts use the lap portion). This has resulted in a number of accidents where the driver or front passenger has been decapitated or paralyzed by the shoulder belt. Ford was sued for $1.3 million in Akron, Ohio, where the driver of a 1990 Escort was paralyzed in an accident in which only the automatic shoulder belt was fastened *(Pflum v. Ford)*. Nissan faces a $10-

million suit in Newnan, Georgia, from the father of a girl who did not have the lapbelt fastened and who was decapitated by her 1989 Sentra's motorized shoulder harness *(Smith v. Nissan).*

Door-mounted seatbelts

U.S. safety agencies are currently looking at the reliability and safety of door-mounted seatbelts in light of accident reports showing a high failure rate and an increased severity of injuries. GM, for example, is being sued in the U.S. for $33 million over the inadequate performance of the driver's door-mounted seatbelt on a 1990 Pontiac Sunbird. The driver was killed when the car door opened, rendering the seatbelt inoperative. The suit claims that GM was negligent in the design that caused the belt to be undone, leaving the driver unprotected and unrestrained.

Three-point seatbelts

Four years ago, in *Garrett v. Ford,* a Baltimore, Maryland, Federal Court jury rendered a $3.2-million verdict against Ford for installing a dangerously designed lapbelt and for not including back seat shoulder harnesses in a 1985 Escort. The lapbelts were designed to cross at the waist instead of the pelvis, and this error contributed to the passengers' paralysis. If shoulder harnesses had been installed the lapbelts would not have aggravated the injuries. Ford is involved in another ongoing trial where the company is being sued for compensatory and punitive damages arising from the death of a 72-year-old nun, Sister Mary Margaret LeGlise. She was riding in the rear seat of a 1987 Ford Tempo with her lapbelt fastened when the accident occurred. At trial, California Superior Court judge Jeffrey Miller lit into Ford for keeping its settlements in other cases secret (referring to a $6-million payout to settle a San Diego case) in order to avoid embarrassment and other lawsuits. Judge Miller noted further that Ford could not claim that the technology to install three-point belts had not been perfected when for years the company had been putting the safer three-point belts in its European models. Judge Miller concluded, "Ford knew that the rear seat lapbelt not only did not provide adequate protection but actually caused injury to its users. Ford also knew through its own internal engineering analysis and experimentation that the three-point restraint system was vastly superior and would save many lives." In another important lawsuit, a Texas court has ordered Hyundai to pay $500,000 in damages to a mother whose daughter was killed while a passenger in a 1986 Excel. The car's lap-only belt increased the severity of the girl's abdominal injuries. The U.S. government is currently investigating shoulder belt failures in all 1987-89 Hyundai Excels. There have been 67 complaints, including 43 injuries and seven deaths.

Steering

Holley v. Ford of Canada, June 18, 1980, Nova Scotia Supreme Court, Judge Cowan. The plaintiff purchased a used 1976 Ford Custom 200 truck that was involved in an accident due to the failure of the steering assembly. The plaintiff was awarded $4100 in damages.

White v. International Harvester (1969), W.W.R. 235 (Alta. T.D.). This new truck's steering assembly had problems and was adjusted by the dealer, but 4200 miles later it suddenly veered out of control due to a defective steering component. The plaintiff was awarded both costs and damages.

Sudden acceleration
Willar v. Ford (1991), 118 N.B.R. (2d) 323. The owner sued Ford after the throttle jammed open twice, causing several accidents. The Court held that Ford, not the dealer, was responsible for the plaintiff's damages.

Tires
Chase v. Goodyear Tire and Rubber Co. and Goodyear Canada Inc., New Brunswick Court of Queen's Bench, Trial Division, No. S/C/513/89, April 12, 1991. The plaintiff was injured when the tire he was inflating exploded. There was no evidence of a manufacturing defect on the original tire or with the retread. Goodyear was found negligent because it failed to warn its customer of the danger inherent in inflating a retreaded tire with worn-out and damaged radial cords, thereby breaching its duty to warn. The plaintiff was awarded $65,000 for his injuries.

Gagnon v. Canadian Tire (1979) C.P. 251, Quebec Provincial Court. The plaintiff was awarded $1310 as compensation for a radial tire that exploded when he was rocking his car out of a snowbank.

Murphy v. D. & B. Holdings (1979) 31 N.S.R. (2d) 380; 52 A.P.R. 380 (S.C). The Court held that the manufacturer was liable for damages for permitting a customer to use its tires in a dangerous manner.

Tire iron placement adding to collision injuries
Gallant v. Beitz (1983), 42 O.R. (2d) 86. This judgment states clearly that automakers are presumed to know that their vehicles will be involved in accidents and must take reasonable steps to minimize injuries caused by flaws inherent in the design of their vehicles.

Transmissions jump from Park to Reverse
McEvoy v. Ford Motor Company et al., Supreme Court of B.C., No. 3841989, September 6, 1989, Judge Hinds. Mr. McEvoy was killed when his new Ford pickup backed over him after the transmission jumped from Park to Reverse. He had left the engine running and was unloading cargo when the right front wheel crushed his chest.

Justice Hinds found Ford 65 percent negligent for the following reasons:

- The RCMP mechanic testified that the gearshift lever could easily be mispositioned into an "unstable Park" position.
- It was determined that Ford was aware of this defect as early as 1971, according to internal company documents presented during the trial.
- Ford had a duty to warn its customers of the hazard caused by the C-6 automatic transmission; the warning in the owner's manual was deemed insufficient to satisfy this duty.
- Ford and its Canadian distributor had breached their duty to the consumer.

Unger v. Ford. In this Bridgeport, Connecticut, out-of-court settlement, Ford paid $700,000 to the family of a man crushed to death when his 1988 F-series pickup went into Reverse while the gearshift lever was in Park. The plaintiff claimed that the automatic transmission and PRNDL indicator were defective. His lawyer also alleged that Ford had received 26,000 complaints about the transmission defect.

Wheels

Nason v. General Motors of Canada Ltd., November 1, 1995, British Columbia Provincial Court (Small Claims Division), No: C93-04200, Judge C. L. Bagnall. Judge Bagnall awarded $5416 plus interest to the plaintiffs for damages arising from an accident caused by their Reatta's faulty right rear wheel knuckle. Damages included $4500 for the decrease in the car's value and $916 for the loss of a safe driving discount offered by the Insurance Corporation of British Columbia.

Michel Beauregard v. Goyette Auto and General Motors, July 3, 1982, Quebec Provincial Court, No. 500-05-011478-763, Judge Aronovitch. A new 1975 Ventura had one wheel suddenly lock up, which caused the vehicle to go out of control. The plaintiff was awarded $3500.

Defects (Performance Related)

New vehicles

The definitive answer to what is a "lemon" is found in U.S. state law, where it's defined as a problem that can't be repaired after four tries, keeps the vehicle out of service for more than 30 days, or renders it unfit for the purpose for which it was purchased.

Bagnell's Cleaners v. Eastern Automobile Ltd. (1991), 111 N.S.R. (2d) 51, 303 A.P.R. 51 (T.D.). This Nova Scotia company found that the new van it purchased had serious engine, transmission, and radiator defects. The dealer pleaded unsuccessfully that the sales contract excluded all other warranties except for those contained in the contract. The Court held that there was a fundamental breach of the implied warranty and that the van's performance differed substantially from what the purchaser had been led to expect. An exclusionary clause could not protect the seller, who failed to live up to a fundamental term of the contract.

Burridge v. City Motor, 10 Nfld. & P.E.I.R., 451. This Newfoundland resident complained repeatedly of his new car's defects during the warranty period, and hadn't used his car for 204 days after spending almost $1500 for repairs. The judge awarded all repair costs and cancelled the sale.

Davis v. Chrysler Canada Ltd. (1977), 26 N.S.R. (2d) 410 (T.D.). The owner of a new $28,000 diesel truck found that a faulty steering assembly prevented him from carrying on his business. The Court ordered that the sale be cancelled and $10,000 in monthly payments be reimbursed. There was insufficient evidence to award compensation for business losses.

Fox v. Wilson Motors and GM, Court of Queen's Bench, New Brunswick, February 9, 1989, File No. F/C/308/87. A trucker's new tractor-trailer had repeated engine malfunctions. He was awarded damages for loss of income, excessive fuel consumption, and telephone charges under the provincial Sale of Goods Act.

Gibbons v. Trapp Motors Ltd. (1970), 9 D.L.R. (3d) 742 (B.C. S.C.). The Court ordered the dealer to take back a new car that had numerous defects that needed 32 hours of repairs. Refund was reduced by mileage driven.

Julien v. GM of Canada (1991), 116 N.B.R. (2d) 80. The plaintiff's new diesel truck produced excessive engine noise. The dealer claimed that the problem was caused by the owner's engine alterations. The plaintiff was awarded the $5000 cost of repairing the engine by an independent dealer.

Johnson v. Northway Chevrolet Oldsmobile (1993), 108 Sask. R. 138 (Q. B.). The Court ordered the dealer to take back a new car that had been brought in for repairs on 14 different occasions. Two years after purchase, the buyer initiated a lawsuit for the purchase price of the car and for general damages. General damages were awarded.

Kravitz v. General Motors, Supreme Court of Canada, January 1979, I.R.C.S., 393. This owner of a new Oldsmobile was never able to have it properly repaired under warranty. When the warranty period was over, General Motors and the dealer refused to do further free work or to give him another vehicle. The presiding judge awarded the car owner damages and a refund of the purchase price. This Quebec case is based on articles 1522 to 1530 of the Quebec Civil Code (hidden defects), but it applies in common-law provinces as well. The Supreme Court ruled that both the dealer and the manufacturer can be held jointly or separately responsible and that the manufacturer's warranty does not negate the implied legal warranty of fitness.

MacDonald GMC v. Gillespie, New Brunswick Court of Appeal, June 3, 1986. Compensation of $7148 was awarded to a new car buyer after the dealer failed to honour his salesman's verbal promises to repair certain defects at no charge.

Magna Management Ltd. v. Volkswagen Canada Inc. May 27, 1988, Doc. No. CA006037, Vancouver (B.C.C.A.). This precedent-setting case allowed the plaintiff to keep his new $48,325 VW while awarding him $37,101—three years after the car was purchased. The problems were centred on poor engine performance. The jury accepted the plaintiff's view that the car was practically worthless with its inherent defects.

Maughan v. Silver's Garage Ltd., Nova Scotia Supreme Court, 6 B. L. R. 303, N.S.C. (2d) 278. The plaintiff leased a defective backhoe. The manufacturer had to reimburse the plaintiff's losses because the warranty wasn't honoured. The Court rejected the manufacturer's contention that the contract's exclusion clause protected the company from lawsuits for damages resulting from a latent defect.

Murphy v. Penney Motors Ltd. (1979) 23 Nfld. & P.E.I.R., 152, 61 A.P.R. 152 (Nfld. T.D.). This Newfoundland trucker found that the repairing of engine problems took his new trailer off the road for 129 days during a seven-month period. The judge awarded all repair costs as well as compensation for business losses, and cancelled the sale.

Murray v. Sperry Rand Corp., Ontario Supreme Court, 5 B.L.R. 284. The seller, dealer, and manufacturer were all held liable for breach of warranty when a forage harvester did not perform as advertised in the sales brochure or as promised by the sales agent. The plaintiff was given his money back and reimbursed for his economic loss based on what his harvesting usually earned. The Court held that the advertising was a warranty.

Oliver v. Courtesy Chrysler (1983) Ltd. (1992), 11 B. C. A. C. 169. This new car had numerous defects over a three-year period, which the dealer attempted to fix to no avail. The plaintiff put the car in storage and sued the dealer for the purchase price. The Court ruled that the car wasn't roadworthy and that the plaintiff couldn't be blamed for putting it in storage rather than selling it and purchasing another vehicle. The purchase price was refunded minus $1500 for each year the plaintiff used the car.

Olshaski Farms Ltd. v. Skene Farm Equipment Ltd., Alberta Court of Queen's Bench, January 9, 1987, 49 Alta. L.R. (2d) 249. This Massey-Ferguson combine caught fire after the manufacturer had sent two notices to dealers informing them of a defect that could cause a fire. The judge ruled under the Sale of Goods Act that the balance of probabilities indicated that the manufacturing defect caused the fire, even though there was no direct evidence proving that the defect existed.

Western Pacific Tank Lines Ltd. v. Brentwood Dodge, June 2, 1975, British Columbia Supreme Court, No. 30945-74, Judge Meredith. The Court awarded the plaintiff $8600 and cancelled the sale of a new Chrysler New Yorker with the following defects: badly adjusted doors, water leaks into the interior, and electrical short circuits.

Paint defects/rusting

New vehicles shouldn't have paint blemishes up to their sixth year of ownership (GM benchmark), and should resist surface rust up to three years and rust perforations up to seven years. Owners of used vehicles have no recourse against the manufacturer (except for recalls and secret warranties). However, they can file suit against the seller if it's obvious that the defects were intentionally covered up, and are substantial enough to make the vehicle worth much less than was paid or to make it unsafe to drive.

Martin v. Honda Canada Inc., March 17, 1986, Ontario Small Claims Court (Scarborough), Judge Sigurdson. The original owner of a 1981 Honda Civic sought compensation for the premature "bubbling, pitting, cracking of the paint and rusting of the Civic after five years of ownership." Judge Sigurdson agreed and ordered Honda to pay the owner $1163.95.

Perron v. Vincent Automobile Ltée. (1979), C.P., 166. The plaintiff had the dealer rustproof her new car at a cost of $115. This dealer's warranty said that any future rusting would be repaired up to a cost of $115, or the purchase price would be refunded. The dealer interpreted this to mean that $115 would be the total amount that could be claimed while the guarantee was in effect. However, the Court agreed with the plaintiff that she could claim up to $115 each time a warranty claim was made.

Prochera v. Sherwood Chevrolet, Saskatoon, November 9, 1978, Judge Clifford Peet. In this Blazer paint case, the plaintiff sued for the correction of a mismatched paint job carried out by the dealer to repair delivery damage and the original mismatching of the paint seen when the vehicle was first delivered. The plaintiff was awarded $75 plus court costs.

Rolland v. Chrysler, November 1979, Third Small Claims Court of Lanark County, Ontario, No. 148/79, Judge Thorpe. After Chrysler admitted it had a secret warranty that paid for the replacement of rusted-out front fenders, Judge Thorpe awarded $896.17 to a couple who purchased a used 1976 Chrysler Volaré in 1978 from a relative.

Thauberger v. Simon Fraser Sales and Mazda Motors, 3 B.C.L.R., 193. This Mazda owner sued for damages caused by the premature rusting of his 1977 Mazda GLC. The Court awarded him $1000. Mr. Thauberger had previously sued General Motors for a prematurely rusted Blazer truck and was also awarded $1000 in the same Court. Both judges ruled that the defects could not be excluded from the carmaker's express warranty or from the implied warranty granted by ss. 20, 20(b) of the B.C. Sale of Goods Act.

Whittaker v. Ford Motor Company (1979), 24 O.R. (2d), 344. A new Ford developed serious corrosion problems in spite of having been rustproofed by the dealer. The Court ruled that the dealer, not Ford, was liable for the damage for having sold the rustproofing product at the time of purchase. This is an important judgment to use when a rustproofer or paint protector goes out of business or refuses to pay a claim, since the decision holds the dealer jointly responsible.

See also:

Danson v. Chateau Ford (1976) C.P., Quebec Small Claims Court, No. 32-00001898-757, Judge Lande.

Doyle v. Vital Automotive Systems, Ontario Small Claims Court (Toronto), May 16, 1977, Judge Turner.

Lacroix v. Ford, Ontario Small Claims Court ((Toronto), April 1980, Judge Tierney.

Marinovich v. Riverside Chrysler, District Court of Ontario, No. 1030/85, April 1, 1987, Judge Stortini.

False Advertising

False sales prices

R. v. Lanthier and Lalonde, Sessions Court (Montreal). A Montreal Ford dealer was fined $300 for placing ads showing tremendous reductions on new cars sold at prices below the manufacturer's suggested retail price. After criminal charges were laid, it was shown that the advertised savings were lies (judgment on file with Consumer and Corporate Affairs). Several dozen suburban Toronto Chrysler dealers were fined by the federal government for similar deceptions.

Odometer tampering

Odometer tampering is a criminal offence under the federal Weights and Measures Act. The Department of Consumer and Corporate Affairs uses the RCMP to investigate all such cases. Many violators have been caught and successfully prosecuted. Nevertheless, the federal law is weak because fines are so low that they practically represent a licence to operate illegally, and an individual can escape prosecution by pleading that the odometer was broken and had to be changed.

Bouchard v. South Park Mercury Sales (1978), 3 W.W.R., 78. The odometer figure written on the contract was incorrect. The dealer pleaded ignorance, but the judge ruled that the car's owner should receive damages to compensate for the extra mileage.

Couturier v. Herman, Quebec Small Claims Court (Montreal North), No. 74-2216, Judge Laurier. The seller of this 1967 Oldsmobile turned back the odometer. Judge Laurier awarded $200 to the buyer as compensation for the additional mileage.

Delmaire v. Westcoast Honda, British Columbia Small Claims Court (Victoria), August 13, 1986. The plaintiff bought a used 1979 Rabbit "as is" and found that the odometer had been turned back. He argued that although he had no proof that the dealer was responsible, the dealer was an expert and should have suspected the low mileage. The Court agreed and awarded $1299 for a rebuilt engine.

Henley v. Bob Barnabe, February 15, 1971, Quebec Provincial Court, No. 384-829, Judge Gold. The dealer turned back the odometer in a Datsun and sold the car for the wrong model year. The vehicle had been sold before to another customer who had been involved in an accident with it. Judgment was rendered in favour of the plaintiff, and the purchase price was reduced by $303.

Zelezen v. Model Auto Sales, November 26, 1971, Quebec Superior Court, No. 722-487, Judge Nicols. Not only did the judge order the car returned and the purchase price refunded because of odometer tampering, he also ordered the dealer to pay compensation for the plaintiff's injuries from an accident caused by the car's defects.

Used car sold as new (demonstrator)
Leblanc v. Frenette and Chrysler Credit, May 27, 1971, Quebec Provincial Court No. 279-772, Judge Laurier. The plaintiff's new demonstrator was actually a used car that had had its odometer rolled back. It had also been in an accident. The Court held the dealer responsible and ordered him to refund the purchase price.

Leasing

Although the state of Florida just got a $4.2-million settlement from its Toyota dealers for leasing misrepresentation, no Canadian government has taken similar action even though the same misleading practices are prevalent here among the major leasing agencies and dealers. Fortunately Canadian courts are more progressive than the government, and have made several significant rulings that give lessees added clout when seeking refunds for deceptive practices and defective vehicles.

Schryvers v. Richport Ford Sales, the Supreme Court of British Columbia, No: C917060, May 18, 1993, Justice Tysoe. The Court awarded

$17,578,47 (including $6000 in punitive damages) plus costs to a couple who paid thousands of dollars more in unfair and hidden leasing charges than if they had simply purchased their Ford Explorer and Escort. The Court found that this price difference constituted a deceptive, unconscionable act or practice in contravention of the Trade Practices Act, R. S. B. C. 1979, c. 406 (the "act").

Judge Tysoe analyzed the price difference using the following method:

Judgment

Explorer Purchase vs. Lease

The difference of these totals and the calculation of the tax consequences as follows:

$32,835.00	–	amount payable by lease method
(28,240.60)	–	amount payable by financing method
597.27	–	PST and GST on difference of above figures
(243.36)	–	saving on PST and GST under lease method
$4,948.31	–	total damages re Explorer

Escort Purchase vs. Lease

The difference of these totals and the calculation of the tax consequences are as follows:

$22,235.96	–	amount payable by lease method
(16,266.40)	–	amount payable by financing method
776.04	–	PST and GST on difference of above figures
(115.44)	–	saving on PST and GST under lease method
$6,630.16	–	total damages re Escort

The total of the general damages in respect of both vehicles is $6,630.16 + $4,948.16 – $11,578.47.

Judge Tysoe concluded that the total of the general damages awarded to the Schryvers couple for both vehicles would be $11,578.47. He then proceeded to give the following reasons for awarding an additional $6000 in punitive damages:

> "… Little wonder Richport Ford had a contest for the salesperson who could persuade the most customers to acquire their vehicles by way of a lease transaction. I consider the actions of Richport Ford to be sufficiently flagrant and high-handed to warrant an award of punitive damages.
>
> There must be a disincentive to suppliers in respect of intentionally deceptive trade practices. If no punitive damages are awarded for intentional violations of the legislation, suppliers will continue to conduct their businesses in a manner that involves deceptive trade practices because they will have nothing to lose. In this case I believe that the appropriate amount of punitive damages is the extra profit Richport Ford endeavoured to make as a result of its deceptive acts. I therefore award punitive damages against Richport Ford in the amount of $6000 …"

Salvador v. Setay Motors/Queenstown Chev-Olds, Hamilton Small Claims Court, Case No.1621/95. Robert Salvador, an Ontario consumer advocate and founder of the Consumer Action Group (CAG), was awarded $2000 plus costs from Queenstown Leasing because the company should have tried harder to sell the leased vehicle at a higher price when the "open lease" expired.

Salvador gave Queenstown a list of offers from independent buyers when he returned the vehicle, but they were never contacted. Instead, the leasing agency auctioned off the van to the highest bidder. You guessed it—Queenstown Leasing.

This judgment can also be helpful in cases where a repossessed vehicle is sold or auctioned off for far less than what it's worth, or where the seller is in a conflict of interest by being the buyer as well. Copies of this judgment can be obtained by calling the Ontario Consumer Action Group at 416-587-0070.

Ford Motor Credit v. Bothwell, December 3, 1979, Ontario County Court (Middlesex), No. 9226-T, Judge Macnab. The defendant leased a 1977 Ford truck that had frequent engine problems characterized by stalling and hard starting. After complaining for one year and driving 22,000 miles, the defendant cancelled the lease. Ford Credit sued for the money owing on the lease. Judge Macnab cancelled the lease and ordered Ford Credit to repay 70 percent of the amount paid during the leasing period. Ford Credit was also ordered to refund repair costs, even though the corporation claimed that it should not be held responsible for Ford's failure to honour its warranty.

See also:

Barber v. Inland Truck Sales, 11 D.L.R. (3D) 469.

Canadian-Dominion Leasing v. Suburban Super Drug Ltd. (1966), 56 D.L.R. (2d) 43.

Neilson v. Atlantic Rentals Ltd. (1974), 8 N.B.R. (2d), 594.
Volvo Canada v. Fox, December 13, 1979, New Brunswick Court of Queen's Bench, No. 1698/77/C, Judge Stevenson.
Western Tractor v. Dyck, 7 D.L.R. (3d) 535.

Misrepresentation

Gas mileage claims
Motorists who fail to get the gas mileage advertised by the manufacturer or dealer can file a criminal complaint for false advertising and initiate a small claims court lawsuit for compensation. Favourable judgments exist for each type of claim.

Dubeau v. Ford of Canada and Ventes Mercury Marie Victorin Ltée., November 20, 1980, Quebec Small Claims Court (Longueuil), No. 505-32-001847-806, Judge Langis. In this judgment, Ford was shown to continue its reign as gas-guzzling champ. The plaintiff was promised by the dealer and by Ford ads that his new car would get an average of 26 mpg. In fact, it got only 17 mpg. Judge Langis forced Ford and the dealer to pay the plaintiff $400 for the difference.

Marchand v. Grondin Auto and Ford Motor Company, October 10, 1975, Quebec Small Claims Court (Thetford Mines), No. 235-32-000387-75-8, Judge Bastien. The owner of a 1974 Bobcat only got 15 mpg, despite Ford's advertising and the dealer's claim that the car would deliver 30 mpg. Judge Bastien awarded the plaintiff $310 as compensation for the difference between what was advertised and the car's actual gas mileage. Both Ford and its dealer were judged responsible.

Late delivery
When the delivery of a new car is delayed, the customer can either demand that the contract be cancelled or ask for special damages. If the delay was caused by the seller's or manufacturer's negligence, both the contract's cancellation and compensating damages can be claimed.

The seller can make a successful argument that no specific delivery date was written on the contract or that the delay was caused by elements beyond his control.

George Archer v. Metro Motor Sales, Quebec Small Claims Court, No. 32-006842-74. The plaintiff was not given his new vehicle at the time promised. He was awarded $300 as compensation for extra expenses, including the cost of an airplane ticket.

Manery v. Kampe (1943), 3 W.W.R. 687, (B.C.C.A.). The seller delivered the goods 18 days after the contracted delivery date. The buyer refused the merchandise and sued for cancellation of the contract. The Court ordered that the buyer's money be refunded.

Mechanical fitness certificate

Belanger v. Fournier Chrysler Dodge Ltée. (1975), 25 N.B.R. (2d), 673. A used car sold in New Brunswick carried an inspection sticker indicating that the body and mechanical components were in good condition. Actually the chassis was rusted through, and the police ordered the vehicle off the road. The plaintiff was awarded the purchase price.

Beliveau v. Duval, November 26, 1973, Quebec Provincial Court, No. 02-046408-72, Judge Casgrain. The plaintiff bought a used Jeep with a spare motor that the defendant said could be used if the original engine failed. It did, but the spare motor was the wrong size. Judgment was awarded against the defendant for misrepresenting the condition of the Jeep and for giving false assurances that the spare engine was adequate. Both parties were private individuals.

Ennis v. Klassen, 70 D.L.R. (4th), 325. Ennis bought a used BMW that was represented as a 1980 733i for $9000. He learned two days later that it was really a 1979 BMW 728—a model without fuel injection that wasn't supposed to be allowed into Canada because of federal safety standards. It was also impossible to find parts for this vehicle. He kept the car in his garage for two years thereafter.

Klassen, a private seller, maintained that the lawsuit was tardy, that Ennis had inspected the vehicle before purchase, and that the whole case revolved around innocent misrepresentation.

Manitoba's Court of Appeal disagreed on the grounds that "the misrepresentation does go to the root of the contract. The plaintiff was led to believe that he was buying a BMW model 733 at a fair retail price for a second-hand vehicle of the advertised model, type and vintage. He received nothing of the kind, and so he may rescind the sale."

As for the action being tardy, the Appeal Court also disagreed, saying that "the plaintiff no longer used the vehicle, and took immediate steps on the path to rescission." Ennis got a complete refund.

See also:

F&B Transport Ltd. v. White Truck Sales Manitoba Ltd. (19675), 49 D.L.R. (2d) 670; *Adams v. Canadian Co-Operative Implements Ltd.* (1980), 20 A. R. 533.

Ferraro v. Marsilio, May 15, 1981, Quebec Provincial Court, No. 500-02-026887-807, Judge Thinel. The plaintiff was awarded $3900, representing a refund of the purchase price of a used car that had been misrepresented as being in good condition by the salesman. Actually, the vehicle had been heavily damaged in an accident. The Court held that the plaintiff's inexperience had been exploited.

Gagnon v. Leveille, May 2, 1975, Quebec Provincial Court (Quebec) No. 103-879, Judge Dussault. The plaintiff was told that his old motor had been replaced with a new one. Actually another old motor had been used. The Court ordered the plaintiff to pay $1 for the old motor and the defendant to pay $850 for a new one.

L.G. Wilson Motors v. Woods (1970), 2 N.B.R. (2d), 581 (S. C.). A safety certification carried out by a provincial inspector doesn't guarantee that a used vehicle is safe or that the inspector was competent. The buyer should have made his own inspection. The plaintiff's claim was rejected.

Presley v. MacDonald (1963), 1 O.R. (2d), 619. In this case an Ontario judge ruled that under s. 49(1) of the Highway Traffic Act, the mechanical fitness certificate made the seller half liable for damages caused in a subsequent accident.

Smith v. Marc Patrick Motors and the Canadian Tire Corporation, September 20, 1984, Ontario Small Claims Court (Niagara North), Judge Kingstone. The plaintiff bought a used 1978 Honda Civic that was sold as having a "new" engine. Shortly thereafter the engine failed. Canadian Tire hadn't put a new engine in the vehicle. Judge Kingstone ordered both defendants to split the cost of the motor repairs ($1000 plus 13 percent interest) for misrepresenting the engine.

Miscellaneous misrepresentation

Beale v. Taylor (1967), 3 All E.R., 253 (C.A.). The seller innocently misrepresented a used car as being in good condition, when it was really two cars welded together. The Court ordered the sale set aside.

Bottcher v. Selig, 26 N.S.R. (2d) 347 (C.A.). A used car was represented as needing only a quart of oil every 1000 miles. The plaintiff was awarded damages for serious oil leaks. In addition to misrepresenting the condition of the vehicle, this Nova Scotia Court held that the seller's promise was an implied warranty.

Hanson and Campbell v. Cornell Chevrolet Oldsmobile Ltd. and Canadian Imperial Bank of Commerce and Weaver (1983), 4 W.W.R. 285. The purchaser of a used car in British Columbia had it seized when he moved to Alberta. He then brought suit against the B.C. dealer who sold him the vehicle, which had a valid chattel mortgage registered against it. The Court held that the British Columbia Sale of Goods Act, s.16, protects consumers whether or not the goods remain in the province. The important element is that the contract was agreed to in British Columbia. As a result, the dealer had to compensate the client for his losses.

Henzel v. Brussels Motors Ltd. (1973), 1 O.R., 339 (C.C.). A used car sold with a mechanical fitness certificate had defective brakes. The Court ordered the purchase price refunded.

Sandilands v. Guelph Datsun 1980 Ltd. (1982), 35 O.R. (2d) 25. The dealer represented a used car as having "good" brakes. Four months after purchase the vehicle was taken off the road by the Ministry of Transportation because of defective brakes and rust perforations. The Court held that the contract should be cancelled because the dealer's misrepresentation was an "unfair practice" according to Section 4(1)(a) of the Ontario Business Practices Act. It was pointed out that the dealer had given false or misleading information when:

1. He supplied a car equipped with brakes that wouldn't stop in an emergency and that hadn't had an adequate mechanical inspection.
2. He supplied a car that hadn't had its rust defects repaired even though he had contracted to do so. The stipulation in the contract that a full body repair job was to be provided was supplementary to the safety check.
3. He concerned himself with outfitting a car that he knew wasn't worth making roadworthy.

The dealer was forced to take back the car and pay storage and transport costs.

"New" car really a used car
Bilodeau v. Sud Auto, Quebec Court of Appeal, No. 09-000751-73, Judge Tremblay. This appeal court cancelled the contract and held that a car can't be sold as new or as a demonstrator if it has ever been rented, leased, sold, or titled to anyone other than the dealer.

Rourke v. Gilmore, January 16, 1928, *Ontario Weekly Notes,* vol. XXXIII, p. 292. Before discovering that his new car was really used, the plaintiff drove it for over a year. For this reason the contract couldn't be cancelled. However, the appeals court instead awarded damages for $500, which was quite a sum in 1928!

Truck misrepresentation
MacDonald v. Equilease Co. Ltd., January 18, 1979, Ontario Supreme Court, Judge O'Driscoll. The plaintiff leased a truck that was misrepresented as having an axle stronger than it really was. The Court awarded the plaintiff damages for repairs and set aside the lease.

Seich v. Festival Ford Sales Ltd., (1978), 6 Alta. L.R. (2d), 262. The plaintiff bought a used truck from the defendant after being assured that it had a new motor and transmission. It didn't, and the Court awarded the plaintiff $6400.

Vehicle not as ordered
Whether you're buying a new or used vehicle, the seller can't misrepresent the vehicle. Anything that varies with what one would commonly expect, or with the seller's representation, must be disclosed prior to signing the contract. Typical scenarios are odometer turnbacks, accident damage, used or leased cars sold as new, new vehicles that are the wrong colour and the wrong model year, or that lack options or standard features that were promised.

Chenel v. Bel Automobile (1981) Inc., August 27, 1976, Quebec Superior Court (Quebec), Judge Desmeules. The plaintiff didn't receive his new Ford truck with the Jacob brakes that were essential for transporting sand in hilly regions. The Court awarded the plaintiff $27,000, representing the purchase price of the vehicle less the money he earned while using the truck.

Lasky v. Royal City Chrysler Plymouth, Ontario High Court of Justice, February 18, 1987, 59 O.R. (2d) 323. The plaintiff bought a 4-cylinder 1983 Dodge 600 that was represented by the salesman as being a 6-cylinder model. After putting 40,000 km on the vehicle over a 22-month period, the buyer was given her money back, without interest, under the provincial Business Practices Act.

White v. Munn Motors, (1960), 45 M.P.R. 253 (Nfld. T.D.). The dealer misrepresented a half-ton truck as having a three-quarter-ton capacity. The owner was given his money back because he didn't get what he paid for.

Wrong model year

Adelaide Motors v. Alexander (1962), 48 M.P.R. 258 (Nfld. T.D.). The customer bought a new 1960 car that was misrepresented as being a 1961 model. The Court ruled that the plaintiff was entitled to damages.

Cohen v. Wilson, January 10, 1973, Quebec Provincial Court, No. 409-793, Judge Tormey. The plaintiff was awarded $958, representing the purchase price and repair costs related to a used Land Rover. The vehicle was advertised in the local paper by its owner as being in good condition and as a 1960 model. In fact, the vehicle was in poor shape and was a 1955 model.

Ginn v. Canbec Auto, Quebec Superior Court (Montreal), No. 500-05-014597-74-4. Relying on expert testimony provided by the APA, the Court awarded $10,000 to the purchaser of a new 1972 BMW that was fraudulently sold as a 1973 model. The case demonstrates beyond a doubt that car retailers are culpable for the misrepresentation of their products.

Woods v. Borstel (1962), 34 D.L.R. (2d) 68 (Alta. C.A.). The customer bought a new 1958 car that was misrepresented as being a 1959 model. The Court ruled that the seller's model year representation was a warranty as defined under s. 2(1)(n) of the Alberta Sale of Goods Act. The plaintiff was entitled to all damages, but the contract remained in force.

In Ontario, two separate, successful lawsuits claimed that Ford systematically cheated consumers by selling 1970 Cortinas as new 1971 models. Each purchaser received $400 in compensation from small claims court. In *Brosseau v. Lewis Motors,* Ottawa-Carleton, and *King v. Paddy Shanahan Ford,* Toronto, the Court pointed to deceptive and misleading sales tactics used to sell the Cortinas.

See also:

Ennis v. Klassen 70 D.L.R. (4th), 325.

Secret Warranties

It's common practice for manufacturers to extend their warranties secretly to cover components with a high failure rate. Customers who complain vigorously get extended warranty compensation in the form of "goodwill" adjustments.

Francois Chong v. Marine Drive Imported Cars Ltd. and Honda Canada Inc. May 17, 1994, British Columbia Provincial Court (Small Claims Division), No: 92-06760, Judge C. L. Bagnall. Mr Chong is the first owner of a 1983 Honda Accord with 134,000 km on the odometer. He's had seven engine camshafts replaced—four under Honda "goodwill" programs, one where he paid part of the repairs, one via the small claims court judgment below, and the latest one pending his signing an out-of-court settlement with Honda (see Honda's letter offering to settle below).

Bull, Housser & Tupper
BARRISTERS & SOLICITORS
Patent & Trade-Mark Agents
3000 ROYAL CENTRE • P.O. BOX 11130 • 1055 WEST GEORGIA STREET • VANCOUVER, BRITISH COLUMBIA • CANADA V6E 3R3
FAX (604) 641-4949 • TELEPHONE (604) 687-6575

Reply Attention of Brent D. Jordan
Direct Line 641-4858
Our File No. 96-6434
July 8, 1996

WITHOUT PREJUDICE

Francois Chong

Dear Sir:

Re: Francois Chong v. Honda Canada Inc.; Carter Motors Ltd.;
Sur-Del Auto Imports Ltd.
Small Claims Action No. 96026393, Vancouver Registry

Offer to Settle

We write to offer to settle your claim as against our clients on the following terms:

1. Honda Canada Inc. will replace your current camshaft with a new camshaft as a **"goodwill gesture"**.
2. There will be **no warranty**, express or implied, with respect to the manufacture, design or fitness for purpose of the new camshaft.
3. The new camshaft **will not** be subject to Honda Canada's Retail Parts Warranty as this is only available for parts sold as a retail item.
4. You will sign a Release provided by the defendants in this action.
5. You will prepare and enter a Notice of Withdrawal for this action.

This settlement looks fair, although I can't see how Honda's lawyer can say that there's no implied warranty. That would elevate Honda above the courts and the legislature.

Mr. Chong claims that the camshaft design is faulty (this is apparently true, judging by the large number of Honda camshaft complaints reported to this author), and rightfully maintains that each replacement under Honda's "goodwill" warranty should last for a reasonable period of time.

In his ruling, Judge Bagnall agreed with Chong and ordered Honda and the dealer to each pay half of the $835.81 repair bill, for the following reasons:

> ". . . The defendants assert that the warranty which was part of the contract for purchase of the car encompassed the entirety of their obligation to the claimant, and that it expired in February 1985. The replacements of the camshaft after that date were paid for wholly or in part by Honda as a "goodwill gesture." The time has come for these gestures to cease, according to the witness for Honda. As well, he pointed out to me that the most recent replacement of the camshaft was paid for by Honda and that, therefore, the work would not be covered by Honda's usual warranty of twelve months from date of repair. Mr. Wall, who testified for Honda, told me there was no question that this situation with Mr. Chong's engine was an unusual state of affairs. He said that a camshaft properly maintained can last anywhere from 24,000–500,000 km. He could not offer any suggestion as to why the car keeps having this problem.
>
> The claimant has convinced me that the problems he is having with rapid breakdown of camshafts in his car is due to a defect, which was present in the engine at the time that he purchased the car. The problem first arose during the warranty period and in my view has never been properly identified nor repaired. . . ."

Desjardins v. Canadian Honda and Du Portage Mercury, February 20, 1981, Quebec Small Claims Court (Hull), No. 550-32-000933-801, Judge Dagenais. The plaintiff bought a used Honda "as is" from a Ford dealership. One year later the head gasket blew and was repaired free of charge by a Honda dealer under a secret warranty extension and the emissions warranty. Ten months later the head gasket blew again and was repaired without charge. A few months later, the part failed again and was repaired at Honda's expense a third time.

The plaintiff brought suit 22 months after purchase for expenses relating to motor adjustments, rental cars, and general inconvenience. Judge Dagenais forced both Honda Canada and the Ford dealer to pay $281 in damages for having made and sold such a defect-ridden vehicle.

See also:

Crevier v. Fiat of Canada (1979), 959.

Danis Mercury v. Société Sanitaire (1979), C.S., 645.

Gascon v. Bonaventure Ford (1974), C.S. (Hull) 550-05-000377-74.

Gerschicoff v. General Motors (1979), C.S., 681.

Marielle Signori v. Toyota Canada Ltée. and St-Laurent Toyota Inc., February 18, 1985, Quebec Small Claims Court (Montreal), No. 505-32-002421-841. Judge Gilles Bélanger. In this case, a 1981 Tercel owner forced Toyota Canada to admit that the company had a secret warranty to cover premature brake wear up to two years or 40,000 km. Judge Bélanger castigated Toyota and its dealer for keeping this warranty secret and awarded $286 to the plaintiff.

Repairs

Estimate not given

St. Arnaud v. Art Auto Body, October 7, 1982, Quebec Provincial Court, No. 500-02-050519-805, Judge Prenoveau. The plaintiff asked the garage for an estimate. The vehicle was repaired without the owner's consent and he was billed $2500. The garage kept the car and sued for its money. The judge ruled that the garage illegally retained the vehicle and violated Article 168 of the Quebec Consumer Protection Act by not giving an estimate. The judge cancelled the $2500 bill and ordered the car returned.

See also:

Gatti v. Gareau (1981) C.P. 400.
David v. Garage P. Breton (1981), C.P. 185.

Ruscitto v. Automag, June 23, 1981, Quebec Provincial Court, No. 500-02-054-215-806, Judge Robitaille. The plaintiff was given a written estimate for repairs, but the garage owner persuaded him to repaint the vehicle without making another written estimate. Judge Robitaille gave the plaintiff all his money back because the garage owner didn't properly note the hour, date, and telephone number called to get a verbal authorization as required by Articles 172 and 272 of the Quebec Consumer Protection Act. Judgment was rendered for $579.

Faulty diagnosis

Let's say that before taking a holiday you have your van checked out and are assured that it's in good condition. While en route to your vacation spot, it dies on the highway and ruins your holiday. When the check-up is incorrect and leads to financial losses (damages), the garage owner is responsible for those losses, as well as for the refund of the diagnostic costs. Of course, you had better show that the defect that caused your troubles was present and detectable at the time the vehicle was checked.

Babcock v. Servacar (1970) 1 O.R., 125. A motorist took a car he was planning to buy to an Ottawa Esso Diagnostic Clinic to determine its condition. He did the recommended repairs, and then had serious problems with the car while on vacation. The judge ruled that the clinic would have to pay for the repairs and reimburse the diagnostic cost as well. The Court held that the garage's advertising claims gave rise to a contractual warranty that promised to root out the car's defects before it was purchased.

Chan v. W. Gordon Inc., October 15, 1981, Quebec Provincial Court, No. 02-000002-811, Judge Page. The plaintiff was awarded $300 to cover repairs to a 1973 Volvo that was taken to Gordon's Service Station prior to purchase. The garage mistakenly diagnosed the car as being sound and roadworthy.

Davies v. Alberta Motor Association, Alberta Provincial Court, Civil Division August 13, 1991, No. P9090106097, Judge Moore. The plaintiff had a used 1985 Nissan Pulsar NX checked out by the AMA's Vehicle Inspection Service prior to buying it. The car passed with flying colours. A month later the clutch was replaced and numerous electrical problems ensued. At that time, another garage discovered that the car had been involved in a major accident, had a bent frame, a leaking radiator, and was unsafe to drive. The Court awarded the plaintiff $1578.40 plus three years of interest. The judge held that the AMA set itself out as an expert and should have spotted the car's defects. The AMA's defence—that it was not responsible for errors—was thrown out. The Court held that a disclaimer clause could not protect the Association from a fundamental breach of contract.

McCormick v. Servacar and Esso, February 9, 1981, Quebec Small Claims Court, No. 500-32-008700-801, Judge Prevost. Before purchasing a used 1978 Ford Fairmont, the plaintiff had it checked out by an Esso Diagnostic Clinic. The clinic said that the car was in good condition except for dirty transmission fluid. Ten days after purchasing the car, the transmission was replaced. The Court ordered Servacar and Esso to pay the $300 for repairs, reasoning that were it not for the clinic's incompetence, negligence, or lack of experience, the defect could have been detected earlier.

Flat-rate abuses

Kesselman v. Chomedy Ford Sales Ltd., September 18, 1975, Quebec Provincial Court, No. 500-02-002113-756, Judge Decary. The plaintiff contested the flat-rate charges for 28.8 hours when the mechanic's clocked time was only 22.8 hours. The Ford dealership raised the defence that the mechanic was following a Ford of Canada flat-rate manual and that this was a common practice. The Court didn't buy this argument. It held the dealer responsible for the excess charges because the customer was never told about the flat-rate method of computing repair time.

See also: *Quebec Consumer Protection Bureau v. Canadian Tire.*

R. v. Birchcliff Lincoln Mercury Ltd., Ontario Court of Appeal, July 7, 1987, 60 O.R. (2d) 610, 220; 220 A.C. 274. This new car dealer advertised a $38 hourly labour charge and then calculated the number of hours using a flat-rate guide that allowed more hours than those actually worked. This was held by the appeal court to be false advertising under the federal Combines Act (Competition Act).

Fuel system fire

Lenz v. J. B.'s Automotive Service Center Ltd. (1987), 51 Alta. L.R. (2d) 16 (Q.B.). The plaintiff's vehicle caught fire three weeks after the fuel system was worked on. The Court held that the garage was liable because the fire was in the same area that had been repaired.

Oil filter improperly installed

Proulx v. Salois Automobile, December 6, 1974, Quebec Provincial Court, No. 02-004322-74, Judge Lacourciere. The plaintiff was awarded damages to pay for motor repairs caused by an improperly installed oil filter. The dealer's mechanic was ordered to pay $1000 in damages.

Repair misrepresentation

Smith v. Marc Patrick Motors and the Canadian Tire Corporation, September 20, 1984, Ontario Small Claims Court (Niagara North), Judge Kingstone. The plaintiff bought a used 1978 Honda Civic that was sold as having a "new" engine. It failed shortly thereafter. Canadian Tire hadn't installed a new engine. Judge Kingstone ordered both defendants to split the cost of the repairs ($1000, plus 13 percent interest) for misrepresenting the engine.

Repairs not done properly

Berta v. Gold Seal Engine Rebuilders, Ontario Small Claims Court (Toronto), No. C217/83, August 22, 1985, Justice Sigurdson. The plaintiff's engine was improperly repaired. Judge Sigurdson awarded $2047.03 to the plaintiff after hearing the garage's employees testify in a "less than truthful" manner.

Canbec Auto v. De Leno, January 18, 1973, Quebec Provincial Court, No. 03-058009-72, Judge Page. The dealer sued the defendant for money owing on a bill for a general inspection and correction of defects. The car owner refused to pay the bill because the vehicle was still running poorly. Judgment was rendered in favour of the defendant. The Court held that the garage had an obligation of results, whereby the repairs would be expected to correct the problems complained of by the car's owner.

Collier v. McMaster's Auto Sales, No. W/C 157/90, New Brunswick Court of Queen's Bench, April 26, 1991. Judge McLellan ruled that the dealer's failure to repair the car properly under warranty justified the owner getting the engine repaired elsewhere at the dealer's expense. The failure to repair the plaintiff's car properly amounted to a breach of the manufacturer's expressed warranty.

Magloire v. Chomedy Toyota, December 1, 1982, Quebec Provincial Court, No. 500-02-014582-824, Judge Hodge. This Toyota dealer installed a defective oil pump that caused $1494.28 in damages to the motor. Judge Hodge awarded the full amount to the plaintiff.

Mudge v. Corner Brooke Garage, 8 Nfld. & P.E.I.R., 374. This truck owner sued the garage successfully for negligent repairs to the rear frame assembly.

Pelleray v. Heritage Ford Sales Ltd., Ontario Small Claims Court (Scarborough), SC7688/91, March 22, 1993. This owner of a 1986 Ford Aerostar was awarded $1691.29 as compensation for repairs to his automatic transmission, which had failed three times after being repaired by the dealer.

Raiches Steel Works v. J. Clark & Son, 16 N.B.R. (2d), 535. The brakes failed three weeks after being repaired. The judge found the mechanic negligent and awarded damages of $6423.

Sigurdson v. Hillcrest Service & Acklands (1977) 1 W.W.R., 740. An accident was caused by a defective brake hose. The garage that installed it claimed that the parts distributor was responsible. The judge ruled that Saskatchewan's Sale of Goods Act made both garage and distributor responsible for damages.

Sylvain v. Carrosseries d'Automobiles Guy Inc. (1981), C.P. 333, Judge Page. The garage had an obligation of results that the paint job on the plaintiff's car would be satisfactory. It was not. The Court held the garage liable for the cost of repainting the car elsewhere.

Tremblay v. Au Grand Salon, September 19, 1973, Quebec Provincial Court, No. 02-054410-73, Judge Bousquet. The plaintiff asked that his brakes be checked and paid $30 for the inspection. After the inspection, the brakes failed and an accident ensued. The Court held the dealer responsible, although no repairs were done.

See also:
Acme v. Coziol (1962) B.R.
Chomedy Ford v. Mash, March 11, 1976, Quebec Provincial Court, No. 500-02-007671-767.
Gagnon v. Ford Motor Co. (1974) C.S., 422.
Lazanick v. Ford Motor Co., June 15, 1965, Quebec Superior Court No. 623504.

Repairs causing other damage/vandalism/theft
Goulet v. Roberval Pontiac Buick, February 11, 1980, Quebec Small Claims Court, No. 155-32-000516-794, Judge Savard. The plaintiff's vehicle was vandalized while being repaired. The Court held the garage responsible because the car was under its care.

Water in fuel

Claridge v. Three Way Motors, Manitoba, July 20, 1987, No. 221/86 (Thompson). The owner of a 1980 Audi 5000 had starting problems and rusty fuel-injection nozzles caused by what he believed to be gasoline contaminated by water. He didn't have any direct proof that the gas station's pumps were contaminated, but the judge ruled that the balance of probabilities indicated this was likely because the station owner had had problems with the storage pumps in the past.

Part Three
NEW VEHICLE RATINGS

"Out of 100 vehicles, we're apt to build 10 that are as good as any that Toyota has ever built, 80 that are okay and 10 that cause repeated problems for our customers."

— Robert Lutz
President, Chrysler U.S.
Chrysler Times, *17 July 1995*

What Makes a Good Vehicle?

Your new vehicle must first live up to the promises made by the manufacturer and dealer. It should be crashworthy, of reasonable durability (at least ten years), cost no more than $500 to $600 a year to maintain, and provide you with a fair resale value a few years down the road. Parts should be reasonably priced and easily available, and servicing shouldn't be given with a shrug or a snarl.

This *Guide* tries to publish up-to-date photographs of each new model rated, but some automakers disagree with our ratings and refuse to cooperate with us in any manner whatsoever, including sending us recent photos and current technical specifications. We regret any errors or omissions that may result. Our independence is more important than a squeaky clean book with pretty pictures.

Under no circumstances are dealers or manufacturers solicited for free "test" vehicles, as is the case with some consumer groups and most auto columnists. When a test vehicle is needed, it's rented from a major rental agency or borrowed from its owner. I've adopted this practice from my early experiences as a consumer reporter twenty years ago. At that time, Nissan asked me to test-drive their new 1974 240Z—no strings attached. I took the car for a week, had it examined by an independent garage, spoke with satisfied and dissatisfied owners, and accessed internal service bulletins. My conclusion: the car's faulty brakes made it unsafe to drive. Nissan sued me and my lawyer for $4 million, fixed the brakes as a "product improvement campaign," and dropped the lawsuit two years later. I never went back for another car.

Definitions of Terms

Ratings

This *Guide* makes use of owner complaints, confidential dealer service bulletins, and test-drives to expose serious factory-related defects, design deficiencies, or servicing glitches. It should be noted that customer complaints alone don't make for a scientific sampling, and that's why they're used in conjunction with other sources of information. On the other hand, owner complaints combined with inside information found in dealer service bulletins are a good starting point to cut through the carmakers' hyperbole and get a glimpse of reality.

Unlike most auto guides, *Lemon-Aid* isn't bedazzled by high-tech wizardry. Almost thirty years of consumer advocacy in the auto industry have taught me that complex components are usually more troublesome during their first few years on the market (airbags and anti-lock brakes in particular). They inflate operating costs, reduce overall reliability, demand better-quality servicing than most dealers can provide, and put extra stress on major and expensive powertrain, fuel system, and emissions components.

Complexity drives up ownership costs. Computerized engine controls and sophisticated fuel-injection systems are impossible to service without specialized training and diagnostic equipment. Although many garages are acquiring this equipment and retraining personnel, few mechanics have a good background in the complex electronics found under the hood of most new cars. As a rule of thumb, a car with fewer electronic accessories will be the cheapest and easiest to maintain.

Depreciation is the biggest—and often ignored—expense you'll encounter when you trade in your vehicle, or when an accident forces you to buy another vehicle before the depreciated loss can be amortized. Most new cars depreciate a whopping 30 to 40 percent during the first two years of ownership. Leasing agents play this depreciation game to their advantage (plus adding in the dealer's profit) in establishing your car's residual value when the lease expires. The only way to use depreciation rates to your advantage is to choose a vehicle listed as being economical to own and keep it for five to ten years.

During a vehicle's first year on the market it takes about six months to acquire enough information as a basis for a fair-minded evaluation, unless it's a hybrid that has been in service under another name or has been only rebadged. Most new vehicles hit the market before all of their bugs have been worked out, so it would be irresponsible to recommend them before they've been owner-driven and before the quality of service from the dealer and manufacturer has been tested by the customer. The Chrysler Caravan is a case in point. Hailed as car of the year by the motoring press upon its introduction in 1984, the vehicle was later known for its poor crashworthiness and has been plagued by engine, transmission, and paint problems since its debut.

Warranties

A manufacturer's warranty is a legal promise that the product it sells will perform in the normal and customary manner for which it was designed. It's an important factor in this *Guide*'s ratings, and is judged by how fairly it's applied—not by what's promised. Extended or supplementary warranties provide extended coverage and may be sold by the manufacturer, dealer, or an independent third party. If a part malfunctions or fails (not due to owner negligence), the dealer will fix, repair, or replace the defective part or parts and bill the automaker for the cost.

Most new vehicle warranties fall into two categories: bumper to bumper for a period of three to five years, and powertrain for up to 6 years/130,000 km. (See the "1997 Warranties" table on p. 87.) Automakers still sometimes charge a $50 to $100 fee to subsequent owners of cars with unexpired base warranties. For snowbirds, the federal and provincial governments can charge GST and sales tax on warranty and non-warranty repairs done south of the border. Beware.

The new longer and more comprehensive warranties are estimated to cost automakers about $100 to $150 per vehicle—a considerable savings over the $1000 rebates automakers have traditionally offered to heat up year-end sales. In spite of this cost savings, Chrysler has gone the other route and abandoned its generous warranty in favour of rebates and low interest rates. The automaker had one of the most comprehensive seven-year warranties one could find up through the 1994 model year. Some of its vehicles were recommended in *Lemon-Aid Guides* for that reason, even though from a quality standpoint they were mediocre choices.

Mazda has a different problem. Although its vehicles are above average in construction quality and its warranty matches the industry average, owners report that warranty authorization takes an inordinately long time to obtain, new vehicles are poorly prepared for delivery, and dealership servicing has deteriorated considerably. No wonder *Consumer Reports'* annual owner survey has put Mazda dealers below average in servicing.

General Motors' warranty performance is part Jurassic, part Marquis de Sade. Ford does much better with an average warranty that's usually applied fairly, giving customers the benefit of the doubt. European automakers have warranties that are stronger than their dealer network.

Tires and batteries aren't covered by most car manufacturers' warranties (except for GM, which began covering tires on its 1996 models); instead they're warranted by their manufacturers on a pro-rated basis. Batteries are covered for at least a year against defects, and then generally for another 24 months on a pro-rated basis. This isn't such a good deal because the manufacturer is making a profit by charging you the full list price. If you were to buy the same replacement battery from a discount store, you'd likely pay less even without the pro-rated rebate. The same applies to tires, because you're given a pro-rated rebate on the suggested list price, which almost nobody pays.

Safety restraints such as airbags and seatbelts usually mirror the basic warranty, with coverage varying between three years/60,000 km and the lifetime of the vehicle/unlimited km. After-market products and services—such as gas-saving gadgets, rustproofing, paint protectors, air conditioning, and van conversions—can render the manufacturer's warranty invalid, so be sure to check with your dealer before purchasing any optional equipment or services from an independent supplier.

This *Guide* emphasizes important new features that add to a vehicle's safety, reliability, road performance, and comfort, and points out those changes that are merely gadgets and styling revisions. Also noted are important improvements to be made in the future, or the dropping of a model line.

Recommended—a Best Buy
This category includes new vehicles that combine a high level of crashworthiness with good road performance, decent reliability, and better-than-average resale value. Service must be readily available, and parts not expensive or difficult to find.

Some vehicles may lose their "Recommended" rating from the previous *Guide* whenever their prices become unreasonable or their warranties inadequate, or when the competition offers less expensive models that offer more standard safety, mechanical, or convenience features.

Above Average
Vehicles in this class exhibit quality construction, durability, and safety features as standard equipment. They may have expensive parts and servicing, an unreasonably high price tag, or only satisfactory warranty performance, which removes them from the "Recommended" category.

Acceptable
Vehicles in this group have some deficiencies or flaws that make them a second choice. In many cases, certain components are prone to premature wear or breakdown, or some other positive aspect of long-term ownership is lacking. An "Acceptable" rating can also be attributed to such factors as substandard assembly quality, lack of a solid long-term reliability record, or some flaw in the parts and service network.

Below Average
This is a rating category that I use less often. It denotes a vehicle that may have had a poor reliability record, but where improvements have been made with regard to durability and/or safety features. It may be a risky buy, but is a cut above "Not Recommended." Ensure that you get an extended warranty with a vehicle in this category.

Not Recommended
Buy at your own risk. Substandard crashworthiness, poor overall reliability, inadequate road performance, poor dealer service, and other factors can make owning one of these vehicles a traumatic and expensive experience. It doesn't necessarily follow that every single vehicle produced in a "Not Recommended" model line will have exactly the same reliability shortcomings, but your chances of having trouble are higher than normal.

Not Rated
Vehicles that haven't been on the road long enough to assess, or that are sold in such small numbers that owner feedback is insufficient, are left unrated.

New for '97

At a glance, you can see what changes have been made to the vehicle over the '96s.

General Comments

Here a brief history of each vehicle is followed by a presentation of the models and trim levels. Engine and powertrain information is generally provided, as well as new safety features.

Cost Analysis/Alternatives

Many of the new 1997 vehicles aren't worth the increased prices over the 1996 versions because safety, performance, comfort, or convenience improvements usually don't add up to that extra $1500 to $3000 you'll have to pay. Each model's cost is analyzed in light of cheaper carryover models, possible rebates, destination charges, servicing, parts cost, depreciation, and fuel consumption. Worthwhile options, as well as those that aren't worth purchasing, are listed along with alternative choices that may be better buys.

Japanese makes usually come with more standard bells and whistles, making them more expensive than their North American counterparts. They come with fewer discounts too, due to a smaller dealer markup, a high-flying yen, and the sustained popularity of Japanese-made vehicles. On the other hand, most Japanese-made vehicles cost less to operate and are worth more at resale time, compensating for their higher upfront cost.

Reliability/Safety

Lemon-Aid bases its reliability evaluations on owner comments, government reports, and confidential manufacturer service bulletins. The *Guide* also draws on the knowledge and expertise of professionals working in the automotive marketplace, including mechanics and fleet owners. The aim is to have a wide-ranging source of unbiased data on reliability, durability, and ownership costs that the carmakers can't refute. Allowances are made for the number of vehicles sold versus the number of complaints, as well as the seriousness of problems reported and the average number of problems reported by each owner.

Manufacturers' service bulletins listed in this section give the most probable cause of factory-related defects on 1995 and some 1996 models. Since these problems are often carried over several years (manufacturers depend on dealer field corrections outlined in their bulletins until a permanent, cost-effective engineering solution is found at the factory), use the service bulletin as your first lead in solving a persistent problem. In the meantime, stay on your guard. Dealers often charge for these repairs, particularly if they think they can convince you that the repair falls under normal maintenance.

Service bulletins cut down considerably the time spent in troubleshooting. In emergencies, independent mechanics can go right to the source of the trouble when dealer servicing isn't available. Warranty repairs are also easier to get done if you can jog the dealer's memory by producing a service bulletin that shows a problem is factory-related and therefore not part of routine maintenance. Bulletins are also great tools for getting consequential compensation, including money spent for towing, a rental car, an interrupted vacation, and lost wages.

Many of the bulletins listed in this *Guide* come from American sources and so their parts numbers may vary somewhat from the Canadian bulletins. Nevertheless, the problems and defects they treat are exactly the same on both sides of the border. Some cars have more DSBs than others, but this doesn't mean they're lemons. It may be that the problems listed affect only a small number of vehicles, or are minor in nature and easily corrected. DSBs should be used to verify that a problem was diagnosed correctly, the correct upgraded replacement part was used, and the labour time was fair.

Safety

The main features weighed in the safety ratings are a model's crashworthiness as assessed by government and insurers, and the availability of adjustable head restraints, airbags, anti-lock brakes, childproof door locks, daytime running lights, integrated child safety seats, safety belts, side impact beams, traction control, and a transmission shift/brake interlock to prevent uncontrolled sudden acceleration.

Crash protection figures are taken from the U.S. National Highway Traffic and Safety Administration's New Car Assessment Program. Vehicles are crashed into a fixed barrier, head-on, at 57 km/h (35 mph) in order to evaluate the forces exerted on specially constructed dummies placed in the two front seats. The latest results—even if they may be several years old—have been included in the ratings.

The NHTSA shows a vehicle's level of crashworthiness by the likelihood, expressed as a percentage, of the belted occupants being seriously injured. The higher the number of stars, the greater the protection:

★★★★★	(five stars)	— a 10% or less chance of serious injury
★★★★	(four stars)	— a 10–20% chance of serious injury
★★★	(three stars)	— a 20–35% chance of serious injury
★★	(two stars)	— a 35–45% chance of serious injury
★	(one star)	— more than a 45% chance of serious injury

NHTSA tests don't necessarily provide an accurate picture as to how a given model will perform in every accident; test figures are valid only if they're used to compare vehicles that are of the same size (i.e., compact, midsize, large). It's also unfortunate that vehicles aren't tested twice to confirm the validity of the first test.

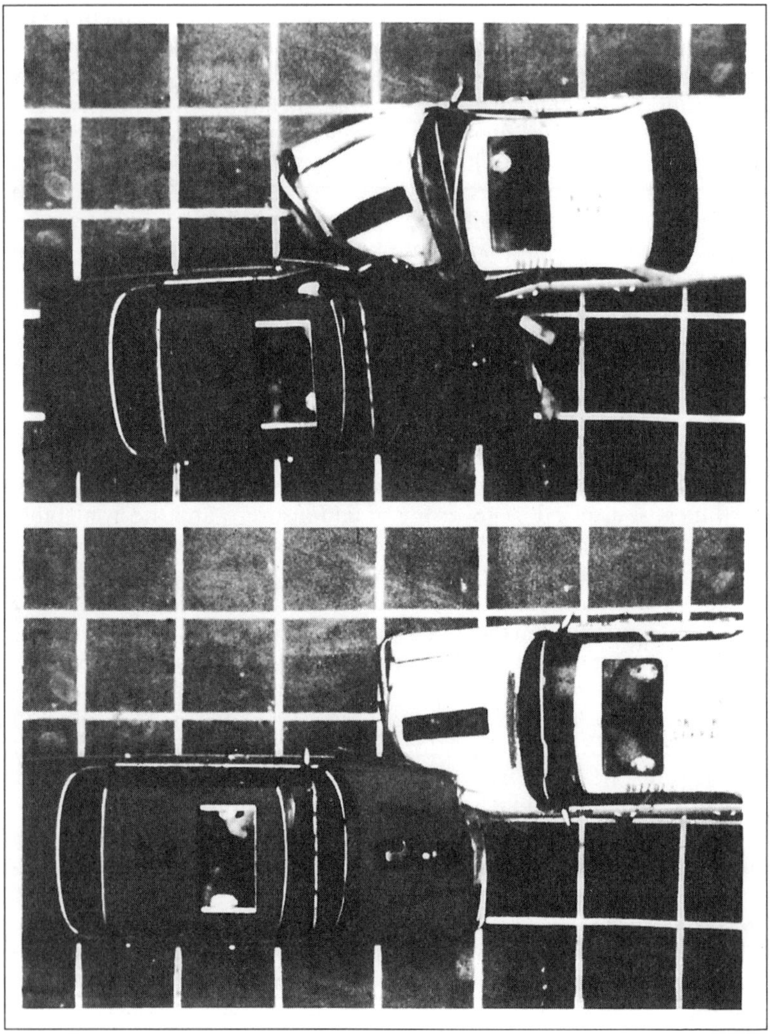

There are other variables too. Mercedes-Benz, proud of its reputation for building crashworthy cars, hasn't always fared well in the NHTSA head-on collisions and so questions the validity of the ratings. The company claims its own crash data show that most frontal collisions occur at an angle, and that this is the kind of test in which its cars excel. NHTSA experts disagree, but the Insurance Institute for Highway Safety (IIHS) sides with Mercedes and crash-tests its own vehicles at an angle and at 40 mph.

The laws of physics dictate that a larger and heavier vehicle will provide better crash protection than a smaller one, and that injuries vary substantially according to the angle of impact. For example, twice as many deaths occur in small cars than in large cars. Furthermore, the frequency of damage claims for small, two-door cars is 35 percent higher than for large two-door cars. The same holds true for four-door cars. This is not only the case when a small car hits a larger vehicle. In single-car crashes the death rate for occupants of small cars is more than double the rate for large cars.

Road (and off-road) Performance

Every vehicle should be able to merge safely onto a highway and have adequate passing power for two-lane roads (not an easy task for Honda's Odyssey and VW's EuroVan). Steering feel and handling should inspire confidence. The suspension should provide a reasonably well-controlled ride on most road surfaces. The passenger compartment should be roomy enough to accommodate passengers comfortably on extended trips. The noise level inside the vehicle shouldn't become tiresome and annoying. As a rule, handling and ride comfort are inversely proportional. Variations from this pattern are reflected in the ratings.

Off-roading requires sufficient low-range power and lots of ground clearance. The suspension has to be adequate to take the punishment of off-roading challenges.

Comfort/Convenience

Driving pleasure is hard to define, but a cramped interior, hard to see or reach controls, engine, road, and wind noise, and poor climate control systems can turn that pleasure into a distressful experience.

This *Guide* points out possible deficiencies that you should check out in the showroom and during the test drive. Obvious deficiencies that are accepted by the customer at the time of sale can't be used later to cancel a sale or to obtain a refund.

Selling Price and Residual Values

The *Guide* lists the estimated manufacturer's suggested retail price applicable to standard-equipped vehicles and whether that price is firm or negotiable, the dealer's markup, and the vehicle's estimated residual value over the next five years. Options, taxes, and other charges are extra. Manufacturers usually increase prices a few times during the year, and these increases may boost prices by 5 to 10 percent. Therefore, the vehicle you've chosen may be selling at a higher price by the time you visit the dealership. If this happens, ask the dealer to show you the manufacturer's notice of the price increase.

The prices are accurate at the time the book goes to press. Space limitations don't allow the inclusion of every price for every level of powertrain or trim for a particular model, but there is a solid representation.

With all the attention created by the so-called "no haggle" sticker prices, keep in mind that there's a substantial gap between the cost of the vehicle to the dealer and the manufacturer's suggested retail price (the "sticker" price). This difference represents the dealer's markup or gross profit. It varies from 8 to 30 percent and is usually augmented by other incentive programs and holdbacks that can add another 2 to 3 percent to the dealer's profit margin. To help you negotiate the best price, the *Guide* indicates those prices that are firm and those that are negotiable, and gives the approximate price markup percentage in parentheses.

Residual values apply to the worth of the vehicle after a lease expires. These values can be a comparative guide to depreciation over the next five years if you plan to sell your car privately.

Destination charges are usually combined with the Pre-Delivery Inspection (PDI) fee, and represent extra profits for the dealer. Don't pay more than 2 percent of a vehicle's MSRP for these charges, no matter what the dealer demands. Note that PDI can run you as much as $300 to $500, and is charged *in addition to* destination charges. These are outrageous extra fees. Don't pay them. Haggle with the dealer, who isn't going to risk losing a sale over these extra charges.

Rebates and dealer incentives are expressed in this *Guide* in U.S. dollars because that's where the programs originate. In Canada, the amounts vary somewhat, but the American figure is the benchmark. Some cars, such as the '96 Lincoln Town car, get a substantial dealer incentive ($4000) followed by a customer rebate ($1500) on the next year's model. Incentives go directly into the dealer's account, while customer rebates are usually sent to the buyer by the automaker.

American Vehicles
CHRYSLER

Chrysler continues to make mostly mediocre cars and trucks and best-selling minivans all at the same time. What few good cars it sells are mostly Mitsubishi-made—and most of them have been dropped for the 1997 model year.

Sayonara Colt, Summit, and Stealth.

In the past, Chrysler compensated for its poor-quality vehicles with a comprehensive seven-year warranty that plugged the quality gaps. Its cars and trucks still broke down frequently but owners didn't holler since the repairs were covered by Chrysler. But several years ago Detroit's bean-counter contingent came up with the bright idea that the company could save millions of dollars by cutting its base warranty down to three years/80,000 km and selling the previous seven-year protection for up to $1000 extra. Even though Chrysler had just turned in a year of record-breaking profits and had already socked away billions in profits from other years, the automaker eagerly embraced the concept that less is more from a warranty standpoint. And you know what? The bean-counters (and P. T. Barnum) were right: customers will pay more for less (and Barnum's adage that there's a sucker born every minute is a conservative figure).

Chrysler's abysmally low quality control and its vehicles' overall poor reliability call for more warranty support, not less. In fact, Chrysler USA's Customer Center confirmed this past July that of the 5000 calls and 500 letters it receives daily, most are complaints. Chrysler Canada complaint figures aren't available, but I'll bet from the complaints I've received from *Lemon-Aid* readers that Canadian car owners are just as incensed. For example, Maryanna Lewyckyj, *Action Line* columnist for the *Toronto Sun*, says that owners are angry that Chrysler has almost

Chrysler owners get the gears

By MARYANNA LEWYCKYJ
Toronto Sun

Chrysler vehicle owners hit with skyrocketing quotes for warranty extensions are wondering how Chrysler Canada can justify the extra costs.

The auto giant — which posted a profit of $83 million in 1995, down from $202 million in 1994 — recently jacked up the cost of warranty extensions without notice to customers.

The change means motorists like Wayne Kurtz of Downsview (who's owned seven Chrysler vehicles) are being quoted $1,300 for a service plan that cost $500 when he bought his 1993 Plymouth Voyageur.

Derek Hand of Mississauga was recently quoted $1,080 for a service plan that cost $450 when he leased his 1993 Dodge Caravan in June 1993. When Hand called Chrysler Canada to complain, he was told nothing could be done.

"I feel I've been cheated," said Hand. "This leaves a bad taste in
mouth and is unbelievable
company of Chrysler's size
ure."

Chrysler Canada spokesman Walt McCall explained, "At the time these customers made their purchase, that was the information that was in force and made in good faith.

"For competitive reasons, we did change some of these programs as we went along and probably still will."

Asked why Chrysler owners weren't notified of the changes, McCall said, "I don't think that was really required."

Service plan hikes

A Chrysler salesman who did
wish to be named, said their
ship had fielded complai
about 50 ticked-off cust
the service plan pric
"One manag
wants to give
of Chrysl
Landry

tripled the price of extended warranty coverage (from $500 to $1300 in some cases), even though many of its dealers guaranteed that the prices wouldn't change if buyers wanted the extra protection after their base three-year warranty expired.

Incidentally, Chrysler's own documents show that costs for warranty-covered repairs have increased by 48 percent over a two-year period, mostly from seven-year warranty claimants. Imagine the number of angry customers that'll build up as more and more warranty claims are refused after the three-year limit is reached.

What's new for '97

A host of redesigned vehicles were launched last year as '96 models: the Breeze, Caravan, Voyager, and Town & Country, the Ram 4500, the Sebring convertible, and the Viper GTS coupe. This year, Chrysler is concentrating on its sport-utilities and pickups by presenting a redesigned Dakota, Wrangler, and Cherokee. The Prowler, a limited production (only 3000 units) "hot rod," will also be launched early in the new year. After retiring the Acclaim, Spirit, LeBaron sedan, Colt, Vista, Laser, Shadow, and Sundance in '95, Chrysler continues the trend this year by axing the Summit, Stealth, and New Yorker. These cuts have reduced the Eagle division to only two vehicles: the Vision and Talon.

Prowler

Coming next spring, this aluminum and plastic, two-seat, purple convertible isn't for introverts. With a $35,000 US base price, the Prowler, much like the $82,000 Viper (another head-turner), is one of Chrysler's most unusual cars. But unlike the Viper, Plymouth's rear-drive Prowler is no high performance muscle car—its 3.5L, 24-valve, 214 hp V6 also powers the Dodge Intrepid and Eagle Vision. The four-speed automatic comes with Autostick (also available on the Vision, Intrepid, and Stratus), which allows you to shift the transmission as you would with a manual gearbox. On climbs it prevents the transmission from changing gears back and forth, and on the downhill you can keep the car in a lower gear to prevent picking up excess speed.

On the downside, the Prowler has a stiff ride, no trunk (you have to buy an optional purple mini-trailer), no spare tire, and room only for two—as long as they're not too tall.

Prowler: a "hot rod" for collectors only.

Viper

This red-hot $82,320 ($56,000 in the U.S.) midsize, two-door, rear-drive roadster breaks all the marketing rules—and wins. Basically a limited production (only 303 were built in 1994) low-tech car, it lacks glass side windows (zip-in plastic windows are used instead), airbags, anti-lock brakes, and outside door handles. Its top should be used only when you absolutely have to. It does have a V-10, 400-hp powerplant, and "in your face" styling that isn't equalled by any other vehicles in its class. Passenger comfort is compromised by excessive wind noise and inadequate protection from the elements. This year, Chrysler has promised to add 15 more horses and outside door handles to the base Viper; to use a lighter, stiffer frame and all-aluminum front and rear suspension systems; and to bring out a hardtop coupe version that offers dual airbags and ABS. Only a hundred or so Vipers have been allocated to Canada. Smart buyers will opt instead for a cheaper, high-tech, and more practical Stealth.

A two-year-old Viper is still worth $45,000-$50,000 US—about the same price as a two-year-old Hummer.

Strengths and weaknesses

Chrysler's good times may be coming to an end as a result of growing competition among all product lines (though its minivans are still going strong), loss of market share, and increasing consumer dissatisfaction over poor-quality vehicles and shorter warranties. Furthermore, unlike the successful launching of its LH cars a few years back, Chrysler's new Neon, Cirrus, and Stratus compacts have been met by a collective yawn.

I don't want to be too repetitive, but Chrysler's decision to cut its much-needed seven-year warranty to three years is an incredibly stupid move that will eventually catch up to it in light of all the serious mechanical (notably powertrain, electrical, and brake defects) and body problems Chrysler has left uncorrected over the previous three model years. Just take a look at this DSB Summary I pulled at random the other day. Incredible as it may seem, these kinds of problems have been afflicting Chrysler's vehicles for years—and are likely to continue, judging by the company's previous actions.

DSB SUMMARY
$15 BULLETIN SUMMARY $5 PER BULLETIN THEREAFTER
FAX CHARGE INCLUDED
1-954-563-2448

1994 DODGE CARAVAN

1.	JUN-95	3.3L/3.8L/ LOWER ENGINE LEAKS
2.	SEP-93	41TE TRANSAXLE RATIO VALUES
3.	APR-95	41TE/42LE TRANSAXLE DOWN/UPSHIFTING IN CRUISE CONTROL
4.	NOV-94	A/C EVAPORATOR FREEZE-UP OR LACK OF COOLING
5.	SEP-93	AC DUCTS EMIT ODOR
6.	JUL-94	AC EVAPORATOR WHISTLE
7.	JUL-94	AC/HEATER BLEND AIR DOOR STICKS
8.	APR-94	ACCELERATION SHUDDER
9.	DEC-93	AIR CONDITIONER RELATED NOISE
10.	MAY-95	AIR CONDITIONING DUCTS EMIT ODOR
11.	APR-94	ANTILOCK BRAKE DIAGNOSIS
12.	DEC-94	ANTILOCK BRAKE SYSTEM (ABS) WARNING LIGHT ILLUMINATED
13.	APR-94	ANTILOCK COMPONENT IDENTIFICATION
14.	OCT-94	BODY CLADDING INTERFERES WITH USE OF JACK
15.	DEC-93	CARBON BUILDUP ON PISTON TOP
16.	JAN-94	CIRCUIT LEAKS LOW/REVERSE ACCUMULATOR COVER
17.	FEB-94	CLEANING ELECTRICAL CONNECTORS
18.	OCT-93	CREAKING NOISE AT LEFT B PILLAR
19.	FEB-95	DELAYED ENGAGEMENT TRANSAXLES 41TE 42LE, START UP
20.	MAY-94	DIAGNOSTIC CONNECTOR CHANGE
21.	DEC-93	DIAGNOSTIC MANUAL REVISION
22.	OCT-93	ELECTRONIC CYCLING CLUTCH SWITCH

23. NOV-93 ENGINE COOLANT RECOMMENDATION
24. JAN-94 ENGINE SPEED SENSING PROBLEM WITH NEW TRANS CONTROLLER
25. FEB-94 ENGINE STALLS ON TAKEOFF
26. MAR-95 EXHAUST NOISES
27. MAR-94 FLOOR PAN TICKING NOISE
28. OCT-93 FRONT COIL SPRING NOISE
29. SEP-94 FRONT DOOR FORWARD HEM SEPARATION
30. JAN-94 FRONT DOOR IMPACT BEAM
31. OCT-94 FRONT MAP/COURTESY LAMP OPERATION
32. MAR-94 FRONT SEAT ADJUSTER LATCH
33. MAR-94 FRONT SEAT BACK NOISE
34. NOV-94 FRONT SUSPENSION RAPPING NOISE WHEN TRAVELING OVER BUMPS
35. JUN-94 FUEL PUMP MODULE CONNECTOR SERVICE
36. OCT-93 FUEL PUMP MODULE WIRING CONNECTOR
37. FEB-94 FUEL PUMP NOISE
38. DEC-93 FUSE BLOCK MOUNTING TABS CRACKED
39. SEP-94 GLUE OOZES OUT A BACKLIGHT OR WINDSHIELD MOULDING
40. DEC-94 HARSH SHIFTING AT LOW SPEED/DIGITAL SPEEDO. FLUCTUATIONS
41. SEPT-94 HARSH, ERRATIC, OR DELAYED TRANSMISSION SHIFTS
42. FEB-94 HEADLINER FASTENER PINS
43. SEP-93 HIGH ALTITUDE KITS
44. DEC-93 IMPROVED SHIFTING
45. JUN-95 IMPROVED TRANSMISSION-SHIFT QUALITY
46. JAN-94 IMPROVED TRANSMISSION SHIFT QUALITY
47. DEC-94 INOPERATIVE SPEEDOMETER
48. MAY-95 INSTALLATION OF RADIO TRANSMITTING EQUIPMENT
49. NOV-93 INSTRUMENT PANEL SQUEAK RIGHT SIDE
50. OCT-94 INTAKE VALVE DEPOSITS
51. SEP-95 INTERACTIVE SPEED CONTROL-41TE/42LE TRANSAXLE
52. OCT-94 INTERMITTENT NO CRANK
53. AUG-94 LEFT B POST EXHAUSTER RETENTION
54. APR-94 LOOSE SPEED CONTROL SWITCH
55. DEC-94 LOW HEATER PERFORMANCE DIAGNOSIS/REPAIR
56. JAN-94 MANUAL REVISIONS
57. JUN-94 MANUAL TRANS SHIFTER SQUEAK
58. FEB-95 MANUAL TRANSAXLE LOCKED IN NEUTRAL OR REVERSE
59. JAN-94 MIDDLE BENCH SEAT OUTER SEATBELT
60. SEP-94 MIDDLE ROW SEAT INTERCHANGEABILITY
61. AUG-94 NOISE WHEN TURNING OR WHEN SHIFTING INTO REVERSE
62. OCT-94 OIL LEAK DIAGNOSIS
63. APR-94 PISTON NOISE ENGINE AT IDLE
64. JAN-94 POOR HEATER PERFORMANCE
65. JUL-93 R-134 REFRIGERANT LEAK DETECTION
66. SEP-94 R-134A REFRIGERANT
67. OCT-93 RADIO LOCKS UP DURING OPERATION
68. DEC-93 RADIO REMOVAL AND INSTALLATION PROCEDURE
69. OCT-94 RATTLING NOISE FROM QUAD SEAT FLOOR ATTACHMENT

70.	APR-94	REAR SEAT ADJUSTER RATTLE
71.	FEB-94	REAR SEAT SLIDING EFFORT
72.	OCT-93	REMOTE KEYLESS ENTRY SYSTEM
73.	DEC-93	REVISED MIDDLE SIDE GLASS LATCHES
74.	APR-94	REVISED SLIDING DOOR AJAR SWITCH ADJUSTMENT
75.	JAN-95	REVISED UNDERBODY REFRIGERANT LINE GASKET
76.	JUL-95	SAG OR HESITATION ON COLD START UP BELOW 20 DEGREES F
77.	DEC-94	SERPENTINE BELT COMES OFF PULLEYS
78.	DEC-94	SERPENTINE DRIVE BELT COMES OFF PULLEYS
79.	OCT-94	SERVICE DIAGNOSTIC PROCEDURE MANUALS
80.	JUN-94	SHIPPING TIE DOWN STRAPS
81.	DEC-93	SLOW FUEL TANK FILL
82.	DEC-94	SMOOTH ROAD VIBRATION AND SHAKE
83.	OCT-94	SMOOTH ROAD VIBRATION/SHAKE/WOBBLE
84.	JAN-94	SNAP RING CHART
85.	FEB-95	SPARE TIRE WINCH OPERATION
86.	OCT-95	SPEED CONTROL OVERSHOOT/UNDERSHOOT
87.	MAR-94	SQUEAK AT BASE OF WINDSHIELD
88.	JAN-94	SQUEAK IN SHOCK TOWER
89.	DEC-93	STOP LIGHT SWITCH WIRING CONNECTOR SERVICE
90.	JUN-94	TAMPER RESISTANT IGNITION KEY CYLINDER
91.	OCT-94	TIRE LEADS/DRIFTS LEFT
92.	DEC-93	TRANSAXLE SHIFT QUALITY IMPROVEMENT
93.	SEP-93	TRANSAXLE VENT OIL LEAK
94.	MAR-94	TSB GROUP CHANGE
95.	OCT-94	UNDER SEAT STORAGE DRAWER CRACKS
96.	AUG-94	VENT WINDOW LATCH POPS OPEN, RATTLES, POPS CLOSED

The company's more comprehensive warranty is the primary reason why defect complaints registered by consumer groups on Chrysler vehicles had begun to decline a few years ago. But they're now on the increase again (a fact confirmed by both *Consumer Reports* and J. D. Power) because of Chrysler's use of cheap body components and failure-prone powertrains. Since the warranty was shortened, all of Chrysler's products have finished at the bottom of the last two J. D. Power quality and customer satisfaction surveys.

In light of the shorter warranty and member complaints, *Consumer Reports* says the company's midsize cars are no longer recommended; other Chrysler vehicles have been similarly downgraded.

Chrysler's dominance of the minivan market continues nonetheless. Its 1996 minivan launching has generated strong sales in spite of being delayed by factory defects, problems in meeting the U.S. government's crashworthiness regulations, failure-prone rear latches, and supplier inefficiency. With its optional driver-side sliding door, roomier interior, and more powerful standard engine, it has kept a leg up on the competition.

Nevertheless, if Chrysler is to be competitive in anything other than minivans, it must spend some of its hefty $1300 profit per vehicle to buy top-quality body and powertrain components, reinstate its previous warranty to bridge the quality gap until reliability is sufficiently improved, and kick out dishonest and incompetent dealers who generate the most customer complaints. If it doesn't take these steps soon, even its minivan dominance won't save the company.

Neon

RATING: Not Recommended. A high-priced, low-quality econobox.

NEW FOR '97: Except for the addition of a cast aluminum oil pan to reduce engine vibrations, redesigned wheel covers, improved sound system, and a centre console with armrest, the Neon is basically unchanged this year. A redesign is planned for 1999.

GENERAL COMMENTS: Until now, Chrysler competed in the subcompact class by rebadging Mitsubishi-built cars and selling them under Chrysler nameplates. Now, with Neon, it has a home-grown competitor that's roomy and reasonably powered.

Neon is no laggard when it comes to horsepower; its base 2.0L engine puts out 132 hp—almost 50 more than the Toyota Tercel. Both the Honda Civic and Nissan Sentra lag considerably behind with 102 hp and 110 hp, respectively. Interior room is where the Neon shines, though, with front and rear seating that easily accommodates six-footers.

Cost analysis/Alternatives: The 1996 Neons are mechanically identical to the 1997 versions; get a '96 and invest the savings in an extended warranty. Other cars worth considering are the Ford Escort, Geo Metro, Honda Civic, and Toyota Corolla. If you're in the market for the sport coupe, make sure that you also check out the Nissan 200SX, SE-R, and the VW Golf GTi. **Rebates**: '96 and '97 Neons get a $1000 rebate until Jan. 6, 1997. **Destination charge** $600. **Recommended options**: Built-in child safety seats (if available) and height adjustment for the steering wheel (for short drivers). Don't invest in the optional

150 hp four-banger—you'll get just as much noise and not much more power. ABS is another option that hasn't got the bugs worked out yet. **Supplementary warranty**: Essential, preferably up to seven years. **Parts supply/Servicing**: Average. **Depreciation**: Below average. **Highway/City fuel economy**: 6-9L/100 km with the base 2.0L engine, and 7-11L/100 km with the high-output powerplant. Owners say that real-world fuel economy is far less than what's hyped, so be wary of Chrysler's fuel economy claims, which are different than the figures listed above.

Reliability/Safety

Pro: Stainless-steel exhaust system. Reinforced doors meet tough U.S. federal side impact standards, years ahead of the standards becoming law. Front adjustable shoulder belt anchors.

Con: It may take longer than three years to correct the Neon's many problems, notably its powertrain, electrical system, and body deficiencies. Hence, Chrysler's shortened warranty is far from reassuring. *Consumer Reports* says that its member survey found that first-year (1995 model) Neons had nearly twice the problems of the average 1995 model car. When *Autoweek*, an American car enthusiast magazine, tested a '96 Neon Sport Coupe after only 16,566 miles for its March 4th edition, it concluded that "aliens" had invaded the test car. Some of the magazine's "close encounters": a "raggedy" shifter, premature front brake pad wear-out, excessive brake fade, a rumbling noise coming from under the car, distorted sound coming from the cassette player, frozen windshield wipers, and a defroster that wouldn't clear the windshield or side windows and that produced a wheezing noise when operating.

A perusal of owner comments confirms that these cars continue to have lots of serious factory-related defects, including an air-conditioning system that often requires expensive servicing, lots of interior noise and leaks, interior window film buildup, uneven fit and finish, poor-quality trim items that break or easily fall off, and exposed screw heads. The finish isn't as good as most other subcompacts, either; the thickness of the coat varies considerably and will chip easily.

Confidential dealer service bulletins also reinforce owners' impressions that they have problem-plagued cars. Bulletins list the following problems that may carry over to the '97s: the engine sags, hesitates, shudders, and surges; a rough idle that's especially bad during cold startup; manual gearshift lever squeaks and vibrates; buzzy manual and automatic gearshift lever; harsh, erratic automatic transmission shifting; rear suspension bottoms out; noisy clutch pedal and wheel cover; oil leaks at the cam position sensor; steering wheel shake; AC freeze-up, poor performance, and evaporator odours; inaccurate fuel gauge readings; instrument panel glare and water leaks; flickering headlights; excessive engine noise intruding into the passenger compartment; exhaust noise/hiss; B-pillar wind noise; power-steering rattles; steering column and right engine mount clicking; chattering steering column tilt lever; accelerator pedal vibrations; front seat rattles and front seatback squeaks; hood prop rod rattle; idle air control motor whistle; front brake moaning; glue oozes out at backlight/windshield moulding; backlight moulding lifts off; poorly fitted deck lid rattles; water leaks into the passenger compartment on lefthand turns; poor AM reception (static); intermittent wiper operation; discharged battery; paint fogging; stained white bumper fascia; and premature front brake pad wear.

Front and rear head restraints are set too low and the headlight switch is a "Hide and Go Seek" affair. NHTSA crash tests of a '95 Neon showed that the driver would sustain severe head injuries in a 57 km/h frontal collision, while the passenger would receive average protection. It was rated: driver, ★★★; passenger, ★★★. A retested '96 four-door Neon did much better. It was rated: driver, ★★★★; passenger, ★★★★.

Road Performance

Pro: The 2.0L engine's 132 horses and Neon's low weight give it acceptable performance in lower gear ranges, which restricts it to mainly urban use. Fewer vibrations are felt in the cockpit with the '97 model. Handling is better than most small cars. The 3-speed automatic transmission should be a 4-speed, but it still performs more smoothly than the manual gearbox.

Con: Base engine runs out of steam in high gear and is buzzy from 4000 rpm on up. It runs particularly roughly after 5000 rpm. This is especially irritating because horsepower and torque peak at 5000 and 6000 rpm. The optional 150 hp 4-cylinder engine isn't much better. Throttle "jerk" in traffic when you barely press the accelerator is probably caused by faulty fuel-injector calibration, because it can also be felt at cruising speed when the accelerator is depressed slightly. The manual transmission is harsh and noisy—no comparison with Honda and Toyota vehicles. The manual gearbox also requires lots of downshifting when going over small hills. The 3-speed automatic transmission lacks sufficient torque in high gear, and shifts abruptly and often. The car cries out for the more economical and efficient 4-speed electronic transmission. The jittery ride becomes fairly rough when traversing anything but the smoothest roads. Ride deteriorates and the suspension bottoms with a vengeance with a full load. Braking is only average.

Comfort/Convenience

Pro: The Neon seats five adults, has a spacious interior, and a surprisingly versatile though narrow trunk with a low sill. Good driving position with easy to operate controls and clear gauges. Seats are firmer and more comfortable than one would expect. Plenty of leg room, head room, and elbow room. Rear seat is roomy enough for three adults. Rear seatbacks can be folded down to increase trunk space. Lots of little storage areas. Large door openings for long legs. Practical cloth bucket seats. Easy-to-use and effective heating and ventilation system (except for the defroster) that's illuminated at night.

Con: Low-quality interior appointments. Noise, noise everywhere. Engine boom, automatic transmission whine, air leaks through the frameless windows, tire thumping, road rumbling, and rattling front-seat shoulder harness mountings. Hard-to-access rear seat doesn't provide enough thigh support. Inadequate rear toe space. Door-mounted power window switches press uncomfortably against the driver's leg. No locks for the inside trunk release or seatback sections that give access to the trunk. Hard-to-operate window cranks and only the front windows are power-assisted. Short, flimsy trunk lid restricts trunk access.

COST

List Price (negotiable)	**Residual Values** (months)			
	24	**36**	**48**	**60**
Base: $14,265 (12%)	$9000	$7500	$6200	$4700
Base sedan: $14,465 (12%)	9300	7900	6700	5200

TECHNICAL DATA

Powertrain (front-drive)
Engines: 2.0L (132 hp)
• 2.0L (150 hp)
Transmissions: 5-speed manual • 3-speed auto.

Dimensions
Length: 171.8 in.
Width: 67.5 in.
Wheelbase: 104 in.

SAFETY FEATURES

	Opt.	Std.
Anti-lock brakes	■	❑
Childproof door locks	❑	■
Driver-side airbag	❑	■
Passenger-side airbag	❑	■

Avenger/Sebring

RATING: Recommended. Sports car thrills, without the bills.

NEW FOR '97: Nothing much has changed this year on the Avenger, except for the ES getting 17-inch wheels and other models getting new wheel covers. The optional 2.5L V6 powerplant is now available with base models. The base Sebring coupe gets a redesigned front and rear end, body cladding, and new wheel covers. Seventeen-inch cast aluminum wheels, an automatic dimming mirror, performance tires, and an improved suspension package are standard on the LXi. Sebring convertibles get the Autostick clutchless manual transmission coupled to the V6 engine, a dash-mounted trip computer on the JXi, and an improved alarm/locking system. The convertible's base 4-cylinder powerplant gets a cast aluminum oil pan to reduce engine vibrations, and an exhaust manifold that's been redesigned to reduce engine noise at low speeds.

GENERAL COMMENTS: The Avenger and its more luxuriously appointed Sebring twin go into their third year on the market as Recommended buys, mainly because these Mitsubishi-built compacts have had fewer-than-average first-year "teething" problems than Chrysler-built cars, and most of their mechanical components have been proven on other Mitsubishi models. Sebring is billed as a reasonably priced luxury coupe equipped with standard amenities including air conditioning, bucket seats, and a tilt steering wheel, while the Avenger fills the sports coupe niche with standard tinted glass and an awesome sound system.

Except for the convertible version, these front-drive replacements for the failure-prone Dodge Daytona and LeBaron coupes are built by Mitsubishi in Normal, Illinois, by the same factory that produces the Talon. They share many safety features and mechanical components with the Talon, including standard dual airbags and a 140-hp 2.0L twin cam 4-cylinder engine. High-performance ES versions are powered by a 164-hp 2.5L V6 coupled to an electronically controlled 4-speed automatic transaxle.

The convertible, made in Mexico, is six inches longer than the Sebring coupe and is powered by a standard 2.0L twin cam, while the upscale JXi gets a performance injection with the 2.5L 6-cylinder powerplant.

Cost analysis/Alternatives: The 1996 Avengers are virtually identical to the *less* expensive 1997 versions. Buy a '97 if the MSRP and the selling price remain reasonable. The redesigned Sebrings are significantly improved from a noise and performance standpoint, however these improvements aren't enough to justify paying more for a '97 model. **Rebates**: '96s get $1000; '97s, $500 until Jan. 1, 1997. **Destination charge**: $350. **Recommended options**: The LXi trim, only if you want the extra performance. **Supplementary warranty**: Not needed. **Parts supply/Servicing**: Very reasonable. **Depreciation**: Below average. **Highway/City fuel economy**: 6-10L/100 km. Sebring shoppers should consider the Ford Thunderbird/Cougar and Nissan Maxima. Avenger shoppers should take a look at other sporty coupes, including the '96 Dodge Stealth Ford Probe, Honda Accord, Mazda Precidia, Nissan 240SX, and Toyota Celica. Convertibles worth a glance: Ford Mustang and Chevrolet Camaro.

Reliability/Safety

Pro: Quality control is above reproach. Body construction and assembly are solid, with few gaps. Even though these cars have been on the market for only a year, parts are easily found. Rear seatback and remote trunk release can be locked. Crash tests of a dual airbag-equipped 1996 Avenger concluded that the driver and passenger would be exceptionally well-protected in a 57 km/h frontal collision. Crash rating: driver and passenger, ★★★★★.

Con: Inadequate base warranty. Confidential dealer service bulletins show a moderate number of problems that may carry over to the '96 versions, including poor engine performance; hard starts and stalling caused by a faulty powertrain control module; a tendency to drift to the left, requiring upgraded compression lower arm assemblies; intermittent or total loss of air conditioning (corrected by installing a revised AC pressure transducer); interior window film buildup; headliner sagging; and difficulty in closing the sunroof due to a faulty lever mechanism. Small horn buttons on the steering wheel spokes may be hard to reach in an emergency.

Some '96 versions have been recalled to fix an improperly installed brake booster vacuum hose, which may, if not corrected, cause increased engine idle speed and loss of power brake assist.

Road Performance

Pro: The base 4-cylinder is thrifty and adequate for most driving tasks. It works well with both the manual and automatic transmission. Handling is exceptional with either engine, and there's little body lean when cornering under speed. Steering is responsive and the ride deteriorates only slightly on bad surfaces due to the car's compliant suspension. Jarring is reduced as the weight of passengers is added. Brakes perform well, with little fading after successive stops. The ES's new 17-inch wheels add to the Avenger's overall handling and performance.

Con: The base 2.0L engine loses power when mated to the 4-speed automatic and, when pushed, it's noisy and less responsive than the V6. Unfortunately the V6 doesn't come with a manual gearbox, so its extra power doesn't translate into performance thrills. Some front-end plow in turns. The car's large turning circle makes parking a chore.

Comfort/Convenience

Pro: These cars have racy styling evocative of the Viper and Stealth, a rigid feel but a soft ride, and a rear seat area more adult-friendly than most sport coupes. Three tall passengers can sit in the rear for short trips, but the seating is really designed for two. Controls and gauges are easily reached and seen. Large doors facilitate entry and exit. Limited trunk cargo area can be extended by folding the split seatback. Cassette radio systems now come with six speakers (I'm not sure if this is a pro feature).

Con: Front seats need additional lateral support, and the seatback bulge is annoying to some drivers. The tilt steering wheel is set too low (almost in the driver's lap). Short drivers may have difficulty with forward vision, even with the seat raised to its maximum setting. With rear-quarter windows that won't open and the optional rear decklid spoiler cutting rear visibility, it's not hard to feel a bit claustrophobic. The climate control system is hampered by a noisy fan and uneven air distribution. The rear defroster leaves some of the glass untouched. Excessive tire noise intrudes into the passenger compartment.

COST

List Price (negotiable)	**Residual Values** (months) 24	36	48	60
Avenger: $18,630 (14%)	$10,500	$9500	$8500	$7500
ES: $20,870 (15%)	12,500	11,000	10,000	9000

TECHNICAL DATA

Powertrain (front-drive)
Engines: 2.0L 4 (140 hp)
• 2.5L V6 (155-164 hp)
Transmissions: 5-speed manual • 4-speed auto.

Dimensions (Avenger/Sebring)
Length: 187.2 in./187.4 in.
Width: 68.5 in./69.7 in.
Wheelbase: 103.7 in./103.7 in.

SAFETY FEATURES

Avenger	Opt.	Std.
Anti-lock brakes	■	❑
Childproof door locks	❑	❑
Driver-side airbag	❑	■
Passenger-side airbag	❑	■
Remote keyless entry	—	—

Sebring	Opt.	Std.
Anti-lock brakes	■	❑
Childproof door locks	❑	■
Driver-side airbag	❑	■
Passenger-side airbag	❑	■
Remote keyless entry	❑	■

Talon

RATING: Recommended. High performance, reasonably priced, and quite durable.

NEW FOR '97: This year's Talon is one mean-looking sports car. It's been dramatically restyled with wide air openings under the front bumper, new body cladding, and a redesigned rear end that includes a spoiler housing the centre-mounted stop lamp. A new, decontented (a fancy word that means it lacks many of the bells and whistles of the ESi, TSi, and TSi AWD) base model has been added. The TSi gets 17-inch wheels and better high performance tires.

GENERAL COMMENTS: This front-drive, Japanese-American hybrid is a high-performance, sporty two-seater made in Illinois by Diamond Star Motors, a joint venture of Mitsubishi and Chrysler. The ESi comes with a 140-hp 2.0L engine (borrowed from the Neon Sport), and the TSi is powered by a 210-hp 2.0L Mitsubishi-bred engine. Two additional powerplants are available: a 2.0L double overhead cam with 135 hp, and a turbocharged version of the same engine rated at a sizzling 195 hp. A manual 5-speed is standard, and an optional 4-speed automatic is available on all models except the Turbo RS. AWD is offered on both '96 model cars, however only the '97 TSi offers AWD.

All high-performance models cost thousands of dollars less than the Japanese competition, without compromising quality or performance. The 16-valve Talon 4X4 is at the top of the trim list and provides five horses more than the turbocharged TSi.

Cost analysis/Alternatives: Except for styling, the 1996 models are identical to the more expensive '97 versions, and are the better buy if they're substantially cheaper. **Rebates**: Waiting can save you money, since '96 models already get a $1000 rebate and '97s, a $500 rebate until January 1997. **Destination charge**: $375. **Options**: The turbo's extra 15 horses aren't that significant and exact a 10 percent fuel penalty. **Supplementary warranty**: Not needed. **Parts supply/Servicing**: Very reasonable. **Depreciation**: Below average. **Highway/City fuel economy**: 7-11L/100 km (non-turbo) and 9-12L/100 km on turbo-equipped AWD Talons. Other cars worth considering are the '96 Dodge Stealth, Ford Mustang and Probe, GM Camaro and Firebird, Nissan 240SX, and Toyota Celica and Supra. The Toyota Celica AWD Turbo is the best alternative to the Talon AWD.

Reliability/Safety

Pro: Mitsubishi products have a reliability record that's above average. Fit and finish are beyond reproach. The AWD system provides sure-footed foul weather stability. A 1996 Mitsubishi Eclipse two-door (identical to the Laser and Talon) was crash tested by NHTSA; it offered ★★★★ protection for both the driver and passenger.

Con: Inadequate base warranty. Dealers may not be capable of adequately servicing these high-tech vehicles. According to the CAA, parts are a bit more expensive than other cars in this class.

Problems reported by owners of previous model years and confirmed by dealer service bulletins: unstable idling, poor idling, and reduced rpm when the AC engages (requires an upgraded powertrain control module); cold weather hard starts and stalling; cold weather transmission shift delays (2-3 and 3-4) that take up to two minutes; transmission defaults into second gear (limp-in mode); vehicle tends to drift or lead to the right, requiring upgraded compression lower arm assemblies; speed control undershoot or overshoot; false theft alarm; centre exhaust pipe heat shield buzz; door buzz and rattle; misadjusted door glass causes water leaks and wind noise; noisy clutch pedal; interior window film buildup; headliner sagging; power seat switch sticks (see illustration below); stress marks on the quarter trim panel; buzz or rattle from the rear quarter trim; inoperative, noisy, and jerky sunroof operation; faulty lever latch pin; sunroof may open by itself.

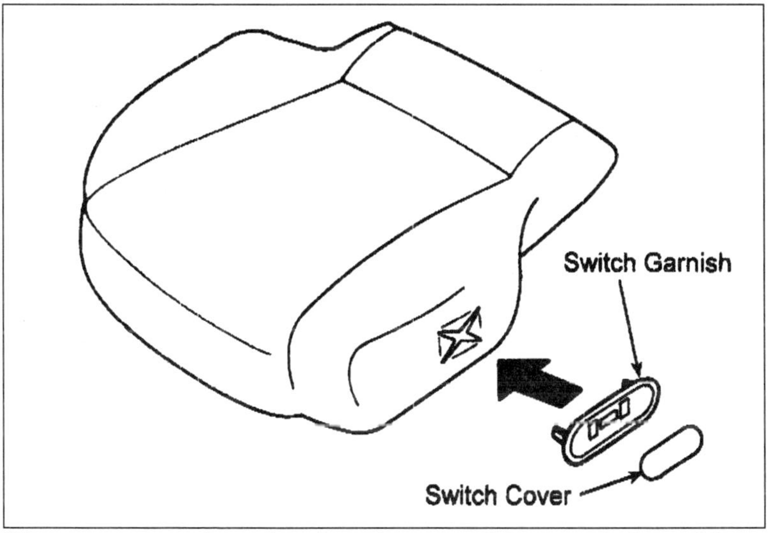

This warranty repair requires the replacement of the seat switch garnish with an upgraded part.

Road Performance

Pro: The base 16-valve 2.0L engine is quite powerful, but the optional 16-valve, turbocharged version gives more horsepower for the dollar than any other front-drive sports coupe and without any irritating turbo lag. The 5-speed manual is the gearbox of choice, especially with its shorter shift stroke and comfortable feel. The addition of 17-inch wheels on the '97 TSi AWD improves overall handling.

Con: Torque steer makes the car appear to try to twist out of your hands when all 195 turbocharged horses are unleashed.

Comfort/Convenience

Pro: Excellent ergonomics, highlighted by a wrap-around dash that makes the good old-fashioned analogue gauges easy to read and the controls easy to adjust. Dashboard air vents provide excellent ventilation. Lots of small storage spaces. Quiet riding, rattle-free construction.

Con: Driving position is set too low and seats are a bit hard. Cramped interior has limited rear room. Small, shallow trunk with a high sill.

COST

List Price (firm)	**Residual Values** (months)			
	24	**36**	**48**	**60**
Talon: $19,725 (15%)	$11,500	$10,500	$9500	$8000
TSi AWD: $29,985 (17%)	15,500	14,000	12,500	11,500

TECHNICAL DATA

Powertrain (front-drive)
Engines: 2.0L 4 (140 hp)
• 2.0L Turbo 4 (210 hp)
Transmissions: 5-speed manual • 4-speed auto.

Dimensions
Length: 172.2 in.
Width: 68.3 in.
Wheelbase: 98.8 in.

SAFETY FEATURES

	Opt.	Std.
Anti-lock brakes	■	❑
Childproof door locks	■	❑
Driver-side airbag	❑	■
Passenger-side airbag	❑	■
Remote keyless entry	■	❑
Traction control	—	—

('96) Stealth

RATING: Recommended. A serious, reasonably priced sports car that's as much go as show.

NEW FOR '97: There is no '97 model.

GENERAL COMMENTS: A pragmatist's dream car, the Stealth screams high performance with its aggressive, low, sleek styling—plus it has door handles, a spare tire, can be driven in any kind of weather, and is within reach of most people's budgets (take that, Viper and Prowler!). But unlike many other sports cars that are more show than go, the Stealth delivers superior performance *and* reliability that matches the promise of its styling. This Chrysler-styled and Japanese-made hybrid is a joint venture of Mitsubishi and Chrysler. Mitsubishi sells the car in the United States as the 3000GT.

Two models are available: the R/T and R/T Turbo, each version offering more equipment and better performance at a higher cost. The R/T comes with lots of standard equipment, comfort, and convenience features, including either a manual or automatic gearbox, anti-lock brakes, and a 24-valve version of the same 222-hp V6 first used by the ES. It doesn't have the twin turbos, four-wheel-steering, electronically adjustable suspension, and extra wide tires found with the top-of-the-line, 320-horsepower R/T Turbo, but it doesn't carry the Turbo's price tag, either.

The R/T Turbo, though, offers only a manual gearbox. It has a top speed of 160 mph plus and uses its twin turbos to provide gobs of torque without any turbo lag and with a minimum of torque steer. Mitsubishi claims 0-to-60 mph acceleration in just under five seconds. Mere mortals are more likely to turn in a six-second time. A full-time all-wheel-drive system also makes the R/T Turbo one of the surest handling sport coupes in bad weather.

Cost analysis/Alternatives: Unsold 1996 models are selling for about 10 percent under MSRP. **Rebates**: Not likely. **Destination charge:** $500. **Recommended options**: None. **Supplementary warranty**: Not needed. **Parts supply/Servicing:** Very reasonable. **Depreciation**: Way below average. **Highway/City fuel economy**: 9-13L/100 km for both the base R/T and the AWD versions. Other cars worth considering are the Eagle Talon, Ford Mustang, GM Camaro and Firebird, Nissan 240SX, and Toyota Celica and Supra.

Reliability/Safety

Pro. Mitsubishi products have an above-average reliability record. Crash tests of an airbag-equipped 1993 Stealth concluded that both the driver and front passenger would be well-protected.

Con: Inadequate base warranty. Dealers may not be capable of servicing these vehicles adequately due to the complexity of the various electronic and mechanical components. The small engine compartment means that some of the simplest jobs will require special tools and take an inordinate amount of time to carry out. Owner complaints have been limited to body glitches (interior window film buildup, some poor fits, fragile trim items, and squeaks and rattles) and electrical short circuits.

Road Performance

Pro: The base V6 engine accelerates well and provides more than enough power for all driving conditions. Twin turbo power on the R/T Turbo is awesome and rivals the engine performance of sports cars selling for far more. Power steering is crisp and predictable and provides just the right amount of road feel. Four-wheel steering kicks in when the car reaches 30 mph, adding to the Stealth's high-speed stability, particularly when cornering. Standard disc brakes work very well, but the ABS is particularly impressive in stopping the car in a short distance without any loss of directional stability or fading after repeated application. The manual and automatic transmissions shift impeccably.

Con: Tall gearing and long clutch travel take getting used to; expect frequent stall-outs when accelerating from a standstill with the manual gearbox. Lots of torque steer upon acceleration. Plenty of tire thumping and V6 growl.

Comfort/Convenience

Pro: Extremely comfortable bucket seats provide plenty of lateral support and come with power controls that have a memory for various settings. Excellent ventilation provided by an efficient and quiet 10-speed fan. Small trunk gets considerably larger with the rear seats folded down. Excellent soundproofing shuts out road and engine noise.

Con: Complex, confusing array of switches, dials, and controls. Inconveniently placed dash controls are confusing and difficult to adjust. Limited head room for tall drivers. Front seatbelts are uncomfortably tight, and the rear belts tend to ride up. The Stealth isn't a car for short drivers, who may have trouble seeing over the hood or reaching the clutch pedal. When the seat is moved forward, a short driver may then be unable to see overhead lights. Rear access and seating is extremely poor, as is the norm with most sports cars. Loading is difficult because of the trunk's high sill. The spare tire is the limited-service kind. Dash control that adjusts exhaust system sound is more gimmick than innovation. The Turbo's excessive weight taxes fuel economy. Some squeaks and rattles emanate from the car's chassis.

COST

List Price (negotiable)	**Residual Values** (months)			
	24	**36**	**48**	**60**
R/T: $35,345 (16%)	$23,000	$19,000	$16,000	$14,500
R/T Turbo: $49,405 (23%)	34,000	27,000	23,000	20,000

TECHNICAL DATA

Powertrain (front-drive/AWD)
Engines: 3.0L V6 (161 hp)
• 3.0L 24-valve V6 (222 hp)
• 3.0L Turbo 6 (320 hp)
Transmissions: 5-speed manual • 4-speed auto. • 6-speed manual (Turbo)

Dimensions (R/T Turbo)
Length: 179.5 in.
Width: 72.4 in.
Wheelbase: 97.2 in.

SAFETY FEATURES

	Opt.	Std.
Anti-lock brakes	❑	■
Childproof door locks	■	❑
Driver-side airbag	❑	■
Passenger-side airbag	❑	■
Remote keyless entry	—	—
Traction control	—	—

Breeze, Cirrus, and Stratus

Cirrus

RATING: Average buy with a below average warranty. Roomy, stylish, well appointed, comfortable, and smooth.

NEW FOR '97: Cirrus and Stratus: an optional dash-mounted trip computer and CD changer in the instrument panel, plus a new floor console that houses an armrest and cupholders for rear passengers. Improved airflow from the heater to the rear passenger compartment. The LXi now comes with standard chrome-plated aluminum wheels. The base 4-cylinder powerplant gets a cast aluminum oil pan to reduce engine vibrations and an exhaust manifold that's been redesigned to reduce engine noise at low speeds. Breeze: redesigned oil pan to reduce engine vibrations, improved shock absorbers and upper mounts that cut noise and smooth out suspension travel, a new floor console that includes an armrest and storage bin, and an optional dash-mounted CD changer.

GENERAL COMMENTS: The Chrysler Cirrus and Dodge Stratus are midsized sedan replacements for the LeBaron. Breeze, Plymouth's entry-level version, won't carry the V6 in order to keep its base price low, and will use an egg-crate, functional grille instead of the more stylish chrome version. Most of these cars' components have been used for some time on other Chrysler models, particularly the Neon subcompact and Avenger/Sebring sports coupes.

Power is supplied by three engines: a 2.0L 4-cylinder engine shared with the Neon powers the Stratus, while a base 2.4L 4-banger and optional 2.5L V6, used by the Avenger, propels the high-performance Cirrus. Carrying Chrysler's "cab forward" design a step further up the evolutionary ladder, these cars have short rear decks, low noses, and massive sloping grilles. A wheelbase that's two inches longer than the Ford Taurus's makes both cars comfortable for five occupants, with wide door openings and plenty of trunk space.

Cost analysis/Alternatives: The 1996 Cirrus and Stratus are practically identical to the '97 versions, and are a better buy if the selling price has been reduced significantly. If not, get a '97 for $270-$500 more. **Rebates**: $1000 for '96s and '97s. **Destination charge:** $375. **Recommended options**: A built-in child safety seat for the rear centre. Get the 2.5L V6. **Supplementary warranty**: Essential. Invest the money you saved in buying a '96 model on an extended seven-year warranty. **Parts supply/Servicing**: Average. **Depreciation**: Average. **Highway/City fuel economy**: Fuel consumption at 9-13L/100 km is higher than competitive models. Other vehicles worth considering: Ford Contour/Mystique, Honda Accord, Nissan Altima, Toyota Camry, and Volvo 850.

Reliability/Safety

Pro: Engine reliability has been pretty good, so far. Even though these cars have been on the market for only three years, parts are easily found and reasonably priced.

Con: The three-year base warranty is clearly insufficient coverage in view of Chrysler's traditionally poor quality control. Owners note the following problems: frequent stalling, myriad body squeaks and rattles, and fragile body hardware.

Confidential dealer service bulletins list the following problems that may carry over to the '97s: engine sag and rough idle, transmission defaults into second gear (limp-in mode), premature front brake lining wear or persistent squeaks or grinding noise, speed control undershoot or overshoot, vehicle drift or lead at highway speeds, inoperable door glass, interior window film buildup, defective air filter element, erratic windshield wiper delay, water leak from behind door trim panel, and cowl or plenum water leaks, causing musty odour or excessive condensation on the inside of windows (see illustration below).

Crash-test results for the '96 Stratus are: driver, ★★★; passenger N/A.

Road Performance

Pro: The base 2.5L V6 provides plenty of power in all gear ranges. This year's improvements have also reduced engine vibration somewhat. A

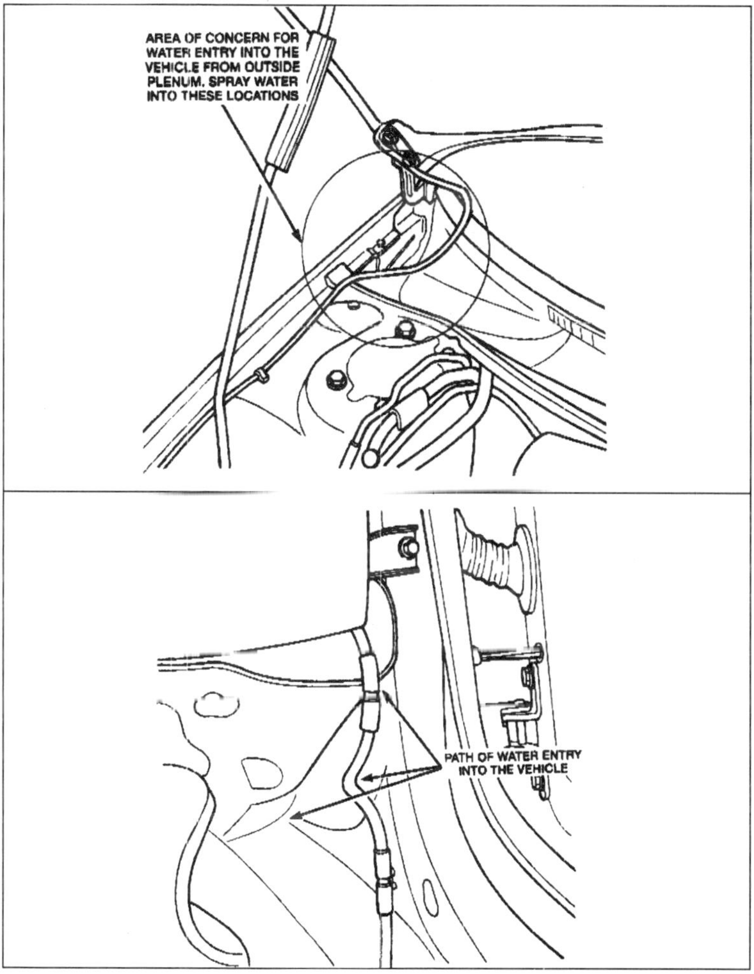

4-speed automatic is the only transmission offered; it shifts smoothly. Although high-performance handling isn't as sporty as the Contour's and the steering isn't quite as sensitive, overall handling is quite competent. Ride quality is generally smooth and pleasant and doesn't deteriorate as the load increases.

Con: Forget about the Neon-borrowed 2.0L 4-banger; it's overwhelmed by this car's size and accessories and is quite noisy in spite of the redesigned exhaust manifold. The V6 is also a bit noisy when pushed and lacks the aggressiveness of the Ford Contour and Mystique V6, particularly when passing. This can be very disconcerting because the powertrain computer kicks the transmission down to second gear, pushing the tachometer to the redline without gaining much more speed. Steering response is a bit vague. Excessive ABS brake fading after successive stops increases stopping distance considerably.

Comfort/Convenience

Pro: Attractive, tasteful interior. Seats are generally comfortable, with nice side bolsters. They aren't quite as snug as the Contour and Mystique seats, but some drivers prefer the extra room. Plenty of front head and leg room. Both tall and short drivers can see and access all controls and gauges. Spacious rear seating can comfortably accommodate three six-footers. Rear seatback folds down, extending the trunk cargo space, which is fairly large to begin with. Rear-seat comfort has been enhanced through better interior heating.

Con: Front seat bottom cushion is a little short on thigh support for tall drivers. In highway cruising between 100-120 km/h the powertrain emits an annoying high-pitched whine. Some suspension noise intrudes into the interior when going over rough surfaces. Narrow rear door armrests and the lack of a centre armrest leave you without much to lean on.

COST

List Price (negotiable)	**Residual Values** (months) 24	36	48	60
Cirrus: $23,730 (16%)	$17,900	$16,500	$12,900	$10,400
Stratus: $18,470 (14%)	13,700	12,200	9200	7200
Breeze: $18,470 (15%)	13,900	12,400	9500	7500

TECHNICAL DATA

Powertrain (front-drive)
Engines: 2.0L 4 (132 hp)
• 2.5L V6 (162 hp)
• 2.4L V6 (132 hp)
Transmissions: 5-speed manual • 4-speed auto.

Dimensions (Cirrus/Stratus)
Length: 187 in./186 in.
Width: 71.7 in./71.7 in.
Wheelbase: 108 in./108 in.

SAFETY FEATURES

Cirrus	Opt.	Std.
Anti-lock brakes	❑	■
Childproof door locks	❑	■
Driver-side airbag	❑	■
Passenger-side airbag	❑	■
Remote keyless entry	❑	■

Stratus	Opt.	Std.
Anti-lock brakes	❑	■
Childproof door locks	—	—
Driver-side airbag	❑	■
Passenger-side airbag	❑	■
Remote keyless entry	■	❑

Concorde, Intrepid, LHS, Vision

Intrepid

RATING: Below Average buy. Reliability is more important than passenger space.

NEW FOR '97: The New Yorker has been dropped in favour of the more luxurious LHS. Major changes are a standard 3.5L multi-valve V6 engine for the Concorde and LHS, redesigned wheel covers, and a supposedly improved automatic transmission (they changed the computer software). The Vision gets an optional 3.5L engine and an improved standard sound system.

GENERAL COMMENTS: These identical full-sized cars share the same LH chassis and offer most of the same standard and optional features. The Intrepid, Vision, and Concorde were launched in early 1993, and the two extended-wheelbase New Yorkers hit dealer showrooms the following summer.

All five models have loads of passenger space and many standard features that usually sell as options, such as four-wheel disc brakes and independent rear suspension. The Concorde is marketed to the more conservative buyer. The Eagle Vision, the newest of the original trio, is aimed at drivers who want higher performance. The Intrepid, the Dynasty's replacement and the most popular model, is the entry-level version.

A standard 3.3L 12-valve 161-hp V6 powers the Intrepid and Vision; the base engine for the Concorde and LHS is a 3.5L 214-hp V6.

Cost analysis/Alternatives: The 1996 models are virtually identical to the slightly more expensive 1997 versions, except for the larger standard engines on the '97 Concorde and LHS. It would be wise to opt for a leftover '96 model with the larger engine and put your savings in an extended seven-year warranty. You'll need it. **Rebates**: Chrysler is giving $3000 dealer incentives to unload '96 New Yorkers/LHS and $1500 on the '96 and '97 Concorde, Vision, and Intrepid. **Destination charge**:

$700. **Recommended options**: The V6 upgrade. The harsh sports suspension, however, is a waste of money. Goodyear GA tires provide better handling, but they're noisy. A similar handicap afflicts the optional 3.5L V6: it's noisier than the base engine and needs medium-grade fuel. On the positive side, its extra power doesn't burn more fuel than does the base V6. Don't choose the no-cost optional front bench seat; it's uncomfortable and lacks side bolstering. The large rear windshield may need tinting to protect rear seat passengers from the sun. **Supplementary warranty**: A wise investment, judging from the serious problems reported on previous models. **Parts supply/Servicing**: Average. **Depreciation**: Below average. **Highway/City fuel economy**: 8-14L/100 km. Seriously consider a Concorde over the New Yorker; it carries most of the same features for less money. Other cars worth considering are the Ford Taurus and Sable, Honda Accord, Nissan Altima, and Toyota Camry.

Reliability/Safety

Pro: Except for some valve train ticking on the '96s, 3.3L and 3.5L engine reliability and durability is pretty good. Plastic front fenders are dent- and corrosion-resistant. NHTSA 57 km/h crash tests have concluded that a 1996 Dodge Intrepid's driver and passenger would be relatively well-protected in a 57 km/h frontal collision. It was rated: driver, ★★★★; passenger, ★★★★. A 1994 New Yorker provided similar crash protection to both the driver and front seat passenger.

Con: Skinflint base warranty. A perusal of dealer service bulletins and comments from owners tells me that these cars continue to have many serious powertrain deficiencies. Chief among these are glitches in the computerized transmission's shift timing, which cause driveability problems (stalling, hard starts, and surging). Amazingly, the 4-speed LE42 automatic transmission—a spinoff of Chrysler's failure-prone A604—appears to be just as problem-plagued as its predecessor, with reports of driveline shudder during 3-4 shifts and frequent transmission defaults into second gear (limp-in mode). The '97 models promise smoother shifting through a software upgrade, but insiders tell me that it's more of a hardware problem that's yet to be addressed by Chrysler.

Body problems abound, with lots of interior noise, uneven fit and finish, poor-quality trim items that break or easily fall off, exposed screw heads, faulty door hinges that make the doors rattle and hard to open, windows that come off their tracks or are misaligned and poorly sealed, power-window motor failures, and steering wheel noise when turning. Other defects specifically addressed in dealer service bulletins: a noisy front suspension (clunking and rattling), a metallic knocking from the front of the vehicle when passing over bumps, interior window film buildup, windshield washer spray is too low, water collecting in the park/turn lamps, and trunk water leaks (see illustration below) or dust accumulation.

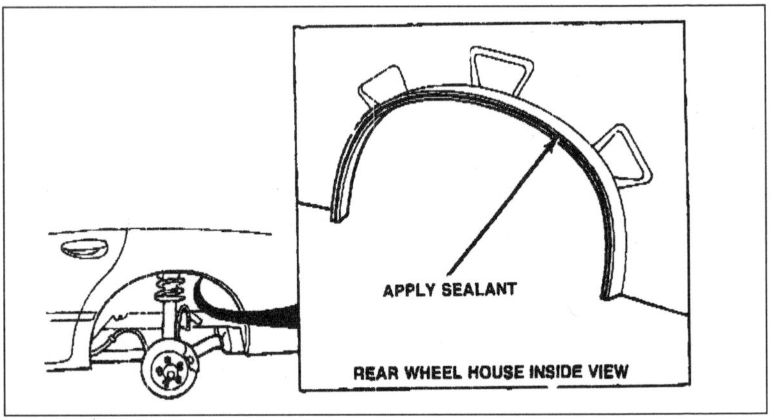

Chrysler has had trunk water leaks for over two decades.

Non-ABS brakes perform poorly, resulting in excessively long stopping distances that exceed other cars in this class. The overhead digital panel is distracting and forces you to take your eyes from the road. The emergency brake pedal catches pant cuffs and shoelaces as you enter or exit. Small, hard-to-find horn buttons. A high rear window sill obstructs rear visibility.

Road Performance

Pro: The 3.3L powerplant is smooth and quiet (except for some valve-train ticking), while providing plenty of power for most driving needs. Both V6 engines provide plenty of low-end torque and acceleration. Smooth-shifting 3-speed automatic transaxle. Good or better handling and steering response than the Taurus, and the optional Autostick clutchless manual transmission available with the Intrepid sports package improves overall performance even more. Independent suspension also maximizes control and provides lots of suspension travel so that you don't get bumped around on rough roads. The ride doesn't deteriorate as the load is increased. The best balance between performance and ride is found with the mid-level touring suspension. It's not as harsh as the optional sport suspension, and it's firmer than the standard settings. Good standard brakes.

Con: The traction control system is noisy when activated. A considerable amount of body roll occurs in tight manoeuvring. The ABS system could use some improvement to reduce noise and improve feel and modulation.

Comfort/Convenience

Pro: A sleeker, more aerodynamic body than the Taurus/Sable, Honda Accord, and Chevrolet Lumina. Chrysler has made these cars the same length as GM's popular H-body cars (Pontiac Bonneville, Buick LeSabre, and Olds 88), which allows for comfortable front bucket seats and a large but shallow trunk with low liftover. Excellent front and rear access. The user-friendly interior features a steering wheel with a solid feel, analogue instruments that are clearly laid out, passenger grab handles for easy access, and lots of storage space, including map pockets in the door. Rear seat sits three abreast with extended front seat tracks for long-legged drivers. Excellent visibility, low front end. Automatic climate-control system is much improved.

Con: Front seat lacks lateral support and the adjustable lumbar support is uncomfortable. Noisy fan. Excessive engine, road, and wind noise comes mainly from the tires and poor sealing around the windows. The trunk has a high decklid, making for difficult loading and unloading, and there's no inside access by folding down the rear seat, as in the Camry.

COST

List Price (negotiable)	**Residual Values** (months) 24	36	48	60
Intrepid: $23,625 (16%)	$11,900	$10,500	$9200	$7600
Concorde: $26,385 (17%)	13,900	12,500	11,500	9500
Vision 4-door: $24,325 (15%)	13,000	11,500	10,500	8500
LHS: $40,130 (20%)	24,000	22,000	19,500	16,500

TECHNICAL DATA

Powertrain (front-drive)
Engines: 3.3L 12-valve V6 (161 hp) • 3.5L 24-valve V6 (214 hp)

Dimensions (Intrepid/Concorde, Vision, New Yorker/LHS)
Length: 201.7 in./201.6 in./207.4 in.
Width: 74.4 in. (all models)
Wheelbase: 113 in. (all models)

Transmissions: 5-speed manual • 4-speed auto.

SAFETY FEATURES

Concorde, LHS	Opt.	Std.
Anti-lock brakes	❑	■
Childproof door locks	■	❑
Driver-side airbag	❑	■
Passenger-side airbag	❑	■
Remote keyless entry	❑	■

Intrepid, Vision	Opt.	Std.
Anti-lock brakes	■	❑
Childproof door locks	❑	■
Driver-side airbag	❑	■
Passenger-side airbag	❑	■
Remote keyless entry	■	❑

Caravan, Voyager, Town & Country

Dodge Caravan: the quintessential familymobile.

RATING: An Above Average buy with a history of below average reliability. There are three factors working against this year's minivans: their base warranty is inadequate, serious powertrain and body defects from previous years may not have been corrected, and Chrysler's redesigned models have a history of being unreliable and poorly put together.

NEW FOR '97: Already loaded with lots of convenience features from last year's redesign, this year's lineup gets a new ABS system that produces less pedal pulsing, a mechanism that releases the power doorlocks and turns on the interior lights when the airbag is deployed, improved cruise control performance, and better body soundproofing with polyurethane foam injected into body cavities (watch those allergies). Other minor standard features include a power outlet in the cargo area, courtesy lights in front and on the liftgate, and an instrument panel-mounted cruise control indicator. The Plymouths now offer an optional eight-way power driver's seat and an overhead console that houses a trip computer, compass, and thermometer.

Town & Country buyers will see all the above, in addition to the return of optional all-wheel-drive coupled with four-wheel disc brakes (instead of the standard rear drums), as well as standard low-speed traction control, and a left-side sliding door.

Last year the redesigned Caravan, Voyager, and Town & Country grew larger; got an optional left-side sliding rear passenger door; a new 2.4L, 16-valve, DOHC 4-cylinder engine; an improved suspension; and detachable rolling seats.

GENERAL COMMENTS: These practical and stylish minivans return after a $2.6-billion redesign that has transformed them from boxy to almost beautiful, and gives buyers a 2.4L 4-banger that's hopefully more reliable than the notorious engine it replaces. In addition to the improvements noted above, these minivans offer a wide array of standard and optional features that include AWD, anti-lock brakes (optional on the Voyager), child safety seats integrated into the seatbacks, flush design door handles, and front windshield wiper/washer controls located on the steering column lever for easier use. Extra care has been taken this year to reduce interior engine and road noise through the new exterior design and additional insulation. The minivan's nose has a softer, more aerodynamic appearance with aero-style headlamps and full lower body fascias. Interior space has been increased by about 25 percent and the volume behind the third seat is about 33 percent greater. The step-in height is an inch and a half lower on the new models. Childproof locks are standard and the front bucket seats incorporate vertically adjustable head restraints. The Town & Country, a luxury version of the Caravan, comes equipped with a 3.8L V6 and standard luxury features that make the vehicle more fashionable for upscale buyers.

Cost analysis/Alternatives: The 1996 Town & Country models are $2000 cheaper than the 1997 versions, but the '97 Caravans are the same price, or a few hundred dollars cheaper than last year's Caravans and are, therefore, the better buy. Take a look at the Ford Windstar. Although far from perfect, it's miles ahead of Chrysler in quality control. Small minivans that may be better suited to your needs include the '96 Eagle Summit, Ford Villager, or Nissan Quest. **Rebates**: Not likely given the '97 Caravan's reduced price. **Destination charge**: $810. **Recommended options**: The 3.3L V6 is a wise compromise for most city-driving situations, but don't hesitate to get the 3.8L if planning lots of highway travel. Stay away from the 4-cylinder engine—it has no place in a minivan, especially when hooked to the automatic transmission. The $600 sliding rear door on the driver's side makes it easy to load and unload children, install a child safety seat directly behind the driver, or remove the rear seat. Child safety seats integrated into the rear seatbacks are convenient and reasonably priced. Remember, the Grand version sacrifices handling for extra interior room. Other important features to consider are the optional defroster, power mirrors, power door locks, and power driver's seat (if you're shorter than 5'9" or expect to have different drivers using the minivan). **Supplementary warranty**: A must-have—preferably a seven-year powertrain warranty. **Parts supply/Servicing**: Average. Chrysler says that its 3.3L and 3.8L engines won't require tune-ups before 100,000 *miles*. **Depreciation**: Below average. **Highway/City fuel economy**: Caravan/Voyager: 9-13L/100 km; Grand Caravan AWD: 10-14L/100 km; Town & Country: 9-14L/100 km; Town & Country AWD: 10-15L/100 km.

Reliability/Safety

Pro: Repair costs are average during the warranty period. The most reliable powertrain is the 3.3L V6 engine coupled to the 3-speed automatic transmission.

Chrysler minivans meet all U.S. passenger car safety standards through 1998. Dual airbags include knee bolsters to prevent front occupants from sliding under the safety belts. Side impact protection is increased with steel beams in door panels. An improved engine compartment layout makes for a larger "crumple zone" in the event of collision. Remote-control power door locks can be programmed to lock when the vehicle is put in gear. The rear wiper is extraordinarily efficient and the Grand Voyager's heated windshield wiper well keeps the blades from icing up in nasty weather.

Convenient, adjustable shoulder height seatbelts and head restraints on all seats (not found on many other minivans). U.S. insurance statistics show that the Caravan and Voyager have substantially fewer accident injury claims than average. The '97s haven't been crash-tested yet, but tests of a 1996 dual airbag-equipped Dodge Grand Caravan carried out by the NHTSA concluded that the driver would receive only average injury protection and that the passenger would receive good protection from serious injury. It's rated: driver, ★★★; passenger, ★★★★. This is a step in the wrong direction. A 1995 Grand Caravan was rated: driver, ★★★★; passenger, ★★★★.

Con: Quality control and reliability have been below average since these vehicles were first launched more than a decade ago. These reliability problems weren't all that serious In the past because Chrysler paid for most repairs up to seven years. Now all that has changed with Chrysler's reduced three-year warranty.

Dealers never serviced these vehicles very well—owners speak of repeated visits to repair dealer "repairs," and a "What, me worry?" attitude expressed by head office customer relations staff. Now that the base warranty has been cut back, owners won't have the luxury of time to get proper warranty servicing through repeat repair bay visits. If your dealer starts to play the waiting game—waiting for the warranty to expire—don't hesitate to use an independent garage if that's where good service can be found.

An advance view of the problems you're likely to have can be seen from owner complaints relating to components that haven't been changed for the new model year, and dealer service bulletins that show which new components are troublesome. For example, I'm told by Chrysler insiders that ABS improvements on the '97s should ameliorate problems that owners have had with the system, but the new transmission module software won't begin to address the multiplicity of deficiencies found in the minivans' automatic transmissions.

Owners report the following problems with earlier minivans: the 2.5L engine head gasket leaks, constant stalling, fuel-injection glitches, and leaky oil pressure sending unit seals. Cruise control often malfunctions, causing excessive downshifting (although it's covered under warranty, dealers try to exclude it from the base warranty). The transmission has a hard time deciding which gear it wants, and when you approach a minor incline it shifts down one or two gears and then shifts up too late—a major cause for complaints of poor fuel economy. Premature wear-out occurs on these parts: cooling system, clutch, front suspension components, wheel bearings, front brake rotors, air-conditioning compressor, and body parts (trim becomes loose and falls off, plastic pieces rattle and break easily, and door handles pull away). The front brakes in particular need constant attention, if not to replace the pads, then to silence the excessive squeaks and squealing when braking. The plastic gas tank is mounted low and is vulnerable to damage from road hazards, and the fuel system develops leaks. Finally, owners report a persistent rotten egg smell caused by poor engine timing or a defective catalytic converter.

The '96s haven't been out a year and they've already collected lots of service bulletins to address major factory-related defects that will surely carry over to Chrysler's '97 minivans.

The ABS system has proved unreliable on older vans and repair costs are astronomical. The ABS control unit on the new vans is located behind a front wheel, where it's susceptible to contamination by road salt and sand.

There's considerable doubt being raised by a former Chrysler engineer as to the overall crashworthiness and rear latch integrity of the 1996 minivans. His allegations are being investigated by the U.S. federal government. The NHTSA is investigating reports of undercarriage fuel leaks from the evaporative emission control canister that cause the vehicle to stall and lead to engine failure. There's also the chance of fire. The dealer will replace the fuel filler tank tube and grounding straps. Two other investigations involve seatbelts on 1991-96 minivans that may not latch properly and power steering belt tensioner fractures.

Chrysler has recalled 1996 model minivans to fix faulty seat bolts that could cause weakening of the rear seat and child safety seat.

Road Performance

Pro: These minivans are the closest thing to a passenger car when it comes to ride and handling. The redesigned chassis and improved steering provide a comfortable ride and excellent road feel with no surprises. Stiff springs greatly improve handling and comfort. Manoeuvrability around town is easy, and the addition of an optional 41TE 4-speed Overdrive transmission, with an Overdrive lockout button on the dash, makes for smoother city driving without the multiple gear shifts found with previous models. Chrysler's top-of-the-line 3.8L engine is smooth and quiet with lots of much-needed low-end torque.

The AWD (not available on the '96) transfers 90 percent of the engine power to the front wheels during normal driving conditions. It's easy to use and performs well. As the front wheels lose traction, the rear wheels get additional power until traction has been stabilized or the 55/45 percent front-to-rear limit is reached. Good brakes, and despite its past failings the ABS appears to operate more smoothly on the '97 model.

Con: Sluggish highway acceleration until you move up to the 3.8L engine. Avoid the 4-speed automatic transmission; it's erratic in city driving. Although it works well, the all-wheel drive option is overrated and not worth the fuel penalty for most driving situations. The stretched wheelbase version gives less than nimble handling. A large turning radius and the long nose can make parking difficult. Furthermore, the brakes tend to heat up after repeated applications, causing considerable loss of effectiveness (fade) and warping of the front discs.

Comfort/Convenience

Pro: This is where Chrysler minivans shine. They offer plenty of comfort and versatility. For example, the step-up height isn't too high for most people, the integrated child safety seat has a reclining back, the instrument panel features easy-to-read gauges and warning lights, and the large glove box and radio and heater controls are set close to the driver. The location of the turn signal indicators is particularly well thought out—they're in the lower portion of your field of vision. A cluster of three large air vents, set above the centre console panel and side window demister outlets located in the outboard ends of the instrument panel, make for a more efficient climate control system. The instrument panel and controls are angled toward the driver's seat. The instruments look less tacky this year, and sit under a curved cowl. Chrysler has copied the Windstar in providing theatre-type seating; each row is set a little higher than the row in front, giving most passengers a better view. A fairly high roofline—about four inches taller than the Ford Windstar—means that a six-foot-tall passenger will sit comfortably in the back seat, but would touch the roof in a Windstar. Another nice touch: grab handles on the rear hatch and sliding door.

Removing the centre and rear seats isn't a problem, thanks to the addition of little wheels on the base of the rear seat. Snap them down and you can roll the seat anywhere. The innovative interior makes for lots of cargo room—just lift the rear seats (still a two-person job) out of the back hatch and roll them away.

Minivan doesn't mean "mini" in terms of passenger space. The aerodynamic exterior design, increased window area, and lower sills make for an attractive, roomier-feeling vehicle, and the interior is large and versatile with excellent outward visibility and plenty of storage space. There is convenient "walk through" access to the rear seating area, and an optional "Convert-a-Bed" package is available with the seven-passenger seating configuration. Drivers are treated to a car-like driving position. Lots of cupholders and interior reading lights.

Dual-zone air conditioning allows for different temperature settings for the driver and front-seat passenger. Overhead heating and ventilation ducts to the rear seat are well placed. Although wind noise at highway speeds is still a problem, Chrysler's soundproofing of the '97 models has cut road noise considerably.

Con: Excessive transmission whine. Driver is faced with 44 switches, dials, and buttons on the dash/door panel/console. Console storage bin for small objects is sometimes hard to open and close. Front seats lack sufficient lumbar support and the seat back comes up short against the shoulder blades. Both sliding side doors are unwieldy to slide and it takes lots of effort to push the buttons that unlatch them. Removable seats aren't as easy to remove as Chrysler would have you believe. Fuel gauge reads E too soon because the fuel tank and fuel pump module are defective. This problem has been confirmed by CompuServe and Internet postings, *Autoweek* (Sept 16, 1996 edition), and Chrysler engineers. The company has a fix and says that dealers will repair the vehicles at no charge (see DSB below).

NO. 14-08-95 Rev. A
GROUP: Fuel
DATE: Jan. 26, 1996
NOTE:
This bulletin supersedes Technical Service Bulletin 14-08-95, dated Jan. 12, 1996, which should be removed from your files.
The labor operation number is revised and lightweighted with "asterisks".
SYMPTOM/CONDITION:
Only 12-13 gallons of fuel are able to be added when the low fuel warning light comes "ON" (normal is 16-17) or 15-16 gallons of fuel are able to be added when the fuel gauge reads "E" (normal is 18-20).
DIAGNOSIS:
Inspect the bottom of the fuel tank. If the fuel tank bottom is bowed upward, perform the Repair Procedure. If it is not bowed upward, this bulletin does not apply and further diagnosis will be needed.
PARTS REQUIRED:

1	4882329	Tank, Fuel
2	4595227	O-Ring, Fuel Pump Module

REPAIR PROCEDURE
This bulletin involves installing a revised fuel tank.

1. Drain the fuel tank into a approved gasoline holding tank.
2. Record the radio station presets and disconnect negative battery cable.
3. Raise the vehicle on an appropriate hoist.
4. Remove the three screws attaching the filler tube blocker and separate the blocker from the vehicle.
5. Disconnect the rollover valve harness to steel vent tube connection at the front of the tank.
6. Disconnect the fuel filter supply line from the steel fuel supply line.
7. Loosen the clamp on the filler tube hose at the tank connection.
8. Slide the fuel pump module electrical connector lock to the unlocked position. Push down on the connector retainer and pull the connector from the module.
9. Use a transmission jack to support the fuel tank. Remove the attaching bolts from the fuel tank retaining straps.
10. Lower the tank slightly. Carefully remove the filler tube hose from the fuel tank.
11. Disconnect the filter vents from the filler tube by squeezing the retainer and pulling the connector off of the steel tube.
12. Lower the fuel tank slowly while feeding the vent lines through the frame rail to remove the fuel tank from the vehicle.
13. Remove the fuel filter attaching screw, disconnect both fuel filter connectors from the fuel pump module and set the fuel filter aside for reuse later.
14. Remove the fuel pump module from the fuel tank and discard the O-ring seal.
15. Install the fuel pump module into the new fuel tank (PIN 4882329) using a new O-ring seal (P/N 4695227). Make sure the locating tab on the fuel pump module is lined up with the notch on the fuel tank.
16. Tighten the fuel pump module lock nut to 40-45 ft. lbs (54-61 Nm).
17. Attach the fuel filter to the fuel pump module by pushing the fittings onto the tubes until the retainers seat. Pull back on the connectors to make sure they are secure.
18. Attach the fuel filter to the fuel tank and torque the screw to 35A5 in. lbs. (4-5 Nm).
19. Place the fuel tank on a transmission jack and slowly raise it into position while feeding the fuel filter vent lines through the frame rail. Make sure the vent lines are not crossed on top of the fuel tank.
20. Line up the fuel filter tube hose with the fuel tank inlet neck and push it on.
21. Raise the tank up to the underbody and install the fuel tank retention straps. Torque the fasteners to 30-50 ft. lbs. (40-68 Nm).
22. Attach the filler vent lines to the filler tubes by pushing the connectors on until they are seated. Pull back on the connectors to make sure they are secure.

Imagine how much money the car rental agencies made when people turned in their Chrysler minivans with less than a full tank. Bet you they charged for 18-20 gallons, even though the tank would take only 15-16 gallons. Let's see, a four-five gallon overcharge on each minivan, converted to litres, multiplied by number of rentals. . . .

COST

List Price (firm)	Residual Values (months) 24	36	48	60
Voyager/Caravan: $19,620 (13%)	$11,900	$10,500	$9000	$8300
Grand Caravan: $21,200 (15%)	12,900	11,500	9900	8900
Grand Voyager LE: $30,550 (16%)	16,900	15,500	13,500	12,500
Town & Country: $40,085 (22%)	25,000	22,000	20,000	16,500
Town & Country AWD: $43,330 (25%)	26,500	23,500	21,000	17,500

TECHNICAL DATA

Powertrain (Front-drive)
Engines: 2.4L 4-cyl. (150 hp) • 3.0L V6 (150 hp) • 3.3L V6 (158 hp) • 3.8L V6 (166 hp) (std. on AWD)

Dimensions (Base/Ext. & AWD)
Weight: 3528 lbs.
Length: 186.3 in./199.6 in.
Width: 75.6 in./75.6 in.
Wheelbase: 113.3 in./119.3 in.
Fuel tank: 76L/reg. unl.
Cargo capacity: 146.2 cu. ft., 3691 lbs./172.3 cu. ft., 4133 lbs.
Towing capacity: up to 3500 lbs
Passengers: 5-7/ 7
Doors: 4 or 5

Transmissions: 3-speed auto. • 4-speed auto. (std. on AWD)

SAFETY FEATURES

	Opt.	Std.
Anti-lock brakes	■	❑
Childproof door locks	❑	■
Driver-side airbag	❑	■
Passenger-side airbag	❑	■
Remote keyless entry	■	❑
Traction control	❑	■
Front/rear head restraints		Yes
Side impact protection		Yes

FORD

Ford's '96 model sales haven't kept pace with those of Chrysler, despite brisk sales of its Explorer 4X4, substantial rebates on the Taurus and Escort, and innovative leasing that keeps monthly payments low and encourages customers to buy another Ford. Nevertheless, Ford is counting on a strong buyer demand this year based on its new model launchings and GM's decision to axe its Caprice, Fleetwood, and Roadmaster rear-drives at the end of the 1996 model year. This gives Ford a virtual monopoly on large rear-drive four-door sedans—principally the Lincoln Town Car, Crown Victoria, and Grand Marquis—long the mainstay of police departments, limousine operators, and retirees.

Ford's vehicles appeal to three types of buyers: those wanting inexpensive front-drive econoboxes; those opting for front- and rear-drive midsize sedans and coupes; and those wanting the comfort and power of traditional rear-drives. The subcompact Escort/Tracer and large-size Crown Victoria/Marquis have been particularly successful in fighting imports at both ends of the market, while keeping Chrysler and GM on their toes. This is all the more ironic because the Escort is a weaker knock-off of the Mazda 323/Protegé, and the rear-drive Crown Victoria/Marquis and Mustang are restyled 1970s products.

Ford has achieved this small miracle by aggressively pushing new and restyled products, cutting prices and dealer markups, and offering special-equipment packages. A total of 18 restyled cars and trucks are due out over the next three years, while the dealer markup has been cut on Ford's popular vehicles.

'97 Model Year Changes: Having launched the Contour, Mystique, and Windstar minivan two years ago, and redesigned its Taurus, Sable, Thunderbird, Cougar, Villager, and F-series trucks last year, Ford's '97 model changes are minimal—except for a redesigned Escort and Tracer and a slightly restyled Lincoln Mark VIII. On the sport-utility and truck side, this year will see the debut of the Expedition and Mountaineer, and redesigned F-150 and 250 pickups.

Strengths and weaknesses: All Fords have a 3 year/60,000 km bumper-to-bumper warranty with no deductible or transfer fee. Rust perforation repairs are covered up to 5 years/unlimited km. Ford's warranty performance is better than Chrysler's and General Motors' in that the company has been more forthcoming when extending its warranty to cover its own manufacturing errors. But it's been less than forthright when dealing with safety-related defects, emission warranty obligations, and secret warranties covering paint defects.

Ford's quality control, although much improved, still lags behind that of Asian automakers. The quality of body components and their assembly and rust resistance are better than GM and Chrysler, but remain far below Japanese and European standards. Poor paint quality, a Ford problem for over a decade, was addressed in 1995 by a changeover in suppliers and the use of improved processes. It'll take at least three years to notice any improvement (keep your fingers crossed). In the meantime, Ford has shut down its Customer Dialogue Program, which repainted, free of charge, vehicles plagued by defective paint.

Article No. 93-8- April 14, 1993
PAINT - EXTERIOR CLEARCOAT "MICROCHECKING," HAZING, OR PEELING

FORD:

1983-93	THUNDERBIRD
1984-93	TEMPO
1985-93	ESCORT
1986	LTD
1986-93	TAURUS
1989-93	CROWN VICTORIA, MUSTANG, PROBE

LINCOLN-MERCURY:

1983-93	COUGAR
1984-92	MARK VII
1984-93	TOPAZ
1985-89	TRACER
1986	MARQUIS
1986-93	SABLE
1988-93	CONTINENTAL, TOWN CAR
1989-93	GRAND MARQUIS
1991-93	TRACER

LIGHT TRUCK:

1983-93	RANGER
1986-93	AEROSTAR
1987-90	BRONCO II
1988-93	F SUPER DUTY, F-47
1991-93	ECONOLINE, EXPLORER
1992-93	F-150-350 SERIES
1993	VILLAGER

ISSUE: The clearcoat layer of the basecoat/clearcoat paint system may "microcheck" (crack and erode), turn white, flake, or peel off the vehicle. This condition is noticeable on the horizontal surfaces only.

ACTION: Inspect the vehicle, and if repair is necessary, see procedure for service details. This is a wet on wet procedure. Sanding is not required after the seal coat is applied.

Keep the above paint bulletin handy. It can serve as proof that Ford's paint problem is factory-related and should be covered by an extended "goodwill" warranty, as it was in the past.

Aspire

RATING: Acceptable. Long on fuel economy, but short on performance.

NEW FOR '97: Nothing much, except for a minor facelift and upgraded side-impact protection.

GENERAL COMMENTS: A far more versatile car than the boxy little Festiva it replaced three years ago, Aspire is the fruit of a cooperative effort by Ford, Mazda, and Kia, a Korean carmaker. Offered in both three- and five-door body styles, it has received well-deserved accolades for its relatively spacious interior and standard safety features. However, there's still lots of Festiva in the Aspire—same engine, same transmissions, and same basic chassis—restricting it to an inner-city environment. The 1997 Aspire returns this year in three- and five-door versions powered by a fuel-injected 1.3L 4-cylinder hooked up to either a standard 5-speed manual transmission or an optional 3-speed automatic.

Cost analysis/Alternatives: The 1996 models are virtually identical to the '97s, and are the better buy. Other cars worth considering are the '96 Eagle Summit, Ford Escort, Geo Metro, Honda Civic, Mazda Protegé, Nissan Sentra, and Toyota Tercel. **Rebates**: Expect $500 rebates on '96 and '97 Aspires until Jan. 1997. **Destination charge**: $250. **Recommended options**: Anti-lock braking and power steering (a must) are available only as options on the four-door automatic version. **Supplementary warranty**: Not essential, but you'll need some extra protection for the inevitable body and electrical problems. **Parts supply/Servicing**: Average. **Depreciation**: Average. **Highway/City fuel economy**: 5.5-8L/100 km. Fuel economy is not all that impressive when compared to Geo Metro/Firefly and Swift, and entry-level Hondas and Nissans.

Reliability/Safety

Pro: The Aspire's long-term reliability has been shown to be better than average. After three years on the Canadian market, the car has elicited few customer complaints, and dealer service bulletins don't show any serious problems. Corrosion protection is enhanced and interior materials are of higher quality. Inasmuch as Ford is responsible for the car's body and interior, these areas will likely deteriorate more quickly than would the Mazda mechanicals.

Crash tests of a 1996 Aspire equipped with a driver-side airbag concluded that the driver and passenger would have better than average protection in a 57 km/h frontal collision. It was rated: driver, ★★★★; passenger, ★★★★. A retested '96 version posted identical results.

Con: Consumer complaints target the front brakes, engine timing belt, and fragile body hardware. True, dealer bulletins don't show any serious factory-related deficiencies, but they do note the following problems on earlier models that may carry over to the '97s: AC failures and excessive compressor noise, brake roughness upon application, inoperative ignition switches, and poor transmission upshifts in cold weather.

Road Performance

Pro: With a manual transmission and fuel injection, the Aspire's base powerplant is noticeably much smoother than the 1.0-litre 3-cylinder engine that powers the Metro and Swift. Very adequate for short city errands. Smooth shifting 5-speed manual transmission. Ride quality is surprisingly supple for a subcompact. The Aspire's 13-inch wheels and tires make for positive and predictable highway handling (only the Geo Metro and Suzuki Swift continue to use 12-inch wheels). Standard brakes exhibit little fade after successive stops, with little directional instability.

Con: The 1.3L engine takes thirteen seconds to reach 60 mph when mated to the manual transmission, and an additional four seconds with the automatic gearbox. It lacks high-end torque, and the widely spaced gear ratios on the manual shifter rob it of much-needed power in the mid-range when passing or pulling long grades. Steering is heavy in city driving and a bit vague at high speeds. Power steering isn't available with the two-door version. Considerable crosswind instability. Although fading is minimal, the brakes don't inspire confidence.

Comfort/Convenience

Pro: Plenty of front seat room with lots of head and leg room for six-footers, and excellent front and rear visibility. The steering wheel feels solid with a thicker rim. Spartan but well laid-out dash. Comfortable seats provide lots of support. Relative absence of wind noise. Cargo capacity, a major shortcoming with the Festiva, is the Aspire's strong suit, particularly in the five-door model. With the rear seatbacks folded forward, it becomes a mini-station wagon. Standard split rear seats make for easy loading.

Con: Styled like a mini-Saab, the Aspire gives new meaning to bland. The two-door's low rear roofline reduces rear head room. Rear seating is restricted to a couple of pliable adults or two well-fed kids. A spoiler on the up-level SE looks ridiculous. Excessive low-speed engine and road/tire noise at higher speeds. No remote hatch release or exterior hatch handle.

COST

List Price (negotiable)	**Residual Values (months)**			
	24	**36**	**48**	**60**
Base: $11,895 (11%)	$6800	$5800	$4300	$3300

TECHNICAL DATA

Powertrain (front-drive)
Engine: 1.3L injected 4 (64 hp)
Transmissions: 5-speed manual • 3-speed auto.

Dimensions
Length: 155.9 in.
Width: 65.7 in.
Wheelbase: 93.9 in.

SAFETY FEATURES

	Opt.	**Std.**
Anti-lock brakes	■	❑
Childproof door locks	■	❑
Driver-side airbag	❑	■
Passenger-side airbag	❑	■

Escort/Tracer

Escort

RATING: Recommended buy. Ford's best-selling small car is a. . . Mazda!

NEW FOR '97: These cars have undergone significant changes this year that make them look more attractive and handle better. They provide 25 percent more horsepower with the 2.0L engine (the 1.8L is gone), additional comfort, a quieter interior, and more standard equipment. The car is four inches longer, mostly taken up by a larger trunk. New standard features include: power steering, rear heat ducts, intermittent wipers, a battery-saver system, a 24-watt, four-speaker stereo unit that can be upgraded to an 80-watt system hooked to a trunk-mounted CD player, and solar glass. Three-door, five-door, and GT models have been dropped; a two-door will come out early next year.

GENERAL COMMENTS: The Escort and Tracer have been using the 323/Protegé platform under its own body for almost six years, and this latest redesign brings it closer to the Mazda than ever before. Mazda's contribution is substantial, accounting for over 70 percent of the car (chassis, body structure, optional engine and transmissions). Ford is responsible for interior and exterior features, the standard 2.0L engine, and the fuel injection and ignition systems. Escorts come with 14-inch wheels and colour-keyed bumpers and trim on the LX sedan. Aluminum wheels, sport suspension, four-wheel disc brakes, a DOHC engine, and seat trim from the '96 GT are offered with the LX-E and Tracer LTS. A power-window option is available on all four-door versions.

Cost analysis/alternatives: The 1997 models are significantly improved over the '96 versions. Furthermore, Ford had pledged to keep this year's prices in the same range as last year's, but just-released data shows an average $900 increase. The discontinued '96 GT, with its 1.8L Mazda four-banger and sportier performance, would be an excellent buy if you can pick one up at a fair price. Escort shoppers may also wish to consider the '96 Eagle Summit, GM Metro and Saturn, Honda Civic, Mazda 323, Subaru Impreza LS wagon, Suzuki Swift, and Toyota Corolla. **Rebates**: '96 Escort: $1000; '97 Escort: $500, until Jan. 1997. **Destination charge**: $250. **Recommended options**: A rear wiper for wagons. Think twice about getting air conditioning; it didn't work well with last year's base engine and the additional 22 horses with this year's engine may not be enough to handle the extra load. AC with last year's optional 1.8L is also a question mark. **Supplementary warranty**: Not a bad idea, since all the changes make this year's Escorts/Tracers practically first-year cars—with the attendant problems associated with first-year vehicles. **Parts supply/Servicing**: Above average. **Depreciation**: Average. **Highway/City fuel economy**: 6-9.5L/100 km on the '96s with the base 1.9L engine. Expect similar or better fuel economy with this year's more efficient 2.0L powerplant.

Reliability/Safety

Pro: This is largely a domestic version of the Mazda 323/Protegé, a vehicle that has been recommended for many years for its overall reliability, responsive handling, and spaciousness. The '97 Escort's increased body rigidity means that doors, windows, trunks, hoods, and body panels fit together better, there's less body flexing, and most wind and road noise—a serious problem denounced in last year's *Lemon-Aid*—is muted fairly successfully. The '96 1.9L 4-cylinder was upgraded last year to require less maintenance—tuneup intervals, for example, were extended to 100,000 *miles*. This year's version continues the low maintenance trend while boosting horsepower substantially. Another plus: the CAA says that Tracer parts are reasonably priced, with heavy discounting by dealers.

Crash tests of a 1994 Escort wagon and a '96 four-door sedan with a driver-side airbag concluded that the driver and passenger would have better than average protection in a 57 km/h frontal collision. It was rated: driver, ★★★★; passenger, ★★★★.

Con: Contrary to its Tracer findings, the CAA says that Escort parts cost more than average. Past overall reliability hasn't equalled the Mazda version. The 1.9L Ford engine has a checkered past, and its rebored revival as a 2.0L may not have addressed the earlier durability problems. In previous years, fuel-injection and EEC IV ignition modules have had a high failure rate, resulting in stalling, hard starting, and poor fuel economy. Owners have also complained of premature cooling system, motor mount, front brake, and paint wear, in addition to the already mentioned excessive interior noise. It's too early to tell if the mechanical and paint deficiencies have been rectified with the latest redesign. There is, however, some interior noise still present, notably a whistling generated by the rain-control channel around the windshield and a gearbox whine.

Confidential dealer service bulletins show the following problems that may carry over to this year's redesigned models: a fuel pump buzz or whine heard in the radio speakers, intermittent horn operation, windshield wipers streak or clean unevenly, and front brake knocking when braking gently (see illustration below).

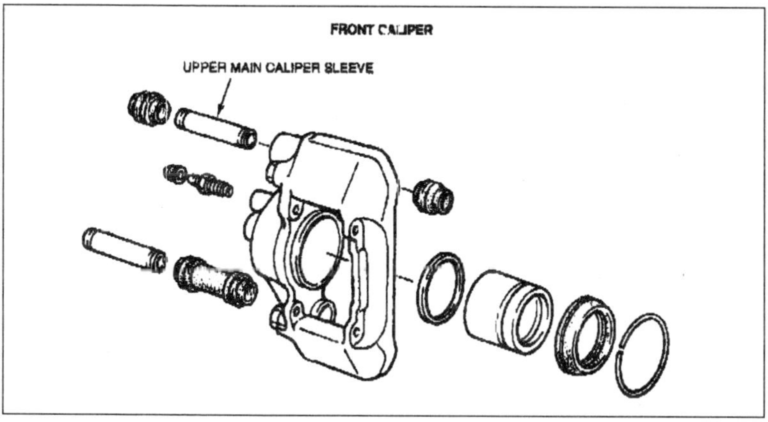

Front brake knocking, afflicting 1991-96 Escorts and Tracers, can be silenced by installing an upgraded caliper sleeve. Ford says that repair is covered under its Bumper to Bumper warranty.

Road Performance

Pro: This year's rebored 2.0L engine makes a big difference from a performance standpoint, pushing peak horsepower from a feeble 88 to a more respectable 110 hp—not quite pocket rocket territory, but a big improvement nonetheless. The sporty '96 GT model uses Mazda's more powerful 1.8L 16-valve powerplant; it has one of the highest redlines in the industry with a whopping 7000 rpm. There's plenty of bottom-end torque for quick acceleration and hill climbing, which aren't hampered by the automatic transmission. A retuned suspension makes for a firmer, more controlled ride with less oversteer. Overall handling and braking have been given a boost with a lighter, more responsive power steering unit, stronger front disc brakes, larger rear drums, and bigger, 14-inch wheels.

Con: Last year's anemic 4-cylinder 1.9L engine is very noisy when accelerating. And when it's hooked to the automatic transmission you have to push it to 6500 rpm to get sufficient horsepower. Hill climbing leads to annoying gear hunting, and the engine stumbles and hesitates at idle with the AC system on.

Comfort/Convenience

Pro: Both cars now have rounded features similar to the Taurus design. The LX model's sports appearance package is a nice touch. Nicely laid-out dash, and instruments are easy to read. Improved sound system. Comfortable front seats with plenty of front leg room. The interior isn't expansive, but it's adequate and well soundproofed. The wagon borrows the most from Mazda and is the practical choice for interior room. Plenty of small storage areas and a reasonably sized trunk. Excellent heating and ventilation system uses four large dash vents.

Con: GT styling is a yawner and the spoiler is out of place on this econobox. Uncomfortable seatbacks (LX), and the GT's seats lack support. Limited front seat access. Radio is hard to tune because of small buttons and a long reach. With the limited head room a sunroof isn't advisable. Rear leg room could be better, and three rear passengers will have a tight fit. The door stops often don't prevent the door from closing. The wagon's raised sill makes cargo loading difficult.

COST

List Price (firm)	**Residual Values** (months)			
	24	**36**	**48**	**60**
LX: $14,995 (13%)	$8500	$7200	$6200	$5300
LX wagon: $14,995 (13%)	9000	7900	6800	5700
'96 GT: $15,295 (14%)	8900	7900	6700	5600

TECHNICAL DATA

Powertrain (front-drive)
Engines: 2.0L injected 4 (110 hp)
• 1.8L injected 4 (127 hp)

Dimensions (4-door/wagon)
Length: 174 in./175.3 in.
Width: 66.7 in./66.7 in.
Wheelbase: 98.4 in./98.4 in.

Transmissions: 5-speed manual • 4-speed automatic

SAFETY FEATURES

	Opt.	Std.
Anti-lock brakes	■	❑
Childproof door locks	❑	■
Driver-side airbag	❑	■
Passenger-side airbag	❑	■
Remote keyless entry	■	❑

Contour/Mystique

Mystique

RATING: Average buy. The main advantages of the Contour and Mystique are exceptional handling and a powerful, limited-maintenance V6 engine. Their drawbacks are an unacceptably high base price, cramped rear seating, an anemic 4-banger, and spotty quality control.

NEW FOR '97: Not much new this year, except for some minor styling tweaks and a new Sport package. A makeover is planned for late in the '97 model year, but may be saved for the '98 version.

GENERAL COMMENTS: These front-drive, midsize twin sedans (the Contour has a more angular nose and different dashboard) are based on the European-designed Mondeo, which has met with respectable sales after many years on the market. The four-door, five-passenger Contour sells for a bit less than its practically identical Mercury counterpart.

Both vehicles are set on a wheelbase that's slightly larger than the Taurus, and come with two engines and transmissions: a base 16-valve 125-hp 2.0L 4-cylinder, and an optional 24-valve 165-hp 2.5L V6. Either engine can be hooked to a standard 5-speed transaxle or an optional 4-speed automatic. A smooth but firm ride and crisp handling are guaranteed by the standard MacPherson strut front suspension, an anti-roll bar, and fully independent rear suspension.

Other interesting standard features include dual airbags, adjustable head restraints, 60/40 split-fold rear seats, rear heater ducts, and a sophisticated air filtration system for the passenger compartment. Four-wheel disc brakes, a sport-tuned suspension, and high-performance tires are standard features on the V6.

Cost analysis/Alternatives: Marketed to fit between the compact Escort and Tracer and the large midsize Taurus and Sable, their high

Manufacturer's Suggested Retail Price (MSRP) have put both vehicles far beyond the budget of former Tempo/Topaz owners (whose cars they replaced). Look for a discounted 1996 model, since the '97s are pretty much identical. The '97s do cost less this year ($200-$800), so look for savings there as well. Mazda's 626 is a worthwhile alternative to the Contour and Mystique. It's a more stylish, highway-proven sedan with a better-than-average warranty, excellent parts supply, and has been powered by a 2.0L and 2.5L V6 for the past several years. **Rebates**: There are plenty of unsold '96 models left on dealers' lots, so the longer you wait to buy the greater your chances of snaring a car that's eligible for both a rebate and dealer incentive bonus. Until Jan. 1997, a $500 rebate is offered with the '96 and '97 models. **Destination charge**: $350. **Recommended options**: The V6 engine, but if you want 4-cylinder economy, stay with the standard 5-speed transmission. You'll get better performance and fuel economy, and you'll save yourself some big bucks. **Supplementary warranty**: Should be seriously considered. **Parts supply/Servicing**: Above average. **Depreciation**: Below average. **Highway/City fuel economy**: 7-11.5L/100 km.

Reliability/Safety

Pro: Ford promises that its new Duratec V6 engine won't require a tuneup before 160,000 km. Would they kid us? U.S. government crash tests of a 1996 Contour with dual airbags concluded that the car would give excellent crash protection to the driver and cause some injuries to the passenger in a frontal collision at 57 km/h. Driver protection was rated ★★★★★; passenger protection, ★★★★.

Con: These cars have had lots of first-year problems that may carry over to this year's models. Owners report frequent AC failures, a fishy smell in the interior, computer module failures, and long waiting periods for parts. One CompuServe member had this to say: "My '95 Mystique ran fine for six months, but has been in the dealer repair shop—still not fixed—for three weeks now. First the 'overlock' froze, so you couldn't shift out of Park—even with a foot on the brake. The dealer said an 'electrical short circuit kept making a module fail.' They told me the part was part of a recall that had not yet been announced. No sooner had they fixed that when the Overdrive on-off button on the automatic gearshift stopped working. That's still not fixed after 11 working days. First the dealer claimed they couldn't 'locate the cause.' They sent the car out to a transmission expert, who found another 'failed module.' The current problem is that the replacement part is 'much in demand,' and they're 'trying to locate one. . . .'"

Confidential dealer service bulletins show the following problems that may carry over to the '97 versions: an inoperative fuel filler door, premature PCV tube wear, automatic transmission produces a whistle noise in Park, and water dripping onto floor (see illustration below).

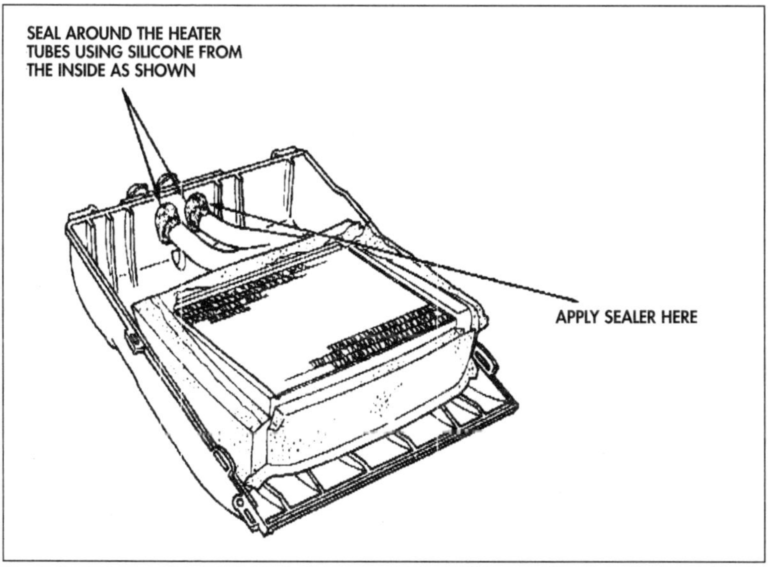

Seal the areas of the AC evaporator case as indicated. Ford will cover the cost under its Bumper to Bumper warranty.

Road Performance

Pro: Ford's 2.5L dual overhead cam 24-valve Duratec V6 is reasonably quiet and smooth and gives plenty of power without hesitation at low and moderate engine speeds. Superb ride and handling qualities. Power steering is quick and precise, and even with an automatic transmission the Contour slices through corners with limited body roll and excellent control. Gear ratios in the 4-speed electronically controlled automatic transmission are well matched to the engine's output. Although traction control is available, the car's front-drive configuration gives good traction on slippery roads without the option. Braking is better than average.

Con: The base 4-cylinder engine is a noisy yawner that isn't suited for passing or hilly terrain, particularly when hooked to the automatic transmission, as the following Contour owners discovered: "The trip was a white-knuckler all the way. Foot on the gas, pushing through the firewall, engine wheezing like crazy. Old VW Westphalias went by like we were standing still. The thing was so slow it was scary!"

Comfort/Convenience

Pro: Fairly good gas mileage—better than Chrysler's Cirrus V6. Contour's bucket seats are snug, supportive, and sporty. The instrument panel is well laid out—a high-mounted coin bin is a thoughtful touch. Contour's front seats are first rate, even in the least expensive GL. Along with the more luxuriously upholstered seats in the Mystique, they're the best in their class. More trunk space than the Accord.

Con: You'll be thoroughly underwhelmed by the Mystique's styling. The dashboard is a busy looking construct that doesn't compare favourably with the one-piece look of the Accord's dash. Plenty of front seat room for a six-footer, but the rear seat is inadequate—even with an extra inch this year. The Mazda Protegé has more rear seat leg room than the Contour. The heads of tall passengers will hit the headliner/roof where it meets the steeply sloped back window, and rear leg room all but disappears with the front seats pushed all the way back. Power-window switches are awkward to use and the radio controls are tiny push buttons requiring the driver's full attention, plus a steady hand, to operate when the car is moving. Lots of road noise.

COST

List Price (negotiable)	**Residual Values** (months)			
	24	**36**	**48**	**60**
Base: $17,395 (15%)	$8900	$7500	$6000	$5000
GL: $18,395 (16%)	7900	6500	5500	9500

TECHNICAL DATA

Powertrain (front-drive)
Engines: 2.0L injected 4 (125 hp)
• 2.5L V6 (170 hp)
Transmissions: 5-speed manual • 4-speed auto.

Dimensions (4-door)
Length: 183.9 in.
Width: 69.1 in.
Wheelbase: 106.5 in.

SAFETY FEATURES

	Opt.	Std.
Anti-lock brakes	■	❑
Childproof door locks	❑	■
Driver-side airbag	❑	■
Passenger-side airbag	❑	■
Remote keyless entry	■	❑

Mustang

Mustang GT

RATING: Recommended. An unsophisticated street brawler.

NEW FOR '97: Standard passive anti-theft system. Ford is standing pat on any major Mustang changes until the 1999 model year, when it's scheduled to get a facelift and engine upgrade.

GENERAL COMMENTS: The Mustang carries a base 3.8L V6 and offers an optional 4.6L V8 along with a high performance, limited-edition Cobra variation that delivers 90 more horses than what the stock 4.6L V8 offers. The single and twin cam V8 options make the Mustang a powerful, if a bit unsophisticated, street machine. V6 models are an acceptable compromise, even though the engine fails to deliver the gobs of power expected of a Mustang by most performance enthusiasts. Base models come equipped with a host of luxury and convenience items. Furthermore, the price is hard to beat, and resale value stays relatively high.

This is definitely not a family car. But for those who want a sturdy and stylish second car, or who don't need room in the back or standard ABS, the Mustang is a pretty good sports car buy.

Cost analysis/Alternatives: Don't waste your money on this year's more expensive Mustang ($800-$1100). The '96 models were substantially improved and can be a real bargain if the dealer will sell you one at a discount, and with a rebate. GM's Camaro and Firebird are the Mustang's traditional competition as far as price and performance are concerned. Ford has the price advantage, with its base Mustang costing about $1300 less than the cheapest Camaro, but it lags from a performance standpoint—10 horses with the V6 and 60 horses with the V8. The GM models offer crisper handling, standard ABS, a 6-speed transmission, and more comfortable rear seats. Other cars worth considering are the '96 Dodge Stealth, Eagle Talon, Mazda MX-3, and Toyota Celica and Supra.

Rebates: $500 rebates on '96 and '97 models, until Jan. 3, 1997. **Destination charge**: $300. **Recommended options**: None. **Supplementary warranty**: Not needed. **Parts supply/Servicing**: Above average. **Depreciation**: Slower than average. For example, a 1994 base Mustang, selling originally for $15,595, will now fetch about $10,100 as a dealer trade-in. Convertibles, with the V6 or V8, do even better. **Highway/City fuel economy**: 7-12L/100 km with the 3.8L; 9-14.5L/100 km with the 4.6L.

Reliability/Safety

Pro: The Mustang's repair history has improved greatly since 1984, and this isn't likely to change with the '97 models, which use parts improved upon from previous years. The engines and transmissions are durable, as are most other components. Body assembly has improved of late, with fewer rattles and a more solid feeling. Parts are cheap and easy to find. Any mechanic is able to fix a Mustang.

Crash tests of a '95 and '96 dual airbag-equipped Mustangs concluded that the driver and passenger would be well-protected in a 57 km/h frontal collision. It was rated: driver, ★★★★; passenger, ★★★★.

Con: The front suspension and steering components remain the only consistent weak spots; MacPherson struts and various steering components are likely to wear out before their time. The parking brake cable seizes easily. The EEC IV engine computer can be temperamental, and electrical problems are common. Assembly quality is still not up to the level of Japanese vehicles. Some premature paint peeling reported. A light rear end makes the car dangerously unstable on wet roads or when cornering at speed.

Confidential dealer service bulletins reveal only two problems that could carry over to this year's models: a coolant leak from the upper radiator hose, and a fuel pump buzz or whine heard through the radio speakers.

Road Performance

Pro: The V8 provides very quick acceleration and smooth power delivery, while the V6 performs fairly well with the automatic 4-speed transmission. The clutch is reasonably smooth. Models equipped with the sport suspension (which includes larger tires) provide sure and predictable handling on dry roads. An improved base suspension makes the car more stable and controllable on most roads.

Con: The 3.8L V6 is rough and noisy when pushed. The V8s are a bit too powerful for the amount of traction available to the rear wheels, making for lots of wheelspin and instability on slippery surfaces. The manual transmission is notchy at times. The rear end tends to slip out under hard cornering. This deficiency is reduced somewhat this year, but it's still a problem. The GT rides harshly on rough roads. These cars are a bit clumsy around town because of a wide turning circle. Brakes are difficult to modulate. ABS is standard only on the Cobra.

Comfort/Convenience

Pro: The LX offers a higher level of ride comfort than does the base model. Comfortable front seats on all models. Complete and well laid-out dual-cowl dashboard and controls. Good ventilation system. The hatchback offers the advantage of a folding rear seat. Improved body rigidity. The V8 convertible's cowl shake has been considerably reduced.

Con: Ugly stubby styling is a rip-off of the Nissan 300ZX. Interior deficiencies and limited room haven't been addressed yet. Front seats need at least an inch more travel; the rear seat is best left to children. The wide doors make for clumsy entry and exit in tight spots. Ride comfort is below average. Very shallow trunk with a small opening.

COST

List Price (firm)	**Residual Values** (months) 24	36	48	60
Base: $19,695 (15%)	$11,500	$10,300	$9000	$7500
Convertible: $28,895 (21%)	19,500	17,500	15,200	13,800

TECHNICAL DATA

Powertrain (rear-drive)
Engines: 3.8L injected V6 (150 hp) • 4.6L injected V8 (215 hp)
Transmissions: 5-speed manual • 4-speed auto.

Dimensions
Length: 181.5 in.
Width: 71.8 in.
Wheelbase: 101.3 in.

SAFETY FEATURES

	Opt.	Std.
Anti-lock brakes	■	❑
Childproof door locks	—	—
Driver-side airbag	❑	■
Passenger-side airbag	❑	■
Remote keyless entry	■	❑

Probe

Probe GT

RATING: Recommended. A refined sports coupe.

NEW FOR '97: Upgraded side-impact protection. Next year's version will undergo a major makeover when it joins the Cougar in adopting the Contour's CDW27 platform.

GENERAL COMMENTS: The four-seater Probe sporty coupe was launched in May 1988 as the front-wheel-drive replacement for the aging Mustang. Don't get the impression that the Mazda MX-6 and Probe are twins. In fact, they differ markedly in handling and appearance. Ford engineers took more control of the chassis tuning and suspension geometry to give the car a smoother and firmer sporty demeanour, while company stylists chopped and pulled the body to give it a more aerodynamic, aggressive personality.

Available only as a two-door hatchback, there are two models, each with its own powerplant: a 2.0L 4-cylinder and a 2.5L V6 engine. These engines give the car much-needed power and smoothness not present in the anemic and brutish powertrains used in the past.

Cost analysis/Alternatives: Buy a discounted '96 Probe, since the '97 version offers little that's different. Other cars worth considering are the Eagle Talon, Ford Mustang, GM Camaro or Firebird, Honda Prelude, '96 Mazda MX-3 and MX-6, and Toyota Celica. **Rebates**: $500 on '96s and '97s until Jan. 3, 1997. **Destination charge**: $350. **Recommended options**: None. **Supplementary warranty**: Not needed. **Parts supply/Servicing**: Above average. **Depreciation**: Below average. **Highway/City fuel economy**: 6.5-10L/100 km with the 2.0L; 7-12L/100 km with the 2.5L.

Reliability/Safety

Pro: Mazdas have had good reliability histories, and the Probe seems to be following that trend as far as the drivetrain and underpinnings are concerned. Except for some piston scuffing problems during cold spells that lead to excessive engine noise and reduced fuel economy, the 2.5L V6 engine has been fairly reliable. Much better body construction is shown by reduced noise intrusion in the passenger compartment. Average servicing access, except for the hard-to-handle oil filter.

Crash tests of a 1996 dual airbag-equipped Probe concluded that the driver would be very well protected and the passenger would have good protection in a 57 km/h frontal collision. It was rated: driver, ★★★★★; passenger, ★★★★.

Con: The GT's electronically adjusted suspension has been troublesome, and replacement parts are very expensive. The front brakes wear out very quickly. Premature paint peeling, poorly aligned interior trim pieces and body panels, and air and water leaks have been commonplace. Complaints of rough engine idling and stalling/starting problems haven't been heard from Mazda MX-6 owners to the same degree, indicating that Ford dealers may not be calibrating the car's electronics correctly.

Confidential dealer service bulletins reveal the following minor problems that could carry over to this year's models: misaligned front door glass, and transmission whistling in Park.

Road Performance

Pro: The 2.0L 4-banger and 2.5L V6 perform smoothly with little noise, vibration, or harshness. The 5-speed manual transmission shifts crisply, and the clutch is exceptionally smooth. An adequate 4-speed automatic is no tire-burner, but it gets the job done and with Overdrive saves fuel. Precise steering and little tendency to wander when accelerating. More sure-footed than the Mustang, with less understeer or fish-tailing when coming off the throttle in corners. Sporty, firm suspension reduces body lean. Handling at moderate speeds is far better than that of other front-drives in the same class. Excellent braking without ABS.

Con: Firm suspension produces a bone-jarring, choppy ride and straight-line instability over uneven roads. The automatic transmission has an unnecessarily complicated shift mechanism. It does a lot of hunting when under load. In the Overdrive setting the transmission will often take more time than it should to select a gear. Steering is a bit too assisted, reducing road feel.

Comfort/Convenience

Pro: Well-appointed and ergonomic interior includes supportive and comfortable front seats. Complete instrumentation enclosed within a wrap-around dash with controls that are easy to reach and see. Large glove compartment. Split rear seatbacks. Roomy trunk and cargo area, especially with the rear seat down. Heating/defrosting/ventilation are first class. Practical liftback design is better than that found on the MX-6.

Con: Cockpit is a bit cramped. Aerodynamic shape forces air and water into the passenger compartment, particularly if the windows aren't rolled up tightly. Airbag in steering wheel causes the steering column to sit at an unusual angle. Electronic trip computer is useless; the readings are unreal, especially on the mpg indicator. The digital speedometer numerals are monstrously large. Factory speakers are far from "premium." Exterior side view mirrors are too small and sacrifice safety for style. The large rear view mirror is mounted too low for maximum visibility. The hatchback's excessive liftover height is a chiropractor's dream, essentially a 2+2 with the rear reserved for children or cargo. The interior is short on head room for tall drivers, especially when equipped with a sunroof; and rear passenger and cargo room are limited.

COST

List Price (firm)	**Residual Values** (months)			
	24	**36**	**48**	**60**
Base: $19,095 (16%)	$12,500	$11,000	$9000	$7500
GT: $22,995 (21%)	14,500	12,800	11,500	9500

TECHNICAL DATA

Powertrain (front-drive)
Engines: 2.0L injected 4 (118 hp)
• 2.5L V6 (164 hp)
Transmissions: 5-speed manual • 4-speed auto.

Dimensions
Length: 178.7 in.
Width: 69.8 in.
Wheelbase: 102.8 in.

SAFETY FEATURES

	Opt.	Std.
Anti-lock brakes	■	❑
Childproof door locks	—	—
Driver-side airbag	❑	■
Passenger-side airbag	❑	■
Remote keyless entry	■	❑

Taurus/Sable

Taurus

RATING: The sedan is a Recommended buy; the wagon is an Above Average buy. The perfect car for anyone wanting a well-equipped sedan with standard dual airbags and plenty of interior room.

NEW FOR '97: A recalibrated transmission for smoother shifting. A minor facelift is scheduled for the 1998 model year. The Sable gets map pockets.

GENERAL COMMENTS: Canada's most popular family car offers a winning combination of safety, reliability, performance, handling, and comfort. The base 3.0L Vulcan V6 is adequate, though dated, and the high-performing 24-valve V6 provides plenty of power for most driving needs. Other nice standard features: heated outside mirrors, a 60/40 split-fold rear seatback for additional cargo space, a driver's foot rest, and reserve power to operate the power windows and moonroof after the engine is shut off.

The SHO high-performance version returns this year with a 3.4L, 32-valve V8 engine. It delivers sparkling performance and sports car handling—at a price. Acceleration rivals the Mustang GT with a top speed of over 140 mph, and it comes with an automatic transmission.

Cost analysis/Alternatives: Want to save a bundle? Stay away from the '97s. The best sedan compromise between a fair retail price, safety, good performance, and fuel economy is found with the second-series '96 version equipped with the base V6 powerplant and optional ABS. Wagons are competent performers, but they're outclassed by some imports and most minivans as far as reliability and overall performance is concerned. The SHO has become a cult car for high-performance fans and its slow depreciation reflects this fact; bargains are hard to find. Other sedans worth considering are the Honda Accord, Mazda 626, Toyota Camry, and Volvo 850. Wagons worth considering are the

Honda Accord EX, Subaru Legacy, Toyota Camry LE V6, and Volvo 850 or 940. **Rebates**: The redesigned '96 Taurus has been a huge sales disappointment. December North American sales were down 35 percent from a year earlier; sales of its arch-rival, the Honda Accord, were up 36 percent. Until Jan. 3, 1997, the '96s get a $1000 rebate; the '97s: $500. The '97 carryovers will also enter a buyer's market, leading to additional generous dealer incentives and customer rebates kicking in by mid- or late-summer. **Destination charge**: $350. **Recommended options**: Expect to spend about $300 more for the flexible-fuel Taurus (ethanol or methanol) currently sold only to fleets. The automatic climate control system, a rear integrated child safety seat, power seats, and a heavy-duty suspension are wise choices. Get the optional DOHC V6 variation, but tell the dealer to forget the wagon's uncomfortable rear-facing third seat. Don't buy the optional leather seats, either; they're slippery and not all that durable. The digital instrumentation is another useless option; it's gimmicky and distracting. **Supplementary warranty**: Not a bad idea if you pick up a first-series '96; not needed with the '97s. **Parts supply/Servicing**: Very reasonable. **Depreciation**: Below average. **Highway/City fuel economy**: 7.5-12L/100 km with the 3.0L; 8-13.5L/100 km with the 24V 3.0L; 9-14L/100 km with the SHO V8.

Reliability/Safety

Pro: Reliability is average for the American Big Three (which is far from being a compliment), and assembly quality depends a lot on where the car was put together: insiders tell me that Atlanta is tops, and Chicago is below average. Paint and body assembly are acceptable and body squeaks are minimal. Parts and service are always easy to find.

Crash tests of a 1996 Ford Taurus sedan concluded that the driver and passenger would be relatively well-protected in a 57 km/h frontal collision. It was rated: driver, ★★★★; passenger, ★★★★.

Con: The underhood area is crowded, making maintenance a little more complicated. Automatic transmission, electrical (lots of blown fuses), steering, fuel system, front suspension, and ignition problems are frequently reported on these cars. Piston scuffing has been a common complaint with the 3.0L V6 engine, but 1996 model refinements may have fixed the problem. Fit and finish vary in quality depending on the assembly plant. Nevertheless, there have been lots of complaints concerning poor paint application (fading, chalking, and peeling) and premature rusting along the door edges, handles, tail light housings, decklid, and inside hood area, as the photo below of a three-year-old Taurus shows.

Trunk and hood edges, door panels and handles, and the rear end are especially prone to early rusting.

Confidential dealer service bulletins show the following relatively minor '96 model year problems that could carry over to the '97 models: cold engine hesitation or stumble, excessive wind noise coming from the windshield or A-pillar, front suspension squeak or groan, Duratec engine no start or stalling, transaxle clicks when going into Reverse, erratic shifting, assorted driveline noise (see bulletin below).

Article No.
96-8-7
04/08/96
• NOISE – AX4S/AX4N TRANSAXLE NOISES – SERVICE TIP
• TRANSAXLE – AX4S/AX4N – DRIVELINE NOISES – SERVICE TIP
FORD: 1991-96 TAURUS
LINCOLN-MERCURY: 1991-96 CONTINENTAL, SABLE
LIGHT TRUCK: 1995-96 WINDSTAR
This TSB is being republished in its entirety to update the procedures.
ISSUE:
There may be concerns of some different driveline noises coming from the transaxle under certain conditions on some vehicles. This TSB article has been written to describe typical noises wxhibited by the AX4N and AX4S transaxles and to assist dealers and technicians in knowing which noises are expected and norma.
ACTION:
Refer to the following text to determine the correct procedure (if any) for the driveline noises.
"BUZZ"/VIBRATION IN "PARK" ON AN INCLINE AX4S AND AX4N
The cause of the concern has been determined to be the park pawl providing a ground parth for normal drivetrain vibrations. This concern can be minimized by making sure the parking brake is applied. Do not attempt to service this condition at this time.
"BUZZ" NOISE IN TRANSAXLE ON ENGINE SHUTDOWN – AX4S AND AX4N
This is due to voltage power being shut off to the Powertrain Control Module (PCM) relay on engine shutdown. With engine rotation still present (which is still driving the rransaxle pump) and the Electronic PRessure Control (EPC) solenoid now off, EPC and line pressure are high (high EPC pressure). This condition is normal hydraulic noise within the pump and valve body. To confirm this symptom, apply the brake, place the transaxle into gear and turn the engine off. If the noise is no longer present then the noise can be considered normal hydraulic noise. Do not attempt to service this condition at this time.
HIGH PITCHED "WHISTLE FROM MAIN CONTROL AT NORMAL OPERATING TEMPERATURE AND TIPPING INTO THROTTLE – AX4S
This condition is normal hydraulic noise and will not cause a malfunction or affect durability of the transaxle. Do not attempt to service this condition at this time. This "whistle" noise could also be caused by the three-port vacuum check valve in the vacuum supply line to the speed control servo.
METALLIC CLICK ON REVERSE ENGAGEMENT – AX4N
When the gear selector is moved from "Drive or "Neutral" into "Reverse," a metallic click noise may be heard. Refer to TSB 96-5-9 for repair procedures.
1996 TAURUS/SABLE WITH ENGINE AND TRANSAXLE NOISES HEARD IN THE PASSENGER COMPARTMENT
These noises may have two sources. The steering column shift cable may be contacting the fuse junction box under the instrument panel on the left side of the steering column. Disconnect the cable from the shift column lever and reroute the cable above the fuse junction box. Reconnect the cable and check the cable adjustment. Refer to the appropriate Service Manual, Page 07-05-22.
This second source may be the NC evaporator housing assembly-to-bulkhead seal. The fasteners may have become loose. Tighten the fasteners from the engine compartment side. Refer to the appropriate Service Manual, Page 12-03A-39 for details.
OTHER APPLICABLE ARTICLES: 95-5-9
SUPERSEDES: 96-3-13
WARRANTY STATUS: INFORMATION ONLY
OASIS CODES: 50400, 50700, 597997, 702000, 702100

Several of the above noise problems still don't have an engineering fix after five years!

Road Performance

Pro: The base 3.0L V6 is a decade-old engine that offers adequate power for most driving situations, while the twin cam, Duratec version provides exhilarating, quiet acceleration equal to the European-influenced chassis dynamics. The 4-speed automatic transmission shifts smoothly and responsively. The sedan's handling, both around town and on the highway, is better than average due primarily to its solid suspension and stiff body construction.

Con: Ford's 3.0L Vulcan V6 is okay for rentals and city commuting, but it's unable to fully take advantage of the car's excellent handling characteristics. The speed-sensitive variable-assist power steering makes the car easier to handle, but not as well as Ford claims. Wagons handle poorly in turns and over uneven terrain. ABS produces strong pedal pulsations.

Comfort/Convenience

Pro: Elliptical styling makes the car look smaller, even though it's more than five inches longer and almost two inches wider than the '95 version. The standard seats are comfortable for most people, however the wagon's fabric-covered seats are more comfortable and supportive than the leather covered sedan seats. The sedans will seat five in comfort, while the wagons offer an optional third seat. A well laid-out, elliptically shaped pod houses the dashboard, and controls are within easy reach. The three-way front-seat console is a nice touch. It's a flip fold affair that's a regular seat, an armrest, or a cup- and coin-carrying console. A tilt steering wheel is a practical idea. Armrest switches make it easy to activate the door locks and power windows. A large glove box is handy up front, and there's lots of cargo area in wagons, plus a huge trunk in the sedan versions. Folding rear seats open to the trunk. The wagon's innovative two-way tailgate allows the entire unit to swing out for large cargo or just the window glass to open for small packages. Powerful climate control system. Reinforced quarter-panels. Ford's optional InstaClear windshield is a boon in Canadian winters.

Con: Short drivers will have to strain to reach the accelerator and see over the dash, and tall drivers will find thigh support lacking. Leather seats offer little lateral support. The massive dash and digital treatment are gimmicky and take getting used to. The radio is set too low and too far forward, and the JBL Premium Sound System's push-button controls require a Ph.D. to understand them. Radio reception quality is disappointing. The rear window defroster is hard to find on the left side of the steering column. Air-conditioning push buttons are difficult to understand and manipulate. The power door locks aren't helpful when loading or unloading a lot of passengers. The trunk has a high sill, making loading/unloading a chore, and the wagon's liftgate doesn't rise high enough to clear most people's heads. The SHO sedan is loaded with exterior styling gimmicks that may not be to everyone's taste. The wagon's interior plastic trim is cheap, and the low-fuel warning light comes on with enough fuel to travel 100 miles. Both the sedan and wagon's noise level is unusually high, with lots of wind noise and tire drumming from the rear.

COST

List Price (negotiable)	Residual Values (months) 24	36	48	60
GL sedan: $22,995 (20%)	$14,500	$12,500	$11,000	$9000
Wagon: $22,995 (20%)	15,000	13,000	11,500	9500
SHO: $32,495 (22%)	22,000	18,500	16,000	14,000

TECHNICAL DATA

Powertrain (front-drive)
Engines: 3.0L injected V6 (145 hp) • 3.0L 24-valve injected V6 (200 hp) • 3.4L 32-valve V8 (SHO)
Transmissions: 5-speed manual • 4-speed auto.

Dimensions (Taurus/Sable)
Length: 197.4 in./199.5 in.
Width: 73.1 in./73.1 in.
Wheelbase: 108.5 in./108.5 in.

SAFETY FEATURES

	Opt.	Std.
Anti-lock brakes	■	❑
Childproof door locks	❑	■
Driver-side airbag	❑	■
Passenger-side airbag	❑	■
Remote keyless entry	❑	■
Traction control	❑	■

SHO	Opt.	Std.
Anti-lock brakes	❑	■
Childproof door locks	❑	■
Driver-side airbag	❑	■
Passenger-side airbag	❑	■
Remote keyless entry	❑	■
Traction control	❑	■

Cougar/Thunderbird

Cougar XR-7

RATING: Recommended. A sport/luxury best buy, if you want a reasonably priced, reliable car with standard airbags, optional ABS, and a choice of two V6s and one V8 engine.

NEW FOR '97: An upgraded four-speed automatic transmission for smoother and quieter shifting, standard four-wheel disc brakes, an easier to read instrument cluster, and revised console. The 1998 model Thunderbird will get only a minor facelift, but the Cougar will be reborn as a front-drive (adopting the Contour platform) and move to the Mazda/Ford joint venture assembly plant in Flat Rock, Michigan.

GENERAL COMMENTS: As in the past, the Thunderbird—with its BMW 535 looks—is oriented to a younger and more "sporting" driver, while the Cougar, with its relatively formal body styling, cultivates a more sedate image. The base 3.8L V6 and Overdrive automatic offer good all-around power and performance, and is more reliable than average in the process. These cars have a history of depreciating less quickly than average, which bodes well for the present lineup. Two trimlines are offered: the base 145-hp V6 and the supercharged 210-hp variant of the same powerplant.

Cost analysis/Alternatives: The 1996 models are practically identical to the more expensive '97 versions and are a real bargain if the selling price has been reduced sufficiently. Other vehicles worth a look: the Eagle Talon, Ford Taurus/Sable, Nissan Maxima, and Volvo 850 and 900 series. Consider this: the Eagle Talon is lighter, more fun to drive, and has an engine half the size of the T-bird SC but with 90 percent of the power. **Rebates**: There are lots of unsold '96s on dealer lots that will likely be cleared away this fall through the judicious use of different rebate programs. Presently Ford is offering $500 rebates on the '96 and

'97 models until Jan. 3, 1997. **Destination charge**: $400. **Recommended options**: None. **Supplementary warranty**: Not needed. **Parts supply/Servicing**: Above average. **Depreciation**: Below average. **Highway/City fuel economy**: 8.5-13L/100 km with the 3.8L; 9-14L/100 km with the 4.6L; 9-13.5L/100 km with the 3.8L High Output.

Reliability/Safety

Pro: Overall reliability has been better than the Big Three average. Some brake and electrical glitches. The base 3.8L V6 and its supercharged variant are well-proven, reliable designs and should remain so despite some minor changes to the mechanical components. Parts and service on the base models are not a problem.

Crash tests of an airbag-equipped 1996 Ford Thunderbird concluded that the driver and passenger would be very well protected in a 57 km/h frontal collision. It was rated: driver, ★★★★★; passenger, ★★★★★.

Con: Ford has had trouble introducing new technology without a lot of teething problems. Front brake computer modules and body components are the main problem areas.

Confidential dealer service bulletins reveal the following problems that could carry over to this year's models: increased power steering effort at low speeds, rough braking, and a fuel pump buzz or whine heard in the radio speakers.

Road Performance

Pro: The new 4.6L V8 engines give strong mid-range performance and plenty of torque in all gear ranges. They perform as well as the supercharged 3.8 V6 without the cost and servicing headaches. The Overdrive automatic shifts smoothly. Variable-assisted power steering. Given the precedent of other recent Ford designs, handling is precise and predictable at moderate speeds. The base models provide a smooth and well-controlled ride, due in part to the all-wheel independent suspension.

Con: The standard V6 has to struggle to pull around the excess weight, which increases the acceleration time and reduces fuel economy. The 4-speed automatic is slow to downshift. The XR-7's ride is firmer and less comfortable on bumpy roads than on the lower-priced versions. A light rear end causes a loss of high-speed stability and makes all models skittish on slippery surfaces and when cornering at high speeds. The standard brakes tend to lock up in hard/emergency braking.

Comfort/Convenience

Pro: Plenty of room for four adults. The Super Coupe and XR-7 have easy-to-read analogue gauges and computerized ride control. Driver seat height is adjustable. Adjustable steering wheel. The excellent optional JBL sound system is borrowed from the Continental. Good access to sound system controls. Comfortable and easily adjusted seats. Trunk area is large and practical. Rear seating is adequate for three adults on a short trip. Excellent soundproofing. Good ventilation system supplies ample air that can be individually controlled.

Con: The accelerator is positioned too far to the left. Front and rear seats lack lower back and side support. Too much emphasis on gimmicky digital instrumentation on the LX. Big, wide, heavy doors. Limited rear seat head room, knee room, and leg room. Rear visibility is very poor. A compact, limited service spare is the only tire available. Excess size and weight result in poor fuel economy.

COST

List Price (firm)	**Residual Values** (months) 24	36	48	60
LX: $24,895 (20%)	$14,500	$12,500	$10,500	$9500
XR7: $24,795 (18%)	14,900	13,000	11,000	9900

TECHNICAL DATA

Powertrain (rear-drive)
Engines: 3.8L injected V6(145 hp) • 3.8L supercharged V6 (205 hp) • 4.6L V8 (205 hp)
Transmissions: 5-speed manual • 4-speed auto.

Dimensions
Length: 200.3 in.
Width: 72.7 in.
Wheelbase: 113 in.

SAFETY FEATURES

	Opt.	Std.
Anti-lock brakes	■	❑
Childproof door locks	—	—
Driver-side airbag	❑	■
Passenger-side airbag	❑	■
Remote keyless entry	■	❑

Crown Victoria, Grand Marquis, Lincoln Town Car

Town Car

RATING: Recommended. Best suited for highway cruising and trailer towing.

NEW FOR '97: Nothing that's substantial, except for a redesigned steering assembly for more precise control. Although a major restyle is scheduled for '98 models, Ford has abandoned its plans to convert these cars to front drive in light of GM's dropping its luxury rear-drives. The Town Car will be redesigned in the 1998 or 1999 model year.

GENERAL COMMENTS: There are still many people around who want the space and road-hugging weight of a large American sedan, and these cars fit the bill much better than the poorly performing '96 Chevrolet Caprice or Chrysler New Yorker and LHS.

The industry's lowest-priced six-passenger V8 sedan, the Crown Victoria, has been such a favourite with police, taxi drivers, farmers, and retirees that Ford's St. Thomas, Ontario, employees have had to work overtime. Now that the model has been updated and improved with the addition of a 4.6L OHC V8, it's likely to stay around a relatively long time without many other changes.

Aside from the sheer wastefulness of the design and the high fuel cost of running one of these boats, they're fairly reliable and predictable highway cruisers. Handling isn't very responsive, but everyone is going to be comfortable inside. The mechanical design is straightforward and easy to troubleshoot (electronic gizmos excepted). The Crown Victoria and Grand Marquis have consistently come out on top in quality surveys of North American cars.

Speed-sensitive variable-assist power steering is a standard feature, as it is with most of Ford's luxury cars. The base model and LX are joined by the Touring Sedan that offers a firmer ride, a more responsive handling package, and different exterior and interior styling touches. An electronically controlled automatic transmission has been around since early 1992.

The Lincoln Town Car still represents the epitome of large car luxury to many people, and it's a popular rear-drive base for Ford's luxury cars. A stretched version of the Crown Victoria/Marquis, its air-spring rear suspension provides a smooth ride and prevents tail-dragging, even when fully loaded.

Cost analysis/Alternatives: Don't waste your money buying a '97 model. A still-new '96 version will cost much less and give you the same features. The Marquis is a slightly more luxurious version that costs more but gives little of consequence for the extra expense. Other cars worth considering: Nissan Maxima, Mazda Millenia, Toyota Avalon, and Volvo 900 series. **Rebates**: Ford is giving out $1500 rebates on the '97 Town Car and $1000 rebates on the '96 and '97 Marquis until Jan. 3, 1997. '96 Town Cars also get an extra $4000 dealer incentive. By using these rebates and incentive programs, you should be able to reduce the '96 MSRP by $1000-$5500 *before* you begin to negotiate the final price. **Destination charge**: $500. **Recommended options**: Invest in a power seat and the "Handling and Performance" option to reduce body roll and increase traction. **Supplementary warranty**: Not needed. **Parts supply/Servicing**: Above average. **Depreciation**: Below average. **Highway/City fuel economy**: 8.5-14L/100 km.

Reliability/Safety

Pro: Overall reliability has been above average for the past several years. Body components and construction are first rate. Parts are available anywhere. Crash tests of a 1996 Crown Victoria concluded that the driver and passenger would be very well protected in a 57 km/h frontal collision. Driver protection was rated ★★★★★; passenger protection, ★★★★★. Surprisingly, crash tests of an airbag-equipped '96 Town Car showed that the driver wouldn't be as well protected as in the Crown Victoria. Driver protection was rated ★★★★; passenger protection, ★★★★★. Towing capacity is 5000 pounds with the Class III Towing or Handling and Performance packages.

Con: Main problem areas are the EEC IV computer module, the electrical system, air-conditioning compressor, prematurely worn brake rotors, faulty seat tracks and door mouldings, and the fuel system. The Lincoln's electrical and mechanical complexity can lead to increased maintenance and repair costs in the long run. According to the CAA, Crown Victoria parts are more expensive than most other cars in this class.

Confidential dealer service bulletins reveal the following problems that could carry over to this year's models: engine squeal during a cold start, delayed 1-2 upshift, and a fuel pump whine heard in the radio speakers.

Other dealer service bulletins show the following problems affecting the '97 Town Car that could also carry over to the '97 models: engine squeal during a cold start, rough idle or stalling at altitudes above 5000 ft., and an inoperative “Power Pull-down” decklid.

Road Performance

Pro: The smooth, quiet-running 4.6L V8 provides more than enough power for a comfortable ride. The Overdrive automatic is flawless. Good four-wheel disc brakes.

Con: These cars handle like the typical full-size sedan of the 1970s: they’re clumsy to manoeuvre and park around town, and provide the driver with little steering feedback on the highway. Cornering is sloppy. Considerable suspension dive when braking.

Comfort/Convenience

Pro: The individual front seats are large, comfortable, and supportive (the power seat option is recommended), particularly in the lumbar region. Very good driving position. Spacious interior: three passengers are comfortable in the back, where there’s lots of head, leg, and shoulder room. Huge trunk on sedan; cavernous cargo area on wagons. Windows roll all the way down. The Town Car’s trunk is an impressive 22 cubic feet. Large doors make entry/exit a breeze. Very quiet interior. Powerful ventilation system.

Con: The split-bench front seat in the Crown Victoria isn’t very comfortable due to its insufficient seatback padding and side support. Rear seats also lack sufficient seatback padding. The dashboard design provides the driver with minimal information, and the control layout is somewhat outdated. Confusing power seat and controls. The driver’s right knee frequently hits the dashboard/radio housing, and no amount of adjusting of the electric seat can remedy the problem. Heater is a bit slow to warm up. The Town Car’s electronic dash is too gimmicky, and its moonroof cuts down on rear head room. One has to do some acrobatics to get at the full-sized spare tire, which is placed far forward in the trunk.

COST

List Price (firm)	Residual Values (months)			
	24	**36**	**48**	**60**
Crown Vic LX: $31,595 (24%)	$19,000	$16,500	$15,000	$12,000
Town Car $45,695 (27%)	26,500	23,500	21,500	18,500

TECHNICAL DATA

Powertrain (rear-drive)
Engine: 4.6L injected
V8 (190 hp)

Transmission: 4-speed auto.

Dimensions (Crown Victoria/ Town Car)
Length: 212 in./218.9 in.
Width: 77.8 in./76.9 in.
Wheelbase: 114.4 in./117.4 in.

SAFETY FEATURES

	Opt.	Std.
Anti-lock brakes	❑	■
Childproof door locks	❑	■
Driver-side airbag	❑	■
Passenger-side airbag	❑	■
Remote keyless entry	❑	■

Lincoln Continental

Continental

RATING: Above Average buy.

NEW FOR '97: Standard traction control, revised accelerator/brake pedal height, and a smoother front suspension (the springs have been changed). A major facelift is planned for the 1998 model.

GENERAL COMMENTS: Reworked two years ago, the Continental rests on a modified front-wheel-drive Taurus chassis, which is one of the most up to date, stylish designs on the road. With the addition of the Lincoln Mark VIII's 4.6L V8 as the standard powerplant, performance has improved immeasurably, to the point that it's now comparable to the Lexus and Infiniti luxury sedans. A sophisticated air cushion suspension allows the driver to dial in different suspension settings for all driving conditions. The 3.8L engine is quieter and allows for more interior space than does the Lexus, Infiniti, or BMW. The interior, however, is much narrower than what you'll find with the Pontiac Bonneville, Buick Park Avenue, or Chrysler Intrepid, Concorde, Vision, and New Yorker/LHS.

Cost analysis/Alternatives: Minor improvements don't justify the higher price tag for the '97 model; go for a '96 instead. Other cars you may wish to consider: the Ford Crown Victoria or Marquis, Infiniti, Lexus, Mercedes-Benz 300 series, or Toyota Avalon. The Continental is less expensive than imported luxury sedans, without sacrificing luxury features or innovative technology. On the other hand, German and Japanese models leave the Continental far behind in handling, braking, engine smoothness, and overall reliability. **Rebates**: $5000 dealer incentives on '96s in effect until Dec. 31, 1996. **Destination charge**: $500. **Recommended options**: A one-touch panic button (RESCU) that alerts the police, ambulance, or tow truck to your whereabouts through a patch between the cellular phone network and global satellites; and run-flat Michelin ZP tires that can be driven up to 50 miles without tire pressure. **Supplementary warranty**: A good idea, not because these cars are failure-prone (they aren't) but because the complicated mechanical and electrical components cost so much to troubleshoot and replace. **Parts supply/Servicing**: Average. **Depreciation**: Below average. **Highway/City fuel economy**: 9-13.5L/km.

Reliability/Safety

Pro: Good assembly and average reliability. Overall quality control is the best of domestic luxury cars, which is far from complimentary. The 3.8L V6 has proven to be reliable. Below-average parts cost, according to the CAA.

Safety is assured with automatically adjusted front head restraints, standard dual airbags and ABS, comfortable, easily adjusted lap-and-shoulder seatbelts, and padded front knee bars. NHTSA crash tests of an airbag-equipped 1991 Continental showed that both the driver and passenger would be well-protected, although some leg trauma would occur. According to the Highway Loss Data Institute, which analyzes real world insurance claims, the Continental is much better than average in overall injury loss, but only average in collision loss payouts.

Con: Front brakes and suspension system aren't very durable. The added complexity of ABS brakes, an electronic air suspension, and all the other high-tech items found on these cars is likely to cause some headaches with age, which is reason enough to buy an extended warranty. The sequential fuel-injection system is difficult to service if problems arise.

Confidential dealer service bulletins show the following relatively minor '96 model year problems that could carry over to the '97 models: a drifting or pulling to one side when driving, a transaxle click when going into Reverse, and assorted driveline noise (see the Taurus/Sable DSB).

Road Performance

Pro: The smooth V8 powerplant provides exhilarating acceleration. The ABS brakes are flawless and will keep wheels from locking even on glare ice. The variable-ratio power steering gives the right amount of road feel and control. The Overdrive automatic transmission shifts smoothly. Air suspension helps both ride and handling; the car is smooth on all but the worst roads, but cornering at highway speeds remains precise and predictable.

Con: The 1995 model's 6-cylinder engine is a dog. Despite its good handling, the Continental does feel clumsy around town. The transmission occasionally has trouble deciding if it wants to be in Overdrive or 3rd gear. The computer-controlled air suspension emits an irritating hissing when it settles after parking. Numb steering.

Comfort/Convenience

Pro: The interior is narrower than other domestic cars in this class, but it's plush and comfortable. Fresh air ventilation is adequate, but the automatic climate controls tend to overcompensate and perform erratically. Large trunk.

Con: Bland styling. The standard leather upholstery is slippery, and it's hot in summer and cold in winter. Seats aren't as comfortable as the competition's. The rear seats need more side and lower back support. The digital dash is hard to read, and the interior lacks storage bins for small objects. Some operating controls are inconvenient and illogical. For example, you'll have to shut off the ignition and blindly grope inside the glove compartment for the trunk lid remote release, and hope you don't hit the fuel-filler door release instead. Confusing power-window switches. Ford's chintzy side is evident when you open the spacious trunk and find that it houses a temporary-service spare tire. Loading the trunk is made difficult by the protruding rear bumper. High speed road/tire/wind noise. Engine is noisy when pushed. Gas tank is too small. Poor phone reception. Handset cradle is not user friendly.

COST

List Price (negotiable)	Residual Values (months) 24	36	48	60
Executive: $49,995 (30%)	$34,000	$28,500	$22,000	$18,500

TECHNICAL DATA

Powertrain (front-drive)
Engine: 4.6L injected V8 (260 hp)
Transmission: 4-speed auto.

Dimensions
Length: 206.3 in.
Width: 73.6 in.
Wheelbase: 109 in.

SAFETY FEATURES

	Opt.	Std.
Anti-lock brakes	❑	■
Childproof door locks	❑	■
Driver-side airbag	❑	■
Passenger-side airbag	❑	■
Remote keyless entry	❑	■
Traction control	❑	■

Lincoln Mark VIII

Mark VIII

RATING: Above Average buy. An exceptional ride and powerful engine make this behemoth a better highway cruiser than city schlepper.

NEW FOR '97: A facelift, high-tech lighting, reduced engine noise, reworked suspension to enhance ride and handling, and new standard features that include traction control, an anti-theft device, and a tilted, telescoping steering column. Ford also says that it will cut prices substantially this year.

GENERAL COMMENTS: Lincoln's Mark VIII is the latest makeover of the series that began in 1955 with the Mark II. It's set on the Thunderbird platform (the Continental shares the Taurus platform) and uses a 4.6L aluminum V8 engine that puts out 280 hp—15 fewer horses than Cadillac's Northstar powerplant.

Cost analysis/Alternatives: The 1997 model is substantially improved and may end up costing less than last year's version, even with the new standard features factored in. Mark VIII shoppers should also consider the Lincoln Town Car or Continental, a fully loaded Ford Crown Victoria/Mercury Grand Marquis, Mazda 929, Nissan Maxima, or Toyota Avalon. **Rebates**: Ford's promised price cut will likely damper any thought of rebates until well into the next year. **Destination charge**: $500. **Recommended options**: None. **Supplementary warranty**: A good idea. **Parts supply/Servicing**: Average. **Depreciation**: Below average. **Highway/City fuel economy**: 9-13.5L/100 km.

Reliability/Safety

Pro: Overall reliability is above average. Comprehensive base warranty. Standard traction control.

Con: Confidential dealer service bulletins reveal the following 1996 model year problems that could carry over to the '97 models: cold start engine squeal, transmission shudder/bump and lower body side paint abrasion.

No crash data is available.

Road Performance

Pro: The smooth, quiet-running 4.6L V8 provides more than enough power for a comfortable ride and effortless passing ability—would you believe 0-to-60 mph in 7.2 seconds? Sensitive steering is a plus around town. Superior ride quality and good emergency handling. Air suspension provides a smooth ride, no matter what the load. Excellent braking, although the ABS pulsing takes getting used to.

Con: Power steering allows for little road feel and is a bit twitchy due to its too-quick response. Clumsy to manoeuvre and park around town. Four-speed automatic shifts abruptly when pushed.

Comfort/Convenience

Pro: Lots of favourable comments highlighting the spacious rear seating, comfortable seating up front, and well-appointed interior. Efficient climate control system. Large doors make entry/exit a breeze.

Con: Controls and gauges are easy to see and reach. Luxurious-looking leather seats don't *feel* luxurious (see "Dumb Options" in Part One). Other irritants: confusing and awkward-to-use trip computer; climate controls and radio buttons that are illogical and too small to adjust easily, and so poorly placed they force you to take your eyes off the road; and parking by ear: it's practically impossible to feel comfortable with the car's real dimensions (the Lumina APV syndrome). Short drivers may have trouble reaching the pedals, while tall drivers may find the leg room insufficient. Easy rear access, but rear seating is surprisingly tight—two average-sized adults can barely squeeze in. Some wind noise.

COST

List Price (negotiable)	**Residual Values** (months)			
	24	**36**	**48**	**60**
Base: $53,695 (30%)	$37,000	$31,000	$24,000	$19,000

TECHNICAL DATA

Powertrain (rear-drive)
Engine: 4.6L injected V8 (280 hp)
Transmission: 4-speed automatic

Dimensions
Length: 207.3 in.
Width: 74.8 in.
Wheelbase: 113 in.

SAFETY FEATURES

	Opt.	Std.
Anti-lock brakes	❑	■
Childproof door locks	—	—
Driver-side airbag	❑	■
Passenger-side airbag	❑	■
Remote keyless entry	❑	■
Traction control	❑	■

JAGUAR

XJ Sedan

RATING: Not Recommended. As far as interior space, reliability, and overall quality are concerned, other automakers offer better products for less.

NEW FOR '97: The launching of the new XK8 and a facelifted XJ6, which will offer the 4.0L V8 used by the XK8. The V12 option and the XJS have been dropped.

GENERAL COMMENTS: Jaguar's name conjures up images of posh sedans and fast sports cars rolling through the English countryside. Jaguars reek of elegance, taste, and money. The car's styling, ride, handling, and comfort still entice motorists full of nostalgia for British cars of the 1960s, but mechanical, electronic, and body problems still persist, though not as many as a decade ago.

There are four XJ variations to choose from: the entry-level XJ6, the more luxurious Vanden Plas, the supercharged XJR sports sedan, and the top-of-the-line XK8.

Cost analysis/Alternatives: Except for the all-new XK8, there isn't any compelling reason to buy a '97 Jaguar instead of a '96 version, unless you feel that the XJ6's V8 and new front end styling are worth the extra expense. Actually, that's debatable when the car is compared with the less expensive convertible/roadsters like the BMW Z3, Mercedes SLK, and Porsche Boxster. It does look like a bargain, though, when compared with last year's more expensive 12-cylinder XJS convertible. Other more reliable luxury cars you may wish to consider are the BMW 7 series, fully loaded Ford Taurus/Sable, Lexus, and Infiniti models, Mazda 929, the Mercedes S class, Nissan Maxima, and Toyota Camry or Avalon. **Rebates**: \$800–\$2400 rebates on all '97 models except XK8; \$800–\$1200 on the '96 Vanden Plas XJ6; \$800–\$2400 on the remaining '96 models. **Destination**

charge: $600. **Recommended options**: None. **Supplementary warranty**: A smart investment. **Parts supply/Servicing**: Below average. **Depreciation**: Above average. Poor resale value. Don't buy into the myth that Jaguars depreciate very little. In fact, a 1993 Vanden Plas that sold originally for $76,000 is now considered by dealers to be worth no more than $35,000! **Highway/City fuel economy**: 9.5-14L/100 km (Vanden Plas); 10.5-16L/100 km (XJR); 13-20L/100 km (XJS); 13.5-20.3L/100 km (XJ12).

Reliability/Safety

Pro: Now that Ford has taken over the company, long-term reliability is still a rather large question mark. Nevertheless, the company does offer a 30-day, money-back guarantee (about 2 percent of the cars have been taken back) and a comprehensive 4 year/80,000 km base mechanical warranty. The automaker also provides a 6 year/unlimited km rust perforation warranty, and Jaguar Club benefits that include no-cost maintenance, roadside assistance, and trip interruption services.

Con: Get used to the "check engine" light coming on. Jaguar says it's normal that it comes on for no apparent reason and that the bug crops up only occasionally. I say the sensors know something that Ford and Jaguar may not.

Confidential dealer service bulletins applicable to the '96 models list the following problems that may carry over to the '97s: Vanden Plas: poor idle quality, interior and fascia panel lighting malfunctions caused by a radio or console wiring harness short circuit (see DSB below); XJ-6: poor idle quality; XJ-S convertible: poor idle quality.

CHECKING CONSOLE WIRING HARNESS FOR CHAFING

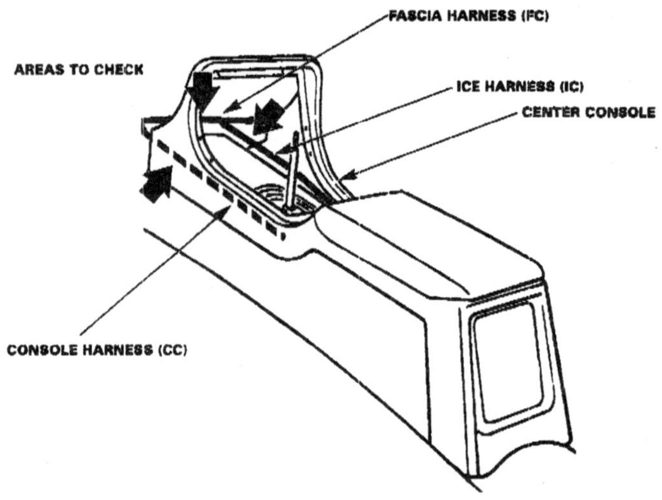

Poor servicing has compounded the quality-control problem. Owners report long delays for service appointments and then even longer waits for the right parts to arrive. Unfortunately, there aren't many Jaguar dealers to choose from, so if you don't find a competent and conscientious one, it's doubtful that you'll be able to go elsewhere for a second opinion.

No crash data available.

Road Performance

Pro: Good choice of motors, except for the superfluous V12. The base V6 engine is smooth and adequate for most driving situations. Nevertheless, the turbocharged V6 is the best performer, considering its price. With 322 horsepower in reserve, it has more than the best from Lexus and Infiniti. Sophisticated suspension provides a smooth ride over all terrain that doesn't deteriorate as the load is increased. Crisp handling. Precise, variable-assisted steering. In slalom tests the XJ12 beats the pants off of its BMW and Mercedes competition. The XJ convertible offers a manual shifter that works well with the car's sport suspension.

Con: Caught in a dilemma similar to that of the Corvette and Nissan 300ZX, the Jaguar's excess weight makes it necessary to install lots of complicated and failure-prone devices, as well as larger engines, in order to make these cars decent highway performers. The base V6 powerplant is a bit overwhelmed by the car's excessive weight. The V12 engine is no tire-burner either. From a performance standpoint, cheaper V6 versions perform almost as well. In fact, the XJ12 has less horsepower and torque than the XJR. Excessive braking distance, although the XJ12 does tie the BMW 750iL and beats the Mercedes S500.

Comfort/Convenience

Pro: Jam-packed with quality standard equipment. Easy-to-read, well laid-out dash. Easy entry/exit. Excellent soundproofing keeps out engine and road noise. Convenient and practical door pouches for storage of small items. Five extra inches of much-needed rear leg room on this year's models.

Con: Cramped front seats, seatbacks could be straighter, and the seat cushion lacks sufficient thigh support. Tall drivers need more leg room. The dash computer requires an engineering degree to understand. Multiple air leaks into the interior. Jaguar styling and small mirrors means that you have to park by ear. Insufficient rear head room. Small trunk. Fuel-thirsty V12. XJ convertible: Poor rear visibility, inadequate rear passenger room, narrow dash, limited distribution.

COST

List Price (very negotiable)	**Residual Values** (months) **24**	**36**	**48**	**60**
XJ6/Plas: $83,000 (25%)	$43,000	$35,000	$30,000	$25,000
XJ-R: $85,000 (25%)	46,000	38,000	33,000	28,000
XJS 4.0: $73,900 (25%)	41,000	33,000	28,000	23,000

TECHNICAL DATA

Powertrain (rear-drive)
Engines: 4.0L injected 6 (245 hp) • 4.0L Super 6 (322 hp) • '96 6.0L V12 (313 hp)
Transmission: 4-speed auto.

Dimensions (Plas/XJR/XJS Coupe)
Length: 197.8 in./197.8 in./191.2 in.
Width: 81.7 in./81.7 in./74.1 in.
Wheelbase: 113 in./113 in./102 in.

SAFETY FEATURES

Vanden Plas/XJR	Opt.	Std.
Anti-lock brakes	❑	■
Childproof door locks	❑	■
Driver-side airbag	❑	■
Passenger-side airbag	❑	■
Remote keyless entry	❑	■

XJS	Opt.	Std.
Anti-lock brakes	❑	■
Childproof door locks	❑	■
Driver-side airbag	❑	■
Passenger-side airbag	❑	■
Remote keyless entry	❑	■
Traction control	❑	■

Ford Aerostar

Aerostar

RATING: Average buy. If you must get a rear-drive minivan, the Aerostar's the one.

NEW FOR '97: Nothing new this year. Having lived on borrowed time for the past three years, the Aerostar will finally be discontinued next year.

GENERAL COMMENTS: The Aerostar is a seven-passenger, aerodynamically styled minivan on a light truck chassis. The Ranger chassis and mechanical components give it a higher floor and make it taller, wider, and more powerful than most other minivans. As a result, the Aerostar has one of the most spacious interiors in its class.

Aerostars come in two sizes: the standard version, which is 174.9 inches long, and the extended edition, which is 15.4 inches longer. All Aerostars are XLT models. Two motors are available: a 145-hp V6 3.0L and a 4.0L V6 that produces 10 more horses. With the 4.0L engine the Aerostar can carry almost a ton of cargo and tow up to 4800 pounds. This large minivan comes with an extended-length version that adds more than 15 inches to the cargo area behind the rear wheels, quick-release latches for easy seat removal, and a 21-gallon fuel tank. AWD capability is offered as an option.

Cost analysis/Alternatives: The '96 models are virtually identical to the more expensive '97 versions and are a real bargain if they're cheap enough. Take a look at the more versatile 200-hp Ford Windstar or Chrysler Caravan/Voyager. Small minivans that may be better suited to your non-towing needs include the Mercury Villager/Nissan Quest. **Rebates**: $500 rebates on the '96s are boosted $1000 on the '97 Aerostar until Jan. 3, 1997. **Destination charge**: $875. **Recommended options**: Be careful in choosing option packages—there's a big spread between the rock bottom price for a basic Aerostar and a loaded version. The 4.0L engine and 4-speed automatic transmission are the best all-round driving/towing combination, except that fuel economy is sacrificed, making the Aerostar one of the most thirsty minivans in its class. A tilt steering wheel, an automatic transmission oil cooler, and the captain's chairs are also recommended. Invest in the optional auxiliary heater, but pass on the electronic instrument cluster option. It's better to have too much space than not enough, so get the extended version, which has a lot more room inside, including a good-size cargo bay behind the third seat. **Warranty**: An extended warranty is a wise investment, particularly if this minivan is dropped next year. **Parts supply/Servicing**: Good supply, but expensive to service. Independent parts suppliers can knock one-third off the cost of a Ford-supplied component. **Depreciation**: Above average. **Highway/City fuel economy**: 9.5-14L/100 km.

Reliability/Safety

Pro: Overall reliability has improved a great deal over the past two years, but that's not much to boast about. No long-term reliability problems have been seen with the 4.0L V6 engine. A large dealer network means that servicing and parts are easily available.

Crash tests of a 1995 Ford Aerostar concluded that the driver and passenger would be very well protected in a 57 km/h frontal collision. Driver and passenger protection were given a four-star rating. The rating for a 1996 Aerostar is driver, ★★★★; passenger, ★★★. Insurance statistics indicate that the Aerostar has had a lower-than-average frequency of collision claims.

Con: Poor quality and badly assembled body hardware, premature front brake wear, ABS malfunctions, defective suspension components, AC failures, and erratic heating/defrosting performance. The electronic engine controls are glitch-prone and are difficult and expensive to repair. Owners have reported engine knocking, coolant leaks, high oil consumption, and fuel-system problems. Automatic transmission breakdowns have been common over the past five years. Paint fading, chalking, and peeling. According to the CAA, parts are more expensive than most other cars in this class. Some reports of stalling with the 3.0L engine.

Stopping distance is unacceptably long with rear-only ABS. Inadequate front defroster leaves the bottom half of the windshield untouched and wipers frozen in their resting place. Tiny horn buttons can't be easily found in an emergency. The hefty B-pillar (where the edge of the door meets the body behind the front seat) obstructs peripheral vision. Tendency to tip over when cornering at moderate speeds.

Confidential dealer service bulletins reveal just four problems with the 1996 model year that could carry over to the '97 models: fuel-pump whine or buzz heard in the speaker; rattle/buzz at the sides of the instrument panel and/or window; and rapping or clanging noise from the steering assembly.

Road Performance

Pro: The V6 4.0L engine (standard on 4X4s) provides plenty of power for most applications. The automatic transmission is computer controlled and changes gears more smoothly. The AWD and traction control combination provides exceptional traction—much superior to the RWD version. Handling is predictable and steering is more precise than with past models.

Con: The 3.0L 6-cylinder engine is barely adequate to haul this heavy vehicle around. The cruise control can be temperamental on hilly terrain. When accelerating, the 4-speed automatic transmission shifts abruptly. The stiff standard suspension gives a busy ride on smooth roads. Owners report excessive body lean and tire squealing when cornering or on uneven surfaces. A full load further compromises handling and causes the suspension to bottom out. Emergency manoeuvres aren't handled very well in city or highway driving. High fuel consumption in city driving.

Comfort/Convenience

Pro: A versatile people or cargo hauler. Easy front access and a middle and rear step makes passenger entry/exit a breeze. Comfortable front seats and high seating position gives good forward visibility. Well laid-out dash and easy-to-read gauges. Except for the front defroster, the climate control system works well. Comfortable centre seats with additional leg room in the extended version. Quiet interior. There's a convenient pull strap for the rear hatch, and cargo liftover height is low.

As far as passenger space and cargo capacity are concerned, the rear-drive Aerostar wins hands down over the front-drive Windstar. There's a lot of head and leg room in all three seating positions, more rear leg room, and the second and third row of seats can be removed to provide a cargo hold of almost 168 cubic feet.

Con: Relatively awkward step-in. The standard driver's seat lacks lateral support and a height adjuster. The rear and centre seats don't move forward or fold flat. As much as the captain's chairs make front seat occupants happy, the same option for the centre seats makes entry/exit fairly difficult. The rear bench seats are quite uncomfortable. The glove compartment is for gloves only. Excess slack develops in the front seatbelt shoulder straps while driving. Access to the engine compartment is difficult. The "limited service" (a euphemism for undersized) spare tire isn't very accessible. Mediocre heating and ventilation are made worse by the limited window openings. Excessive road noise and driveline vibration.

COST

List Price (very negotiable)	Residual Values (months) 24	36	48	60
4X2: $19,395 (19%)	$12,500	$10,500	$9500	$8000
4X4 Ext.: $27,295 (21%)	15,000	13,000	11,500	9900

TECHNICAL DATA

Powertrain (rear-drive/AWD)
Engines: 3.0L injected V6 (135 hp) • 4.0L V6 (155 hp)
Transmissions: 5-speed manual • 4-speed auto.

Dimensions (Base/Extended)
Weight: 3650 lbs./3800 lbs.
Length: 174.9 in./190.3 in.
Width: 71.7 in./72 in.
Wheelbase: 118.9 in./118.9 in.
Fuel tank: 79L/reg. unl.
Cargo capacity: 13-57 cu. ft.
Towing capacity: 4800 lbs.
Passengers: 7

SAFETY FEATURES

	Opt.	Std.
Anti-lock brakes (rear)	❑	■
Childproof door locks	❑	■
Driver-side airbag	❑	■
Passenger-side airbag	—	—
Remote keyless entry	■	❑
Traction control	■	❑
Front/rear head restraints	No	Yes
Side impact beams	Yes	

Mercury Villager/Nissan Quest

Mercury Villager

RATING: Recommended. Maxima reliability and Ford styling.

NEW FOR '97: Side door intrusion beams and improved side impact protection. Styling changes, including a sliding, powered fourth door, are scheduled for the 1999 model year.

GENERAL COMMENTS: Launched in the summer of 1992, the Mercury Villager and Nissan Quest minivans are the first product offering of the Ford/Nissan joint project begun in 1986. Manufactured by Ford at its truck factory in Avon Lake, Ohio, and sized comfortably between the regular and extended Chrysler minivans, these front-drive, five- or seven-passenger minivans come without aero-styling gimmicks, having adopted a bit of Chrysler's boxy look and interior dimensions.

Of all the small minivans, the Mercury Villager/Nissan Quest is the most economical to maintain, the least expensive to purchase, and the most fun to whip around the city in. Their strongest assets are car-like handling, modular seating, and reliable mechanical components that have been tested for years on the Maxima.

Mercury, unlike Nissan, offers a cargo version in addition to its five- and seven-passenger models. It's also quite different from the lighter weight, truck-like Ford Aerostar because its front-drive setup and 151-hp 3.0L V6 engine give the Villager car-like handling, ride, and cornering. Nissan borrowed the powertrain, suspension, and steering assembly from its Maxima, mixed in some creative sheet metal, and left the job of outfitting the sound system, climate control, dashboard, steering column, and wheels to Ford. This has resulted in an attractive and not overly aero-styled minivan.

Cost analysis/Alternatives: The '97 models are practically identical to the cheaper '96 versions, which are the better buy. Other minivans worth considering are the Ford Windstar or Toyota Previa. **Rebates**: $1000 on the '97s. **Destination charge**: $875. **Recommended options**: The integrated child safety seat is a must-have and the seat height adjuster will benefit short drivers. A separate rear air conditioner/heater and power side windows are also worth considering. The optional performance handling equipment makes little improvement to the standard suspension, and the Nautica option is simply a high-priced cosmetic makeover. **Warranty**: An extended warranty isn't needed. **Parts supply/Servicing**: Good supply. Above average servicing. **Depreciation**: Slower than average. **Highway/City fuel economy**: 9.5-13.5L/100 km.

Reliability/Safety

Pro: The engine and drivetrain are borrowed from the Nissan Maxima, a very reliable vehicle. Excellent fit and finish. A large dealer network means that servicing and parts are easily available. According to the CAA, parts are less expensive than most other cars in this class. Plenty of glass provides excellent front and rear visibility.

The Villager and Quest offer a large array of standard safety features that include airbags, side-impact beams, reinforced centre pillars, front and rear impact absorbing zones, rear outboard three-point safety belts, ABS, and a childproof doorlock in the sliding door. An integrated child seat is optional. A 1996 Mercury Villager did fairly well in government crash tests; the driver is well-protected while the front passenger has average protection. It's rated: driver, ★★★★; passenger, ★★★.

Con: Most owner-reported problems involve interior and exterior noise and driveline vibrations. Interestingly, confidential dealer service bulletins confirm the noise problem and reveal the following '96 model-year problems that could carry over to the '97s: airbag lamp flashes constantly, body side windows fail to stay closed, carpet lifts at right sliding seat track, fuel pump noise heard in the radio speakers, horn produces a chirping sound, rear suspension crunch/grunt noise, and a noisy sliding door requires a high closing effort (see illustration below).

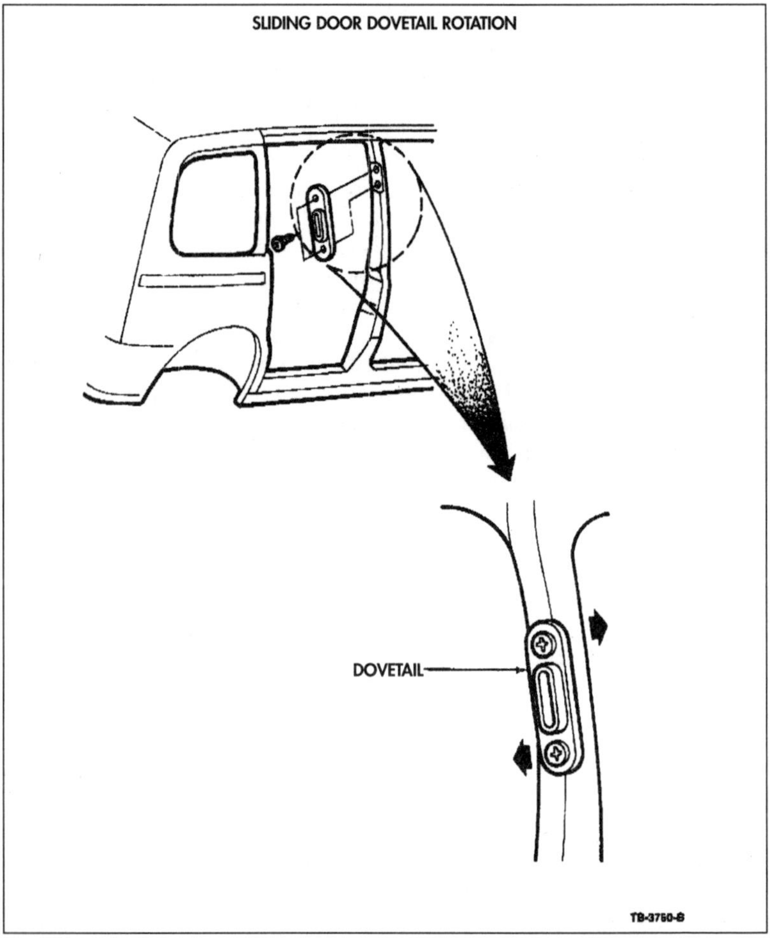

The sliding door noise and high closing effort is simple to correct.

Safety investigators are looking into reports of electric door lock and power window failures that have trapped occupants in the vehicle.

Road Performance

Pro: Smooth V6 engine delivers plenty of power for city and most highway driving needs. Agile (the short wheelbase helps in this area) and easy to drive, the Villager delivers a no-surprise, smooth, quiet ride on the highway that isn't compromised by a full load. Precise steering makes the Villager quite responsive at highway speeds and in emergency manoeuvres. Impressive highway stability. The 4-speed automatic transmission is particularly smooth and quiet—you can switch from Economy to Power shift mode by pressing a dashboard button. Fourth gear can be locked out to prevent constant gear hunting when going over hilly terrain. Braking performance is excellent, because ABS on the Villager improves directional control by eliminating wheel lockup.

Con: Passing ability with the V6 engine is not impressive. Rough terrain or uneven pavement makes for a busy to rough ride. Don't make too much of the Villager's car-like handling. Sure, it handles much better than truck-based minivans like the GM Astro and Ford Aerostar, but it isn't superior to other front-drive minivans. It requires a rather wide turning circle. High gas consumption. Long-legged drivers may find the leg room a bit short. Towing capacity of 3500 pounds is possible only with an optional towing package.

Comfort/Convenience

Pro: Car-like driving position; comfortable seats, including a power lumbar support in the driver's seat; and controls and instruments that are generally easy to use and read, with a few exceptions. The front captain's chairs are easily removed, and the modular interior allows 14 possible seating and cargo configurations, making for better seating for three adults in the rear than with most other small vans or wagons. Flexibility and the easy-to-use sliding rear seat make up for the Villager's modest cargo-carrying capacity. Middle seatback folds flat, and the rear seats have tracks that allow them to slide forward all the way to the front. Rear seat can be folded flat and converted to a serving area for tailgate parties. Low liftover height makes for convenient loading from the rear. Helpful assist grab handles over the front and sliding doors. All side windows can be opened for maximum ventilation. Efficient, powerful climate control system; you can turn on the AC and control the air outlet location separately. The standard radio gives great sound.

Con: The Villager is less well-appointed than the Nissan Quest, and provides about one-third less interior space than the base Caravan. Steering wheel blocks the view to many operating controls. Front seats could use more lateral support. The seven-passenger configuration leaves little room for cargo. Middle seat is optional on the GS. Tiny controls on the Villager's climate control system are distracting and hard to adjust. Some of the indicator lights fade out in sunlight. The radio controls require a long reach and nimble fingers. Some wind and road noise accompanies the previously mentioned interior squeaks and rattles.

COST

List Price (firm)	**Residual Values** (months)			
	24	**36**	**48**	**60**
GS: $23,995 (19%)	$15,800	$13,200	$11,500	$9500
LS: $32,145 (21%)	18,900	16,500	14,500	12,500

TECHNICAL DATA

Powertrain (front-drive)
Engine: 3.0L V6 (151 hp)
Transmission: 4-speed auto.

Dimensions
Weight: 4015 lbs.
Length: 189.9 in.
Width: 73.7 in.
Wheelbase: 112.2 in.
Fuel tank: 76L/reg. unl.
Cargo capacity: 14.1 cu. ft.
Towing capacity: 3500 lbs.
Passengers: 5-7

SAFETY FEATURES

	Opt.	Std.
Anti-lock brakes	❑	■
Childproof door locks	❑	■
Driver-side airbag	❑	■
Passenger-side airbag	❑	■
Remote keyless entry	■	❑
Traction control	—	—
Front/rear head restraints	Yes	Yes
Side impact beams		Yes

Ford Windstar

Windstar

RATING: Above Average buy. More crashworthy than the Chrysler minivans.

NEW FOR '97: Nothing really new this year, but next year's models will get a minor facelift. Hoping to correct one of its worst product decisions in years, Ford will spend $615 million to add an enlarged driver-side door on its 1998 models and then follow that move with a rear sliding-door on the driver's side on the next year's models. These moves have been made to compete with the four-door minivans launched last year by Chrysler, and this year by GM.

GENERAL COMMENTS: Launched as a 1995 model in March 1994, the Windstar is a front-drive minivan that looks a bit like a stretched Mercury Villager. It's longer, larger, and lower than most other minivans. It's also one of the few minivans not built on a truck platform (it uses the Taurus platform instead), and so it has some of the car-like handling characteristics of Chrysler's minivans. It's offered in two body styles—a seven-passenger people-hauler and the less expensive basic cargo van. Buyers have the choice of two 6-cylinder engines: a standard 147-hp 3.0L V6 or a 200-hp 3.8L V6. Both motors are hooked to a 4-speed electronic automatic transmission.

Cost analysis/Alternatives: This has been a terrible year for Windstar sales, so lots of '96 models are being liquidated at fire-sale prices. Inasmuch as they're practically identical to the more expensive '97 versions, they represent a real bargain if discounted enough. Toyota Previa, Mercury Villager/Nissan Quest, and Chrysler Caravan/Voyager are recommended alternatives. **Rebates**: Last December, Ford had a 100-day-plus supply of Windstars on dealer lots across the country, while Chrysler was selling every minivan it could produce. Why? Ford ignored its own internal market data, which showed that a third of its customers wanted another sliding door on the new minivan. Ford nixed the idea and Chrysler reaped the benefits. If you must have a '97 Windstar, take advantage of Ford's $1000 rebate on the '97s until Jan. 5, 1997. **Destination charge**: $875. **Recommended options**: Dual integrated child safety seats for the middle bench seat; middle bucket seats (more comfortable and easier to remove); power side windows; and rear air conditioner, defroster, and heater. **Warranty**: An extended warranty is a good idea. **Parts supply/Servicing**: Parts are widely available, but pricy. **Depreciation**: Slower than average. **Highway/City fuel economy**: With the 3.8L V6: 9.5-14L/100 km.

Reliability/Safety

Pro: Good assembly quality and a nice array of standard safety features. Unlike Chrysler and GM minivans, Windstars don't depend on shims, slots, and toytabs on sheet metal to permit inexact parts to be manoeuvred into a fit (akin to putting a round peg into a square hole). This ensures a quiet interior with little engine or road noise. The '96 Windstar meets all safety standards that apply to cars. In a 57 km/h frontal crash, it was rated: driver, ★★★★★; passenger, ★★★★★.

Con: Long-term reliability is unproven. Mechanical components are based on the old Ford Taurus, which had a below average reliability rating after the third year. Expect coolant leaks, premature tie-rod wear, and a noisy power steering pump. I've received letters outlining some serious concerns with the Windstar: rear windows that break suddenly because of auxiliary rear heater overheating; a rear heating duct behind the driver's seat that gets so hot it can burn an unsuspecting driver's fingers; and a front windshield that cracks from the base upwards due to faulty mounting or sudden temperature changes. Ford—not your insurance company—should pay the damage claim.

Still on the safety issue, some '96 versions have been recalled to inspect and retorque the driver's seat bolts.

Confidential dealer service bulletins reveal the following problems that could carry over to the '97 models: intermittent no starts, transaxle and driveline noises, floor pan clunk when accelerating or decelerating, clunk when moving gearshift out of Park, AC produces a persistent musty odour, carpets may produce a fishy odour (no kidding! See the DSB below).

Article No.
96-7-16
03/25/96
INTERIOR TRIM – OBJECTIONABLE ODOUR (FISHY) FROM CARPET – VEHICLES BUILT THROUGH 3/4/96
LIGHT TRUCK:
1995-96 WINDSTAR
ISSUE:
An objectionable odour may be emitted from the carpet under certain conditions.
ACTION:
Replace the underpadding and carpet after verifying customer concern. The new underpadding, Myrabond(R), will not produce the odour.

Funny, Chrysler's Cherokees and minivans had the same problem with their headliners.

Road Performance

Pro: A 30 percent increase in horsepower (55 more horses) this year improves acceleration greatly. The electronic 4-speed automatic responds well and shifts smoothly. Smooth and supple ride under most driving conditions that doesn't deteriorate as the load increases. Easy to drive. Emergency handling and braking are exceptional, with little loss of directional stability or fading in successive applications. Fourth gear can be locked out for towing.

Con: The Windstar's city manners aren't impressive: heavy steering makes driving less car-like than the new Chrysler minivans; it has a large turning radius; and it's hard for the driver to see the nose of the vehicle in parking manoeuvres. Lots of wind noise on the highway.

Comfort/Convenience

Pro: Excellent driving position gives any size of driver a commanding view of the road. Efficient climate control system. Superior sound system. Rear hatch is easy to open and shut, and the low floor improves cargo handling. Another nice touch is the optional power lock switch just inside the rear hatch, which saves you from having to walk to the front of the van to lock up. Quiet interior.

Con: The Windstar's driver's seat isn't comfortable for big, tall drivers who complain of the lack of leg room, seat contouring, and support. Rear window wiper and washer controls are obscured by the steering wheel. Small buttons on the Windstar's radio make it hard to use. Although the seats are easily removed, getting them in and out of the vehicle is more of a chore than it is for the Chrysler minivans. The right side sliding door takes a lot of effort to open and close.

COST

List Price (firm)	**Residual Values** (months) 24	36	48	60
Base: $22,195 (18%)	$14,000	$12,000	$10,500	$8000
GL: $24,195 (19%)	15,000	14,000	12,000	9500
LX: $30,895 (21%)	18,500	16,500	14,000	12,500

TECHNICAL DATA

Powertrain (front-drive)
Engine: 3.0L V6 (150 hp)
• 3.8L V6 (200 hp)
Transmission: 4-speed auto. OD

Dimensions
Weight: 4000 lbs.
Length: 201.2 in.
Width: 74.3 in.
Wheelbase: 120.7 in.
Fuel tank: 75L/94L/reg. unl.
Cargo capacity: 22.1 cu. ft.
Towing capacity: 3500 lbs.
Passengers: 7

SAFETY FEATURES

	Opt.	Std.
Anti-lock brakes	❑	■
Childproof door locks	❑	■
Driver-side airbag	❑	■
Passenger-side airbag	❑	■
Remote keyless entry	■	❑
Traction control	■	❑
Front/rear head restraints	Yes	Yes
Side impact beams	Yes	

GENERAL MOTORS

Auto buyers are well aware of GM's reputation for making low-quality vehicles (except for the Saturn), which is the main reason why GM's U.S. market share has plummeted from nearly 50 percent in the late 1970s to its current 32 percent. Nevertheless, the company has made record profits selling fewer cars and trucks by cutting production costs through closing plants, slashing jobs, reducing the number of parts, and using common parts across several product lines. But GM's labour costs to build a single car are still the highest of the Big Three. The automaker spends almost 30 hours per vehicle—20 percent longer than the time it takes Ford.

Average time required to assemble a vehicle:	
General Motors	30 hours
Ford Motor Co.	25 hours
Chrysler	27.2 hours

Trimming production costs will be GM's biggest challenge in the next decade.

New '97 products

This is a year of big changes for GM, as the automaker struggles to make sense of its sprawling portfolio of overlapping vehicle brands (midsize cars in particular) by emphasizing each model's uniqueness (tough job; most are clones of each other). Instead of radically paring the number of vehicles down to a more understandable and manageable level, GM is simply repositioning them, merging its divisions (watch out Saturn!), and putting its PR people into overdrive. With 32 percent of the new vehicle market, GM sells 82 models (down from 89 in 1994) while Ford, with 26 percent of the U.S. market, keeps its market share with half as many vehicles.

GM's New Vehicle Portfolio

Some vehicles GM is adding:

Midsize cars:

- Oldsmobile Cutlass
- Oldsmobile Intrigue
- Chevrolet Malibu
- Oldsmobile Alero
- Saturn Innovate

Other new models:

- Oldsmobile Eighty Eight full-size car
- Chevrolet Venture minivan
- Cadillac Catera entry-level luxury car
- EV1 (GM's electric vehicle)

Some vehicles GM will eliminate:

- Buick Skylark
- Buick Roadmaster
- Cadillac Fleetwood
- Chevrolet Caprice
- Oldsmobile Cutlass Ciera
- Oldsmobile Cutlass Supreme
- Chevrolet Corsica, Beretta
- Oldsmobile Achieva
- Oldsmobile Ninety Eight
- Chevrolet Lumina minivan

Vehicles under review for elimination:

- Coupes (two-door models) including Cadillac Eldorado

In addition to the above changes, GM is redesigning this year's Park Avenue, Corvette, DeVille and Concours, and Saturn coupe.

Cadillac Catera

Cadillac Catera: it's spelled with a "C," as in Cimarron.

RATING: Not Recommended; first year on the market.

GENERAL COMMENTS: Assembled in Germany and based on a the Opel Omega, the rear-drive, midsize Catera comes with a 200-hp V6 engine, four-speed automatic transmission, 16-inch alloy wheels, four-wheel disc brakes, a limited-slip differential, traction control, and standard dual airbags (side airbags will be added next year). Designed to compete with the BMW 328i, Lexus ES 300, and Mercedes Benz C280, GM hopes that its conservatively-styled Catera—the uninspired styling has Lumina written all over it—won't drive away its more traditional "empty-nesters" (guess that's a polite term for "old folks") while luring more baby boomers to its higher performance variations. Preliminary reports say that the car will be priced in the high 30s and embody "European" ride and handling.

The last time Cadillac introduced an entry level model was in 1981 when the automaker launched the Cimarron, a fully-loaded, Chevrolet Cavalier-derived Cadillac that carried a $4000 premium over a comparably equipped Cavalier. Back then, most auto critics and consumer advocates considered the Cavalier to be at the back of the pack as far as performance and quality control were concerned. The Catera, on the other hand, has gotten good reviews from the European press for its quiet, spacious, and comfortable interior, responsive handling, precise steering, fine-tuned suspension, and almost nonexistent lean or body roll when cornering. Without a doubt this is one Cadillac that's meant to be driven. On the downside, though, when you pass over a large expansion joint the floorpan vibrates annoyingly; drive over a bump when turning and the steering wheel kicks back in your hands.

A few other points you may wish to consider: GM dealers are notoriously bad when it comes to understanding and repairing European transplanted cars (just ask any Saab owner). Secondly, first-year cars don't generally have an adequate supply of replacement parts in the pipeline until their second or third year on the market. So get ready for long service waits and high parts costs for those repairs not covered under warranty. Finally, the fact that they're European-built doesn't necessarily mean that these Cadillacs will be reliable or durable. GM first learned that lesson with the British-built Vauxhall Firenza it unleased on an unsuspecting Canadian public in the '70s. A few years later it settled out of court several class actions that were piloted by this author, and paid a $20,000 fine to the federal government for misleading advertising. (On a nationally advertised roadtrip across Canada, GM said the cars excelled. Truth is, they were a mess. They required a team of engineers just to get started.)

Olds Cutlass/Chevrolet Malibu

RATING: Not Recommended; first-year sedans.

GENERAL COMMENTS: The '97 Oldsmobile Cutlass is a new front-drive, five-passenger, midsize sedan that replaces the 14-year-old Ciera. It's a conventionally-styled car that uses a more rigid body structure to cut down on noise and improve handling. Standard mechanicals include a tad noisy 3.1L V6, a four-speed automatic gearbox, ABS, and a split folding rear seat. The ignition switch is mounted on the dash (a throwback to your dad's Oldsmobile).

Other points to consider: outside mirrors are too small, the stiffer suspension may be too firm for some, and there's no traction control.

The Malibu, a close cousin of the Cutlass, is also a midsize sedan that offers a base twin cam, 2.4L 4-cylinder powerplant and an optional 3.1L V6, a stiff body, European-like handling, plenty of passenger and luggage space, and contemporary styling.

1997 Olds Cutlass

1997 Chevrolet Malibu

Chevrolet Venture/Olds Silhouette

RATING: Not Recommended; first-year minivans. These new minivans are a definite step up from the Lumina and Trans Sport and should be even more improved later in the year. You might consider the FE3 suspension option for the best handling and comfort combination. Other vehicles worth considering: Chrysler minivans, Ford Windstar, Mercury Villager, Nissan Quest, and Toyota Previa.

GENERAL COMMENTS: The Venture and Silhouette will eventually replace GM's Lumina and Trans Sport ("Dustbuster"), minivans noted for their plastic body panels, elongated front ends, and football-field-size dash tops that gobble up keys and small change, force you to lay on the dash and reach out with a mop handle to clean the front windshield, and teach you to park by ear.

Both the Venture and Silhouette come in regular and extended wheelbase versions. The extended wheelbase models get more bells and whistles, such as an optional power slide-open passenger-side door first offered last year (and unavailable from Chrysler), and an optional driver-side manual slide-open door. They aren't as sleek as the wider Chrysler competition, the view through the front windshield isn't as expansive, and they don't have half as many convenience items, but they are less rattle-prone than most minivans due to a more rigid body structure.

Minivan Comparison Chart

Name	Length	Width	Wheelbase	Sliding Doors	Horsepower (base engine)
Chrysler					
Caravan/Voyager	186.3 in.	75.6 in.	113.3 in.	2	150
Grand Caravan/ Grand Voyager	199.6 in.	75.6 in.	119.3 in.	2	150
Ford (Nissan)					
Aerostar	174.9 in.	71.7 in.	118.9 in.	1	135
Aerostar (ext.)	190.3 in.	72.0 in.	118.9 in.	1	135
Villager/Quest	189.9 in.	73.7 in.	112.2 in.	1	151
Windstar	201.2 in.	74.3 in.	120.7 in.	1	150
General Motors					
Astro/Safari	189.8 in.	77.5 in.	111 in.	1	190
Lumina/Trans Sport	191.5 in.	74.6 in.	109.8 in.	1	180
Venture	200.9 in.	72.0 in.	120 in.	2	180

You don't get as many option choices with the entry-level Venture as you do with the pricier Silhouette, which offers optional traction control, a power sunroof, a power passenger seat, and leather trim.

Both minivans use the same quiet-running, V6 powerplant that harnesses 14 more horses than the Chrysler minivans' top-line 3.8L 6-cylinder, providing good mid-range and top-end power. Unfortunately, the GM engine is hampered by less torque, making for less grunt when accelerating and frequently downshifting out of Overdrive when climbing moderate grades (there's no Overdrive on/off switch). This is the main reason why owners feel that the GM minivans are underpowered when compared with Chrysler's. Handling is better than most of the competition, particularly when equipped with the touring suspension, although the steering effort is quite high.

Dual airbags and ABS are standard. Other notable features and convenience items: Sungate, a metallic-coated windshield that blocks the sun's rays and acts as a radio antenna; easy-to-fold seats that drop down to increase storage space; the second seat flips forward for access to the third seat; lots of storage bins and compartments; an anti-glare dashtop covering; and huge side mirrors. One convenience item that can easily become an inconvenience: the two cargo nets found between the front seats and behind the rear seat are easily entangled and complicate the removal of the rear seats. Also, be wary of the power-assisted sliding side door—although it moves slowly and re-opens when contacting a foreign object, you wouldn't want to catch your hand between the door and pillar (it's not a painless experience).

1997 Chevrolet Venture

Value pricing

GM continues to take advantage of the higher-priced Japanese imports by expanding the number of models that are "value priced." This practice involves cutting dealer discounts and pricing vehicles more realistically (closer to anticipated transaction prices) in exchange for a no haggling policy. With value pricing, automakers say they build a package of options into a model and sell it at a set reduced price that reflects the lower invoice profit and reduced dealer discounts. This can be a good deal as long as the options are what you really need and a lot of fluff isn't thrown in to increase the base price. As for the no price haggling stipulation, haggle away. *Lemon-Aid* readers report that salespeople often ignore the no haggle edict if they feel that the customer is a serious prospect.

Your best bet is to consider how the bottom line price, essential options, dealer incentives, rebates, and included taxes measure up against comparable domestic and Japanese makes. Remember, the bottom line price should include all the little "extras" that dealers like to tack on just before getting your signature (administration fee, acquisition fee, destination and pre-delivery charges). You might be surprised to learn that dealers selling Japanese vehicles will bargain more than they did last year, because there's more profit built into their MSRP (already priced more realistically than the '96s) due to the deteriorating value of the yen.

Warranty woes

GM continues to pile up customer complaints over the way it handles customer complaints. When reimbursing customers for factory-related defects, GM acts as if its customers are asking for charity. It then charges a deductible or part of the cost for the repair needed to correct the company's original mistake. To add insult to injury, the company's 800 hotline for customer assistance systematically avoids divulging GM's many secret warranties covering a host of expensive, factory-related problems including paint defects, transmission/engine failures, and emission component defects. Instead, hotline staffers play a variation of "Let's Make A Deal" whereby the helpless customer is given a spiel designed to extort as much money as possible for a repair caused by a factory mistake.

Aware that it's losing customer loyalty by the lousy way it handles customer complaints, in April 1995 GM adopted a new policy that gives dealers in the United States almost complete authority in handling customer complaints and carrying out "goodwill" repairs for all kinds of factory-related defects. GM says that this new policy shouldn't be confused with "Special Policy Adjustments" (a euphemism used to describe secret warranties).

The following bulletin from April 1995 was sent to all of GM's U.S. divisions and dealers. It clearly sets out far-reaching (dare I say, *generous*) guidelines on how GM expects U.S.-based dealers to handle customer complaints related to paint defects and other generic factory-related problems. Although it specifically excludes Canadian dealers and customers, these new guidelines impact favourably upon GM's Canadian customers' claims because it's doubtful that provincial consumer affairs staffers, arbitrators, or small claims court judges would accept second-class treatment for Canadian car owners. Interestingly, the bulletin also includes a spiel similar to the one used by GM's customer relations hotline staffers to get some of the repair cost from the car owner.

This service bulletin goes under the nomenclature: BULLETIN No: 57-05-01, SUBJECT: Dealer/Retailer Administration of Case-by-Case Individual Goodwill Adjustments, MODELS: General Motors Passenger Cars and Trucks, All General Motors Marketing Divisions (Except GM of Canada), ATTENTION: Service Manager/Warranty Claims Administrator. This is an important reference if you don't want to copy the whole document, but wish to impress the service manager or factory rep that you know what's going on.

FILE IN SECTION: Warranty Administration
BULLETIN NO.: 57-05-01 **DATE:** April 1995
SUBJECT: Dealer/Retailer Administration of Case-by-Case Individual Goodwill Adjustments
MODELS: General Motors Passenger Cars and Trucks
All General Motors Marketing Divisions (Except GM of Canada)

ATTENTION: Service Manager/Warranty Claims Administrator

This bulletin contains additional details of the authorization empowerment change described in the March 3, 1995, letter mailed to all General Motors dealers/retailers on the subject of common case-by-case goodwill adjustment empowerment, effective March 15, 1995. The new common maximum authorization empowerment limit supersedes any prior divisional claim authorization empowerment levels that may have exceeded the new maximum authorization empowerment limit described in this bulletin.

Moving in the direction of common dealer/retailer goodwill, adjustment claim authorization empowerment is part of General Motors' continuing effort to eliminate waste and make administration easier for dealers/retailers and divisions. In addition, dealers/retailers have requested a more common approach to authorization empowerment and guidelines. While the maximum level of dealer/retailer goodwill adjustment authorization empowerment has been uniformly implemented, the criteria for establishing authorization empowerment will continue to be different by division at this time.

Listed below is the definition for goodwill adjustments, general administrative guidelines identifying the facts, and division claim authorization empowerment information.

DEFINITION

Individual, case-by-case goodwill adjustments are intended to recognize that circumstances outside the parameters of the written warranty may exist where special consideration is in order to enhance customer satisfaction and loyalty.

Such good will adjustments should not be confused with special policy adjustments provided to all involved owners through a special bulletin and direct mail. Case-by-case individual goodwill adjustments are not legal obligations as are the terms of General Motors warranties.

GENERAL ADMINISTRATIVE GUIDELINES

- Maximum dealer/retailer authorization empowerment, common to all GM divisions, is up to 2 years/24,000 miles for non-paint conditions and up to 2 years/unlimited mileage for paint, beyond the limits of the Bumper to Bumper base new vehicle warranty. Maximum authorization empowerment regarding GMC and Chevrolet medium duty truck authorization empowerment will be two years unlimited mileage for both non-paint and paint due to the unlimited mileage base warranty.
- Some dealers/retailers may be empowered to limits less than the maximum while a few select dealers/retailers may not be empowered at all. Individual dealer/retailer authorization empowerment levels are subject to change upon divisional notification.
- Any claim involving "individual goodwill adjustments" submitted after the effective date of March 15, 1995, which exceeds the dealer/retailer goodwill adjustment authorization empowerment limit will require wholesale review and authorization. This includes work in progress which you may have already committed to perform.
- Bumper to Bumper base new vehicle warranty coverage does not include current and past model year warranty coverage on specific components that carry warranty coverage longer than the base new vehicle warranty coverage, i.e., "Federal and California Emissions Warranties," "Sheet Metal Coverage," or "Diesel Engine Coverage."
- Paint Labor Operations excluded from authorization empowerment - See Below:
  Dealer/retailer authorization empowerment for paint claims covers exterior body panels

only. The following paint labor operations are excluded from the unlimited mileage paint empowerment that applies to exterior panels:

- A0110 - Finesse Sand and Buff
- A3740 - A4260 Replace Paint Stripe
- A4340 - A4700 Replace Decal Stripe
- A5020 - A5127 Replace Wood Grain Transfer
- A5541 - A5560 Paint - Chemical Spotting
- A5575 - A5580 Rail Dust Removal
- A7000 - A8200 Interior Paint

IDENTIFYING THE FACTS

Your authorization empowerment should be exercised when it appears that the condition could be the result of a defect in materials or workmanship rather than conditions occurring from aging, physical damage, lack of proper maintenance or owner abuse. Vehicle concerns should be assessed on their own merits within the context of the current owner's reasonable expectations and with appropriate concern for the cost to General Motors.

In exercising your judgment in each case, the following questions should be considered:

- Is the vehicle covered by other service or extended warranty contracts? If "yes," repairs must be performed under that contract.
- Does the vehicle show a lack of proper care and maintenance?
- Is the overall condition of the vehicle such that the cost to repair will approximate the vehicle's value?
- Did the condition occur after the vehicle was purchased used by the current owner? Is it likely the vehicle exhibited the condition before purchase?
- Did the condition occur while the vehicle was in the possession of a second or third owner and no vehicle history is available?
- Could the customer have done anything to prevent or cause the condition?
- Has the vehicle been used in ways for which it was not intended?
- Did the condition result from an after-market conversion or alteration?
- Did the condition result from the use of non-GM parts or accessories?
- Is there evidence of vehicle mileage alteration?
- Is the vehicle condition a normal operating characteristic?
- Is the condition largely a result of normal aging, wear and usage?
- Is the condition a result of unusual localized environmental, geographical, or climate factors?
- Additional Questions When Paint Condition Is the Concern:

Is the condition largely the result of normal paint aging or environmental damage (fading, gloss loss, chalking, cracking, flaking, yellowing)?
Is the condition only on a physically damaged panel that the customer declines to repair?

The above list is not intended to be all-inclusive. However, if the answer to any of these or similar questions is "yes," then it probably is not a concern you should address at General Motors' expense.

PARTIAL PARTICIPATION

In situations beyond the warranty period, but within your claim authorization empowerment, customers have received value from use of the vehicle. It would be reasonable to consider partial payment by the customer. The judgment belogs to you.

- Determine what the customer expects before making an offer to assist.
- Evaluate the reasonableness of the customer's expectations.
- Determine what offer would satisfy the customer as a fair and equitable adjustment.
- Make your evaluation of the situation through direct communication with the customer.
- Always strive for a mutually acceptable agreement.

Here's the kind of interrogation you can expect when asking for "goodwill" warranty repairs to correct a factory mistake.

Before making your complaint a federal case, start negotiations with GM by presenting excerpts from the April '95 bulletin to the dealer's service manager, one of GM's service reps, or before the small claims court, if need be. Take your copy of *Lemon-Aid* with you.

Metro/Firefly

Firefly

RATING: Above Average buy. The best small car GM doesn't make!

NEW FOR '97: This Suzuki Swift clone only gets a new LSi convenience package that includes dual outside rear-view mirrors, a passenger seat-back pocket, remote trunk release, standard 1.3L engine and cargo cover (LSi coupe), and split folding rear seats (sedans).

GENERAL COMMENTS: Excellent city and commuter cars that are capable of fitting into the tiniest of parking spaces and nipping through narrow city streets. But they still provide sufficient room inside for two adults and their cargo (there's little room for either with the rear seat up, especially in the two-door version).

These cars deliver outstanding fuel economy because of an unusual aluminum 1.0L 3-cylinder engine, which is a little rough around the edges but gets the job done efficiently. People who would like a little more zest from their city scooter can order the fuel-injected 1.3L 4-banger. Power steering isn't needed.

Cost analysis/Alternatives: The 1996 Metro and Firefly are essentially identical to the more expensive '97 versions ($500) and represent the better buy if you can't get the '97 rebate and intend to keep the car at least five years to amortize the extra year's depreciation. The XFi bare-bones Metro is the fuel economy champion, but it sacrifices an automatic transmission and a host of other amenities. Actually, a better-equipped model would be almost as economical. Convertibles are the best choice for ragtop thrills that won't break your budget. Compare prices with the Suzuki Swift, the Metro's twin; it may offer a better warranty and more standard features for less. Other cars to consider are the Honda Civic and Toyota Tercel. **Rebates**: $300 rebate on '96s and '97s. **Destination charge**: $525. **Recommended options**: A remote trunk release and split folding rear seats (sedans). **Supplementary warranty**: Not needed. **Parts supply/ Servicing**: Above average. **Depreciation**: Slower than average. For example, a 1994 base hatchback, selling originally for $8995, will now fetch about $5000 as a dealer trade-in. **Highway/City fuel economy**: 4.5-5.4L/100 km with the 1.0L and 5-speed manual; 5-6.5L/100 km with the 1.3L and 5-speed manual; 6.2-8L/100 km with the 1.3L and 3-speed automatic.

Reliability/Safety

Pro: This is a low-cost and low-maintenance econobox with a better-than-average repair record that goes back many years. The trend seems to be continuing, judging by the absence of significant problems mentioned in dealer service bulletins. Parts and service are easy to come by, and maintenance is made simple by an uncluttered underhood layout. Also, the paint and body assembly are of surprisingly high quality for such an inexpensive car. Parts are relatively inexpensive (except for powertrain components), but you may wish to shop around at different dealerships for parts since Suzuki dealers often charge less than GM dealers.

Crash tests of a 1996 Metro hatchback concluded that the driver and passenger would be relatively well-protected in a 57 km/h frontal collision. It was rated: driver, ★★★★; passenger, ★★★★. Chassis rigidity and crash safety have been increased with the placement of a steel beam behind the instrument panel.

Con: Noisy front metallic brake pads, and front discs that warp easily. Poorly performing fuel-injection system. If not checked often for corrosion and leaks, the cooling system will eventually fail, causing much damage to the aluminum engine. Some complaints concerning excessive oil consumption, premature clutch and piston wear, paint peeling, early rusting, fragile body hardware, and sloppy body assembly leading to air and water leaks.

Very sensitive to crosswinds and passing trucks on the highway.

Road Performance

Pro: The tiny 1.0L 3-cylinder powerplant has no trouble keeping up with city traffic, but the optional 1.3L 4-cylinder handles the automatic gearbox and highways much better. The 5-speed manual with Overdrive shifts easily. The non-power steering is fairly precise and always predictable. Handling is acceptable in most situations, thanks partly to independent suspension, but cornering becomes sloppier and less predictable as speed increases. Spectacular fuel economy, even when driven hard.

Con: Even with the optional 4-cylinder engine, these cars are not great highway or long-distance cruisers. Highway acceleration is glacial, producing a 14-second 0-to-60 mph time. The base 3-cylinder engine provides little power for highway passing when the vehicle is fully loaded and hooked to an automatic transmission. It's loud and vibrates excessively due to the absence of balance shafts. The clutch is abrupt, and the automatic transmission robs the engine of what little power it produces. The absence of an Overdrive gear on the automatic makes for excessive engine noise at highway speeds.

Comfort/Convenience

Pro: Despite its diminutive proportions, these cars will easily accommodate tall occupants in front. Standard seats are reasonably comfortable. All models come with a standard rear window wiper and washer. Convenient controls. The plunging hood, sweeping window glass, and thin side pillars give the interior an airy look that heightens visibility in all directions. Fairly large trunk for such a small car.

Con: The rear seat is a bit cramped on two-door models. Mediocre heating and ventilation. Some radios furnished by GM dealers are poorly calibrated, producing an irritating, tinny sound. The interior is quite noisy, due mainly to poor soundproofing and the car's small size.

COST

List Price (firm)	**Residual Values** (months)			
	24	**36**	**48**	**60**
Coupe: $11,495 (9%)	$6900	$6000	$5100	$4100

TECHNICAL DATA

Powertrain (front-drive)	**Dimensions** (coupe)
Engines: 1.0L 3 (55 hp)	Length: 149.4 in.
• 1.3L 4 (70 hp)	Width: 62.6 in.
	Wheelbase: 93.1 in.

Transmissions: 5-speed manual • 3-speed auto.

SAFETY FEATURES

	Opt.	Std.
Anti-lock brakes	■	❑
Childproof door locks*	❑	■
Driver-side airbag	❑	■
Passenger-side airbag	❑	■
Remote keyless entry	—	—
Traction control	❑	❑

* sedan only

Saturn

Saturn SW1

RATING: Above Average buy. Fair quality supported by superior servicing.

NEW FOR '97: Sedan and wagon: upgraded engine mounts promise less noise and vibration. Coupe: this year the coupe shares the sedan's 102-inch wheelbase, providing additional leg room, particularly in the rear. More effective silencing materials have been added forward of the dash, and the air inlet is redirected away from the passenger compartment. Upgraded seatbelts are less prone to trip up passengers trying to access the rear seat. Both the SC1 and SC2 use plastic body panels. The SC2 gets a front roll bar that's thicker than the SC1's.

GENERAL COMMENTS: Strict quality control at the factory level, posted sticker prices, no haggling over prices, and a 30-day money-back guarantee have all contributed to Saturn's sales success, but it has yet to make a profit from GM's $5-billion investment. Consequently, GM announced earlier this year that it will be merging Saturn's operations into one of its other operations. What this means is that General Motors is cutting Saturn's umbilical cord and will force the company to sink or swim depending on its own balance sheet. In other words, Saturn will henceforth be like all of GM's other car divisions.

Launched four years ago as an all-American effort to beat the Japanese in the small-car market, the Saturn compact was GM's first totally new car rated as being practically as reliable as the Japanese competition. Is almost as good as Toyota good enough? No, not when GM has its own Prizm, Suzuki, and other captive imports and hybrids to market at less cost and risk.

Nevertheless, the Saturn is a better car than GM's other homegrown compacts we've learned to be wary of over the past 20 years. Rust protection is maximized with the stainless-steel exhaust system and plastic body panels. Another positive step that should have been taken years ago is GM's offer of a complete refund or exchange if the buyer brings the car back within 30 days or 2400 km (a pro-rata deduction is made in the U.S. but not in Canada). So far, about 2 percent of owners have turned in their Saturns under this program. GM is so pleased that it has extended the buy-back to its U.S. Oldsmobile division. Marketing strategy is another improvement. Following Japanese pricing practice, the base Saturn comes with a wide range of standard equipment.

Cost analysis/Alternatives: The 1997 Saturns are virtually identical to the less expensive '96 versions, which are a real bargain if the selling price has been reduced sufficiently and the smaller interior and extra noise don't bother you. The Honda Civic LX and EX and Toyota Corolla perform well and offer better quality. The Corolla and Subaru Legacy/Impreza LS wagons are good wagon alternatives. **Rebates**: Not likely before mid-summer. **Destination charge**: $455. **Recommended options**: None. **Supplementary warranty**: A good idea in view of the Saturn's uncertain future at the hands of GM. **Parts supply/Servicing**: Above average. **Depreciation**: Below average. **Highway/City fuel economy**: 6-9L/100 km with the manual 5-speed and automatic transmission; the High Output engine adds another litre to the figure.

Reliability/Safety

Pro: Corrective repairs are usually carried out quickly, competently, and with a smile. Side body panels are made of rust-proof, dent-resistant polymer. Except for some cases of excessive engine vibration at idle and AC odour at startup, dealer service bulletins give the '96 Saturns a fairly good review. Paint quality and body assembly are much better than other Big Three competitors, but not up to Japanese car standards. According to the CAA, parts are reasonably priced, with heavy discounting by dealers. Crash tests of a 1996 Saturn SL2 sedan concluded that the driver and passenger would be well-protected in a 57 km/h frontal collision. It was rated: driver, ★★★★; passenger, ★★★★.

Con: Owners note some engine coolant and power steering leaks, premature brake wear, and excessive brake noise.

Reliability and dealer servicing have been overhyped, but why not? They're still much better than what you'll find among GM's other car divisions. You may be surprised to learn that Saturns aren't built that much better than other vehicles. It's just that when problems occur, they're dealt with quickly and repair costs are frequently covered by GM.

Saturn dealers say that GM is no longer as generous in paying warranty goodwill claims. They're worried that this may be a harbinger of a new "tough love" approach that's been urged by GM dealers in other divisions who are frustrated by the special treatment given Saturn customers. Another cloud on the horizon: if GM carries out its plan to merge Saturn with its other car divisions and add larger Saturn models to the lineup, it's unlikely that Saturn dealers and customers will get the same high level of service that Saturn ads profess.

Road Performance

Pro: The double-cam 1.9L powerplant is no neck-snapper, but it delivers fuel economy and performance as good as the best sedans and wagons in its class. The manual transmission lever is precise and easily shifted. The automatic has a useful performance setting. Steering is fairly precise and predictable, with plenty of assist and road feedback. Handling is impressive, particularly when it comes to emergency manoeuvres. The firm suspension gives a comfortable ride. Nimble handling with only a slight tendency to understeer. There's no torque steer because of the use of equal-length driveshafts. Impressive fuel economy, even when driven hard. Good braking.

Con: The base single-cam engine gives barely adequate acceleration times (12.2 seconds to reach 60 mph) with the manual transmission. This time is increased to a near glacial 13.7 seconds with the 4-speed automatic gearbox that robs the engine of what little power it produces. Engines are noisy at high revs. The 5-speed manual sometimes has trouble going into Reverse. Long clutch travel. Excessive automatic gearbox shudder when the kickdown is engaged while passing. Some wallowing in tight turns, and ride quality deteriorates if the car is loaded.

Comfort/Convenience

Pro: Interior trim is first class. Large glove box and convenient door pockets. Good radio performance. Comfortable front seats, with a fair amount of head and leg room. Excellent visibility in all directions. Excellent climate control system. The rear seats fold down 60/40 for cargo flexibility. Huge trunk also has a large opening and low liftover height. Very little engine noise at cruising speed.

Con: Steering wheel is too close for comfort. The rear is not the place to be—door sills are high, seat cushions are short and hard, and the seatbacks are too upright. Lots of road and wind noise.

COST

List Price (firm)	**Residual Values** (months)			
	24	**36**	**48**	**60**
SL sedan: $13,948 (10%)	$7900	$6700	$5900	$5100

TECHNICAL DATA

Powertrain (front-drive)
Engines: 1.9L inline 4 (100 h)
•1.9L 16-valve (124 hp)
Transmissions: 5-speed manual • 4-speed auto.

Dimensions (sedan/coupe)
Length: 176.8 in./173.2 in.
Width: 66.7 in./67.6 in.
Wheelbase: 102.4 in./99.2 in.

SAFETY FEATURES

	Opt.	Std.
Anti-lock brakes	■	❑
Childproof door locks	❑	■
Driver-side airbag	❑	■
Passenger-side airbag	❑	■
Remote keyless entry	■	❑
Traction control	—	—

Cavalier/Sunfire

Sunfire

RATING: An Above Average buy. Crash safety and quality control still need some improvement.

NEW FOR '97: Nothing that's significant. An RS trim level returns to the coupe, giving it a sportier look, and a ho-hum 2.2L powerplant. Convertible Sunfires get a standard 4-speed automatic transmission. An upgraded body structure meets U.S. government side-impact standards.

GENERAL COMMENTS: These twins are two of the lowest priced cars to come equipped with standard ABS and dual airbags. They have exceptional styling (especially the coupe) and lots of interior room, with a better-tuned suspension (making for an improved ride) than their predecessors. The ride and handling have also improved markedly over the past two years with power rack and pinion steering, a longer wheelbase, and wider track. The Sunfire is identical to the Cavalier, except for its more rakish look.

The Cavalier Z24/Sunfire GT are performance versions of the compacts introduced two years ago. They use a reworked version of the failure-prone Quad 4, 2.4L DOHC 16-valve 4-cylinder powerplant. GM promises that its past problems have been cured through the addition of a balance shaft for smoother engine performance and a longer operating life.

Cost analysis/Alternatives: Save money by purchasing the practically identical '96 version. Also consider buying a '96 Chrysler Spirit/Acclaim, Ford Taurus/Sable, Honda Civic, Mazda Protegé, or Nissan Stanza. **Rebates**: Not likely before mid-summer. **Destination charge**: $620. **Recommended options**: The suspension upgrade and air conditioning. If you want performance, the best combination is the 2.4L engine hooked to a 5-speed transmission. Of course, you'll have to deal with the engine's uncertain reliability. **Supplementary warranty**: A wise investment. **Parts supply/Servicing**: Above average. **Depreciation**: Average. **Highway/City fuel economy**: 6-10L/100 km with the 2.2L and manual 5-speed; 7-10L/100 km with the 2.2L and automatic 3-speed; 7.5-12L/100 km with the 2.4L and manual 5-speed; 7.5-11.5L/100 km with the 2.4L and automatic 4-speed.

Reliability/Safety

Pro: Overall reliability has been better than average. Maintenance on 4-cylinder models is reasonably straightforward and parts are easy to find. According to the CAA, parts are reasonably priced, with heavy discounting by dealers.

Con: The Quad 4 engine, despite its new refinements, has had a poor reliability history. Computer modules have also been one of the most common sources of complaints; symptoms include stalling and a shaky idle. Fuel-injection and cooling systems are temperamental as well. The power steering may lead or pull, and the steering rack tends to deteriorate quickly, usually requiring replacement sometime shortly after 80,000 km. The front MacPherson struts also wear out rapidly, as do the rear shock absorbers. Many owners complain of rapid front brake wear and warped brake discs after a year or so. Quality control is variable, often leading to poor paint application, inside and outside body panel gaps, and lots of exposed screw heads. Most body hardware is fragile.

Confidential dealer service bulletins list the following problems affecting the '96 models that could carry over to the '97s: loose door trim panels, faulty fuel tank filler door rest, interior water leaks, and excessive road noise heard from the rear quarter panel area, especially when the road is wet (see illustration below).

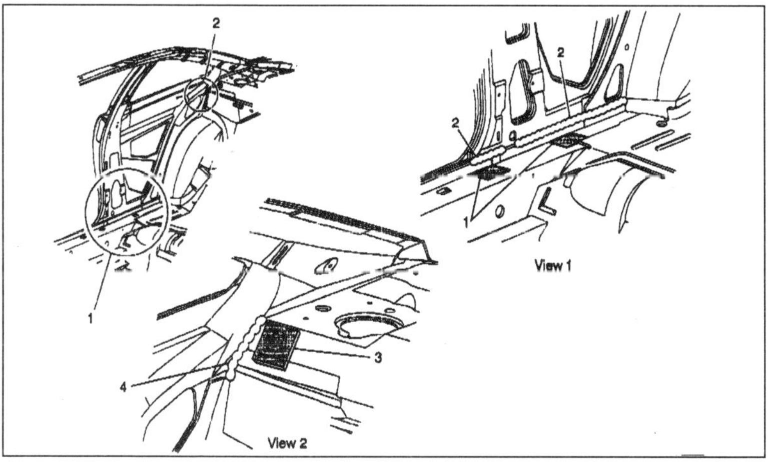

Excessive road noise can be silenced by installing "sound barriers" at these key locations.

Crash tests of a 1996 Chevrolet Cavalier dual airbag-equipped sedan concluded that the driver and passenger would get only average protection in a 57 km/h frontal collision. It was rated: driver, ★★★; passenger, ★★★. The lower control arm—which links the steering mechanism to the wheels—may lack a weld and this may cause a sudden steering loss. Dealers will inspect and repair the component for free.

Road Performance

Pro: The fuel injected 2.2L 4-cylinder engine provides adequate power when used with the manual transmission or the smoother, more responsive 4-speed automatic. The 150-hp 2.4L Quad 4 produces lots more torque, shaving 0-to-60 mph times by over a second (to 8 seconds). Models equipped with an optional suspension package offer the best handling at highway speeds and ride control on bad roads.

Con: When hooked to the 3-speed transaxle, the 2.2L 4-cylinder lacks sufficient power to distinguish these J-cars from the competition. The 5-speed manual transaxle has an abrupt clutch. The 3-speed automatic strains to get into the proper gear range. Base models don't handle or ride as well as most other vehicles do in this class. Power steering feels over-assisted, resulting in insufficient road feel. Standard tires corner poorly. Excessive brake distances.

Comfort/Convenience

Pro: Well laid-out dashboard and controls. Plenty of interior room. Quiet interior with improved defrosting. Quad 4 engine noise is reduced considerably. Good-sized trunk with a low liftover.

Con: Tall drivers may find the driving position a bit confining. Interior ventilation is feeble without the air-conditioning option. Lots of engine resonance invades the car's interior. Poor visibility (Z24).

COST

List Price (firm)	**Residual Values** (months)			
	24	**36**	**48**	**60**
Cavalier: $14,390 (11%)	$7900	$6500	$5500	$4700
Sunfire: $15,340 (11%)	8500	7100	6200	5400

TECHNICAL DATA

Powertrain (front-drive)
Engines: 2.2L injected 4 (120 hp) • 2.4L Quad 4 (150 hp)

Dimensions
Length: 180.3 in.
Width: 67.4 in.
Wheelbase: 104.1 in.

Transmissions: 5-speed manual • 3-speed auto. • 4-speed auto.

SAFETY FEATURES

	Opt.	Std.
Anti-lock brakes	❑	■
Childproof door locks	❑	■
Driver-side airbag	❑	■
Passenger-side airbag	❑	■
Remote keyless entry	■	❑
Traction control (LS)	—	—

('96) Corsica/Beretta

Corsica

RATING: Not Recommended. Gone, and best forgotten

NEW FOR '97: Nothing new; both cars will be dropped after the 1996 model year.

GENERAL COMMENTS: The Corsica and Beretta compacts sit on a front-wheel-drive platform that will seat four comfortably while providing decent ride and handling. The Beretta is a high-performance two-door, powered by a 2.2L 120-hp engine or optional 3.1L V6, and comes with a raft of performance and cosmetic extras. The GTZ has a shorter axle ratio for quicker acceleration.

From a performance and pricing perspective, these cars represented a small step in the right direction. Nevertheless, General Motors still has a long way to go to deliver the high level of assembly and materials quality found on similarly priced and equipped Japanese and European vehicles.

Cost analysis/Alternatives: The 1996 Corsica and Beretta may be a real bargain if the selling price is low enough. Other cars to consider are the Chrysler Spirit and Acclaim, Honda Accord, Mazda 626, or Toyota Camry. **Rebates**: $500 customer rebates on '96s. **Destination charge**: $620. **Recommended options**: You can still get hatchback convenience if you can find one of these cars that has the optional split folding rear seats. Stay away from the 4-banger hooked to the automatic transmission. The optional V6 powerplant provides more torque and is smoother and more reliable than the 4-cylinder version. **Supplementary warranty**: Essential if you want to save money in the long run. **Parts supply/Servicing**: Below average. **Depreciation**: Above average. **Highway/City fuel economy**: 7-10L/100 km with the 2.2L and automatic 3-speed; 8.5-10.3L/100 km with the 3.1L and automatic 4-speed; Beretta: 6-10L/100 km with the 3.1L and manual 5-speed.

Reliability/Safety

Pro: Parts are widely available at reasonable cost. Stainless-steel exhaust system.

Con: Long-term durability is a question mark, and GM isn't likely to invest more money for improvements since the cars have been dropped this year. Mechanical and body components aren't very reliable. The engines haven't proven themselves in the long term. Defective alternators, electronic engine modules, power-steering hoses, and power-steering pump pulleys are common problems. Many owners have complained about failing latches, numerous rattles and squeaks, and fragile interior hardware. The electronic engine computer is temperamental on the 3.1L engine, causing chronic stalling. Shock absorbers and MacPherson struts often begin leaking or go soft around 40,000 km. Body assembly is poor. Servicing is made difficult by the tight engine compartment. Expensive body parts.

Confidential GM bulletins show that 1996 models may have one or more of the following problems: AC odour upon startup, faulty power door locks and rear defogger, rattle between defroster grill and instrument panel, and interior water leaks.

Crash tests of a 1996 Corsica equipped with a driver-side airbag concluded that the driver and passenger would be poorly protected in a 57 km/h frontal collision. It was rated: driver, ★★★ (20 to 35 percent chance of serious injury); passenger, ★★ (35 to 45 percent chance of serious injury). These results also apply to the Beretta and Tempest. According to the U.S. Highway Loss Data Institute, 1989-91 Berettas had collision losses that were 31 percent higher than average. Traction control isn't available. The front brakes rust and wear out quickly, and there've been many complaints of sudden brake loss. No ABS-equipped model has been crash tested, but Transport Canada is investigating the excessive pedal effort required to stop these cars.

Road Performance

Pro: The 3.1L engine is the best choice for these cars. It has lots of reserve power and responds well to all driving conditions. Smooth-shifting transmission. Precise and predictable steering. The base suspension has been much improved this year, but the optional sport suspension option (standard on some models) offers better handling and a firm but comfortable ride.

Con: The 2.2L base powerplant is a disappointment when hooked to an automatic transmission. Its 110 horses quickly tire out on hills and when passing other vehicles. The automatic transmission is harsh and cuts into fuel economy when hooked to the 2.2L engine. Its lockup feature hesitates occasionally in city driving. Braking is a scary experience: ABS prevents the wheels from locking, but stopping distance and pedal effort are excessive.

Comfort/Convenience

Pro: Plenty of interior space and a much improved dash layout. Comfortable front seats. Good heating/defrosting and ventilation system. Large trunk. Reduced engine noise with the addition of dual-intake resonators.

Con: Exterior styling is boring and the interior is spartan at best. Dash instrumentation and layout are confusing, archaic, and cheap. Overall trim looks embarrassingly cheap. The driver's seat is set too low. Large adults will be cramped in back. Limited rear seat access in the Beretta. Poor support in rear seats. Climate controls are hard to see. Excessive wind and road noise intrusion into the interior. Seatbelts are most uncomfortable.

COST

List Price (negotiable)	**Residual Values** (months) 24	36	48	60
Corsica LT sedan: $17,685 (14%)	$9800	$8600	$7700	$5800
Beretta coupe: $17,275 (14%)	9500	8300	7300	5300

TECHNICAL DATA

Powertrain (front-drive)
Engines: 2.2L injected 4 (120 hp) • 3.1L injected V6 (155 hp)

Dimensions (Corsica/Beretta)
Length: 183.5 in./187.3 in.
Width: 68 in./67.9 in.
Wheelbase: 103.4 in./103.4 in.

Transmissions: 5-speed manual • 3-speed auto. • 4-speed auto.

SAFETY FEATURES

	Opt.	Std.
Anti-lock brakes	❑	■
Childproof door locks	—	—
Driver-side airbag	❑	■
Passenger-side airbag	—	—

Achieva, Grand Am, Skylark

Achieva

RATING: Acceptable. Quality control has improved, but long-term reliability is still a question mark.

NEW FOR '97: Minimal changes this year. Achieva gets a new traction control dash light, while the Skylark gets an improved headliner with passenger-assist handles, lighted visor vanity mirrors, a front-seat storage armrest, and a four-position manual seat adjuster. AC is standard on all Grand Ams. A compact sedan is scheduled to replace the Skylark and Grand Am in 1998.

GENERAL COMMENTS: The Achieva uses the Grand Am and Skylark platform, Quad 4 powerplant, and suspension. The base car uses a 150-hp Quad SOHC engine, a 5-speed transaxle, and ABS. The basic front-wheel-drive platform continues to be a refined version of the Sunbird and Cavalier J-body. These cars are too cramped to be family sedans, too sedate for sporty coupe status, and too ordinary for inclusion in luxury car ranks.

In their basic form, these cars are unreliable, unspectacular, and provide barely adequate performance. An upgraded and more reliable 3.1L V6 powerplant is available, but it gives you only five more horsepower than the Pontiac's four. There's been a lot of hype about the new Quad 4 16-valve engine, available with all models, but little of this translates into benefits for the average driver. Multi-valve motors produce more power than a standard engine, but always at higher rpms and with a fuel penalty. The Quad 4 is rougher than most multi-valve engines when revved to cruising speed, and so does little to encourage drivers to get the maximum power from it.

Cost analysis/Alternatives: The 1996 models are essentially identical to the more expensive '97 versions and are a real bargain if you can get them cheap enough. Other cars worth considering are the Chrysler Spirit/Acclaim, Eagle Talon, Ford Taurus/Sable, Honda Accord, Nissan Stanza, or Toyota Camry and Avalon. **Rebates**: $1500 rebate on the '96 Skylark; $750 for the '97 Skylark and Grand Am. **Destination charge**: $620. **Recommended options**: The best engine choice for power, smoothness, and value retention is the 155-hp 3.1L V6. Stay away from the Computer Command Ride option: true, it allows you to choose your own suspension setting, but the settings are not quite what they pretend to be. Also be wary of the infamous Quad 4 engine. **Supplementary warranty**: A good idea, particularly in view of these cars' past failings. **Parts supply/Servicing**: Below average. **Depreciation**: Average. **Highway/City fuel economy**: Skylark: 7.5-11.5L/100 km and 8.5-12.5L/100 km with the 3.1L; Achieva: 7.5-12L/100 km with the 2.4L and manual 5-speed, 7.5-11.5L/100 km with the 2.4L and automatic 4-speed, 7.5-12L/100 km with the 3.1L and automatic 4-speed; Grand Am: posted fuel figures similar to the Achieva's.

Reliability/Safety

Pro: The 4-speed automatic and 5-speed manual have had few major mechanical problems. The stainless-steel exhaust system is impervious to rust. Parts are available anywhere at reasonable prices, according to the CAA.

Crash tests of an airbag-equipped 1995 Oldsmobile Achieva concluded that the driver would be relatively well-protected in a 57 km/h frontal collision but that the passenger would sustain some injuries. It was rated: driver, ★★★★; passenger, ★★★. One may assume that the Grand Am and Skylark would do just as well.

Con: The Quad 4 has proven to be unreliable in the past and parts are often in short supply. Defective power-steering hoses and pump pulleys and electrical problems have been reported. Body assembly and paint application are substandard.

Confidential GM bulletins show that 1996 models, and possibly some '97s, may have one or more of the following (relatively minor) problems: engine overheating or inoperative cooling fan, AC odour upon startup, and a fuel filler door that won't open.

Road Performance

Pro: The Quad 4 runs a lot smoother than does the base engine. Acceleration is improved a bit with the 3.1L V6 engine, but it's no dazzler. The standard power steering is reasonably accurate, but it lacks road feel. Suspension improvements have made for better handling and have smoothed out the ride a bit, but an optional heavy-duty or sport suspension still makes a big difference. On the other hand, the Grand Am handles well even in standard form.

Con: The Quad 4 powerplant accentuates the harsh shifting of the 4-speed automatic; it's overeager to enter lockup mode in high gear, causing sluggish response in city driving. Poor fuel economy with the 3.1L engine. The manual transmission lacks precision. Soft springs make for lacklustre handling and a floaty ride, particularly during hard cornering. All these models have ride deficiencies: the base Buick and Oldsmobile are too softly sprung, tossing passengers about on bad roads, while the Grand Am and other models equipped with an upgraded suspension are a bit too firm. Even with ABS, braking is unimpressive.

Comfort/Convenience

Pro: The Skylark is the more remarkable of the N-cars for its interior and exterior styling. Well laid out, user-friendly dash and controls include round heater and air-conditioning knobs and rockers for radio controls, cup holders, and remote fuel-filler door and trunk releases. The Skylark's rear windows roll all the way down. Comfortable driving position. Efficient heating/defrosting and ventilation system. Well-proportioned trunk.

Con: Driver's seat is set too low. Limited interior and trunk space. Large occupants will find their rears pinched by the Grand Am's front seats. The rear seat is uncomfortable, even for just two adults. The doors on two-door models are heavy and awkward to open in tight spaces. The front seatbelts interfere with getting in and out. Excessive road/engine noise. Limited rear visibility. High trunk sill makes loading difficult.

COST

List Price (negotiable)	**Residual Values** (months) 24	36	48	60
Achieva S coupe: $20,735 (15%)	$10,800	$9500	$8200	$7300
Grand Am SE: $19,035 (13%)	9900	8700	7500	6500
Skylark coupe: $21,220(15%)	11,500	10,200	9000	8000

TECHNICAL DATA

Powertrain (front-drive)
Engines: 2.4L 16-valve 4 (150 hp) • 3.1L injected V6 (155 hp)

Dimensions (Skylark/Grand Am/ Achieva)
Length: 189.1 in./186.9 in./ 187.9 in.
Width: 67.5 in./67.5 in./67.2 in.
Wheelbase: 103.4 in. (all)

Transmissions: 5-speed manual • 4-speed auto.

SAFETY FEATURES

Achieva	**Opt.**	**Std.**
Anti-lock brakes	❑	■
Childproof door locks	■	❑
Driver-side airbag	❑	■
Passenger-side airbag	❑	■
Remote keyless entry	■	❑
Traction control	■	❑

Grand Am/ Skylark	**Opt.**	**Std.**
Anti-lock brakes	❑	■
Childproof door locks	❑	■
Driver-side airbag	❑	■
Passenger-side airbag	❑	■
Remote keyless entry	■	❑
Traction control	❑	■

Century/('96) Ciera

Ciera wagon

RATING: A Below Average buy. Mediocre performance and low quality.

NEW FOR '97: Ciera will be discontinued, while the Century moves over to the W platform that serves the Chevrolet Lumina, Pontiac Grand Prix, and 1998 Oldsmobile Intrigue. It will have some important improvements, including gobs of room and trunk space that rival the Taurus, Concorde, Accord, and Camry; sleeker styling; an incredibly quiet interior; and an upgraded, quieter, standard ABS system that produces minimal pedal pulsation. Engine noise has also been deadened. Other new features: the starter has an anti-grind feature in case you turn the key with the engine running, upgraded door seals, steering wheel mounted radio controls, and additional heating ducts for rear passengers.

On the downside, you can get only the 160 hp 3.1L V6 engine; the new Century's speed-dependent power steering is too light and vague; and its suspension and handling are more tuned to comfort than performance.

The Ciera has been replaced by the Olds Cutlass, a new midsize sedan similar to the new Malibu. Be careful not to confuse the new Cutlass with the Cutlass Supreme, a 10-year-old model that will be replaced next year by the Intrigue, which will be similarly equipped as the Century.

GENERAL COMMENTS: The A-body line, long a mainstay in GM's family sedan market, is quickly disappearing. This is good news, because these cars are outclassed by the competition and are in desperate need of high quality components and fresher styling. Overall quality has improved somewhat since the introduction of these cars in 1982, but with the arrival of the Ford Taurus eleven years ago and better-quality Japanese imports, these derivatives of the X-bodies aren't really in the running. Within the next two years they'll either be radically restyled or axed.

Cost analysis/Alternatives: The '96 Century isn't in the same league as the more expensive, revised '97 version. You'll probably find a cheaper '96 Ciera, but you won't have the important mechanical and body upgrades offered by its '97 replacement, the Cutlass. Consider the Acura Integra, Chrysler Spirit/Acclaim, Ford Taurus/Sable and Thunderbird/Cougar, Honda Accord, Nissan Stanza and Maxima, and Toyota Camry and Avalon. **Rebates**: $1500 customer rebate on the '96 Century until Dec. 31, 1996. 1996 Cieras will probably be eligible for a customer rebate in addition to the normal dealer incentive. **Destination charge**: $785. **Recommended options**: The rear-mounted child safety seat. **Supplementary warranty**: A must-have. **Parts supply/Servicing**: Below average. **Depreciation**: Average. **Highway/City fuel economy**: 8-13L/100 km with the 3.1L. Add an additional litre for the station wagon.

Reliability/Safety

Pro: Servicing can be performed by most neighbourhood mechanics. Crash tests of a 1996 Buick Century concluded that the driver and passenger would be relatively well-protected in a 57 km/h frontal collision. It was rated: driver, ★★★★; passenger, ★★★★. The '97 version hasn't been tested.

Con: The 3.1L V6 engine has had more than its share of fuel system and engine computer problems. The 4-speed automatic is easily damaged if left in Overdrive during prolonged city driving or when pulling heavy loads. Electrical system problems are common on cars loaded with power accessories. The front brakes wear out early and the discs warp far too easily. Shock absorbers and MacPherson struts wear out or leak prematurely. The power rack-and-pinion steering system degenerates quickly after three years and is characterized by chronic leaking. Poor body fit, particularly around the doors, leads to excessive wind noise and water leaks into the interior. Door locks freeze up easily.

Confidential GM bulletins show that '96 models, and possibly some '97s, may have a disagreeable AC odour upon startup and a noisy steering column (see below).

File in Section: 3 - Steering/Suspension
Bulletin No.: 56-32-02A
Date: April 1996
Subject:
Intermittent Steering Column Snap or Click Noise when Turning (Install New Upper Bearing Spring)
Models:
1994-96 Buick Century, LeSabre, Park Avenue, Regal, Roadmaster
1995-96 Buick Riveria
1994-96 Cadillac Concours, DeVille, Eldorado, Fleetwood, Seville
1994-96 Chevrolet Camaro, Caprice, Corvette, Lumina. Lumina APV
1995-96 Chevrolet Monte Carlo
1994-96 Oldsmobile Cutlass Ciera, Cutlass Supreme, Eighty Eight, Ninety Eight, Silhouette
1995-96 Oldsmobile Aurora
1994-96 Pontiac Bonneville, Firebird, Grand Prix, Trans Sport with Tilt Steering Columns
1995-96 Chevrolet and GMC C/K, M/L, S/T Models with Tilt Steering Columns
This bulletin is being revised to add the passenger cars and update parts information. Please discard Corporate Bulletin Number 56-32-02 (Section 3 - Steering/Suspension).
Condition
Some owners may comment on an intermittent steering column snap or click noise while turning. The snapping or clicking may also be felt in the steering wheel.
Cause
The upper bearing race seat may, under some turning conditions, move in an axial direction along the upper steering shaft. The noise is a result of the inner race seat hanging up on the shaft and then suddenly releasing causing a snapping or clicking noise.
Correction
A new upper bearing spring with increased stiffness has been developed and should be installed in the steering column. The new spring will increase the preload between the upper bearing inner race seat and the upper steering shaft. To accommodate the new spring with increased stiffness, the cancel cam will also need to be replaced. The new spring and cancel cam, along with a retainer ring and an upper bearing inner race seat are included in the parts kit listed below.

Excessive steering noise affects almost all of GM's product line.

Road Performance

Pro: The 3.1L V6 engine produces sufficient power for smooth acceleration and works well with the 4-speed automatic transmission. Predictable handling. Highway ride is a bit floaty, but comes into its own on winding roads.

Con: With the V6 power you also get some unwanted noise intrusion into the interior. Handling and ride are sloppy and bumpy without a heavy-duty or sport suspension. Otherwise, passengers get tossed about on bumpy roads. Undersized, original-equipment tires compromise handling. The over-assisted power steering gives little road feel. Excessive body lean when cornering under power. The ABS brakes are hard to modulate and sometimes lock up, causing long stopping distances and some loss of directional stability.

Comfort/Convenience

Pro: The cockpit area is much more user friendly, with improved instrumentation and easy to read gauges and controls. A tilt steering wheel is standard. Front seats are fairly comfortable. Rear seats have enough space for three adults. The wagons add an optional third seat, and can seat six to eight adults. The sedans have large trunks. Excellent heating/defrosting/ventilation system.

Con: Luxury models use tacky imitation wood and cheap cloth covers. Large decklid hinges reduce space further in the right and left front corners. Cramped rear leg room. Absence of interior storage areas. High trunk sill makes for difficult loading and unloading.

COST

List Price (negotiable)	**Residual Values** (months)			
	24	**36**	**48**	**60**
'96 Century Special: $23,820 (13%)	$12,500	$10,500	$9300	$8300
'96 Ciera S sedan: $23,625 (16%)	11,800	10,800	9900	9000

TECHNICAL DATA

Powertrain (front-drive)
Engine: 3.1L injected V6 (160 hp)
Transmission: 4-speed auto.

Dimensions (Century/Ciera)
Length: 190.9 in./193.2 in.
Width: 69.4 in./69.5 in.
Wheelbase: 104.9 in./104.9 in.

SAFETY FEATURES

Century	Opt.	Std.
Anti-lock brakes	❑	■
Childproof door locks	—	—
Driver-side airbag	❑	■
Passenger-side airbag	❑	■
Remote keyless entry	■	❑
Traction control	—	—

Ciera	Opt.	Std.
Anti-lock brakes	❑	■
Childproof door locks	—	—
Driver-side airbag	❑	■
Passenger-side airbag	—	—
Remote keyless entry	❑	■

Cutlass Supreme, Grand Prix, Lumina, Monte Carlo, Regal

Regal

RATING: Not Recommended. Different bodies but the same poor quality components.

NEW FOR '97: Supreme: no more high-performance, 3.4L twin-cam V6; it'll be replaced by the '98 Intrigue in the spring of next year. Grand Prix: the new sport sedan, cousin to the Buick Century and Olds Intrigue, comes as a two- or four-door model and is powered by the Chevy Lumina's 3.1L V6 and an optional 3.8L V6—or supercharged variation—borrowed from the Pontiac Bonneville. Larger brakes, upgraded power steering, a two-inch longer body, a three-inch longer wheelbase, and a two-inch wider track. Lumina and Monte Carlo: all versions of Luminas equipped with the 3.1L V6 engine get an upgraded rear stabilizer bar with revised spring rates for a smoother ride. An LTZ trim package debuts, offering a standard 3.1L V6 and an optional 3.4L V6, rear spoiler, sporty side mouldings, and larger aluminum wheels. LS and LTZ versions get a sunroof option, solar-control front and rear windshield glass, and a leather-wrapped steering wheel with radio controls. Regal: essentially a '96 model carryover, next summer GM will launch a redesigned '98 Regal, based on the W platform shared with Lumina, Grand Prix, Century, and the 1998 Intrigue.

GENERAL COMMENTS: These cars are identical, except for some sheet metal variations, and are set to replace the aging A-bodies (Century and Ciera) as GM's prime family movers. They also represent a change in philosophy. The automotive giant used to design one platform and have each division sell a version of it. Very often, the cars looked and felt nearly identical, making customers wonder why they had to pay more for a Buick than an equivalent Chevrolet. Now, each car has been given a slightly different exterior appearance and a distinct "personality." The Buick version is aimed at the older, more traditional buyer who wants safety, comfort, and luxury first; the Cutlass Supreme strives for a "sophisticated" look with its swoopy body and 3.4L engine; the Grand Prix offers a new sport sedan, with an optional engine upgrade and all the high performance accoutrements. On the other Gran Prix models, stylish colours and aluminum wheels, and an LE sedan with STE styling, all contribute to Pontiac's performance image.

A 3.1L V6 is the standard engine, while the 3.4L DOHC V6 and 3.8L V6 power are the more upscale versions. These cars are pleasant to drive and provide comfortable accommodation for four people. The Buick is a throwback to the mid-1970s in road feel, as well as interior decor.

The Lumina and Monte Carlo are popular two- and four-door versions of Chevy's mid-size cars, featuring standard dual airbags, ABS, and 160-hp V6 power. The Monte Carlo is the Lumina's coupe twin that was formerly sold as the Lumina Z34. Powertrain enhancements have increased horsepower and fuel efficiency. Engine performance is also smoother and quieter, thanks to the addition of dual hydraulic engine mounts. Although styling is rather plain, a more rigid body structure, thicker side windows, and additional soundproofing material have reduced interior rattles as well as wind and road noise. **Lumina alternatives**: Ford Taurus, Honda Accord, and Toyota Camry. **Monte Carlo alternatives**: Honda Accord coupe, Ford Thunderbird and Taurus, and Toyota Camry.

Cost analysis/Alternatives: The 1997 models much improved when compared with the '96 versions. As alternatives, consider the Ford Taurus/Sable, Honda Accord, Mazda 626, and Toyota Camry and Avalon. **Rebates**: '96 Grand Prix: $800; Regal: $1500. **Destination charge**: $785. **Recommended options**: Braking is the pits on these cars without ABS, so spring for the $500 or so extra cost. The sunroof option isn't a good idea if you're taller than 5'11". **Supplementary warranty**: A good idea. **Parts supply/Servicing**: Average. **Depreciation**: Average. **Highway/City fuel economy**: Cutlass Supreme: 8-13L/100 km; Grand Prix: 8-13L/100 km; Lumina: 8-13L/100 km; Monte Carlo: 8-13L/100 km; Regal: 8-13L/100 km and 9-14.5L/100 km with the High Output engine.

Reliability/Safety

Pro: These cars have benefited from GM's mistakes on earlier models and appear to be assembled with more care. Still, their overall reliability is below Ford front-drives and Japanese competitors. Parts are relatively inexpensive and easy to find.

A 1992 two-door Regal provided excellent crash protection. Crash tests of a 1996 Grand Prix equipped with dual airbags concluded that the driver would be well-protected in a 57 km/h frontal collision, while the passenger would receive average protection. It was rated: driver, ★★★★; passenger, ★★★. Similar tests of a 1996 Lumina sedan concluded that the driver and passenger would be fairly well protected. It was rated: driver, ★★★★★; passenger, ★★★★. Tests of a 1996 Monte Carlo showed that the driver and passenger would also be fairly well protected. It was rated: driver, ★★★★; passenger, ★★★★.

Con: In spite of some noise reduction progress, body construction is still below par with loose door panel mouldings, poorly fitted door fabric, and misaligned panels. Other common problems: frequent stalling, vague steering, premature paint peeling on the hood and trunk, heavy accumulation of hard-to-remove brake dust inside the honeycomb design wheels, and front tires that scrape the fenders when the wheel is turned. The redesigned 3.8L V6 (3800 TPI) engine is difficult to service due to its highly sophisticated fuel system and difficult-to-diagnose electronic controls. In spite of its own recent redesign, the 3.1L engine isn't entirely problem-free. Electronic fuel-injection systems and engine controls have created many problems for GM owners. The 4-speed automatic transmission still has bugs. The front brakes wear quickly, as do the MacPherson struts and shock absorbers. Steering assemblies tend to fail prematurely. The electrical system is temperamental. The sunroof motor is failure-prone. Owners report water leaks from the front windshield. Front-end squeaks may require the replacement of the exhaust manifold pipe springs with dampers.

Confidential GM bulletins show that '96 models, and possibly some '97s, may have a disagreeable AC odour upon startup, excessive noise when accelerating or driving up medium grades, a front suspension popping noise, a noisy steering column, and interior water leaks.

Crash tests of a 1994 Buick Regal concluded that the airbag-protected driver would have good protection, while the passenger would sustain serious head injuries. It was rated: driver, ★★★★; passenger, ★. Some '96 Luminas and Monte Carlos have been recalled to inspect and correct a faulty brake booster tab.

Road Performance

Pro: The 3.1L V6 is the engine of choice for reliability, but it doesn't have enough grunt to handle all highway situations (particularly passing power). The 3.8L powerplant is smoother and more powerful, but reliability and long-term durability still haven't been nailed down. The 3.4L motor runs well and dealer service bulletins don't show any serious problems. An upgraded rear suspension on the Lumina and Monte Carlo two years ago has made considerable improvements to both ride and handling under either a light or full load.

Con: The 4-speed automatic occasionally has less trouble choosing the right gear with this year's refinements, but it's still a bit quirky. Highway handling is sloppy on base models. A fully loaded car causes the back end to sag and makes for a poor ride. The ride is firm and hyperactive on bumpy roads, especially in the Grand Prix. ABS brakes control directional stability by preventing wheel lockup, but take an unacceptably long time to work under normal conditions.

Comfort/Convenience

Pro: Spacious interior has more room than the Taurus/Sable. Cockpit area is much more ergonomically oriented. The comfortable front bench seats will accommodate just about anyone. Good visibility. Quiet interior. Interior controls are fairly user friendly, but some instrument panel gauges are hard to read. On the Grand Prix SE, useful convenience features include radio controls in the steering wheel, remote keyless entry, and a switch for 2nd gear starts in inclement weather. Large trunk.

Con: The Grand Prix sports sedan's head room has been sacrificed to give the car a sleeker appearance. Uncomfortable driving position without the optional power seat, and the bucket seats are best suited for bucket bottoms. The low-cut side bolstering leaves much of the back unsupported. The seat can't be lowered sufficiently to prevent your head from touching the roof. The interior is too "space age," with omnipresent small buttons and paddle switches that are distracting and difficult to fiddle with, particularly when adjusting the AC system. Instruments and controls are fussy, poorly laid out, and fragile. Getting in and out of this car takes real effort and determination, particularly due to the heavy, stiff front doors. The rear seat is not very comfortable; getting into it is a chore, and there's marginal room for adults. Mediocre heating/defrosting.

COST

List Price (negotiable)	**Residual Values** (months)			
	24	**36**	**48**	**60**
Cutlass Supreme: $25,855 (17%)	$15,800	$13,800	$12,000	$10,800
Grand Prix SE: $26,305 (18%)	16,500	14,800	13,100	12,000
Lumina: $22,340 (16%)	13,500	12,100	11,000	9500
Monte Carlo: $24,275 (18%)	14,300	13,500	11,600	10,300
'96 Regal Custom: $25,035 (19%)	15,300	13,300	11,500	10,300

TECHNICAL DATA

Powertrain (front-drive)
Engines: 3.1L injected V6 (160 hp) • 3.4L injected V6 (215 hp) • 3.8L injected V6 (195 hp) • 3.8L supercharged V6 (240 hp)
Transmission: 4-speed auto.

Dimensions (Lumina/Regal)
Length: 200.9 in./193.7 in.
Width: 72.5 in./72.5 in.
Wheelbase: 107.5 in./107.5 in.

SAFETY FEATURES

	Opt.	Std.
Anti-lock brakes	❑	■
Childproof door locks	❑	■
Driver-side airbag	❑	■
Passenger-side airbag	❑	■
Remote keyless entry	■	❑

88, Bonneville, LeSabre

88 Royale

RATING: Not Recommended. These luxurious family sedans are outclassed by more reliable and better-performing competitors.

NEW FOR '97: Nothing much new. 88: a front bench seat fold-down storage arm and additional overhead handles for easier entry/exit. Bonneville: the supercharged engine gets an improved electronically-controlled four-speed automatic transaxle with smoother, quieter shifting and an upgraded power steering assembly. LeSabre: a restyled exterior last January gave the '97 LeSabre a smoother look.

GENERAL COMMENTS: Set on a modified Seville/Eldorado platform, these large, front-wheel-drive sedans represent the state of the art in GM's concept of family motoring, which in turn exemplifies the malaise afflicting the company these days. The LeSabre is the bargain of the group. It offers all the technical features of the more expensive Park Avenue but in a smaller package. The 88 Royale is the best-looking car of the bunch, and it performs quite well with the 3.8L V6. Pontiac continues this year to break away from the pack by offering its stylish Bonneville SSE to those buyers who want more bark and bite.

The SSEi uses the same supercharged 240-hp 3.8L engine that powers the Buick Ultra.

Although the interiors will seat six in a pinch, and the decor is suitably "upscale," these large cars still feel as though they got stuck in the 1970s when conservative styling, uninspiring handling, and a floaty, cushiony, extra-quiet ride were the norm. The Bonneville SSE interior is stylish without a lot of steering wheel mounted controls, and its dash layout makes for easy reading of the gauges and controls. A retuned 3800 TPI 3.8L V6 engine and electronically controlled 4-speed transmission form the base drivetrain for all models.

Cost analysis/Alternatives: The 1996 models are essentially identical to the more expensive '97 versions, and are a real bargain if the selling price has been reduced sufficiently. The Olds 88 Royale LS and Bonneville SE with a V6 and optional sport suspension are cheaper alternatives to the Bonneville SSEi. Other cars worth considering include Ford Taurus/Sable, Crown Victoria, and Lincoln Town Car. **Rebates**: $750 on the '96 Bonnevilles. These slow sellers generally get $1500 rebates toward the end of the year. When dealer incentives are added next fall, you could double that figure. **Destination charge**: $895. **Recommended options**: Stay away from the optional digital cluster—all you get are large digital read-outs and bar graphs. You must buy the optional firmer suspension to counteract the base suspension's unsettling jiggle. It includes quicker-ratio steering, firmer shocks, thicker sway bars, and high-performance Goodyear tires. **Supplementary warranty**: Essential for a car this expensive. **Parts supply/Servicing**: Below average. The LeSabre's accident repair costs are much lower than average. **Depreciation**: Below average. **Highway/City fuel economy**: 88: 8.5-14L/100 km and 9-14.5L/100 km with the High Output engine; Bonneville: 8.5-14L/100 km and 9-14.5L/100 km with the High Output engine; LeSabre: 8-13L/100 km.

Reliability/Safety

Pro: Comprehensive roadside assistance warranty. The failure-prone Quad 4 engine has been replaced by the smoother and more powerful 3.8 V6 engine. Crash tests of a 1996 Bonneville concluded that the driver would have excellent protection in a 57 km/h frontal collision, while the passenger would receive average protection. It was rated: driver, ★★★★★; passenger, ★★★. Test results for a Buick LeSabre indicate that the front passenger would be well-protected; data was inconclusive for the driver.

Con: If consumer complaints can be believed, most people who bought one of these cars wish they hadn't—overall reliability has hovered between average and below average. The electronic controls and sequential fuel-injection system are unreliable. The electrical system in general is plagued by an alarming frequency of short circuits and other failures, and it's difficult to troubleshoot. Front shock absorbers and steering assembly are likely to wear out quickly. Body hardware is fragile. Many mechanics, including GM's own, find the underhood systems a mystery—even when there's no problem. Paint application is substandard.

Confidential GM bulletins show that all three 1996 models, and possibly some '97s, may exhibit the following problems: an AC odour upon startup, excessive noise when accelerating or driving up medium grades, a front suspension popping noise, wind noise at the lower front moveable glass area, and poor appearance or retention of the header portion of the glass runner channel on front and rear doors. 88 and LeSabre: whistling from the heater and AC system.

Road Performance

Pro: The base 3.8L V6 engine is quiet, smooth, and relatively more economical than some competitive V6 powerplants. It provides lots of power through the lower gear ranges, but runs out of steam as it gets to the top end of its power curve. Smooth and quiet shifting with the 4-speed automatic. Quiet ride on smooth roads. The Olds' suspension is calibrated more on the firm side than most cars in this class. One major improvement: you can leave the car in Overdrive and drive around town without the transmission constantly shifting up and down.

Con: The power steering transmits very little road feel and highway handling is clumsy, particularly when cornering. Excessive body lean in corners. The ride deteriorates rapidly as the suspension bottoms out on rough roads. This effect is made worse as the passenger and cargo load increases. The Bonneville SSE handles well but rides harshly for such a large car.

Comfort/Convenience

Pro: User-friendly instruments, climate-control system, and radio. Improved climate controls and a higher efficiency AC compressor provide excellent ventilation. The Bonneville has a well designed, though busy, dashboard. Climate controls provide different temperature settings for either side of the car. Good driving position if your buttocks fit the predefined indents. The 88's aerodynamic lines are cleaner and use little chrome trim. A more pleasing and practical half-eyebrow dash copies that of the Japanese and European automakers. There's plenty of rear seat leg room, thanks to the limited rearward travel of the front seats. The interior feels spacious and airy. Large trunk. Long objects can be passed from the trunk through the rear seat armrest port. The SSEi's trunk contains a road emergency kit and a trunk-mounted air compressor.

Con: Styling is fairly bland, except for the 88 and Bonneville. Limited rear travel on the front seats can put the driver too close to the steering wheel. The optional power seat is essential for a comfortable driving position. Be wary of GM's claims of a six-passenger carrying capacity; only four passengers will ride in comfort. Rear seats offer little thigh support and aren't sufficiently padded. Front quarter windows don't open.

COST

List Price (negotiable)	**Residual Values** (months) 24	36	48	60
88 LS: $32,185 (21%)	$17,300	$15,300	$12,900	$11,000
Bonneville SSE: $36,030 (22%)	20,000	17,600	15,500	13,500
LeSabre Custom: $32,370 (19%)	17,500	15,900	13,700	11,700

TECHNICAL DATA

Powertrain (front-drive)
Engines: 3.8L V6 (205 hp)
• 3.8L V6 supercharged (240)
Transmission: 4-speed auto.

Dimensions (Bonneville/LeSabre)
Length: 199.5 in./200 in.
Width: 74.5 in./74.9 in.
Wheelbase: 110.8 in./110.8 in.

SAFETY FEATURES

	Opt.	Std.
Anti-lock brakes	❑	■
Childproof door locks	❑	■
Driver-side airbag	❑	■
Passenger-side airbag	❑	■
Remote keyless entry	❑	■
Traction control	■	❑

SAAB

No one can accuse GM of opportunism in buying Saab for $600 million in late 1989—just before the Swedish automaker announced a $380-million operating loss for that year, followed by stunning 1990-91 losses exceeding a billion dollars. North American sales fell 30.7 percent during the first half of 1993, despite the huge effort put into attractive leasing and low financing deals. In 1994 Saab made a small profit for the first time since GM bought the company, and in 1995 it earned a profit of $22.3 million. Unfortunately, these profits were wiped out when sales plunged for the first quarter of 1996, causing a pretax loss of $50.15 million—more than double what it had earned for the entire previous year. Saab says that it will stay in the red for all of 1996, and has petitioned GM to inject more money to help it sell new products already in the pipeline.

Saab's growth has been undeniably slowed by increased competition from European and Japanese luxury sedans that are more smartly styled, have greater market penetration than the rather dated 900 and 9000, and are marketed through attractive and innovative leasing plans that Saab is only beginning to adopt.

What's so special about Saabs? Their unusual, aerodynamic styling is (to put it mildly) distinctive; passenger comfort is unbeatable; and they handle very well with precise steering and lots of road feel. Unfortunately, a lot of less expensive cars offer just as much road performance and are more reliable and easier to repair.

Saab's much ballyhooed '93 redesign was carried out to increase performance and raise quality control. However a leaked Saab video, which aired on Swedish TV earlier this year, says that neither goal was achieved. The video outlines the problem areas, which include brakes that may weaken when wet. Saab officials confirmed that the car had defects from the start and is still rife with them.

Peter Moeller, Saab's technical development chief, told the Swedish press shortly after the story aired that "we were extremely pressed when we developed this model. We anticipate that customers will feel the '95 model will be close to average in quality." Moeller may be right, judging from the few problems addressed in '96 service bulletins. On the other hand, U.S. and Canadian safety investigators have been probing an unusual number of safety-related complaints targeting the 1995-96 Saab 900 and 9000 models.

900 Series

900 Coupe

RATING: Not Recommended. Good highway performer; poor servicing backup.

NEW FOR '97: Bigger brakes, an upgraded gearshift mechanism, new wheels (on the 900S and SE), and minor interior changes. Next year the 900 gets a wider stance, a restyled rear end, and a new grille and headlamps.

GENERAL COMMENTS: Like the Volvo 850, the front-wheel-drive Saab 900 is a carefully evolved version of a model that was launched over 20 years ago. Unlike Volvo's boxy and upright sedans, the Saab counterparts offer a look that's been unique since the day they were first put on the market. Primarily an airplane builder, Saab has always laid strong emphasis on aerodynamics. This is why the older Saabs such as the 900 have always looked as though they were drawn by someone other than an automotive artist dedicated to style over function.

Three engines are offered with the 900 series: a 2.3L 16-valve 150-hp powerplant; a 2.0L 185-hp turbo 4-cylinder; and, for drivers wanting good overall performance without the extra turbocharging hardware, a 2.5L 170-hp V6. The base 4-banger is smooth and almost as fast as the V6, and it provides good fuel economy to boot. The turbo version is a bit slower than the V6 and exacts a heavy fuel penalty.

These models feature a number of impressive safety features, including dual airbags, standard ABS, an ignition key that's still located on the floor (Saab believes that a little inconvenience is worth a saved kneecap), integrated child safety seats built into both outboard rear positions (borrowed from Chrysler minivans and made by Magna in Ontario), and three-point rear seatbelts.

Cost analysis/Alternatives: The 1996 900 is essentially identical to the more expensive '97, therefore you'd do well buying last year's Saab and investing the savings in an extended warranty if you plan to keep the car after the base warranty expires. Saabs depreciate much more quickly now that GM has bought the company, so if you plan to keep it for only a few years and don't want to lose much money through depreciation, choose the 900 drop-top (a '92 convertible is worth $18,500, almost half its original value), or some other car or multipurpose vehicle (minivan van, sport-utility, or pickup) that's likely to keep its value. Both the 4- and 6-cylinder engines provide lots of power along with sporty handling, but there are cheaper cars that offer the same level of performance at lower prices. Other cars worth considering are the BMW 3-series, Ford Taurus/Sable, Lexus ES 300, Mazda Millenia, and Toyota Avalon. **Rebates**: $1500 for the base '96 900 series; $2000 for the '96 convertible. **Destination charge**: $770. **Recommended options**: Traction control. If you get the sunroof, be prepared to lose lots of head room. **Supplementary warranty**: Essential for a car this expensive and served by a weak and warring dealer network. **Parts supply/Servicing**: Below average. **Depreciation**: Average to above average. For example, a 1994 900S sedan, selling originally for $30,578, will now fetch about $17,000 as a dealer trade-in. **Highway/City fuel economy**: 8-12L/100 km. The turbo models add about two litres to city driving.

Reliability/Safety

Pro: The 900s have an acceptable reliability record that's comparable to Volvo's. The non-turbocharged 2.0L engine and the manual transmission have proven to be quite reliable. Saab owners report numerous automatic transmission failures and electrical, brake, and exhaust-system problems. Seals and gaskets will often leak prematurely. The turbocharger will self-destruct if special maintenance isn't followed, although Saab turbo units at most times have an excellent reputation. Body hardware complaints are common.

Both the driver and passenger were judged to be well-protected in government crash tests of a 1996 two-door 900. It was given a ★★★★ rating. Night driving dash distractions are reduced with the aircraft-inspired Black Panel, which shuts down all instrument panel lights except for the speedometer. Rear head restraints are stylish and effective.

Con: Owners report multiple electrical problems, poor quality body hardware, automatic transmission and other powertrain failures, and premature disc brake wear. Parts are moderately expensive and servicing is a major liability (the dealership network is spotty and relatively inexperienced) due to GM's inept administration of its Saab franchises. GM threw out many Saab dealers when it bought the company, and gave the Saab franchise to inexperienced Passport dealers who serviced primarily Isuzus. After fielding a deluge of customer complaints, GM realized this was a mistake two years ago, closed one-third of its 60 dealerships, and is now trying to lure back disgruntled former Saab franchisees. Many of them, though, are fed up with what they call GM's "duplicity," and have taken GM to court for unjust termination. No wonder service quality remains the weakest link in GM's Saab connection in Canada.

Road Performance

Pro: Smooth acceleration with all engines. Versatile automatic transmission has setting for Normal, Sport, and Winter driving conditions, allowing the driver to start out in third gear for more traction in the Winter setting. Good high-speed cornering with minimal body roll and plowing.

Steering is sensitive and precise at cruising speed. Effective traction control system. Good braking on wet and dry pavement, with no loss of directional control or fading after successive stops.

Con: Busy dash/climate controls. Considerable turbo lag. Steering is ponderous in city driving and sudden acceleration produces serious torque steer (twisting). Too much wheelspin without traction control. Stiff ride becomes uncomfortable over rough terrain.

Comfort/Convenience

Pro: Excellent driving position and comfortable front seating. Seats can be adjusted and settings memorized for three different drivers. Leather upholstery and seat heaters are a nice touch. Climate control system performs flawlessly. Above average front and rear access. Quiet interior. Lots of trunk space, particularly with the rear seatbacks folded down. Snug convertible top is a breeze to operate.

Con: Only two adults can sit comfortably in the rear because of the limited head room and flat cushions. Some road and wind noise intrudes into the interior. Some squeaks and rattles (surprising in a European car this expensive).

COST

List Price (negotiable)	**Residual Values** (months)			
	24	**36**	**48**	**60**
900S: $29,900 (21%)	$15,000	$13,000	$11,000	$ 9500
Convertible: $47,500 (28%)	22,200	20,000	18,000	15,000

TECHNICAL DATA

Powertrain (front-drive)
Engines: 2.3L injected 4 (150 hp) • 2.5L V6 (170 hp) • 2.0L Turbo 4 (185 hp)
Transmissions: 5-speed manual • 4-speed auto.

Dimensions
Length: 182.6 in.
Width: 67.4 in.
Wheelbase: 102.4 in.

SAFETY FEATURES

	Opt.	Std.
Anti-lock brakes	❑	■
Childproof door locks	❑	■
Driver-side airbag	❑	■
Passenger-side airbag	❑	■
Remote keyless entry	❑	■
Traction control	❑	■

9000 Series

9000

RATING: Not Recommended. A higher price doesn't buy better reliability or servicing.

NEW FOR '97: A new sedan, with a possible name change, will make its debut early in the new year.

GENERAL COMMENTS: Roomier and more conventionally styled than the 900, the upscale 9000 returns this year relatively unchanged. The base turbocharged 2.3L engine powering the CS comes in three variants, reaching a maximum of 225 hp, while the 3.0L engine does very well with 15 fewer horses. Traction control can be turned on or off. Styling changes have produced a more aerodynamic front end, in addition to many interior and exterior refinements.

Saab's Ecopower base engine is competent, handling is first rate, and anti-lock braking inspires confidence. The interior is exceptionally well laid out, with every inch of space used to functional advantage. This creates an extremely quiet, luxurious, aviation-type cockpit that will hold five passengers in remarkable comfort.

All of this luxury comes at a very high price—one that's not easy to justify by name and performance alone.

Cost analysis/Alternatives: The 1996 9000 is essentially identical to the more expensive '97, and represents the better buy. The new sedan may be launched as a '98 model, and is a risky buy during its first year on the market judging by the many first-year problems these cars encountered the last time they were revamped. Both the 4- and 6-cylinder engines provide lots of power along with sporty handling, but there are cheaper cars that offer the same level of performance at lower prices. Other cars worth considering are the BMW 3-series, Ford Taurus/Sable, Lexus ES 300, Mercedes 300 series, Mazda Millenia and 929, Nissan Maxima, Toyota Avalon, and Volvo 900 series. **Rebates**: $2000 dealer incentive. **Destination charge**: $770. **Recommended options**: Traction control. **Supplementary warranty**: A wise investment. **Parts supply/Servicing**: Below average. **Depreciation**: Average. For example, a 1994 900S sedan, selling originally for $30,578, will now fetch about $17,000 as a dealer trade-in. (A 1994 9000 Aero, selling originally for $45,995, will now fetch about $30,000 as a dealer trade-in.) **Highway/City fuel economy**: 8-12L/100 km. The turbo models add about two additional litres to city driving.

Reliability/Safety

Pro: The 9000 series has only an average reliability history. A 1993 airbag-equipped four-door Saab 9000 provided excellent injury protection for the driver and front passenger in the U.S. government's 57 km/h frontal crash tests. Rear head restraints are stylish and effective. In emergencies, the standard Bosch ABS-3 anti-lock brakes stop the sedan in an impressively short distance without the brakes pulsating as they do in other ABS systems.

Con: GM/Saab dealers can't handle cars this complex, and competitive vehicles are more reliable. As with the 900 series, major problem areas are multiple electrical problems, poor-quality body hardware, automatic transmission failures, and premature disc brake wear. Dealer servicing has been substandard and is likely to get worse as these cars age and dealer/GM relations continue to erode.

Road Performance

Pro: All engines provide plenty of power and smooth acceleration, without the turbo lag that's common with most turbocharged engines. Normal, Sport, and Winter transmission settings are convenient and effective. Good high-speed cornering with minimal body roll. Steering is sensitive and precise at cruising speed. Effective traction control system. Good braking on wet and dry pavement. Firm, controlled ride doesn't deteriorate as the load increases.

Con: Stiff, uncomfortable ride. Without the optional traction control found on the Aero, the 9000 tends to spin its wheels when accelerating from a stop.

Comfort/Convenience

Pro: Excellent driving position and comfortable front seating. Seats can be adjusted for different drivers. Leather upholstery and seat heaters are nice touches. Above-average front and rear access. Quiet interior. Lots of trunk space, particularly with the rear seatbacks folded down.

Con: Front seats could use additional lateral support. Automatic climate system makes for cold feet in the winter. If you turn up the heat, hot air blows in your face while your feet remain cold. Inadequate air recirculation. Only two adults can sit comfortably in the rear.

COST

List Price (negotiable)	**Residual Values** (months)			
	24	**36**	**48**	**60**
9000CS: $37,100 (25%)	$17,800	$16,200	$14,000	$12,000

TECHNICAL DATA

Powertrain (front-drive)
Engines: 2.3L Turbo 4 (200 hp) • 2.3L Turbo 4 HO (225 hp) • 3.0L V6 (210 hp)
Transmissions: 5-speed manual • 4-speed auto.

Dimensions
Length: 187.4 in.
Width: 67.4 in.
Wheelbase: 105.2 in.

SAFETY FEATURES

	Opt.	Std.
Anti-lock brakes	❑	■
Childproof door locks	❑	■
Driver-side airbag	❑	■
Passenger-side airbag	❑	■
Remote keyless entry	❑	■
Traction control	■	■

Aurora/Riviera

Aurora

RATING: Not Recommended. Performance upgrades are no match for poor quality drivetrain components.

NEW FOR '97: This year's Riviera has been revised to provide smoother shifts and run more quietly. Handling has been improved by an upgraded suspension with increased travel, and by recalibrated steering to give more road feel and produce less body roll. New standard features: an improved theft-deterrent system, and a programmable keyless entry device. Aurora gets larger front brakes; the Bosch sound system now includes an in-dash CD player; and a compass is now built into the rear-view mirror (to tell you where you've been, perhaps?).

GENERAL COMMENTS: This luxury coupe shares its G-platform with the Oldsmobile Aurora, also introduced in 1995. Its main claim to fame is the availability of a 225-hp (up from 205 hp) 3.8L V6 supercharged engine that provides 0-to-60 mph (97 km/h) acceleration in 8.2 seconds. Optional in the U.S., GM Canada has made the supercharged version its standard powerplant in Canada.

The Aurora is the epitome of ugly styling. Built on the Riviera platform and similar in size to the Lexus LS 400, Aurora is a five-passenger sports sedan that targets Lexus, Infiniti, Mazda's new Millenia, and Toyota's Avalon. GM is shooting at moving targets, however, and has missed the mark with Aurora. For example, its five-passenger seating can't compete with Avalon's six-passenger capacity; its failure-prone front-drive (based on past complaints when used with other vehicles) competes poorly in a market that has more reliable powertrains and includes rear-drives; and exterior fit and finish just don't compare.

Aurora is powered by a 250-hp 4.0L V8 Northstar engine—a smaller version of the Cadillac powerplant—coupled to a standard 4-speed automatic transmission. Standard features include dual airbags, four-wheel ABS, traction control, adjustable shoulder height manual seatbelts, cruise control, keyless remote entry and security system, and power-assisted everything.

Cost analysis/Alternatives: The 1996 Aurora and Riviera are essentially identical to the more expensive '97 versions, except for some transmission, handling, and suspension upgrades on the latter. Try both versions, because it's a toss-up as to whether the improvements on the '97 version are worth the extra cost. Other cars worth considering are the Ford Crown Victoria and Mercury Marquis, Lexus SC400, Lincoln Mark VIII, Mazda 929 and Millenia, Nissan Maxima, and Toyota Avalon. **Rebates**: The '96 Riviera gets a $3000 customer regate until Dec. 31, 1996. **Destination charge**: $895. **Recommended options**: Original-equipment speakers are disappointing; consider buying an after-market product from an independent retailer. Bucket seats provide more comfortable support. **Supplementary warranty**: A wise investment. **Parts supply/Servicing**: Average. **Depreciation**: Below average. **Highway/City fuel economy**: 9-14.5L/100 km.

Reliability/Safety

Pro: Good base warranty and few major reliability problems reported, due to the short time this reworked version has been on the market. Improved structural integrity cuts flexing and reduces squeaks and rattles. Crash tests of a 1996 dual airbag-equipped Aurora concluded that the driver and passenger would get only average protection in a 57 km/h frontal collision. It was rated: driver, ★★★; passenger, ★★★.

Con: Reliability for previous years' models was below average. The supercharged engine may be a source of problems, and can't be repaired at your corner garage.

Confidential GM bulletins show that 1996 models, and possibly some '97s, may have a loss of oil pressure or loss of power, oil leaks, reduced heater performance on the driver's side, an AC odour upon startup, excessive noise when accelerating or driving up medium grades, a "loose lumber" or rubber thumping noise coming from the rear of the vehicle, cupholders that are too small or inoperable, poor retention of the door trim lace, a faulty rear compartment lid assist rod, a wet or smelly carpet caused by water leaks, and a gap between the door opening and roofline causing wind noise and appearance concerns (see below).

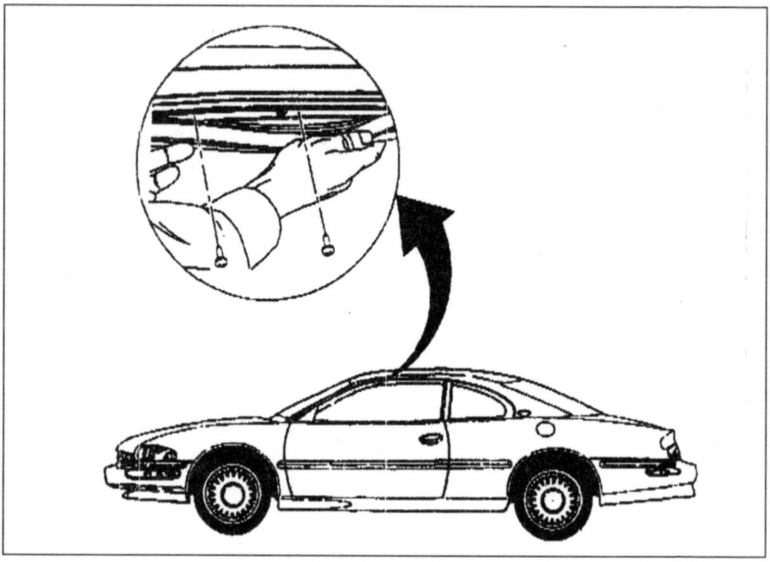

Road Performance

Pro: Acceptable acceleration with the base 3.8L engine and impressive performance with the supercharged powerplant. A rigid body makes for first-class handling without depriving the driver of good road feel. Excellent braking.

Con: Inadequate power steering road feel at high speeds. An early kick-down on the auto transmission is annoying. The downside of the car's rigid body structure is its tendency to hop about when cruising over rough roads.

Comfort/Convenience

Pro: Impressive styling combined with a roomy interior. Well-appointed interior includes comfortable front seats. Very good climate controls. Excellent soundproofing and few vibrations.

Con: Interior ergonomics provide comfort, but the Saab-like dash and console feel a bit confining. The far from stylish, large, flat dash is set too high, gauges are positioned too far apart to be read quickly, radio controls are difficult to use, and the ashtray is intrusive to the extreme. Rear centre seat passenger lacks sufficient room to be comfortable. Lots of interior trim rattles; a high trunk liftover makes for difficult loading; and it's hard to lift the handle-less trunk lid except when it's opened by remote control.

COST

List Price (negotiable)	Residual Values (months) 24	36	48	60
Aurora: $46,045 (27%)	$30,500	$27,500	$23,500	$18,500
Riviera: $42,415 (25%)	26,500	22,500	18,500	12,500

TECHNICAL DATA

Powertrain (front-drive)
Engines: 4.0L V8 (250 hp)
• 3.8 V6 supercharged (240 hp)

Transmission: 4-speed auto.

Dimensions (Aurora/Riviera)
Length: 205.4 in./207.2 in.
Width: 74.4 in./75 in.
Wheelbase: 113.8 in./113.8 in.

SAFETY FEATURES

	Opt.	Std.
Anti-lock brakes	❑	■
Childproof door locks	—	—
Driver-side airbag	❑	■
Passenger-side airbag	❑	■
Remote keyless entry	❑	■
Traction control	❑	■

('96) Olds 98, Park Avenue, Ultra

Olds 98

RATING: An Average buy. A host of luxury features can't compensate for poor reliability.

NEW FOR '97: The Olds 98 is replaced this year by the Regency, a white-walled clone of the 88 and 98 that epitomizes luxury and comfort. It gets some transmission and powertrain computer module refinements. Like the LeSabre, the Park Avenue and Ultra were redesigned last January (sharing GM's G platform with the Buick Riviera and Oldsmobile Aurora), so most of what's available has already been seen. Some of the most important changes are a reworked powertrain, a stiffer body, improved interior amenities, upgraded four-wheel disc brakes, and an upgraded ventilation system.

GENERAL COMMENTS: Full-size luxury sedan aficionados love the flush glass, wrap-around windshield and bumpers, and clean body lines that make for an aerodynamic, pleasing appearance. But these cars are more than a pretty package; they provide lots of room, luxury, style and, dare I say, performance. Plenty of power is available with the Park Avenue's 205 hp 3.8L V6 engine and the Aurora's 240 hp supercharged version of the same powerplant. It does a 0-to-60 mph time in under 9 seconds (impressive, considering the heft of these vehicles), and improves low and mid-range throttle response. Power is transmitted to the front wheels through an electronically controlled transmission that features "free-wheeling" clutches designed to eliminate abrupt gear changes. Both the Park Avenue and Ultra use a stretched version of the more rigid Buick Riviera and Olds Aurora platform.

Cost analysis/Alternatives: Except for the above-noted improvements found in the Regency, last year's cheaper Olds 98 may be a better buy if the selling price has been reduced sufficiently. As far as the Park Avenue and Ultra are concerned, the sum total of their improvements makes the purchase of a '97 version the better deal. Other cars worth considering: a fully equipped Ford Taurus/Sable, Crown Victoria, Lincoln Continental, or Town Car, Mercury Marquis, Nissan Maxima, or fully equipped Toyota Camry and Avalon. **Rebates**: Likely on the Olds 98 sometime near the end of the year. The '96 Park Avenue and Ultra get $2000 customer rebates until Dec. 31, 1996. **Destination charge**: $895. **Recommended options**: The Grand Touring suspension is a good middle ground between sporty firmness and luxo cruising comfort. **Supplementary warranty**: A good idea. **Parts supply/Servicing**: Average. **Depreciation**: Below average. **Highway/City fuel economy**: 8-13L/100 km; 9-14.5L/100 km with the High Output engine.

Reliability/Safety

Pro: Quality control has improved a lot during the past two years. Parts are relatively inexpensive and easy to find. A personalized vehicle security system disables the starting and fuel systems if a non-matching key is used. Rear shoulder belts have a strap to pull the belt away from the neck of small passengers and children. More secure seat-mounted seatbelts.

Con: Frequent engine, transmission, and electronic module malfunctions. Confidential GM bulletins show that 1996 models, and possibly some '97s, may exhibit the following problems: an AC odour upon startup, whistling from the heater and AC system, excessive noise when accelerating or driving up medium grades, a noisy power steering unit, wind noise at the lower front movable glass area, and poor appearance or retention of the header portion of the glass runner channel on front and rear doors.

A 1988 Park Avenue was crash-tested and showed that the driver would sustain severe head injuries and the passenger would suffer serious leg trauma. Insurance claim rates for injuries are lower than average for the Park Avenue and Olds 98. Insurance claim rates for injuries are lower than average for the Park Avenue and Olds 98.

Road Performance

Pro: The 3.8L V6 engine is competent, quiet, and smooth running, with lots of low-end torque. The supercharged version is impressive. The F31 electronic 4-speed transmission works imperceptibly. Cruise control is much smoother without all those annoying downshifts we've learned to hate in GM cars. Handling is acceptable, with variable-assist power steering and shocks that are a bit firmer than usual. Body roll has been reduced with the retuned suspension found on the '97s. Good braking with or without ABS.

Con: Acceleration isn't breathtaking with the base 3.8L engine; at higher revs torque falls off quickly. Power steering is a bit vague at highway speeds. Excessive body roll with the '96 versions. "Gran Touring" suspension is too soft.

Comfort/Convenience

Pro: Modern, aerodynamic styling (similar to the Riviera's) maximizes front and rear visibility. More front head room, and front and rear hip room. Plenty of storage areas. Plenty of interior room and trunk space. Much improved interior ventilation and AC performance with the '97 models. Climate controls allow the driver and passenger to choose different temperature settings for their own comfort. Minimal road and engine noise. This year the entire body has a more solid feel than what one normally finds with GM. Excellent soundproofing. Rear shoulder belts are a lot more comfortable than in previous versions.

Con: Some driver-side window wind noise and excessive tire vibration.

COST

List Price (negotiable)	Residual Values (months) 24	36	48	60
'96 98 Elite: $36,610 (23%)	$22,500	$19,500	$16,000	$13,500
Park Avenue: $40,865 (24%)	24,500	21,600	18,000	15,500
Ultra: $46,865 (27%)	27,500	24,600	21,000	18,500

TECHNICAL DATA

Powertrain (front-drive)
Engines: 3.8L V6 (205 hp)
• 3.8L super V6 (240 hp)

Transmission: 4-speed auto.

Dimensions (98/Park Avenue)
Length: 205.5 in./205.2 in.
Width: 74.6 in./73.6 in.
Wheelbase: 110.8 in./110.8 in.

SAFETY FEATURES

	Opt.	Std.
Anti-lock brakes	❑	■
Childproof door locks	❑	■
Driver-side airbag	❑	■
Passenger-side airbag	❑	■
Remote keyless entry	❑	■
Traction control	■	❑

('96) Caprice, Roadmaster, Fleetwood

Caprice

RATING: Not Recommended, going, going, gone!

NEW FOR '97: There are no '97 models.

GENERAL COMMENTS: Best suited for trailer towing, a powerful engine, spacious interior, and comfortable ride are marred by poor reliability and clumsy handling. These survivors of GM's large rear-wheel-drive car line are living on borrowed time—that will run out by early spring. The Cadillac is included in this group because it rides on a stretched version of the same chassis and shares its powertrain with the B-bodies as well.

These cars are really old models dressed up with a larger, curvaceous, aerodynamic body set on the traditional rear-drive chassis. They're sold with two drivetrains, a base 4.3L V6 engine, and a 180-hp 5.7L fuel-injected V8 powerplant coupled to a 4-speed automatic transmission and standard cruise control. These sedans can carry a full load of passengers and baggage without compromising speed or fuel economy. A full complement of six to eight passengers (eight in the wagon, of course) will find the interior to be roomy and relatively comfortable. Depreciation is average, and servicing has posed no problem. The Impala SS (the nameplate is a throwback to a bygone era), a sporty version of the Caprice sedan powered by a 5.7L 260-hp V8 motor, came online in the spring of 1994 and will suffer the same fate as its big brother.

Cost analysis/Alternatives: The '96s can be picked up pretty cheaply now that they've been discontinued. Other cars worth considering are Ford Taurus/Sable or Crown Victoria/Grand Marquis, Mazda 929 and Millenia, Mercury Marquis, Nissan Maxima, and Toyota Avalon. **Rebates**: '96 Roadmaster: $1500 dealer incentive. **Destination charge**: $870. **Recommended options**: It's too late to order any special options, but look for cars that have the following optional features already installed: a trailer-towing package to conserve low-end power and provide better handling, and the Sport suspension for its extra road feel and firmer ride. **Supplementary warranty**: A good idea, not only because these cars have been dropped, but because they've had lots of powertrain, electrical, brake, and body problems that cost wads of money to correct if you don't have warranty coverage. **Parts supply/Servicing**: Below average and likely to get worse all the more reason to frequent an independent garage for everything but warranty work. **Depreciation**: Above average and accelerating. **Highway/City fuel economy**: 8.5-13.5L/100 km with the 4.3L and 9-14L/100 km with the 5.7L engine.

Reliability/Safety

Pro: Factory defects are less expensive to repair than front-drives because these cars are a cinch to service due to their simple, old, rear-wheel-drive design, underhood accessibility, uncomplicated components, and easily found parts that are reasonably priced. Independent mechanics should have no problem servicing everything but the electronics.

The Fleetwood provides standard traction control and less hazardous plastic fuel tanks. Crashworthiness was rated above average after a review of injury claims by the Highway Loss Data Institute. This contradiction of the government crash test results given below is apparently caused by the difference between real-world statistics and tests that measure a car's crashworthiness in a frontal collision only.

Con: Overall reliability, though better than GM front-drives, has declined markedly lately. The electrical system is failure-prone and computer electronics are tough to troubleshoot. GM has acknowledged that its Hydramatic 4L60E automatic transmissions may have a misadjusted shift linkage, causing loss of Reverse or lack of power in second gear.

Confidential GM bulletins show that 1996 models may exhibit the following problems: engine overheating, the steering wheel may lose chunks of the wheel (GM calls it "chunking"), an AC odour upon start-up, and a noisy power steering unit.

Crash tests of a 1996 dual airbag-equipped Caprice concluded that the driver would be well-protected but the passenger would receive below average protection in a 57 km/h frontal collision. It was rated: driver, ★★★★; passenger, ★★.

Road Performance

Pro: Acceleration has been improved due to the 4.3L engine's extra horsepower and increased low-end torque. The electronic 4-speed automatic transmission shifts smoothly through all gear ranges. Ride comfort is exceptional due to the upgraded shocks, four-wheel coil spring suspension, and rubber-cushion body-to-frame mounts. Larger wheels and tires improve handling. Braking is flawless with ABS.

Con: Rack and pinion steering is a bit slow and vague. The standard soft suspension gives the Caprice a wallowing, boat-like ride. ABS is difficult to modulate.

Comfort/Convenience

Pro: Modern, aerodynamic styling maximizes front and rear visibility. Practical and easy-to-understand instrumentation and controls. Much improved side mirrors. Standard air conditioning is much more efficient and quieter this year. Plenty of storage areas. Good amount of head room. Excellent soundproofing. Increased interior room. The seats—a major source of complaints from police and fleet managers in the past—now give good lateral and lumbar support for all passengers. Three passengers can sit comfortably in the rear.

Con: Seats lack dialed-in lumbar support and the seatbacks lack sufficient padding. Uncomfortable seating for the front middle passenger.

Access is hindered by the small door openings. Radio reception is below par. Front leg room is a bit disappointing. The sharply sloped rear deck and front hood make it necessary to park by ear. The large trunk is compromised by its impractical shape and the optional full-service spare tire.

COST

List Price (very negotiable)	**Residual Values** (months) 24	36	48	60
Classic sedan: $28,345 (23%)	$13,000	$11,000	$9500	$8000
Roadmaster wagon: $36,315 (24%)	17,000	15,000	13,000	11,000
Fleetwood: $46,695 (26%)	22,000	19,500	17,500	15,500

TECHNICAL DATA

Powertrain (rear-drive)
Engines: 4.3L injected V6 (200 hp) • 5.7L injected V8 (260 hp)
Transmission: 4-speed auto.

Dimensions (Caprice/Fleetwood)
Length: 214.1 in./225.1 in.
Width: 77.5 in./78 in.
Wheelbase: 115.9 in./121.5 in.

SAFETY FEATURES

Caprice	Opt.	Std.
Anti-lock brakes	❑	■
Childproof door locks	❑	■
Driver-side airbag	❑	■
Passenger-side airbag	❑	■
Remote keyless entry	❑	■

Fleetwood	Opt.	Std.
Anti-lock brakes	❑	■
Childproof door locks	❑	■
Driver-side airbag	❑	■
Passenger-side airbag	❑	■
Remote keyless entry	❑	■
Traction control	❑	■

Cadillac DeVille, DeVille Concours

DeVille

RATING: Not Recommended.

NEW FOR '97: Both cars get styling changes that include new front fenders and front and rear ends, standard side airbags, and an optional OnStar cellular/GPS tracking system. The Concours gets a new version, the d'Elegence, aimed at more traditional buyers with loads of standard luxury features. Other Concours features: a new centre console making for five-place seating, redesigned front bucket seats, a new instrument panel, and dual climate controls. Powertrain configurations remain the same on all vehicles.

GENERAL COMMENTS: Now that the rear-drive Fleetwood is gone, these two Cadillacs step in to fill the void. There are really two DeVilles: the Sedan DeVille, GM's most popular Cadillac, aimed at traditional Cadillac buyers, and the Concours, which offers sportier performance. Essentially a front-drive clone of the rear-drive Fleetwood, the sedan is a chrome-ridden, overly large luxury car whose new Northstar powerplant blurs the distinction between it and the Concours. It uses a "brake only" traction-control system, which counters wheelspin at low speeds by applying the front brakes, and a softer suspension. Michelin whitewalls are standard.

The Concours version carries the powerful 4.6L 305-hp Northstar engine and 4-speed automatic transmission, improved traction control, electronic variable-dampening suspension (programmed for a firmer ride), four-wheel anti-lock disc brakes, and 225/6016 Eagle GA touring tires. Both Cadillacs have moved from GM's C platform—which they used to share with the Buick Park Avenue and Olds Ninety Eight—to a K-Special chassis, a stretched version of the Seville/Eldorado platform.

Cost analysis/Alternatives: The 1996 models are virtually identical to the '97 versions and represent the better buy if discounted sufficiently.

Last year's Olds 88 Royale LS and Bonneville SE with a V6 and optional sport suspension are cheaper alternatives to the DeVille. Other cars worth considering: Ford Crown Victoria and Lincoln Town Car, Mazda 929 and Millenia, Mercury Marquis, Nissan Maxima and Infiniti, and Toyota Avalon. **Rebates**: Probably around mid-summer. **Destination charge**: $895. **Recommended options**: Stay away from the optional digital cluster; all you get are large digital read-outs and bar graphs. Buy the optional firmer suspension to counteract the base suspension's unsettling jiggle. It includes quicker-ratio steering, firmer shocks, thicker sway bars, and high-performance Goodyear tires. **Supplementary warranty**: Essential for cars this expensive. **Parts supply/Servicing**: Below average. The DeVille's accident repair costs are much lower than average. **Depreciation**: Below average. **Highway/City fuel economy**: 9-16L/100 km; DeVille Concours: 9-14.5L/100 km.

Reliability/Safety

Pro: Comprehensive base warranty with a special VIP hotline.

Con: Long-term ownership of any of these models doesn't look promising; their reliability histories are replete with major faults, constant malfunctions, and mind-spinning depreciation. Worst of all, the engine control and electrical systems are too complicated for most garages to service. Assembly quality isn't anywhere near luxury car standards, and paint is often poorly applied. Fragile body hardware. Large gaps between sheet metal panels and doors. The front brakes and shock absorbers wear out quickly. Serious fit and finish deficiencies. Intermittent stalling, rough idling, hesitation, and no-starts.

Crash tests of a 1996 dual airbag-equipped DeVille concluded that the driver would receive average protection but the passenger would receive severe or fatal injuries in a 57 km/h frontal collision. It was rated: driver, ★★★; passenger, ★.

Confidential GM bulletins show that 1996 models, and possibly some '97s, may exhibit the following problems: oil leaks, loss of oil pressure, an AC odour upon startup, inaccurate fuel gauge display, poor heat distribution or lack of air flow, lack of AC in traffic or at high ambient temperatures, rattle or "loose lumber" noise from the front of the vehicle, front seat clicking, a noisy power steering unit, exhaust rattling, radio clock stuck on 12:00, slow Park brake release or slow heater and AC mode changes, and wet or smelly carpet from water leaks.

Road Performance

Pro: Plenty of power with the base 275-hp 4.6L V8 engine, with less harshness and reduced vibration and noise on this year's version. The Concours variant has improved acceleration over last year's version, thanks to its 30 extra horses and other engine/transmission refinements. The 4-speed automatic with Overdrive is responsive, despite occasional confusion about which gear it should be in. The Dynaride suspension provides a soft ride. Steering is crisp, with little body roll and more responsive handling. Road Sensing suspension prevents excessive body lean in turns. Excellent anti-lock brakes.

Con: The 4.6L V8 overpowers the front-drive chassis. Some torque steer is evident.

Comfort/Convenience

Pro: These cars come equipped with just about every imaginable electrical and power-assisted gadget. Quiet, plush interiors. Fairly large trunk.

Con: Front seats lack adequate thigh support and the leather covering doesn't breathe. Dashboard controls are too fussy for safe operation; the driver must often look away from the road to do such simple things as tune the radio or adjust the climate controls. Imitation wood dash.

COST

List Price (negotiable)	**Residual Values** (months)			
	24	**36**	**48**	**60**
DeVille: $49,400 (26%)	$22,800	$19,800	$17,800	$15,800
Concours: $56,985 (27%)	27,500	23,500	22,500	19,500

TECHNICAL DATA

Powertrain (front-drive)	**Dimensions**
Engine: 4.6L OHC V8 (275 hp)	Length: 209.7 in.
• Concours: 4.6L OHC V8 (300 hp)	Width: 76.6 in.
Transmission: 4-speed auto.	Wheelbase: 113.8 in.

SAFETY FEATURES

	Opt.	Std.
Anti-lock brakes	❑	■
Childproof door locks	❑	■
Driver-side airbag	❑	■
Passenger-side airbag	❑	■
Remote keyless entry	❑	■
Traction control	❑	■

Eldorado/Seville

Eldorado

RATING: Not Recommended.

NEW FOR '97: Eldorado gets a stiffer suspension. Seville's new features: brake, suspension, and structural improvements. Optional OnStar cellular phone/GPS global positioning system.

GENERAL COMMENTS: These overweight luxo toys return with a few important changes that improve ride and handling. Eldorado and its sporty Sports Coupe twin are both equipped with the Northstar V8 and built on identical platforms with the same components. This provides a quiet, comfortable ride along with impressive acceleration.

Both Cadillacs come with GM's PASS KEY theft-deterrent system that shuts down the starter and fuel system if the right key isn't used. The Eldorado has clean, more aerodynamic lines enhanced by body overhangs.

Like most of GM's front-drives, these models have amassed a terrible reputation for being unreliable and expensive to maintain. In all, there is little to recommend them; there are cheaper vehicles that offer better performance and interior comfort.

Both cars are offered with some sort of performance suspension, usually in a special model. This makes them more pleasant to drive, but these are half hearted efforts when compared to the sterling performance offered by the more expensive Japanese and German imports. On the whole, there doesn't seem to be much hope for this model line, and we're just going to have to wait until GM can redesign it from the tires up. For anyone planning to spend big bucks on one of these two Cadillacs, the likelihood of multiple reliability and body problems should make you think twice.

Cost analysis/Alternatives: Except for the improvements noted above, which may appear marginal to some, the 1997 Eldorado and DeVille are essentially identical to the less expensive '96 versions. Before opting for the cheaper models, drive a '97 to see if the changes are worth the extra cost. Consider the purchase of a BMW 325i, Lexus SC400, Mazda 929 and Millenia, Nissan Maxima or Infiniti, or the Toyota Avalon. **Rebates**: Not likely before mid-summer. **Destination charge**: $895. **Recommended options**: None. **Supplementary warranty**: A must-have. **Parts supply/Servicing**: Below average. **Depreciation**: Below average. **Highway/City fuel economy**: 9-14.5L/100 km for both vehicles.

Reliability/Safety

Pro: Below-average parts cost, according to the CAA. Plastic fuel tanks improve Seville and Eldorado crashworthiness. A 1992 Seville performed exceptionally well in NHTSA's 57 km/h crash tests; both driver and passenger came out unscathed.

Con: Little has escaped the gremlins' hands on these cars. The Overdrive automatic is prone to premature failure. Assembly quality isn't anywhere near luxury car standards, and paint is often poorly applied. Fragile body hardware. Large gaps between sheet metal panels and doors that are poorly hung and not entirely square.

The front brakes and shock absorbers wear out quickly. The Seville and Eldorado have serious fit and finish deficiencies. Some sample problems: cracking of front outside door handles; door rattles (Eldorado); poor bumper fit; loose sun visor mounting; rear taillamp condensation (Seville); interior window fogging; "creaking" body mounts; water leaks into trunk from licence plate holder (Eldorado); noisy roof panels and seatback lumbar motors; and excessive brake pedal travel to disengage the cruise control or activate the brake lights. Intermittent stalling, rough idling, hesitation, and no-starts.

GM bulletins show that 1996 models, and possibly some '97s, may exhibit the following problems: oil leaks, loss of oil pressure or lack of power, coolant temperature gauge shows vehicle is running hot, cup holder won't latch/excessive gaps, an AC odour upon startup, a whistling noise comes from the AC, inaccurate fuel gauge display, poor heat distribution or lack of air flow, lack of AC in traffic or at high ambient temperatures, front seat clicking, a noisy power steering unit, exhaust rattling, radio clock stuck on 12:00, slow Park brake release or slow heater and AC mode changes, and wet or smelly carpet from water leaks.

Drivers complain that the shoulder belt chafes the neck. The Eldorado's wide rear pillars obstruct the driver's view to the right rear. Traction control lacks an override feature.

Road Performance

Pro: Plenty of power with the 4.6L V8 engine, with less harshness and reduced vibration and noise on this year's version. The 4-speed automatic with Overdrive is responsive, despite occasional confusion about which gear it should be in. The Dynaride suspension provides a soft ride. Road Sensing suspension prevents excessive body lean in turns. Steering is crisp and suspension improvements make for much less body roll and more responsive handling. Excellent anti-lock brakes.

Con: The 4.6L V8 engine overpowers the Eldorado's front-drive chassis. Some torque steer is evident.

Comfort/Convenience

Pro: These cars come equipped with just about every imaginable electrical and power-assisted gadget. Quiet, plush interiors. Fairly large trunk. The Seville's extra length and width offer rear passengers considerable room. The Seville offers the advantage of four doors. Large trunk.

Con: Front seats lack adequate thigh support and the leather covering doesn't breathe. The Eldorado's steering wheel is too close. Limited interior space; the huge dashboard makes people feel as though they're sitting in a bathtub. The Eldorado's rear seat won't accommodate two adults comfortably, and getting back there takes very inelegant contortions. There are too many distracting and fussy controls on the dashboard for safe operation; the driver must often look away from the road to do such simple things as tune the radio or adjust the climate controls. Imitation wood dash.

COST

List Price (negotiable)	**Residual Values** (months) 24	36	48	60
Eldorado: $52,015 (26%)	$28,000	$24,000	$21,000	$18,000
Seville SLS: $57,010 (28%)	31,500	26,500	23,500	20,500

TECHNICAL DATA

Powertrain (front-drive)
Engines: 4.6L V8 (270 hp)
• 4.6L OHC V8 (300 hp)

Transmission: 4-speed auto.

Dimensions (Eldorado/Seville)
Length: 202.2 in./204.1 in.
Width: 75.5 in./74.2 in.
Wheelbase: 108 in./111 in.

SAFETY FEATURES

	Opt.	Std.
Anti-lock brakes	❑	■
Childproof door locks	❑	■
Driver-side airbag	❑	■
Passenger-side airbag	❑	■
Remote keyless entry	❑	■
Traction control	❑	■

Camaro/Firebird

Camaro

RATING: Recommended. Safer, better-performing muscle cars with above-average crash protection and high resale value. It takes the lead over Ford Mustang with its standard ABS and slightly better reliability record.

NEW FOR '97: A 30th birthday styling package for the Camaro; and some interior upgrades, V6 engine dampening for smoother running at high speeds, optional Ram Air induction, and racier-looking ground-effects body trim for the Firebird.

GENERAL COMMENTS: These sporty convertibles and coupes are almost identical in the features they offer (the Firebird has pop-up headlights, a more pointy front end, a narrower middle, and a rear spoiler) and in their pricing. Both cars were completely made over two years ago, making them more powerful and aerodynamic with less spine-jarring performance. They were given new plastic skins, dual airbags, standard anti-lock brakes, new suspension and steering systems, a new 5-speed manual transmission, a reworked interior, and minor cosmetic improvements.

As one moves up the scale overall performance improves considerably. The V8 engine gives these cars lots of sparkle and tire-spinning torque, but there's a price. A 4-speed automatic transmission is standard on the 5.7L-equipped Z28; other versions come with a standard 5-speed manual gearbox or an optional 6-speed. All cars can be ordered with lots of extra performance and luxury options, including a T-roof package guaranteed to include a full assortment of creaks and groans.

Both cars are equipped with an impressively effective PASS KEY theft-deterrent system similar to the one used successfully in the Corvette. A resistor pellet in the ignition disables the starter and fuel system when the key code doesn't match the ignition lock.

Cost analysis/Alternatives: The 1996 Camaro and Firebird are essentially the same as the more expensive '97 versions. Get a firm delivery date; long delivery delays have been caused by the huge demand for these cars. Insurance will cost you about $2500, or three times the cost of a Japanese econobox. A V8-equipped Camaro or convertible is the best choice for retained value a few years hence. But you can do quite well with the base coupe equipped with the performance handling package (about $500) and 235 tires. Other cars worth considering are the Eagle Talon and '96 Stealth, Nissan 240SX, and Toyota Celica and Supra. **Rebates**: Not likely; there's a lot of pent-up demand for these popular cars. **Destination charge**: $680. **Recommended options**: GM's Performance Handling Package and 235/55 tires on 16-inch aluminum wheels. **Supplementary warranty**: Not needed. **Parts supply/Servicing**: Above average. **Depreciation**: Below average. **Highway/City fuel economy**: 8-12.5L/100 km with the base 3.4L and manual 5-speed; 8-12.5L/100 km with the 3.4L and 4-speed automatic; 9-15L/100 km with the 5.7L and manual 6-speed; 9-14L/100 km with the 5.7L and 4-speed automatic.

Reliability/Safety

Pro: Most repairs are simple to perform and relatively inexpensive. The new plastic body panels are dent- and rust-resistant. Body construction is better than average. Dual airbags and ABS are standard. Traction control is optional. Crash tests of a 1994 Chevrolet Camaro concluded that the driver and passenger would have excellent protection in a 57 km/h frontal collision. It was rated, for both driver and passenger, ★★★★★.

Con: The 5.7L V8 fuel and electrical systems have been troublesome in the past. Engine cooling and ignition systems are also bug-plagued. Poor air-conditioner performance is a common complaint. The front brakes and MacPherson struts wear out quickly. The automatic transmission has a better reliability history than does the manual. Servicing the fuel-injection system is an exercise in frustration. Body problems include door rattles, poor fit and finish, misaligned doors and hatch, and a sticking hatch power release.

Confidential GM bulletins show the following problems affecting either vehicle equipped with the V6 or V8 engines: transmission fluid leak from the pump body; an AC odour upon startup; a noisy power steering unit; steering lead or pull, usually to the right; and uneven brake pad wear requires the replacement of the rear caliper mounting brackets (see chart below). Rear compartment lid water leaks (see illustration below).

File In Section: 5 - Brakes
Bulletin No: 53-50-20
Date: November, 1995
Subject:
Taper Wear and/or Uneven Wear on Rear Disc Brake Pads (Replace Caliper Mounting Brackets)
Models:
1993-96 Chevrolet Camaro
1993-96 Pontiac Firebird
Condition
Some of the above vehicles may exhibit taper wear and/or uneven wear on the rear disc brake pads. (Taper wear is defined as uneven wear of the pad from end to end or inboard versus outboard uneven wear.) Maximum taper allowed is 0.15 mm (0.006 inch).
Cause
Wear of the caliper guide pins and the bores on the caliper anchor brackets may result in the caliper not sliding freely.
Correction
Replace the caliper anchor bracket, the guide pins and the brake pads. Refer to Section 5B2 of the Service Manual.

Description	P/N
Rear Caliper Mounting Bracket (2 required)	18020432
Bracket Mount Bolt (4 required)	10229606
Rear Caliper Guide Pin (4 required)	18022147
Boot - Rear Caliper Guide Pin (4 required)	14067552
Caliper Mounting Bolts (2 required)*	14067559
Pads - Rear Brakes (1 required)	18021875

* (4 bolts required, but 2 bolts come with new pads)

File In Section: 10 - Body
Bulletin No.: 53-10-32
Date: December, 1995
Subject:
Water Leaks at Rear Compartment Lid When Parked on an Incline (Add Sealer to Weatherstrip Carrier)
Models:
1993-96 Chevrolet Camaro
1993-96 Pontiac Firebird
Condition
Some vehicles may exhibit water leaks at the rear compartment lid. This condition is most likely to occur when the vehicle is parked on an incline during a period of rain with the front end being lower than the rear of the vehicle.
Cause
This condition may be due to a collection of water in the rear compartment lid gutter. Water may collect in the gutter and finds a path into the vehicle at the flange mounted weatherstrip.
Correction

Figure 1

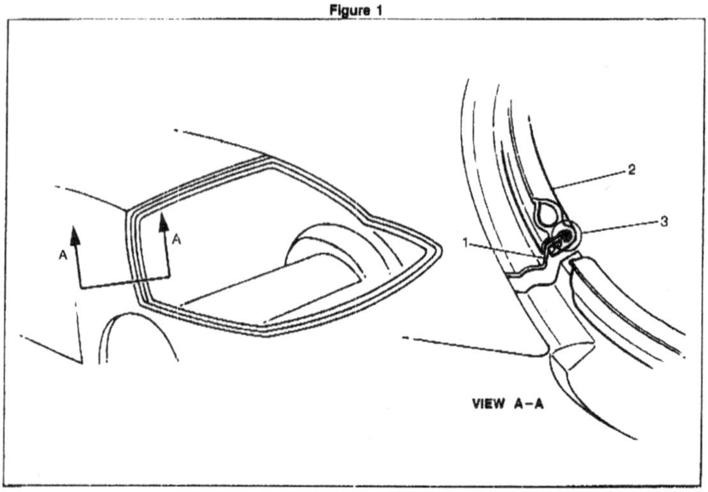

Road Performance

Pro: Engines start well in cold weather, give ample pulling power, and provide fast acceleration. Handling is best on the sports models, but even the base coupes perform respectably on the road, and the stiffer suspension makes for much tighter cornering. The rack and pinion steering is responsive and precise. Excellent ABS brakes.

Con: The 6-speed manual transmission's clutch is heavy and gets tiring in city driving—the shifter takes getting used to due to the pattern of the gear throws. The upgraded 4-speed automatic with Overdrive tends to shift late, putting extra strain on the engine. Without traction control, the tires lose traction and directional stability is compromised on wet pavement. Due to the rear axle suspension, the ride is constantly busy and particularly bouncy on poor roads. A stiffer suspension adds to this effect. These cars cry out for independent rear suspension. V8-equipped coupes have poor traction on slippery surfaces (just like the Mustang).

Comfort/Convenience

Pro: Most people find the Firebird's front seats more comfortable, but they're comfortable and supportive on both cars. The rear buckets are just that—buckets. Dash is well laid out with easy-to-read gauges. Complete instrumentation. Good fresh air ventilation system. A dent-resistant body copies that of the Saturn. A tighter chassis eliminates a lot of the creaks and groans that have accompanied these cars for decades.

Con: Driving position is too low for short drivers. The hard, cheap-looking, plastic dash maximizes glare on sunny days. Control knobs are primitive when compared with the digital controls offered by the Japanese, and the ignition key takes two hands to remove. The front windshield has only a single demister vent. The obtrusive centre console gets in the way when shifting. The split rear seat is a joke—or a place to put people whom you don't like. Limited rear seat access. The cargo area is small and awkwardly shaped. Large objects won't fit under the hatch. Excessive road and engine noise. Poor heating/defrosting. Door detents are too weak to keep the heavy doors open. The convertible's front spoiler is unnecessary and set too low.

COST

List Price (firm)	Residual Values (months) 24	36	48	60
Base: $20,910 (15%)	$13,500	$12,500	$10,000	$8500
Z28: $27,270 (18%)	17,000	15,500	13,500	12,000
Firebird: $23,120 (15%)	14,900	12,900	10,900	9900
Formula: $27,555 (15%)	18,000	16,500	13,900	12,500
Trans Am: $30,780 (16%)	19,000	17,700	15,500	13,500

TECHNICAL DATA

Powertrain (rear-drive)
Engines: 3.8L injected V6 (200 hp) • 5.7L injected V8 (285 hp)

Dimensions (Camaro/Firebird)
Length: 193.2 in./195.6 in.
Width: 74.1 in./74.5 in.
Wheelbase: 101 in./101.1 in.

Transmissions: 5-speed manual • 6-speed manual • 4-speed auto.

SAFETY FEATURES

	Opt.	Std.
Anti-lock brakes	❑	■
Childproof door locks	—	—
Driver-side airbag	❑	■
Passenger-side airbag	❑	■
Remote keyless entry	■	❑
Traction control	■	■

Corvette

Corvette convertible

RATING: Not Recommended. A Jurassic sports coupe that proves more *can* mean less. Perfect for guys who want to show off their big "thing." In French we say, "grosse Corvette petite quequette."

NEW FOR '97: Scheduled to make its debut at the Detroit Auto Show next January, insiders say that the new "Vette" will have a a longer wheelbase, more rigid chassis, upgraded suspension and steering, and a totally new 5.7L 340 hp V8 engine.

GENERAL COMMENTS: Introduced in 1953 as a futuristic show car, and the first American car to use fuel injection (in 1957), the Corvette has never made money for GM. Over the past 40 years more than a million units have been sold, and an estimated 500,000 are still on the roads. But the car has fallen on hard times, with declining sales accompanied by increased production costs. Its peak year was 1984, when over 84,000 units were sold in North America for about half of today's price. GM is optimistic that sales will improve, and plans to revamp the high-performance, two-seater next year. It's likely to be offered then as a cheaper, rear-drive, fibreglass-bodied stripped-down sports car carrying a V6 powerplant—burying forever the car's muscle image.

This year we see the return of the base 300-hp L98 powerplant, harnessed to either a 4-speed automatic or a 6-speed manual transmission. An optional powerplant gives 30 additional horses.

Cost analysis/Alternatives: The cheaper 1996 Corvette won't have the cachet or the mechanical and body refinements of the '97 version. If you choose the '97 model, try to get a second-series car that was made after June 1997. Keep in mind that premium fuel and astronomical insurance rates will further drive up your operating costs. Other sporty models worth considering are the Eagle Talon and Stealth, Ford Taurus SHO, and Toyota Supra. **Rebates**: Not likely. **Destination charge**: $895. **Recommended options**: None. **Supplementary warranty**: A good idea. **Parts supply/Servicing**: Below average. The convertible's accident repair costs are much higher than average. **Depreciation**: Below average. **Highway/City fuel economy**: 9 15L/100 km with the 6-speed manual, 9-14L/100 km with the 6-speed manual hooked to the High Output engine, and 9-14L/100 km with the automatic.

Reliability/Safety

Pro: Key-controlled lockout feature discourages joy riding by cutting engine power in half. Both Corvette versions are equipped with an impressively effective PASS KEY theft-deterrent system that uses a resistor pellet in the ignition to disable the starter and fuel system when the key code doesn't match the ignition lock. According to the CAA, parts are reasonably priced.

The tires have built-in low-pressure sensors that warn the driver through a light on the centre console. ABS, traction control, and dual airbags are standard. Excellent driver and passenger protection, according to NHTSA tests.

Con: Poor heating/cooling. Electronically controlled suspension systems have been glitch-plagued over the past several years. All the Corvette's squeaks and rattles are due to the car's structural deficiencies. The car was built as a convertible, and therefore has too much body flex. Servicing the different sophisticated fuel-injection systems isn't easy, even (especially) for GM mechanics.

Confidential GM bulletins show the following 1996 model year problems, possibly carried over to '97 models: noisy power steering, armrest lid hard to open or close, lack of power, early or late shifts, and transmission fluid leak from the pump body.

Although the redesigned '97 version hasn't been crash-tested yet, the Insurance Institute for Highway Safety found that fatality rates from all kinds of crashes involving Corvettes between 1985-89 was the highest of any car. Another organization, the Highway Loss Data Institute, compiles statistics relative to the actual frequency of insurance claims filed for personal injury and collision loss per vehicle. It found that '88 and '89 Corvettes scored better than average in injury claims, and worse than average in collisions.

Road Performance

Pro: Gobs of torque and horsepower. The Bilstein FX-3 Selective Ride Control suspension can be preset to touring, sport, or performance. Under acceleration, an electronic module automatically varies the suspension as the speed increases. No oversteer, wheelspinning, breakaway rear ends, or nasty surprises. The 6-speed gearbox performs well in all gear ranges, and makes shifting smooth with short throws and easy entry into all gears. The ABS-vented disc brakes are easy to modulate, fade-free, and incorporate a Bosch system that GM engineers claim will pull over 1.0 G deceleration rates.

Con: In addition to an irritating engine boom, there's excessive tire noise, wind whistling through the car's A- and C-pillars, and the all-too-familiar fibreglass body squeaks caused by excessive body flexing on rough surfaces.

Comfort/Convenience

Pro: Attractively styled and full of power-assisted accessories. Rust-resistant fibreglass body. Simple to operate convertible top. Innovative Passive Keyless Entry System.

Con: The massive front snout detracts from the car's sporty styling. There's not a great deal of comfort or convenience with this sporty brute. The electronic dash never quite works right (speedometer lag, for example). There's no room in the engine compartment for a sophisticated climate-control system. All you get is the basic air conditioner and heater, and they're quite noisy. Excessive tire/road noise invades the passenger compartment.

COST

List Price (negotiable)	**Residual Values** (months) 24	36	48	60
'96 Sport Coupe: $48,080 (28%)	$29,000	$25,000	$21,000	$17,000
'96 Convertible: $56,335 (31%)	32,500	27,000	23,000	19,000

'96 TECHNICAL DATA

Powertrain (rear-drive)
Engines: 5.7L injected V8 (300 hp) • 5.7L injected V8 (330 hp)
Transmissions: 6-speed manual OD • 4-speed auto. OD

Dimensions
Length: 178.5 in.
Width: 70.7 in.
Wheelbase: 96.2 in.

SAFETY FEATURES

	Opt.	Std.
Anti-lock brakes	❑	■
Driver-side airbag	❑	■
Passenger-side airbag	❑	■
Remote keyless entry	❑	■
Traction control	❑	■

Astro/Safari

Safari

RATING: Not Recommended. More a utility truck than a comfortable minivan.

NEW FOR '97: Some transmission refinements and leather-clad seats (whips and chains are optional).

GENERAL COMMENTS: These boxy, rear-drive minivans are built on a reworked S-10 pickup chassis. As such, they offer uninspiring handling, trouble-prone mechanical and body components, and relatively high fuel consumption. Both Astro and Safari come in a choice of either cargo or passenger van. The cargo van is used either commercially or as an inexpensive starting point for a fully customized vehicle. The Safari is identical to the Astro, except for a slightly higher base price.

The engine is a 4.3L 190 hp V6. Dual airbags are standard. Also offered are an optional rear door and rear bench seats that can be adjusted fore and aft. Carried-over standard features are a 4-speed automatic transmission with Overdrive, power steering, a front stabilizer bar, a 102L fuel tank (by comparison, Lumina offers 76L), and anti-lock brakes. All-wheel-drive with a single-speed transfer case with viscous-controlled differential (no switches to throw) is available on the regular length and extended models. The sport package includes louvred rear-quarter body panels, two-tone paint, fog lights, and a front air dam. With the right options, the Astro and Safari have the advantage of being versatile cargo haulers when equipped with a heavy-duty suspension. Depreciation is moderate.

Cost analysis/Alternatives: The 1996 Astro and Safari are essentially identical to the '97 versions, and represent the better buy if they're discounted enough. You might try the rear-drive Ford Aerostar, but make sure you get Ford's supplementary warranty. Front-drive minivans made by Ford/Mercury and Nissan are better handling and more reliable and economical people carriers; unfortunately, they lack the grunt needed for cargo hauling and trailer towing. **Rebates**: Look for substantial rebates in the $1000 range early next year. **Destination charge**: $845. **Recommended options**: None. **Supplementary warranty**: A wise investment. Repairs won't cost a lot, but they'll be frequent. **Parts supply/Servicing**: Below average. **Depreciation**: Above average. **Highway/City fuel economy**: 11-15.5L/100 km for 2-wheel drive and 11.5-16L/100 km with AWD.

Reliability/Safety

Pro: The engine is durable. An extensive dealer network and plenty of independent parts suppliers combine to keep repair costs down. In fact, parts are less expensive than they are for other cars in this class, according to the CAA.

Con: Below-average reliability. Owners have reported frequent problems with engine head gaskets, automatic transmission, steering, electrical system, heating and defrosting system, and suspension components. Poor body construction and sloppy paint application also figure prominently among owner beefs. Reports of bench seat squeaks and rattles. In order to prolong the life of the automatic transmission, it's a good idea to lock out Overdrive in city driving and when pulling a trailer or heavy load.

Confidential GM bulletins show that the 1996 models, and possibly some '97s, may have the following problems: frequent transmission fluid leaks from the pump body and elsewhere, an AC odour upon startup, a noisy power steering unit, lack of power, and erratic shifting.

Insurance industry claims statistics compiled by the Highway Loss Data Institute show that the 1986 Astro cargo van had a much higher than average claim frequency when compared to other vehicles in its class. Crash tests of a 1994 Astro concluded that the driver would have average protection in a 57 km/h frontal collision, while the passenger would sustain serious injuries. It was rated: driver, ★★★; passenger, ★.

Road Performance

Pro: The V6 engine offers peppy performance and enough reserve power for trailer towing and heavy hauling. The 4-speed automatic transmission's '97 refinements make it smoother and easier-shifting. Very light power steering. The all-wheel drive gives sure-footed traction.

Con: The V6 is thirsty in city driving. Busy, harsh ride caused by stiff springs. Interior noise levels rise sharply at highway speeds. Handling isn't very precise; overall behaviour is predictable but sloppy. A heavy-duty suspension will improve both ride and handling.

Comfort/Convenience

Pro: Spacious interior leaves lots of room for passengers or cargo. Can seat up to eight people in a pinch. All seats are comfortable, although the front two are the best. The rear seat can be removed easily by a single person.

Con: The driving position is awkward for most drivers—more like a truck than a passenger car. Tall drivers will find the pedals too close. Obtrusive engine makes for very narrow front footwells. Some dashboard controls are hard to reach. Swing-out cargo doors don't allow for either a rear window defroster or wiper/washer. Engine and transmission located under the dashboard make maintenance and repairs a chore. Excessive engine noise.

COST

List Price (negotiable)	**Residual Values** (months) 24	36	48	60
Astro passenger: $26,920 (20%)	$13,800	$11,500	$9500	$8000

TECHNICAL DATA

Powertrain (rear-drive)
Engine: 4.3L injected V6 (190 hp)
Transmission: 4-speed auto. OD

Dimensions
Length: 189.8 in.
Width: 77.5 in.
Wheelbase: 111 in.

SAFETY FEATURES

	Opt.	Std.
Anti-lock brakes	❑	■
Childproof door locks	❑	■
Driver-side airbag	❑	■
Passenger-side airbag	❑	■
Remote keyless entry	■	❑

Lumina/Trans Sport

Lumina APV

RATING: Not Recommended. Space-age design marred by medieval engineering; poor outward visibility; and a mediocre, poor-quality drivetrain and underpinnings taken from GM's front-drives.

NEW FOR '97: These minivans are living on borrowed time now that the new Venture and Silhouette minivans have made their debut. They're '96 carryovers until the new minivans get a market toe-hold, and then they're history. In the meantime, these minivans get a nose job, a larger wheelbase, standard front AC, and an extra sliding door.

Envying Subaru's success with the Outback (a sport-utility treatment of its station wagon similar to the long-gone AMC Eagle), GM will equip about half of its '97 Trans Sport production with a Montana package, which the automaker hopes will transform its comical "Dustbuster" image into a lean, mean, 4X4 machine. Unfortunately, new paint, extra body side cladding, driving lights, and other amenities do not a 4X4 sport-utility make, although traction control and the sport suspension do help. In its defence, GM says that its traction control actually saves fuel while delivering 75 to 80 percent of the traction of an all-wheel-drive vehicle.

GENERAL COMMENTS: These are the weakest selling domestic minivans of the Big Three, and are largely responsible for the drop in GM's U.S. domestic market share last year. Launched only five years ago, they're striking in their rakish and rounded space-age design that uses plastic panels impervious to dents and rust. Unfortunately, GM's creativity stops at the drivetrain and underpinnings, which are borrowed almost entirely from its front-drive compacts and intermediates. A 3.4L V6 powerplant will hopefully improve acceleration, compared to the inadequate (and discontinued) 3.1L V6.

These plastic-bodied, front-drive vehicles look more like oversized Dustbusters than traditional minivans, as exemplified by the popular

Chrysler Caravan and Ford Windstar. These vehicles use the Chevrolet Lumina (W-body) platform, and therefore have more car-like handling than does GM's Astro/Safari. They don't offer 4X4 capability, however, leaving this option to GM's more utilitarian rear-drive minivans.

The plastic panels absorb engine and road noise very well. This combination of high-tech plastics, space frame design, and adhesive bonding has never been used before in any mass-produced vehicle. On the downside, body shops complain that the innovative plastic panels are in short supply and damaged panels can't be recycled, driving up the cost of repairs and causing insurance adjusters to simply write off vehicles that might otherwise be repaired. That's probably one of the reasons why GM is dropping the panels next year.

Cost analysis/Alternatives: The 1996 Lumina/Trans Sport are essentially identical to this year's carried-over versions. Seriously consider a more reliable Ford Windstar, Mercury Villager, or Nissan Quest. A second-series Chevrolet Venture or the Chrysler minivans are also credible alternatives, as long as you get the supplementary warranty. **Rebates**: '96 models are covered by a $1000 rebate. **Destination charge**: $845. **Recommended options**: The integrated child safety seat. **Supplementary warranty:** A good idea. **Parts supply/Servicing**: Average. **Depreciation**: Above average. **Highway/City fuel economy**: 10.5-13L/100 km.

Reliability/Safety

Pro: Body panels are impervious to rusting, dents, and dings. Standard stainless-steel exhaust system. Mechanical components are easily obtained at very reasonable prices. Extensive dealer network and lots of independent parts suppliers cut repair costs. Standard anti-lock brakes, driver-side airbag, and child safety seat. Crash tests of a 1996 Trans Sport equipped with dual airbags concluded that the driver would be very well protected and the front passenger would receive average protection in a 57 km/h frontal collision. It was rated: driver, ★★★★★; passenger, ★★★.

Con: The chassis and mechanicals have all been borrowed from GM's failure-prone W-bodies (Lumina, Regal, Cutlass Supreme, and Grand Prix). Some complaints of electronic module (PROM) and starter failures, sliding door malfunctions, and defective modular rear seat latches that will be replaced at no charge. Other problem areas have been a sliding side door glass that pops open, squeaks in the instrument panel cluster area, and a wind buffeting noise around the front doors. Front-end squeaks may require the replacement of the exhaust manifold pipe springs with dampers.

Confidential GM bulletins show that 1996 models (it's too early to get bulletins on the '97s), may exhibit the following, relatively minor, problems: an AC odour upon startup, a noisy power steering unit, and rattles in the rear compartment area of the roof console.

Road Performance

Pro: The 3.4L V6 engine should provide smooth acceleration and plenty of power for most driving conditions. Very stable and responsive on the highway. Four-speed automatic transmission with Overdrive saves fuel and shifts more smoothly than does the manual. Load-levelling suspension automatically adjusts for additional passenger or cargo weight. Low centre of gravity makes the APV more stable at high speeds. Good ABS.

Con: Old technology and conventional front-drive mechanicals have proven to be unreliable on GM's midsize sedans. The long nose makes city driving a bit scary.

Comfort/Convenience

Pro: The dash is ultra-modern and laid out to facilitate readability and accessibility. The large windshield contains a special reflective coating that keeps the interior cool by reflecting 60 percent of the sun's radiation. Long 24-inch wiper blades incorporate washer nozzles. Defrosting system uses two plastic vents to direct air to the 17-square-foot windshield and two side windows. Comfortable front and rear seats outclass what's offered by other domestic automakers. Seating is limited to five adults (two up front and three on a removable bench seat) on the standard models, but this can be increased to seven if optional modular seats are ordered. Seats can be folded down flat, creating additional storage space.

Lightweight (34-pound) seats have quick-release latches and can be shifted easily into a variety of configurations. Easy to increase cargo room by smart seating arrangement. No high step-up into the vehicle. Plenty of space to walk from front to rear. Many storage bins and drink wells. Seatbacks fold flat to form tables. Rear hatch flips open for better storage access. The rear hatch and sliding side door also outclass domestic minivans in providing easy access to the vehicle's interior. Good heating/ventilation system only if the optional rear heater and air conditioner are included. Built-in air pump can inflate anything from tires to rafts.

Con: Serious visibility problems during cornering and parking. When the driver's seatback is upright, the seat-mounted right armrest tilts downward at an uncomfortable angle. Parallel parking is problematic with this minivan because the swoopy front end makes it difficult to judge the vehicle's position. The dash slopes so far down toward the windshield that objects would be impossible to retrieve should they slide down. The expansive windshield makes air conditioning quasi-essential. The steering wheel is offset about five centimetres to the right of the driver's seat. The pedals match the seat and are five centimetres to the left of the steering column—too far from the centre console for it to be used as a leg rest. The steering wheel rim blocks access to the climate control cluster and hides the instrument panel. Side door is often hard to open. Excessive wind noise.

COST

List Price (negotiable)	Residual Values (months)			
	24	36	48	60
Base: $23,475 (17%)	$11,500	$9500	$8000	$7500

TECHNICAL DATA

Powertrain (front-drive)
Engine: 3.4L V6 (180 hp)
Transmission: 4-speed auto. OD

Dimensions (Lumina/Trans Sport)
Length: 191.5 in./192.2 in.
Width: 73.9 in./74.6 in.
Wheelbase: 109.8 in./109.8 in.

SAFETY FEATURES

	Opt.	Std.
Anti-lock brakes	❑	■
Childproof door locks	❑	■
Driver-side airbag	❑	■
Passenger-side airbag	❑	❑
Remote keyless entry	■	❑
Traction control	■	❑

Asian Vehicles

This year, Asian automakers will give you less car for less money. It's called "decontenting."

It started with that handy little vent window that American carmakers dropped as a cost-cutting and fuel-saving measure two decades ago. Then they adopted itsy-bitsy spare tires, guaranteed for at least 200 kilometres. Then plastic bodies that didn't rust (they cracked instead). But although content was reduced, prices continued to rise.

Japanese automakers know that their cars are already outrageously overpriced, especially considering that many models are now made in North America where production costs are far less onerous than they are in Japan. But their decontenting savings, and the fact that over the past year the American dollar's value has gained considerably over the yen, have meant that their margin of profit is greater now. This has allowed them to cut MSRP prices this year as a means to gain market share. And that's their marketing plan.

Japanese vehicles have been cheapened through fewer standard features, smaller platforms, and the dropping of quality base components in favour of cheaper parts. For example, the revamped '97 Infiniti Q45 should be called the Q41 now that its engine has been downsized to a 4.0L size. The car's also shorter, narrower, and 180 pounds lighter than last year's version. On the plus side, Infiniti has dropped its MSRP price by about 10 percent.

The reworked '97 Toyota Camry's cheapening is more subtle: for example, the antenna is now part of the windshield, fold-back side-view mirrors are gone, and doors are no longer triple-sealed. As a result of its decontenting efforts, Toyota has announced Camry price reductions of an average 4.4 percent.

Hyundai, the Korean automaker, is stuck with a huge inventory of unsold, discontinued cars. As a result, it's counting on sizeable rebates this year rather than on cheaper production costs. The company's offering of $1000-$2000 rebates on unsold '95s and '96s works out to a MSRP reduction of more than 10 percent.

In a nutshell, the cheaper (both literally and figuratively) '97 Japanese cars will undoubtedly drive down the prices of last year's unsold models, meaning that buyers will get a great deal on either model year. Furthermore, important rebate and dealer incentive programs (a rarity with most Asian imports) will likely be announced early in the new year.

The only losers? Last year's buyers who paid full price for their Japanese or Korean cars.

ACURA

When Acura first came to Canada in 1986 it did very well in selling reasonably priced compact cars that many considered to be no more than all-dressed Honda clones. Then the company got cocky, and rather than counting on lower profits and more sales they raised prices (over dealer objections) to what the market would bear. Fortunately, competitive pressures—not the least from Lexus and Nissan—forced the automaker to cut Acura prices with cash rebates and low-interest financing programs. Nevertheless, this move was too little, too late. Acura sales have been way off since 1991, when they peaked at almost 16,000 units.

Although they've been somewhat pacified through higher dealer profit margins and an improved product lineup, Canadian Acura dealers are still ticked off by what they consider to be the company's "take it or leave it" attitude toward them. In a recent Canadian Federation of Automobile Dealer Associations dealer survey they blasted Acura management for being insensitive to their concerns. Dealers want an entry-level model that would sell in the $14,000 range instead of the current $19,500, but no such product is in sight.

Six 1997 models are sold under the Acura nameplate: the Integra, CL coupe, TL, RL, SLX sport-utility, and NSX sports car. Except for the SLX sport-utility, which is based on the Isuzu Trooper, Acura's lineup comprises overpriced, upscale Honda variants that have been sold and serviced by a separate Acura network since 1986. Maintenance costs are low, reliability is way above average, and Acura's warranty performance has been more generous than that of most automakers.

2.2 CL/3.0 CL

RATING: Not Recommended; a first-year luxury coupe.

GENERAL COMMENTS: Launched last summer, the most distinctive features of the $27,800 2.2L CL and its 3.0L CL twin are the engine and wheels. These cars are both stylish, front-drive, five-passenger, American-built and designed luxury coupes. They have a flowing, slanted back end, and no apparent trunk lock (a standard remote keyless entry system opens the trunk from the outside and a lever opens it from the inside). And while other Japanese automakers are taking content out of their vehicles, Acura has put content into the CL, making it one of the most feature-laden cars in its class.

Sure, we all know that the coupe's mechanicals and platform aren't that different from the Accord's, but when you add up all of its standard bells and whistles you get a fully-loaded small car that costs thousands of dollars less than such competing luxury coupes as the BMW 318is and the Lexus SC300. Consider this array of standard features: power windows, power mirrors, power moonroof, six-way power driver seat, a remote keyless entry system, ABS, leather-wrapped steering wheel, simulated wood trim, automatic climate control, dual airbags, tilt steering wheel, cruise control, CD player, and an AM/FM stereo with six speakers.

Although no one would consider the CL a high performance car, it gets plenty of power from an all-new 3.0L 24-valve sohc Variable Valve Timing and Lift Electronic Control (VTEC) V6, in addition to the Accord's 2.2L, single overhead cam 4-cylinder VTEC engine. That engine's 145 horses (same as the Accord) takes the CL from 0 to 100 km in a respectable nine seconds. Handling is better than average, thanks to the Accord's upgraded suspension, variable-assisted steering, and 16-inch wheels that are an inch larger than the Accord's (I told you there was a lot of Accord in the CL).

On the minus side, this is not a car for passengers in the rear. Back-seat room is insufficient, unless the front seats are pushed all the way forward and the rear windows don't roll down.

Cost analysis/Alternatives: The only difference between these two coupes is the 3.0/CL's larger engine, different wheels, and larger exhaust tip. Other vehicles worth considering, but with fewer standard features: the BMW 318, Honda Accord, Lexus SC300, Nissan Maxima, and Toyota Camry. **Rebates**: No incentives or rebates are likely. **Destination charge:** $350. **Recommended options**: None. **Supplementary warranty**: Not needed. **Parts supply/Servicing**: Above average. **Depreciation**: Expected to be below average. **Highway/City fuel economy**: 8.5-12L/100 km.

Acura 2.2 CL: an Accord clone with lots of extra features.

TL Series

RATING: Not Recommended.

NEW FOR '97: Insignificant, minor changes.

GENERAL COMMENTS: Retailing for about $36,600 ($5000 less than the 3.2L), this isn't a particularly impressive car, with its conservative, Legend-like styling and unusual 2.5L 176-hp 5-cylinder powerplant carried over from previous years. Last year it was joined by a 3.2L 200-hp V6 variant.

The base engine provides smooth but less than dazzling acceleration. It feels sportier, though, because the 2.5TL isn't loaded down with the extra weight that hampers its big brother. Despite its extra horses, the optional V6 can't compare with most sports sedans, and performs decently only on the open road.

Although the TL is roomier than the Vigor, its rear seat still feels cramped. Fuel economy with a manual transmission is 9.8L/100 km; with a 4-speed automatic transmission it should get 10.1L/100 km.

The Vigor had a better-than-average repair record, so the TL variants should be just as reliable. The only areas that have proven troublesome in the past have been poor body fits and premature brake wear.

Be wary of Acura's claim that the TL is "a personal performance sports sedan . . . with a higher level of performance than that available in the Integra." For despite its five cylinders, the TL lacks vigour (no pun intended) and smoothness when compared with the old Integra, and is seriously outclassed by the competition.

Standard safety features include ABS, dual airbags, childproof door locks, three-point seatbelts, and a transmission/brake interlock. Traction control is offered as an option on the 3.2L version. Crash tests of a 1996 TL four-door Integra found that the driver and passenger would be relatively well-protected in a frontal collision. It was rated: driver, ★★★★; passenger, ★★★★.

Cost analysis/Alternatives: Get last year's TL if it's discounted sufficiently; this year's version doesn't have enough changes to justify its higher cost. Also consider a CL coupe; it's not as expensive, and is as close as you can get to the Accord with lots of standard bells and whistles thrown in. Other cars worth considering are the Infiniti I30, Lexus ES 300, Mazda Millenia, and Toyota Camry V6. **Rebates**: No incentives or rebates are likely before next summer. **Destination charge**: $350. **Recommended options**: None. **Supplementary warranty**: Not needed. **Parts supply/Servicing**: Above average. **Depreciation**: Below average. **Highway/City fuel economy**: 8.5-12L/100 km.

NSX

NSX

RATING: Above Average buy. Acura has allocated only a few hundred NSXs to this country, and will likely drop the model if sales don't pick up.

NEW FOR '97: Acura's high-priced exotic sports car, the NXS returns this year with its VTEC engine upgraded from a 3.0 to a 3.2L, boosting its horsepower and torque. This year's model also features an improved chassis for better handling, and a minor facelift.

GENERAL COMMENTS: Selling for about $125,000 and touted by the automotive press as the world's best-handling car, this 3.2L 300-hp V6, rear-drive, mid-engine, aluminum-bodied sports car goes from 0 to 60 mph in less than six seconds and covers the quarter-mile in just under 14 seconds. These are impressive figures, but they're matched by lots of other sports cars that cost much less. Without its roof, wind turbulence and road noise invade the NXS-T's cramped interior. And forget about carrying luggage.

Fuel economy for the NSX is 10.9L/100 km with a manual gearbox, and 11.3L/100 km with an automatic. Standard safety features include ABS, dual airbags, traction control, three-point seatbelts, and a transmission/brake interlock. The car hasn't been tested by the NHTSA for crashworthiness.

Cost analysis/Alternatives: The 1997 NSX is substantially changed and is the better buy if Acura keeps a lid on prices. Other two-seaters worth considering are the Corvette and the Porsche 911 Carrera. **Rebates**: Not likely before mid-summer. **Destination charge**: $350. **Recommended options**: None. **Supplementary warranty**: Not needed. **Parts supply/Servicing**: Above average. **Depreciation**: Below average. For example, a 1994 NSX base coupe, selling originally for $90,000, will now fetch about $62,000 as a dealer trade-in. **Highway/City fuel economy**: 9.5-13.5L/100 km.

Integra

Integra

RATING: An Above Average buy. Overpriced, but performance and reliability are worth the extra cost.

NEW FOR '97: The 1997 Integra is carried over virtually unchanged. In mid-summer a new high-performance model will join the Integra line.

GENERAL COMMENTS: The Integra doesn't quite fit into any category; it's a comfortable and practical small sedan with a high price. Its sporty pretensions lack the sizzle you'll find with the Eagle Talon, Ford Probe, or Mazda MX-6. On the whole, there's little that can be said against the Integra and little to be said for it. One can get the same size four-door compact with a bit less performance for a lot less money—or a similar car with a lot more performance for just a little more money.

Cost analysis/Alternatives: The 1996 Integra is substantially identical to the 1997 version, and is the better buy if its selling price has been reduced sufficiently. Incidentally, a used '94 Accord has more interior space, is more reliable, and holds its value better than does the Integra. Other cars worth considering are the Ford Probe LX and Mustang 5.0, Honda Accord, Mazda MX-6, and Toyota Camry V6. **Rebates**: $300 dealer incentive on the '96 Integras. **Destination charge**: $400. **Recommended options**: None. **Supplementary warranty**: Not needed. **Parts supply/ Servicing**: Above average. **Depreciation**: Below average. **Highway/City fuel economy**: 7-10L/100 km. VETEC 4-banger requires premium fuel.

Reliability/Safety

Pro: Acura has a comprehensive standard warranty. There have been few occasions where warranty disputes have had to be settled by third parties. The Integra has earned a good reliability record because it shares half of its components with the indestructible Civic. According to the CAA, parts are reasonably priced, with heavy discounting by dealers.

Crash tests of a 1996 four-door Integra found that the driver and passenger would be relatively well-protected in a frontal collision. It was rated: driver, ★★★★; passenger, ★★★.

Con: Limited dealer network, so make sure that your community has a Honda dealer nearby. Dealer service bulletins show that fit and finish deficiencies and malfunctioning accessories are common. Some examples: moonroof chatter while opening or closing, window rattles, a hard-to-close hatch, and poor radio reception. Owners complain of clutch failures and premature front brake wear. Squeaks and rattles frequently crop up on both the coupes and sedans. The sedan's frameless windows often have sealing problems.

Crash tests of a 1993 four-door Integra found that the driver and passenger would suffer severe leg trauma. Horn buttons may be hard to find in an emergency.

Road Performance

Pro: Brisk acceleration. The GS-R VTEC 1.8L engine cranks out 170 hp. The standard 5-speed manual transmission shifter and clutch mechanism are substantially beefed up, giving slightly higher ratios in 3rd and 4th and a taller 5th gear. An optional electronic 4-speed automatic uses "fuzzy logic" to reduce the annoying shifting back and forth over hilly terrain. Variable-assisted power steering is quick and precise. Good handling under almost all circumstances. Gas shocks and improved body rigidity create a smooth and firm ride. Ride doesn't deteriorate as load is increased. Acceptable standard brakes.

Con: Engine whines at high speed. Steering exhibits a bit of understeer and excessive lean when cornering. Base tires just don't have sufficient grip. Standard braking is a bit long. ABS brakes are slow to engage.

Comfort/Convenience

Pro: The coupe's seat cushions provide good thigh support, its windows have frames for better sealing, and a reinforced body has made for a stiffer body shell. The four-door sedan carries four passengers in comfort and has a spacious trunk. The cloth-covered seats are fairly comfortable and supportive for short drives. The attractive interior includes an easy-to-read dashboard layout with large analogue gauges that are complete and clear, and climate and radio controls that are easy to operate. The climate control system works flawlessly. The sedan has comfortable rear seating for two adults, and the rear seats fold down completely.

Con: The coupe's four small headlights are a throwback to the Isuzu Impulse, and the side-view mirrors resemble those of both the Prelude and Civic. The sunroof switch is too far from the sunroof, the radio controls aren't easily reached, and the sun visors are cheap-looking. Entry/exit is made difficult by the curved windows and the doors' awkward design. The three-door model's rear seat is cramped and suitable only for luggage on trips longer than to the corner grocery store. The steering column, even when tilted to the max, practically rests on your kneecaps. Seats are lower than usual and tend to be uncomfortable on long trips. The trunk on the coupe and sedan is awkward to load because of its narrow opening and extra height. Poor sealing around the sedan's side windows. Lots of road and engine noise, especially at full throttle.

COST

List Price (firm)	**Residual Values** (months)			
	24	**36**	**48**	**60**
RS: $19,500 (11%)	$9500	$8400	$7500	$6000

TECHNICAL DATA

Powertrain (front-drive)
Engines: 1.8L 16-valve 4-cylinder (142 hp) • 1.7L 16-valve 4 GS-R (170 hp)
Transmissions: 5-speed manual • 4-speed auto.

Dimensions (coupe/sedan)
Length: 172.4 in./178.1 in.
Width: 67.2 in/67.3 in.
Wheelbase: 101.2 in./103.1 in.

SAFETY FEATURES

	Opt.	Std.
Anti-lock brakes	❑	■
Driver-side airbag	❑	■
Passenger-side airbag	❑	■
Remote keyless entry	■	❑

HONDA

With Toyota rolling back prices, look for Honda to do the unthinkable and sell its '97 models at a discount too. If the yen continues to slide, and if American automakers' price increases aren't rolled back, Honda will have a unique opportunity this year to snatch market share from the American Big Three while Honda customers pocket their savings.

Civic/del Sol

del Sol

RATING: Recommended. The overweight del Sol is Not Recommended, because of its poor handling and its exorbitant price for what is essentially a two-seater commuter car with sporty pretensions.

NEW FOR '97: After a major rework last year, the Civic returns with 14-inch wheels and standard wheel covers for the DX. The del Sol is unchanged.

GENERAL COMMENTS: Having last year undergone its sixth design change since 1973, the Civic has become one of the most refined and competent subcompacts on the market today. Few larger and costlier cars can match its quality, performance, and roominess. The hatchback line is available in a wide range of models: a base CX, mid-level DX, a VX econobox, and the high-performance Si. Sedans are designated in a fashion similar to that of the Accord's, with a base DX, mid-level LX, and a high-performance EX that carries the most powerful Civic powerplant.

The Civic DX hatchback lacks many of the luxury items that are standard on the LX, but it also lacks the 200 to 300 pounds in extra curb weight, giving it the performance and handling edge. Civics are easy to resell as used cars and command premium prices. Unfortunately, Civics in any form are now very expensive, especially when compared with domestic offerings. On the other hand, they're stylish, have lots of interior room, and are tops in fuel efficiency thanks to Honda's new VTEC system.

Imported from Japan, the del Sol is a semi-convertible sporty coupe that's less fuel-efficient and less responsive than the CRX it replaced four years ago. It comes with a sporty twin-cam VTEC 160-hp variant of the 1.6L powerplant, standard ABS, power door locks, an interior trunk release, low fuel warning light, and driver-side vent control.

Cost analysis/Alternatives: Cheaper second-series '96 models are a better buy if the '97s' prices aren't sufficiently cut. Choose the reasonably priced Civic CX or DX for the best combination of comfort, performance, and fuel economy. Other cars worth considering are the '96 Eagle Summit, Geo Metro, Nissan Sentra, Suzuki Swift, and Toyota Paseo and Tercel. Mazda's Miata or the '96 MX-3 are good del Sol alternatives. **Rebates**: Not likely. **Destination charge**: $300. **Recommended options**: The "fuzzy logic" automatic transmission is a wise investment. Steer clear of the standard-issue radio. These cars are popular with thieves; buy an anti-theft system device from an independent retailer. Remember, Honda dealers have higher-than-average markups on options, so this is the best area to bring the retail price down. **Supplementary warranty**: Not needed. **Parts supply/Servicing**: Above average. **Depreciation**: Below average. For example, a '94 base Civic that retailed for $10,595 is now worth about $7400 wholesale; a '94 Chevrolet Cavalier sold new for $10,998 now has a wholesale value of $6900. Overall savings: almost $1000. **Highway/City fuel economy**: 6.5-9.5L/100 km.

Reliability/Safety

Pro: Assembly, as well as the quality of materials used in the cars, is first class. Civics have proven to be almost trouble-free, with a sound base warranty, good dealer backup, and easily found parts. Independent repair shops find most Civics easy to repair, except for some engines, like the CVCC.

Crash tests of a 1996 dual airbag-equipped Civic sedan showed that the driver would have better than average protection and the front passenger would receive excellent protection in a 57 km/h frontal collision. It was rated: driver, ★★★★; passenger, ★★★★★.

Con: Main problem areas have been engine timing belts, constant velocity joints, steering components, premature front brake wear, and excessive brake noise. The 16-valve engine's extra mechanical and electronic complexity means that the corner mechanic won't have a good idea what to do if a problem occurs. According to the CAA, parts are a bit more expensive than for most other cars in this class.

Air-conditioner condensers frequently fail after a few years. Honda will pick up the approximate $300 cost if you threaten to take the company to court. The two-piece tailgate is a paradise for rattles, and is complicated without any reason to be. Metallic paint problems.

Confidential dealer service bulletins reinforce owners' impressions that the Civic is a top-quality car. Bulletins list the following minor problems that may carry over to the '97s: a sticking fuel gauge; the cupholder lid sticks open or closed; and a rattling noise from the driver's side lower dash cover and rear headliner, just above the rear windshield (see illustration below).

Bulletin No. 95-026
Issue Date: NOV 6, 1995
Model [New] 1992-96 CIVIC
Applicable To: ALL OHIO-PRODUCED 4-DOORS
File under: BODY
Rattle From rear of headliner (Supersedes 95-026, dated May 8, 1995).
SYMPTOM
A rattling noise is coming from the rear of the headliner, just above the rear window.
PROBABLE CAUSE
The rear window upper fasteners are rattling.
CORRECTIVE ACTION
Remove the rear window upper fasteners.

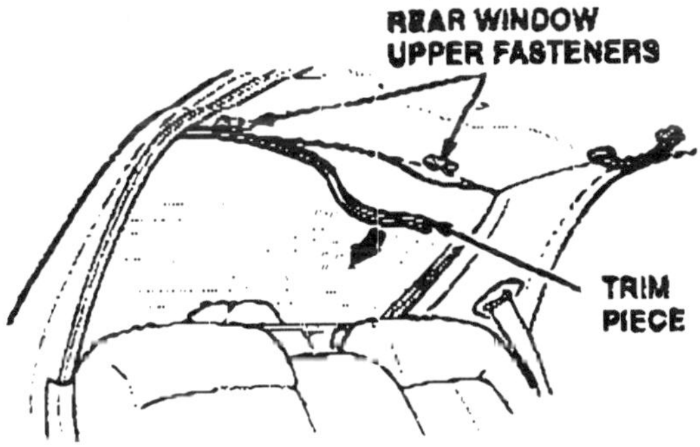

This headliner rattling is a common problem that affects 1992-96 Civics and is normally covered by the warranty. For repairs on cars that are out of warranty, most Honda dealer service bulletins include a "goodwill" paragraph telling the dealer that "any repair performed after warranty expiration may be eligible for goodwill consideration by the District Service Manager or your Zone Office. You must request consideration, and get a decision, before starting work."

Road Performance

Pro: The 1.6L engine is smooth and responsive once it attains cruising speed. The only disadvantage with these multi-valve engines is that peak power is developed at high engine rpm. Handling is excellent, and the ride, though stiff, is among the best in the subcompact class. The del Sol's VTEC engine gives the car a much-needed acceleration boost, particularly when shifting through the higher gear ranges. All Civics give a ride that's smoother over uneven terrain than last year's version, thanks to a retuning of the double-wishbone suspension.

Con: The base engine loses its pep when the Overdrive gear on the automatic transmission engages in city driving, and the VTEC variant is noisy. The 4-speed automatic transmission jerks into gear during hard acceleration, and the 5-speed manual is hard to shift when it's cold. Optional power steering is imprecise and doesn't communicate much road feel. The VX gets its impressive fuel economy by sacrificing acceleration power through its extremely tall gearing. Get used to using second gear for cornering under speed or passing other cars unless you want to stall out. It's hard to modulate the throttle without having the car surge or lurch. Moderate body roll when cornering. Skinny tires add to overall noise and harshness.

Comfort/Convenience

Pro: This year the coupe and sedan are two inches longer, while the hatchback is four inches longer. All three body styles are also three inches taller. These changes, along with interior refinements and the large window area, make for excellent visibility and a feeling of spaciousness. Good driving position. The Civic's front seats are comfortable and supportive. Excellent dashboard design, with easily read gauges and accessible controls. Versatile and spacious cargo areas or trunk space. DX and LX models are nicely trimmed inside. Heating and ventilation are first class. Engine/road noise has been cut considerably.

Con: VX styling makes the car appear unusually heavy. The del Sol's front seats are a bit too firm and set too low to permit short drivers to see over the hood, and its tiny horn buttons may be hard to find in an emergency. The ignition switch is hidden away under the steering wheel. Uncomfortable back seat will hold only two adults. The basic Civic is very plasticky inside. Dual cup-holders aren't very accessible.

The del Sol's body produces more squeaks and rattles than you will find in other, more structurally rigid Civics. The confining interior and low seating make for difficult entry and exit, and restrict overall visibility. The trunk has limited cargo space and a high sill, the tiny sun visors are practically useless, and the Targa-style top is tough to remove. Cheap-sounding doors.

COST

List Price (firm)	Residual Values (months) 24	36	48	60
CX: $12,995 (9%)	$8000	$7000	$6000	$5000
del Sol : $20,495 (12%)	12,000	10,500	9000	8000

TECHNICAL DATA

Powertrain (front-drive/4X4)
Engines: 1.6L 16-valve 4 (106 hp) •1.6L 16-valve 4 (127 hp)• 1.6L DOHC 16-valve 4 (160 hp)
Transmissions: 5-speed manual • 4-speed auto. • 4-speed auto. "fuzzy logic"

Dimensions (Sedan/del Sol)
Length: 173 in./157.3 in.
Width: 66.9 in./66.7 in.
Wheelbase: 103.2 in./93.3 in.

SAFETY FEATURES

Civic	Opt.	Std.
Anti-lock brakes	■	■
Childproof door locks	❑	■
Driver-side airbag	❑	■
Passenger-side airbag	❑	■
Remote keyless entry	❑	■

del Sol	Opt.	Std.
Anti-lock brakes	❑	■
Driver-side airbag	❑	■
Passenger-side airbag	❑	■
Remote keyless entry	❑	■

Accord

Accord wagon

RATING: Recommended. Accord represents the state of the art in family sedans. It's smooth, quiet, competent, and has excellent engineering backed by excellent assembly.

NEW FOR '97: Revised alloy wheels for the EX. A major redesign is scheduled for 1998.

GENERAL COMMENTS: The Accord doesn't really excel in any particular area; it's just very, very good at everything. It's smooth, quiet, mannerly, and competent, with outstanding fit and finish inside and out. Every time Honda redesigned the line it not only caught up with the latest advances, but went slightly ahead. Strong points are comfort, fit and finish, ergonomics, impressive assembly quality, reliability, and driveability.

Fast and nimble without a V6, this is the car of choice in the compact sedan class for drivers who want maximum fuel economy and comfort along with lots of space for grocery hauling and occasional highway cruising. With the optional 16-valve 4-cylinder engine or V6, the Accord is one of the most versatile compacts you can find. It offers something for everyone, and its high resale value means there's no way you can lose money buying one.

Cost analysis/Alternatives: The 1996 Accords are practically identical to the 1997s, and are a real bargain if you can find one with a reduced price. There are also lots of reliable and cheaper cars in this class that come with a V6, handle just as well, and give as much interior space. Some vehicles worth considering: Ford Taurus and Sable, BMW 325i, Mazda Protegé and 626, Nissan Altima and Stanza, Toyota Camry, and VW Golf and Jetta. **Rebates**: '96 V6 Accords get $1000 dealer incentives; 4-bangers get $700. **Destination charge**: $500. **Recommended options**: If you're likely to do a lot of driving in the snow or over wet pavement, don't let the dealer sell you Michelin MXV4 tires. They're terrible snow performers. Choose instead one of the brands recommended in Part One. **Supplementary warranty**: Not needed. **Parts supply/Servicing**: Above average. **Depreciation**: Below average. **Highway/City fuel economy**: 7-9.5L/100 km with the base 2.2L; 7.5-10L/100 km with the 16-valve 2.2L; 9-13L/100 km with the V6 engine.

Reliability/Safety

Pro: The standard Honda warranty is one of the best. Reliability is excellent for the first five years. These cars are built with care; rarely is a misaligned piece of trim or a crooked seam to be found. Corrosion-prone overlapping metal panels have been eliminated and galvanized steel used instead. Honda has also made efforts to improve customer relations in the last few years, and the results are good: CAA surveys show that customer satisfaction is an impressive 88 percent, compared to 85 percent for both the Toyota Camry and Mazda 626. A large dealer network means that parts and service are never far away, and parts prices are very reasonable. Honda will replace at no charge faulty seatbelts in the rear.

Crash tests of a 1996 dual airbag-equipped Accord concluded that the driver would be relatively well-protected and a passenger would receive average protection in a 57 km/h frontal collision. It was rated: driver, ★★★★; passenger, ★★★.

Con: Air-conditioner condensers frequently fail after a few years. Some body glitches and premature front brake wear are the more common problems reported by owners and confirmed by internal bulletins.

Dealer service bulletins list the following three problems that may carry over to the '97s: instrument panel creaks (see first DSB illustration below), poor fit of the wheel centre cap, and a screeching noise heard when lowering the driver's window (see second DSB illustration below).

Bulletin No. 93-049
Issue Date: OCT 30, 1995
Model [New] 1994-96 ACCORD
Applicable to [New]: See VEHICLES AFFECTED
File Under: BODY
Instrument Panel Creak
(Supersedes 93-049, Gauge Panel Creak, dated November 28, 1994)
SYMPTOM [New]
The noise can be caused by any of the following:

- The instrument panel rubs against the dashboard.
- The instrument panel rubs against the clear plastic cover of the gauge assembly.
- A gauge assembly wiring harness rubs against the top of the dashboard.

VEHICLES AFFECTED [New]
1994: All
1995: Coupe-All
Sedan-All
Wagon-Thru VIN 1HGCE1...SA013764
1996: Coupe-Thru VIN 1HGCD7...TA001439
Sedan-Thru VIN 1HGCD5...TA007151
DIAGNOSIS [New]
While driving on a rough road, press on the gauge assembly, then push up on the top of the dashboard where it meets the instrument panel. If neither action eliminates the noise, continue with CORRECTIVE ACTION.
RECOMMENDED MATERIALS
EPT 3T: P/N 06990-SA5-000, H/C 2086643
Wool felt: P/N 06993-SA5-000, H/C 2086676
PARTS INFORMATION
Nylon washer, 1.5 mm (two required):
P/N 90295-A140, H/C 4683850
CORRECTIVE ACTION [New]
Make sure there is clearance between the instrument panel and the gauge assembly. Relocate and apply EPT to the wiring harnesses. Apply wool felt around the outer edge of the instrument panel.
Use a business card to check for clearance between the instrument panel and the gauge assembly.

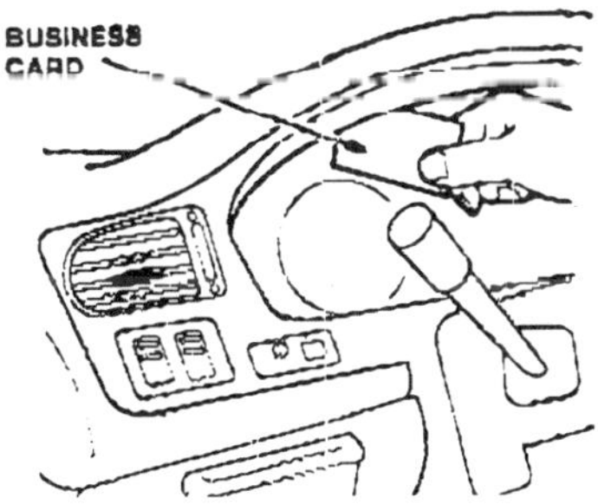

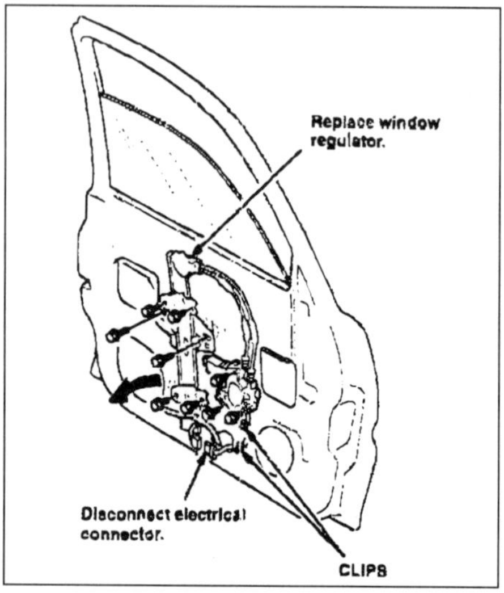

Window-screeching affects all 1994-96 Accords and is normally covered by the warranty. Cars that are out of warranty fall under Honda's "goodwill" warranty guidelines (see Civic).

Road Performance

Pro: The 2.2L 4-cylinder engines are essentially the same as last year's offerings. They give sparkling performance with minimal noise. An optional V6 provides plenty of grunt for a full load. The 5-speed manual transmission works very well with smooth and light clutch action. The 4-speed automatic has Overdrive to help save fuel. It also has a Grade Logic feature that reduces gear hunting when climbing hills and automatically downshifts when descending, using engine compression to brake. Excellent handling in town or on the highway. Excels in smoothness when passing over freeway expansion joints and potholes, where it damps out the jolts better than most cars in its class. Although its power ratings aren't much higher than that of the Ford Contour's slightly smaller engine, it feels considerably stronger. It's also amazingly smooth and quiet. There's not a trace of vibration throughout the operating range, including at idle.

The emphasis on comfort also dominates the Accord's ride and handling. Although its chassis is as good as any, Honda's suspension settings aren't as firm as those of the other cars in this group. A firm but well-controlled ride is achieved through increased body rigidity, a reworked suspension, and wider, larger-diameter wheels. Improved variable-assist power steering provides excellent road feel.

Con: No all-wheel drive option, available on many cars in the Accord class. The four-door and wagon have a less rigid suspension and less precise road handling than does the coupe. Firm suspension makes for tiresome journeys over rough roads. Slight tendency to understeer and excessive body lean when cornering. Braking is just adequate, with longer stops and some loss of directional control.

Comfort/Convenience

Pro: The well-designed dashboard looks like it's one big moulding, rather than a lot of pieces thrown together. Everything is right where it should be, easily seen and easily reached. Comfortable front seats are well padded and supportive. The Accord's rear seat measurements are virtually identical to those of the Contour. Flush side windows, improved bodywork, and better-positioned windshield wipers make for a more aerodynamic and quiet-running vehicle. Clear gauges and instruments. User-friendly controls and instrumentation. The radio and AC controls have been moved closer to eye level. Excellent driving position. Very comfortable, sporty front seating. Redesigned front seat bases provide more rear foot room. Easy entry and exit. Large trunk on sedans, and versatile hatchback design. The LX and DX sedans' pass-through rear seats allow for more convenient cargo handling. Excellent visibility.

Con: Conservative interior styling. The dash was reworked last year, but it still needs improving. Shoulder space is a bit cramped. Front and rear seats provide poor thigh support. The driver's seat could use a height adjuster. Rear seating is too low. Room for three is fairly tight and the middle passenger will be squeezed from both sides. Rear door armrests are useless. Limited ventilation. Poor insulation leads to excessive engine and road noise, particularly at full throttle.

COST

List Price (firm)	**Residual Values** (months) 24	36	48	60
LX: $20,995 (14%)	$13,200	$10,500	$ 9000	$ 8000
EX: $23,495 (16%)	15,000	12,000	11,000	9500

TECHNICAL DATA

Powertrain (front-drive)
Engines: 2.2L 4 (130 hp)
• 2.2L 16-valve 4 (145 hp)
• 2.7L V6 (170 hp)
Transmissions: 5-speed manual • 4-speed auto.

Dimensions (sedan)
Length: 185.6 in.
Width: 70.1 in.
Wheelbase: 106.9 in.

SAFETY FEATURES

	Opt.	Std.
Anti-lock brakes	■	❑
Childproof door locks	❑	■
Driver-side airbag	❑	■
Passenger-side airbag	❑	■
Remote keyless entry	❑	■

Prelude

Prelude

RATING: An Above Average buy. Performance upgrades leave last year's model in the dust.

NEW FOR '97: This is the year for big Prelude changes. The car has been restyled, repowered, and given handling upgrades that make it a better performing, more comfortable-riding sports coupe. The base 2.2L VTEC engine gets five additional horses, a new Automatic Torque Transfer System (ATTS), an upgraded suspension, standard ABS, air conditioning, 16-inch wheels, and a CD player with six speakers. The Sequential SportShift automatic transmission (a variation of the one used in the NSX) is now available with the base Prelude. This year's car is roomier (the extended wheelbase gives added stability and provides more room in the rear seating area), has a more solid body structure, and includes a totally redesigned, user-friendly dash with analogue gauges.

GENERAL COMMENTS: This fifth generation Prelude is complete, functional, and rational without any hint of aggression in its styling or performance components. In fact most of its performance upgrades won't be noticed by the average driver. The 2.2L 195-hp VTEC engine, Honda's most powerful, is the only engine offered this year. There are two trim levels available, the base Prelude and the Prelude Type SH, due out next summer.

Cost analysis/Alternatives: If you don't know it already, the 1997 Prelude is substantially improved over last year's version, and is a real bargain if Honda doesn't get greedy. Other worthwhile cars to consider are the Acura Integra, Eagle Talon, Ford Mustang and Probe, Mazda '96 MX-3 and '96 RX-7, Nissan 240SX and '96 300ZX, and Toyota Celica. **Rebates**: Likely around mid-summer. **Destination charge**: $300. **Recommended options**: None. **Supplementary warranty**: Not needed.

Parts supply/Servicing: Above average. **Depreciation**: Below average. **Highway/City fuel economy**: 8.5-11L/100 km.

Reliability/Safety

Pro: As far as performance and reliability go, the Prelude is one of the best sports coupes on the market. Like other Hondas it's pricy, but the extra cost is easily justified by what the car can deliver—and you get the money back through the car's high resale value. Preludes usually give their owners excellent service for the first five years. Even later on, the few problems that surface aren't difficult to diagnose or expensive to repair.

Crash tests of a 1994 Prelude concluded that the driver and passenger would be relatively well protected in a 57 km/h frontal collision. It was rated: driver, ★★★★; passenger, ★★★★★.

Con: Air-conditioner condensers frequently fail after a few years and often need cleaning to eliminate disagreeable odours. Owners have complained about minor electrical problems, brake squealing, and prematurely warped front brake rotors. Most corner mechanics are ill-equipped to service these cars, and the new Automatic Torque Transfer System (ATTS) won't make their job any easier. According to the CAA, parts are a bit more expensive than for other cars in this class.

The U.S. Highway Loss Data Institute says that 1989-91 Preludes had collision losses that were 26 percent higher than average. Without ABS, wheels tend to lock up easily during emergency braking.

Road Performance

Pro: The 2.2L 195-hp 4-cylinder engine is smooth, quiet, and powerful. Handling is very responsive and the ride is quite comfortable, due mainly to suspension refinements and 4-wheel disc brakes.

The manual and automatic transmissions are precise, smooth shifting, and require little effort. Steering is direct and predictable. The new Automatic Torque Transfer System (ATTS) is an interesting gizmo that transfers torque to the outside wheel in a turn, making for quicker high-speed cornering. Suspension travel is long enough to reduce bottoming out when fully loaded or when encountering irregular terrain. This year's suspension upgrade gives a better feel of the road while reducing throttle-lift oversteer, bump, and torque steer (high performance enthusiasts, rejoice!). Body roll is minimal, due partly to the stiffer chassis. Handling is excellent in all conditions. Very good standard ABS brakes.

Con: The 2.2L's five extra horses are felt only in the top end of the power range, as when passing at high speed. Even though the 195-hp engine is ideal for sporty performance, this car cries out for a V6 powerplant that provides more torque in all gears.

Comfort/Convenience

Pro: Greatly improved, user-friendly dash. More rigid body cuts down on wind and road noise. The extended wheelbase increases rear head room by 1.5 inches, knee room by 2.5 inches, and foot room by almost 3 inches. Comfortable front seats are well padded and supportive. Tilt steering wheel. Competent climate control system. Large trunk for a sporty car. Excellent visibility.

Con: Short or tall drivers may not find the driving position entirely to their liking because the seat is low and set relatively far back. Tall drivers may find head room lacking, especially with a sunroof.

COST

'96 List Price (firm)	**Residual Values** (months)			
	24	**36**	**48**	**60**
SR: $27,395 (16%)	$15,200	$12,700	$11,700	$10,500

TECHNICAL DATA

Powertrain (front-drive)	**Dimensions**
Engine: 2.2L VTEC 4 (195 hp)	Length: 174.8 in.
	Width: 69.5 in.
	Wheelbase: 101.7 in.

Transmissions: 5-speed manual • 4-speed auto.

SAFETY FEATURES

	Opt.	Std.
Anti-lock brakes	❑	■
Driver-side airbag	❑	■
Passenger-side airbag	❑	■
Remote keyless entry	❑	■

Odyssey

Odyssey

RATING: Below Average. This minivan cries out for a much-needed V6 engine.

NEW FOR '97: Nothing significant. Numerous luxury features will be available late in the model year.

GENERAL COMMENTS: Anybody want an Accord masquerading as a minivan? Not likely, when you consider all the other minivan variants on the market today. Sure, the Odyssey is more reliable and handles more easily than the American-built, rear-drive, truck-inspired minivans. But its high price, modest 2.2L engine, and small dimensions can't compete with the Big Three's newest front-drive offerings.

About the same size as the Nissan Quest/Mercury Villager, the Odyssey uses four sedan-type doors, a rear liftgate, second-row bench seating, and a third seat that folds flat. The Odyssey is more like a tall station wagon than a minivan. Step-in height is one of the lowest of all the minivans. Seat layout is tops in terms of cargo adaptability. The middle seat can be removed in a flash, and the third seat flips down into a storage well.

The Odyssey sits on a modified Accord chassis with several extra cross-members added for extra strength and rigidity. It's powered by a slightly modified 140-hp Accord 4-cylinder engine hooked to a 4-speed automatic transmission. The Odyssey is offered in two trim levels: LX and upscale EX. Seats for seven are standard.

Cost analysis/Alternatives: Get a cheaper, left-over '96 Odyssey; it has the same features as the '97 model. Mercury Villager and Nissan Quest are worth considering. **Rebates**: $400 dealer incentives. **Destination charge**: $350. **Recommended options**: Power mirrors and door locks. **Supplementary warranty**: Not needed. **Parts supply/Servicing**: Supply is better than average. Parts can be expensive. **Depreciation**: Slower than average. **Highway/City fuel economy**: With the 2.2L engine: 9.5-13L/100 km.

Reliability/Safety

Pro: Comprehensive base warranty. Component quality and assembly are similar to the Accord—first class. A minimum of buzzes and rattles. Hinged doors are a good idea from a reliability standpoint; sliding doors often malfunction or wear out prematurely. Crash tests of a 1996 Odyssey concluded that the driver and passenger would be well protected from injury. It was rated: driver, ★★★★; passenger, ★★★★★.

Con: Premature brake wear and noise from the front brakes. Trim and accessory items that come loose, break away, or don't work. Timing chain has to be frequently replaced. The transmission may be failure-prone.

Road Performance

Pro: The 4-cylinder engine delivers respectable freeway performance when it gets up to speed. Road manners are very car-like; steering is light to the touch and responsive. The Odyssey is quiet at most operating speeds. It performs pretty well in terms of all-around handling, but ride quality, like the Accord, is a bit on the firm side. Good brakes. Good fuel economy, most of the time.

Con: The 4-cylinder engine is short on getaway power from a standing start; it has to work extra hard to produce acceptable two-lane passing times, and too much noise accompanies the wide-open throttle. If you want enough power to tow light trailers, or for a big cargo capacity, look elsewhere. It's too easy to click the shifter into third gear rather than Drive when you're starting up. Busy, choppy ride over rough pavement, and excessive body lean when cornering.

Comfort/Convenience

Pro: Controls and displays are easy to reach and read. The transmission lever is located on the steering column. The Odyssey provides car-like room in the front two rows of seats; getting in is no more difficult than climbing into an Accord. Having two hinged rear doors makes it easier to climb in and out of the second row, and having those seats extend right out to the doors, as in a station wagon or sedan, also has its advantages. The bench seat in the centre row is more practical than the captain's chairs, which can't be removed. It's more like a seven-seater station wagon than a minivan. The interior is quiet in most situations, save for engine noise at full-throttle acceleration. It's easy to strap a child seat into the Odyssey because there's far less lifting and reaching. Not a lot of room behind the rear seat, but there's space enough for groceries, and the edging around the storage area will help keep your apples from rolling around. If you need to expand the cargo area, the third seat folds flat into the floor.

Con: Original equipment air conditioner is barely adequate; get the optional rear AC. Seats could use additional thigh and side support. Long drives are fatiguing. Climbing into the third row requires some agility, and it's a fairly tight fit for adults. Most youngsters simply climb over the middle seat rather than fold down the seatbacks. Although the hinged doors open wide, they're still a hassle to get around in a garage or tight parking space. Can't compete with the long-wheelbase minivans in terms of cargo capacity. Tinny-sounding radio. Heating/ventilation is below par with marginal defrosting and slow heating. Check the system out before purchasing the vehicle.

COST

List Price (firm)	**Residual Values** (months)			
	24	**36**	**48**	**60**
Base: $28,795 (20%)	$16,500	$14,000	$12,000	$10,000

TECHNICAL DATA

Powertrain
Engines: 2.2L 4-cyl. (140 hp)
Transmission: 4-speed auto.

Dimensions
Weight: 3500 lbs.
Length: 186.7 in.
Width: 70.5 in.
Wheelbase: 111.4 in.
Cargo capacity: 10 cu. ft.
Towing capacity: 1000 lbs.
Passengers: 6-7
Fuel tank: 65L/reg. unl.

SAFETY FEATURES

	Opt.	**Std.**
Anti-lock brakes	❑	■
Childproof door locks	❑	■
Driver-side airbag	❑	■
Passenger-side airbag	❑	■
Remote keyless entry	■	❑
Front/rear head restraints		Yes/Yes
Rollover resistance		Excellent
Side impact protection		No

HYUNDAI

Hyundai doesn't make top-quality cars—a fact repeated time and again by consumer groups on both sides of the Canadian border. But its cars are relatively inexpensive, and this is their main appeal. For the 1997 model year, the company launches its new Tiburon sport coupe and presents a reworked Sonata. Both the Accent and Elantra are carried over this year without any significant changes.

Quality control and competent servicing are the two areas where Hyundai has come up short in the past. And the company's latest attempts to streamline its Canadian management don't bode well for the company's future success. Last year Hyundai closed down its Vancouver warehouse division, and scaled back its Canadian head office in Markham, Ontario, by 21 people. In the past six years it has laid off 950 workers.

Hyundai's quality control also took a heavy hit south of the border last year when a U.S. customer satisfaction poll ranked Hyundai dead last and *Consumer Reports* rated the Excel and Sonata as unreliable.

Tiburon

RATING: Not Recommended; a first-year sporty coupe based on the 1993 HCD-II concept car.

GENERAL COMMENTS: Although the Tiburon (it means Shark in Spanish) is a two-door spinoff of the Elantra sedan, its stylish exterior promises sports car thrills in a compact coupe. Powered by a base 130-hp 1.8L or an optional 140-hp 2.0L, and mated to a four-speed electronically controlled automatic or a five-speed manual transmission, the Tiburon appears at first glance to be a competent, but not impressive performer. It handles well, with gas-charged shocks inside coil springs at all four corners, and front MacPherson struts. Steering is light and responsive with a minimum of body flex. Standard brakes consist of discs up front and drums in the rear; the FX package includes four-wheel discs and ABS.

Cost analysis/Alternatives: Other vehicles worth considering: the Chrysler Neon, Ford Probe, Honda Civic, Mazda MX-6, Nissan 240SX, and Toyota Corolla and Celica. **Rebates**: No incentives or rebates are likely. **Destination charge**: $350. **Recommended options**: The FX package with better-gripping tires, four-wheel disc brakes, and ABS. **Supplementary warranty**: A wise investment. **Parts supply/Servicing**: Expected to be average. **Depreciation**: Expected to be below average. **Highway/City fuel economy**: N/A.

Accent

Accent

RATING: An Above Average buy with lots of standard features.

NEW FOR '97: Nothing of any significance.

GENERAL COMMENTS: An upgraded Excel masquerading as an Accent, this front-drive 4-cylinder sedan retains most of the Excel's underpinnings while dropping the Mitsubishi powerplant in favour of its own home-grown 1.5L 4-cylinder. It's better than the old Excel, though, with its upgraded, smoother-shifting automatic transmission; stiffer, better-performing suspension; stronger and quieter-running engine; optional dual airbags; and ABS. The three-door matches the Excel in length; the four-door is six inches shorter. Interior space has been increased by an inch. Although Hyundai's new engine produces 11 more horses than does the Excel version, fuel economy hasn't changed.

Cost analysis/Alternatives: The 1996 Accent is substantially identical to the more expensive 1997 and should cost about 20 percent less. Other vehicles worth considering: the '96 Eagle Summit, Geo Metro, Honda Civic, Nissan Sentra, Suzuki Swift, Toyota Corolla, and VW Golf. **Rebates**: $1000 rebate on the '96 Accent; $500 on the '97. **Destination charge**: $350. **Recommended options**: Power steering is essential. **Supplementary warranty**: A good idea. **Parts supply/Servicing**: Average. **Depreciation**: Average. **Highway/City fuel economy**: 6-8.5L/100 km.

Reliability/Safety

Pro: Repair is straightforward because of a fairly simple design, and parts are less expensive than average. Crash tests of a 1996 Accent showed that the driver would receive average protection while the passenger would have better than average protection in a 57 km/h frontal collision. It was rated: driver, ★★★; passenger, ★★★★.

Con: Excels have always had a checkered reliability and servicing history, so the Accent has a lot of bad karma to overcome. Hyundai says the timing chain should be replaced every 100,000 km. Past problem areas include the engine cooling system and cylinder head gaskets, transmission, premature front brake wear and excessive noise when braking, wheel bearings, and fuel system and electrical components. Mediocre body assembly and poorly applied paint. A perusal of dealer service bulletins and comments from owners confirms that these cars have some serious automatic transmission glitches, described by Hyundai as "shift shock," and delayed shifting.

Horn controls may be hard to find in an emergency, rear head restraints appear to be too low to protect occupants, and the rear seatbelt configuration complicates the installation of a child safety seat.

Road Performance

Pro: The 5-speed manual transmission shifts smoothly and is well adapted to the engine's power range. Good braking, with short stopping distances on dry pavement and minimal fade. The non-power steering is precise and predictable. The ride is reasonably soft on good roads.

Con: The 4-speed automatic transmission shifts roughly under full throttle. Uneven pavement makes for a busy, jittery ride that's accentuated as passengers are added. Steering takes a lot of effort without the power-assist option. Highway handling is a bit mushy and vague. Poor braking on wet pavement.

Comfort/Convenience

Pro: Well laid-out dashboard and controls. Fairly comfortable but very firm and narrow front seats. Multiple front seat adjustments and a well-appointed interior. Plenty of front head room. Front and rear access is impressively easy. Room for three adults in the rear. Efficient, easy-to-understand climate control system. Reasonable amount of luggage space, but the hatchback is more versatile with its folding rear seatbacks.

Con: Limited front leg room for tall passengers. Temperature controls aren't within easy reach. Plenty of engine, road, and wind noise.

COST

List Price	Residual Values (months) 24	36	48	60
L (3-door): $10,995 (11%)	$5300	$4200	$3400	$2700
L (4-door): $11,895 (12%)	6500	5400	4400	3500

TECHNICAL DATA

Powertrain (front-drive)
Engines: 1.5L SOHC 4 (92 hp)

Dimensions (sedan)
Length: 162.1 in.
Width: 63.8 in.
Wheelbase: 94.5 in.

Transmissions: 5-speed manual • 4-speed auto.

SAFETY FEATURES

	Opt.	Std.
Anti-lock brakes	■	❑
Driver-side airbag	❑	■
Passenger-side airbag	❑	■

Elantra

Elantra

RATING: Not Recommended.

NEW FOR '97: This is a '96 model carryover.

GENERAL COMMENTS: Introduced six years ago, this Italian-designed, front-drive, conservatively styled sedan is only marginally larger than the discontinued Excel. Nevertheless, its larger 16-valve

1.6L engine supplies the much-needed power that you won't find with the Excel. The ride and handling are also improved, due mainly to the Elantra's longer wheelbase and more sophisticated suspension.

Elantra comes in two body styles: the base model and the GLS. As with most Asian cars, the base Elantra is loaded with standard equipment, including intermittent wipers, full centre console, dual remote-control outside mirrors, remote fuel-filler door and trunk release, reclining bucket seats, and tinted glass. Upgrading to the GLS will get you more instruments, power accessories, better tires, a tilt steering wheel, and a premium sound system.

Cost analysis/Alternatives: Last year's Elantra is practically identical to this year's version and is a better buy if you can find a discounted second-series model. Other cars worth considering are the GM Saturn SL, Honda Civic, Nissan Sentra, and Toyota Corolla. **Rebates**: $1000 on the '96 sedan and $2000 on the wagon. '97s get $500 rebates. **Destination charge**: $300. **Recommended options**: None. **Supplementary warranty**: A good idea. **Parts supply/Servicing**: Average. **Depreciation**: Below average. **Highway/City fuel economy**: 6-10L/100 km.

Reliability/Safety

Pro: Good base warranty. According to the CAA, parts are reasonably priced, with heavy discounting by dealers.

Con: Overall reliability has been slightly below average. The Elantra's brethren have racked up a sorry history of factory-related defects. If it follows in the Excel's footsteps, overall reliability is likely to be considerably below average. Crash tests of a 1994 Elantra equipped with a driver-side airbag concluded that the driver would be well-protected but the passenger would be severely injured in a 57 km/h frontal collision. It was rated: driver, ★★★★; passenger, ★.

Road Performance

Pro: The 16-valve 1.6L 4-cylinder engine is smooth, efficient, and adequate when mated to the 5-speed manual transmission. It produces 32 more horses than does the Excel. The 1.8L powerplant is the engine of choice for an automatic transmission. Good handling under almost all circumstances. Definite suspension improvement with the four-wheel independent suspension.

Con: The optional 4-speed automatic transmission robs the base engine of at least 10 horses and isn't as smooth as it should be. Brakes are difficult to modulate.

Comfort/Convenience

Pro: The seats are comfortable and supportive. The attractive interior includes an easy-to-read dashboard with large analogue gauges that are complete and clear, and climate and radio controls that are easy to operate and effective. The climate control system works without a hitch. Comfortable rear seating for two adults.

Con: Conservative styling makes the Elantra look a bit like an underfed Accord. The car is available only as a four-door hatchback. Interior room is limited. Head room is a bit tight for tall drivers.

COST

'96 List Price (negotiable)	**Residual Values** (months) **24**	**36**	**48**	**60**
Base: $13,495 (12%)	$7200	$5900	$4900	$3900

TECHNICAL DATA

Powertrain (front-drive)
Engine: 1.8L 16-valve
4-cylinder (130 hp)

Dimensions
Length: 174 in.
Width: 66.9 in.
Wheelbase: 100.4 in.

Transmissions: 5-speed manual • 4-speed auto.

SAFETY FEATURES

	Opt.	Std.
Anti-lock brakes	■	■
Childproof door locks	■	❑
Driver-side airbag	❑	■
Passenger-side airbag	❑	■

Sonata

Sonata

RATING: Below Average buy. There's lots of car for little money, but long-term reliability is still problematic.

NEW FOR '97: The Sonata has been restyled; additional sound-deadening materials plus a new engine and transmission mounts provide a smoother, quieter ride; and optional ABS is now available.

GENERAL COMMENTS: The 1997 Sonata compact sedan returns with lots more standard features, standard air conditioning, power steering, and a 2.0L 16-valve 4-cylinder engine. It also features an optional 3.0L V6 Mitsubishi engine and ABS.

If you don't want to risk a "Stellar" experience, plan on selling your Sonata before its warranty ends and depreciation takes its toll. Even during the warranty period owners report horrendous experiences. One Regina, Saskatchewan, owner of a 1990 Sonata with only 35,000 km wrote me the following litany of disappointments:

> ". . . . Now that the dealer has closed, I have to travel more than 500 km to change the oil to keep the warranty valid. And there is no 1-800 number so I have to pay the long-distance telephone calls myself. After several months they opened a dealership in Regina, but the service coupons given by the previous dealer were not honoured.
>
> I still keep asking myself how the 1990 Sonata was selected as 'Car of the Year'. . . . The only thing I can say to you, Mr. Lemon-Aid, and to the many thousands of potential buyers of Hyundai cars today and in the years to come, is NEVER BUY A HYUNDAI PRODUCT because you will really get a LEMON. If you are willing to expend your money, your own time, and have your health deteriorate due to stress, then go ahead. . . . The car may be gone in a few more years (if not before), but the memories of this

> nightmare will remain in our mind for the rest of our life, and every time and anywhere that somebody starts talking about cars, I will relate my Hyundai experience. I think I got screwed and there is nothing I can do, but I don't want other innocent people to have the same misfortune as I did, and to finish the letter, the only thing I can say is, look before you even think of buying a HYUNDAI."

Cost analysis/Alternatives: The styling of the 1997 versions has been altered significantly, but it's a toss-up as to whether these improvements merit paying more. My suggestion is to buy a deeply discounted '96 version, plan to keep it at least five years to shake off the additional year's depreciation, and put some of the savings on the purchase price on a comprehensive supplementary warranty to protect you during that period. Other cars worth considering are the Ford Taurus, Honda Accord, Mazda 626, and Nissan Altima. **Rebates**: $1000-$2500 rebates on the '96s and some '95s are likely before year's end. **Destination charge**: $300. **Recommended options**: The V6 engine; if you get the 4-banger version, keep in mind that good fuel economy means putting up with an engine that's rougher and noisier than the V6. Be wary of the sunroof; it eats up a lot of head room. **Supplementary warranty**: A wise choice, particularly if you opt for a discounted '96 version. **Parts supply/Servicing**: Below average. **Depreciation**: Average to below average. For example, a 1993 GL, selling originally for $13,495, will now fetch about $6200 as a dealer trade-in. **Highway/City fuel economy**: 7.5-11L/100 km with the 2.0L; 9-13L/100 km with the 3.0L engine.

Reliability/Safety

Pro: No serious problems reported with the 3.0L Mitsubishi powerplant. Repair is straightforward because of the Sonata's simple design. Parts are less expensive than average and easy to find, according to the CAA.

Crash tests of a 1996 Sonata concluded that the driver and passenger would be relatively well protected in a 57 km/h frontal collision. It was rated: driver, ★★★; passenger, ★★★★. The Sonata meets 1997 side-impact safety standards.

Con: *Consumer Reports* magazine says that 1990-92 Sonata owners found their cars to be 120 percent worse than average in terms of complaints. Sonatas have had body assembly and preparation deficiencies that show that Hyundai doesn't yet have a firm grip on quality control. For example, sloppily applied paint shows an orange peel effect, and the sun visors and headliner look cheap and fragile. If the Stellar and Pony experience is any guide, the third and fourth year of ownership will show serious deficiencies.

Hyundai dealer service bulletins indicate that the Sonata's automatic transmission may exhibit what Hyundai describes as "shift shock," as well as delayed shifting.

Problems reported by owners in the past: poor engine performance (hard starting, poor idling, stalling); engine runs hot and, when you're stopped at a traffic light, it shakes like a boiling kettle; #3 spark plug often needs replacement or cleaning; rough engine rattle; high oil consumption (one litre every two to three months); excessive front brake pulsation and premature wear; steering defects (when the steering wheel is turned to either extreme, it makes a sound like metal cracking); cruise control malfunctions and electrical short circuits, battery life of only 18 months, malfunctioning lights; radio failures; falling interior roof liner; faulty hood locks; a rotten egg smell coming from the catalytic converter; broken muffler; faulty resonator; defective exhaust pipe; poor door and window sealing (water leaking into the interior when the car is washed); and premature paint peeling and rusting.

NHTSA crash data for a 1994 four-door Sonata indicate that the driver would sustain severe or fatal head injuries, and the passenger would receive massive leg trauma.

Road Performance

Pro: The 2.0L engine provides adequate acceleration, and the 3.0L V6 powerplant is fairly smooth. The 4-speed automatic transmission with Overdrive (a fuel-saving feature) works smoothly and is well adapted to the engine's power range. An improved electronic automatic transmission uses "fuzzy logic" to make shifting smooth and predictable. Surprisingly effective disc/drum brakes provide good braking with short stopping distances and minimal fading after successive stops.

Con: V6 engine still a bit rough-running and noisy despite this year's improvements. Poor handling due to imprecise steering, little road feel. Lots of body lean in turns. This car doesn't handle bumps well, transmitting the slightest road imperfection to the vehicle's occupants. Ride quality deteriorates as load increases.

Comfort/Convenience

Pro: Well equipped for the price. Great visibility. Well laid-out dashboard and controls. Easily read gauges. The comfortable, fairly supportive standard bucket seats are set high off the floor. One of the roomiest midsize vehicles around—almost as wide as the Accord and as tall as the Altima, which are the benchmarks for width and height for vehicles this size. Ample front knee room. It seats five adults, has a spacious interior, and surprisingly large but shallow trunk. Good heating/defrosting/ventilation system. Many storage bins. Large engine compartment for easy servicing.

Con: Excessive engine whine and road/wind noise. Limited-use spare tire. Mediocre fuel economy.

COST

List Price (negotiable)	**Residual Values** (months) 24	36	48	60
GL: $19,595 (13%)	$10,500	$8700	$7400	$6000

TECHNICAL DATA

Powertrain (front-drive)
Engines: 2.0L injected 4 (137 hp) • 3.0L injected V6 (142 hp)
Transmissions: 5-speed manual • 4-speed auto.

Dimensions (4-door)
Length: 185 in.
Width: 69.7 in.
Wheelbase: 106.3 in.

SAFETY FEATURES

	Opt.	Std.
Anti-lock brakes	■	❑
Childproof door locks	❑	■
Driver-side airbag	❑	■
Passenger-side airbag	❑	■

INFINITI

Nissan's luxury car division soldiers on this year without any major changes, due to a series of budget cuts made necessary by a 20 percent drop in Nissan sales. Infiniti has historically stressed performance over comfort and opulence. Lately, though, it's become a more mainstream luxury carmaker and has lost its performance edge.

Infiniti makes four vehicles: the entry-level G20 sedan, the top of the line Q45 four-door sedan, the J30 V6 four-seater sedan, and its latest entry-level luxury sedan, the I30.

The I30's $41,000 base price slots it between the G20 and J30. It's viewed as the world's most expensive Maxima, incorporating many of its chassis and drivetrain components, including the 190-hp 24-valve 3.0L V6 engine and rear multi-link suspension. So far there are no indications that the I30 suffers from the defects afflicting first-year cars.

Apart from the Maxima, there are two classes of alternative vehicles that compete with the I30: those costing $40,000 to $50,000 like the BMW 328, Mazda Millenia, Mercedes-Benz C230, and Volvo 960; and those costing $50,000 or more, such as the Lexus ES 300. For my money, the Maxima looks to be the better buy.

Infinitis are sold and serviced by dozens of dealers across Canada. This small number doesn't affect the quality servicing, because Infinitis are luxury spinoffs of other Nissan models routinely serviced by Nissan dealers. All Infinitis come fully equipped and offer owners the prestige of driving a reliable and nicely styled luxury car.

('96) G20

G20t

RATING: Recommended.

NEW FOR '97: 1996 was the last model year.

GENERAL COMMENTS: The $31,440 G20 is a front-drive luxury four-door sedan that uses a base 2.0L 140-hp 16-valve twin-cam 4-cylinder powerplant to accelerate smoothly, albeit noisily, through all gear ranges. It does this while delivering 24 miles to a gallon of gasoline. Cruise control is a bit erratic, particularly when traversing hilly terrain. The automatic transmission is silent, and engine power is reduced automatically when shifting, making gear changes imperceptible. Steering is precise and responsive under all conditions. All Canadian versions come with a limited-slip front differential. The G20t model comes with sport-tuned suspension, leather seats, rear spoiler, 60/40 split-fold rear seatbacks, and foglamps.

Overall, however, this Infiniti isn't as well refined as is the Lexus in interior space, drivetrain, or convenience features. It still offers quite a lot of features that include a 4-speed electronically controlled automatic transmission, four-way power front seats, a keyless remote entry system, an upgraded audio system, polished cast alloy wheels, all-season tires, and stylish bumpers and mouldings. Safety is assured with standard dual airbags, seatbelt pretensioners, adjustable head restraints, childproof door locks, easily adjusted three-point seatbelts, anti-lock brakes, and an automatic transmission shifter interlocked with the ignition and brakes. No crash data are available.

Owners have complained that the automatic transmission shifts roughly from first to second gear, the power steering needs more assist during parking, dealer-installed foglamps cost an exorbitant $500 to replace, and the armrest-mounted trunk and filler release are inconvenient to operate. Tall drivers may find leg room insufficient. The trunk is spacious, but its small opening is limited by the angle of the rear window. The temporary-service tire is an anomaly for this class of vehicle.

Cost analysis/Alternatives: Since there is no '97 model, the 1996 G20 is your only choice. Other cars worth considering are the BMW 540i and 740i, Lexus series, Mercedes-Benz 300 series, Mazda Millenia, Toyota Camry LE V6 and Avalon, and Volvo 850. **Rebates**: Not likely. **Destination charge**: $350. **Recommended options**: None. **Supplementary warranty**: Not needed. **Parts supply/Servicing**: Above average. **Depreciation**: Below average. **Highway/City fuel economy**: 7-10L/100 km; add another litre if using an automatic transmission.

Q45

Q45

RATING: Recommended. Not quite a Japanese BMW or your father's Oldsmobile.

NEW FOR '97: There are lots of changes that make this year's $65,000 Q45 smaller and cheaper (both figuratively and literally). The V8 engine's displacement has been reduced to 4.1 litres and variable timing has been added for a net horsepower loss of 12. Yet performance remains practically the same due to the engine's greater efficiency and the car's weight loss of 200 lbs. plus. The wheelbase is chopped by two inches, and the car is shorter and narrower overall. Although front passenger space has been reduced to make room in the back, total interior volume has been increased. Traction control and 10-way power seats for the driver and front passenger are now standard, the Bose audio system has been upgraded, and the wheels and tires are an inch larger (16 inches).

Some of the changes that have cheapened the Q45 don't appear to be all that important: the independent, multilink suspension has been dropped, the wood console and dash trim has been replaced by wood-pattern plastic, and the analogue clock is now digital, which is actually an improvement, judging by *Lemon-Aid* readers' comments last year that the clock was hard to read.

GENERAL COMMENTS: As you can see from the changes noted above, Infiniti has shifted the Q45's emphasis from performance to luxury and comfort. This is unfortunate, because it reduces the distinction between the Q45 and Lexus' LS 400. In fact, now that the engine has been downsized from a 4.5 to a 4.1L one wonders if the the Q45 moniker isn't misleading advertising. Nevertheless, in spite of its downsized engine, this luxury sedan is faster and more glitzy than many cars in its category.

Retailing for $7,000 less this year, the Q45 uses a 32-valve 266-hp 4.5L V8 not frequently found on Japanese luxury compacts. It's a refined powerplant that has been both reliable and durable over the years. The car accelerates from 0 to 60 mph in 7.1 seconds without a hint of noise or abrupt shifting, giving it a slight edge over the Lexus. The engine supplies plenty of upper-range torque as well.

Steering is precise and this year's standard traction control should go a long way in preventing the car's rear end from sliding out on slippery roads. Forget about the active suspension option, though; it doesn't improve the handling or ride very much. Other niggling little irritants: power-window controls are scattered between the centre console and doors; and owners report tire thumping and excessive wind noise around the A-pillars. Parts are more expensive than other cars in this class, according to the CAA.

No NHTSA crash data are available, but insurance injury claim statistics give the Q45 a better than average rating for occupant protection.

Cost analysis/Alternatives: The 1997 Q45 is quite different from the '96; its lower price also sets it apart. Inasmuch as most drivers won't mind the '97 changes, it represents the better buy. **Rebates**: Not likely. **Destination charge**: $350. **Recommended options**: None. **Supplementary warranty**: Not needed. **Parts supply/Servicing**: Above average. **Depreciation**: Slower than average, but not as slow as you might think. For example, a 1994 Q45, selling originally for $72,000, will now fetch about $38,000 as a dealer trade-in—only $14,000 more than a '94 J30 that sold originally for $27,000 less! **Highway/City fuel economy**: 10-14.5L/100 km with the 4.5L engine.

I30/J30

J30

RATING: An Above Average buy. Long on luxury and comfort for two, short on rear seating and handling.

NEW FOR '97: The J30, and its entry-level cousin the I30, return this year relatively unchanged except for some added colours and interior refinements. The J30 also gets better side-impact protection.

GENERAL COMMENTS: Resembling the Mazda 929 Serenia and selling for about $52,600, this V6, four-seater, rear-drive sports sedan fills the gap between the entry-level and now discontinued G20 and the high-priced Q45 (why do I keep wanting to write "Q41"?). The I30, introduced last year, sells for $41,000, or $11,600 less than the J30.

In spite of their rather bland Nissan Altima styling, these "J" cars come with a long list of standard features, including the 3.0L 24-valve 210-hp V6 engine borrowed from the 300ZX (also recently departed), standard dual airbags and ABS, an electronically controlled 4-speed automatic transmission, and a fully appointed—even elegant—interior that includes comfortably supportive front seats and a soft light mounted in the headliner that illuminates the dashboard at night.

The engine performs better at high speed than low, where it lacks torque and tends to stumble. Don't take Infiniti's 130 mph pretensions seriously, though; the car's weight works against the horses. Still, it handles acceptably and provides a quiet, comfortable ride when cruising. The automatic transmission is imperceptible, and the viscous limited-slip differential assists traction over slippery roads. Nevertheless, this car needs traction control badly; its slalom performance is unimpressive, and both the tires and engine loudly protest against rapid acceleration. Steering lacks precision, but braking is particularly good, with little fading or loss of directional stability.

Crash tests of a 1996 Infiniti J30 equipped with dual airbags concluded that the driver and passenger would be relatively well-protected in a 57 km/h frontal collision. It was rated: driver, ★★★★; passenger, ★★★★. The I30 can be expected to post similar results.

Excellent driving position and interior accommodation is fine up front, although leg room is limited for tall people. Rear seat passengers will have trouble seeing the J30 as a legitimate luxury car, due to its small rear bench seat and skimpy head and leg room. Rear leg room, for example, is two and a half inches shorter than that of the Lexus ES 300, making the J30 more a four- than a five-passenger conveyance. Style also dominates function when it comes to the low roof and narrow rear opening, which makes getting in and out more difficult than need be. Function takes a back seat to style again with the poorly lit analogue clock and an inexcusably small trunk that offers less space than the small trunk of the Mazda 929. Adding insult to injury, its high sill complicates loading and unloading. Power-window switches operate in reverse to that of other cars.

Unusual as it may seem for a luxury sports sedan, the J30 is remarkably unsophisticated and gimmick-free. It's *not* front-drive, the lights and mirror *don't* dim automatically, and forget about an oil gauge, controlled traction, rear-seat air conditioning ducts, heated seats, and a memory for seat adjustments. Also, don't expect to feed this filly just any fuel; premium only, if you please.

Buyers wishing more sporty performance may purchase the J30t touring package for a tauter ride and more responsive, tighter steering. That money will get you anti-roll bars, 10 percent stiffer springs, 143-44 Goodyear Eagle GA tires with a "performance" tread on improved wheels, a ubiquitous decklid spoiler, and four-wheel steering. On the downside, J30t buyers should know that engineers have cranked up the shock and damping rates on the suspension, which results in severe axle hop and harsh jolts over rough pavement that feel as though the suspension is bottoming out.

Although reputation counts for a lot in attracting buyers, thereby keeping values high, estimating the J30's depreciation precisely is difficult since it hasn't been on the market that long. Nevertheless, preliminary indications of cars coming off three-year leases show that it does as well as the Infiniti Q45, a car with a bit better than average rate of depreciation (see below).

Cost analysis/Alternatives: The 1996 J30 is virtually identical to the '97 version and is a real bargain if the selling price has been reduced sufficiently. Be sure to test-drive the I30 as well; it gives you 20 fewer horses, a smaller body, and an $11,000 discount. Other cars worth considering are the Acura Legend, BMW 540i and 740i, Lexus series, Mercedes-Benz E420, Mazda Millenia, Toyota Avalon, and Volvo 850 and 900 series. **Rebates**: Not likely, now that the MSRP has been discounted. **Destination charge**: $350. **Recommended options**: None. **Supplementary warranty**: Not needed. **Parts supply/Servicing**: High parts cost but better than average servicing. **Depreciation**: A bit slower than average, but not as slow as dealers pretend. For example, a 1994

J30, selling originally for $45,000, will now fetch about $24,500 as a dealer trade-in. **Highway/City fuel economy**: 9.5-13L/100 km.

LEXUS

Lexus has become a luxury carmaker on its own merits, even though it started out selling dressed-up Camrys as upscale models (only the ES 300 fits that description now). But so did Acura and Infiniti, right? Unlike Infiniti, though, Lexus isn't morphing into anything other than what it's always been: the epitome of luxury and comfort, with a small dab of performance thrown in. While Infiniti engineers see the highway as a challenge Lexus sees it as an irritant, successfully isolating the driver from the driving experience. And guess what? It's a winning formula. No matter how much car enthusiast magazines say drivers want "road feel," "responsive handling," and "high performance" thrills, the truth of the matter is that most drivers simply want to travel from point A to point B in safety and comfort, without interruption. Infiniti bucked that concept, and lost.

Lexus has scheduled some major changes for this year that include a reworked ES 300, fresh styling for the SC 300 and SC 400 coupes, and extra airbag protection plus an upgraded security system on the top-of-the-line, V8-powered LS 400.

Although these luxury imports do set advanced benchmarks for quality control (see the chart on the following page), they're not engineering perfection (well, they do average about half a defect per car during the first 90 days of ownership). Cheaper luxury cars like the Acura 3.0L CL, Mazda Millenia, Nissan Maxima, and Toyota Avalon give you almost as much comfort and reliability, but without the Lexus cachet.

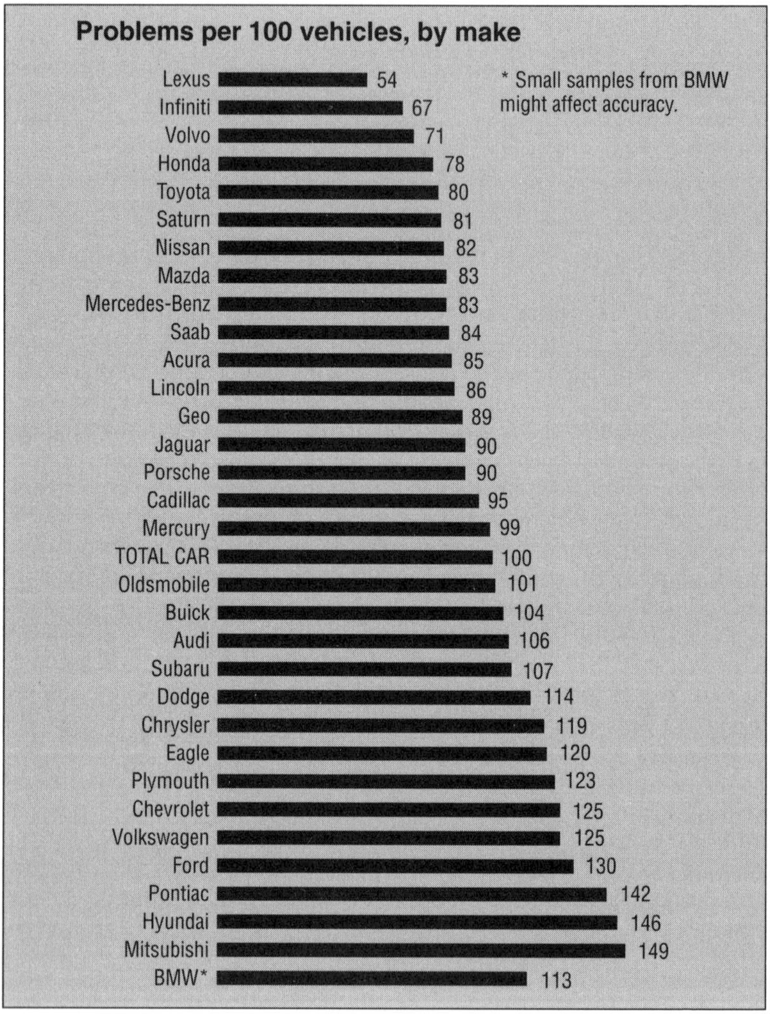

This J. D. Power Initial Quality Survey was taken last spring and includes defects reported only during the first 90 days of ownership. J. D. Power is one of a dozen survey firms measuring car quality. Although the 90-day period is seemingly too early to catch the serious defects that crop up much later, the relative placement of different companies in the 90-day survey is, surprisingly, confirmed (except for Jaguar and Saab) by additional two- and three-year surveys carried out by Power, its competitors, and consumer associations.

Dealer service bulletins show that these cars are affected by some minor body fit and trim glitches. Most owners haven't heard of these problems, because Lexus dealers have been particularly adept at fixing many of them before they become chronic. In summary, as much as the Infiniti appeals to sporty car enthusiasts, particularly with its J30t, the Lexus lineup is geared more to the luxury cruiser crowd that prefers comfort over performance thrills. All models come with such important standard safety features as standard dual airbags, automatically adjusted head restraints, an automatic transmission shifter interlocked with the ignition and brakes, childproof door locks, airbags, easily adjusted three-point seatbelts, anti-lock brakes, and optional traction control.

ES 300

ES 300

RATING: Recommended. A dressed-up Camry.

NEW FOR '97: This second-generation Lexus has undergone significant changes. The base engine has picked up 12 additional horses; restyling touches give the ES 300 a more wedge-like body that's more rigid than last year's model; and a 2-inch-longer wheelbase and upgraded suspension improve the ride, make for more responsive handling, and create more passenger room.

GENERAL COMMENTS: A Camry clone with some additional features, this $42,900 entry-level Lexus front-drive returns this year with more refinement, more horsepower, more front seat room, and fresher styling. The sole engine is a 200-hp V6 mated to an electronically controlled 4-speed automatic transmission that handles the 3.0L engine's 12 extra horses effortlessly—making for 0 to 60 mph times in the low eights—without sacrificing fuel economy. All ES 300s feature dual airbags, anti-lock brakes, improved double-piston front brake calipers, 60/40 split folding rear seats, and one of the rarest features of all, a conventional spare tire. According to the CAA, parts cost a bit less than for other cars in this class.

NHTSA crash tests of a 1996 airbag-equipped ES 300 have concluded that the driver would receive excellent crash protection, while the passenger would have only average protection in a frontal collision. It was rated: driver, ★★★★★; passenger, ★★★.

Cost analysis/Alternatives: With all its improvements, the 1997 ES 300 is a better buy than the 1996 version. Other cars worth considering are the BMW 540i and 740i, Infiniti series, Mercedes-Benz E420, Mazda Millenia, Toyota Avalon, and Volvo 850 and 900 series. **Rebates**: Not likely. **Destination charge**: $350. **Recommended options**: None. **Supplementary warranty:** Not needed. **Parts supply/Servicing**: Above average. **Depreciation**: Below average. **Highway/City fuel economy**: 8-12L/100 km.

GS 300

GS 300

RATING: An Above Average buy. Comfortable, rather than thrilling, performance.

NEW FOR '97: Nothing that's important.

GENERAL COMMENTS: Launched in the spring of 1993, the GS 300 fills the gap between the entry-level ES 300 and the top end LS 400. A $71,400 rear-drive four-door sedan powered by an in-line 24-valve 6-cylinder engine coupled to a 4-speed automatic transmission, this luxury sedan is a smooth performer that shares the same base engine with the high-performance SC 300. Drivers wishing a more sporty performance should go directly to the SC version. Crash tests of a 1996 model concluded that the driver and passenger would receive average protection in a 57 km/h frontal collision. It was rated: driver, ★★★; passenger, ★★★.

Cost analysis/Alternatives: The 1996 GS 300 is practically identical to the '97 model and is a real bargain if the selling price has been reduced sufficiently. Other cars worth considering are the BMW 540i and 740i, Infiniti series, Mercedes-Benz E420, Mazda Millenia, Toyota Avalon, and Volvo 850 and 900 series. **Rebates**: $2000 dealer incentives on the '96. **Destination charge**: $350. **Recommended options**: None. **Supplementary warranty**: Not needed. **Parts supply/Servicing**: Average. **Depreciation**: Below average. **Highway/City fuel economy**: 9.5-13.5L/100 km.

SC 300/400

SC 400

RATING: Recommended. Heavy on performance and handling, light on gadgets. The SC 300 isn't available in Canada.

NEW FOR '97: More aggressive body cladding and minor interior refinements.

GENERAL COMMENTS: The SC 300/400 luxury sport coupes are great for long-distance cruising, and really come to life on winding back roads. The SC 300's 225-hp in-line V6 taken from the GS 300 (and the Toyota Supra) isn't as powerful as the $82,100 SC 400's 260-hp V8, but it's the only Lexus with a clutch, it uses its horses more efficiently, and it shifts smoothly. Zero to 60 mph times for both cars differ by only one second. No NHTSA crash data are available.

Cost analysis/Alternatives: Except for the small styling refinements already noted, the '96 SC 400 is substantially identical to the '97 version. Other cars worth considering are the BMW 540i and 740i, Infiniti series, Mercedes-Benz E420, Mazda Millenia, Toyota Avalon, and Volvo 850 and 900 series. **Rebates**: $3000 dealer incentive on the '96. **Destination charge**: $350. **Recommended options**: None. **Supplementary warranty**: Not needed. **Parts supply/Servicing**: Above average. **Depreciation**: Below average. **Highway/City fuel economy**: 9.5-13L/100 km.

LS 400

LS 400

RATING: Recommended. Luxury high-performance and plenty of gadgets. This is no Camry.

NEW FOR '97: Front side airbags.

GENERAL COMMENTS: This attractive, $78,700 rear-drive luxury sedan returns this year considerably improved. Designed using a traditional European approach, Lexus outclasses Cadillac and Lincoln both in styling and function. The long wheelbase makes for a comfortable ride, lots of interior room (exceeding that of the Mercedes S class and BMW 7 series) and easy entry/exit.

The base engine is a 260-hp 4.0L V8 that provides impressive acceleration and superior highway passing ability at all speeds. Its transmission is smooth and efficient. The suspension provides an easy ride without body roll or front-end plow during emergency stops, thereby delivering a major comfort advantage over other luxury compacts. There's an absence of engine or wind noise, and parts are reasonably priced. The $1000 optional memory feature resets the driver's seat, steering wheel, head rest, mirrors, and safety belt. It's particularly useful if several people will be driving the car.

LS 400 models were rated better than average overall for injury claims by the Highway Loss Data Institute, an insurance industry-sponsored safety group. No NHTSA crash data are available.

Cost analysis/Alternatives: The 1996 LS 400 is substantially identical to the more expensive '97 model, and is a real bargain if the selling price has been reduced sufficiently. Other cars worth considering are the BMW 540i and 740i, Infiniti series, Mercedes-Benz E420, Mazda Millenia, Toyota Avalon, and Volvo 850 and 900 series. **Rebates**: Not likely before mid-summer. **Destination charge**: $350. **Recommended options**: None. **Supplementary warranty**: Not needed. **Parts supply/Servicing**: Above average. **Depreciation**: Below average. **Highway/City fuel economy**: 9.5-13L/100 km.

MAZDA

Mazda has always been regarded as an innovative and technically advanced automaker, but it may have bitten off more than it can chew with an overly broad range of products. Since its orgy of new product launchings during 1991-92, Mazda's vehicles now cover the entire mainstream of the automobile spectrum, including the MPV minivan and sporty Miata. Although Mazda has cut its model lineup by ditching the 323 hatchback, MX-3, RX-7, and 929 Serenia, all of this model musical chairs hasn't helped the company's bottom line.

Mazda is more vulnerable than other Japanese automakers because it doesn't have the huge cash reserves of Toyota (almost $30 billion), and has only one overseas plant (a Michigan plant co-owned by Ford) to which it can shift production. The company has been hit hard by a softening in the entry-level market that has sent Protegé sales spinning downward. It also produces such specialty-niche vehicles as the Miata roadster and the recently axed RX-7, which are often the first to head south in an economic downturn.

Mazda's misery represents a buying opportunity for smart shoppers who can take advantage of the company's many rebates and dealer incentives to pick up some good quality cars and trucks. The only caveat is the abysmal servicing and high parts cost, both of which can be overcome through the purchase of a supplementary warranty or servicing by an independent repair facility.

Protegé

Protegé

RATING: Recommended. Top-notch performance and reliability.

NEW FOR '97: Slightly restyled grille and headlights.

GENERAL COMMENTS: Now that the 323 has been dropped the Protegé is Mazda's least costly model. It shares platforms with the Escort and Tracer, but keeps its own sheet metal, engine, and interior styling. Powered by a standard, fuel-efficient 1.5L engine mated to a manual 5-speed transmission, the Protegé is one of the most responsive and roomiest small cars around.

Cost analysis/Alternatives: The 1996 models are virtually identical to the '97 version and are a real bargain. Chrysler's Neon easily outruns the Protegé, but its engine is noisier, the interior isn't as user-friendly, and its overall reliability is questionable. Other cars worth considering are the Ford Escort and Tracer (Protegé clones), Geo Metro and Saturn, Honda Civic, Suzuki Swift, Toyota Tercel and Corolla, and VW Golf and Jetta. **Rebates**: $850 rebate on the '96 Protegé; $750–$1000 dealer incentives on the '96 Protegé. **Destination charge**: $400. **Recommended options**: Get a regular-sized spare tire; it'll fit in the trunk. **Supplementary warranty**: A wise investment. **Parts supply/Servicing**: Below average. **Depreciation**: Below average. **Highway/City fuel economy**: 6.5-9.0L/100 km with the 1.8L engine and manual transmission; 7-9.5L/100 km with the 1.8L and automatic transmission.

Reliability/Safety

Pro: Better than average reliability; both the 323 and Protegé have generated few quality-control complaints. Parts aren't difficult to find and the cars are easily serviced by dealers or independents. In fact, most Ford dealers have parts that can be used on Mazda products because the Ford Escort uses lots of Mazda mechanicals. This knowledge may be useful if you find your Mazda dealer jacking up parts prices to an unreasonable level.

Crash tests of a 1996 airbag-equipped Protegé concluded that the driver would receive average protection in a 57 km/h frontal collision; passenger results weren't usable. It was rated: driver, ★★★. There's a valet lock that locks the folding rear seatbacks to prevent access to the trunk's contents. ABS is standard on the ES and optional on the LX.

Con: According to the CAA, Mazda parts cost far more than average. The front brakes tend to wear out too quickly, and MacPherson struts and rear shock absorbers don't last as long as they should. Some complaints of poor fit and paint defects. Mazda dealer service bulletins say that engine knocking on 1995-96 Protegés equipped with a Z5 engine may require the replacement of the powertrain control module.

Road Performance

Pro: The 1.5L twin-cam 4-cylinder engine is surprisingly responsive and quiet; the multivalve 1.8L engine has power to spare with plenty of torque in all gear ranges, and is quick and smooth when revved. Both transmissions shift smoothly. The 5-speed manual has a handy "Hold" feature that allows the driver to select and hold any of three lower gears through the shift lever. Two other advantages: the automatic transaxle can be driven away in second gear, an asset on snow and ice; and you can lock out Overdrive with the push of a button, allowing you to traverse hilly terrain or urban traffic without constant shifting. Although the suspension is on the firm side, handling is excellent at all times, especially since the original-equipment tires have been upgraded. Comfortable, firm ride doesn't deteriorate as passenger load increases. Excellent braking, with little loss of directional stability and no fading after successive stops.

Con: The automatic transmission robs the base engine of much-needed power. Some body roll in turns.

Comfort/Convenience

Pro: The driver and front passenger are pampered with firm, comfortable front bucket seats and multiple-seat steering wheel adjustments. Clear and well laid-out controls. Good heating and defrosting. Easy entry/exit to the front and rear. Lots of interior space to store large and small items. Trunk space, already impressive, is expanded with locking, folding rear seatbacks.

Con: The sunroof drastically reduces head room. Cheap-looking, sober interior. The rear seating is marginally tolerable for three adults. Rear seatbacks are hard, offer little side support, and are too vertical. The gear shift lever is a bit too far away when shifting into fifth gear. Some engine and tire noise intrusion into the interior. Climate controls aren't user-friendly.

COST

'96 List Price (firm)	**Residual Values** (months)			
	24	**36**	**48**	**60**
Protegé SE: $14,695 (10%)	$8000	$6700	$5400	$4700

TECHNICAL DATA

Powertrain (front-drive/4X4)
Engine: 1.5L 16-valve DOHC (92 hp) •1.8L 16-valve DOHC (122 hp)
Transmissions: 5-speed manual • 4-speed auto.

Dimensions (hatchback/sedan)
Length: 171.7 in./171.7 in.
Width: 65.8 in./65.8 in.
Wheelbase: 96.5 in./98.4 in.

SAFETY FEATURES

	Opt.	Std.
Anti-lock brakes	■	■
Childproof door locks	❑	■
Driver-side airbag	❑	■
Passenger-side airbag	❑	■
Remote keyless entry	■	❑

626/MX-6

626

RATING: Recommended. An outstanding midsize performer.

NEW FOR '97: A rear spoiler (MX-6 LS) and four more horses.

GENERAL COMMENTS: The 626 is a stylish front-drive compact sedan that does everything well. It comes in several different body styles, including the base 626 sedan—similar in appearance to the discontinued 929 luxury sedan—and the sporty MX-6.

Mazda knows how to build great sports cars, as the Miata and RX-7 prove. But the MX-6's muted styling belies its sports car capability, even though its platform is shared with the Ford Probe. Two obvious improvements are a Ferarri-type allure with side front hood humps and a low roof, plus the elimination of torque steer (the body's tendency to twist and turn in one direction under hard acceleration).

These sedans and coupes provide room for five, along with either a high level of luxury and comfort or a sporty demeanour. In spite of all the gimmicks, the 626 and MX-6 are among the best midsize cars currently available on the market. It's too bad these cars have become so expensive; Mazda's poor sales over the past few years will presumably generate substantial price discounting this year.

Cost analysis/Alternatives: The '96 models are almost identical to the '97 versions and offer the most savings. Equipped with the optional 164-hp 2.5L V6 offered with the LS package, the MX-6 competes with the Honda Prelude, Nissan 240SX, and Toyota Celica. The standard 2.0L 4-banger competes with Accord, Stanza, and Camry. **Rebates**: $1000 rebate on the '96 626; $1000 dealer incentives on the '96 MX-6. **Destination charge**: $400. **Recommended options**: Performance tires on the ES provide poor traction in snow. Order all-season tires instead. **Supplementary warranty**: A must-have. **Parts supply/Servicing**: Below average. **Depreciation**: Below average. MX-6s have the bese resale value. **Highway/City fuel economy**: 7-9.5L/100 km with the base engine and manual transmission; 7.5-11L/100 km with the automatic; 9-12L/100 km with the 2.5 and manual transmission; 9.5-13L/100 km with the automatic.

Reliability/Safety

Pro: The 626 has compiled an excellent repair history. Assembly and component quality are high. Body rigidity has been increased, making the car more comfortable and preventing many of the creaks and groans common to all small cars. Better than average reliability; both the 626 and MX-6 have generated few quality control complaints. Parts aren't difficult to find and the cars are easily serviced by dealers or independents. In fact, most Ford dealers have parts that can be used on Mazda products because the Ford Probe uses lots of Mazda mechanicals. This knowledge may be useful if you find your Mazda dealer too greedy when it comes to parts prices (more than cost, plus 50 percent).

Crash tests of a '96 626 DX equipped with dual airbags concluded that the driver and passenger would be very well protected in a 57 km/h frontal collision. It was rated: driver, ★★★★; passenger, ★★★★★.

Con: According to the CAA, parts for the 626 cost twice as much as other cars in its class. Complex electronics might cause trouble with age. There's only one DSB-covered problem affecting '96 626 and MX-6 models: front strut squeaking on turns due to faulty strut or strut bearings. Owners report air-conditioning defects, head gasket leaks, automatic transmission malfunctions, excessive hydraulic lifter noise, sunroof rattles, and premature wear-out of the front brakes. The electronically controlled shock absorbers haven't been durable, and they cost a lot to replace. Mazda suggests replacing the engine timing chain after 100,000 km.

Tiny horn buttons may be difficult to find in an emergency, and the rear head restraints appear to be too low to be effective.

Road Performance

Pro: The standard 2.0L 4-cylinder engine is smooth and peppy and works best with the manual gearbox. The V6 powerplant is a road burner once it gets up to speed. The manual transmission and clutch work very well, and the 4-speed Overdrive automatic shifts smoothly most of the time. Power steering is a bit light but very accurate and predictable. Nimble handling. Reasonably steady, soft ride outclasses that of the Accord and Camry and doesn't deteriorate as passenger load increases. Excellent braking on wet or dry pavement.

Con: The 4-speed automatic has an unnecessarily complicated gear selection scheme. This gearbox, when left in the fully automatic Overdrive mode, will often take too much time to decide which gear it wants to be in, and will downshift abruptly. The electronic shock absorbers make precious little difference in normal driving. Excessive body roll when cornering. MX-6's overly soft suspension seems almost like the Miata's.

Comfort/Convenience

Pro: The front seats are exceptionally comfortable, and there's lots of head and leg room for tall drivers. The MX-6's sunroof doesn't rob head room. Driver's left footrest prevents cramping. Well-positioned gauges and instruments. The rear seat will hold two adults easily and comfortably. The hatchback version has a versatile cargo area. Large trunk and lots of handy storage bins. The sedan's locking, folding rear seatbacks add to the trunk's versatility and overall capacity. Heating and ventilation are above reproach.

Con: The driver's seat may be too low for some. Leather seats lack heating. Rear seats will sit three with minimal comfort. Getting in and out of the rear seat on the MX-6 is difficult, and the small rear bucket seats are barely usable. Steering wheel is too large. Some engine and road noise in the passenger compartment. The defroster is a bit weak in very cold or damp weather.

COST

'96 List Price (negotiable)	**Residual Values** (months)			
	24	**36**	**48**	**60**
LX $22,400 (16%)	$13,500	$11,800	$ 9500	$8000
MX-6 RS: $22,780 (15%)	14,500	12,700	11,300	9800

TECHNICAL DATA

Powertrain (front-drive)
Engines: 2.0L 4 (118 hp)
• 2.5L V6 (164 hp)

Dimensions (626 sedan/MX-6)
Length: 184.4 in./181.5 in.
Width: 68.9 in./68.9 in.
Wheelbase: 102.8 in./102.8 in.

Transmissions: 5-speed manual • 4-speed auto.

SAFETY FEATURES

	Opt.	Std.
Anti-lock brakes	■	❑
Childproof door locks	❑	■
Driver-side airbag	❑	■
Passenger-side airbag	❑	■

Millenia

Millenia

RATING: Above Average buy. Lots of power and sophisticated mechanicals.

NEW FOR '97: Minor refinements. Halogen headlamps, new sound system, and a windshield-embedded antenna.

GENERAL COMMENTS: This entry-level, $36,500 luxury car competes with the Mercedes-Benz C class and the Lexus ES 300. Millenia was originally intended to be the flag bearer for a new Amati luxury car division that was abandoned two years ago. Despite its late entry into the luxury market—Lexus and Infiniti have had years to fortify their position—the car has been a hit, with surprisingly strong first-year sales.

Smaller than the Mazda 929, the front-drive Millenia carries the same 2.5L 170-hp V6 used by the 626. An optional 2.3L Miller-Cycle "S" 6-cylinder engine, although smaller than the base powerplant, still manages to pump out 210 horsepower. Both engines use a standard 4-speed automatic transmission.

As with all luxury cars, the Millenia comes with a wide array of standard features that would normally cost thousands of dollars more. Although billed as a five-passenger car, the middle occupant in the rear seat would be cramped and have to sit on a hump—a problem with which 929 owners are familiar.

Cost analysis/Alternatives: The 1996 Millenia is practically identical to the '97 version and is the better buy if you can find one that's cheap enough. From a performance standpoint, the Camry V6, with its less complicated powertrain, outruns the Millenia. Other cars worth considering are the BMW 540i and 740i, Infiniti series, Lexus series, Mercedes-Benz E420,

Mazda 929, and Volvo 850 and 900 series. **Rebates**: $2500–3500 dealer incentive on the '96. **Destination charge**: $450. **Recommended options**: Be wary of the sunroof option if you're a tall driver; it takes away much-needed head room. The 4-Seasons Package is a must for leather seat heating. Get the dealer to change the limited spare tire for a full-service tire that can easily fit in the trunk well. **Supplementary warranty**: Almost essential. **Parts supply/Servicing**: Average. **Depreciation**: Below average. **Highway/City fuel economy**: 8.5-12.5L/100 km with either engine.

Reliability/Safety

Pro: Assembly and component quality are high, despite the few problems mentioned in Mazda DSBs. Parts and service aren't difficult to find or perform. Crash tests of a 1996 Millenia equipped with dual airbags concluded that the driver and passenger would be relatively well protected in a 57 km/h frontal collision. It was rated: driver, ★★★★; passenger, ★★★★★.

Con: According to the CAA, Mazda parts are more expensive than parts for most other automakers. Dealer service bulletins list the following three '96 model problems that may carry over to the '97s: rear package tray rattling, a creaking or knocking noise coming from the rear of the vehicle and caused by loose diagonal braces behind the rear seat, and a cracked centre sun visor holder.

Road Performance

Pro: The 170-hp V6 engine provides plenty of power in most driving situations, but the supercharged version is a real road burner. A comfortable ride that doesn't deteriorate as passenger load increases. Electronic traction control performs flawlessly. Excellent braking with short stops, no loss of directional stability, and minimal fading after successive stops. Smooth, precise steering.

Con: The 4-speed automatic transmission shifts a bit roughly at times. Excessive body lean when cornering.

Comfort/Convenience

Pro: Firm, comfortable driver's seat has lots of control for height and tilt. Quiet interior.

Con: Tall drivers may find head and leg room a bit limited. Insufficient thigh support with the bucket seats. Controls aren't sufficiently lit. Radio controls aren't user-friendly. Rear seating isn't very comfortable for three. Erratic temperature control can't keep a consistent setting. Entry/exit is complicated by the low seat, high, large doors, and limited foot room. Narrow trunk opening.

COST

'96 List Price (negotiable)	**Residual Values** (months)			
	24	**36**	**48**	**60**
Base: $42,900 (28%)	$27,500	$23,500	$19,500	$16,000

TECHNICAL DATA

Powertrain (front-drive)
Engines: 2.5L V6 (170 hp)
• 2.3L (210 hp)

Transmission: 4-speed auto.

Dimensions
Length: 189.8 in.
Width: 69.7 in.
Wheelbase: 108.3 in.

SAFETY FEATURES

	Opt.	Std.
Anti-lock brakes	❑	■
Childproof door locks	❑	■
Driver-side airbag	❑	■
Passenger-side airbag	❑	■
Remote keyless entry	❑	■

MX-5 (Miata)

Miata

RATING: Recommended. Now that the RX-7s have been dropped, the Miata represents Mazda's best sportster.

NEW FOR '97: Minor refinements.

GENERAL COMMENTS: The Miata is a stubby, rear-drive, two-seater sports car that combines new technology with old British roadster styling reminiscent of the Triumph, Austin-Healy, and Lotus Elan. Built on a shortened 323 platform, the Miata is shorter than all other sports cars except the Porsche 911 (although it's almost eight inches longer than the old Honda CRX). The 1.8L twin-cam 4-cylinder engine, borrowed from the Protegé, is coupled to a 5-speed manual gearbox, and the rear suspension is a copy of the RX-7's.

Cost analysis/Alternatives: Not much difference between the 1996 and '97 models; buy whichever one fits your budget. Other cars worth considering are the Ford Mustang and Probe (another Mazda), Honda Prelude, Nissan 240SX, and Toyota Celica. **Rebates**: $1000 dealer incentives on the '96. **Destination charge**: $300. **Recommended options**: None. **Supplementary warranty**: Not needed. **Parts supply/Servicing**: Average. **Depreciation**: Below average. **Highway/City fuel economy**: 8.5-11L/100 km.

Reliability/Safety

Pro: Assembly and component quality appear to be first rate, and the comprehensive base warranty is fairly applied.

Con: According to the CAA, Mazda parts cost more than average. Owner feedback tells me that servicing has deteriorated considerably.

Oil filter is hard to reach. Seat fabric isn't very durable. Dirt and debris can clog up side door sill holes, allowing water to collect and corrosion to occur. The dealer will drill larger drain holes and repaint the area under the car's base warranty. Replacement batteries can be hard to find. Owners complain that the shoulder belts chafe their necks.

Crash tests at 57 km/h of a 1996 Miata concluded that the driver would be well protected while the front seat passenger would receive average protection. It was rated: driver, ★★★★; passenger, ★★★. Tiny horn buttons aren't easily found.

Road Performance

Pro: The 1.8L engine delivers plenty of power and accelerates smoothly with a 115 mph top speed. Lightness and 50/50 weight distribution make it an easy car to toss around corners. Steering is crisp and predictable. Very effective vented front disc brakes. Excellent braking.

Con: Acceleration from 0 to 60 mph is in the high eight-second range—not impressive for a sports car. The Miata is quite jittery on uneven roads and its stiff suspension can be punishing on long trips—just like those old English roadsters we loved to hate. The rear end tends to swing out when cornering under speed. Fourth-to-fifth gear shifts sometimes get caught on the gate between third and fourth.

Comfort/Convenience

Pro: The base model is well equipped. The round dash air vents heighten the sports car image, giving the cockpit a 1960s British roadster allure. Gauges are simple. Excellent heating and defrosting system. Plenty of head room. The convertible top is a breeze to put up, and the optional hardtop is quite practical and easy to install. A rigid chassis gives the car a solid feeling.

Con: Bucket seats could use a bit more padding. Interior is a bit small for tall occupants, who must sit bolt upright when pushing their seat all the way back. The steering wheel is set too close to the driver, and the seats are set too low for short drivers. Insufficient lower back and thigh support. Storage space is practically nonexistent; there's almost no room behind the rear seats, and the trunk is small and shallow. Lots of noise from the tires, engine, wind, and exhaust. Door handles are too small and user-hostile. Radio controls are hard to read and use.

COST

'96 List Price (firm)	**Residual Values** (months) 24	36	48	60
MX-5, Miata: $24,695 (15%)	$15,800	$13,800	$12,000	$10,500

TECHNICAL DATA

Powertrain (rear-drive)
Engine: 1.8L 16-valve (133 hp)
Transmissions: 5-speed OD manual • 4-speed auto.

Dimensions
Length: 155.4 in.
Width: 65.9 in.
Wheelbase: 89.2 in.

SAFETY FEATURES

	Opt.	Std.
Anti-lock brakes	■	❑
Driver-side airbag	❑	■
Passenger-side airbag	❑	■

MPV

MPV

RATING: Not Recommended. Outclassed by Chrysler, Ford, and Nissan.

NEW FOR '97: Just a few additional colours and a revised model line-up. Standard ABS and foglamps.

GENERAL COMMENTS: Mazda's only minivan quickly became a best-seller when it first came on the market, but during the past four years its popularity has fallen off. The competition is building roomier and more versatile minivans and selling them for less. In an effort to reclaim lost ground, Mazda redesigned the MPV last year to offer more interior room, dual airbags, 4-wheel ABS, and four swing-out doors.

The MPV's length was increased by 7.7 inches to 183.5 inches over the 1995 version. The hood and fenders are redesigned and wrap around a new grille. There are two trim levels: LX and ES (luxury). The ES and LX are available with optional on-demand 4-wheel drive.

The MPV offers seating for eight (seating for seven is optional), and the vehicle easily handles a 4' by 8' sheet of plywood. In rear-drive mode, when equipped with the towing package, it can tow up to 4300 pounds.

The MPV's innards are borrowed from the 929 luxury sedan, so it's not surprising that it handles quite well, although not as well as the front-drive Caravan/Voyager. Overall, the MPV is a more expensive and less reliable challenger to the Chrysler Caravan and Ford Villager and Windstar.

Cost analysis/Alternatives: The 1996 MPV is practically identical to the 1997 edition and is the better buy, if you can get a second-series version (made after March '96) that had some of the reworked '96's kinks ironed out. Other minivans worth considering are Ford Windstar, Mercury Villager/Nissan Quest, and Chrysler Caravan/Voyager. **Rebates**: $1000 rebate and $1000 dealer incentive on the '96. **Destination charge and PDI**: $895. **Recommended options**: Power seat adjustment, windows and door locks, and a rear heater. Rear AC depending on your needs. **Supplementary warranty**: An extended warranty is worth having. **Parts supply/Servicing**: Weak dealer network outside major centres. This affects parts supply and servicing. Expensive parts. **Depreciation**: Just a bit better than average. For example: a 1994 base MPV, selling originally for $20,515, will be worth only about $13,500 as a dealer trade-in. **Highway/City fuel economy**: 2WD: 10.2-14.3L/100 km; 4WD: 12.1-16.6L/100 km.

Reliability/Safety

Pro: High-quality workmanship and rugged construction. Enlarged crush zone. Crash test of a 1996 MPV concluded that the driver and front passenger would be relatively well protected. The vehicle was rated: driver, ★★★★; passenger, ★★★★.

Con: Inadequate base warranty. Early MPV models experienced expensive transmission failures due to inadequate cooling, and some ABS malfunctions caused by water infiltration. Rear-wheel ABS compares poorly with 4-wheel ABS performance. According to the CAA, Mazda parts cost more than average. Servicing has deteriorated a great deal over the past few years. Owners have complained about excessive oil consumption, premature front brake wear, AC leaks, and paint discolouration and peeling.

Road Performance

Pro: The base 6-cylinder engine, borrowed from the 929, provides adequate power in all gear ranges considering the MPV's heft, but it's no tire burner. Rear-drive set-up makes for easy load carrying and trailer towing. The versatile 4X4 Multi-Mode System goes from 2WD to 4WD at the touch of a button on the column shifter. Another button locks up the centre differential when needed to drive in deep snow or mud. Overdrive can be locked out at the touch of a switch. The driver has a good view of the road.

Con: Excessive engine noise. This minivan's highway performance doesn't inspire confidence with its poor emergency handling, especially on wet roads. (*Consumer Reports* recommends that the all-wheel-drive be engaged all the time for safe driving.) Unacceptable ride and braking. The rear end tends to swing out when cornering under speed. Automatic transmission sometimes shifts roughly. The automatic 4-speed gearbox takes its toll on fuel economy. Unacceptable braking is characterized by long stops and loss of directional control. Low ground clearance limits off-road excursions. High fuel consumption.

Comfort/Convenience

Pro: Instrumentation on the car-like dash is easily read, and all controls are within easy reach. The comfortable, plush interior seats seven or eight and offers many storage areas. Easy entry/exit up front. Centre bench seat flips forward to become a table. The third row seat can be folded or removed for additional cargo space. The swing-out side door is easier to operate and less complicated to service than a sliding door. Rear door windows roll all the way down. Excellent heating/defrosting/ventilation system.

Con: The MPV is less roomy than some other minivans, mainly because of thick walls that rob the interior of space. The 2-3-3 package is an attempt to squeeze eight people into a space adequate for only seven. Limited access and leg room for rear seat passengers. Swing-out side door hampers access in tight places. Cargo room is sacrificed with the hard-to-remove third seat in place.

COST

'96 List Price (firm)	**Residual Values** (months)			
	24	**36**	**48**	**60**
L: $27,845 (25%)	$16,500	$13,000	$10,500	$9000
LX 4X4: $30,590 (27%)	20,000	17,000	13,500	11,500

TECHNICAL DATA

Powertrain
Engine: 3.0L V6 (155 hp)
Transmission: 4-speed auto. OD

Dimensions (2WD/part-time 4WD)
Weight: 3790 lbs./4105 lbs.
Length: 183.5 in.
Width: 71.9 in.
Wheelbase: 110.4 in.
Fuel tank: 74L/75L/reg. unl.
Cargo capacity: 11.1 cu. ft.
Towing capacity: 2600-4300 lbs.
Turning circle: 36.1 ft./39.6 ft.
Passengers: 5-8

SAFETY FEATURES

	Opt.	Std.
Anti-lock brakes	❑	■
Childproof door locks	❑	■
Driver-side airbag	❑	■
Passenger-side airbag	❑	■
Remote keyless entry	■	❑
Front/rear head restraints	Yes/No	
Rollover resistance	Good	
Side impact protection	Yes	

NISSAN

Nissan has expanded its position in the midsize family sedan market with the Altima, a compact that fits in between the Sentra and Maxima. It's also making inroads into the minivan niche with its Quest, a co-venture with Mercury that also produces the Villager. Unfortunately, the company is saddled with a debt of about three trillion yen ($37.2 billion), a larger debt load than that of the U.S. Big Three combined. This debt hasn't been reduced much by Nissan's unsuccessful attempt to buy market share by offering rebates and free air conditioning and automatic transmissions. The company has also been hurt by the devaluation of the Mexican peso. It can't afford to expand beyond its Tennessee plant, which is already running at full capacity.

Nissan intends to gain market share and increase profits by taking four simple steps: cut the number of variations per model; slow down the model-change race to better amortize development costs; standardize parts so that 55 percent will be interchangeable; and offer innovative six-year leasing plans to bolster sales and service.

1997 models return this year relatively unchanged, except for refreshed styling and better side-impact protection. This year Nissan is standing pat on prices, pushing its comprehensive warranty, and using innovative long-term leasing programs to regain market share.

Sentra/200SX

Sentra

RATING: Recommended.

NEW FOR '97: No significant improvements, except for the 200SX's new rear spoiler and interior refinements.

GENERAL COMMENTS: Nissan redesigned the Sentra and decided to market a two-door version of the car as the sporty 200SX, which is more expensive and comes loaded with such important features as dual airbags, power steering, side-door impact beams, and other items that were once optional. Three body styles are offered: a two-door coupe, a three-door hatchback, and a four-door sedan. Unlike many bare-bones economy cars, entry-level Sentras offer solid, dependable motoring at little cost. The 200SX is sold as the Sentra coupe in the U.S.; it sits on the Sentra sedan's wheelbase and is a bit wider than the smaller Canadian coupe. All models are powered by a 1.6L 115-hp 16-valve 4-cylinder engine.

Cost analysis/Alternatives: The last two model years are practically identical; get the less expensive second-series '96. Other worthwhile cars to consider are the '96 Eagle Summit, Ford Escort, Honda Civic, Mazda Protegé, and Toyota Tercel. Fully equipped Sentras can often be bought for less than many other Japanese subcompacts, making them particularly good buys. **Rebates**: Expect $500 dealer incentives to clear out the leftover '96s. **Destination charge**: $300. **Recommended options**: Extra equipment on the XE is worth the $1500 expense. Spend extra money for better-grade, quieter tires. **Supplementary warranty**: Not needed. **Parts supply/Servicing**: Above average. **Depreciation**: Below average. **Highway/City fuel economy**: 6-8.5L/100 km with a manual transmission, and about a half-litre more with an automatic.

Reliability/Safety

Pro: Sentras are almost trouble-free. Overall reliability with the 1.6L powerplant is good. Good body assembly. Uncluttered underhood layout makes servicing easy. Parts are easily found from independent suppliers, and according to the CAA they're reasonably priced, with heavy discounting by dealers.

Crash tests of a 1996 airbag-equipped Sentra sedan concluded that the driver and front passenger would be well protected in a 57 km/h frontal collision. It was rated: driver, ★★★★; passenger, ★★★★.

Con: Some reports of 1.6L engine cylinder head and gasket failures. Clutch, exhaust system, and fuel system problems are fairly common after the first three years. Front brakes aren't very durable either. Internal service bulletins say that Nissan dealers will apply a sealing compound around door hinges to prevent premature rusting at no cost to owners.

Rear vision is partially blocked by the rear pillars on the coupe.

Road Performance

Pro: The 16-valve 1.6L 4-cylinder provides plenty of power for all driving situations, thanks to variable-valve timing. Both manual and automatic transmissions shift very smoothly. Good manoeuvrability around town. The steering is direct and predictable. Firm but well-mannered ride on most roads. Good brakes. Excellent fuel economy.

Con: Engine surges in stop-and-go traffic. Highway handling is a bit sloppy, and emergency handling is sluggish. Standard tires perform poorly while cornering.

Comfort/Convenience

Pro: Firm but comfortable front seats. The four-door sedan and wagon should accommodate four people without too much trouble. Easy-to-read dash gauges and convenient controls. Neatly finished interior. Spacious trunk has a low liftover. Excellent heating, defrosting, and ventilation. Good fuel economy.

Con: Antiquated, boxy styling; the 200SX's spoiler looks cheap and silly. The front driver's seat is set a bit too low. Rear seating is uncomfortable, especially with the coupe. It's a chore getting in and out of the rear seat on two-door models. Excessive road and engine noise in the passenger compartment. Very sensitive to side winds.

COST

'96 List Price (negotiable)	**Residual Values** (months)			
	24	**36**	**48**	**60**
DLX 4-door: $13,725 (9%)	$7500	$6200	$5100	$4300

TECHNICAL DATA

Powertrain (front-drive)
Engine: 1.6L (115 hp)

Dimensions
Length: 170.1 in.
Width: 66.6 in.
Wheelbasc: 99.8 in.

Transmissions: 5-speed manual • 4-speed auto.

SAFETY FEATURES

	Opt.	Std.
XE		
Anti-lock brakes	■	❑
Childproof door locks	❑	■
Driver-side airbag	❑	■
Passenger-side airbag	❑	■
Remote keyless entry	■	❑

	Opt.	Std.
GXE		
Anti-lock brakes	❑	■
Childproof door locks	❑	■
Driver-side airbag	❑	■
Passenger-side airbag	❑	■
Remote keyless entry	■	❑

Altima

Altima

RATING: Above Average buy. The competition has overrun this competent compact, which is short on power, handling, and comfort.

NEW FOR '97: Upgraded side-impact protection and a Limited Edition package for the GXE.

GENERAL COMMENTS: Nissan's latest midsize sedan, this Yuppie-mobile is a four-door, front-drive, 4-cylinder aimed at Chrysler's LH series and GM's best-selling Cavalier/Sunfire. The engine is a spinoff of the 240SX 16-valve 2.4L four-banger that delivers 150 hp.

Cost analysis/Alternatives: Don't buy a 1997 Altima if a cheaper '96 model is available. Although the SE gives the sportiest performance, the less-expensive GXE is the better deal. Other cars worth considering are the Ford Probe, Mazda 626, and Toyota Camry. **Rebates**: At year's end, Nissan will likely offer $500 to $700 dealer incentives to clear out the '96 models. **Destination charge**: $400. **Recommended options**: Get the optional automatic transmission; the manual is imprecise and not refined enough for pleasurable shifting. Overall, the GXE version is well worth the extra $2500. **Supplementary warranty**: Not needed. **Parts supply/Servicing**: Above average. **Depreciation**: Below average. **Highway/City fuel economy**: 7.5-10L/100 km with the manual transmission and 8-11.5L/100 km with an automatic.

Reliability/Safety

Pro: No reliability problems have been reported with the 16-valve powerplant. Good body assembly. Uncluttered underhood layout makes servicing easy. Parts are easily found from independent suppliers at discount prices. Only the SE upgrade gives you disc brakes at all four corners.

Crash tests of an airbag-equipped 1996 Altima concluded that the driver and front passenger would be well protected in a 57 km/h frontal collision. It was rated: driver, ★★★★; passenger, ★★★★.

Con: According to the CAA, parts are more expensive than most other cars in this class. Tiny horn buttons may be hard to locate in an emergency.

Road Performance

Pro: The automatic transmission shifts very smoothly through all gear ranges. Good manoeuvrability around town. Good braking.

Con: Noisy, rough engine performance; this car cries out for a V6 like the one used in the Maxima. The 4-banger has insufficient top-end torque and gets buzzier the more it's pushed. The 5-speed manual transmission is sloppy. The Altima's sporty handling is way overrated; there's excessive body roll and front-end plow in hard cornering, tires squeal at moderate speeds, and steering isn't as precise or responsive as befits a car with performance pretensions. In spite of the car's independent suspension, it gives a busy, uncomfortable ride that's punishing over bumps—and the ride deteriorates as the passenger load increases. Lots of engine, road, and tire noise intrudes into the passenger compartment.

Comfort/Convenience

Pro: Infiniti J30 styling. Instruments are easy to read and to understand. User-friendly controls. Comfortable, supportive seats. Good all-round head room and rear leg room for four. Good heating, defrosting, and ventilation. Well-appointed interior and large trunk. Good fuel economy. Trunk allows for pass-through storage of long items.

Con: Tall drivers will find that the pedals are set too close. Front seats are low and can't be adjusted for height. The ignition switch and power mirror controls aren't easily accessed. The small cabin seats only four. Rear seat access is difficult to master due to the slanted roof pillars, inward-curving door frames, and narrow clearance. Rear seatbacks don't fold down to expand trunk room.

COST

List Price (negotiable)	Residual Values (months) 24	36	48	60
Base: $20,795 (15%)	$12,000	$10,500	$9000	$7500
SE: $25,998 (21%)	15,000	13,000	12,000	10,000

TECHNICAL DATA

Powertrain (front-drive)
Engine: 2.4L 16-V 4 (150 hp)
Transmissions: 5-speed manual • 4-speed auto.

Dimensions (4-door sedan)
Length: 180.5 in.
Width: 67.1 in.
Wheelbase: 103.1 in.

SAFETY FEATURES

	Opt.	Std.
Anti-lock brakes	■	❑
Childproof door locks	❑	■
Driver-side airbag	❑	■
Passenger-side airbag	❑	■

240SX

240SX

RATING: An Above Average buy. Expensive reliability.

NEW FOR '97: Restyled front and rear end.

GENERAL COMMENTS: This rear-drive sporty coupe has moved away from its sports car heritage toward what Nissan describes as a luxury sports coupe. Translation: you can get some standard luxury features to compensate for the engine's limited power range when compared to the cheaper Mustang and Camaro rear-drives.

Cost analysis/Alternatives: Get a cheaper 1996 model; it's identical to the '96 version and can be a real bargain if the selling price is reasonable. Other cars worth considering are the Eagle Talon, Ford Mustang and Probe, GM Camaro, Honda Prelude, Mazda MX-6, Miata, Porsche 944, and Toyota Celica. **Rebates**: Early in the year, expect $1500 to $2000 dealer incentives to clear out the leftover '96s. **Destination charge**: $500. **Recommended options**: None. **Supplementary warranty**: Not needed. **Parts supply/Servicing**: Above average. **Depreciation**: Below average. **Highway/City fuel economy**: 8-11L/100 km.

Reliability/Safety

Pro: Above average reliability, and comprehensive base warranty. Crash tests of a 1996 240SX equipped with dual airbags concluded that the driver wouldn't be as well protected as the passenger in a 57 km/h frontal collision. It was rated: driver, ★★★; passenger, ★★★★.

Con: Reports of numerous electrical problems causing hard-to-diagnose engine, AC, radio, and headlight malfunctions. Rear-drive layout makes the car hard to control on icy, wet roads because the rear end tends to suddenly swing out upon hard acceleration.

Road Performance

Pro: Brisk acceleration with the 2.4L 155-hp engine that outclasses all of the other 4-cylinder import powerplants, except those that are turbo-boosted. The 5-speed manual transmission shifts with minimal effort. Exceptional handling and a surprisingly comfortable ride that's not a kidney-pounder and doesn't deteriorate as the roadway roughens or passengers are added. Steering is direct, predictable, and transmits lots of road feel. All of this combines to make emergency manoeuvres a breeze. Hard acceleration produces no torque steer, which is more characteristic of front-drives. Great brakes, with little fading after successive applications

Con: Engine loses torque in the higher gear ranges, producing a not very-impressive 0 to 60 mph acceleration time of 8.1 seconds—just a bit ahead of the glacial Celica—and runs roughly when hitting the 2500 to 3500 rpm range. When decelerating—i.e., coming to an exit after sustained highway cruising—the engine sometimes dies out.

Comfort/Convenience

Pro: Well-appointed interior is comfortable, with elegance nicely complementing sportiness. Intimate cockpit includes a wraparound dash that has easily read and accessed instruments and controls. Little wind noise, and overall visibility is excellent.

Con: Engine is noisy when pushed. Rear seating is an oxymoron; it's a torture chamber for the average-sized adult. Some road noise invades the interior. Extremely small trunk.

COST

List Price (negotiable)	**Residual Values** (months)			
	24	**36**	**48**	**60**
Base: $26,998(17%)	$15,000	$13,000	$11,000	$10,000
SE: $28,398 (19%)	16,000	14,000	12,500	11,000

TECHNICAL DATA

Powertrain (rear-drive)
Engine: 2.4L 4 (155 hp)

Dimensions
Length: 177.2 in.
Width: 68.1 in.
Wheelbase: 99.4 in.

Transmissions: 5-speed manual • 4-speed auto.

SAFETY FEATURES

	Opt.	Std.
Anti-lock brakes	■	❑
Driver-side airbag	❑	■
Passenger-side airbag	❑	■
Remote keyless entry	■	❑

('96) 300ZX

300ZX

RATING: Not Recommended. Overweight and overpriced.

NEW FOR '97: 1996 is the 300ZX's last model year.

GENERAL COMMENTS: Last redesigned in 1990, the 300ZX has a Porsche 928 body style with a carp-like nose. The base engine is a 3.0L 24-valve V6 rated at 222 hp. Add turbocharging to this motor and you get an estimated 300 hp. Available as a two-seater coupe, convertible, or extended-length 2+2 version, the 300ZX has a body style to please almost everyone.

Cost analysis/Alternatives: The last two model years are practically identical; choose whichever is the cheaper one left over on dealers' lots. Chevrolet's Z28 convertible offers 50 additional horsepower and costs thousands less. Other cars worth considering are the Eagle Talon, Ford Mustang and Probe, Honda Prelude, Mazda MX-6 and Miata, Porsche 944, and Toyota Celica. **Rebates**: Look for $3000 dealer incentives early next year to clear out the '96 models. **Destination charge**: $500. **Recommended options**: None. **Supplementary warranty**: A smart buy, considering this car's complexity. **Parts supply/Servicing**: Average. **Depreciation**: Below average. **Highway/City fuel economy**: 9.5-13.5L/100 km with the Turbo or 2+2.

Reliability/Safety

Pro: Average reliability. Crash tests of a 1991 300ZX showed that both the driver and passenger would be unharmed.

Con: Underhood layout is nightmarishly crowded and complicated. Expensive parts. Removable T-roof panels are likely to leak. Reports of minor electrical malfunctions. Convertible rear sport bar doesn't provide rollover protection.

Road Performance

Pro: Once the turbo kicks in, the 24-valve 3.0L V6 engine accelerates exceptionally well with the manual transmission. Some body roll in corners (due partly to the car's weight), but overall handling, particularly for a rear-drive, is above reproach. The high-tech suspension is firm but supple enough to allow the car to be tossed about in corners. Steering is quick and light. Anti-lock brakes perform flawlessly.

Con: Acceleration is handicapped by the car's weight and further dulled by the 4-speed automatic. Drivers report that the manual can be a bit notchy, especially when shifting from fourth to fifth gear. Considerable turbo lag when accelerating from low speeds. The power steering doesn't communicate enough road feel.

Comfort/Convenience

Pro: Good array of standard equipment, including a versatile and comfortable power-assisted driver's seat. Quiet engine. Wind noise is minimal and forward visibility is excellent. Easy to use, practical convertible-top storage system. Excellent heating and defrosting.

Con: Small interior. No-tilt steering option is available. Dash controls are illogical; the windshield wiper is activated by a dash-mounted rotary switch, but the rear wiper is controlled by a steering-wheel stalk. Rear and side visibility are seriously compromised by a mail slot rear window and thick side pillars. The rear seat on the 2+2 is for small children, not adults. Convertible top eliminates usable trunk space and is hard to operate. Atrocious fuel consumption caused by excessive weight.

COST

List Price (negotiable)	**Residual Values** (months)			
	24	**36**	**48**	**60**
Base: $53,698 (26%)	$30,000	$24,500	$18,000	$15,000
Convertible: $61,398 (29%)	34,000	28,000	23,000	19,000

TECHNICAL DATA

Powertrain (rear-drive)
Engines: 3.L multivalve V6 (222 hp) • 3.0L Turbo V6 (300 hp)
Transmissions: 5-speed manual • 4-speed auto.

Dimensions (2-seater)
Length: 169.5 in.
Width: 70.5 in.
Wheelbase: 96.5 in.

SAFETY FEATURES	Opt.	Std.
Anti-lock brakes	❑	■
Driver-side airbag	❑	■
Passenger-side airbag	❑	■
Remote keyless entry	❑	■

Maxima

Maxima

RATING: Recommended. A high quality, reasonably priced luxo-sedan that's hidden by all the Infiniti hype.

NEW FOR '97: Restyled front and rear end.

GENERAL COMMENTS: The front-wheel-drive Maxima soldiers on as Nissan's luxury flagship, one step removed from the discontinued Infiniti G20. The 190-hp 24-valve DOHC V6 is a real dazzler. With its impressive array of standard features, the Maxima becomes a full-fledged member of what Nissan calls the "executive sports" luxury sedan class that includes the base Infiniti and Lexus models, as well as European entries like the Volvo 900s, Audis, and smaller BMWs. In fact, the Maxima "borrowed" its aerodynamic shape from BMW's 5-series. There's not much risk involved in buying a Maxima; it's a pleasure to drive and much cheaper than most of the competition.

Cost analysis/Alternatives: If you can get an identical but cheaper '96 version, you'll be smiling all the way to the bank. Other cars worthy of consideration are the BMW 3-series; Ford Taurus and Sable, Thunderbird, Grand Marquis and Crown Victoria; Lexus ES 300; Mazda Millenia; Toyota Camry and Avalon; and Volvo 850 and 900 series. **Rebates**: Early next year, Nissan will likely offer $1000 dealer incentives to clear out the '96 models. **Destination charge**: $400. **Recommended options**: None. **Supplementary warranty**: Not needed. **Parts supply/Servicing**: Above average. **Depreciation**: Below average. **Highway/City fuel economy**: 8.5-11.5L/100 km.

Reliability/Safety

Pro: Maximas have always had an impressive reliability history. Parts are relatively inexpensive and easy to find. Servicing is simple. Excellent body construction.

NHTSA crash tests of a 1996 Maxima concluded that the driver would be well protected, while the passenger would have average protection in a 57 km/h frontal collision. It was rated: driver, ★★★★; passenger, ★★★.

Con: Some electrical problems are likely as the car ages. There are some reports of manual transmission and electrical-system malfunctions, as well as paint defects (paint chips easily). The optional sonar suspension found on the GXE is an unnecessary gadget; it will give the average mechanic nightmares. Parts are more expensive than the Japanese average. The trunk lid and latch are hazardous when raised.

Road Performance

Pro: The powerful and smooth standard V6 engine provides substantial power without excessive noise. The smooth-shifting automatic transmission has an Auto position that switches the transmission from normal to power mode when accelerating. It also has a switch to let you lock out fourth gear to assist in trailer towing and prevent frequent gear changes over hilly terrain. The standard 5-speed manual gearbox has a good shift linkage. Very good handling. The ride is fairly firm, but comfortable due to the refined suspension that handles rough roads well if the car is lightly loaded. Excellent braking.

Con: The power steering doesn't transmit road feel very well. Transmission whine.

Comfort/Convenience

Pro: Although some controls are a bit fussy, the dashboard is well designed with easily read analogue gauges that don't wash out in sunlight. Firm, supportive, and comfortable front seating. The optional, form-fitting SE seats are especially good buys. Excellent defrosting and defogging system. Lots of little storage bins for odds and ends. Better fuel economy than the Acura Legend or Mazda 929. Impressive theft-deterrent system sounds an alarm, flashes the lights, and disables the car if the vehicle is disturbed. The system is armed automatically whenever the Maxima's doors are locked with a key.

Con: High-tech luxury interior with emphasis on electronic gadgets. Don't buy the optional instrument panel; it's distracting, confusing, and more suitable to a video arcade than a luxury automobile. Power-window switches are difficult to operate. Inside door pull blocks the two rear window switches. Rear seat comfort is compromised by flat seats that give inadequate thigh support, and obtrusive side wing bolsters that push passengers into the middle. Head restraints in the rear are too low for average-sized adults. The trunk isn't very deep. Wind and road noise intrude into the passenger compartment.

COST

List Price (firm)	**Residual Values** (months)			
	24	**36**	**48**	**60**
Base: $27,998 (19%)	$15,500	$13,500	$12,000	$11,000

TECHNICAL DATA

Powertrain (front-drive)	**Dimensions**
Engine: 3.0L 24-valve V6 (190 hp)	Length: 187.7 in.
	Width: 69.7 in.
	Wheelbase: 106.3 in.

Transmissions: 5-speed manual OD • 4-speed auto. OD

SAFETY FEATURES

	Opt.	Std.
Anti-lock brakes	■	❑
Childproof door locks	❑	■
Driver-side airbag	❑	■
Passenger-side airbag	❑	■
Remote keyless entry	❑	■

Quest (Villager)

Quest

RATING: Recommended. Both the Quest and the Mercury Villager are about the size of a short-wheelbase Dodge Caravan. See the Mercury Villager for additional details.

NEW FOR '97: Upgraded side-impact protection.

Reliability/Safety

Pro: Despite its short time on the market, the Quest has had an impressive reliability record. Body construction is above reproach. Servicing is simple to perform and parts are relatively inexpensive and easy to find. Crash tests of a 1994 Quest equipped with a driver side airbag concluded that the driver would be relatively well-protected and the passenger would receive average protection in a 57 km/h frontal collision. It was rated: driver, ★★★★; passenger, ★★★.

Con: Some minor electrical problems and premature front brake wear.

COST				
List Price (firm)	**Residual Values** (months)			
	24	**36**	**48**	**60**
XE: $25,998 (21%)	$16,500	$14,500	$13,000	$11,500

SAFETY FEATURES	**Opt.**	**Std.**
Anti-lock brakes	■	■
Childproof door locks	❑	■
Driver-side airbag	❑	■
Passenger-side airbag	❑	■
Remote keyless entry	■	❑

SUBARU

Subaru's making money hand over fist, and it owes its Aussie sport-utility wannabe "Outback" spokesman, Paul Hogan, a large measure of thanks for an incredible sales turnaround. U.S. sales profits for 1996 promise to be second only to a record $94 million set 10 years ago on much greater volume.

Subaru's overall product lineup for 1997 marks a return to the company's four-wheel-drive roots with the repackaging of its Legacy and Impreza 4X4 lineup as Outbacks. (Half of all Legacys sold are Outbacks.) A Legacy 2.5L GT all-wheel-drive sporting sedan or wagon variant also joins the group this year. In addition to these redesignated models—and the squeezing out of a bit more horsepower from its limited range of engines Subaru hopes that it can continue to tap the sport-utility craze through lower prices for its AWD and ABS options and by offering a greater variety of AWD vehicles.

Are Subarus good buys? Devotees will insist that there's no other car as versatile; and the manufacturer is justifiably proud of the high J. D. Power owner satisfaction rating earned in the U.S. Canadian owners, on the other hand, are not all that satisfied with the company's weak dealer network.

A word of warning: *Consumer Reports* says that the Outback upgrade isn't worth the extra $3000 US. They point out that Subaru's ads are misleading when they show Paul Hogan zipping around off-road. They also say that handling isn't as competent as that of the regular Legacy (something to do with the higher centre of gravity, no doubt).

SVX

SVX

RATING: An Above Average buy.

NEW FOR '97: This year's car is basically a carried-over '96, except for a new grille and slightly narrower tires.

GENERAL COMMENTS: Subaru's only vehicle equipped with a 6-cylinder engine, this $47,495 front-drive/4X4 two-door sports coupe is a competent performer once you get beyond its oddball styling and lack of a manual transmission. A forgiving and predictable car that's reminiscent of a German sports sedan, the SVX is a limited-production model designed by Giugiaro. It comes equipped with a 3.3L DOHC flat 6-cylinder engine that produces 230 hp. Set on a 103-inch wheelbase and modified strut/parallel arm suspension system, the SVX uses an automatic transmission with Overdrive and permanent AWD to propel this 2+2's 3525 pounds. There are plenty of goodies offered as standard equipment, including a power sunroof, ABS (on the AWD version), and electronics galore.

With unusually low interior noise levels for a sports coupe, the SVX embodies radically different styling that gives new meaning to "weird." The goofy-looking side windows are really a window within a window—a standard feature on show cars. It allows you to get fresh air during a rainstorm without getting wet or blasted by wind at high speeds. Unfortunately, it also severely restricts your peripheral vision.

Cost analysis/Alternatives: The '96 SVX is almost identical to the more expensive '97 version and is a real bargain if the selling price has been reduced sufficiently. Other models worth considering are the Acura NSX, Lexus SC 400, and Toyota Supra. **Rebates**: $1500 customer rebates and $1500 dealer incentives on the '96. **Destination charge**: $350. **Recommended options**: None. **Supplementary warranty**: Not needed. **Parts supply/Servicing**: Average. **Depreciation**: Below average. **Highway/City fuel economy**: 13.5L/100 km.

Impreza

Impreza

RATING: An Above Average buy.

NEW FOR '97: An Outback Sport model and standard ABS.

GENERAL COMMENTS: The Impreza is essentially a shorter Legacy with additional convenience features, and a bit more interior room than the discontinued Loyale. It comes with either a front-drive or 4X4 drivetrain and is available as a two-door coupe, a four-door sedan, a wagon that resembles the old American Motors Pacer and, *surprise*, an Outback Sport wagon powered by a gutsier 2.2L engine and dressed more aggressively in GT cladding.

The base engine is a peppy 1.8L 110-hp 4-cylinder that occasionally stumbles after cold starts. An optional 2.2L powerplant provides an extra dose of power for highway passing and additional torque when traversing rough or hazardous terrain. Buyers may choose either a 5-speed manual or a 4-speed automatic transmission. The manual transmission's "hill holder" clutch prevents the car from rolling backwards when starting out. This advantage is small compensation for the transmission's rough behaviour. The electronically controlled automatic (which I recommend) has a power mode and a manual button that holds the lower gears a bit longer to reduce irritating gear hunting.

Cost analysis/Alternatives: The '96 Impreza is substantially identical to the more expensive '97 version, except for the addition of standard anti-lock brakes. Try to get an unsold '96 with the ABS included. The '96 Eagle Summit, Saturn, and Toyota Corolla are good wagon alternatives. **Rebates**: Expect some hefty rebates and dealer incentives on the non-Outback variants by early spring. **Destination charge**: $350. **Recommended options**: ABS, but it's available only with the AWD version. **Supplementary warranty**: A good idea. **Parts supply/Servicing**: Below average. **Depreciation**: Average. **Highway/City fuel economy**: 7-

10L/100 km with the base version and manual transmission; 8-11L/100 km with the 4X4 variants and 2.2L engine.

Reliability/Safety

Pro: There haven't been any major problems reported by owners. Servicing and repairs are made easier due to a very straightforward design. According to the CAA, parts are reasonably priced due to heavy discounting by dealers.

Con: Some complaints concerning poor engine idling, frequent cold weather stalling, manual transmission malfunctions, premature exhaust system rust-out, catalytic converter failures, and paint peeling. Mediocre servicing is hard to overcome because independent garages can't service key 4X4 powertrain components. Parts shortages, a problem in the past, are likely to get much worse.

Road Performance

Pro: The manual transmission shifts smoothly. The all-wheel-drive system is a boon for people who often need extra traction, and it works well with either a manual or automatic transmission. The CVT transmission is quiet and efficient. Smooth and nimble handling. Precise and predictable steering. Excellent braking with ABS.

Con: The base engine is anemic, harsh, and noisy; cold weather makes it run even more roughly. Annoying steering wheel vibrations are caused by the rough-running engine. Non-assisted steering requires maximum effort when parking. Uncomfortable ride with a full load. Some loss of directional stability with hard braking. Cornering at highway speeds feels tippy on the all-wheel-drive. The ride is buckboard-bumpy. Larger tires would improve handling. Unacceptably long non-ABS braking that causes the car to spin out of control.

Comfort/Convenience

Pro: Clear and simple dashboard and gauges. Very firm and supportive front seats. Versatile hatchback design.

Con: This is not a quiet car. The clutch pedal and the dash click, the engine roars, and the fan whirs. Front shoulder belts are uncomfortable and rear seatbelts are hard to buckle up. Rear seating is uncomfortable and limited to two small passengers. The heater is insufficient and air distribution is inadequate. Small trunk. The 4X4 version uses more fuel.

COST

List Price (negotiable)	Residual Values (months) 24	36	48	60
Base AWD: $21,395 (19%)	$14,000	$12,000	$10,000	$8500

TECHNICAL DATA

Powertrain (front-AWD)
Engines: 1.8L 4 (105 hp)
• 2.2L 4 (137 hp)
Transmissions: 5-speed manual • 4-speed auto.

Dimensions
Length: 172.2 in.
Width: 67.1 in.
Wheelbase: 99.2 in.

SAFETY FEATURES

	Opt.	Std.
Anti-lock brakes	■	❑
Driver-side airbag	❑	■
Passenger-side airbag	❑	■

Legacy

Legacy

RATING: An Above Average buy as a front-drive. Recommended with its 4X4 capability.

NEW FOR '97: An additional ten horses, a new 5-speed manual transmission, and a Limited Edition Outback with a faux-wood-trimmed leather interior, new alloy wheels, a weatherband radio, and 4-speed transaxle.

GENERAL COMMENTS: A competent, full-time 4X4 performer for drivers who want to move up in size, comfort, and features, this front-drive and AWD compact represents a clean break with the past. Available as a four-door sedan or five-door wagon, the Legacy is clean and conventionally styled, with even a hint of the Acura Legend in the rear end. Added this year is the 2.5L GT AWD sports sedan and wagon, offered with new 16-inch alloy wheels, a restyled nose, and 5-speed manual transmission.

Owners who prize Subaru's rugged reliability and distinctive styling may find the Legacy too "modern." Nowhere is there any sign of the excessive reliance upon chrome moulding and oddball styling that has turned off buyers in the past. Another plus is that the Legacy's interior dimensions are similar to the Accord's—the benchmark for comfortable four-door sedans.

The mechanicals are modern as well—a standard 137-hp 2.2L 16-valve 4-banger hooked to a standard 5-speed or optional 4-speed gearbox and an optional 165-hp, 2.5L 4-cylinder. Wagons are about 600 pounds heavier; nevertheless, they accentuate high performance with all-wheel-drive, anti-lock brakes, a firmer suspension, 15-inch aluminum wheels, and top-quality tires.

Cost analysis/Alternatives: Except for some trim items, the '96 models are practically identical to the '97 versions, making the '96 models the better buy if they're sufficiently discounted. The base front-drive models are outclassed by the Honda Accord, Toyota Camry, and Nissan Maxima. **Rebates**: Expect substantial dealer incentives and customer rebates by mid-summer. **Destination charge**: $350. **Recommended options**: ABS. **Supplementary warranty**: A wise investment. **Parts supply/Servicing**: Below average. **Depreciation**: Average. **Highway/City fuel economy**: 7-10.5L/100 km with the base model and either transmission; 8-11L/100 km with the 4X4 variants.

Reliability/Safety

Pro: No major mechanical or body problems. Overall assembly quality is better than average. According to the CAA parts are reasonably priced, due principally to heavy discounting by dealers.

Crash tests of a 1996 Legacy sedan concluded that the driver and passenger would be relatively well protected in a 57 km/h frontal collision. It was rated: driver, ★★★★; passenger, ★★★★.

Con: The 2.2L 4-cylinder motor is much more complicated than previous engines and is, therefore, a prime candidate for the minor failures that plagued older designs. Minor electrical, fuel system, and automatic transmission problems are common. Owners report that the front brakes require more attention than average. Premature surface rust and exhaust system rust-out are common. Servicing can be awkward because of the crowded engine compartment, particularly on turbocharged versions. Other expected drawbacks are high maintenance costs, a weak dealer network, and occasional parts shortages. Small horn buttons may be hard to find in an emergency.

Road Performance

Pro: With the base 2.2L engine, acceleration is average but more than adequate for most conditions, particularly when coupled to the 5-speed manual transaxle. The 2.5L engine is much peppier, but it also needs the manual gearbox to really "strut its stuff." Manual transmission throws are short and precise. Acceptable steering response and predictable handling. Fairly soft and comfortable ride isn't affected as passenger load is increased. Excellent ABS braking.

Con: The 2.2L engine is not as fast off the mark as is the Accord or Mitsubishi/Chrysler 2.0L 16-valve powerplant. The 2.5L engine doesn't give GT performance when hooked to an automatic transmission. Steering is a bit heavy at times. Rear end tends to swing out when the Legacy takes corners under speed.

Comfort/Convenience

Pro: Low but comfortable driving position, with plenty of head and leg room. The left footrest prevents cramping. Adjustable driver's seat on the deluxe model. Well designed, sweeping dashboard (similar to the Accord's) and control layout. Easy-to-read analogue gauges. Comfortable cloth-covered seats with plenty of side and shoulder support. Excellent climate control system. Seating for four adults offers good leg room, and cargo capacity puts the Legacy up in the Taurus, Camry, and Accord class. A cavernous trunk is expandable with the split rear seatbacks.

Con: Seat height adjuster is available only on the Outback variants. Limited rear head room. Extremely sensitive to cross winds. Limited-service spare tire.

COST

List Price (negotiable)	**Residual Values** (months)			
	21	**36**	**48**	**60**
Base: $25,695 (20%)	$17,000	$13,500	$11,000	$9500

TECHNICAL DATA

Powertrain (front-AWD)
Engines: 2.2L 4 (137 hp) • 2.5L DOHC 4 (165 hp)
Transmissions:5-speed manual • 4-speed auto.

Dimensions (wagon/sedan)
Length: 180.9 in./183.9 in.
Width: 67.5 in./67.5 in.
Wheelbase: 103.5 in./103.5 in.

SAFETY FEATURES	Opt.	Std.
Anti-lock brakes	■	■
Childproof door locks	❑	■
Driver-side airbag	❑	■
Passenger-side airbag	❑	■
Remote keyless entry	■	❑

SUZUKI

Having made its reputation by building quality motorcycles, Suzuki has been making very good entry-level small cars and sport-utility vehicles for over a decade. But most buyers aren't familiar with the company's products because they're sold under GM's name. In fact, the company makes only three mainstream vehicles: the Swift (GM's Metro twin), the Esteem, and the 4X4 Sidekick—a vehicle sold by General Motors of Canada as the Tracker.

Chastened by the poor reputation garnered by its first 4X4, the Samurai—which captured the hearts and smiles of the young and trendy set and then made all the newspaper headlines when *Consumer Reports* showed it rolling over in low-speed turns—Suzuki has quietly gone about making its revamped Sidekick, Tracker, Swift, and Esteem a success. Its latest entry, the X-90 4x4, has been well received.

Swift

Swift

RATING: Recommended, but not a car for long journeys.

NEW FOR '97: Nothing significant. The Swift will be revised in 1999.

GENERAL COMMENTS: This is a very small car. How small? Smaller than the Subaru Justy. The price is also small, and that's what makes this 50-mpg econobox so popular. It gives you one more cylinder and a more refined suspension for $500 less than what a Metro costs ($10,995 vs. $11,495).

With the introduction of the Swift and Esteem, Suzuki has made a bold move into the small-car niche controlled by American and Japanese automakers. Although the Swift shares many body and mechanical components with the Metro and Pontiac Firefly, it features its own drivetrain. These little cars are lots of fun to drive around town. They'll go anywhere with a minimum of fuss and still carry both front seat passengers in relative comfort.

Cost analysis/Alternatives: Buy a discounted 1996 version; it's identical to the 1997 Swift. Other cars to consider are the '96 Eagle Summit, GM Metro and Firefly, and Honda Civic. **Rebates**: Suzuki is offering $350 dealer incentives to clear out the '95s. **Destination charge**: $275. **Recommended options**: None. **Supplementary warranty**: Not needed. **Parts supply/Servicing**: Above average. **Depreciation**: Average. For example, a 1994 base Swift, selling originally for $8995, is now worth about $4600 as a dealer trade-in. **Highway/City fuel economy**: 4.9-6.4L/100 km with the manual transmission; 6.3-7.7L/100 km with the automatic. Fuel economy is often exaggerated by dealers.

Reliability/Safety

Pro: The Swift has an excellent repair record. According to the CAA, parts are reasonably priced with heavy discounting by dealers. Parts and service are easy to come by (quality is a concern), and maintenance is made simple by an uncluttered underhood layout and the availability of two dealer networks for servicing.

Con: Owners complain about mediocre servicing. The rear hatch vibrates when windows are down and it seems to want to fly open. Push-buttons for the lights and wipers tend to pop off the dashboard. Poor fuel-injection system. The brakes are often squeaky and wear quickly; the front discs warp easily. Noisy front metallic brake pads. Some complaints concerning premature clutch wear, paint peeling, and sloppy body assembly.

NHTSA crash tests of a 1989 Swift concluded that the passenger in the two-door version would sustain severe or fatal head injuries; in the crash of a four-door, the driver was on the receiving end of massive head trauma. Test results may not apply to later models, particularly in view of the '96 Geo Metro's ★★★★ crash rating (the Metro is the Swift's twin).

Road Performance

Pro: The tiny 1.3L 4-cylinder powerplant produces enough power to keep up with city and most highway traffic. The 16-valve engine provides genuinely sporty performance. The manual transmission shifts smoothly. Light but precise steering. Handling is nimble and stable most of the time. Four-wheel independent suspension works well under most highway conditions. Impressive fuel economy, particularly in city driving.

Con: Some stalling and hesitation under full throttle. If you hear a constant knocking when accelerating or decelerating, blame it on the unusually pliable engine mounts that allow the engine and exhaust system to knock against the floor pan. The Swift is a bit harder riding on the highway than is Honda, because its four struts can't handle the road as well as Honda's A-arm suspension. The suspension thumps and bounces in hard turns. The added weight of the 4-cylinder engine makes for hard steering while parking. Swifts get tossed about by side winds and passing trucks on the highway.

Comfort/Convenience

Pro: Front seats are comfortable and provide good support for short trips. Six-footers can sit in comfort in the front. Well-appointed interior with easy-to-read and easy-to-access dash controls. Complete instrumentation. Very little road or wind noise in the passenger compartment. Excellent all-round visibility due to the car's thin pillars.

Con: The area behind the front seats is a compromise; either you get limited space for two people and no room for cargo, or a spacious cargo area with the rear seat folded down. Seats become cramped and generally uncomfortable during long trips. Excessive engine noise due mainly to poor soundproofing and the car's small size.

COST

List Price (firm)	**Residual Values** (months)			
	24	**36**	**48**	**60**
Base: $11,595 (11%)	$7500	$6500	$5500	$4700

TECHNICAL DATA

Powertrain (front-drive)	**Dimensions** (3-door)
Engine: 1.3L 16-valve 4 (70 hp)	Length: 149.4 in.
	Width: 62.6 in.
	Wheelbase: 93.1 in.

Transmissions: 5-speed manual • 3-speed auto.

SAFETY FEATURES	Opt.	Std.
Anti-lock brakes	■	❑
Childproof door locks	❑	■
Driver-side airbag	❑	■
Passenger-side airbag	❑	■

Esteem

Esteem

RATING: Acceptable. Nevertheless, the car has lots of potential, once it goes through its first-year shakeout.

NEW FOR '97: The GL gets a standard AM/FM cassette stereo system. The GLX option package now includes an automatic transmission.

GENERAL COMMENTS: The Esteem, Suzuki's largest car, is a small four-door sedan that's a step up from the Swift. Smaller than the Honda Civic and Dodge Neon, it has a fairly spacious interior, offering comparable or better rear accommodation for two full-sized adults than most cars in its class.

Both the base GL and upscale GLX come loaded with standard features that cost extra on other models. The GL, for example, comes with power steering, rear-window defroster, remote trunk and fuel filler door releases, tinted glass, and a fold-down rear seat (great for extra cargo space). GLX shoppers can look forward to standard ABS, power windows and door locks, and a host of other interior refinements.

Cost analysis/Alternatives: Consider getting a second-series (made after March 1996) '96 Esteem rather than a '97, since they're practically identical and the '96 should be much cheaper. Other cars worth considering are the '96 Eagle Summit, GM Metro and Firefly, Honda Civic, and Nissan Sentra. **Rebates**: Expect Suzuki to offer $500 dealer incentives by mid-summer to clear out its '96 models. **Destination charge**: $300. **Recommended options**: ABS. **Supplementary warranty**: Not needed. **Parts supply/Servicing**: Average. **Depreciation**: Average. **Highway/City fuel economy**: N/A.

Reliability/Safety

Pro: Many of the mechanical components have been used on Suzuki's other models with few reliability problems reported. According to the CAA, Suzuki parts are reasonably priced and not that hard to find. Servicing can be done by any independent garage and maintenance is made simple by an uncluttered underhood layout. Body panels and trim look flimsy, and wind and water leaks may be a problem.

Con: Noisy front metallic brake pads. Reports of wind and water intrusion into the passenger compartment. Fragile body panels and trim items. NHTSA crash tests haven't yet been carried out.

Road Performance

Pro: Overall performance is better than average, with the Esteem's 4-wheel independent suspension giving just the right balance between a comfortable ride and no-surprise handling. Good braking.

Con: The 98-hp 4-cylinder engine could use a bit more grunt.

Comfort/Convenience

Pro: In spite of sitting on a smaller wheelbase, interior space beats out most of the competition, including that of the Honda Civic.

Con: Boring, bland styling.

COST

List Price (firm)	**Residual Values** (months)			
	24	**36**	**48**	**60**
Base: $13,495 (11%)	$8500	$7000	$6000	$5000

TECHNICAL DATA

Powertrain (front-drive)	**Dimensions** (4-door)
Engine: 1.6L 4 (98 hp)	Length: 165.2 in.
	Width: 65.7 in.
	Wheelbase: 97.6 in.

Transmissions: 5-speed manual • 4-speed auto.

SAFETY FEATURES

	Opt.	Std.
Anti-lock brakes	■	❑
Driver-side airbag	❑	■
Passenger-side airbag	❑	■

TOYOTA

Toyota, a price cutter? That's right, if we can believe the automaker's announcement to the U.S. motoring press that it will cut prices on its 1997 lineup by an average of 4.4 percent. The company's Canadian subsidiary refuses to confirm that the price reduction will be as great in Canada, but if past pricing is any guide Canadians are looking at some lower prices this fall. Toyota can well afford to cut prices. With almost $30 billion in cash reserves—more than that of the U.S. Big Three automakers combined—Toyota is in better shape than any other automaker to capture additional market share with reduced prices, lower production costs, and cheapening content.

Toyota's frugality and team spirit are legendary. In its Japanese factory the company shuts off the lights at lunchtime and has posted regulations on the thrifty use of toilet paper. In the U.S., Toyota workers buy only Wild Turkey bourbon made in Kentucky, where it has a factory. Jack Daniels bourbon is distilled in Tennessee, home to the factory of its arch-rival, Nissan.

Changes for the 1997 model lineup include a totally reworked Camry and Supra, the addition of a Paseo convertible, the dropping of the Corolla wagon, and more power for the Avalon.

There's no longer much difference between Toyota, Honda, Suzuki, and Nissan when it comes to the overall reliability and durability of their products. True, Toyotas hold up very well over the years, but Nissan has a much more comprehensive base warranty and Honda is on the cutting edge of new technology relating to fuel economy and performance. Nevertheless, Toyotas are especially forgiving of owner neglect and cost very little to service at independent garages. But the kicker for most buyers is the high resale value for most Toyotas; it's not unusual to see a five-year-old sedan selling for almost half its original selling price.

As for customer dissatisfaction with Toyota's salespeople and service managers—a *Lemon-Aid* criticism for the last few years—the company concurs that poor treatment by dealers is a problem, and says that it has taken steps to sensitize dealers to customers' needs.

Persistent problems with all Toyota vehicles are premature brake wear, excessive noise, and vibrations. Stung by consumer criticism that these problems haven't been fixed for over a decade and that owners are charged for useless repairs, Toyota published a "Brake Repair" service bulletin #POL94-18 in October 1994 that finally defines those repairs that will be done under warranty. Toyota has promised that premature brake wear and noise will be fixed under warranty for the first 12 months/12,500 *miles* (it's a U.S. bulletin) and that vibrations will be attended to, under warranty, for up to 3 years/38,000 miles.

NO: POL94-18
DATE: 10/1094
SUBJECT: BRAKE REPAIR

When a brake repair is required on a vehicle that is still covered by the applicable warranty, the repair should be performed using proper repair procedures at minimum cost. Based on this rule, brake repairs shall be performed by replacing or repairing the defective component parts only. Therefore, when the replacement of any hardware, such as shims, wear indicators and anti-squeal springs is necessary when replacing brake pad kits (only four pads), the cost for such additional replacements may be also be included for reimbursement under warranty. If the cost of the individual hardware used plus the pads exceeds the cost of the full kit, or the pad kit is not available, then the full kit should be used.

Condition	Warranty Policy	Claim Processing
Abnormal or Fast Wear Generally, pads/shoes should be replaced when the remaining material is 1.0mm thick or less or if the pads/shoe has uneven wear. Refer to repair manuals for exact replacement criteria.	• Covered under warranty for 12 months from the vehicle date-of-first use or 12,500 miles. ***NOTE:*** Wear is *not warrantable* on vehicles with greater than 12 months or 12,500 miles. • Brake rotor/drum grinding is not required and is not warrantable unless the pad/shoe has worn to the metal and caused damage to the rotors/drum.	Operation Code Replace Front Pads - 473301 Replace Rear Pads - 473311 Replace Rear Shoes - 472021 OPN -Pads Front 04465-XXXXX Pad Only Kit 04491-XXXXX Full Pad Kit Rear 04466-XXXXX Pad Only Kit 04492-XXXXX Full Pad Kit 04495-XXXXX Brake Shoe Kit T1 - 99 (Others) T2 - 19 (Wear)

Condition	Warranty Policy	Claim Processing
Disc brake squeak or abnormal noise (front or rear)	• Covered under warranty for 12 months from the vehicle date-of-first use or 12,500 miles. ***NOTE:*** Wear is *not warrantable* on vehicles with greater than 12 months or 12,500 miles. • Brake adjustment (clean and/or lubrication is recommended). • Pads/shoes generally are not required. Check Technical Service Bulletins for exceptions. • Brake rotor/drum grinding should not be required to complete this repair.	Operation Code Front Disc Brake CL/LU - 046043 Rear Disc Brake CL/LU - 046083 Rear Drum Brake CL/LU - 046073 OPN -Pads Front 04465-XXXXX Pad Only Kit 04491-XXXXX Full Pad Kit Rear 04466-XXXXX Pad Only Kit 04492-XXXXX Full Pad Kit 04495-XXXXX Brake Shoe Kit T1 - 36 (Squeaking, Squealing) T2 - 99 (Others)

Condition	Warranty Policy	Claim Processing
Brake vibration caused by excessive rotor thickness variation or excessive lateral run-out of the rotor.	• Covered under warranty for 3 years from the vehicle date-of-first use or 38,000 miles. • If rotor thickness allows, on-car rotor grinding is strongly recommended to achieve best long-term results, as compared to rotor replacement or off-car resurfacing. • Pads generally are not required. Check Technical Service Bulletins for exceptions.	Operation Code Front Disc Grind Off Vehicle - 473015* OR Front Disc Grind On Vehicle - 473025* Rear Disc Grind Off Vehicle - 473065* OR Rear Disc Grind On Vehicle - 473075* OR Rear Brake Drum Grind - 472155 OPN -Rotor (43512-XXXXX - Front) (42431-XXXXX - Rear) -Drum (42431-XXXXX - Rear) T1 -21 (Shuddering, Vibration, Pulsation) T2 -13 (Deformed, Warped)

**** Repair is dependent on the equipment available at the dealership.***

The tables illustrate warrantable conditions, applicable operation and T-codes, and original part numbers to be used in submitting a warranty claim to TMS.

Tercel

Tercel

RATING: Acceptable. A competent, reliable, but mediocre subcompact.

NEW FOR '97: Standard trip odometer, dual outside mirrors, and 14-inch wheels. Only the CE trim level is offered this year.

GENERAL COMMENTS: The entry-level, front-drive Tercel represented the best of what the subcompact car market had to offer when it was introduced in Canada in 1979. Since then, the competition has caught up and passed the Tercel in terms of standard features and overall performance. Tercels are available as either two- or four-door sedans.

The main disadvantages of a Tercel are its high price and lack of comfort/convenience features. The base model is in chronically short supply and, for the price, one has to settle for a spartan interior and a rudimentary 4-speed manual transmission. In general, though, a Tercel performs decently, has room for four people and their luggage, and is likely to be more dependable than most cars.

Cost analysis/Alternatives: The '96 Tercel is virtually identical to the '97 version, making it the better buy if its price is low enough. Last year's DX models gave the most features for the best price. Other cars worth considering are the '96 Eagle Summit, Geo Metro, Honda Civic, Mazda Protegé, Mercury Tracer, Nissan Sentra, Suzuki Swift, Toyota Corolla, and VW Golf. **Rebates**: Not likely before mid-summer. **Destination charge**: $250. **Recommended options**: The 60/40 split seatback on the '96 DX version or the '97's CE package. Cloth upholstery instead of vinyl. **Supplementary warranty**: Not needed. **Parts supply/Servicing**: Above average. **Depreciation**: Resale value is higher than average. **Highway/City fuel economy**: 6-8L/100 km.

Reliability/Safety

Pro: No major mechanical or body problems have been reported, and last year's redesign hasn't made these cars less reliable. A large dealer network assures quick servicing.

Crash tests of a 1996 Tercel sedan concluded that the driver would receive average protection, while the passenger would be very well protected in a 57 km/h frontal collision. It was rated: driver, ★★★; passenger, ★★★★.

Con: According to the CAA, parts are more expensive than those of most other cars in this class. Tercel front brakes wear out very quickly and the exhaust system is rust-prone. Toyota recommends replacing the timing chain every 100,000 km. Lately there's been a sharp rise in complaints concerning excessive rusting and paint chipping on body panels. Customer service has declined to the point where Honda and Nissan do a much better job. Rear head restraints are set too low.

Road Performance

Pro: The 1.5L 4-cylinder engine provides plenty of power in the lower gear ranges, primarily because of the car's light weight and the well matched, smooth-shifting manual and automatic transaxles. Handling on smooth roads is quite acceptable for a car in this class.

Con: The engine is overworked when pulling a full load. Sloppy handling and jittery road manners when going over small bumps. Manual steering is vague and takes lots of effort when cornering, but the power-assist over-corrects, giving little road feel. Rough pavement makes this car dance all over the highway. Suspension bottoms out easily, and there's lots of body lean around corners. Braking is exceptionally bad, with long stopping distances and loss of directional control (you can easily spin out).

Comfort/Convenience

Pro: Attractive, rounded styling. Well laid-out dashboard and controls. The front seats are fairly comfortable. The sedan has a very large trunk, and long items are easily handled with the folding rear seatback. Good heating and ventilation.

Con: Base model is very austere and noisy. The overly sensitive gas pedal requires a light touch, resulting in constant leg cramping. Forget about putting five passengers in this car—it's strictly a four-passenger subcompact. The back seat holds only two adults; it's unbelievably small and uncomfortable, with limited head and shoulder room, inadequate knee and foot room, and a low cushion that firms up uncomfortably in the middle. The vinyl covering (on the basic hatchback) is slippery all the time and clammy in hot weather. No side-window defogging vents. Very small trunk with the coupe. Difficult rear seat access on the two-door model. Excessive road noise.

COST

'96 List Price (firm)	**Residual Values** (months)			
	24	**36**	**48**	**60**
SD: $11,948 (9%)	$7700	$6700	$5600	$4300

TECHNICAL DATA

Powertrain (front-drive)
Engine: 1.5L 4 (93 hp)

Dimensions (4-door sedan)
Length: 161.8 in.
Width: 65.3 in.
Wheelbase: 93.7 in.

Transmissions: 4-speed manual • 5-speed manual • 3-speed auto. • 4-speed auto.

SAFETY FEATURES

	Opt.	Std.
Anti-lock brakes	❑	■
Childproof door locks	❑	■
Driver-side airbag	■	❑
Passenger-side airbag	❑	■

Paseo

Paseo

RATING: Above Average buy.

NEW FOR '97: A new convertible with a glass rear window.

GENERAL COMMENTS: A two-door, nicely styled, economy/sports 2+2 coupe, the Paseo is easy to drive, performs smoothly, and is reasonably priced. It comes with an impressive list of standard features, including a Paseo-exclusive DOHC 1.5L 16-valve 4-cylinder rated at 93 horsepower. This engine gives the car a higher power-to-weight ratio than that of most competitors. Four-wheel independent suspension, with MacPherson struts up front and a trailing torsion beam in back, is another noteworthy standard feature. There are also stabilizer bars in front and back. The brakes are power-assisted front disc and rear drum.

If you're looking for a cheaper, sporty alternative to the Celica, the Paseo is the car to buy. Although the interior is a bit bare, this entry-level sporty coupe has the styling and engine to meet all competition in its class. It's a Tercel spinoff, but it distinguishes itself with a powerplant that accelerates more quickly than does the NX 1600. This speed is achieved mainly because of the Paseo's light weight.

Cost analysis/Alternatives: The 1996 Paseo isn't much different from the '97 version, which represents the better buy if you can find one on dealers' lots that's priced right. Other cars worth considering are the Honda Civic Coupe, '96 Mazda MX-3, Nissan 200SX, and Toyota Tercel. **Rebates**: Not likely. **Destination charge**: $275. **Recommended options**: None. **Supplementary warranty**: Not needed. **Parts supply/Servicing**: Above average. **Depreciation**: Below average. **Highway/City fuel economy**: 6-8L/100 km with a manual transmission; 7-9.5L/100 km with the automatic.

Reliability/Safety

Pro: Toyota's legendary reliability has been one of the main reasons its vehicles have been so popular despite their high cost. Other Japanese carmakers, however, have overtaken Toyota and are offering just as much quality and reliability for less money. Parts and service are easy to obtain because the Paseo shares most of its parts with other Toyotas. Below average parts cost, according to the CAA.

Con: Premature front brake wear, electrical problems, and exhaust system rust-out are the more common problems. Complaints concerning excessive paint chipping. The quality of customer service has declined, especially when it comes to getting dealer and manufacturer support with brake and paint/rusting claims. No crash data are available.

Road Performance

Pro: While not a neck-snapper, the basic 93-hp 1.5L engine is a model of smoothness and economy. It can cruise quietly at 55 mph while turning less than 2400 rpm. Both the 5-speed manual and electronically controlled 4-speed automatic transmissions shift smoothly. Responsive steering. Steady, quick, and accurate handling under normal driving conditions. Excellent braking.

Con: The lethargic, 16-valve 4-cylinder powerplant, despite its growling when pushed, is weak in low-end torque; it takes a while to attain cruising speed. The 4-speed automatic robs the engine of power. The ride is stiff and choppy on anything other than the smoothest roads.

Comfort/Convenience

Pro: Overall fit and finish are impressive. Excellent instrument panel and control layout. Quiet, rattle-free interior. Very comfortable front seats. Sober interior highlighted by analogue gauges and easily accessible controls. Map pockets are located in the doors. The back seat folds down to provide an impressive amount of storage space. First-class heating, defrosting, and ventilation system. Reasonably-sized trunk.

Con: Drivers over six feet tall will find it hard to adjust the seat sufficiently to be comfortable. The base interior is practical but bland. No centre console. Glove box is too small. Uncomfortably upright rear seats.

COST

'96 List Price (firm)	**Residual Values** (months)			
	24	**36**	**48**	**60**
Base: $17,608 (14%)	$11,000	$9500	$8000	$6300

TECHNICAL DATA

Powertrain (front-drive)
Engines: 1.5L carbureted 16-valve 4 (93 hp)
Transmissions: 5-speed manual • 4-speed auto.

Dimensions
Length: 163.2 in.
Width: 65.2 in.
Wheelbase: 93.7 in.

SAFETY FEATURES

	Opt.	**Std.**
Anti-lock brakes	■	❑
Childproof door locks	❑	■
Driver-side airbag	❑	■
Passenger-side airbag	❑	■
Remote keyless entry	■	❑

Corolla

Corolla

RATING: Recommended. Both the sedan and wagon are top in their class.

NEW FOR '97: No more wagon. Enhanced side-impact protection, new door trim, and repackaged options.

GENERAL COMMENTS: The Corolla has long been Toyota's standard-bearer in the subcompact sedan class. Over the years, however, the car has grown in size, price, and refinement to the point where it can now be considered a small compact.

All Corollas ride on a front-wheel-drive platform with independent suspension on all wheels. Four-wheel drive has been dropped as an option on the four-door sedan. There are two wagon versions available: a conventional front-wheel-drive model and a special four-wheel-drive edition that made its debut in late 1988. This second version features a tall body and an update of the unusual styling that Toyota used on the now-defunct Tercel wagon.

Cost analysis/Alternatives: The 1997 Corollas are identical to the '96 versions and are the better buy if you can find one on dealers' lots. Other small cars that represent good investments are the '96 Eagle Summit, Ford Escort, Honda Civic, Mazda Protegé and '96 MX-3, Mercury Tracer, and Nissan Sentra. Other wagon choices: Saturn and the Subaru Impreza LS. **Rebates**: Not likely. **Destination charge**: $300. **Recommended options**: The optional 1.8L engine's five extra horses may not justify the extra expense. Try both engines before deciding. A built-in rear child seat in the DX model, and a rear wiper and a full-sized spare tire for the wagon version (it has the storage space). **Supplementary warranty**: Not needed. **Parts supply/Servicing**: Average. **Depreciation**: Below average. **Highway/City fuel economy**: 6.5-8.5L/100 km with the 1.6L engine and a manual transmission; the

3-speed automatic eats up another litre. 6.5-8.5L/100 km with the 1.8L engine and a manual transmission; the 4-speed automatic uses only a half-litre more.

Reliability/Safety

Pro: Toyota parts are easy to find, and a large dealer network keeps waits to a minimum. The Corolla is one of the most reliable cars sold. First-class component and assembly quality.

Crash tests of a 1996 dual airbag-equipped Toyota Corolla concluded that the driver and passenger would be well protected in a 57 km/h frontal collision. It was rated: driver, ★★★★; passenger, ★★★★.

Con: According to the CAA, parts are more expensive than most other cars in this class. Premature rusting and front brake wear, electrical problems, and exhaust system rust-out are the more common problems. The front brakes need frequent servicing. Customer service has declined, particularly when it comes to settling disputes as to what is normal maintenance and what is a warranty item on brake repairs.

Road Performance

Pro: The standard 1.6L engine is smooth and economical, and the optional 1.8L engine, offered with the DX, LE, and '96 wagon, provides a much needed, though minimal, five extra horses. Acceptable handling under normal driving conditions, and the ride is busy but comfortable. Both manual and automatic transmissions shift smoothly. The automatic permits you to lock out fourth gear for towing or when climbing long grades. The manual transmission gives the Corolla extra pep. Light clutch. Soft but well-controlled ride for a small car. Very good brakes, with the wagon registering shorter stopping distances than does the sedan.

Con: Steering doesn't give much road feel. Handling is a bit clumsy with lots of body roll, and sometimes the car plows straight ahead in hard cornering. Soft suspension makes for a busy highway ride. Ride quality deteriorates as the load increases. The sedan's ABS braking isn't impressive—too much weaving and veering to one side.

Comfort/Convenience

Pro: Except for some confusing climate controls, the instrument panel and control layout are exceptionally user-friendly. Very comfortable front seats. The rear seat will hold two comfortably in the sedan, and especially so in the wagon. The rear seatback can be folded down. First-class heating, defrosting, and ventilation system. Large trunk on the sedan and spacious cargo area on the wagon.

Con: In models equipped with a sunroof, tall drivers may find the front head room inadequate and thigh support lacking. Short drivers may have trouble seeing over the wagon's hood. Climate controls aren't user friendly. DLX models don't have a deluxe interior. Tight rear seating for three and limited foot room. No automatic shutoff for the rear defroster. Excessive engine, road, and wind noise—driving over rough pavement produces an annoying rumbling noise.

COST

'96 List Price (firm)	**Residual Values** (months)			
	24	**36**	**48**	**60**
Base: $13,118 (13%)	$8000	$7100	$6000	$5000

TECHNICAL DATA

Powertrain (front-drive)
Engines: 1.6L injected 16-valve 4 (100 hp) • 1.8L injected 16-valve 4 (105 hp)
Transmissions: 5-speed manual OD • 3-speed auto. • 4-speed auto. OD

Dimensions (sedan)
Length: 172 in.
Width: 66.3 in.
Wheelbase: 97 in.

SAFETY FEATURES

	Opt.	**Std.**
Anti-lock brakes	■	❑
Childproof door locks	❑	■
Driver-side airbag	❑	■
Passenger-side airbag	❑	■

Camry

Camry

RATING: An Above Average buy (1997); a Recommended buy (1996). This year's Camry has been so reworked that it should be considered a first-year car. Even if it's sold at a reduced MSRP you'd be wise to see how the cheapening of the car's components affects its overall reliability and performance. And this you won't know until well into the new year.

NEW FOR '97: Totally redesigned this year, the Camry is taller, longer, wider, quieter, more powerful, and cheaper, both in a literal and a figurative sense. The wheelbase has been extended by two inches, giving back seat passengers more room. Other changes: ABS is standard on all but the base 4-cylinder version, traction control is standard on all V6-equipped Camrys, rear seats have shoulder belts for the middle passenger, brighter low beam lights, optional heated mirrors, more cupholders, a sunglasses holder, and an additional power port in the centre console.

Decontenting has hit Toyota's '97 lineup hard, resulting in many changes that cheapen the Camry in subtle ways the average driver may not notice. They are: less expensive S-rated tires on models with 4-cylinder engines, less expensive heating/ventilation system components, no more assist handles for front occupants, no more chrome trim around the windshield, one door seal instead of three (greater chance for wind and water leaks), fewer airbag sensors, an LCD odometer, distributorless ignition with the 4-cylinder, a windshield-embedded antenna, and no coupe or wagon variants.

GENERAL COMMENTS: The Camry is available only as a four-door sedan—gone are the coupe and station wagon variants. It's powered by a base 2.2L 133-hp 16-valve 4-cylinder engine (taken from the Celica), and an optional 3.0L 24-valve V6 that unleashes 194 horses. Either engine can be coupled to a 5-speed manual or an electronically controlled 4-speed automatic. The suspension features MacPherson struts up front, dual-link mounted struts at the rear, gas pressurized shocks for better damping, and stabilizer bars in the front and rear. Control is further maintained through speed-sensing variable power steering.

No longer can we say that the Honda Accord or Ford Taurus offer little more than what a Camry CE provides for less. For example, all 4-cylinder Camrys still use rear drum brakes while most of the competition uses disc brakes; variable intermittent wipers are found only on top-of-the-line Camrys while the competition spreads them throughout their lineup; the Camry's MacPherson strut suspension is no match for the Accord's double-wishbone suspension at all four corners; and Camrys now have single-seal doors while the the Accord uses double seals and the Taurus uses triple.

Cost analysis/Alternatives: The '96 Camry is a better buy at the moment because the revamped '97's upgrades and cheaper base price may not equal the impact of Toyota's cheapening of the car's components. Other cars worth considering are the Ford Taurus and Sable, Honda Accord, '96 Infiniti G20, Lexus ES 300, Mazda 626, and Nissan Stanza. **Rebates**: Expect $500 dealer incentives to clear out the '96s. **Destination charge**: $300. **Recommended options**: The built-in child safety seat ($150). If you get the '96 wagon's optional rear-facing third seat, you'll also have to replace the full-size spare with a space-saver tire. Stay away from the optional sunroof; it robs you of much-needed head room. Toyota's base radio and tape player are failure-prone; buy a better sound system from an independent supplier. **Supplementary warranty**: Not a bad idea. **Parts supply/Servicing**: Above average. Fortunately, parts are easily found and independent servicing is a breeze. **Depreciation**: Below average. **Highway/City fuel economy**: 7-10.5L/100 km with the 2.2L and manual transmission; an automatic burns up an additional litre. 8-12L/100 km with the 3.0L and an automatic transmission (only one available); the '96 station wagon version uses about a half-litre more fuel.

Reliability/Safety

Pro: No telling how this redesigned and cheapened Camry will hold up over the years. Bulletproof reliability for previous years, though. Owners can neglect routine servicing without paying a heavy penalty. Exceptionally durable drivetrain hasn't been modified much with this year's changes. First-class body assembly and component quality. Good parts availability.

Crash tests of a 1996 airbag-equipped Toyota Camry sedan concluded that the driver would be well protected in a 57 km/h frontal collision but the passenger would receive only average protection. It was rated: driver, ★★★★; passenger, ★★★. A crash-tested two-door posted much better results for the passenger. It was rated: driver, ★★★★; passenger, ★★★★★. These scores may not be applicable to the reworked '97 Camry, which sits on a different chassis.

Con: Automatic transmission and power steering have been trouble-prone with previous model years. Owners also report that the front brakes and exhaust system aren't durable. According to the CAA, parts are more expensive than most other cars in this class (alternator and ignition module, for example). Lots of complaints concerning dealership sales and servicing.

Dealer service bulletins address the following '96 Camry problems that may carry over to the revamped '97 versions: transmission check-ball wear causing hard shifting, moonroof panel wind noise, rear suspension squeak or groan, rear disc brake moan, and front brake groaning (see brake pad illustration below).

REF.: BRAKES
NO.: BROO2-96
DATE: MARCH 29, 1996
MODEL: CAM & AVL
CAMRY & AVALON FRONT BRAKE GROAN NOISE
To reduce front brake groan noise on Camrys and Avalons, the brake pad material has been changed.
IDENTIFICATION OF NEW PARTS:

Previous Pads

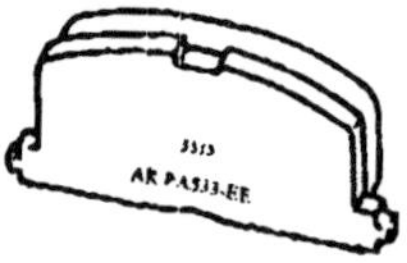

4 digit lot number (Example "5315")

New Pads

6 digit lot number (Example "5618E2")

Check the lot number embossed on the metal backing plate of the brake pads, as shown.

Toyota says that the excessive front brake noise affects all Avalons, Camrys, and ES 300s, but that the automaker will pay for the repair up to only 12 months or 12,000 miles. The same bulletin goes on to say that coverage is extended, however, to 24 months or 18,000 miles under New York's Lemon Law. VEERY interesting.

Road Performance

Pro: Both the 4- and 6-cylinder powerplants are more powerful and offer better fuel economy than do last year's engines. The smooth and flexible 2.2L 4-cylinder engine is best mated to the 5-speed manual transmission and should be relegated to city commuting, although it's surprisingly peppy in the lower gear ranges. This car shines on long drives, and for that you must have the exceptionally quiet-running 3.0L V6 mated to the smooth-shifting automatic gearbox with a dual-mode feature that allows the driver to choose either a power or economy setting. You can get the manual transmission and V6, but only with the CE model. Nimble and predictable handling, enhanced by light and precise steering. This year's additional horsepower doesn't produce any noticeable torque steer. Supple but steady ride on all but the worst roads. Excellent brakes on the sedan.

Con: Neither the 4-banger nor the V6 are high performance engines, but the Camry doesn't pretend to be a high-performance car. The torque converter disengages noisily when traversing hilly terrain. Overly compliant suspension makes for a busy ride when passing over bumps. Little road feel with power steering.

Comfort/Convenience

Pro: Much improved Harmon Motive Stereo system. Heater and climate controls are well situated and easy to use, with large buttons and logical placement. Huge glove box and lots of little storage bins and door map pockets. Firm and supportive seats. Large rear seats will easily sit three people, and on the '96 wagon the seats can be easily folded flat once the head restraints are removed and stored. The wagon also comes with an optional rear-facing third seat that pops out of a recess in the trunk floor. Well-designed instrument layout is more practical and attractive. Huge but narrow cargo area on the wagon. Efficient heating, defrosting, and ventilation. Reasonably-sized trunk has a low liftover sill and carries a full-size spare tire.

Con: Squarish, angular, and conservatively styled, the Camry lacks distinctiveness. Rear taillights look to be the wrong size for the allocated space. In fact, the integrated plastic bumper and grille flashes Lumina while the flat sloping hood whispers Thunderbird. The side-view mirrors can't be adjusted from inside unless you go for the power option. Front seat centre console armrest is set too far back to be comfortable. The tall rear suspension towers cut into luggage space. Rear head room is still a bit tight for six-footers. Side-view mirrors don't spring back (if you clip your garage door, kiss your insurance deductible goodbye). Noisy suspension transmits lots of shock absorber clunk and tire rumble into the passenger cabin.

COST

'96 List Price (firm)	**Residual Values** (months)			
	24	**36**	**48**	**60**
Coupe: $19,998 (15%)	$13,000	$11,500	$10,500	$9500
DX : $20,488 (16%)	14,000	12,000	11,500	10,500
LE: $25,188 (20%)	17,000	15,500	14,000	12,500

TECHNICAL DATA

Powertrain (front-drive)
Engines: 2.2L injected 4 (133 hp) • 3.0L injected V6 (194 hp)
Transmissions: 5-speed manual OD • 4-speed auto. OD

Dimensions (sedan)
Length: 188.5 in.
Width: 70.1 in.
Wheelbase: 105.2 in.

SAFETY FEATURES

	Opt.	Std.
Anti-lock brakes	■	■
Childproof door locks	❑	■
Driver-side airbag	❑	■
Passenger-side airbag	❑	■
Remote keyless entry	■	❑
Traction control	■	■

Avalon

Avalon

RATING: Above Average buy. Essentially an all-dressed Camry with lots more rear seat room.

NEW FOR '97: Eight more horses, a windshield-embedded antenna, standard ABS on the XL, and optional traction control.

GENERAL COMMENTS: Toyota's largest model, this near-luxury four-door offers more value, interior space, and reliability than do other cars in its class that cost thousands of dollars more. A front-engine, front-drive midsize sedan, based on a stretched Camry platform, the Avalon is similar in size to the Ford Taurus and bigger than the rear-drive Cressida it replaced.

Avalon offers a 200-hp version of the Camry's 3.0L V6 powerplant coupled to a 4-speed electronically controlled automatic transaxle. Base models give a nice array of standard comfort/convenience features, including air conditioning, power windows, power door locks, cruise control, and an AM/FM cassette sound system. Safety features include standard ABS and a three-point shoulder belt for the rear centre seat passenger.

The base price nudges the more expensive Camry, but when you start adding extras—ABS, for example—the Avalon's price is a bargain. For thousands less you could drive home in a comparably equipped Bonneville SSE, Eagle Vision TSi, or Oldsmobile Eighty Eight LSS, but you won't get Toyota's legendary quality or high resale value.

Cost analysis/Alternatives: Except for a slight horsepower boost, the '96 and '97 Avalons are practically identical. If Toyota holds the line on prices this year, as it has pledged to do, you'd probably be better off with a '97 version. If you want a more driver-involved experience in a Toyota, consider a Supra or Lexus ES 300 or GS 300. Other cars worth considering: Ford Crown Victoria and Mercury Grand Marquis; Mazda

626, MX-6, and Millenia; Nissan Maxima; and Toyota Camry V6. **Rebates**: Not likely. **Destination charge**: $350. **Recommended options**: A bench seat if you crave additional passenger seating, but the middle passenger won't be comfortable. **Supplementary warranty**: Not needed. **Parts supply/Servicing**: Above average. **Depreciation**: Below average. **Highway/City fuel economy**: 8-12L/100 km.

Reliability/Safety

Pro: The Avalon uses conventional mechanical components employed on Toyota's other models, which explains why there are no major reliability or durability problems. Much improved brake components.

Crash tests of an airbag-equipped 1996 Avalon concluded that the driver and front passenger would be very well protected in a 57 km/h frontal collision. It was rated: driver, ★★★★; passenger, ★★★★★.

Con: Owners report excessive wind noise intruding into the passenger compartment and some fragile trim items. Confidential dealer service bulletins list the following three problems that may carry over to the '97 Avalon: transmission checkball wear causing hard shifting, front brake groan, and rear disc brake moan.

Road Performance

Pro: The V6 engine is smooth, powerful, and quiet, and the electronically controlled 4-speed automatic transmission is well matched to its power without any performance penalty. Better than average handling, thanks to the Camry's stiffened suspension. Ride quality is flawless, providing living-room comfort on virtually any kind of road. Excellent braking.

Con: Power steering is over-assisted at all speeds, and the car has a tendency to oversteer. Wallows a bit, and tends to plow ahead when cornering at high speed.

Comfort/Convenience

Pro: Well-designed instrument layout is both practical and attractive, with controls that are both easy to see and well within reach (instruments are similar to the Camry's, with controls placed in all the familiar places). Front and rear seats are exceptionally comfortable with plenty of thigh support. Large rear seat will easily sit three people. User-friendly heater and climate controls. Easy entry/exit. Enormous trunk has a low liftover sill. Powerful climate control system—efficient heating, defrosting, and ventilation. Lots of sound insulation makes for an interior that's quieter, generally speaking, than the Camry's.

Con: Bland styling, with a hint of Lexus' GS 300. Tire noise and drumming. Radio controls are busy, with lots of identical buttons that are difficult to operate while driving. The cup holders are flimsy, and the fuzzy headliner has a cheap appearance. The car doesn't have fold-down rear seats for trunk access and hauling long objects. Keyless entry sometimes opens the trunk inadvertently.

COST

'96 List Price (firm)	**Residual Values** (months) 24	36	48	60
XL: $33,698 (24%)	$23,000	$18,500	$15,500	$13,000

TECHNICAL DATA

Powertrain (front-drive)	**Dimensions** (sedan)
Engine: 3.0L (200 hp)	Length: 190.2 in.
	Width: 70.3 in.
	Wheelbase: 107.1 in.
Transmission: 4-speed auto.	

SAFETY FEATURES

	Opt.	Std.
Anti-lock brakes	■	❑
Childproof door locks	❑	■
Driver-side airbag	❑	■
Passenger-side airbag	❑	■
Remote keyless entry	■	❑
Traction control	■	■

Celica

Celica Liftback

RATING: An Above Average buy.

NEW FOR '97: The GT coupe is gone; the hatchback remains.

GENERAL COMMENTS: The front-wheel-drive Celica offers benchmark reliability, good handling, and great fuel economy in an attractive sports car package. The GT and GTS have a firm suspension, well-equipped interior, ABS brakes, and a more sporting feel than do other versions. All handle competently and provide the kind of sporting performance expected from a car of this class. The extra performance in the higher-line versions does come at a price, but this isn't a problem given the high resale value and excellent reliability for which Celicas are known. Overall, it's one of the best choices in the sporty car field.

Cost analysis/Alternatives: The 1996 and 1997 models are practically identical; choose the cheapest version. The Eagle Talon 4X4 matches the Celica's features for thousands of dollars less. Other cars worth considering are the '96 Dodge Stealth, Eagle Talon, Ford Mustang and Probe, GM Camaro and Firebird, Mazda Miata, and Toyota's Supra. **Rebates**: Not likely. **Destination charge**: $300. **Recommended options**: Go for the larger 2.2L engine. **Supplementary warranty**: Not needed. **Parts supply/Servicing**: Average. **Depreciation**: Below average. **Highway/City fuel economy**: 6.5-8.5L/100 km with the 1.8L and manual transmission; about a half-litre more with an automatic. 7.5-10.5L/100 km with the 2.2L and manual transmission; an automatic actually uses a bit less fuel.

Reliability/Safety

Pro: The Celica uses the conventional mechanical components that are employed on Toyota's other models, and this explains why there are no major reliability or durability problems. Parts cost less than average, according to the CAA.

Con: Dealer servicing has gone to the dogs during the past few years. The front brakes are troublesome (see Toyota intro); some audio systems and trim items have also been troublesome.

Crash tests of a 1993 Celica concluded that the driver would be well protected in a 57 km/h frontal collision, while the passenger would sustain serious leg trauma.

Road Performance

Pro: The 2.2L powerplant coupled to the smooth-shifting 5-speed manual gearbox is the best choice for overall performance. Precise and predictable handling in all conditions—sportier on GT and GTS models. The power steering provides plenty of road feel. Firm but not uncomfortable ride. Excellent brakes.

Con: The base 1.8L engine is short on acceleration and power and is no match for many of its V6 and V8 competitors. The 4-speed automatic is ill-suited to this kind of machine.

Comfort/Convenience

Pro: Long on features. Restyled exterior resembles a Lexus coupe from the front and a Supra from the rear. Complete and well-designed controls. Exceptionally comfortable front seats, especially on the GT and GTS. The hatchback offers a larger and more versatile cargo area. Quiet, well-insulated interior. The 10-speaker 200-watt "System 10" radio is one of the most advanced systems currently on the market.

Con: Models equipped with the sunroof offer minimal head room for tall front seat passengers. Limited outward vision. The high beltline and low seating position induce claustrophobia. The rear seat is very cramped and the trunk on the '96 coupe isn't very large.

COST

'96 List Price (firm)	**Residual Values** (months)			
	24	**36**	**48**	**60**
GT: $27,998 (20%)	$16,000	$14,000	$12,500	$11,000

TECHNICAL DATA

Powertrain (front-drive)
Engines: 1.8 injected 4
(105 hp) • 2.2L 4 (130 hp)

Dimensions (3-door hatchback)
Length: 174.2 in.
Width: 68.9 in.
Wheelbase: 99.9 in.

Transmissions: 5-speed manual • 4-speed auto.

SAFETY FEATURES

	Opt.	Std.
Anti-lock brakes	■	❑
Driver-side airbag	❑	■
Passenger-side airbag	❑	■
Remote keyless entry	■	❑

Supra

Supra Turbo

RATING: Above Average buy. A reliable but overpriced sports car that replaces finesse with forgiveness.

NEW FOR '97: The return of the 6-speed manual transmission, a sturdier structure, premium cassette stereo radio, restyled front and rear lights, slightly restyled front fascia, a rear spoiler, a standard sunroof on the turbo models, and more sound-deadening material.

GENERAL COMMENTS: The rear-drive Supra comes with an in-line 6-cylinder engine that's available with or without turbocharging. The non-turbo base version uses the Lexus SC 300's 220-hp 3.0L 6-cylinder DOHC 24-valve powerplant, while the high-performance Supra Turbo produces an incredible 320 horsepower from the same in-line 6-cylinder. A unique, optional 4-speed automatic uses "fuzzy logic" to figure out which gear is best suited for each driving situation. The turbo also comes with standard traction control.

Equipped in the tradition of large and powerful grand touring coupes, but with fewer gimmicky gadgets (AWD, 4-wheel steering, etc.), the rear-drive Supra provides seating for four people, but only the two front passengers will be happy. The base price is very high, but you do get a lot for the money. There's very little to criticize on the Supra, aside from excesses in power and equipment—the same characteristics that make it popular. Those who can afford a Supra will get the renowned dependability of all Toyotas, and the assurance that they'll get their money back through the car's high resale value.

Cost analysis/Alternatives: Buy an upgraded '97 version, if the price is reasonable. If not, go for a '96 version without the 6-speed manual or extra soundproofing. Other cars worth considering are the '96 Dodge Stealth, Eagle Talon, Ford Mustang and Probe, GM Camaro and Firebird, '96 Nissan 300ZX, and Toyota Celica. **Rebates**: Not likely, considering the

Supra's popularity. **Destination charge**: $500. **Recommended options**: None; this car comes fully loaded. **Supplementary warranty**: A good idea, considering the car's complexity. **Parts supply/Servicing**: Average. **Depreciation**: Below average. For example, a 1994 Supra, selling originally for $59,800, is now worth about $40,000 as a dealer trade-in. **Highway/City fuel economy**: 9-14L/100 km with the manual 6-speed and about a litre less with the automatic in city driving.

Reliability/Safety

Pro: No major problems have been reported. Excellent component and assembly quality. Large dealer network. Sticky high-performance Michelin MXX3 tires.

Con: Ownership costs are higher than on most other cars in this class because of the complex design and high insurance premiums. Owners report frequent electrical glitches, problems with the brakes, and some instances of intercooler overheating. The quality of dealership servicing has declined remarkably over the years. Rear spoiler obstructs rear vision. No crashworthiness data are available.

Road Performance

Pro: Faster acceleration than the Porsche 968. Zero to 60 mph in 4.6 seconds with a top speed of 155 mph (250 km/h). No turbo lag or torque steer. Very agile and sure-footed. Smooth-shifting 5-speed manual and exceptionally responsive 6-speed. The progressive, speed-sensitive power-steering system changes assist as road speed increases. This makes for precise and predictable steering, although some road feel is lost. Suspension absorbs rough terrain without bouncing, making for a comfortable though somewhat firm ride. The anti-lock brakes perform exceptionally well.

Con: The car is way too heavy, in spite of a recent 10 percent weight reduction. Jarring ride at low speeds. As with most rear-drives, the rear end is a bit twitchy on slippery roads.

Comfort/Convenience

Pro: Excellent cockpit ergonomics. Very comfortable, supportive front seats should suit everyone (as long as you're not too short). The removable roof panels provide the strong body structure of a sedan with the open-air feeling of a convertible. This year's stiffer body has eliminated many of the shakes and rattles present in previous versions.

Con: Low front seats make it hard to see out, and there's no power height adjustment for the seats or telescoping steering wheel. Some controls are a bit complicated. Interior needs a bit more room. The rear seat isn't suited for adults. Limited trunk room for bulky objects. Despite this year's additional soundproofing, there's still lots of interior engine, wind, and road noise. Excessive fuel consumption.

COST

'96 List Price (negotiable)	**Residual Values** (months) 24	36	48	60
Base: $80,758 (30%)	$45,000	$40,000	$34,000	$30,000

TECHNICAL DATA

Powertrain (rear-drive)
Engines: 3.0L injected 6 (220 hp) • 3.0L turbocharged 6 (320 hp)
Transmissions: 5-speed manual OD • 6-speed manual • 4-speed auto. OD • 4-speed auto. "fuzzy logic"

Dimensions
Length: 177.8 in.
Width: 71.3 in.
Wheelbase: 100.4 in.

SAFETY FEATURES

	Opt.	Std.
Anti-lock brakes	❑	■
Driver-side airbag	❑	■
Passenger-side airbag	❑	■
Remote keyless entry	❑	■
Traction control	❑	■

Previa

Previa

RATING: Acceptable.

NEW FOR '97: An expanded choice of interior fabrics. Toyota plans to replace the Previa next year with an all-new front-wheel-drive minivan, based on the midsize Camry and built in Kentucky.

GENERAL COMMENTS: This seven-passenger, four-door, rear-drive/4X4 is Toyota's latest entry in the hot minivan market dominated since 1984 by Chrysler. It's bigger, lower, sits on a longer wheelbase, and is more aerodynamically styled than its predecessor, the LE. Body lines are clean and more rounded than before, with a roof that's lower than the Mazda MPV and Ford Aerostar, and a body that's shorter than GM's Lumina APV.

Only the supercharged engine is available (it's laid on its side and sits under the front seats), hooked to a 4-speed automatic transmission with Overdrive. It has enough power to tow a 3500-pound trailer, but not without some difficulty. Larger wheels and tires, a reworked suspension, and a more efficacious braking system have reduced the erratic braking performance and instability at moderate speeds that have plagued Toyota minivans over the years.

Cost analysis/Alternatives: In addition to AWD versatility and electronic gadgets galore, this minivan comes with a host of options that can drive up its base price to well over $35,000 if the optional cooler/ice maker is included. All things considered, the LE All-Trac with anti-lock brakes looks like the best choice. The 1996 Previa is substantially identical to the '97 version, and can be a bargain if the selling price has been reduced sufficiently. On the other hand, if Toyota does cut its MSRP prices across the board this year you may find the '97 Previa to be a bargain after all. Other minivans worth considering are the Ford Windstar, Mercury Villager/Nissan Quest, and Chrysler Caravan/Voyager. **Rebates**: Not likely if the base price is cut. **Destination charge**: $850 (est.). **Recommended options**: Anti-lock brakes, power windows and door locks, rear heater and AC unit. Eliminating the 4-wheel-drive All-Trac system drops the price by $3000. Second-row bench seats are essential for hauling cargo; the optional captain's chairs can't be removed. **Supplementary warranty**: An extended warranty is a wise decision, considering the drivetrain's complexity. **Parts supply/Servicing**: Average to good supply. Parts are expensive. Servicing has been acceptable. **Depreciation**: Slower than average. For example, a 1994 base Previa DX, selling originally for $24,748, is now worth about $18,000 as a dealer trade-in. **Highway/City fuel economy**: 10-13.3L/100 km; add another half-litre per 100 km for the 4X4 version.

Reliability/Safety

Pro: The Previa was the top-scoring minivan in J. D. Powers and Associates' initial quality survey, with just 0.71 problems per van. Body construction and trim items are first class; all the interior and exterior surfaces come together imperceptibly. "Sedan-like" driveability.

Crash tests of a 1996 dual airbag-equipped Previa concluded that the driver would be very well protected in a 57 km/h frontal collision, while the passenger would have average protection. It's rated: driver, ★★★★; passenger, ★★★.

Con: Engine malfunctions, premature front brake wear, and chassis rusting have been reported. Although routine service jobs such as checking the coolant, washer fluid, or oil can be easily done by raising the short hood, anything more complicated is time-consuming and costly. Expensive brake service. Parts are more expensive than those for other vehicles in this class, according to the CAA. Many parts are available only at dealerships. Head restraints create blind spots, and styling makes it hard to judge the vehicle's size when parking.

Road Performance

Pro: Car-like performance. Good handling and moderate body lean when cornering due to the mid-engine design. Comfortable ride under normal conditions. Fairly resistant to side wind buffeting. Excellent braking. All-wheel drive helps on slippery roads.

Con: Noisy, anemic base engine is particularly slow when hooked to the heavy 4X4 drivetrain. Even with supercharging, engine performance is not this vehicle's strong suit. Four-speed automatic transmission is a bit rough-shifting. Handling and fuel economy also suffer with the 4X4 option. Shocks are overly soft, producing a wallowing feel. Constant shifting and a jarring ride when fully loaded.

Comfort/Convenience

Pro: Plenty of head room and interior space for passengers. The third seat splits in two and folds up against the sides of the van to increase cargo space. Excellent climate control and sound system. Overdrive lockout switch.

Con: Instrument panel is a bit overdone with gadgets and video arcade gauges. Awkward slide-type climate controls, and five different control stalks stick out of the steering column. Huge front windshield wipers are distracting and noisy when hit by cross winds. No support for the driver's right foot. The engine, located in the middle of the van, is separated from the interior by just a fibreglass cover and a few layers of insulation, allowing lots of engine noise into the interior. Some wind noise reported as well.

Getting into the Previa is as difficult as climbing into a sport-utility vehicle. The combination of the front roof pillar's steep angle and the relatively narrow opening into the front seat (based on the Hi Ace,

Toyota's popular cargo van sold only in Japan) make it easy for taller drivers to whack their heads when climbing in. The engine sits beneath the passenger compartment, with an engine housing that separates the front seats from the rest of the interior. This means that Mom and Dad have to climb out of the van and walk around to the sliding rear door in order to attend to the little ones. As a cargo hauler the Previa comes up short; although the rear seats fold up flat against the sides of the van, the second-row captain's chairs can't be removed.

COST

List Price (negotiable)	**Residual Values** (months)			
	24	**36**	**48**	**60**
Base: $36,998 (23%)	$24,900	$19,000	$16,500	$14,000
LE: $41,598 (25%)	26,000	22,500	18,000	15,500
LE 4WD: $44,438 (27%)	27,500	23,900	19,500	17,500

TECHNICAL DATA

Powertrain (rear-drive/ full-time AWD)
Engine: 2.4L supercharged 4-cyl. (161 hp)
Transmission: 4-speed auto. OD

Dimensions (FWD/AWD)
Weight: 3750 lbs./3950 lbs.
Length: 187.0 in.
Width: 70.9 in.
Wheelbase: 112.8 in.
Fuel tank: 75L/reg. unl.
Cargo capacity: 33.1 cu. ft.
Towing capacity: 3500 lbs.
Turning circle: 37.4 ft.
Passengers: 7

SAFETY FEATURES

	Opt.	Std.
Anti-lock brakes*	■	■
Childproof door locks	❑	■
Driver-side airbag	❑	■
Passenger-side airbag	❑	■
Remote keyless entry	■	❑
Front/rear head restraints		Yes
Side impact beams		Yes

**ABS standard on LE models*

European Vehicles

European hatchbacks and sedans are back in favour with Canadian motorists. These cars are more fun and comfortable to drive than most American vehicles; they're loaded with high-tech gadgets; most have a relatively slow rate of depreciation; and during the past several years their prices have been more reasonable than those of the Japanese and American competition.

Volkswagen has managed to do relatively well as a result of both its comprehensive warranty and its adherence to the mid-price range, where Japanese imports are too pricy and American cars don't perform as well. Luxury car importers such as Audi and BMW have also made a remarkable comeback through price cuts and the launching of less expensive entry-level models (for example, this year's Audi A4 1.8T, a spinoff of the A4 2.8).

On the other hand, some European carmakers have abandoned the U.S. and Canadian markets altogether, while others are barely hanging on. Fiat, Renault, and Peugeot were the first to turn tail, while Jaguar and Saab continue to struggle with huge losses that are draining GM and Ford's cash reserves. Saab reported a $65 million loss in the first half of 1996 (about $1300 US per car), and says that it expects to continue losing money over the next two years.

Why? Because buyers are wary of European carmakers' reputation for poor quality and weak dealer networks. Some of the luxury makes have indeed proved to be surprisingly problematic. One MIT report, for example, concludes that German carmakers have gotten lazy and now fail to build quality into every step of the production process, as do Japanese manufacturers. Researchers found that these carmakers instead waste time and money correcting mistakes at the end of the assembly line rather than preventing them at the beginning.

This conclusion is echoed by Canadian drivers. *Lemon-Aid* readers who own pricy European imports invariably tell me of nightmarish electrical glitches that run the gamut from the annoying to the life-threatening (see the Saab section). Other problems noted by owners include premature brake wear and excessive brake noise, AC malfunctions, faulty computer modules leading to erratic shifting, poor driveability, hard starts, and frequent stalling.

Although the servicing problem is usually more acute with vehicles that are new on the market, it has long been the Achilles tendon of European importers. Owners give them low ratings for mishandling their complaints, inadequate service training, and hiring an insufficient number of service representatives—not to mention the abrasive, arrogant attitude typified by some automakers and dealers who bully customers because they have a virtual monopoly on servicing in their region. Look at their dealer networks and you'll see that most European carmakers are crowded into Quebec and Ontario, leaving their eastern and western Canada customers to fend for themselves. This makes the chance of finding competent repairs somewhat akin to winning the lottery.

In light of all these shortcomings, why are European vehicles so popular? Because they make driving so much fun and so comfortable that you quickly forget about Franz, Ingmar, and Luigi waiting for your return to their service bay.

AUDI

Audi has made considerable progress in raising the quality of its vehicles, a fact that's reflected in the company's improved sales in Canada over the past several years. Through a limited lineup of just four vehicles (the A4, A6, S6, and A8), Audi has gained the reputation for making sure-footed, comfortable, all-wheel-drive luxury cars that are loaded with lots of high-tech bells and whistles.

As with most European makes, Audis excel in comfort and performance. But servicing remains problematic, especially now that Volkswagen VW/Audi has closed down its Canadian headquarters and runs its Canadian operations from the U.S. and Germany.

A4/A6 Series

Audi A4

RATING: Above Average buy. Servicing remains Audi's Achilles' heel.

NEW FOR '97: Significant A4 engine changes: the new entry-level A4 1.8T carries a turbocharged 150-hp 4-cylinder engine, incorporating 5 valves per cylinder (similar to the Ferrari's engine setup). The uplevel 2.8L V6 returns with new 5-cylinder heads, boosting horsepower to 193.

This year's improvements to the A6 are minimal: an upgraded locking system and an enhanced value package.

GENERAL COMMENTS: The A4 targets BMW's 3-Series by featuring increased interior room (about two inches), standard multi-link suspension, upgraded automatic climate control, a light body, low-speed traction enhancement, a 5-speed automatic transmission, and all-wheel-drive for about an extra $2000. Selling for $37,500, equipped with standard dual airbags, ABS, and a 150-hp 1.8L turbo or a 193-hp 2.8L V6 engine coupled to an electronic 4-speed automatic transmission, this entry-level four-door is powerful, easy to handle, and lavishly appointed.

The A6 sells for $49,270 and is packed with plenty of standard features in a sedan or wagon format. It too is a comfortable, spacious, front-drive or all-wheel-drive luxury sedan that comes with dual airbags and ABS. It uses the same V6 powerplant as its smaller sibling, the A4.

Audi introduced the S6 sports sedan in Canada last year. It offers a turbocharged 2.2L 20-valve 5-cylinder engine that produces 227 hp. The transmission is a 5-speed manual.

The $89,840 A8, Audi's new all-aluminum luxury sedan, makes its debut this year. Set on an aluminum-alloy frame, it has standard 4-side airbags and a 230-hp, 3.7L V8 engine mated to a 5-speed manual transmission. The Quattro variant comes with a 300-hp, 4.2L V8.

The A4 and A6 have identical shortcomings. They're conservatively styled, and slow off the mark in spite of the turbocharger and V6 additions. The 4-speed automatic shifts erratically and the 2.8L V6 engine needs full throttle for adequate performance. Handling is acceptable, but the ride is a bit firm and the car still exhibits considerable body roll, brake dive, and acceleration squat when pushed. Handling is on a par with the BMW 300 series, and acceleration times beat out those of Mercedes. Quattro's AWD is extended to entry-level models at a time when most automakers are dropping the option on passenger cars.

Overall quality control has improved markedly over the past several years, with fewer body, trim and accessories, brake, and electrical glitches than exhibited by previous models. A perusal of this year's internal service bulletins shows the following '96 model problems that may carry over to the '97s: front speaker buzzing, CD changer skips, cruise control fails to maintain set speed, radio volume goes to maximum when adjusted, binding rear ashtray lid, and a loose rear reading lamp.

A crash-tested, airbag-equipped, 1996 four-door A4 showed that the driver would have a bit less injury protection than would the passenger. It was rated: driver, ★★★★; passenger, ★★★★★. A similarly tested 1996 four-door A6 showed that both the driver and passenger would be well protected. It was rated: driver and passenger, ★★★★★.

Cost analysis/Alternatives: The 1997 A4's engine downgrade and upgrade offer you more money in your pocket on the one hand, and more horses in your engine on the other. As for the A6, consider buying last year's near-identical version if it's discounted sufficiently. Other vehicles worth taking a look at: the BMW 328, Lexus ES 300, Mazda 929 and Millenia, Mercedes C-series, Toyota Avalon, and Volvo 850 turbo and 960. **Rebates**: Likely by mid-summer. **Destination charge**: $500. **Recommended options**: None; these cars come fully loaded. **Supplementary warranty**: Essential, given the cost of repairs and parts once the base warranty expires. **Parts supply/Servicing**: Below average. There's no guarantee that the dealer body and Audi's American administrators can service customers adequately and apply the warranty in a fair and efficient manner. **Depreciation**: Fairly slow during the two years since their debut. Historically, Audi values plummet when the base warranty expires and high repair costs become the owner's responsibility. **Highway/City fuel economy**: 8.5-12.5L/100 km for the A4 and an automatic transmission; 9.5-13.5L/100 km for the A6. Add another half-litre for the Quattro version.

BMW

BMW has long made well-appointed cars that excel at handling and driving comfort. Its vehicles have excellent road manners, depreciate slowly, and have a cachet that only money can buy. Unfortunately, they also have limited interior room (except for the high-end models) and are difficult and expensive to service. But these drawbacks haven't discouraged BMW's loyal following of young professionals and people who want something prestigious but not priced entirely beyond reach. Tapping this growing popularity, over the past several decades BMW has brought out a larger and much more expensive line of sedans known as the 3.0, the Bavaria and, since 1976, different combinations of the 5-Series, 6-Series, 7-Series, and 8-Series.

All BMWs have improved technically and aesthetically over the years. But even so they still lag behind the Japanese competition in terms of resale value, interior comfort, and high-tech componentry.

Take the entry-level 318i, for example. Apparently its only *raison d'être* is to bring down the base price to a level where more people can afford to buy a BMW. It's embarrassingly slow compared to other cars in its class, and it can't keep up with sporty coupes that cost half as much. And if you make the mistake of putting an automatic transmission in the car, you'll be lucky to beat a Lada.

Servicing has always been problematic with Bimmers. Three years ago BMW Canada set up an innovative program in Montreal, Toronto, and Vancouver to improve servicing. They made house calls, and their dealerships provided service technicians on a rotating basis to man a fully equipped BMW service vehicle. Although it may be too early to have a definite opinion about the efficacy of this program, reader feedback to *Lemon-Aid* has been very negative. For example, one 318i owner from Vancouver attached these comments to his *Lemon-Aid* survey sheet:

> "The problems started almost immediately with the malfunctioning clock, then the door seal, then the muffler, then missing heating ducts, faulty window switches, a faulty heater control unit, faulty radio, another faulty window switch (three in total now), faulty coin holder lid, no heat again, faulty clutch assembly, faulty parking brake handle, no heat again, then no heat again, then no heat again. . . . At present I am waiting for the repair of the fan unit (settings 2 and 3 of the heat/air conditioning both provide the same level of air flow). . . ."

BMW's Canadian dealers also have complained about the way they've been treated by BMW Canada. Dealers claim that the company's president, Ed Robinson, is obsessed with sales and could care less about customer service or dealer rights. Called "The Terminator" by BMW dealers, Robinson closed down three dealerships (Northwest Motors and Beach Auto in the Toronto area, and Chapman Performance Cars in Nova Scotia). Others have been threatened with termination because they weren't selling enough cars. Robinson says that his tough action has pushed BMW sales to record levels, despite the more than 500 letters and 1700 calls of protest. Disagreeing with Robinson's downplaying of the criticism, Canadian dealer associations have called the controversy a "national problem."

The only justifications for buying one of these German cars are prestige value and (hopefully) a low rate of depreciation. There are plenty of other cars that cost less, offer more interior room, and are safer, more reliable, and better performing. So if you're buying a BMW, keep in mind that the entry-level versions of these little status symbols are more show than go. The larger, better-performing high-end models are more expensive and don't give you the same standard features as do many Japanese imports. Also, be prepared to endure some poor servicing; brake, electrical, and accessory problems; as well as body and trim glitches.

3-Series

3-Series

RATING: Above Average buy.

NEW FOR '97: Standard traction control; refreshed front-end styling that includes a new steering wheel; and the M3 coupe gets a four-door brother, the Z3 roadster.

GENERAL COMMENTS: Combining power, performance, and aerodynamic styling, the entry-level 318i and 318ti return this year accompanied by a convertible and a high-performance coupe. The 318ti is cheaper because it comes only as a hatchback, is 8.8 inches shorter overall, carries a smaller fuel tank and limited-service spare tire, uses a cheaper rear suspension, and offers a no-frills dashboard and instruments. Six different versions are offered: the base two- and four-door sedans; a convertible; the 325iS (a high-performance two-door); a high-performance 4-wheel-drive model; and a four-door 325iX.

With its recent styling changes and increased exterior and interior dimensions the 325i has come to resemble its more expensive big brothers. The 2.8L 4-valves-per-cylinder 190-hp in-line 6-cylinder engine is borrowed from the 525i. The less expensive 318i is powered by a 16-valve DOHC in-line 4-cylinder with 138 horsepower. Its convertible twin is a budget version of the 325 convertible, priced at $9000 less. It has a manual top and a smaller 1.9L engine. A BMW 320i is available only in Canada. Its 150-hp, small 6-cylinder powerplant is the first Canadian application of BMW's optional 5-speed automatic. The 320i comes only as a sedan. The sporty M3 carries a 3.2L in-line 6-cylinder engine that puts out an impressive 240 hp when hooked to a 5-speed manual transmission.

Cost analysis/Alternatives: Don't waste your money on a 1997 3-Series (unless you want a Z3 roadster); you can find a practically identical '96 for less. If not, go for the cheaper, entry-level 318ti and use the extra money to buy better-performing Michelin MXV2 tires. Other cars worth considering are the Eagle Talon; Ford Taurus and Sable; Mazda Miata HT and MX-6 GT; Lexus and Infiniti models; VW Cabriolet, Golf GTi, and Jetta GTi; and Toyota Camry and Celica GTS. **Rebates**: Not likely. **Destination charge**: $525. **Recommended options**: Upgraded Michelin tires. If you buy the 325i convertible, invest $1500 in the rollover protection system that pops up from behind the rear seat. **Supplementary warranty**: A wise investment. **Parts supply/Servicing**: Below average. **Depreciation**: Below average. **Highway/City fuel economy**: 318ti: 7.5-11L/100 km; 318/320i/325i/318iS/325iS: 8-12L/100 km.

Reliability/Safety

Pro: The engines and transmissions are sturdy. Parts are less expensive than for other cars in this class, according to the Canadian Automobile Association. Excellent quality control and factory rustproofing.

All 3-Series models are pre-wired for an alarm system and use a Coded Driveaway Protection system that won't allow the car to start unless the ignition key matches the ignition switch code, which changes each time the car is started. Automatic seatbelt tensioners draw up slack for maximum collision protection. A crash-tested, airbag-equipped, '96 328i showed that both the driver and passenger would be well protected. It was rated: driver and passenger, ★★★★.

Con: Average reliability. Body assembly and workmanship have declined over the years. Expect to pay close to $2500 per year to keep your Bimmer on the road. Parts are scarce outside major metropolitan areas, and independent mechanics are rare. Brakes, electrical system, and body trim and accessories are the most failure-prone components.

Road Performance

Pro: Impressive off-the-line acceleration with the 1.9L 4-cylinder engine, and a manual transmission oriented toward driving enthusiasts. Responsive optional 2.8L in-line 6-cylinder engine and transmissions are the essence of harmonious cooperation. The M3's 3.0L 6-cylinder motor is a real tire-burner. Light and precise gear shifting with easy clutch and shift action. Competent and predictable handling on dry surfaces. No-surprise suspension and steering makes for crisp handling. Braking is exceptionally good, particularly with Michelin MXV2 tires.

Con: The 318i's acceleration is embarrassingly slow with an automatic transmission. Traction is notoriously poor on slippery surfaces. A throttle-shift delay takes getting used to for smooth takeoffs. Second gear is a bit short. The ride is firm and occasionally uncomfortable on rough roads. The Z3 roadster could use a 6-cylinder's additional firepower.

Comfort/Convenience

Pro: Comfortable driving position and supportive seats. Excellent control layout and design. Wiper action automatically drops from constant to intermittent when you slow down or stop. All power windows have an express down and up. The 325i's additional room and separate driver and passenger climate controls make for a more hospitable interior. A rigid body design keeps rattles and clunks to a minimum.

Con: Bland styling and very austere interior. Limited head room when equipped with a sunroof. Insufficient number of gauges. Sober interior. Confusing switches on the dual climate-control system. Interior plastics look tacky. The four-door model offers marginally improved access to the rear seat, which is too firm. Rear seating is comfortable only for two adults. Limited trunk space.

COST

List Price (negotiable)	**Residual Values** (months) **24**	**36**	**48**	**60**
318ti: $26,900 (17%)	$21,000	$17,000	$13,500	$11,000
318i: $32,300 (19%)	23,000	19,000	15,500	13,000
328i: $46,900 (27%)	31,000	27,500	23,000	21,000
'96 Cabriolet: $ 57,900 (29%)	38,000	33,000	29,000	26,000

TECHNICAL DATA

Powertrain (rear-drive)
Engines: 1.9L injected 4 (138 hp) • 2.8L injected 6 (190 hp) • 3.2L injected 6 (240 hp)
Transmissions: 5-speed manual • 4-speed auto.

Dimensions (4-door)
Length: 174.5 in.
Width: 66.8 in.
Wheelbase: 106.3 in.

SAFETY FEATURES

	Opt.	Std.
Anti-lock brakes	❑	■
Childproof door locks	■	❑
Driver-side airbag	❑	■
Passenger-side airbag	❑	■
Remote keyless entry	■	❑
Traction control	❑	■

5-Series

525i

RATING: An Above Average buy.

NEW FOR '97: The 5-Series is more conservatively styled, with a longer, wider, and taller body. It offers a quieter and more spacious interior; uses a lighter, all-aluminum suspension and chassis; and features rack-and-pinion steering, standard traction control, ABS, and six airbags to protect the chest, head, and side. Power is supplied by a 190-hp 2.8L 6-cylinder and a 282-hp, 32-valve 4.4L V8 engine.

GENERAL COMMENTS: The 528i ($54,900) soldiers on with its in-line 6-cylinder engine, while the 540i ($68,900) comes with a standard automatic transmission and a 4.4L V8 powerplant. The wagon's engine puts out seven more horsepower than does the in-line 6-cylinder motor, and uses a more sophisticated automatic transmission that has a torquier first gear. King of the sporty luxury car hill are the $61,900 M3 coupe and its sedan variant ($81,900).

These medium-sized sedans have proven to be fairly reliable in the short term, although accident repair costs for the 525i's and 535i's are much higher than average. Featuring a modern, rounded body, they offer an impressive package that combines great performance (except for some excessive body roll in turns) and good comfort. They're pre-wired for an alarm system and remote telephone controls and offer a number of trim and electronic upgrades. The M5's standard features include a 3.73:1 axle (for better fuel economy) and Servotronic power steering. All BMWs, from the 5-Series on, have standard dual airbags, anti-lock brakes, childproof door locks, three-point seatbelts, and transmission/brake interlocks.

740i, 750iL

7-Series

RATING: Above Average buy.

NEW FOR '97: The V8 engine gets bumped up to a 282-hp 4.4L, and the standard wheelbase 740i joins its long wheelbase brethren.

GENERAL COMMENTS: These large sedans are indulgence on wheels, with a large, aerodynamic body, two powerful engines (a base V8 and a high-performance 322-hp 5.4L V12), key-controlled remote unlocking system, a revamped interior with improved steering wheel controls, quad headlights under glass, side-impact airbags, and a 5-speed automatic transaxle. Except for a horsepower boost and more airbags, there's little that's new this year to justify the '97 model's higher cost. Shop around at Infiniti, Lexus, Lincoln, or Mercedes dealerships before you sign for the Bimmer.

The '96 740iL sells for a little over (but who's counting?) $89,900, while this year's 750iL, with its longer body and V12 engine, will set you back a cool $129,500. It comes with an electronically adjustable steering column, an electronic damping control system, and a number of trim and electronic upgrades. Only the S-Class Mercedes-Benz can rival the solidity, performance, and comfort of these luxury touring cars. The sophisticated electronics found on the 7-Series have caused owners a few problems, the AC is noisy, and the climate controls aren't user-friendly.

8-Series

8-Series

RATING: Above Average buy.

NEW FOR '97: These cars are carried-over '96s.

GENERAL COMMENTS: BMW's '96 850i flagship ($124,900) is in its last year on the Canadian market. Compared to the 12-cylinder motor, the $130,900 840Ci's V8 powerplant delivers just the right amount of low-end torque. Amenities include a cellular phone with voice-activated dialing, and steering wheel stalk controls. The only import with a 6-speed automatic gearbox, the 850Ci carries the same V12 5.4L engine used by the 750iL. Its disadvantages are a rear seat that won't hold passengers in comfort, 4123 pounds of weight to move, and a cachet that says "Take my money, please."

LADA

LadaCanada should be given some kind of prize for sheer tenacity. While bigger and richer European automakers have turned tail and abandoned the Canadian market when their sales declined, Lada has weathered a second Russian revolution, near-bankruptcy, an Ontario NDP government, and a Not Recommended label from *Lemon-Aid*—all in the 19 years since these primitive econoboxes first hit our shores.

Initially no more than a Russian-built Fiat 124, sales were good in the late 1970s when the Canadian public began to turn away from gas-guzzling land yachts and embraced inexpensive economy cars—no matter their origin. In its zeal to promote inexpensive economy cars, even the APA briefly put the Lada on its recommended list.

But quality-control problems and Lada's refusal to honour warranty claims in the mid-'80s gave these low-priced and low-tech cars an uncertain future. Buyers deserted Lada showrooms in droves. Lada never recovered fully from all the bad publicity, despite having considerably improved its cars' overall quality control. It has since been reduced to selling just two vehicles—the Samara and the Niva 4X4.

Lada gives a 3 year/72,000 km bumper-to-bumper base warranty, anti-rust-through protection for the life of the car, and 24-hour roadside assistance. Like Chrysler, Lada's warranty is way too limited to be of much help to customers who experience powertrain malfunctions after the third year. Furthermore, many Lada dealerships have gone bankrupt or changed their franchises over the years, leaving a weak support system for parts and servicing. True, the company has a respectable 80-plus dealers across Canada, but they're concentrated mainly in major urban areas. And forget about Lada service in the U.S. LadaCanada advises owners to take their cars to the nearest service station ("Hey, Clem, we got one of those Ruskies"), and the repair cost will be settled under warranty back in Canada—after you pay Canada Customs duty.

Another problem is the lack of safety features in Lada's vehicles. Apart from the inclusion of three-point seatbelts, neither the Samara nor the Niva offer anti-lock brakes, airbags, childproof locks, or a transmission/brake interlock. No crashworthiness data are available.

LadaCanada now sells about 1500 cars annually, half of these in Quebec, where its warehouse was relocated last year. The Russian manufacturer, a joint-stock company called Avtovaz Inc., is the successor of the state-owned Volga Automobile Works. LadaCanada says that it plans to expand its base to 120 dealers and sell 12,000 to 14,000 units annually through aggressive pricing within the next few years. Sure—and Elvis is working at McDonald's.

Samara

Samara

RATING: Below Average buy.

NEW FOR '97: Nothing significant.

GENERAL COMMENTS: Launched in 1989, the first 1.3L three-door hatchback sold for $15,000 in the Soviet Union and $5595 in Canada. The 1997 lineup includes a base Samara retailing for $9445, and a $10,845 1.5L 66-hp four-door Samara/Sagona equipped with fuel injection made by General Motors.

The Samara is modern—for the '70s. It doesn't offer the sleek, aerodynamic body of today's cars, or their mechanical sophistication. The design is (for lack of a better term) utilitarian, with a large rear seating area and trunk. In terms of performance, the car is predictably unpredictable. Glacial acceleration in the 0-to-60 mph range is about 14 seconds. The 1.5L engine is often hard to start, and noisy when revved. Once started, it tends to stumble and stall. Even the hard starting is unpredictable, with drivers endlessly cranking the starter on warm days but having the engine start right up at minus 35 degrees. Steering is imprecise, and excessive torque steer causes the car to jerk unexpectedly to the right and even to lift up the inside right wheel when negotiating curves under heavy throttle. The 5-speed manual transmission—the only one offered—has a vague and somewhat balky shifter that's oriented more toward saving fuel than easy shifting. The shift linkage is imprecise, and clutch takeup is far from smooth. The body leans heavily in cornering. Braking performance is barely adequate. The ride is always busy and uncomfortable on secondary roads. Interior accommodations are good. There's a tire pump in the trunk.

The quality of mechanical and body components is generally poor; however, not as poor as in the past. Expect fuel and electrical system failures and premature brake wear. Major problems usually start after the third year, and it may be difficult to find parts and service. According to the CAA, however, parts cost much less than average. If the past is any guide, the Samara is a poor investment. Ladas all depreciate very quickly, because no one wants to buy a used one. The body is sloppily assembled and highly vulnerable to premature rusting and paint peeling. Doors are poorly hung. These cars have never been crash tested by the U.S. or Canadian governments.

Cost analysis/Alternatives: The 1996 Samaras are virtually identical to the '97 versions, but these cars are priced so low it's unlikely that buying an earlier model will save you what the extra year's depreciation will cost. (And, you might find it too costly to keep the car long enough to amortize its early depreciation losses.) Other cars worth considering are the '96 Eagle Summit, Ford Escort or Tracer, Geo Metro, and Suzuki Swift. **Rebates**: Not likely. **Destination charge**: $300. **Recommended options**: None. **Supplementary warranty**: A must-have option. **Parts supply/Servicing**: Below average. **Depreciation**: Above average. **Highway/City fuel economy**: 6-9.5L/100 km with the 1.5L; 7-10L/100 km with the 1.3L.

MERCEDES-BENZ

Like buying a minivan or pickup, you can't lose money buying a Mercedes-Benz if you keep it long enough. The German automaker has long made it a point to design and engineer cars at the forefront of technology and safety, and to clothe them in conservative, though attractive garb.

Yet one gets the impression that for the past decade Mercedes-Benz has coasted on its reputation, losing market share to Infiniti and Lexus in the process. Its cars once had excellent reliability records (tarnished somewhat by electrical system, brake, engine cooling, air conditioning, and body hardware defects) and astonishingly low depreciation rates. They also lasted longer than did most American-made passenger cars. But this couldn't make up for high prices; low-tech, poorly styled entries like the 190 Series; and a small dealer network.

In an attempt to respond to critics' charges that its cars were priced out of most buyers' reach and that its styling was antiquated, Mercedes tried out its own new aero look about five years ago with the entry-level 190 ("baby Benz") Series. It was a flop.

But the aero look was retained, and is now what makes these luxury imports distinctive. As well, more realistic prices in the past several years, and a revamped model lineup full of high-tech safety and convenience features, have brought the company back to profitability.

SLK

RATING: Not Recommended during its first year on the market.

GENERAL COMMENTS: Taking its cue from BMW's 318ti and Audi's new 1.8t, this year Mercedes-Benz is launching its entry-level SLK230 ("simple luxury that's kind to your wallet"), a rear-drive roadster that's almost half the cost of M-B's other roadsters. In addition to a great price, there are a number of amenities one would expect to find only with a far costlier SL, including a one-button full-power top, roll-over protection, side airbags, ABS, and traction control. Add to this a 191-hp 2.3L supercharged in-line four hooked to a 5-speed automatic transmission pulling only 3000 pounds, and you can expect swift performance and superb handling.

On the downside, the entire model year is sold out, they went for full sticker price, and the first series is likely to be more troublesome than units made six months later, which you can't buy anyway. But even if you did buy one of the first ones out, chances are the depreciation will be so slight that you won't have to keep the vehicle long to get a good resale price.

C-Class

C-Class Sedan

RATING: An Above Average buy.

NEW FOR '97: Twelve more horses for the 2.3L engine, a 5-speed automatic transmission, and redesigned headlights.

GENERAL COMMENTS: Three entry-level versions based on the 190 platform are offered this year: a $36,950 148-hp 2.3L-equipped Special Edition C230; a $42,950 standard 2.3L-equipped C230; and an upscale $50,995 C280 offered with a 194-hp 2.8L V6 engine. An awesome 276-hp 3.6L in-line 6-cylinder powers the top-of-the-line $72,365 C36.

The base 2.3L engine is acceptable around town, but highway cruising requires more grunt to handle the car's heft and accessories. And speaking of grunt, the 2.8L powerplant is a real powerhouse in this small car. Although its power is used most effectively when coupled to the new 5-speed manual transmission, its performance with the new 5-speed automatic is quite acceptable. On '96 models, some owners have complained that the 4-speed automatic requires a lot of throttle effort to downshift.

Keep in mind that owner surveys give the entry-level cars "just" a better than average rating, while the 300 and higher series have always scored way above average in owner satisfaction. Parts costs are below average, according to the CAA.

Crash tests of a 1996 C220 sedan equipped with dual airbags concluded that the driver and passenger would be very well protected in a 57 km/h frontal collision. It was rated: driver, ★★★★; passenger, ★★★★.

Cost analysis/Alternatives: Consider buying a '97 C-Class only if you feel you need its extra horses and improved automatic gearbox. Keep in mind, though, that you'll have to keep the car at least five years in order to amortize the extra year of depreciation. Other cars worth considering are the Ford Thunderbird/Cougar, Infiniti J30, Lexus GS 300, '96 Mazda 929 and Millenia, Mercedes-Benz 300, Nissan Maxima, Toyota Camry and Avalon, and Volvo 850 and 900 series. **Rebates**: Not likely. **Destination charge**: $400. **Recommended options**: Traction control and anti-theft alarm. **Supplementary warranty**: A good idea. **Parts supply/Servicing**: Average. **Depreciation**: Below average. **Highway/City fuel economy**: 8-11L/100 km with the 2.3L; 8-10.5L/100 km with the 2.8L V6. No information available for the 3.6L.

E-Class

E-Class Sedan

RATING: Recommended.

NEW FOR '97: Lots of chassis, mechanical, and styling changes. Set on a chassis that's over an inch longer and wider, Mercedes' conservative image is transformed with new aerodynamic styling that uses ovoid headlamps and a moulded hood to accentuate the car's more aerodynamic shape. Additional mechanical and safety features include active ride control, automatic damping control, side airbags, and a rain sensor for windshield wipers. The new 5-speed manual transmission is a big improvement over last year's 4-speed automatic, which is known for requiring a lot of throttle effort to downshift.

GENERAL COMMENTS: Most of the midsize E-Class sedans offer inline 6-cylinder engines, although a V8 powerplant is offered on the E300D ($59,950) with its 134-hp 3.0L turbodiesel, the E320 ($65,900) with the new 217-hp 3.2L, and the E420 ($73,300) with its 275-hp 4.2L V8.

Redesigned twice in the past seven years, the E-Class is considered to be the state of the art in German auto technology. These cars do everything well, and manage to hold five people in relative comfort. They're first class in combining performance, road manners, and comfort. True, they're not the best riding, handling, or accelerating cars available, but they're able to perform each of these tasks almost as well as the best cars in each specific area without sacrificing some other important element in the driving equation. And on top of all that, the CAA reports that parts are fairly inexpensive.

The E-Class continues to offer standard traction control that prevents wheelspin upon acceleration. Another interesting feature is the remarkably smooth and quiet base 24-valve 217-hp high-performance version of the in-line 6-cylinder engine that powers the 300 Series. All this has its price, though. If you'd like to drive one of these cars but are of an economical frame of mind, choose the '96 280; it offers everything the E320 does but for about $15,000 less. The E300CE is a coupe version, appealing to a sportier crowd, while the E300TE is the station wagon variant. Both the 300E sedan and 300TE station wagon carry the 4Matic all-wheel drive.

A 1984 300SD four-door was crash tested by the NHTSA and didn't fare very well; the driver was judged to have sustained severe or fatal chest and leg injuries. But since that time Mercedes-Benz has campaigned for a review of the crash test method, arguing that its cars are engineered to protect occupants from frontal collisions that are at an angle, rather than straight on. This year the U.S. Congress agreed to spend the money to include this kind of test in subsequent NHTSA crashworthiness tests.

Cost analysis/Alternatives: The 1997 models are substantially improved over last year's models, and are the better buy. Other cars worth considering are the Infiniti series, Lincoln Town Car and Mark series, Lexus series, Mazda 929 and Millenia, Mercedes-Benz 300, Nissan Maxima, Toyota Camry wagon and Avalon, and Volvo 850 and 900 series. **Destination charge**: $500. **Recommended options**: None. **Supplementary warranty**: A good idea. **Parts supply/Servicing**: Average. **Depreciation**: Below average. **Highway/City fuel economy**: 9-13L/100 km with most of the gasoline engines; 7-9.5L/100 km with the 3.2L V6 diesel powerplant.

S-Class

S320 Sedan

RATING: Recommended.

NEW FOR '97: A less expensive SLK roadster; door-mounted, side airbags; ASR traction control; bichromatic taillights; restyled alloy wheels, xenon gas discharge headlights; Parktronic parking (in-bumper sensors and dash indicators that aid in parking); and rain sensor wipers.

GENERAL COMMENTS: These S-Class cars are the Mercedes-Benz flagships. They range from the entry-level $87,500 S320 and S350 Turbodiesel to the most exclusive $175,900 S600 coupe and sedan. Designed to incorporate a more aerodynamic, flowing style with understated power, the base powerplant is a 3.2L 228-hp 6-cylinder engine. The $101,900 S420 is essentially an S320 equipped with a 4.2L 275-hp V8 engine. The 560 version has been replaced by the $132,950 S500 and continues to be powered by a 5.0L 315-hp V8 motor. The S600 returns with a standard 6.0L 389-hp V12 engine with a top speed of 150 mph.

Reliability and durability have never been a problem with any of these models, although the new electronic wizardry has had some initial glitches. All S-Class models feature sound-insulating double-pane side windows. All Mercedes cars have very high resale values, but the SL320 does especially well. The SL Series' accident repair costs are much higher than average.

Cost analysis/Alternatives: How much do you feel the extra side airbags and traction control are worth? That's what the higher cost '97 version offers you. Other cars worth considering are the Infiniti series, Lincoln Town Car and Mark series, Lexus series, Mazda 929 and Millenia, Mercedes-Benz 300, Nissan Maxima, Toyota Camry wagon and Avalon, and Volvo 850 and 900 series. **Rebates**: Not likely. **Destination charge**: $450. **Recommended options**: None. **Supplementary warranty**: A wise investment. **Parts supply/Servicing**: Average. **Depreciation**: Below average. **Highway/City fuel economy**: 8-14L/100 km with the 3.2L L6 DOHC; 8-11.5L/100 km with the 3.5L L6 SOHC turbo diesel; 11-15.5L/100 km with the 4.2L V8 DOHC; 11.5-14L/100 km with the 5.0L V8 DOHC; and 13.5-19L/100 km with the 6.0L V12 DOHC.

VOLKSWAGEN

Like most European cars, Volkswagens are practical and offer excellent handling and great fuel economy without sacrificing interior comfort. While overall reliability isn't spectacular, the entry-level models are reasonably priced. And they're not all that difficult to service at independent garages, which have grown increasingly popular as owners flee more expensive and harder to find dealerships. Although VW parts are fairly expensive, independent repair agencies usually have no trouble finding them.

However, in an effort to keep its service customers and to find a marketing hook to lure wary customers into its showrooms, Volkswagen offers an optional 10-year comprehensive warranty that goes a long way in protecting owners from the many electrical, brake, and trim problems long associated with VWs.

The only continuing concern is how the closure of its Canadian headquarters will affect Volkswagen's supply of new vehicles, its warranty administration, and parts availability. In a recent Canadian Federation of Automobile Dealer Associations dealer survey, taken before VW relocated, VW dealers blasted Volkswagen management as being insensitive to their concerns. VW's move to the U.S. reinforces that impression.

Golf, Jetta, Cabrio

Jetta

RATING: Recommended. A taxi-fleet workhorse.

NEW FOR '97: New colours and trim. The rear brake light has been moved from the spoiler to the rear window. Golfs and Jettas equipped with the 115-hp 4-cylinder engine get a redesigned cylinder head that cuts engine noise. The Golf GTI VR6 rides lower, thanks to new shocks, springs, and anti-roll bars. The Cabrio Highline gets standard AC, 14-inch alloy wheels, halogen driving lights, and leather upholstery. The base convertible loses standard ABS and a few other goodies in order to keep a lid on prices.

GENERAL COMMENTS: Reasonably priced, practical, and fun to drive. That pretty well sums up the main reasons why these VWs continue to be so popular. Yet they offer much more, including lots of interior room, a peppier engine than what you'll find in most cars this size, responsive handling, great fuel economy, and better than average reliability.

The Jetta is a more expensive Golf with a trunk, and the Cabrio is a Golf without a roof that costs thousands more. The Golf GTI V6 is a sporty performer that comes with lots of standard equipment, including air conditioning, an upgraded sound system, and a split folding rear seat. Jettas offer standard cruise control, power mirrors, and alloy wheels.

Three engines are available: a 115-hp 2.0L base 4-cylinder, a 90-hp turbo diesel variant, and a 172-hp 2.8L V6 borrowed from the Corrado and Passat. A manual 5-speed transmission is also offered as a standard feature, along with an optional 4-speed automatic. Power steering is optional on base-level models.

Although the entry-level Golf's engine is no tire burner, it's well mated to the base manual transmission and handles most driving conditions with ease. From the standpoint of driveability and purchase price, the Jetta is an overlooked bargain.

Cost analysis/Alternatives: The 1996 models and the '97s are pretty much the same, making a leftover '96 the bargain of the two if it's sufficiently discounted. Other cars worth considering are the '96 Eagle Summit and Talon, Honda Civic, '96 Mazda MX-3 and Protegé, Nissan Sentra, and Toyota Corolla. **Rebates**: Not likely. **Destination charge**: $525. **Recommended options**: Stay away from the electric sunroof; it costs a bundle to repair and offers not much more than the well-designed manual sunroof. **Supplementary warranty**: VW's 10-year warranty is essential. **Parts supply/Servicing**: Below average. **Depreciation**: Below average. **Highway/City fuel economy**: 7-9.5L/100 km with the 1.8L; 6-7.5L/100 km with the 1.9L SOHC diesel; 7-10L/100 km with the 2.0L; and 9-13L/100 km with the 2.8L V6.

Reliability/Safety

Pro: Major components are relatively trouble-free. Standard three-point safety belts and anti-theft alarm (thieves just adore these cars; they steal the VW badges from the grille and rear panel, and there are a dozen thieves for each Blaupunkt radio). Internal service bulletins don't show any factory-related defects that require correction.

Crash tests of a 1996 Jetta concluded that the driver and passenger would receive average protection from serious injuries in a 57 km/h frontal collision. It was rated: driver, ★★★; passenger, ★★★.

Con: Inadequate base warranty. Now made in Mexico, the quality control on these vehicles isn't comparable to German workmanship. The brakes and the electrical, fuel, and exhaust systems are especially troublesome. Owners report that doors are poorly hung, rattles are omnipresent, and dashboard controls and interior and exterior trim items aren't very durable. Paint defects and premature rusting have been common. According to the CAA, parts are more expensive than most other cars in this class.

Road Performance

Pro: The standard 2.0L 4-cylinder engine is acceptable for city driving and leisurely highway cruising with the manual gearbox, thanks mainly to the car's light weight and improved fuel injection. The V6, however, is the prerequisite engine for performance thrills. Both the standard and automatic transmissions function flawlessly. Precise and predictable steering. Excellent handling. Ride quality is less firm than with previous models. Very good brakes.

Con: The base 4-cylinder engine provides sluggish acceleration when hooked to an automatic transmission. Diesel engines equipped with cruise control can't handle small hills well, and usually drop 10 to 15 km/h. The soft suspension produces lots of body roll when turning.

Comfort/Convenience

Pro: Ergonomics are impressive. The dash is well laid-out, and gauges are easy to read. Controls are easy to find and use. Although the interior is very austere, it's well finished and fairly spacious. Comfortable and versatile front bucket seats help to make driving a pleasure. Excellent driving position. Front seat head room is adequate for most drivers, even with a sunroof. Tilt steering column. The rear seats include headrests and will hold two people in relative comfort. The Golf's hatchback design is a bit more versatile for diverse cargo than is the Jetta's huge enclosed trunk. Rear seating is adequate for two adults.

Con: Despite additional sound deadening, the 2.0L engine is fairly noisy and tends to produce excessive vibrations. The front seats are too firm for some. The Cabriolet's top takes some effort to handle, and its trunk is too small. The odd way the trunk opens compromises loading. Heating is barely sufficient.

COST

List Price (firm)	**Residual Values** (months)			
	24	**36**	**48**	**60**
Golf CL: $14,690 (13%)	$8700	$7500	$5800	$5000
Jetta GL: $18,050 (16%)	11,500	10,000	8000	7000
GTi: $ 20,045 (15%)	13,500	12,000	9800	8800
Cabrio: $25,230 (18%)	19,500	16,000	13,500	12,000

TECHNICAL DATA

Powertrain (front-drive)
Engines: 1.9L turbo diesel 4 (90 hp) • 2.0L in-line 4 (115 hp) • 2.8L V6 (172 hp)
Transmissions: 5-speed manual • 4-speed auto.

Dimensions (Golf/Jetta)
Length: 160.4 in./173.4 in.
Width: 66.7 in./66.7 in.
Wheelbase: 97.3 in./97.3 in.

SAFETY FEATURES

Golf	Opt.	Std.
Anti-lock brakes	■	❑
Childproof door locks	■	❑
Driver-side airbag	■	■
Passenger-side airbag	❑	■
Traction control	■	❑

Jetta	**Opt.**	**Std.**
Anti-lock brakes	❑	■
Childproof door locks	❑	■
Driver-side airbag	❑	■
Passenger-side airbag	❑	■
Traction control	■	❑

Passat

Passat

RATING: A Below Average buy.

NEW FOR '97: No significant changes.

GENERAL COMMENTS: The Passat's narrow-angle (15-degree) 2.8L V6, tweaked suspension, and sticky performance tires provide a smooth ride combined with exceptional handling. The GLS, equipped with a turbo-boosted 2.0L 115-hp engine, is outclassed by the 2.8L powerplant. Nevertheless, this is an attractive midsize car with a more aerodynamic design than that of the Golf or Jetta. It offers a comfortable, roomy interior and gives good all-round performance for highway and city driving. The car's large wheelbase and squat appearance give it a massive, solid feeling, while its aerodynamic styling makes it look sleek and clean. Most Passats, except for the CL version, come with air conditioning, tinted glass, power-assisted disc brakes on all four wheels, front and rear stabilizer bars, full instrumentation, and even a roof rack with the wagon.

Cost analysis/Alternatives: The 1996 Passats are substantially identical to the '97s, and are a better buy if the selling price has been reduced sufficiently. Other cars worth considering are the BMW 328, Eagle Talon, Ford Probe and Taurus, Mazda Protegé and MX-6 GT, Nissan Maxima, and Toyota Celica GTS and Camry V6. **Rebates**: Likely around mid-summer. **Destination charge**: $500. **Recommended options**: The 2.8L V6, and a good anti-theft system. **Supplementary warranty**: A wise investment. **Parts supply/Servicing**: Below average. **Depreciation**: Average. **Highway/City fuel economy**: 6-8L/100 km with the diesel engine, and 9-13L/100 km with the 2.8L.

Reliability/Safety

Pro: The Passat uses mechanical parts borrowed from other VW models, so overall reliability and problem areas should be similar to those of the Golf, Jetta, and Corrado. Internal service bulletins don't show any factory-related defects that require correction.

A crash-tested airbag-equipped '96 four-door Passat showed that both the driver and passenger would be well protected. It was rated: driver and passenger, ★★★★.

Con: Base warranty is inadequate, considering this car's reliability history. Maintenance costs are higher than average once the warranty expires, which is all the more reason to buy the optional 10-year warranty. Problems with the automatic transmission, steering, front brakes, MacPherson struts, and the fuel and electrical systems. Interior trim and controls are fragile. Parts and service are much more expensive than average, reports the CAA. Insurance rates are higher than average because these cars are favourites with thieves—whether for radios, wheels, VW badges, or the entire car. Rear headrests limit visibility.

Road Performance

Pro: The 2.8L V6 provides lots of power when revved, but as far as overall performance goes the Passat is in the middle of the pack. Diesel power is relatively quick and quiet. Handling is superior to most of the competition, however. The Synchro 4X4 shifts effortlessly into gear. Power steering is quick, precise, and predictable. Suspension is firm but not unpleasant. Acceptable braking.

Con: Forget about the wimpy base 115-hp 2.0L 4-cylinder motor that powers the Golf, Jetta, and Cabrio. The 5-speed manual transmission gear ranges are too far apart; there's an enormous gap between third and fourth gears. The vague 4-speed automatic downshifts erratically, upshifts protesting all the way, and severely limits the car's acceleration.

Comfort/Convenience

Pro: This is VW's most luxurious car, so it comes fairly well appointed with a user-friendly instrument panel, lots of sound-deadening material, and a dust-and-pollen filter in the ventilation system. Aerodynamic styling gives it a slippery 0.29 drag coefficient, which means less fuel consumption. Spacious interior rivals the Mazda 626, Hyundai Sonata, and Ford Taurus and Sable. Heated outside mirror. The front seats are supportive and comfortable. Fairly good dashboard layout. Many small storage spaces. Large and accessible trunk. Innovative trunk latch.

Con: Italian-style straight-arm driving position is not for all. The front seats need a bit more side bolstering. Lots of interior road and wind noise. No gas tank warning light when fuel drops to 8 or 10 litres.

COST

List Price (very negotiable)	**Residual Values** (months)			
	24	**36**	**48**	**60**
GLX: $32,270 (22%)	$18,000	$14,500	$12,000	$10,000

TECHNICAL DATA

Powertrain (front-drive)	**Dimensions**
Engines: 1.9L turbo diesel 4 (90 hp) • 2.0L in-line 4 (115 hp) • 2.8L V6 (172 hp)	Length: 180 in. Width: 67.5 in. Wheelbase: 103.3 in.

Transmissions: 5-speed manual • 4-speed auto.

SAFETY FEATURES

	Opt.	Std.
Anti-lock brakes	■	■
Childproof door locks	❑	■
Driver-side airbag	❑	■
Passenger-side airbag	❑	■
Remote keyless entry	❑	■
Traction control	■	■

EuroVan

EuroVan

RATING: Not Recommended. Outclassed by the competition.

NEW FOR '97: No significant changes this year.

GENERAL COMMENTS: Introduced to North Americans in the late 1950s, the rear-engine Microbus was the first North American minivan. During the 1960s it was considered to be both car and home by the so-called hippie generation. The Westfalia Camper version came later, and appealed mostly to retirees wanting to "rough it" in comfort.

A new EuroVan is in the works, likely to feature the 2.8L V6 and four swing-out doors. EuroVans are available in three models: the GLS, CV, and Transporter panel van. A 2.5L 5-cylinder powerplant is standard, and a 2.4L 5-cylinder diesel engine is optional on the GLS and Transporter.

The Camper van is converted by Winnebago, and features a pop-up roof, two beds, a battery-powered refrigerator, and a propane stove. There's a closet, kitchen sink, dining tables, and mosquito netting for the rear hatch—all for about $43,000.

The camper gears add about 1000 pounds that the already overburdened engine has to pull around. Acceleration is glacial.

Cost analysis/Alternatives: The 1996 Eurovans are virtually identical to the '97s, and are a better buy if the selling price has been reduced sufficiently. An inflated base price makes customized domestic full-sized vans, or more powerful V6-equipped minivans, better buys. Look at Ford Windstar, Chrysler Caravan/Voyager, Toyota Previa, and Mercury Villager/Nissan Quest. **Rebates**: Likely at the end of the year. **Destination charge**: $800. **Recommended options**: ABS, and power mirrors and door locks. **Supplementary warranty**: Essential, considering VW's precarious position in Canada and the EuroVan's past servicing history. Try to get VW's 10-year warranty protection. **Parts**

supply/Servicing: Average supply; exorbitant prices. **Depreciation**: Believe it or not, depreciation is about average for a minivan or van. For example, a 1994 base EuroVan, selling originally for $27,545, will now fetch about $17,000 as a dealer trade-in. **Highway/City fuel economy**: Automatic transmission and gas engine: 11.1-13.5L/100 km. Manual transmission and diesel engine: 8.8-8.9L/100 km.

Reliability/Safety

Pro: Body assembly and paint quality are acceptable. VW internal service bulletins don't list any factory-related problems on the 1996 EuroVan that may afflict the '97s.

Con: Weak base warranty. Overall reliability deteriorates quickly with age. Parts are much more expensive than for other cars in this class, reports the CAA. Owners report problems with the air conditioning, brakes, drivetrain, engine cooling, heating and defrosting systems, and electrical and fuel systems. Surface rust is a common complaint. Service quality at VW dealerships is variable and expensive. Parts shortages and delivery delays are commonplace. Maintenance costs are high once the warranty expires.

Now that the EuroVan has been restyled the NHTSA crash test figures may no longer apply. Nevertheless, crash tests of a 1994 EuroVan concluded that the driver would likely sustain serious injuries in a 57 km/h frontal collision, while the passenger would have average protection. It was rated: driver, ★; passenger, ★★★.

Road Performance

Pro: Fairly comfortable ride for this type of vehicle. Good steering response. Front engine placement makes for crisp response in handling and steering. Adequate braking.

Con: Although the 2.5L 5-cylinder engine gives 20 percent more power than the Vanagon, acceleration is still unacceptably slow. The diesel engine is pushed to get up to highway speed. Very sensitive to even mild cross winds.

Comfort/Convenience

Pro: Aerodynamically styled up front. Well laid-out dash and analogue gauges are easy to read. Controls are within easy reach. Wide door openings make the front seats more accessible. Very comfortable seats come with adjustable armrests. The sliding side door is particularly easy to use and safe for unwary fingers. Centre seats are easily removed to increase cargo space. The rear bench seat can be folded in two different ways to further increase cargo room.

Con: Same old boxy shape in the rear. Bus-like driving position is short on driver leg room. Gas pedal placement requires that your foot be held at an awkward and quickly tiring angle. Seats lack a finished appearance. Overwhelming engine, wind, and road noise. Difficult engine access. Rearward visibility hampered by head restraints.

COST

List Price (very negotiable)	**Residual Values** (months)			
	24	**36**	**48**	**60**
'96 Base GLS: $28,770 (25%)	$14,000	$12,000	$9800	$8000

TECHNICAL DATA

Powertrain (front-drive)
Engine: 2.5L in-line 5-cyl. (110 hp) • 2.4L in-line 5-cyl. diesel (77 hp)
Transmissions: 5-speed man. • 4-speed auto. OD

Dimensions
Weight: 4750-4960 lbs.
Length: 202.3 in.
Width: 72.4 in.
Wheelbase: 130.7 in.
Fuel tank: 80L/reg. unl.
Cargo capacity: 35 cu. ft.
Towing capacity: Up to 4400 lbs.
Turning circle: 39.2 ft.
Passengers: 6-8

SAFETY FEATURES

	Opt.	Std.
Anti-lock brakes	■	❑
Childproof door locks	❑	■
Front/rear head restraints	Yes	Yes
Side door beams		No

VOLVO

This is a quiet year for Volvo; most of its product line is sold in advance and the company sees no reason why it should change a winning hand. The 850 and the 900 series continue with minor revisions.

The main shortcomings of all of Volvo's products are bland styling and an inconsistent quality control that affects long-term reliability. Owners bitterly complain of major and minor defects that aren't corrected properly by the small dealer network. Volvo is currently working to improve service and warranty relations by allowing its dealers to carry out warranty and extra-warranty repairs without obtaining prior authorization from the company.

850

850

RATING: Recommended. Bland but reliable. Practical to the extreme, with plenty of power, good handling, and lots of carrying capacity. The side-impact airbags and built-in child safety seats are reason enough to buy an 850, as long as Volvo resists the temptation to boost prices.

NEW FOR '97: The 850 GLT gets a bit more lower end torque, while the turbo version is upgraded with electrically adjusted front-passenger seats and an in-dash CD player.

GENERAL COMMENTS: The base 850 sedan uses a 2.4L 24-valve 168-hp 5-cylinder engine hooked to a front-drive powertrain. An all-wheel-drive version is available only in Canada and Europe. Wagons use the same base powerplant, hooked to a 5-speed manual or optional 4-speed electronic automatic. GLTs have a torquier, turbo variant of the same powerplant that boosts horsepower to 190.

The "sports" sedan T5 is a rounder, sportier-looking Volvo that delivers honest, predictable performance but comes up a bit short on the "sport" side. Volvo's base turbo boosts horsepower to 222, but its new T-5R variant uses an upgraded turbocharger that boosts power to 240 horses—for up to seven seconds.

Cost analysis/Alternatives: Don't waste your money on a '97 850: the 1996 models are virtually identical to the more expensive '97 versions and are a real bargain if the selling price has been reduced sufficiently. Other cars worth considering are the Mazda 626, the '96 929, and Millenia; Nissan Maxima; and Toyota Camry and Avalon. A fully equipped '96 Taurus or Sable wagon would save you over $10,000, is fairly reliable, performs almost as well, and is easier to repair at independent garages. Other wagons you may wish to consider in relation to the 850 R Sportswagon: the BMW 5-Series Touring, Audi S6, and Mercedes-Benz E Class wagon, due out early next year. **Rebates**: Not likely. **Destination charge**: $350. **Recommended options**: Integrated child safety seats, seat heaters, and a full-sized spare tire (tell the dealer that the full-sized tire well in the trunk shouldn't house a skimpy limited-service spare, if Volvo honestly believes in highway safety). The optional turbo's traction control and additional 22 horses aren't worth the extra cost. If you get the 850 R wagon, change the skimpy, low-profile tires (they don't wear well and are noisy) for 5-spoke 16-inch rims with Michelin MXM 205-50s, used with the standard turbo. Volvo says that the substitution will be made free of charge. **Supplementary warranty**: A good idea if you plan on keeping your Volvo longer than the standard warranty. **Parts supply/Servicing**: Average. **Depreciation**: Below average. **Highway/City fuel economy**: 8-12.5L/100 km with the 2.4L; 9-14L/100 km with the turbocharged engine. Station wagons get about the same gas mileage.

Reliability/Safety

Pro: Good base warranty. Body assembly and paint quality are better than average. The 850 is well serviced by Volvo's small dealer body, and parts aren't hard to find. CAA research also shows that Volvo parts are less expensive than other cars in this class.

Standard side-impact airbags and standard traction control with the T-5R version. Other safety features include rear head restraints, reinforced anti-roll bars, front and rear crumple zones, a practical, roof-mounted interior cargo net that protects passengers from being hit by objects stored in the rear, and rear three-point seatbelts. Volvo's attention to safety has paid off in crash tests of a 1996 dual airbag-equipped 850 sedan. The driver and passenger would be well protected in a 57 km/h frontal collision. It was rated: driver, ★★★★★; passenger, ★★★★.

Con: Problem areas are limited to the front brakes, electrical system, and minor body faults. Base tires on the 850 R Sportswagon wear out prematurely and are noisy. Owners complain of insufficient rear travel for the front seats. Servicing quality is acceptable, but choice is limited due to the small dealer network.

Road Performance

Pro: Plenty of high-range power with the base engine, especially with a manual gearbox. With an automatic transmission, the normally aspirated base engine has a 0-to-60 km/h time of 9.5 seconds—about 2.5 seconds slower than the turbo version. No turbo lag. Nimble handling and predictable, rapid steering response. Braking on dry and wet pavement is exemplary.

Con: Base engine could use more grunt in the lower gear ranges. There's no manual transmission for the turbo version. Moderate torque steer when accelerating. Both the wagon and sedan's soft ride deteriorates progressively as the road gets rougher and passenger weight is added.

Comfort/Convenience

Pro: Excellent driving position and plenty of seat adjustments to accommodate almost any size of driver. Easy front and rear access. Passenger space, seating comfort, and trunk and cargo space are unmatched by the competition. Excellent climate control. The wagon's rear seatbacks fold flat and the seat cushion can be removed for additional cargo space.

Con: Lumbar support knob is decidedly low-tech, requiring lots of effort to adjust. Windshield wiper and power mirror controls aren't user-friendly. Excessive engine noise upon acceleration. Some wind and tire noise at highway speeds.

COST

List Price (very negotiable)	**Residual Values** (months)			
	24	**36**	**48**	**60**
GTO: $32,995 (23%)	$21,000	$18,000	$14,000	$12,000

TECHNICAL DATA

Powertrain (rear-drive/4X4)
Engines: 2.4L injected 5 (168 hp) • 2.4L turbo 5 (190 hp) 2.3L turbo 5 (222 hp) • 2.3L turbo 5 (240 hp)
Transmissions: 5-speed manual • 4-speed OD auto.

Dimensions (sedan/wagon)
Wheelbase: 104.9 in./104.9 in.
Length: 183.5 in./185.4 in.
Width: 69.3 in./69.3 in.

SAFETY FEATURES

	Opt.	Std
Anti-lock brakes	❑	■
Childproof door locks	❑	■
Driver-side airbag	❑	■
Passenger-side airbag	❑	■

960

960

RATING: Recommended.

NEW FOR '97: Nothing significant; a major makeover is planned for the '98 model.

GENERAL COMMENTS: Slightly larger than a Ford Taurus, the 960 rear-drive sedans and wagons are practically identical in offering exceptional roominess, superb handling, and loads of standard safety and convenience features. Both versions are capable of carrying five people in comfort, and the wagon variant provides lots of cargo space.

Cost analysis/Alternatives: The 1996 models are substantially identical to the '97 versions and represent the better buy. If Volvo holds the line on 1997 prices (not likely, judging by the '97 850's higher price), however, the savings from buying a year-old version may not be worth the extra year's depreciation if you sell your 960 after only a few years. Other cars worth considering are the Ford Crown Victoria/Marquis, Mazda Millenia, Nissan Maxima, and Toyota Avalon. **Rebates**: Not likely. **Destination charge**: $350. **Recommended options**: Built-in child safety seats and seat heaters. **Supplementary warranty**: Not needed. **Parts**

supply/Servicing: Average. **Depreciation**: Below average. **Highway/City fuel economy**: 8.5-12.5L/100 km with last year's 2.3L, and 9-14L/100 km with this year's base 2.9L 6-cylinder.

Reliability/Safety

Pro: Good base warranty. CAA says that parts cost less than average. These cars haven't been crash-tested, but insurance injury claim data indicate that they offer better than average crash protection. Safety belt pretensioners take up slack in a frontal collision. Reinforced side panels and side airbags.

Con: Repair and maintenance costs are significantly higher than average, even though parts are reasonably priced. Body assembly and finish can't match the Japanese competition. Owners report problems with the air conditioning, brakes, and electrical and fuel systems. Parts shortages and delivery delays are commonplace. Stalk-mounted horn buttons could be hard to find in an emergency.

Road Performance

Pro: The 960's 2.9L 181-hp 6-cylinder puts out plenty of low-end and mid-range torque that meets all driving conditions with a minimum of strain or engine noise. Its multi-link rear suspension and front engine placement make for crisp handling and steering response. Braking is short and straight with minimal fading after successive brake application.

Con: Some torque steer upon acceleration.

Comfort/Convenience

Pro: Front and rear seats are supportive and comfortable. Three passengers can sit in the rear in comfort. Well laid-out dash and analogue gauges are easy to read. Controls are within easy reach. Easy front and rear access. Climate control system is efficient and unobtrusive. Wagons have plenty of cargo space.

Con: Bland exterior and interior styling. 940 drivers may find it necessary to lower the seat in order to extend the leg room to reach the accelerator comfortably. This makes it difficult to see over the steering wheel.

COST

List Price (very negotiable)	**Residual Values** (months) **24**	**36**	**48**	**60**
960: $47,400 (29%)	$32,000	$28,000	$23,000	$18,000

TECHNICAL DATA

Powertrain (rear-drive/4X4)
Engine: 2.9L injected 6 (181 hp)
Transmissions: 5-speed manual • 4-speed OD auto.

Dimensions
Wheelbase: 109.1 in./109.1 in.
Length: 191.7 in./191.8 in.
Width: 69.3 in./68.9 in.

SAFETY FEATURES

	Opt.	Std.
Anti-lock brakes	❑	■
Childproof door locks	❑	■
Driver-side airbag	❑	■
Passenger-side airbag	❑	■
Remote keyless entry	■	❑

Appendix I

Use the following three dealer pricing sheets to find out which dealer will give you the most features for the least amount of money.

DEALER PRICE REPORT #1

Dealership #1: ______________________________

Salesperson: ______________________________

Phone/Fax: ______________________________

Vehicle: ______ ______ ______ ______
Year Brand Model Engine

Optional Equipment

Item	Dealer Price	Agreed Price
______	$______	$ ______
______	$______	$ ______
______	$______	$ ______
______	$______	$ ______
______	$______	$ ______
______	$______	$ ______
______	$______	$ ______

Cost of Options: $ ______

Manufacturer's suggested price (MSRP):______ $ ______

Dealer's price: ______ $ ______

Destination charge/Predelivery inspection:______ $ ______
Rebates/Incentives:______ $ ______
Price negotiated with dealer:______ $ ______
Trade-in allowance:______ $ ______

Notes/Comments (taxes, other fees, vehicle in stock/ordered, date of mfg. plate, warranty, etc.):

____
____
____

DEALER PRICE REPORT #2

Dealership #2: ______________________________

Salesperson: ______________________________

Phone/Fax: ______________________________

Vehicle: ______ ______ ______ ______
Year Brand Model Engine

Optional Equipment

Item	**Dealer Price**	**Agreed Price**
____________	$__________	$ __________
____________	$__________	$ __________
____________	$__________	$ __________
____________	$__________	$ __________
____________	$__________	$ __________
____________	$__________	$ __________
____________	$__________	$ __________

Cost of Options: $ __________

Manufacturer's suggested price (MSRP):______ $ __________

Dealer's price: ______________________ $ __________

Destination charge/Predelivery inspection:_____ $ __________
Rebates/Incentives:______________________ $ __________
Price negotiated with dealer:______________ $ __________
Trade-in allowance:______________________ $ __________

Notes/Comments (taxes, other fees, vehicle in stock/ordered, date of mfg. plate, warranty, etc.):

____

____

____

____

DEALER PRICE REPORT #3

Dealership #3: ______________________________

Salesperson: ______________________________

Phone/Fax: ______________________________

Vehicle: ______ ______ ______ ______
Year Brand Model Engine

Optional Equipment

Item	Dealer Price	Agreed Price
____________	$____________	$ ____________
____________	$____________	$ ____________
____________	$____________	$ ____________
____________	$____________	$ ____________
____________	$____________	$ ____________
____________	$____________	$ ____________
____________	$____________	$ ____________

Cost of Options: $ ____________

Manufacturer's suggested price (MSRP):______ $ ____________

Dealer's price: ____________ $ ____________

Destination charge/Predelivery inspection:_____ $ ____________
Rebates/Incentives:____________ $ ____________
Price negotiated with dealer:____________ $ ____________
Trade-in allowance:____________ $ ____________

Notes/Comments (taxes, other fees, vehicle in stock/ordered, date of mfg. plate, warranty, etc.):

____
____
____
____

Appendix II

TEST-DRIVE REPORT

Use the form below to evaluate up to three vehicles that you're interested in purchasing. Rank each category by a score of 1 to 10.

1 - 2	3 - 4	5 - 6	7 - 8	9 - 10
Poor	Fair	Average	Good	Excellent

	#1	#2	#3
Safety Features (Yes/No)			
Anti-lock brakes			
Anti-theft ignition/fuel cut-off			
Childproof door locks			
Comfortable seatbelts			
Crashworthy? (NHTSA)			
Driver-side airbag			
Integrated child safety seats			
Passenger-side airbag			
Passenger-side airbag disabler			
Rear head restraints: high/low			
Side airbags			
Side impact beams			
Spare tire (full-sized)			
Traction control			
Entry/Exit (1 to 10)			
Door: too narrow/heavy			
Rear seat access			
Step-up height: low/high			
Seating Comfort (1 to 10)			
Ease of seat adjustment			
Seats firm and supportive?			
Interior Convenience (1 to 10)			
Centre console: cupholders, etc.			
Door pockets			
Easy access spare tire storage			
Easy access trunk			
Efficient heating/defrosting/AC			
Head/leg room			
Seats fold/remove: ease of use			
Sunroof: ease of use/noise			

	#1	#2	#3
Dashboard/Controls (1 to 10)			
Climate control system controls: ease of use			
Gauges: large and clear/complete			
Power windows/locks: location/ease of use			
Sound system: ease of use/volume/clarity			
Steering wheel: height/adjustable			
Turn signals, horn: location/ease of use			
Windshield wipers: location/ease of use			
Visibility (1 to 10)			
Forward vision			
Headlight illumination			
Rearward vision			
Cargo space (1 to 10)			
Size of opening			
Size: with rear seat up			
Size: with rear seat folded/removed			
Engine (1 to 10)			
Acceleration			
Ignition: easy/hard start			
Noise			
Smoothness			
Transmission (1 to 10)			
Clutch pedal: position/height			
Shifts smoothly in all gear ranges?			
Handling/Ride (1 to 10)			
Responsive steering/road feel			
Stable ride/cornering at speed			
Braking (1 to 10)			
Brake pedal: position/height			
Stopping distance/noise/fade			
Noise (1 to 10)			
Road/wind/exhaust noise			
Squeaks/rattles			
Style/Finish (1 to 10)			
Interior finish: quality of components			
Welds, paint/hood, trunk alignment			
Total Points (400 maximum)			

Appendix III

1996-97 PRICES AND RATINGS

Part Three listed the strengths and weaknesses of individual models; now let's compare costs and see how prices can be cut by using rebates and the seasons to your advantage. Two prices are listed: the 1996 Manufacturers' Suggested Retail Price (MSRP) as of the date of this *Guide*'s publication, and the MSRP for '97 models. Don't be distressed if the same model isn't listed from one year to the next, since the model name often changes for what is essentially the same vehicle.

You won't see the latest '97 prices for many of the imports because their new prices aren't announced until late fall. However, the September '96 prices included in this edition shouldn't be that far off. Nevertheless, use the MSRP figures only as a starting point for negotiating a final price. If the dealer says that this *Guide*'s MSRP prices are too low, ask for proof of when and by how much the MSRP was raised (the automaker sends a letter each time there's a price increase). If you don't get independent confirmation of a price increase, reject the higher figure. You can always get the latest MSRP figures, transportation costs, and PDI fees from the auto manufacturer's PR staff at each company's head office.

The dealer's markup, indicated as a percentage of the MSRP for each model, varies somewhat among importers. Japanese carmakers give their dealers less generous markups than do American manufacturers, while Europeans give a bit more. Dealer profit from pre-delivery inspection (PDI) and transportation fees, in addition to the 1 to 3 percent holdback allowance, represent additional profit areas that aren't counted in the markup percentage.

Expect to pay the full MSRP for any '97 bought between September and December. During the winter (January through March) rebates and the weather start to work in your favour, allowing you to split the dealer's profit and knock 5 to 10 percent off the MSRP. As you get into the late summer and early fall, a 2 to 3 percent increase in the MSRP is usually accompanied by additional rebates on leftover models that more than make up for the MSRP boost.

Each vehicle's price/quality rating is extrapolated from Part Three's evaluations. Similar models may be rated differently due to their dissimilar costs and extra equipment. Ratings are summarized using the following symbols:

❶	❷	③	④	⑤
Not Recommended	Below Average	Average	Above Average	Recommended

Company/ Model	Page #	1996 ($)	1997 ($)	Dealer %	Rating
Acura					
2.2TL	312	$34,900	—	23	④
2.5TL	312	$34,000	$36,600	23	④
3.2TL	312	$39,900	$41,600	24	④
3.5RL	310	$52,300	$54,600	27	④
Integra GS-R	314	$26,345	$26,900	20	③
LS		$23,245	$23,800	19	④
Sedan		$23,645	—	19	③
RS		$18,795	$19,500	17	③
Sedan		$20,495	—	17	③
NSX-T	313	$125,000	$125,000	30	④
Audi					
A4	422	$36,250	$37,500	23	④
Quattro		$38,830	—	20	④
A6	423	$48,670	$49,270	30	④
Quattro		$51,250	—	30	④
Wagon		$53,024	$53,510	30	④
S6 Quattro	423	$61,400	—	30	④
A8 Quattro	423	—	$89,840	30	④
BMW					
318ti	426	$25,900	$26,900	17	⑤
318i		$30,900	$32,300	19	⑤
318iC		$42,900	$43,900	27	⑤
318iS		$31,900	$33,300	20	⑤
328iS	426	$45,900	$48,900	27	⑤
328i		$43,900	$46,900	27	⑤
328iC		$55,300	$57,900	29	⑤
M3 Coupe			$61,900	29	⑤
Sedan		—	$81,900	29	⑤
Z3		$38,900	$40,500	29	⑤
528i	429	—	$54,900	29	③
540i		—	$68,900	29	③
740iL	430	$87,900	$89,900	30	⑤
750iL		$126,900	$129,500	30	⑤
840i Conv.	431	$98,900	—	30	⑤
840Ci		—	$100,900	30	⑤
850Ci		$128,900	$130,900	30	⑤
Buick					
Century					
Custom	259	$24,535	—	14	❶
Special		$23,820	—	13	❶
Wagon		$24,995	—	14	❶
LeSabre					
Custom	267	$29,560	$32,370	19	③
Limited 4d		$32,640	$35,210	22	③
Park Avenue	281	$38,150	$40,865	24	③
Ultra		$43,260	$46,865	27	③
Regal					
Custom	263	$25,035	—	19	③
4d		$25,550	—	20	③
Limited 4d		$27,625	$27,265	21	③
Gran Sport		$28,695	$28,695	21	③
Riviera	278	$40,700	$42,415	25	③
Roadmaster	284	$34,230	$36,315	24	③
Limited		$34,345	—	24	③
Wagon		$35,015	—	25	③
Skylark					
Custom	256	$20,035	$21,220	13	③
4d		$20,035	$21,220	13	③
Cadillac					
Catera	288	—	$42,200	26	③
DeVille	288	$48,125	$49,400	26	③
Concours		$54,340	$56,985	27	③
Eldorado	291	$50,745	$52,015	26	③
Touring					
Coupe		$53,380	$54,735	27	③
Fleetwood	284	$46,965	—	26	③
Seville SLS	291	$55,635	$57,010	28	③
STS		$57,560	$58,930	28	③
Chevrolet					
Astro	302	$22,640	—	20	❷
Passenger CS		$23,295	—	20	❷
Passenger CL		$25,720	$26,920	20	❷
CL AWD	302	$28,170	$29,370	20	❶
Beretta	253	$12,698	—	14	③
GT		$15,398	—	17	③
GTZ		$18,300	—	17	③
Blazer		$25,635	$27,160	20	❷
4X4		$27,690	$29,015	21	❷
4d		$25,615	$28,205	21	❷
4X4		$28,645	$30,335	23	❷
Camaro	294	$20,195	$20,910	15	⑤
Convertible		$28,365	$29,080	18	⑤
Z28		$25,530	$27,270	17	⑤
Convertible		$32,330	$34,070	20	⑤
Caprice	239	$28,345	—	23	③

Company/ Model	Page #	1996 ($)	1997 ($)	Dealer %	Rating
Wagon		$30,980	—	25	③
Cavalier	249	$13,030	$14,390	11	④
Sedan		$13,530	—	11	④
LS sedan		$16,840	$17,015	13	④
Convertible		$22,925	$24,285	16	④
Z24		$17,643	$19,000	14	④
Z28		—	$27,270	14	④
Convertible		—	$34,070	14	④
Corsica	253	$17,685	—	14	④
Corvette	298	$48,635	$48,635	28	❷
Convertible		$56,335	—	31	❷
Impala SS		$32,685	—	26	❶
Lumina	263	$21,455	$22,340	16	❶
LS		$22,705	$23,810	16	❶
LTZ		—	$25,145	17	❶
Lumina Minivan	305	$20,110	—	16	❷
CS		$22,730	—	17	❷
Monte Carlo	263	$23,625	$24,275	18	❶
Z34		$25,850	$26,500	19	❶
Series S P/up		$14,510	$15,300	11	❷
LS		$17,005	$17,890	12	❷
4X4		$19,845	$20,115	13	❷
Cab+		$21,450	$22,540	14	❷
Sub. ½ ton		$30,115	$33,335	21	❷
4X4		$32,885	$36,105	22	❷
Sub. ¾ ton	—	$34,435	21	❷	
4X4		—	$37,135	22	❷
Tahoe 2d		$27,930	$30,595	20	❷
4X4		$30,700	$33,365	26	❷
4d		$35,135	$37,800	23	❷
4X4		$37,905	$40,570	26	❷
Chrysler					
Cirrus LX	165	$23,235	$23,730	16	❷
LXI		$25,695	$26,200	17	❷
Concorde LX	170	$26,005	$26,385	17	❷
LXi		$28,710	$28,960	18	❷
Intrepid	170	$22,980	$23,625	16	❷
ES		$29,050	$28,485	18	❷
LHS	170	$38,420	$40,130	20	❷
New Yorker		$34,490	$34,490	23	❷
Sebring LX	155	$19,514	$19,514	—	⑤
LXI		$25,538	$25,565	—	⑤
JX		—	$26,730	—	⑤

Company/ Model	Page #	1996 ($)	1997 ($)	Dealer %	Rating
JX Conv.		$25,490	$26,730	—	⑤
JXi		—	$25,565	—	⑤
JXi Conv.		$31,985	$33,355	—	⑤
Town & Country	174	$38,280	$40,085	25	④
AWD		—	$43,330	25	③
Dodge					
Avenger	155	$18,954	$18,290	13	⑤
ES		$22,544	$20,695	15	⑤
Caravan	174	$18,840	$18,840	13	④
ES		$29,460	$29,135	19	④
LE		$27,355	$26,865	17	④
SE		$22,235	$22,235	17	④
Dakota		$14,705	$14,705	12	③
4X4		$18,725	—	13	❷
Club Cab		$18,140	—	13	③
4X4		$21,675	$22,385	16	❷
Club Sport		$19,035	—	13	③
4X4		$22,845	—	13	③
Grand Caravan	174	$20,320	$21,200	15	④
LE		$28,355	$30,550	21	④
LE AWD		—	$31,945	19	③
SE		$23,235	$24,615	17	④
ES		$31,075	$32,790	19	④
Neon 2d	151	$12,635	$14,465	11	❶
4d		$12,835	$14,265	12	❶
Highline 2d		$14,420	—	12	❶
4d		$13,950	$15,425	12	❶
Sport		$15,315	—	13	❶
4d		$15,515	—	13	❶
Stratus	165	$18,200	$18,470	14	❷
ES		$20,110	$20,970	14	r
Stealth R/T	162	$35,345	—	16	⑤
RT turbo		$49,405	—	23	⑤
Viper RT 10	147	$82,320	$82,320	30	⑤
Eagle					
Talon	159	—	$19,725	13	⑤
ESi		$20,695	$22,495	15	⑤
TSi AWD		$29,985	$29,985	17	⑤
Vision ESi	170	$23,770	$24,325	15	❷
TSi		$29,315	$30,270	18	❷

Company/ Model	Page #	1996 ($)	1997 ($)	Dealer %	Rating
Ford					
Aerostar					
Cargo	223	$18,495	$19,395	19	❷
XL		$19,995	—	20	❷
Club XL		—	$27,095	20	❷
Club XLT		—	$30,195	20	❷
XLT					
(extended)		$23,395	$27,295	21	❷
4X4		$24,395	$27,295	21	❷
Aspire	184	$11,295	$11,895	13	③
SE		$11,895	—	13	③
5d		$11,395	—	14	③
Bronco XL		$26,495	—		❶
XLT		$28,295	—	20	❶
Eddie Bauer		$33,095	—	24	❶
Club Wagon					
XL		$26,495	—	19	③
XLT		$28,595	—	21	③
Contour GL	191	$17,595	$18,395	20	③
LX		$18,395	$21,895	21	③
SE		$20,395	$22,795	21	③
Crown					
Victoria	210	$28,295	$28,295	23	⑤
LX		$29.895	$30,995	23	⑤
Escort GT	187	$15,295	—	14	⑤
GL		—	$14,395	14	⑤
LX 3d		$13,595	—	13	⑤
4d		$14,095	$14,995	13	⑤
5d		$14,095	—	13	⑤
Wagon		$14,095	$14,995	13	⑤
Expedition					
XLT		—	$34,895	23	❶
4X4		—	$37,895	23	❶
Explorer XL		$24,395	—	23	④
4X4		$27,095	$29,795	25	④
XLT		$29,495		27	④
4X4		$31,995	—	27	④
Limited		—	$43,495	25	④
Mustang	195	$18,595	$19,695	15	⑤
Convertible		$25,895	$28,895	23	⑤
GT		$21,895	$23,595	22	⑤
Convertible		$29,795	$33,695	26	⑤
Probe	198	$18,395	$19,095	16	⑤
GT		$22,195	$22,995	21	⑤
Ranger XL		$14,395	—	13	⑤

Company/ Model	Page #	1996 ($)	1997 ($)	Dealer %	Rating
4X4		$19,695	$20,795	17	⑤
XL Super		$17,495	—	16	⑤
4X4		$22,995	—	22	⑤
Taurus GL	201	$22,195	$22,995	20	⑤
Wagon		$22,195	$22,995	20	⑤
LX 4d		$25,095	$25,995	22	⑤
Wagon		$25,095	$25,995	21	⑤
SHO 4-door					
sedan		$31,095	$32,495	23	⑤
T-Bird LX	207	$23,595	$24,895	21	⑤
Super Coupe		$28,695	—	24	⑤
Windstar	231	$20,495	$22,195	22	⑤
GL		$22,495	$24,195	22	④
LX		$27,495	$30,895	23	④
Geo					
Metro	243	$10,995	$11,495	9	⑤
Sedan		$12,095	$12,495	11	⑤
LSI		$11,245	—	10	⑤
Sedan		$12,345	—	11	⑤
Tracker 4X2		$15,665	$16,855	13	⑤
4X4		$16,940	$18,130	14	⑤
LSi		$18,385	$19,750	15	⑤
GMC					
Jimmy SL		$25,710	$27,235	24	❷
4X4		$27,765	$29,090	25	❷
SLE		$26,590	$28,280	25	❷
4X4		$28,875	$30,565	25	❷
Safari		$23,475	$25,110	24	❷
Passenger		$25,285	$27,560	24	❷
AWD		$27,735	—	24	❷
Sonoma SL		$14,510	$15,300	20	❷
4X4		$19,225	$20,015	20	❷
SLS 4X4		—	$22,635	21	❷
Yukon 2d		$27,030	$30,595	24	❷
4X4		$30,700	$33,365	25	❷
4d		$35,135	$37,800	27	❷
4X4		$37,905	$40,570	27	❷
Honda					
Accord EX	321	$22,995	$23,495	16	⑤
LX		$20,295	$20,995	14	⑤
EX-R		$26,595	$27,395	19	⑤
V6		$31,595	$31,995	24	⑤

Company/ Model	Page #	1996 ($)	1997 ($)	Dealer %	Rating
SE		—	$26,995	24	⑤
Civic CX	317	$12,995	—	9	⑤
DX		$15,295	$15,595	11	⑤
EX		$16,195	$16,695	11	⑤
LX		$14,895	$15,395	10	⑤
Si		$17,895	$17,995	11	⑤
del Sol	317	$20,495	—	12	③
VTEC		$23,495	—	13	③
Odyssey	329	$28,795	$28,795	17	❷
Prelude SR	326	$27,395	$27,395	16	④
SR-V		$29,995	—	17	④
Hyundai					
Accent L	333	$10,495	$10,995	11	③
Sedan		$11,395	$11,895	11	③
GL		$11,795	$12,295	12	③
GT		$12,995	$13,495	12	③
Elantra GL	335	$13,495	—	12	③
GLS		$16,745	$17,245	12	③
Wagon		$18,995	$19,495	14	③
Sonata	338	$16,595	—	13	❷
GL		$18,995	$19,595	14	❷
GLS		$22,495	$23,095	14	❷
Tiburon	332	—	$16,995	13	❶
FX		—	$19,845	14	❶
Infiniti					
G20	342	$31,440	—	25	⑤
I30	345	$40,600	$41,000	27	⑤
I30i		—	$43,600	27	⑤
J30	345	$51,600	$52,600	29	⑤
J30t		—	$54,600	29	⑤
Q45	343	$72,000	$65,000	30	⑤
Q45T		—	$67,500	30	⑤
QX4		—	$44,500	30	⑤
Jaguar					
Vanden Plas	219	$86,500	$83,000	30	❷
XJ6	219	$75,000	$83,000	30	❷
XJ12		$99,900	—	30	❷
XJ-R		$87,900	$85,000	30	❷
XJS Conv.	219	$84,500	—	30	❷
XK8		—	$89,900	30	❷
Convertible		—	97,900		
Sovereign		$75,500	—	30	❷

Company/ Model	Page #	1996 ($)	1997 ($)	Dealer %	Rating
Jeep					
Cherokee SE		$19,065	$19,810	15	④
4d		$21,100	$21,845	16	④
4X4 3d		$21,285	$22,030	17	④
V6		$22,465	—	19	④
Sport		$20,680	$21,845	18	④
4d		$22,715	—		④
4X4 3d		$22,900	$23,645	19	④
4X4 4d		$24,080	—	20	④
Country		$25,095	—	19	④
4X4 3d		$26,460	$27,255	22	④
Grand SE		$28,660	—	24	④
4X4		$30,555	—	25	④
Laredo		$30,830	$34,260	25	④
4X4		$31,730	—	25	④
Limited		$36,240	—	27	④
4X4		$37,580	$42,305	28	④
Lada					
Samara 1500	432	$8995	$9445	10	❷
Sagona		$10,395	$10,845	12	❷
Niva		$9995	$10,645	12	❶
Cossack		$10,895	$11,595	12	❶
Lexus					
ES 300	349	$45,600	$42,900	25	⑤
GS 300	350	$71,400	$71,400	28	⑤
LS 400	352	$75,900	$78,700	29	⑤
SC 400	351	$80,800	$82,100	29	⑤
Lincoln					
Continental	213	$51,895	$49,995	30	④
Mark VIII	216	$51,895	$53,695	30	⑤
Town Car Ex.	210	$44,895	$45,695	29	⑤
Signature		$46,995	$47,695	29	⑤
Cartier		$50,095	$50,795	30	⑤
Mazda					
626 DX	356	$19,995	$19,995	14	⑤
LX		$22,400	$22,400	15	⑤
ES		$30,295	$30,295	22	④
B2300		$14,285	$14,285	16	⑤
4X4		$20,700	$20,700	18	⑤
Cab Plus		$17,875	$17,875	20	⑤
Millenia	360	$42,035	$42,900	28	④

Company/ Model	Page #	1996 ($)	1997 ($)	Dealer %	Rating
MPV L	365	$27,845	—	21	❷
V6		$27,020	—	25	❷
4X4		$30,590	—	27	❷
LX		$30,900	$31,520	25	❷
4X4		$34,350	$35,335	28	❷
MX-5 (Miata)	363	$24,210	$24,695	12	⑤
MX-6 RS	356	$22,780	$22,780	15	⑤
LS		$27,220	$27,220	18	⑤
Protegé SE	354	$13,895	$14,685	10	⑤
LX		$17,450	$17,205	13	⑤
Mercedes Benz					
C220 SE	435	$35,995	—	23	④
C230 Special	435	—	$36,950	26	④
C230		—	$42,950	26	④
C280	435	$49,995	$50,995	26	④
C36	436	$70,600	$72,365	26	④
E300 Diesel	436	$58,500	$59,950	30	⑤
E320	436	$64,750	$65,900	30	⑤
E420	436	$71,550	$73,000	30	⑤
S320	438	$86,600	$87,500	30	⑤
S350 Turbo	438	$89,000	—	30	⑤
S420	438	$90,850	$101,900	30	⑤
S500	438	$127,600	$132,950	30	⑤
Coupe		$132,500	$132,000	30	⑤
S600	438	$171,350	$175,000	30	⑤
Coupe		$174,900	$181,000	30	⑤
SL320		$101,500	$101,900	30	⑤
SL500		$125,500	$128,500	30	⑤
SL600		$154,500	$154,900	30	⑤
Mercury					
Cougar XR7	207	$23,495	$24,795	19	⑤
Marquis GS	209	$30,295	$31,995	23	⑤
LS		$31,395	$33,095	23	⑤
Mystique GS	191	$17,995	$18,795	16	③
LS		$19,595	$23,295	18	③
Sable GS	201	$22,595	$23,395	18	⑤
Wagon		$22,595	$23,395	18	⑤
LS		$25,495	$26,395	20	⑤
Wagon		$25,495	$26,395	20	⑤
Villager GS	226	$23,695	$23,995	19	⑤
LS		$28,095	$32,145	21	⑤
Nautica		$29,895	$33,045	23	⑤

Company/ Model	Page #	1996 ($)	1997 ($)	Dealer %	Rating
Nissan					
200SX	369	$15,598	$15,598	9	⑤
SE		$17,198	$17,198	10	⑤
SE-R		$20,698	—	12	⑤
240SX	374	—	$26,998	17	④
SE		$22,598	$28,398	19	④
LE		$29,598	$31,398	15	④
300ZX	377	$53,698	—	26	❷
2+2		$56,198	—	26	❷
Convertible		$61,398	—	29	❷
Twin Turbo		$60,698	—	29	❷
Altima XE	372	$20,598	$20,795	15	④
GLE		$29,298	—	21	④
GXE		$23,298	$23,498	14	④
SE		$25,798	$25,998	21	④
Hardbody		$13,498	$13,798	11	⑤
4X4		$17,990	$20,498	15	⑤
King Cab XE		$14,990	$16,898	11	⑤
4X4		$21,690	$20,498	16	⑤
SE		—	$23,998	16	⑤
Maxima	379	$27,998	$27,998	19	⑤
GLE		$33,498	$33,998	21	⑤
SE		$30,998	$31,598	21	⑤
GLE A4		—	$33,998	21	⑤
Pathfinder		$29,698	$29,998	22	④
LE		$37,298	$37,798	23	④
SE		$35,998	$37,198	23	④
Quest XE	382	$25,598	$25,998	21	⑤
GXE		$29,290	—	22	⑤
Sentra DLX	369	$12,498	$13,725	9	⑤
4d		$13,448	$13,725	9	⑤
GXE		$16,848	$17,098	11	⑤
XE		$14,548	$14,798	10	⑤
GLE A4		$20,248	$20,498	13	⑤
Oldsmobile					
Achieva S/SL	256	$19,950	$20,735	14	❷
Sedan		$19,925	$20,710	14	❷
Aurora	278	$43,695	$46,045	27	❷
Ciera SL	259	$23,625	—	16	❶
Wagon		$24,560	—	16	❶
Supreme S	263	$25,285	$25,855	17	❷
Sedan		$24,955	$26,185	16	❷
Olds 88 LS	267	$30,190	$32,185	21	❷

Company/ Model	Page #	1996 ($)	1997 ($)	Dealer %	Rating
Plymouth					
Breeze	165	$18,200	$18,470	15	❷
Voyager	174	$18,840	$19,620	13	④
SE		$22,235	$23,515	16	④
LE		$26,865	$29,450	21	④
Grand					
Voyager	174	$20,320	$21,200	15	④
SE		$23,235	$24,615	17	④
LE		$24,865	$30,550	16	④
Pontiac					
Bonneville					
SE	267	$29,440	$31,175	19	❷
SLE		—	$33,695	22	❷
SSE		$33,260	$36,030	22	❷
Firefly	243	$10,995	$11,495	9	④
SE		$11,245	$12,495	10	④
Firebird	294	$19,795	$23,120	13	⑤
Convertible		$28,590	$30,625	18	⑤
Formula		$25,080	$27,555	15	⑤
Convertible		$32,500	$34,850	18	⑤
Trans Am GT		$27,390	$30,780	16	⑤
Convertible		$35,130	$37,645	18	⑤
Grand Am					
GT	256	$20,050	$22,035	13	❷
Sedan		$20,155	$22,135	13	❷
SE		$18,000	$19,035	12	❷
Sedan		$18,100	$19,135	12	❷
Grand Prix					
SE		$25,525	—	16	❷
Sedan		$23,940	$26,305	17	❷
Sunfire SE	249	$13,380	$15,340	11	④
Sedan		$14,380	$15,640	12	④
GT		$17,875	$19,335	13	④
Convertible		$23,260	$24,720	16	④
Sunrunner					
4X2		$15,665	—	13	③
Convertible		—	$16,855	14	③
4X4 Conv.		$16,940	$18,130	14	③
GT Conv.		$18,385	—	14	③
Trans Sport	305	$23,475	—	18	❷
Saab					
900S 3d	272	$28,500	$29,900	21	❷
5d		$28,500	$29,900	21	❷
Convertible		$46,100	$47,500	29	❷
900SE		$36,400	$37,500	25	❷
5d		$36,400	$37,500	25	❷
Convertible		$53,350	$55,500	30	❷
9000 CS	275	$36,400	$37,100	25	❷
Aero		$48,600	$49,200	30	❷
CDE		$47,000	$48,000	29	❷
CSE		$45,500	$47,600	29	❷
Saturn					
Saturn SC1	246	$15,348	$16,028	13	④
SC2		$18,048	$18,998	15	④
SL		$12,998	$13,948	11	④
SL1		$14,398	$14,948	13	④
SL2		$16,148	$16,758	14	④
SW1		$14,898	$15,658	14	④
SW2		$16,748	$17,448	15	④
Subaru					
Impreza L	385	$17,995	$21,395	19	④
Sedan		$17,996	$21,695	18	④
Wagon		$18,595	$21,995	16	④
Outback		$23,995	$24,995	20	④
Legacy L	387	$23,195	—	21	④
AWD		$25,195	$25,695	20	④
Wagon		$25,995	$26,995	23	④
LS		$29,095	$28,995	26	④
Wagon		$29,895	$29,995	26	④
LSI		$33,595	$32,995	26	④
Wagon		$31,495	$33,995	26	④
GT		—	$29,995	26	④
Outback 2.2L		$28,995	—	25	④
2.5L		—	$30,695	26	④
Limited		—	$33,695	26	④
SVX	384	$47,495	$47,495	30	④
Suzuki					
Esteem CL	393	—	$13,495	11	③
GL		$13,495	$13,495	11	③
GLX		$14,495	$14,995	12	③
CLX		—	$14,995	12	③
Sidekick JA		$14,495	$15,495	13	⑤
JX		$16,995	—	14	⑤
4d		$17,495	$17,995	14	⑤
JLX		$18,995	—	15	⑤

Company/ Model	Page #	1996 ($)	1997 ($)	Dealer %	Rating
4d		$20,895	—	17	⑤
Super Deluxe		—	$25,495	17	⑤
Swift DLX	390	$10,995	$10,995	9	⑤
DLX		$11,295	$11,595	11	⑤
X-90		—	$17,995	13	③
Toyota					
4Runner SR5		$28,428	$28,428	19	④
V6		$31,958	$31,958	22	⑤
Avalon XL	410	$33,368	$31,058	24	④
XLS		$35,778	$34,458	27	④
Camry DX	405	$20,488	—	16	⑤
Sedan		$21,138	—	18	⑤
CE		—	$21,178	19	⑤
LE		$25,188	—	20	⑤
LE sedan		$25,458	$25,268	19	⑤
LE wagon		$29,208	—	21	⑤
LE V6		$29,218	—	22	⑤
LE V6 sedan		$29,858	—	22	⑤
LE V6 wagon		$32,178	—	22	⑤
XLE V6		—	$30,488	22	⑤
Celica	412	$24,358	—	19	⑤
GT		$27,968	$27,998	20	⑤
Corolla	403	$13,508	$13,968	13	⑤
DX		$16,238	$16,748	13	⑤
DX 1.8		$16,778	$17,308	14	⑤
Wagon		$21,838	—	15	⑤
Paseo	400	$17,218	$17,608	14	④
Previa	417	$35,908	$36,998	23	④
LE		$40,378	$41,598	25	④
4X4		$43,238	$44,438	27	④
Rav4 2X4		—	$20,348	17	④
4d 4X4		—	$23,078	17	④
Supra Turbo	415	$78,738	$80,758	30	④
T100 Pickup		$23,598	$24,718	17	④
XtraCab		$25,768		19	④
XtraCab SR-5		$32,208	$33,218	22	④
Tacoma 4X2		$16,578	$16,808	13	④
XtraCab		$20,098	$20,358	16	④
4X4		$22,018	$22,228	17	④
XtraCab		$24,268	$24,498	19	④
V6		$25,398	$25,748	19	④
SR-5 V6		$30,548	$30,848	23	④
Tercel	398	$11,948	—	9	④
DX		$12,958	$13,068	10	④

Company/ Model	Page #	1996 ($)	1997 ($)	Dealer %	Rating
Sedan		$13,188	$13,790	10	④
Volkswagen					
EuroVan GLS	446	$28,770	$28,770	25	④
Golf CL	440	$14,325	$14,690	13	④
5d		$14,825	$15,190	12	④
GL		$16,695	$16,730	13	④
Diesel		$16,620	$16,665	13	④
GTi		$19,645	$20,045	15	④
VR6		$25,710	$25,745	18	④
Cabriolet		—	$25,230	18	④
Jetta GL	440	$17,650	$18,050	16	④
Diesel		$17,575	$17,975	16	④
VR6		—	$27,885	19	④
GLS		$19,165	$19,930	16	④
GLX		$24,855	—	16	④
Passat GLS	443	$27,230	—	22	❷
Wagon		$29,245	—	20	❷
GLX		$32,270	$32,270	22	❷
Wagon		$32,895	$32,895	24	❷
Volvo					
850 GLE	449	$31,995	—	23	⑤
Wagon		$33,295	—	23	⑤
GTO		—	$32,995	23	⑤
GLT		$37,495	$40,495	26	⑤
Wagon		$38,795	$41,795	26	⑤
Turbo sedan		$41,695	43,995	28	⑤
Turbo Wagon		$43,095	$45,395	28	⑤
R		$54,495	$55,495	28	⑤
AWD		—	$48,495	28	⑤
960 sedan	452	$46,400	$47,400	29	⑤
960 wagon		$48,075	$49,075	30	⑤

Appendix IV
SURVEY AND BULLETIN SEARCH

Rate Your Vehicle

Information found in this book has been garnered from motorists' responses to surveys like the one on the facing page. Your answers to the survey below will help us to protect others from sales scams and bad products. Include any photographs (especially of paint defects), diagrams, contracts, or work orders that expose a defect or dishonest practice. Your survey comments also help me to zero in on bulletins useful to you when I prepare a bulletin summary.

I pull the computer bulletin summaries myself (it keeps me in touch with readers like you), and usually have them faxed back within a few days. Sorry, I can only process Visa cards.

Phil Edmonston
lemonaid@earthlink.net
102344.1253@compuserve.com

Cut Repair Costs • Fight Fraud and Incompetence With . . .

Lemon-Aid's $15 Bulletin Summary

If you plan to buy a vehicle, have just bought one, or want to know everything about your present vehicle before the warranty expires, you need a bulletin summary computer print-out.

Nothing gives you a stronger argument with a service manager or mechanic than pulling out a confidential dealer service bulletin (DSB) that says a failure is factory-related or is covered by an extended warranty.

Fill out the Request on the next page. You'll receive an exhaustive summary of DSBs (published in the U.S.) that concern your post-1980 vehicle.

Bulletins show repair shortcuts, labour time, lists of upgraded parts, probable defects, recall campaigns, and secret warranties. With your order, we'll also give you your vehicle's present wholesale and retail value.

Order by fax or mail. There's no difference in price, although fax is much quicker. Set your fax to receive. The fax will be sent in the evening.

- FAX (Visa only): (954) 563-2448 (24 hours a day).

- MAIL: Make your cheque out to "Lemon-Aid DSB," 2805 E. Oakland Park Blvd., Suite 211, Ft. Lauderdale, FL 33306.

Lemon-Aid Survey/DSB Summary Request

❑ I don't need a DSB summary; my survey comments are below.
❑ Please mail me a DSB summary for my car ($15 Cdn fee enclosed) and an estimate of its worth.
❑ Please fax me the above information ($15).

FAX # ______________ VISA (ONLY) # ______________
Signature: ______________
Name: ______________
____
Address: ______________
____
Province: ______________ Postal code: ______________

MY VEHICLE'S PROFILE

Make: ______________ Model: ______________ Year: ______________
Engine (litres): ______________ Mileage: ______________

GENERAL COMMENTS

(Include a photo, diagram, or bill.)

Safety: ______________
Reliability: ______________
____
____
Performance: ______________
____
____

JOY OF OWNERSHIP

(Recommended ⑤, Above Average ④, Average ③, Below average ❷, Not recommended ❶)

OVERALL RELIABILITY

Air conditioning	Ignition system
Automatic transmission	Rust resistance
Body integrity	Steering
Braking system	Suspension
Electrical system	**Dealer service**
Engine	**Maintenance**
Exhaust/converter	**Parts availability**
Fuel system	**Repair costs**